D0086744

Exploring
Economics

Exploring Economics

PATHWAYS TO PROBLEM SOLVING

Robert L. Sexton

PEPPERDINE UNIVERSITY

THE DRYDEN PRESS
HARCOURT BRACE COLLEGE PUBLISHERS
FORT WORTH   PHILADELPHIA   SAN DIEGO   NEW YORK
AUSTIN   ORLANDO   SAN ANTONIO
TORONTO   MONTREAL   LONDON   SYDNEY   TOKYO

Publisher
George Provol
Acquisitions Editor
Gary Nelson
Product Manager
Debbie K. Anderson
Developmental Editor
Amy Porubsky
Project Editor
Rebecca Dodson
Art Director
Linda Beaupré
Production Manager
Lois West
Photo/Permissions Editor
Linda Blundell

ISBN: 0-03-018329-4
Library of Congress Catalog Card Number: 98-73566

Copyright © 1999 by The Dryden Press

All rights reserved. No part of this publication may be reproduced or transmitted in any form or by any means, electronic or mechanical, including photocopy, recording or any information storage and retrieval system, without permission in writing from the publisher.

Requests for permission to make copies of any part of the work should be mailed to: Permissions Department, Harcourt Brace & Company, 6277 Sea Harbor Drive, Orlando, FL 32887-6777.

Address for editorial correspondence:
The Dryden Press
301 Commerce Street, Suite 3700
Fort Worth, TX 76102

Address for domestic orders:
The Dryden Press
6277 Sea Harbor Drive
Orlando, FL 32887-6777
1-800-782-4479

Address for international orders:
International Customer Service
The Dryden Press
6277 Sea Harbor Drive
Orlando, FL 32887-6777

Web site address: http://www.hbcollege.com

THE DRYDEN PRESS, DRYDEN, and the DP Logo are registered trademarks of Harcourt Brace & Company.

Printed in the United States of America
7 8 9 0 1 2 3 4 5 6   048   9 8 7 6 5 4 3 2 1

The Dryden Press
Harcourt Brace College Publishers

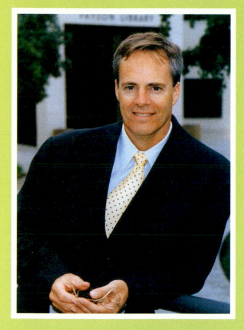

About the Author

Robert L. Sexton is currently Professor of Economics at Seaver College, Pepperdine University, and the Pepperdine School of Public Policy. Professor Sexton has also been a Visiting Professor at the University of California at Los Angeles in the Anderson Graduate School of Management and the Department of Economics.

Professor Sexton's research ranges across many fields of economics: labor economics, environmental economics, law and economics, economic education, and economic history. He has written several books and has published more than 35 research papers, many in top economic journals such as *The American Economic Review, Southern Economic Journal, Economics Letters, Journal of Urban Economics,* and *The Journal of Economic Education.* Professor Sexton has also written more than 100 other articles that have appeared in books, magazines, and newspapers.

Professor Sexton received the Pepperdine Professor of the Year Award in 1991 and 1997, and the Howard A. White Memorial Teaching Award in 1994; he was named a Harriet and Charles Luckman Teaching Fellow in 1994.

Professor Sexton resides in Agoura Hills, California, with his wife, Julie, and their three children, Elizabeth, Katherine, and Tommy.

In memory of my father
1913–1996

Thanks Dad,
I love you.

THE DRYDEN PRESS SERIES IN ECONOMICS

Baldani, Bradfield, and Turner
Mathematical Economics

Baumol and Blinder
Economics: Principles and Policy
Seventh Edition
(also available in Micro and Macro paperbacks)

Baumol, Panzar, and Willig
Contestable Markets and the Theory of Industry Structure
Revised Edition

Breit and Elzinga
The Antitrust Casebook: Milestones in Economic Regulation
Third Edition

Brue
The Evolution of Economic Thought
Fifth Edition

Edgmand, Moomaw, and Olson
Economics and Contemporary Issues
Fourth Edition

Gardner
Comparative Economic Systems
Second Edition

Gwartney and Stroup
Economics: Private and Public Choice
Eighth Edition
(also available in Micro and Macro paperbacks)

Gwartney and Stroup
Introduction to Economics: The Wealth and Poverty of Nations

Heilbroner and Singer
The Economic Transformation of America: 1600 to the Present
Third Edition

Hess and Ross
Economic Development: Theories, Evidence, and Policies

Hirschey and Pappas
Fundamentals of Managerial Economics: Theories, Evidence, and Policies
Sixth Edition

Hirschey and Pappas
Managerial Economics
Eighth Edition

Hyman
Public Finance: A Contemporary Application of Theory to Policy
Fifth Edition

Kahn
The Economic Approach to Environmental and Natural Resources
Second Edition

Kaserman and Mayo
Government and Business: The Economics of Antitrust and Regulation

Kaufman
The Economics of Labor Markets
Fourth Edition

Kennett and Lieberman
The Road to Capitalism: The Economic Transformation of Eastern Europe and the Former Soviet Union

Kreinin
International Economics: A Policy Approach
Eighth Edition

Lott and Ray
Applied Econometrics with Data Sets

Mankiw
Principles of Economics
(also available in Micro and Macro paperbacks)

Marlow
Public Finance: Theory and Practice

Nicholson
Intermediate Microeconomics and Its Application
Seventh Edition

Nicholson
Microeconomic Theory: Basic Principles and Extensions
Seventh Edition

Puth
American Economic History
Third Edition

Ragan and Thomas
Principles of Economics
Second Edition
(also available in Micro and Macro paperbacks)

Ramanathan
Introductory Econometrics with Applications
Fourth Edition

Rukstad
Corporate Decision Making in the World Economy: Company Case Studies

Rukstad
Macroeconomic Decision Making in the World Economy: Text and Cases
Third Edition

Samuelson and Marks
Managerial Economics
Second Edition

Scarth
Macroeconomics: An Introduction to Advanced Methods
Third Edition

Stockman
Introduction to Economics
(also available in Micro and Macro paperbacks)

Walton and Rockoff
History of the American Economy
Eighth Edition

Welch and Welch
Economics: Theory and Practice
Sixth Edition

Yarbrough and Yarbrough
The World Economy: Trade and Finance
Fourth Edition

A MODULAR APPROACH TO PROBLEM SOLVING (MAPS)

As you can see from a cursory flip, this book is different. I designed it to be different. This book differs from traditional economics texts in two important ways: (1) its modular presentation, and (2) its *focus* on economics as a problem-solving science.

The two goals of *Exploring Economics* are encapsulated in one mnemonic, MAPS: a **M**odular **A**pproach to **P**roblem **S**olving. As you will see, these ideas are not mere constructs; rather, they are complements that work together to create a unique learning experience for your students.

THE MODULAR APPROACH: WHAT AND WHY?

Exploring Economics uses a modular approach in its presentation of economic ideas and concepts. Information is presented in small, self-contained sections rather than in large blocks of text. My enthusiasm for and dedication to this approach stems from a study of learning theory research, which indicates that students retain information much better when it is broken down into short, "digestible" sections. Students *will* be more successful in mastering and retaining economic principles through this approach.

Unlike standard textbook construction, the modular approach is distinctly more compatible with the modern communication style with which most students are familiar and comfortable: short, intense, and exciting bursts of information. Rather than being distracted and discouraged by the seeming enormity of the task before them, students are more likely to work through a short, self-contained concept before getting up from their desks. The student is more likely to read and process the material before he or she proceeds to the next concept, a point that is particularly important in economics, where one idea is often a building block that serves as the foundation for the next.

In executing the modular approach in *Exploring Economics*, every effort has been made to take the intimidation out of economics. The idea of sticking to the basics and reinforcing student mastery, concept by concept, coupled with the careful display of pictures, charts, and graphs, has been done with the student in mind. But students aren't the only ones to benefit from this approach. The modular presentation allows instructors greater flexibility in planning their courses. More importantly, instructors benefit from having a student population that has actually read the textbook and prepared for class!

THE MODULAR APPROACH: HOW?

The philosophy of the modular approach takes form in the basic structure and organization of *Exploring Economics* and is also embodied in the accompanying Student Workbook.

The Text Organization

Exploring Economics is presented in 26 Modules, each of which is comprised of approximately 6–8 short Concepts. These Concepts are self-contained learning units, typically presented in 2–4 page, bite-size sections that include all of the relevant graphs and tables as well as numerous colorful photos for the topic at hand. Each Concept begins with a number of key questions designed to introduce the important ideas to be presented. These questions serve as landmarks for students: If they can answer these questions after reading the material, they have prepared well. This tool is reinforced by the Concept Check points and questions that appear at the end of each Concept. Key points summarize concisely the major ideas that the student should have retained, and short questions, the answers to which can be found in the back of the book, give students an opportunity to check their mastery before proceeding.

The Student Workbook

At the end of each Concept, students are encouraged to turn to the related section in the Student Workbook. The Student Workbook for use with *Exploring Economics* is an extension of the text, both in philosophy and in execution. Like the text, the workbook is designed on a Concept-by-Concept basis. After reading each Concept in the text, the student can turn to the Workbook and test his or her mastery of the material with true-false, multiple-choice, and discussion and application questions that cover only the topics covered in that Concept. If students can answer these questions, they can be confident that they have mastered the topic. In addition to these Concept-based questions, additional exercises are provided at the end of each Module that draw on and integrate all of the material in the Module. In short, the Workbook, like the text, is designed at every step to instill your students with confidence in their own abilities to master the tools of economics.

THE PROBLEM-SOLVING APPROACH: WHAT AND WHY?

Economics is a collection of problem-solving tools that can be applied to many social, political, and business issues. Even everyday issues can be more easily understood when one has a good handle on the "economic way of thinking." However, in the words of a Lake Wobegon philosopher Garrison Keillor, "Just because you sleep in a garage doesn't make you a car." In other words, picking up the terminology of economics is not enough; students have to learn when and how to use their new tools. Economic principles aren't just definitions to memorize; they are valuable tools that can help students analyze a whole host of issues and problems in the world around them. It is this philosophy that serves as the focus for the problem-solving approach in *Exploring Economics,* which is designed to serve two key purposes: (1) to facilitate student mastery of concepts both theoretically and in application, and (2) to communicate a sense of relevancy to students.

THE PROBLEM-SOLVING APPROACH: HOW?

The problem-solving approach is evident throughout *Exploring Economics*—in the basic organization of the text and in the supporting pedagogical elements. This approach is also embodied in the well-integrated student ancillary materials that are packaged with the text, collectively known as the Integrated Learning System.

The Text Organization

By presenting material in a Concept-by-Concept, building-block format that encourages and reinforces students at every step, the modular approach directly supports the problem-solving focus of the text. The modular approach breaks difficult concepts into digestible parts and then offers students opportunities to evaluate their level of understanding before proceeding. In this way, students are provided with an optimal format in which to master the economic tools that they will need and to develop confidence in their own abilities and understanding of these ideas.

Learning Tools

Key Questions. Each Concept begins with a list of questions that highlight the primary ideas that the student should learn from the material. These questions are intended to serve as a preview and to pique students' interest in the material to come.

Text Heads. Many paragraphs in the text have headings that are structured as questions. The philosophy be-

hind this approach is that if students develop the habit of asking themselves such questions, they will become much more effective learners; that is, they will begin to learn to ask the right questions themselves.

Tune Up. Tune Up boxes are scattered throughout the text as a way of reinforcing and checking student comprehension of important or more difficult concepts. These elements provide students with an opportunity to test their mastery of new tools through short applications. Students can then check their work immediately against the answer given at the bottom of the box, providing them immediate feedback and encouragement in the learning process.

Applications. There are numerous applications to everyday life situations scattered throughout the text. These applications were chosen specifically with students in mind, and they are designed to help students find the connection between economics and their lives. With that, economic principles are applied to everyday problems and issues, such as classroom cheating, sexually transmitted diseases, teenage drug use, juvenile crime, on-line betting, road kill, and the cost of raising children.

In addition to the large number of in-text examples, one integrative application is presented in the last Concept of each Module as a platform for tying together some of the primary ideas presented in the Module. Also, there are two special boxed applications, "In the News" and "Global Watch," scattered throughout each Module.

In the News. "In the News" applications focus primarily on current news stories that are relevant and thought-provoking. These articles are placed strategically throughout the text to solidify particular concepts. In an effort to emphasize the breadth and diversity of the situations to which economic principles can be applied, these articles have been chosen from sources that range from *National Geographic* to *Wired* magazine.

Global Watch. Whether we are concerned with understanding yesterday, today, or tomorrow, and whether we are looking at a small, far-away country or a large next-door neighbor, economic principles can strengthen our grasp on many global issues. "Global Watch" articles were chosen to help students understand the magnitude and character of the change occurring around the world today and to introduce them to some of the economic causes and implications of this change. To gain a greater perspective on a particular economy or the planet as a whole, it is helpful to compare important economic indicators around the world. For this reason, "Global Watch" applications will sometimes be used to present relevant comparative statistics.

Concept Checks. Each Concept in a Module ends with a Concept Check box. This element contains 4–6 short sentences emphasizing the important points in each section. It also includes 4–6 questions designed to test students' comprehension of the basic points of the Concept just covered. If students can answer these questions, they can feel confident about proceeding to the next topic.

Memory Devices. Mnemonic devices are used where appropriate as an extra aid to help students remember certain important ideas. For example, "PYNTE," the old-English spelling of *pint,* is used to help students remember the major demand shifters: *P,* price of related goods; *Y,* income; *N,* number of buyers; *T,* tastes; and *E,* expectations.

Photos. The text contains hundreds of colorful pictures. They are not, however, mere decoration; rather, these photos are an integral part of the book, for both learning and motivation purposes. The photos are carefully placed where they reinforce important concepts, and they are accompanied with inquisitive captions designed to encourage students to extend their understanding of particular ideas.

Exhibits. Graphs, tables, and charts are important economic tools. These tools are used throughout *Exploring Economics* to illustrate, clarify, and reinforce economic principles. Text exhibits are designed to be as clear and simple as possible, and they are carefully coordinated with the text material.

THE INTEGRATED LEARNING SYSTEM

The Integrated Learning System is more than an extension of the problem-solving approach to student success that characterizes *Exploring Economics*; it is, in fact, an integral part of that approach. Individually, the elements of this system—the Student Workbook, EconActive CD-ROM, and Student Web Site—can help your students take the small steps toward a mastery of microeconomics. Collectively, these elements serve as a key to your students' ultimate goal: their mastery of the economic way of thinking and the development of a confidence in their abilities to use those tools elsewhere. This, I believe, is the ultimate success, but it is a success that must come gradually, one step at a time. The Integrated Learning System helps students take those steps by reinforcing basic concepts and ensuring student mastery at every point, using the same basic student-friendly and interactive style that characterizes the text.

Student Workbook

The Student Workbook for use with *Exploring Economics* reinforces the basic problem-solving approach of the text. On a Concept-by-Concept basis, the Student Workbook guides the student through various exercises designed to test their comprehension and mastery, including true-false, multiple-choice, and application-type questions. These exercises proceed from the relatively easy to the more difficult, thus allowing students to experience success and generate feelings of confidence as they proceed. Then, at the end of each Module, students can enjoy and learn from

"The Lowells," a cartoon strip that illustrates a key concept from the Module and then tests student understanding of that idea. The answers to all Student Workbook activities are included in the Workbook, so that students can get immediate feedback on their work.

EconActive CD-ROM

The EconActive CD-ROM is designed to allow your students to get even more interactive and involved in their own learning process. In addition to guided tutorials with new examples and graphs, the EconActive CD-ROM also includes Java-powered, interactive graphs. The power of Java allows students to manipulate a variable or variables on a graph and immediately see the effects of those changes on the graph. The hands-on interaction that these Java-powered graphs provide illustrates and reinforces economic relationships in a way that a static graph and explanation cannot. As with the Student Workbook, the interactive graphs and the other materials on the EconActive CD-ROM are designed to reinforce student mastery and success at each point.

Student Web Site

A Student Web Site has been developed to accompany *Exploring Economics*. In addition to providing students with a secondary access to many of the learning tools that appear on their EconActive CD-ROM (including the Java-powered interactive graphs), the Student Web Site gives students access to other resources they can use to test their understanding of key economic concepts. These tools include online, interactive quizzes (multiple-choice, matching, and true-false) that provide students with immediate feedback, cyberproblems with links to relevant data or Web sites, and additional applications.

SUPPLEMENTS FOR THE INSTRUCTOR

The following ancillaries are available to instructors:

Test Bank

Computerized Test Bank

Instructor's Resource Manual

Electronic Resource Manual

Power Point Presentation

Instructor Web Site

Video Lecture Starters

WALL STREET JOURNAL EDITION

One goal in teaching the principles of economics is to provide students a better understanding of the world around them. Many instructors, therefore, encourage students to read about economic issues in the newspaper as they take the course. Those instructors may want to consider the special *Wall Street Journal Edition* of this text. The edition is the same as the standard edition but includes a ten-week subscription to *The Wall Street Journal*. Students can activate their subscriptions simply by completing and mailing the business reply card found in the back of the book. Talk to your Dryden Press sales representative for more information, or call 1-800-237-2665.

The Wall Street Journal is a registered trademark of Dow Jones & Company, Inc.

ACKNOWLEDGMENTS

I would like to extend special thanks to the following colleagues for their valuable insight during the manuscript phase of this project. I owe a debt of gratitude to Philip Graves, University of Colorado; Gary Galles, Pepperdine University; Richard Vedder, Ohio University; Dwight Lee, University of Georgia; Robert M. Escudero, Pepperdine University; Ron Batchelder, Pepperdine University; Steve Jackstadt, University of Alaska, Anchorage; Lee Huskey, University of Alaska, Anchorage; Robert Clower, University of South Carolina and Gary M. Walton, University of California, Davis.

Without the devotion and creativity of several people at The Dryden Press, this book would not have been possible. My appreciation goes to Gary Nelson, without whom this project would never have materialized and Amy Winston, whose detail and motivation improved the book tremendously. Also thanks to George Provol, Becky Dodson, Linda Beaupré, Linda Blundell, Lois West, Rosemarie Console, Brad Balaban, Debbie K. Anderson, Amy Porubsky, Barrett Lackey, and Kimberly Powell.

In addition, my family deserves special gratitude—my wife Julie, daughters Elizabeth and Katherine, and my son Tommy. They are an inspiration to my work. Also, special thanks to my mother Willa and my brother Bill.

Thanks to all of my colleagues who reviewed the project. From very early on in the writing phase all the way up to publication, your comments were very important to me.

Jack Adams, University of Arkansas, Little Rock

James Q. Aylsworth, Lakeland Community College

G.E. Breger, University of South Carolina

Gilbert L. Christopher, Jr., Wingate University

Andrew J. Dane, Angelo State University

John W. Dorsey, University of Maryland

David Eaton, Murray State University

Mary E. Edwards, St. Cloud State University

Robert M. Escudero, Pepperdine University

Gary Galles, Pepperdine University

Phil Graves, University of Colorado

Stanley Keil, Ball State University

Ronald Kessler, British Columbia Institute of Technology

Saleem Khan, Bloomsburg University

Philip King, San Francisco State University

Thomas Maloy, Muskegon Community College

Pete Mavrokordatas, Tarrant County Junior College

Thomas Porebski, Trinton College

Tom Potiowsky, Portland State University

Sue Lynn Sasser, William Woods University

Mark Strazicich, University of Central Florida

Howard Whitney, Franklin University

The Dryden Press conducted a national survey of professors who offered tremendous feedback on the ideas and teaching style presented with this text. A special thanks to all participants, including the following:

Steve Abid, Grand Rapids Community College

Fatma Wahdan Antar, Manchester Community College

Donald C. Balch, University of South Carolina

Randall Barnes, San Diego Miramar College

Cihan Bilginsoy, University of Utah

Barbara L. Brogan, Northern Virginia Community College

George W.M. Bullion, Indiana University–Purdue

Dennis Byrne, University of Akron

James E. Clark, Wichita State University

Joe B. Copeland, University of North Alabama

Kenneth M. Cross, Southwest Virginia Community College

John P. Dahlquist, College of Alameda

David E. Davis, University of Oregon, USDA

Richard Deitz, Rochester Institute of Technology

Mike Dunton, Delmar College

David H. Eaton, Murray State University

Dipak Ghosh, Emporia State University

Spencer R. Graf, University of Virginia

Paul F. Haas, Bowling Green State University

Peter W. Harman, Rhode Island College

Barry Haworth, University of Louisville

Wei-Chiao Huang, Western Michigan University

Paul A. Joray, Indiana University–South Bend

Patrick Joyce, Michigan Technological University

Saleem M. Khan, Bloomsburg University of Pennsylvania

Ghebre Y. Keleta, Grambling State University

Syrous Kooros, Nicholls State University

Rose M. LaMont, Modesto Junior College

Michael B. Lehmann, University of San Francisco

Stephen E. Lile, Western Kentucky University

Vernon Lynch, Fort Lewis College

Dayle Mandelson, University of Wisconsin–Stout

James M. McQuiston, University of Southern Mississippi

Green R. Miller, Morehead State University

Masoud Moghaddam, St. Cloud State University

Marie T. Mora, New Mexico State University

Amlan Mitra, Purdue University–Calumet

William R. Pedersen, Southeastern Louisiana University

Chris Phillips, Somerset Community College

Etienne E. Pracht, Louisiana State University

Rarahmand Rezvani, Montclair State University

Mark Strazicich, University of Central Florida

Thomas A. Swanke, West Virginia State College

Robert E. Tansky, St. Clair County Community College

Neil Terry, West Texas A&M University

Jesus M Valencia, Slippery Rock University

John R. Wagner, Westfield State College

Karen T. Wilson, Delta College

Willard E. Witte, Indiana University–Bloomington

Lewis Woodruff, Sinclair Community College

Douglas Woolley, Radford University

Edward G. Young, University of Wisconsin–Eau Claire

Brief Table of Contents

Contents

Exploring Economics

Economics:
Ten Powerful
Ideas

A. Economics: A Definition
What is economics?

B. Wants and Desires
Can all of our wants and desires
be satisfied?

C. Scarcity
Did nature provide enough
for all of our wants?

D. Choices
Can we have our cake and eat it too?

E. Marginal Thinking
What is the rule of rational choice?

F. Incentives Matter
Do people respond to incentives?

G. Specialization and Trade
How can specialization and trade lead to greater economic growth?

H. Markets and the Price System
Can markets and the price system make consumers
and producers better off?

I. Government Policies
Can appropriate government policies improve our economic well-being?

J. Economic Growth
Can economic growth improve overall standards of living?

K. Price Stability
Will price stability enable producers and consumers
to make better plans and decisions?

L. Application: Laws and Enforcement Costs
How can strict laws function as incentives to influence behavior?

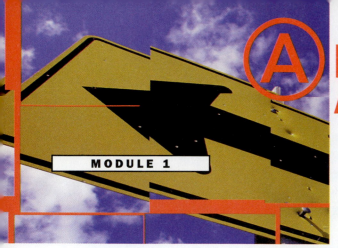

(A) Economics: A Definition

MODULE 1

- What is economics?
- Do our wants and desires grow over time?

ECONOMICS—A WORD WITH MANY DIFFERENT MEANINGS

The term "economics" means different things to different people. Even the pronunciation of the word varies; some pronounce it with a long *e,* while others combine the *e* with the *c* into *ec* (as in *tech* or *wreck*). As to the meaning of the word, some individuals think economics involves the study of the stock market and corporate finance, and it does—in part. Others think that economics is concerned with the wise use of money and other matters of personal finance, and it is—in part. Still others think that economics involves forecasting or predicting what business conditions will be in the future, and again, it does—in part. The word economics is, after all, derived from the Greek word *oeconomicus,* which refers to the management of household affairs.

The front page of a newspaper is usually filled with articles that are related to economics either directly or indirectly.

A Unique Way of Looking at Human Behavior

Economics is a unique way of analyzing many areas of human behavior. Indeed, the range of topics to which economic analysis is applied is quite broad! As a result, many researchers have discovered that the economic approach to human behavior sheds light on social problems that have been with us for a long time: discrimination, education, crime, divorce, political favoritism, and many more. In fact, economics is front-page news almost every day, whether it involves politicians talking about balancing budgets, business executives talking about restructuring to cut costs, or the average citizen trying to figure out how much it will cost taxpayers to reduce crime. Economics is all of this and more.

Growing Wants and Scarce Resources

Precisely defined, **economics** is the study of the allocation of our scarce resources to satisfy our unlimited wants for goods and services. **Resources** are those things, such as tools, machinery, and factories, that are used to make goods and services. Water, land, and trees are **natural resources.** The problem is that our wants exceed what our resources can produce, a fact that we call **scarcity.** Scarcity forces us to make choices on how to best use our limited resources. We want more things; we want different things. We want materialistic things that we can touch and hold. We also want intangible things like friendship, love, spirituality, knowledge, and so on. Because resources are scarce, however, no one can have all of the goods and services he or she desires. Scarcity forces us all to make choices. And whenever we have to choose, we must do without something else that we also desire. This want that we choose not to satisfy cannot be recovered—it is a lost opportunity. This lost opportunity is the cost of the choice we actually make. This is the economic problem: *Scarcity forces us to choose, and choices are costly because we must give up other opportunities.* This economizing problem is evident in every aspect of our lives, even those things that appear decidedly non-economic in nature.

"O.K., who can put a price on love? Jim?"

Drawing by Ziegler: Copyright 1991 *The New Yorker* Magazine, Inc.

ECONOMICS IS ALL AROUND US

Although many things that we desire in life are considered to be "non-economic," economics concerns anything that is considered worthwhile to some human being. For instance, love, sexual activity, and religion have value for most people. However, even these have an economic dimension. Consider religion, for example. Concern for spiritual matters has led to the development of institutions such as churches and temples that provide religious and spiritual services. These services are goods that many people desire. Love and sex likewise have received economists' scrutiny. One product of love, the institution of the family, is an important economic decision-making unit. Also, sexual activity results in the birth of children, one of the most important "goods" that humans desire.

Even time has an economic dimension. In fact, perhaps the most valuable single good we possess is time. We all have the same limited amount of time per day, and how we divide our time between work and leisure (including perhaps study, sleep, exercise, etc.) is a distinctly economic matter. Virtually everything we decide to do, then, has an economic dimension.

THE 10 POWERFUL IDEAS OF ECONOMICS

Most of economics is really knowing certain principles well and knowing when and how to apply them. We think that there are 10 powerful ideas that serve as the

Economics can make us look at everything—even the value of our time—differently.

foundation of economics. These few basic ideas will repeatedly occur throughout the text and are presented in this Module as a preview of what is to come. If you develop a good understanding of these principles and master the problem-solving skills inherent in them, they will serve you well for the rest of your life. As Bill Gates, CEO of Microsoft, has said, just being intelligent is not enough for success: "To succeed, you also have to know how to make choices and how to think more broadly." As you will see, Mr. Gates's tools for success are the cornerstones of the economic way of thinking!

1. Economics is a problem-solving science.
2. Economics is the study of the allocation of scarce resources to satisfy unlimited wants.

3. Our wants exceed our resources, so we must make choices.

1. What is the definition of economics?
2. Why does scarcity force us to make choices?
3. Why are choices costly?

4. Why do even "non-economic" issues have an economic dimension?
5. If a genie gave you three wishes, would that solve the problem of scarcity for you?

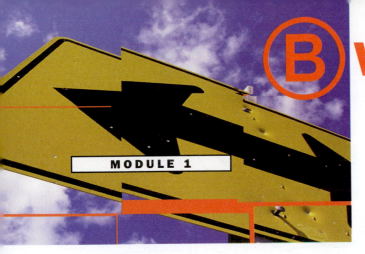

B Wants and Desires

- What are resources?
- What are goods and services?
- What are tangible and intangible goods?
- What are economic goods?

WHAT ARE RESOURCES?

As you already know, economics is concerned primarily with how we satisfy our unlimited wants and desires in a world of limited resources. As we noted earlier, resources are the scarce inputs that are used to produce the goods and services that we want. Resources, both "man"-made and natural, can include such things as machinery, tools, time, air, water, trees, land, and the knowledge of how to productively employ them (technology). These resources, however, are finite. Only so much knowledge, so many trees, so much water, and so many tools are available for our use at any given time. It follows, then, that because these resources are limited, the things that can be produced from them—goods and services—are also limited.

WHAT ARE GOODS AND SERVICES?

"Goods" and "services" are those things that we value or desire. **Goods** tend to be tangible things—objects that can be seen, held, heard, tasted, or smelled. But there are also goods that we cannot reach out and touch, called **intangible goods.** Intangible goods include such things as fairness for all, friendship, knowledge, security, intelligence, and health. While some intangible goods have no price tags, a *USA Today* poll showed that the wealthy would be willing to pay top dollar, if they could, for a place in heaven ($640,000), true love ($487,000), and a great intellect ($407,000). **Services** are intangible because they are less

An airplane is a good, but taking a trip on an airplane involves a service.

overtly visible, but they are no less valuable than goods. An airplane is a good, but taking a trip on an airplane involves the provision of a service.

All goods and services, whether they are tangible or intangible, are scarce and can be subjected to economic analysis. In fact, these scarce goods that are created from scarce resources are called **economic goods.**

WHAT ARE BADS?

In contrast to goods, **bads** are those items that we do not desire or want. For most people, garbage, pollution, weeds, and crime are bads. People tend to want to eliminate or minimize bads, so they will often pay to have bads, like garbage, removed. Then, the elimination of the bad—garbage removal, for example—becomes a good.

ARE THOSE WHO WANT MORE GREEDY?

We all want more tangible and intangible goods and services. In economics, we assume that more goods lead to greater satisfaction, or **utility,** and that bads lead to dissatisfaction, or **disutility.** However, because we assume that people want more goods and wish to eliminate or minimize bads does not mean that economics presumes that people are selfish and greedy. For example, Mother Teresa spent much of her time helping others because that is what she wanted to do with her time. Many people give much of their income and time to charitable or religious organizations. That is, they commit their time, and other scarce resources, to achieving the "good" of charitable giving. Clearly, then, many desires, like building new friendships

or helping charities, can hardly be defined as selfish, yet these are desires that many people share. In other words, "self-interest" is not the same as "selfishness."

"Christmas shopping is going to be easy for this year, Mom. There's hardly anything I don't want!"

CLINTON MOURNS THE LOSS OF TWO REMARKABLE WOMEN

Last year, when President Clinton was mourning the passing of two remarkable women, he made the following observations. "While both Mother Teresa and Princess Diana had vastly different backgrounds and lived in very different worlds, both were committed to providing compassion to those who needed it most—the desperately poor, the abandoned, the sick, and the dying. Each woman in her own way demonstrated what it is to live a life of meaning, with concern for others. They both will be remembered for the gifts they left for others."

CONSIDER THIS:
Providing charity is a desire or want to some.

CONCEPT CHECK

1. Resources are the scarce inputs used to produce goods and services.
2. Goods and services are things that we value.
3. Goods can be tangible (physical) or intangible (love, compassion, and intelligence).
4. Economic goods are goods created from limited resources.

1. What are resources?
2. How do finite resources impact our ability to produce goods and services?
3. What must be true for something to be an economic good?
4. Does wanting more tangible and intangible goods and services make us selfish?
5. Why might sunshine be scarce in Seattle but not in Tucson?

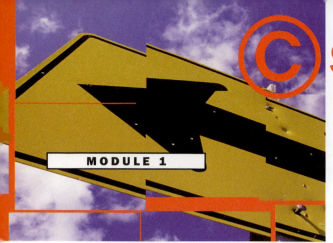

©Scarcity

■ Do we all face scarcity?
■ Do our wants and desires change over time?

DOES EVERYONE FACE SCARCITY?

We all face scarcity, because no one can have all of the goods and services that he or she desires. However, because we all have different wants and desires, scarcity affects everyone differently. For example, a child in an underdeveloped country may face a scarcity of food and clean drinking water, while a rich person might face a scarcity of garage space for his growing antique car collection. Likewise, a harried middle-class working mother may find time for exercise particularly scarce, while a pharmaceutical company may be concerned with the scarcity of the natural resources it uses in its production process. Clearly, then, while its effects vary, no one can escape scarcity.

CAN PEOPLE BECOME SO RICH THAT THEY DON'T HAVE TO CHOOSE?

We often hear it said of rich people that "He has everything" or "She can buy anything she wants." Actually, even the richest person must live with scarcity and must, at some point, choose one want or desire over another, and, of course, we all have only 24 hours in a day! The problem is that as we get more affluent, we learn of new luxuries to provide us with satisfaction. Wealth, then, creates a new set of wants to be satisfied. There is no evidence that people would not find a valuable use for additional income, no matter how rich they become. Even the wealthy individual who decides to donate all of her money to charity faces the constraints of scarcity. If she had greater resources, she could do still more for others.

Clearly, though, the concepts of scarcity and choice are relative in nature. For example, in the extreme case of a person with very limited resources, the cost that he might pay for, say, a nice shirt or sweater might be starvation. That is, his limited resources can support nothing beyond the basic necessities of life. For a multimillionaire, on the other hand, the cost of a shirt or sweater would be imperceptibly small. Scarcity for that individual might mean

Does Donald Trump face the problem of scarcity?

choosing between a plane and a yacht. The point here is that even though the choices that the wealthy are forced to make may seem less crucial than those made by a relatively poor person, they are still choices and they still reflect a scarcity of resources.

ARE SCARCITY AND GROWING EXPECTATIONS HERE TO STAY?

It is probably clear by now that scarcity never has and never will be eradicated. The same creativity that permits new methods to produce goods and services in greater quantities also reveals new wants. Thus, the small black-and-white television set that provided so much enjoyment for viewers raised on radio would now be considered an inadequate form of entertainment by most. Two generations ago, only the well-to-do had telephones; today telephones are provided to some welfare recipients on the grounds that they are a "necessity." It is also possible that while people seem to be happier at a point in time the more goods and services they can buy, over a period of time, a rising quantity of goods and services may not increase human happiness. Why? There are several possibilities, but it is very possible that our wants grow as fast, if not faster, than our ability to meet those wants, so we still feel scarcity as much or more than we did before.

New wants quickly replace old ones.

CONCEPT CHECK

1. Scarcity will always be with us.
2. Our wants grow over time, so scarcity will never be eliminated.
3. Scarcity is a fact for everyone.

---

1. Does everyone face scarcity?
2. Why does scarcity affect each of us differently?
3. Why can't a country become so technologically advanced that its citizens won't have to choose?
4. If Penny Pincher became a billionaire after winning the largest lottery ever, would she still face scarcity?

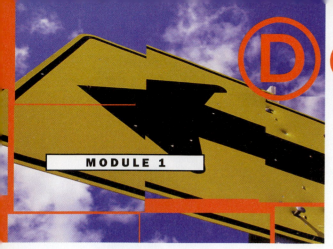

D Choices

- Why do we have to make choices?
- What do we give up when we have to choose?
- Why are "free" lunches not free?
- Are prices and costs the same thing?

DOES SCARCITY FORCE US TO MAKE COSTLY CHOICES?

We may want two luxury cars in every garage, nice homes, good tasting and wholesome food, all enjoyed in a pristine environment with zero pollution. If we had unlimited resources, and thus an ability to produce all of the goods and services anyone wanted, we would not have to choose among those desires. If we did not have to make meaningful economic choices, the study of economics would not be necessary. The essence of economics is to fully understand the implications that scarcity has for wise decision making. This suggests another way to define economics: Economics is the study of the choices we make among our many wants and desires.

WHAT WOULD YOU HAVE TO GIVE UP TO TRAIN FOR A MARATHON?

We all have to make important choices with our time every day. Suppose you were a marathon runner. Would your training be a scarce good? Of course it would, because you would have to give up other things to run. The time you spend working out has a cost, because it comes at the expense of that same time spent at other valued activities like studying, socializing, watching TV, or sleeping.

WHENEVER WE CHOOSE, DO WE LOSE?

We are all faced with the fact of scarcity, and as a consequence, we must make choices. Because none of us can "afford" to buy everything we want, each time we do decide to buy one good or service, we reduce our ability to buy other things we would also like to have. If you buy a new car this year, you may not be able to afford your next best choice—the vacation you've been planning. You must choose. The cost of the car to you is the value of the vaca-

Time spent running costs time spent doing something else.

tion that must be foregone. The highest or best foregone opportunity resulting from a decision is called the **opportunity cost**. Another way to put this is that "to choose is to lose." To get more of anything that is desirable, you must accept less of something else that you also value.

WHAT IS THE OPPORTUNITY COST OF GOING TO COLLEGE OR HAVING A CHILD?

The average person often does not correctly consider opportunity costs when thinking about costs. For example,

© 1981 by King Features Syndicate, Inc. World rights reserved

the cost of going to college is not just the direct costs of tuition and books. It also includes the opportunity cost of your time, which for many people is the greatest part of their costs. Specifically, the time spent going to school is time that could have been spent on a job earning, say, $25,000 a year. What is the cost of rearing a child to the age of 18? There are the obvious costs: clothes, piano lessons, time spent at soccer practices, food, visits to the doctor, and so on. But there are also other substantial opportunity costs incurred in rearing a child. For example, consider the opportunity cost if one of the parents chooses to give up his or her job to stay at home. Then, the time spent in child rearing is time that could be used making money and pursuing a career. These opportunity costs must be included in the total costs of raising a child.

EXHIBIT 1	WOMEN'S SHAVING OVER A LIFETIME

SOURCE: Schick

Time spent shaving is time that could have been used for something else, but you must value "hair-free surfaces" more than other uses of that time, or you would not shave.

IS THAT REALLY A FREE LUNCH, A FREEWAY, OR A FREE BEACH?

The expression *"there's no such thing as a free lunch"* clarifies the relationship between scarcity and opportunity cost. Suppose the school cafeteria is offering "free" lunches today. While the lunch is free to you, is it really free from society's perspective? The answer is no, because some of society's scarce resources will have been used in the preparation of the lunch. The issue is whether the resources that went into creating that lunch could have been used to produce something else of value. Clearly, the labor and materials (food-service workers, lettuce, meat, plows, tractors, fertilizer, and so forth) that went into the production of the lunch could have been used in other ways. They had an opportunity cost, and thus were not free. Whenever you hear the word "free"—freeways, free beaches, free libraries, free admission, and so on—an alarm should go off in your head. Very few things are free, in the sense that they use none of society's scarce resources. So what does a free lunch really mean? It is, technically speaking, a "subsidized" lunch—a lunch using society's scarce resources, but one for which you personally do not have to pay.

ARE PRICES AND COSTS DIFFERENT?

Prices and costs are not the same thing. A **price** reflects the monetary value of a good or service; it is an objective fact. However, costs are personal and subjective. Costs reflect the relative value of foregone goods or services to individuals. For example, would a $100,000 BMW cost more to a richer rather than a poorer person? The price is the same—both would have to give up $100,000 of other goods and services to buy the car—but the costs are likely to be different. Even if the poorer person, by selling everything he had, could buy it, he still might view a BMW as frivolous because he would likely place a higher value on the things he would have to give up for the BMW—like food, clothing, and shelter. That is, although the price of

© 1987 Thaves/Reprinted with permission. Newspaper dist. by NEA, Inc.

Are kittens free? Raising a kitten certainly isn't free; it requires lots of scarce resources, including vaccinations, food, and time.

the car does not change, the cost may be greater to the poorer person because of the value he places on the sacrificed goods. Because costs are personal and subjective, we cannot objectively compare the values individuals place on goods and services. However, we can say that different people are likely to place different values on the same goods and services, even if they have the same price tag.

Is the price of a BMW the same to different buyers? How about the cost?

CONCEPT CHECK

1. Because of scarcity we have to make choices.
2. When we are forced to choose, we give up the highest valued alternative.
3. Opportunity cost is what you give up when you make a choice.

---

1. Would we have to make choices if we had unlimited resources?
2. What is given up when we make a choice?
3. What do we mean by opportunity cost?
4. Why is there no such thing as a free lunch?
5. How are prices and costs different?
6. Why was the opportunity cost of staying in college higher for Tiger Woods than for most undergraduates?
7. Why is the opportunity cost of the time spent getting an MBA typically lower for a 22-year-old straight out of college than for a 45-year-old experienced manager?

(E) Marginal Thinking

- What do we mean by marginal changes?
- What is the rule of rational choice?
- Why do we use the word "expected" with marginal benefits and costs?

CHOICES ARE PRIMARILY MARGINAL— NOT ALL OR NOTHING

Most choices involve how much of something to do, rather than whether or not to do something. It is not whether you eat, but how much you eat. Hopefully, the question is not whether to study but instead how much to study this semester. For example, "If I studied a *little* more, I might be able to improve my grade," or "If I had a *little* better concentration when I was studying, I could improve my grade." This is what economists call marginal thinking because the focus is on the additional, or marginal, choices. Marginal choices involve the effects of adding or subtracting from the current situation. In trying to make themselves better off, people alter their behavior if the expected marginal benefits to them from doing so outweigh the expected marginal costs they will bear. This is what economists call **the rule of rational choice.** The term *expected* is used with marginal benefits and costs because the world is uncertain in many important respects, so the actual result of changing behavior may not always make people better off—but on average it will. However, as a matter of rationality, people are assumed to engage only in behavior that they think ahead of time will make them better off. That is, they will only pursue an activity if expected marginal benefits are greater than the expected marginal costs, or $E(MB) > E(MC)$. This fairly unrestrictive and realistic view of individuals seeking self-betterment can be used to analyze a variety of social phenomena.

DO JAYWALKERS USE RATIONAL DECISION MAKING?

Imagine that a friend of yours crosses a busy street without using the designated crosswalk at the traffic signal. Is her decision to jaywalk a rational one?

Weighing the expected marginal benefits and costs, your friend might recognize that it is prohibitively costly

---

| EXHIBIT 1 | SCALES OF ECONOMICS |

Is this decision to jaywalk a rational one?

for the police and the legal system to monitor the behavior of the thousands of pedestrians that live in her city. As a result, the chance of her being caught is small. She also probably knows that, even if she did get caught, the penalty for jaywalking for a first offense is likely to be a warning. The costs, then, don't look too high. Also, your friend recognizes that the value of her time is a limited resource. The time she saves by jaywalking rather than waiting for the light can be spent pursuing other activities. After weighing the expected costs and benefits of waiting for a long light versus jaywalking, she decides to take a chance. While it is important to note that her decision might ultimately be a bad one—she might receive a citation or, worse, she could get hit by a car—people make decisions based on what they *expect* to happen, not on what actually happens. Clearly, then, your friend's decision to jaywalk was rational from her perspective. Similarly, because both benefits and costs are subjective (individual specific), a more cautious person with a lower value of time might rationally have chosen not to jaywalk.

IS THE GOAL OF ZERO POLLUTION RATIONAL?

What would we have to give up—that is, what costs would we have to incur—in order to achieve *zero* pollution? A lot! You could not drive a car, fly in a plane, or even ride bikes, especially if everybody else is riding bikes too (because congestion is a form of pollution). How would you get to school, go out on a date, or go to the grocery store? Everyone would have to grow his or her own food, because foods are transported, stored, and produced using machinery and equipment that pollute. And even growing your own food would be a problem because many plants emit natural pollutants. We could go on and on. The point is not that we shouldn't be concerned about the environment; rather, it is that we have to weigh the expected marginal benefits of a cleaner environment against the expected marginal costs of a cleaner environment. It is the net, or difference, that is important. In this case, given the large expected marginal costs, a decision to pursue a state of zero pollution would not be rational.

What would you be willing to give up to eliminate the rush-hour congestion you face?

CONCEPT CHECK

1. Economists are usually interested in the effects of additional, or marginal, changes in a given situation.
2. People try to make themselves better off.
3. People make decisions based on what they *expect* to happen.

4. The rule of rational choice states that individuals will pursue an activity if they expect the marginal benefits to be greater than the marginal costs, or $E(MB) > E(MC)$.

---

1. What are marginal choices? Why does economics focus on them?
2. What is the rule of rational choice?
3. Why does rational choice involve expectations?
4. Why do students often stop taking lecture notes when a professor announces that the next few minutes of material will not be on any future test or assignment?

5. If you decide to speed to get to a doctor's appointment and then get into an accident as a result, does your decision to speed invalidate the rule of rational choice?

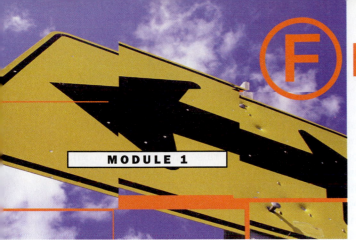

F Incentives Matter

- Can we predict how people will respond to changes in incentives?
- What are positive incentives?
- What are negative incentives?

DO PEOPLE RESPOND TO INCENTIVES?

In acting rationally, people are responding to incentives. That is, they are reacting to fluctuations—both positive and negative—in the relevant cost–benefit structure. In fact, much of human behavior can be explained and predicted as a response to incentives. Consider the economic view of crime. Why do criminals engage in their "occupation"? Presumably because the "job," even with its risks, is considered to be preferable to alternative forms of employment. For criminals, the benefits of their actions are higher and/or the opportunity costs of them are lower than is the case for non-criminals. In some cases, the criminal cannot get a legitimate job at a wage he or she would find acceptable, so the cost of engaging in crime in terms of other income foregone may be quite low. At other times, the likelihood of being caught is small, so the expected cost is negligible. Also, for some, the moral cost of a crime is low, while for others it is high. The benefits, in terms of wealth gained, are clear. If the expected gains or benefits from committing a crime outweigh the expected costs, the activity is pursued.

If the unemployment rate rose significantly, what would you expect to happen to crime rates?

For most policy purposes, the primary concern is not what causes the level of crime to be what it is but, rather, what causes the level of crime to change. The changes in the crime rate in recent decades can be largely explained in terms of such a benefit–cost framework. If the benefits of crime rise, say, in the form of larger real "hauls," and/or if the costs fall due to a reduced likelihood of being caught or of being imprisoned if caught, then economists would expect the amount of crime to rise. Likewise, economists would expect the crime rate to fall in response to increased police enforcement, stiffer punishments, or an increase in the employment rate. Whether this analysis tells the complete story is debatable, but the use of the economic framework in thinking about the problem provides a plausible explanation.

WHAT ARE POSITIVE AND NEGATIVE INCENTIVES?

Almost all of economics can be reduced to incentive [$E(MB)$ versus $E(MC)$] stories, where consumers and producers are driven by incentives that affect expected costs or benefits. Prices, wages, profits, taxes, and subsidies are all examples of economic incentives. Incentives can be classified into two types: positive and negative. **Positive incentives** are those that either increase benefits or reduce costs and thus result in an increase in the level of the related activity or behavior. **Negative incentives,** on the other hand, either reduce benefits or increase costs, resulting in a decrease in the level of the related activity or behavior. For example, a tax on cars that emit lots of pollution (an increase in costs) would be a negative incentive that would lead to a reduction in the amount of pollution emitted. On the other hand, a subsidy to electric cars (an increase in benefits) would be a positive incentive that would encourage greater consumption and production of electric cars. Human behavior is shaped and influenced in predictable ways by such changes in economic incentives, and economists use this information to predict what will happen when the benefits and costs of any choice are changed.

WILL BIRTH RATES FALL IF THE TAX DEDUCTION FOR DEPENDENTS IS REMOVED?

Although it would not change everyone's behavior, overall we would expect birth rates to fall if the tax deduction for dependents was eliminated, because it would then be more expensive for couples to raise children. We would also predict that couples would choose to have fewer children if the government imposed a birth tax on couples. Clearly, both of these policy changes would serve as negative incentives to having children, because both increase the costs of having kids. In essence, what either of these policies would do is change the benefit–cost equation, and altering this equation typically leads to predictable results.

A subsidy on electric cars would be a positive incentive that would encourage greater consumption and production of these vehicles.

T U N E   U P

DO INCENTIVES MATTER?

Q: Do you think there are fewer drug traffickers in Singapore than there would be if the mandatory sentence was five years with parole for good behavior?

A: Singapore's tough drug-trafficking penalty—death—would clearly impact the cost–benefit ratios of would-be smugglers. Lighter sentences would probably result in more drug smuggling, because the overall cost of breaking the law would be reduced.

IMPORTANT NOTICE

Please DO NOT remove this portion of the form from your passport/ travel document. You are required to surrender this portion of the form to the Immigration Officer at the check point at the time of your departure.

WARNING
DEATH FOR DRUG TRAFFICKERS
UNDER SINGAPORE LAW

(1)

SURVEY FINDS CHEATING NOT UNCOMMON AMONG TOP U.S. HIGH SCHOOL STUDENTS

WASHINGTON (CNN)—Cheating, risky sexual behavior, and drug and alcohol use are activities found among high achievers in the nation's high schools, according to the 26th annual survey of students listed in "Who's Who among American High School Students."

However, students who took part in the survey named the "decline of moral and social values" as the greatest crisis confronting the nation and the number one problem facing teenagers.

Cheating: 89 percent of the students said cheating is common at their schools, and 76 percent admitted they had cheated on schoolwork themselves. Of those who cheated, 94 percent said they never got caught, and only 5 percent of those caught said they were punished. "In theory, we all want this to be a better world," said Jackie Knoll, 17, a senior in Montrose, Michigan. "In reality, we have to get this test done and we have to get an A. I think the bright kids are honest, but there is a lot of pressure to excel."

Drugs and alcohol: About half of students surveyed said drugs and alcohol are "easy or not very difficult" to obtain at school, while 8 out of 10 students said there is a lot of alcohol use among students in their schools. About 1 in 10 of the students surveyed admitted driving after drinking and about one in four said they have been in cars with drivers who had too much to drink.

Guns: About 28 percent knew someone who had brought a weapon to school, and 45 percent said they own or have access to some kind of gun.

Note: The Who's Who annual survey was conducted among 3,351 16- to 18-year-old students around the country who have an "A" or "B" average. Of those surveyed, 98 percent plan to attend college after high school graduation.

SOURCE: http://cnn.com/US/9601/student_survey/

CONSIDER THIS:
Can we predictably alter human behavior by changing the incentive structure—the expected marginal benefits and/or the expected marginal costs? For example, what do you think would happen to the amount of cheating if more effective ways of catching cheating were implemented or if the penalties were increased? What if drugs, alcohol, and guns all became more difficult to obtain? In each of these situations, we have changed the cost–benefit ratio and would expect behavior to change in predictable directions.

DRUNK DRIVING DRAWS GLOBAL WRATH

PETER GRIER

Alcohol and automobiles are a combustible combination all over the world. Cultural attitudes towards drinking and driving do differ from nation to nation. Penalties vary widely, too: In Bulgaria and El Salvador, driving under the influence can bring the death penalty. In Turkey, offenders may be simply driven 10 miles from town, dumped, and forced to walk home under police escort. . . .

Americans may think that Europe has a more relaxed attitude towards drinking and driving than does the United States. In general, that is not the case. . . . Most U.S. states set the level at which a driver is declared legally drunk at 0.10 percent alcohol in his or her bloodstream. Fifteen have a lower limit of 0.08. . . .European nations tend to have lower blood-alcohol limits. Countries that set the bar at 0.08 include Austria, Canada, Denmark, Great Britain, Ireland, and Spain. France's legal limit is 0.05 (0.08 percent risks time in jail). Other nations with this relatively low limit include Belgium, Finland, Greece, the Netherlands, and Norway.

And while research is sketchy, it appears fewer drivers get behind the wheel drunk in Europe than do in the United States. One study conducted in the late 1980s indicated that about 8 percent of U.S. drivers on the road at night had blood-alcohol levels of 0.05 or higher. The comparable number from France was 5 percent; for Britain, 3 percent; and for the Nordic countries, a remarkably low 1 percent.

SOURCE: http://plweb.csmonitor.com/plweb-turbo/cg

EXHIBIT 1	WHEN YOU'RE LEGALLY DRUNK

When you're legally drunk
(by blood–alcohol level)

.10%

.08%

.05%

Norway   Canada   34 U.S.States

CONSIDER THIS:
The Nordic countries (Finland, Norway, and Sweden) all have lower legal blood-alcohol limits than the United States, and at least one study shows that lower blood-alcohol rates and tougher punishments are deterring many from drinking and driving. How many drunk drivers do you think are on the road in Bulgaria and El Salvador?

CONCEPT CHECK

1. People respond to incentives in predictable ways.
2. A negative incentive increases costs or reduces benefits, thus discouraging consumption or production.
3. A positive incentive decreases costs or increases benefits, thus encouraging consumption or production.

---

1. What is the difference between positive incentives and negative incentives?
2. According to the rule of rational choice, would you do more or less of something if its expected marginal benefits increased?
3. According to the rule of rational choice, would you do more or less of something if its expected marginal costs increased?
4. How does the rule of rational choice imply that young children are typically more likely to misbehave at a supermarket checkout counter than at home?
5. Why do many parents refuse to let their children have dessert before they eat the rest of their dinner?

Specialization and Trade

MODULE 1

- What is the relationship between opportunity cost and specialization?
- What are the advantages of specialization in production?

WHY DO PEOPLE SPECIALIZE?

As you look around you, you can see that people specialize in what they produce. They tend to dedicate their resources to one primary activity, whether it be child-rearing, driving a cab, or making bagels. Why is this? The answer, short and simple, is opportunity costs. By concentrating their energies on the activity to which they are best suited, individuals incur lower opportunity costs. This allows them to make the best use of (and thus gain the most benefit from) their limited resources. If a person, a region, or a country can produce a good or service at a lower opportunity cost than others, we say that they have a **comparative advantage** in the production of that good or service.

DO WE ALL SPECIALIZE?

We all specialize to some extent and rely on others to produce most of the goods and services we want. The work that we choose to do reflects our specialization. For example, we may specialize in selling or fixing automobiles. The wages for that work can then be used to buy goods from a farmer who has chosen to specialize in the production of food. Likewise, the farmer can use the money earned from selling his produce to get his tractor fixed by someone who specializes in that activity.

Specialization is evident not only among individuals but among regions and countries as well. In fact, the story of the economic development of the United States and

TUNE UP

COMPARATIVE ADVANTAGE

Q: Should an attorney who types 100 words per minute hire a secretary to type her legal documents, even though he can only type 50 words per minute? If the attorney does the job, she can do it in 5 hours; if the secretary does the job, it takes him 10 hours. The attorney makes $100 an hour, and the secretary earns $10 an hour. Which one has the comparative advantage (the lowest opportunity cost) in typing documents?

A: If the attorney types her own documents, it will cost $500 ($100 per hour x 5 hours). If she has the secretary type her documents, it will cost $100 ($10 per hour x 10 hours). Clearly, then, the lawyer should hire the secretary to type her documents, because the secretary has the comparative advantage (lowest opportunity cost) in this case, despite being half as good in absolute terms.

Cranberries are cultivated in bogs found primarily in the northeastern United States. Is this an example of regional specialization?

the rest of the world involves specialization. Within the United States, the Midwest with its wheat, the coastal waters of the Northeast with their fishing fleets, and the tall timbers of the Northwest are each examples of regional specialization.

WHAT ARE THE ADVANTAGES OF SPECIALIZATION?

In a small business, employees may perform a wide variety of tasks—from hiring to marketing. As the size of the company increases, each employee can now be used in a more specialized job, with a consequent increase in output per worker. The primary advantages of specialization are that employees acquire greater skill from repetition, they avoid wasted time in shifting from one task to another, and they do the types of work for which they are best suited.

The advantages of specialization are seen throughout the workplace. For example, in larger firms, personnel relations can be conducted by specialists; accounting is put in the hands of full-time accounting experts instead of someone with half a dozen other tasks. The owner of a small retail store selects the location for the store primarily through guesswork, placing it where she believes sales would be high or where an empty, low-rent building is available. In contrast, larger chains have store sites selected by experts who have experience in analyzing the factors that make different locations relatively more desirable like traffic patterns, income levels, demographics, and so on.

Specialization is also possible with capital equipment. As a firm increases its scale of operations, it can replace nonspecialized equipment capable of performing a wide number of tasks with specialized equipment designed for various specific operations. This also increases a firm's productivity.

CAN SPECIALIZATION AND TRADE LEAD TO GREATER WEALTH AND PROSPERITY?

Voluntary exchange directly increases wealth by making both parties better off (or they wouldn't trade). It is the prospect of wealth-increasing exchange that leads to productive specialization. That is, trade increases wealth by allowing a person, a region, or a nation to specialize in those products that it produces better and to trade for those products that others produce better. For example, say the United States is better at producing wheat than Brazil, and Brazil is better at producing coffee than the United States. So the United States and Brazil would benefit if the United States produces wheat and trades some of it to Brazil for coffee. Coffee growers in the United States could grow coffee in expensive greenhouses, but it would result in higher coffee costs and prices, while leaving fewer resources available for employment in more productive jobs, such as wheat production.

MICHAEL JORDAN SIGNS NEW CONTRACT

In late August of 1997, the Chicago Bulls basketball organization signed superstar Michael Jordan to a one-year contract. The agreement was apparently reached after a quick meeting in Las Vegas between Jordan and Bulls owner Jerry Reinsdorf.

The *Chicago Tribune* reported that Jordan was seeking a one-year deal worth at least $36 million. Jordan has led the Bulls to their fifth NBA crown in seven years. In addition, he is reported to make millions more in commercial endorsements.

> **CONSIDER THIS:**
> Michael Jordan is a decent golfer and a good baseball player, and he may even enjoy these sports better than basketball. In fact, Michael did quit basketball to play baseball for the Chicago White Sox organization. What did it cost Michael to play baseball?

CONCEPT CHECK

1. We all specialize.
2. Specialization is important for individuals, businesses, regions, and nations.
3. Specialization and trade increase wealth.
4. The person, region, or country that can produce a good or service at a lower opportunity cost than other producers has a comparative advantage in the production of that good or service.

---

1. Why do people specialize?
2. What do we mean by comparative advantage?
3. Why does the combination of specialization and trade make us better off?
4. If you can mow your lawn in half the time it takes your younger brother to do it, do you have a comparative advantage in mowing the lawn?
5. If you became far more productive than before in completing yard chores, could that eliminate your current comparative advantage in doing the dishes?
6. Could a student who gets a C in one class but a D or worse in everything else have a comparative advantage in that class over someone who gets a B in that class but an A in everything else?
7. How can Michael Jordan help feed more poor people by playing basketball than by serving meals in a homeless shelter?

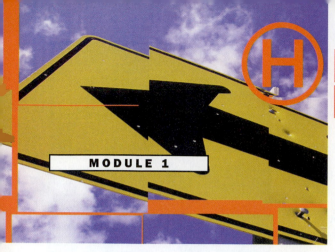

Markets and the Price System

MODULE 1

- How does a market system allocate scarce resources?
- What are the important signals that market prices communicate?
- What are the effects of price controls and price supports?
- What causes miscommunication in the market system?

HOW DO WE DETERMINE WHO GETS WHAT?

Our collective wants far outweigh what the scarce resources nature has provided can produce. So how should we allocate those scarce resources? Some methods of resource allocation might be perceived as bad and counter-productive, like the "survival of the fittest" competition that exists on the floor of the jungle. Physical violence has been used since the beginning of time, as people, regions, and countries attack one another to gain control over resources. One might argue that government should allocate scarce resources on the basis of equal shares or according to need. However, this approach poses problems because of diverse individual preferences, the problem of ascertaining needs, and the negative work and investment incentives involved. In reality, society is made up of many approaches to resource allocation. However, for now, let us take a closer look at the predominant form of allocating goods in most countries—the market system.

In countries that do not use a free market system, there is no clear communication between consumers and suppliers. Bottlenecks, inefficiency, low-quality goods, and shortages often result.

HOW DOES THE MARKET SYSTEM WORK TO ALLOCATE RESOURCES?

The market system provides a way for producers and consumers to communicate about the allocation of scarce resources. Individuals indicate their wants and desires through their actions and inactions in the marketplace, and it is this collective "voice" that determines how resources are allocated. But how is this information communicated? Market prices serve as the language of the market system. By understanding what these market prices mean, you can get a better understanding of the vital function that the market system performs.

HOW DO MARKET PRICES PROVIDE IMPORTANT INFORMATION?

Market prices communicate important information to both consumers and producers. These prices communicate in-

formation about the relative availability of products to consumers, and they provide producers with critical information about the relative value that consumers place on those products. In effect, market prices provide a way for both consumers and producers to communicate about the relative value of resources. This communication results in a shifting of resources from those uses that are less valued to those that are more valued. We will see how this works beginning in Module 4.

WHAT EFFECT DO PRICE CONTROLS HAVE ON THE MARKET SYSTEM?

Government policies sometimes force prices above or below what they would be in a market economy. These are called **price controls.** Unfortunately, these controls often impose harm on the same people they are trying to help, in large part by short-circuiting the market's information transmission function. That is, price controls effectively strip the market price of its meaning for both consumers and suppliers. Consider the following examples: agricultural price supports and the minimum wage.

Agricultural Price Supports

Consider the effects of agricultural price supports on those whose low incomes make proper nutrition a genuine problem. Is a dairy farmer allowed to supply milk to a poor family (or any other family) at prices lower than the government allows? No! That action is currently illegal in the United States because of government restrictions on the prices of dairy products. These government price supports can destroy the communication between farmers and consumers that is provided by the market system, and can lead to the creation of huge stockpiles of some food products.

Minimum Wage

Consider how minimum-wage legislation censors effective communication from teenagers to employers. Many teenagers would like to tell prospective employers, "I have few skills and college is not possible for me. But I am willing to work hard for a low wage now, while I have only a few financial responsibilities, in order to acquire the experience and training necessary for a better paying job later." It is true that in the absence of minimum-wage legislation, some teenagers will express their willingness to work for wages many might consider "obscenely" low.

But an increase in the minimum wage has two effects on teenage employment: (1) The higher minimum wage increases the number of teenagers who want jobs, sometimes even causing them to drop out of school; and (2) the higher minimum wage for low-skilled workers discourages hir-

ing. Together these effects can lead to a large surplus of teenage workers that are actively seeking jobs. That is, the price control can prevent thousands of unemployed youths from preparing productively for their future. Journalists and broadcasters could fill the news with stories of jobless teenagers and the need to expand employment opportunities for our nation's youth. But the effectiveness of this information would be very small in comparison with the information conveyed by lower wages, which would serve to tell employers that teenagers are willing and able to work for less.

CAN THE MARKET FAIL?

The market mechanism is a simple but effective and efficient general means of allocating resources among alternative uses. However, those same markets can sometimes lead to problems as well. For example, a steel firm, as a byproduct of making steel, might put soot and other forms of "crud" into the air. When it does this, it imposes costs on others not connected with using or producing steel from the steel mill. For example, the soot may require homeowners to paint their homes more often, entailing a cost. And studies show that respiratory diseases are greater in areas with more severe air pollution, imposing costs and often shortening life itself. In addition, the steel mill might discharge chemicals into a stream, thus killing wildlife and spoiling recreational activities for the local population. Economists call this type of situation, where the economy fails to allocate resources efficiently on its own, a **market failure**. The case of market failure will be taken up in more detail in Module 6.

In addition, we cannot depend on the market economy to always communicate honestly and accurately. Some firms may have **market power** to distort prices in their favor. For example, the only regional cement company in the area has the ability to charge a higher price and provide lower-quality services than if the company was in a highly competitive market. In this case, the lack of competition can lead to higher prices and reduced product quality. And without adequate information, unscrupulous producers may be able to misrepresent their products to the disadvantage of unwary consumers. This, too, is considered in more depth in Module 6.

If the government subsidizes farmers, they may produce more than consumers want at that price, leading to inefficiency.

The government may be able to correct some market failures through regulation and the dissemination of information. The function of government in the marketplace will be discussed in greater detail in the next Concept.

Sometimes markets fail because producers have too little incentive to clean up their wastes.

CONCEPT CHECK

1. Scarcity forces us to allocate our limited resources.
2. Market prices provide important information to buyers and sellers.
3. Price controls distort market signals.
4. Markets do not always communicate all information accurately.

---

1. Why must every society choose some manner by which to allocate its scarce resources?
2. How does a market system allocate resources?
3. What do market prices communicate to others in society?
4. How do price controls undermine the market as a communication device?
5. Why can markets sometimes fail to allocate resources efficiently?

I Government Policies

MODULE 1

- Why do we need government at all?
- Why can't we rely exclusively on the "invisible hand" of the market to determine economic decisions?
- Why is it so important that the government protect our property rights?

CAN APPROPRIATE GOVERNMENT POLICIES IMPROVE OUR WELL-BEING?

Political scientists, economists, and philosophers have theorized for centuries about the role of the government in society. Governments are institutions devised by humans to serve the collective or group will. According to Nobel laureate Douglass North, the rise in government's role since the Middle Ages reflects changes in perceptions as to the benefits or rewards from such activity relative to the costs of carrying out the activity. At least seven reasons have been used to justify government involvement into the economic decision-making process: (1) government provides a legal framework that enforces and protects property rights; (2) some goods and services are inherently "public"

One of the key functions of government is to provide a legal framework that protects and enforces property rights and contracts.

in character, like national defense; (3) a lack of competition in some cases has led markets to operate inefficiently; (4) by providing information, government can help participants in market activity make better decisions; (5) the existence of externalities—like pollution—can cause inappropriate market signals; (6) the market-determined income distribution may be considered unfair or inequitable; or (7) the overall level of output, employment, or prices may be viewed as being inappropriate if determined by the market mechanism alone.

WHY ARE PROPERTY RIGHTS SO IMPORTANT?

When consumers buy a house, a car, or a pizza, they have purchased the right to use these goods in a way they, not someone else, sees fit. (Of course, the use must also be within the existing legal system; that is, just because you own a car does not give you the right to drive it recklessly.) These rights are called property rights.

Property rights give individuals broad powers to use, sell, rent, dispose of, or enhance the value of goods. If property rights are well defined and respected, then the owner of a resource has confidence that he or she will, by maintaining ownership, benefit from any increase in the future value of the resource. Property rights, then, serve as a powerful incentive for individuals to maintain and conserve their resources.

Why does graffiti cover the walls of public rest rooms but is seldom seen on the walls of bathrooms in private homes? Probably because people are more concerned with the future value of property they own than of property they do not own. In the same sense, if you own your car, you have an incentive to keep the car in good condition with regular oil changes. Do you think this incentive might be less strong if you lease your car rather than buy it?

Why don't we see graffiti in our bathrooms at home?

WHAT IS THE LAW OF UNINTENDED CONSEQUENCES?

When considering the role of government in economic affairs and decisions, it is wise to remember that the actual results of actions are not always as initially intended. This is called the **law of unintended consequences.** As economists, we must always look for the secondary effects of an action that may occur along with the initial effects. In the area of public policy, the government is often well intentioned when it adopts policies to help unskilled workers, poor farmers, or tenants in search of affordable housing; however, such policies can also cause unintended consequences, which may completely undermine the intended effects. For example, rent controls may have an immediate effect of lowering rents, but secondary effects may well include very low vacancy rates, discrimination against low-income and large families, and deterioration of the quality of rental units. Similarly, minimum-wage increases may help many unskilled workers or apprentices, but will result in higher unemployment and a reduction in fringe benefits, such as vacations and discounts to employees. And agricultural price supports may initially help stabilize farmers' incomes, but may eventually lead to unused surpluses of foodstuffs for which the taxpayers will have to pay. As we will learn in the following modules, society has to make tough decisions, and if the government subsidizes some program or groups of people in one area, then something must always be given up somewhere else. The "law of scarcity" can not be repealed!

1. Government can improve our well-being.
2. Property rights provide important incentives.
3. Government policies can correct (and prevent) problems in the market system.

4. The law of unintended consequences states that the results of certain actions may not always be as clear as they initially appear.

---

1. What justifications are there for government involvement in the economic decision-making process?
2. What are property rights?
3. How do different property rights alter incentives?

4. What is the law of unintended consequences?
5. Why is the law of unintended consequences so important in making public policy?
6. Why is the shared, common area of a dormitory often messier than the students' individual rooms?

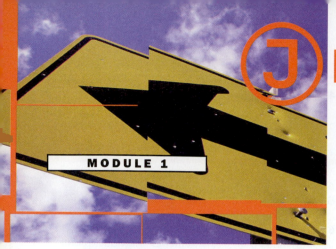

J Economic Growth

MODULE 1

- Why is economic growth desirable?
- Can there be negative side effects of economic growth?
- How can a nation improve its economic growth rate?

ECONOMIC GROWTH CAN IMPROVE STANDARDS OF LIVING

The desire to bring about a long-term increase in the output of goods and services has been expressed with varying degrees of intensity in nearly every economy. The richest nations today have perhaps 50 to 100 times the output levels per person of the poorest countries.

IS ECONOMIC GROWTH GOOD OR BAD?

To be sure, there is not unanimous agreement that economic growth is desirable; some have been outspoken about negative impacts that often accompany economic growth, such as increased environmental problems, growing inequalities, higher crime, a decline in moral standards, and so on. Still, economic growth is proclaimed as a "good" thing by most people, and in many countries it has been the primary concern with respect to public policy. Economic growth, of course, enhances the potential amount of individual consumption; the greater the economic growth, the more goods we and our descendants will have to consume in the future. Economic growth also increases a nation's potential military and political power and enhances prestige.

WHAT CAN A COUNTRY DO TO INCREASE ITS ECONOMIC GROWTH?

Nations engage in a variety of policies designed to increase output over time. Some of these policies are designed to increase capital formation—the construction of tools and machinery today, which increases output in future time periods. In addition, new technology and the adoption of more efficient methods of doing things will lead to higher economic growth rates. Nations with high investment and capital formation have higher average annual economic growth rates (measured in gross domestic product, or GDP), while nations devoting smaller amounts of their output to capital formation have lower growth rates.

Investment in factories and equipment can lead to greater economic growth in the future.

EXHIBIT 1   CORRELATION OF INVESTMENT AND GROWTH

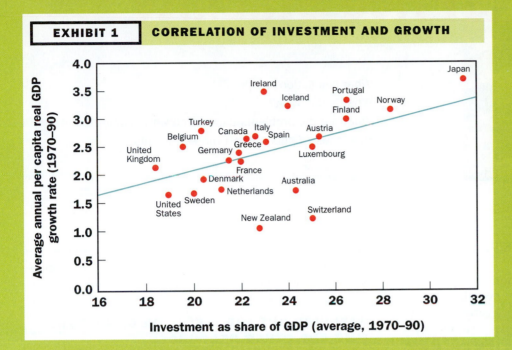

Investment as share of GDP (average, 1970–90)

CONSIDER THIS:
Exhibit 1 shows that there is a close correlation between investment and economic growth. Most economists agree that investment (like new machinery and technology) is an important component of economic growth.

CONCEPT CHECK

1. Economic growth can improve living standards.
2. There can also be negative effects from economic growth, including higher crime and increased environmental problems.
3. A country can increase its economic growth through technology and investing in physical capital (machines and tools) and human capital (education and training).

1. Why do we want economic growth to take place?
2. Can economic growth have negative side effects?
3. What sorts of policies can encourage economic growth?
4. Is it possible for economic growth to increase the quality of the environment?
5. If a country is building a bridge or road that nobody uses, will that kind of investment contribute to economic growth?

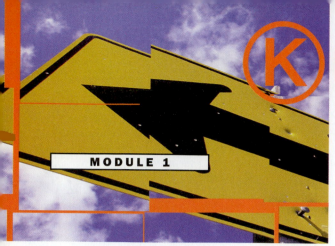

Ⓚ Price Stability

MODULE 1

- What is inflation?
- What is deflation?
- What are the problems associated with inflation?
- How does inflation distort market signals?

WHAT IS INFLATION? WHAT IS DEFLATION?

When overall prices are rising (even though some prices may be falling), we have **inflation.** When overall prices are falling (even though some prices may be rising), we have **deflation.** In either case, the purchasing power of money is changing. With inflation, the purchasing power of money is falling; with deflation, it is rising. Ideally, an economy would have a stable monetary environment—a situation in which the economy is experiencing neither inflation nor deflation.

DOES A STABLE MONETARY ENVIRONMENT LEAD TO BETTER DECISION MAKING?

A stable monetary environment leads to price stability and enables producers and consumers to better coordinate their plans and decisions through the market. Inflation brings about changes in incomes of persons, and these changes may be undesirable. The redistributional impact of inflation need not be the result of conscious public policy; it just happens. Moreover, inflation can raise one nation's prices relative to prices in other countries, which will either lead to difficulties in financing purchases of foreign goods or to a decline in the value of the national currency relative to that of other countries. In its extreme form, inflation can lead to a complete erosion of faith in the value of money. After both World Wars, prices in Germany rose so fast that, in some cases, people finally refused to take paper money, insisting instead on payment in goods or metals.

DOES INFLATION DISTORT PRICE SIGNALS?

In periods of high and variable inflation, households and firms have a difficult time distinguishing changes in the relative prices of individual goods and services from changes in the general price level of all goods and services. Inflation distorts the information that flows from price signals. Does the good have a higher price because it has become relatively more scarce, and therefore more valuable relative to

other goods, or did the price rise along with all other prices because of inflation? This muddying of the information reflected in prices undermines good decision making.

WATCHING OUT FOR INFLATION CAN WASTE TIME AND OTHER RESOURCES

Households nervous about higher inflation rates in the future that may never materialize may decide to reduce their current saving and increase their current consumption instead. In an inflationary climate, investors nervous about hikes in wages and interest rates might pass up investments, particularly long-term investments that might have been pursued if prices were stable. In addition, households, producers, and investors will spend costly resources looking for ways to guard their assets and wealth from inflation. If it were not for unpredictable prices, these resources could be used more productively from society's perspective.

Unanticipated changes in overall prices increase uncertainty for decision makers.

1. When overall prices are rising, we have inflation.
2. When overall prices are falling, we have deflation.
3. A stable monetary environment allows consumers and producers to do a better job coordinating their plans and decisions.
4. Consumers, producers, and investors spend costly resources guarding their assets against inflation.

---

1. What is inflation?
2. What is deflation?
3. Why is price stability useful?
4. How can inflation distort price signals?
5. Why is the mere *possibility* of inflation costly to society?
6. Why does writing a five-year supply agreement for coal become more difficult when the future price level becom33es more uncertain?

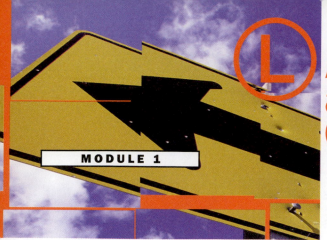

Application: Laws and Enforcement Costs

Most of economics comes down to the fifth powerful idea—incentives matter. Can you see how the concepts of (1) incentives matter and (2) scarcity are demonstrated in this article?

MONTANA RAISES FINES FOR VIOLATORS

JOHN HOLT

Violators of Montana fish and game laws will pay at least twice as much in fines under a bill signed into law by Governor Marc Raciot. Senate Bill 210 increases the minimum fine for violations from $50 to $100 and the maximum fine from $1,000 to $2,000.

Other increases include the following:

1. The fine for illegally killing a black bear has been doubled to $2,000.

2. The fine for illegally catching a bull trout has increased from $10 to $500.

3. The fine for illegally killing an arctic grayling has increased from $10 to $300.

SOURCE: *Outdoor Life,* August 1995.

Sometimes it is less expensive to substitute tougher statutes and fines for increasing state or federal budgets to enforce laws more vigorously. In this case, an alternative to charging higher fines would be to add additional rangers, game wardens, and the like. However, this might prove to be prohibitively expensive because costly scarce resources would have to be used to comb the vast wilderness, which is not easily patrolled. Because the probability of being detected is lower, the higher fine should deter some from illegal hunting and fishing activities without adding additional and costly wildlife personnel. That is, substituting fines for monitoring is a relatively inexpensive method for deterring illegal behavior. For example, if the fine for illegally killing a black bear was raised to $100,000 and a five-year mandatory prison sentence, we would expect that the Department of Fish and Game would only have to enforce the laws casually; that is, because incentives matter, most hunters would be deterred by the stringent fine. This line of reasoning can be used in other areas of public policy. For example, a lower blood-alcohol level requirement on drinking and driving can be substituted for more costly choices like sobriety checkpoints and increasing the number of police officers.

IN THE BLEACHERS   By Steve Moore

© 1998 Universal Press Syndicate

"It's a Fed! ... Act natural."

Are laws against fishing without a license tough to enforce?

SOURCE: Moore, Universal Press Syndicate, May 19, 1998. Also see http://www.uexpress.com

Do incentives matter? You bet! Need an incentive to check out your Workbook? The problems and questions you will find in the Workbook and on your EconActive CD-ROM will help to reinforce your understanding of key concepts and ideas for each Module. Check them out!

1. Which of the following is an example of a positive incentive?

   A. Your dad says he will ground you if you flunk your high school physics class.

   B. The police in your town give a speeding ticket to anyone who drives over 25 miles per hour.

   C. Your math teacher says she will give a free laptop computer to each student who scores over 90 percent on the midterm exam.

   D. Your piano teacher raps you on the knuckles every time you hit a wrong note.

2. Which of the following is an example of a negative incentive?

   A. The Seattle Mariners give Ken Griffey, Jr. $10,000 for every home run he hits.

   B. The Chicago Bulls fine Dennis Rodman $10,000 every time he is late for practice.

   C. The New York Liberty give Rebecca Lobo $10,000 each time she scores over 30 points in a game.

   D. Mercury Records give Hanson an extra $300,000 for each week any of their songs is number one on the Billboard charts.

PHOTO CREDITS MODULE 1

Page **4:** © Ken Chernus/FPG International; Page **5:** top, Jack Ziegler © 1991 from The New Yorker Collection. All Rights Reserved; bottom, © PhotoDisc; Page **7:** © PhotoDisc; Page **8:** Reprinted with permission of Hank Ketchum and North American Syndicate; Page **9:** © Bebeto Matthews/AP Wide World Photos; Page **10:** © AP/Wide World Photos; Page **11:** © D. Stoecklein/The Stock Solution; Page **12:** © PhotoDisc; Page **13:** Reprinted with special permission of King Features Syndicate; Page **14:** top, © Thaves/Reprinted with permission; bottom, BMW Corporation; Page **15:** © Alan Schein/The Stock Market; Page **16:** © PhotoDisc; Page **17:** © Terry Qing/FPG International; Page **18:** © PhotoDisc; Page **22:** © Peter Southwick/Stock, Boston/PNI; Page **23:** © Ron Vesely Photography; Page **24:** © Erica Lansner/Tony Stone Images; Page **25:** © Edith Haun/Stock, Boston/PNI; Page **26:** © T/Maker Company; Page **27:** © J. Neubauer/H. Armstrong Roberts; Page **28:** © 1998 Don Couch Photography; Page **30:** © Vladimir Pcholkin/FPG International; Page **32:** U.S. Treasury Department; Page **34:** © Tim Fitzharris/Masterfile; Page **35:** © Steve Moore. Reprinted with permission of UNIVERSAL PRESS SYNDICATE. All rights reserved.

The Role and Method of Economics

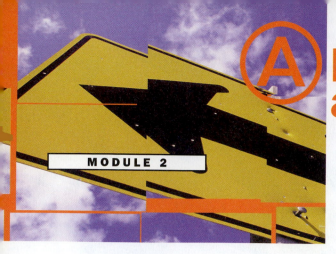

(A) Economics as a Science

- How is economics similar to other social sciences?
- What are macroeconomics and microeconomics?
- Are microeconomic tools important to macroeconomists?
- Why study economics?

WHY IS ECONOMICS A SOCIAL SCIENCE?

Like psychology, sociology, anthropology, and political science—the social sciences—economics is concerned with reaching generalizations about human behavior. Because the social sciences all have the same primary focus, it should not come as a surprise that the investigations in these spheres often overlap and can complement one another. For example, an economist might analyze the impact of a given tax policy, while a political scientist might examine the process that led to the adoption of the policy. Or an economist might study the change in the crime rate, while a psychologist may try to figure out what makes the criminal mind work. Social scientists, then, may be studying the same issue but from different perspectives.

MACROECONOMICS AND MICROECONOMICS

Conventionally, we distinguish two main branches of economics, macroeconomics and microeconomics. **Macroeconomics** deals with the total economy; it looks at economic problems as they influence the whole of society. For example, topics covered in macroeconomics include discussions of inflation, unemployment, business cycles, and economic growth. **Microeconomics,** by contrast, deals with the smaller units within the economy, attempting to understand the decision-making behavior of firms and households and their interaction in markets for particular goods or services. Microeconomic topics include discussions of health care, agricultural subsidies, the price of energy or running shoes, the distribution of income, and the impact of unions on wages.

We Look at the Small to Understand the Large

While macroeconomics and microeconomics might emphasize different topics, they are both ultimately striving to understand people's behavior. Microeconomics analyzes smaller pieces of the economy, in part to better understand the large. The study of microeconomics has

Microeconomics helps us understand why ice cream costs what it does, while macroeconomics increases our understanding of inflation, unemployment, and economic growth.

helped economists gain a greater understanding about many macroeconomic topics, including interest rates, economic growth, unemployment, and the price level. However, both are concerned with social coordination—how humans interact with each other in a dynamic world.

WHY STUDY ECONOMICS?

While there are many good reasons to study economics, perhaps the best reason is that so many of the things of concern in the world around us are at least partly economic in character. A quick look at newspaper headlines reveals the vast range of problems that are related to economics—global warming, welfare reform, health care, education, and Social Security. The study of economics improves your understanding of these concerns. A student of economics becomes aware that, at a basic level, much of economic life involves choosing among alternative possible courses of action—making choices between our conflicting wants and desires in a world of scarcity. Economics provides some clues as to how to intelligently evaluate these options and determine the most appropriate choices in given situations. But economists learn quickly that there are seldom easy, clear-cut solutions to the problems we face—the easy problems were solved long ago!

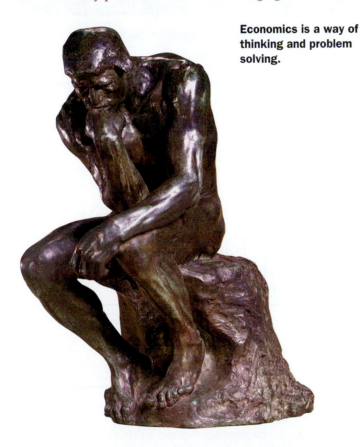

Economics is a way of thinking and problem solving.

Of course, there are other reasons to study economics. Many students take introductory college-level economics courses because they are required to as part of a general education curriculum or breadth requirements. But why do the committees that establish these requirements include economics? In part, because economics helps develop a disciplined method of thinking about problems. You see, while economics may not always give you clear-cut answers, it will give you something very useful: the

economic way of thinking. The problem-solving tools you will develop by studying economics will prove valuable to you both in your personal and professional life, regardless of your career choice.

Will You Ever Really Use This Stuff?

The basic tools of economics are valuable to people in all walks of life and in all career paths. Newspaper reporters benefit from economics, because the problem-solving perspective it teaches trains them to ask intelligent questions whose answers will better inform their readers. Engineers, architects, and contractors usually have alternative ways to build. Architects learn to combine technical expertise and artistry with the limitations imposed by finite resources. That is, they learn how to evaluate their options from an economic perspective. Clothing designers face similar problems, because costs are a constraint in both creating and marketing new apparel. Will the added cost of a more expensive fabric be outweighed by the added sales revenues that are expected to result? Economists cannot answer such questions in a general sense because the answers depend on the circumstances. Economists can, however, pose these questions and provide criteria that clothing designers can use in evaluating the appropriateness of one fabric as compared to another. The point is that the economic way of thinking causes those in many types of fields to ask the right kinds of questions. As John Maynard Keynes once remarked:

> The object of our analysis is not to provide a machine or method of blind manipulation, which will furnish an infallible answer, but to provide ourselves with an organized and orderly method of thinking out particular problems; and, after we have reached a provisional conclusion by isolating the complicating factors one by one, we then have to go back on ourselves and allow, as well as we can, for the probable interactions of the factors amongst themselves. This is the nature of economic thinking."[1]

Will an Understanding of Economics Make You a Financial Wizard?

Some people think that economics may be a useful course of study, hoping that it will tell them how to become successful in a financial sense. If this is your goal in studying economics, you may be disappointed. While most economists make a good living, few have gotten very rich from their knowledge of economics. In fact, if economists had some secret for making money in, for example, the stock market, they would likely be using those secrets to their own financial advantage rather than making less money doing things such as teaching. Moreover, if economists did have some secret for making money, they would not be

---

[1] See J. M. Keynes, *General Theory of Employment Interest and Money* (New York: Harcourt Brace, 1936), p. 297.

likely to let non-economists in on it, because economic theory suggests (as will be clear later) that disclosure of the secret would reduce or eliminate the possibility of the economists' earning further income from this knowledge. Still, having some knowledge of the workings of market forces is likely to help individuals make more informed and appropriate decisions, including financial decisions. In short, economics won't necessarily make you rich, but it may keep you from making some decisions that would make you poorer.

While economics is a problem-solving science, it probably won't make you a stock market genius.

CONCEPT CHECK

1. Economics is concerned with reaching generalizations about human behavior.
2. Economics provides tools to intelligently evaluate and decide on choices.
3. Macroeconomics deals with the aggregate, or total, economy.
4. Microeconomics focuses on smaller units within the economy—firms and households.

1. What makes economics a social science?
2. What distinguishes macroeconomics from microeconomics?
3. Why is it worth studying economics?
4. Why is the market for running shoes considered a microeconomic topic?
5. Why is inflation considered a macroeconomic topic?

B Economic Behavior

MODULE 2

- What is self-interest?
- What is rational behavior?
- Why is observation more difficult in the social sciences?
- Can economists predict human behavior?

SELF-INTEREST AND RATIONAL BEHAVIOR

Is it rational for people to try to improve their own situation? Economists think so. We call this **self-interest.** Economists assume that self-interest is the motivation behind economic behavior. To economists, individuals are acting "rationally" if they are striving to do their best to achieve their goals with their limited income, time, and knowledge. That is, economists believe that when individuals act to advance their own self-interest, it is rational behavior.

ACTION AND INACTIONS HAVE CONSEQUENCES

Most economists also believe that rational behavior includes *trying* to anticipate the likely future consequences of one's behavior. For example, if someone with a suspended driver's license chooses to illegally drive an automobile, we presume that the individual considered the consequences of this action before he made that decision. That does not necessarily mean that he will not drive illegally, merely that he will consider the consequences of that action—perhaps a serious jail sentence or an impounded car—before he makes his choice. Or if someone decides to take up smoking, she is presumed by economists to have thought about the consequences of that action. An individual may still decide to smoke, but he or she will have at least considered the potential results of that action. Actions (even inactions, which are choices to not make changes) have consequences!

WHY ARE OBSERVATION AND PREDICTION HARDER IN THE SOCIAL SCIENCES?

Working from observations, scientists try to make generalizations that will enable them to predict certain events. However, observation and prediction are more difficult in the social sciences than in physical sciences such as physics, chemistry, and astronomy. Why? The major reason for the difference is that the social scientists, including economists, are concerned with *human* behavior. And human behavior is more variable and often less readily predictable than the behavior of experiments observed in a laboratory. However, by looking at the actions of a large group of people, economists can still make many reliable predictions about human behavior.

WHY DO ECONOMISTS PREDICT ON A GROUP LEVEL?

Economists' predictions usually refer to the collective behavior of large groups rather than to that of specific individuals. Why is this? Looking at the behaviors of a large group allows economists to discern general patterns of actions. For example, consider what would happen if the price of air travel from the United States to Europe was reduced drastically, say from $500 to $200, because of the invention of a more fuel-efficient jet. What type of predictions could we make about the effect of this price reduction on the buying habits of typical consumers?

Actions have consequences!

What Does Individual Behavior Tell Us?

Let's look first at the responses of individuals. As a result of the price drop, some people will greatly increase their intercontinental travel, taking theater weekends in London or week-long trips to France to indulge in French food. Some people, however, are terribly afraid to fly, and the price reduction will not influence their behavior in the slightest. Others might detest Europe and, despite the lowered airfares, prefer to spend a few days in Aspen, Colorado, instead. A few people might respond to the airfare reduction in precisely the opposite way from ours: At the lower fare, they might make fewer trips to Europe, because they might believe (rightly or wrongly) that the price drop would be accompanied by a reduction in the quality of service, greater crowding, or reduced safety. In short, we cannot predict with any level of certainty how a given individual will respond to this airfare reduction.

What Does Group Behavior Tell Us?

While we cannot say what each individual will do, within a group of persons, we can predict with great accuracy that more flights to Europe will be sold at lower prices than at higher prices, holding other things such as income and preferences constant. We cannot predict exactly how many more tickets will be sold at $200 than at $500, but we can

Flug Flight		nach to	über via	planm. scheduled	verspätet delayed	Schalter Counter
LG	302	LUXEMBURG		930		113-33
AZ	419	TURIN		935		339-34
LH	1122	NEAPEL		935		113-33
LH	1906	MADRID		935		113-33
LH	1022	STUTTGART HBF.		935		-
AF	1701	LYON		940		683-68
AY	822	HELSINKI		940		113-33
AA	071	SFRANCISCO-DALLAS		945		731-73
AF	743	PARIS		945		683-68
LH	1116	VENEDIG		945		113-33
DL	023	DALLAS		950		478-48
GA	892	AMSTERDAM		950		721-72

Abflug

If airfares to Europe rise, what would you expect to happen to the number of people traveling to Europe by plane?

predict the direction of the impact and approximate the extent of the impact. By observing the relationship between the price of goods and services and the quantities people purchase in different places and during different time periods, it is possible to make some reliable generalizations about how much people will react to changes in the prices of goods and services. Economists use this larger picture of the group for most of their theoretical analysis.

CONCEPT CHECK

1. It is rational for people to act in their own self-interest and try to improve their situation.
2. People try to anticipate the likely consequences of their actions.
3. Economists generally predict group behavior rather than individual behavior.

1. What do economists mean by self-interest?
2. What does rational behavior involve?
3. Why are observation and prediction more difficult in the social sciences?
4. Why do economic predictions refer to the behavior of groups of people rather than individuals?
5. Why is it typically rational for students to make some mistakes (get less than 100 percent) on a test?
6. Can you sometimes get a high grade on a test without studying? Does that mean that additional studying does not lead to higher grades?

© Economic Theory

- What are economic theories?
- What can we expect out of our theories?
- Why do we need to abstract?
- What is a hypothesis?
- What is empirical analysis?

WHAT ARE ECONOMIC THEORIES?

A theory is an established explanation that accounts for known facts or phenomena. Specifically, **economic theories** are statements or propositions about patterns of human behavior that are expected to take place under certain circumstances. These theories help us to sort out and understand the complexities of economic behavior. People ask many things of theories. But most of all, we expect a good theory to explain and predict well. A good economic theory, then, should help us to better understand and, ideally, predict human economic behavior.

WHY IS ABSTRACTION NECESSARY?

Economic theories cannot realistically include every event that has ever occurred. This is true for the same reason that

How is economic theory like a map?

a newspaper or history book does not include every world event that has ever happened. We must abstract. A road map of the United States may not include every creek, ridge, and gully from Los Angeles to Chicago—indeed, such a map would be too large to be of value—but it will provide enough information for a traveler to reach Chicago if traveling by car from Los Angeles. Likewise, an economic theory provides a broad view, not a detailed examination, of human economic behavior.

HOW DO ECONOMISTS DEVELOP THEIR THEORIES?

The beginning of any theory is a hypothesis, a testable proposition that makes some type of prediction about behavior in response to certain changed conditions. A hypothesis in economic theory is a testable prediction about how people will behave or react to a change in economic circumstances. For example, if the prices charged for compact discs (CDs) increase, we might hypothesize that fewer CDs would be sold or if the price of CDs fell we might hypothesize that more CDs would be sold. Once a hypothesis is stated, it is tested by comparing what it predicts to what actually happens.

Why Do We Use Empirical Analysis?

To see if our hypothesis is valid, we must engage in an empirical analysis. That is, we must examine the data to see if our hypothesis fits well with the facts. If the hypothesis is consistent with real-world observations, it is accepted; if it does not fit well with the facts, it is "back to the drawing board."

Determining whether an economic hypothesis is acceptable is more difficult than is the case in the natural or physical sciences. A chemist, for example, can observe chemical reactions under laboratory conditions. He or she can alter the environment to meet the assumptions of the hypothesis and can readily manipulate the variables (chemicals,

Economists are not so fortunate to have controlled experiments like this.

temperatures, and so on) crucial to the proposed relationship. Such controlled experimentation is seldom possible in economics. The laboratory of economists is usually the real world. And unlike a chemistry lab, economists cannot easily control all the other variables that might influence human behavior.

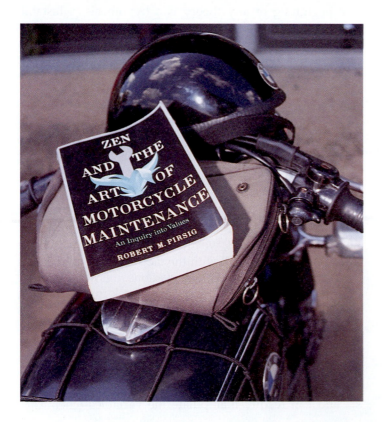

FROM HYPOTHESIS TO THEORY

After gathering his or her data, an economic researcher must then evaluate the results to determine whether the hypothesis is supported or refuted. If it is supported, the hypothesis can then be tentatively accepted as an economic theory.

Zen and the Art of Scientific Thinking

Economists, like motorcycle mechanics, interweave theory and observations to solve problems. For example, an economist might hypothesize that people tend to buy more oranges at lower prices than higher prices. He then might test that hypothesis; and if he then observed in one region after another that when the price of oranges increased, people bought fewer oranges and that when the price of oranges fell, people bought more oranges, he would conclude that people tend to buy more oranges at lower prices than at higher prices. This is the pathway to scientific thinking that leads to problem solving. Robert Pirsig, in his classic book, *Zen and the Art of Motorcycle Maintenance,* maps out this pathway in the following excerpt.

> Part Three, [is] that part of formal scientific method called experimentation . . . A motorcycle mechanic, . . . who honks the horn to see if the battery works is informally conducting a true scientific experiment. He is testing a hypothesis by putting the question to nature . . . An experiment is never a failure solely because it fails to achieve predicted results. An experiment is a failure only when it also fails adequately to test the hypothesis in question, when the data it produces don't prove anything one way or another. Skill at this point consists of using experi-

ments that test only the hypothesis in question, nothing less, nothing more. If the horn honks, and the mechanic concludes that the whole electrical system is working, he is in deep trouble. He has reached an illogical conclusion. The honking horn only tells him that the battery and horn are working. To design an experiment properly he has to think very rigidly in terms of what directly causes what . . . The horn doesn't make the cycle go. Neither does the battery, except in a very indirect way. The point at which the electrical system *directly* causes the engine to fire is at the spark plugs, and if you don't test here, at the output of the electrical system, you will never really know whether the failure is electrical or not.

To test properly the mechanic removes the plug and lays it against the engine so that the base around the plug is electrically grounded, kicks the starter lever and watches the spark-plug gap for a blue spark. If there isn't any he can conclude one of two things: (a) there is an electrical failure or (b) his experiment is sloppy. If he is experienced he will try it a few more times, checking connections, trying every way he can think of to get that plug to fire. Then, if he can't get it to fire, he finally concludes that (a) is correct, there's an electrical failure, and the experiment is over . . .

. . . skill comes in stating no more than the experiment has proved. It hasn't proved that when he fixes the electrical system the motorcycle will start. There may be other things wrong. But he does know that the motorcycle isn't going to run until the electrical system is working . . ."[1]

[1] Robert Pirsig, *Zen and the Art of Motorcycle Maintenance* (New York: William Morrow and Company, Inc.), pp. 93–96.

Was Dinkins' hypothesis tested empirically?

THE FAR SIDE   By GARY LARSON

**"Oh, and *that* makes me feel even worse! ...
I laughed at Dinkins when he said his
new lenses were indestructible."**

CONCEPT CHECK

1. Economic theories are statements about patterns of human behavior.
2. We must abstract.
3. A hypothesis makes a prediction about human behavior.

4. We use empirical analysis to examine the data and see if our hypothesis fits well with the facts.

1. What are economic theories?
2. What is the purpose of a theory?
3. Why must economic theories be abstract?

4. What is a hypothesis? How do we determine if it is tentatively accepted?

Problems with Scientific Thinking

- What is the *ceteris paribus* assumption?
- If events are associated with each other, does that mean one event caused the other to happen?
- What is the fallacy of composition?

In our discussion of economic theory and model building, we have not yet mentioned that there are certain problems that may hinder scientific and logical thinking. We will discuss several problems of concern in this Concept.

WHAT IS THE *CETERIS PARIBUS* ASSUMPTION?

One condition common to virtually all theories in economics is usually expressed by use of the Latin expression *ceteris paribus.* This roughly means "let everything else be equal" or "holding everything else constant." In trying to assess the effect of one variable on another, we must isolate their relationship from other events that might also influence the situation that the theory tries to explain or predict. To make this clearer, we will illustrate this concept with a couple of examples.

Suppose you develop your own theory describing the relationship between studying and exam performance: If I study harder, I will perform better on the test. That sounds logical, right? Holding other things constant (*ceteris paribus*), this is likely to be true. However, what if you studied harder but inadvertently overslept the day of the exam, or were so sleepy during the test that you could not "think straight," failing it? Or what if you studied the wrong material? While it may look like additional studying did not improve your performance, the real problem may lie in the impact of other variables such as sleep deficiency or how you studied.

Researchers must be careful to hold other things constant (*ceteris paribus*). For example, in 1936, cars were inexpensive by modern standards, yet few were purchased; in 1949, cars were much more expensive, but more were bought. This

It Needs No Breaking-In

You can take a Ford V-8 right out of the dealer's showrooms and drive it across the country. For it needs no breaking-in. You can drive it 60 miles an hour the day you buy it. . . . This means more efficient, useful service for every one—more enjoyable motoring because you do not have to drag along for 500 or 1000 miles. . . . The reason for this fine-car feature is as important as the result. . . . The Ford V-8 needs no breaking-in because of unusual accuracy in the manufacture of moving parts and the smoothness of bearing surfaces. Clearances are correct when you buy the car. You do not have to depend on a long wearing-in period to eliminate tightness and insure smooth running. . . . Formerly, only the most expensive cars could be driven at normal speed from the beginning. That still holds true today—except in the case of the Ford V-8. . . . Fine-car construction means fine-car performance.

NEW FORD V·8 FOR 1936

$25 A MONTH, WITH USUAL DOWN-PAYMENT, BUYS ANY NEW FORD V-8 CAR ON UCC ½ PER CENT PER MONTH FINANCE PLANS

'49 Ford

See it today at your Ford Dealers!

Between 1936 and 1949, car prices increased and sales increased. Does this mean that people are willing to buy more at higher prices than at lower prices?

statement appears to imply that people prefer to buy more when prices are higher. However, we know from ample empirical observations that this is not the case—buyers are only willing to buy more at lower prices, *ceteris paribus*. Several other important variables, particularly the purchasing power of dollars, the income of potential car buyers, and the quality of cars, were not constant over this period.

IS ASSOCIATION ALWAYS CAUSATION?

Without a theory of causation, no scientist could sort out and understand the enormous complexity that occurs in the real world. But one must always be careful not to confuse **association** with **causation.** In other words, the fact that two sets of phenomena are related does not necessarily mean that one caused the other to occur. For example, say a ground hog awakes after a long winter of hibernation, climbs out of his hole, sees his shadow—and then six weeks of bad weather ensue. Did the groundhog cause the bad weather? Similarly, Cal Ripkin's consecutive game streak in baseball started at the same time that the Weather Channel was introduced on television. Does that mean that the two events are systematically related? It is highly unlikely.

Confusing association and causation can lead to three different types of misinterpretations. First, there may be no causation between the two variables. Second, there may be a third variable that is responsible for causing both events.

Cal Ripkin's consecutive game streak started at the same time the Weather Channel went on the air. Did one cause the other to happen?

Third, the causality may run in the opposite direction. Let us look at each of these problems separately.

No Causation between the Two Variables

Although two variables may appear to be interrelated, they may not be related at all. For example, if students sitting in the back of the classroom get lower grades on a particular test, does that mean that sitting in the back of the classroom causes lower grades? Clearly, the answer is no.

It is also important to remember that the reoccurrence of a certain relationship between two variables does not necessarily strengthen the argument for causation. That is, because two things happen together more than once does not necessarily make it more likely that one causes the other. Similar events, or clusters, often happen by chance. For example, the pockets of cancer that occur around power lines may not be related to the power lines at all—they may just be clusters.

THE WALL STREET JOURNAL

"I have some good news. While your cholesterol level has remained the same, the research findings have changed."

Additional Variable Causing the Relationship

Although two variables may appear to be causally related, it may be that a third, unidentified factor is in fact responsible for the relationship. For example, the Food and Drug Administration proposed banning the artificial sweetener saccharin for human use in 1978 because studies indicated that the substance caused bladder cancer in rats. However, in 1992, researchers discovered that it was saccharin's interaction with the rat urine, a third variable, rather than saccharin itself, that made rats susceptible to bladder cancer.

Sometimes a third variable is responsible.

Causality May Run in the Opposite Direction

Sometimes it may appear that one variable causes another, when, in fact, just the opposite is true. For example, the fact that overweight individuals drink diet soda does not mean that diet soda causes obesity. It is much more likely that the opposite is true: Overweight individuals drink diet soda to help them control their weight. Likewise, although a rooster always crows before the sun comes up, it does not cause the sun to rise; rather, the light from the sunrise causes the rooster to crow.

WHAT IS THE FALLACY OF COMPOSITION?

One must also be careful with problems associated with aggregation, particularly the **fallacy of composition.** That is, even if something is true for an individual, it is not necessarily true for many individuals as a group. For example, say you are at a Green Bay Packer game and you decide to stand up to get a better view of the playing field. This works as long as no one else stands up. But what would happen if everyone stood up at the same time? Then, standing up would not let fans see better. Hence, what may be true for an individual does not always hold true in the aggregate. The same can be said of arriving to class early to get a better parking place—what if everyone arrived early? Or studying harder to get a better grade in a class that is graded on a curve—what if everyone studied harder? All of these are examples of the fallacy of composition.

Why Is There an Association between Ice Cream Sales and Crime? Did you know that when ice cream sales rise, so do crime rates? What do you think causes the two events to occur together? Some might think that the higher crime rate might be caused by the sugar "high" in the ice cream. Excess sugar in a snack was actually used in court testimony in a murder case—the so called "twinkie defense." However, it is more likely that crime peaks in the summer because of weather, more people on vacations (leaving their homes vacant), teenagers out of school, and so on. It just happens that ice cream sales also peak in those months because of weather. The lesson: One must always be careful not to confuse *association* with *causation*.

Can you get a better view by standing up?

HEAVY METAL MUSIC AND TEEN SUICIDE

KAREN R. SCHEEL

Many parents and mental health professionals have watched the rising rate of adolescent suicide and the growing popularity of heavy metal music among teenagers and wondered, with some concern, if there is any connection between the two phenomena. A new study . . . offers the first direct assessment of the suicidal risk of American adolescent heavy metal fans compared to that of peers who do not like heavy metal music.

For the study, 121 midwestern public high school students (mean age 17.2) were given two psychological assessments, the Reasons for Living Inventory (RFL) and the Suicide Risk Questionnaire (SRQ) (both measures of risk for suicide), and their musical preferences were assessed.

Compared with fans of country, pop/mainstream, rock, and rap music, heavy metal fans had lower scores on the RFL (indicating greater risk of suicide) and they were more likely to say they occasionally or seriously thought about killing themselves (74 percent versus 35 percent for females; 42 percent versus 15 percent for males).

But the author cautions that while these findings "do suggest that a teenager's liking of heavy metal music may be a useful 'red flag' for suicidal vulnerability for psychologists and other professionals who work with adolescents," she adds that these findings should not be thought of as indicative of imminent suicidal risk and that they "are not suggestive of any important causal effects of heavy metal listening on suicidality."

Does heavy metal music cause increases in teen suicide rates?

CONSIDER THIS:
Note how the researcher cautions against any determination of causality. Perhaps the causality runs in the other direction: Kids that are at greater risk for suicide may like heavy metal music. Perhaps some other variables are causing the association, like genetic predisposition, peer pressure, environment, or a host of other things.

SOURCE: http://cybertowers.com/selfhelp/boards/teen/board1.shtml. December 12, 1997.

CONCEPT CHECK

1. In order to isolate the effects of one variable on another, we use the *ceteris paribus* assumption.
2. The fact that two events are related does not mean that one caused the other to occur.
3. What is true for the individual is not necessarily true for the group.

---

1. Why do economists hold other things constant *(ceteris paribus)*?
2. What is the relationship between association and causation?
3. To what types of misinterpretations does confusing association and causation lead?
4. What is the fallacy of composition?
5. If U.S. consumers bought more gasoline in 1998, when prices averaged $1.20 per gallon, than they did in 1970, when prices averaged $0.30 per gallon, does that mean that people buy more gas at higher prices? Why or why not?
6. If rain dancing is correlated with rain, does that mean that rain dancing causes rain? Why or why not?
7. Why could getting up earlier to beat the other fishermen to the fish lead anglers to catch the same number of fish at 5 A.M. as they would at noon?

E Positive and Normative Analysis

■ What is positive analysis?
■ What is normative analysis?
■ Why do economists disagree?

WHAT IS POSITIVE ANALYSIS?

Most economists view themselves as scientists seeking the truth about the way people behave. They make speculations about economic behavior, and then (ideally) they try to assess the validity of these predictions based on human experience. Their work emphasizes how people behave, rather than how they should behave. In the role of scientist, an economist tries to objectively observe patterns of behavior without reference to the appropriateness or inappropriateness of that behavior. This objective, value-free approach, utilizing the scientific method, is called **positive analysis.** In positive analysis, we want to know the impact of variable A on variable B. We want to be able to test a hypothesis. For example, the following is a positive statement: If rent controls are imposed, vacancy rates will fall. This statement is testable. A positive statement does not have to be a true statement, but it does have to be a testable statement.

However, keep in mind that it is doubtful that even the most objective scientist can be totally value-free in his or her analysis. An economist may well emphasize data or evidence that supports his hypothesis, putting less weight on other evidence that might be contradictory. This, alas, is human nature. But a good economist/scientist strives to be as fair and objective as possible in evaluating evidence and in stating conclusions based on the evidence.

WHAT IS NORMATIVE ANALYSIS?

Economists, of course, have opinions and make value judgments. When economists, or anyone else for that matter, express opinions about some economic policy or happening, they are stating in part how they believe things should be, not just facts as to the way things are. Opinions expressed about the desirability of various actions are called **normative statements.** Normative statements in-

Because of normative analysis, it is not unusual, as in 1996, for two presidential candidates with different policy beliefs to each receive the support of Nobel Prize winners in economics.

volve judgments about what should be or what ought to happen. For example, one could judge that incomes should be more equally distributed. If there is a change in tax policy that makes incomes more equal, there will be positive economics questions that can be investigated, such as how work behavior will change. But we cannot say, as scientists, that such a policy is good or bad; rather, we can point to what will likely happen if the policy is adopted.

WHY DO I NEED TO KNOW THE DIFFERENCE?

The distinction between positive and normative analysis is important. It is one thing to say that everyone should have universal health care, a normative statement, and quite another to say that universal health care would lead to greater worker productivity, a testable positive statement. It is important to distinguish between positive and normative analysis because many controversies in economics revolve around policy considerations that contain both. When economists start talking about how the economy *should* work rather that how it does work, they have entered the normative world of the policymaker.

IS DISAGREEMENT IN ECONOMICS UNIQUE?

While professional economists differ frequently on economic policy questions, there is probably less disagreement than the media would have you believe. Disagreement is common in most disciplines—seismologists trying to predict earthquakes or the eruption of volcanoes differ; historians can be at odds over the interpretation of historical events; psychologists differ on proper ways to rear children; nutritionists debate the merits of large doses of vitamin C; and so on.

The majority of disagreements in economics stem from normative issues, as differences in values or policy beliefs result in conflict. As we discussed earlier in this Module, an economist inevitably emphasizes specific facts over others when trying to develop support for his or her own hypothesis. As a result, disagreements can result when one economist gives weight to facts that have been minimized by another, and vice versa.

Is Freedom More Important Than Fairness?

Some economists are very concerned about individual freedom and liberty, thinking that any encroachment on individual decision making is, other things equal, bad. Persons with this philosophic bent are inclined to be skeptical of any increased government involvement in the economy, unless the objective evidence is overwhelming that the intervention will have profound beneficial economic consequences.

On the other hand, some economists are very concerned with what they consider an unequal, "unfair," or unfortunate distribution of income, wealth, or power, and view governmental intervention as desirable in righting injustices that they believe exist in a market economy. To these persons, the threat to individual liberty alone is not sufficiently great to reject governmental intervention in the face of perceived economic injustice.

Just as there are differences in opinions among individuals, so too are there differences of opinion among scientists.

Which Economic Theory Is Valid?

Aside from philosophic differences, there is a second reason why economists may differ on any given policy question. Specifically, they may disagree as to the validity of a given economic theory for the policy in question. Suppose two economists have identical philosophical views, and that those views have led them to the identical conclusion that unemployment should be reduced to end injustice and hardship. The first economist believes that the government should lower taxes and increase spending to reach the objective, while the second economist believes that the lower unemployment goal can be reached with fewer undesirable consequences by increasing the amount of money in public hands by a variety of banking policies.

The two economists differ because the empirical evidence relating to economic theories dealing with the cause of unemployment appears somewhat conflicting. Some evidence suggests government taxation and spending policies are effective in reducing unemployment, while other evidence would suggest that the prime cause of unnecessary unemployment lies with faulty monetary policy. Still other evidence is consistent with the view that, over long periods, neither approach mentioned here is of much value in reducing unemployment, and that unemployment will be part of our existence regardless of what macroeconomic policies we follow.

What Makes One Theory Come to Be Accepted over Others?

Some economists do a recognizably better job of holding constant other appropriate variables. Also, information tends to become better over time, either because we have longer time periods to analyze or because databases can be assembled to answer a specific question. And statistical techniques for analyzing the available data are improving as well, and certain of those techniques are becoming more accepted than others. Finally, it may sometimes be the case that human behavior actually changes over time, so that a theory that explained behavior fairly well in the past comes to be replaced by another theory that is more relevant to current behavior.

DO ECONOMISTS EVER AGREE WITH EACH OTHER?

Although you may not believe it after reading the previous discussion, economists don't always disagree. In fact, according to a survey among members of the American Economic Association, most economists agree on a wide range of issues, including rent control, import tariffs, export restrictions, the use of wage and price controls to curb inflation, and the minimum wage (Exhibit 1). Often, economists argue that if market forces are allowed to work freely, economic analysis can predict certain phenomena with a high degree of success. For example, if Florida suf-

Could you predict what would happen to the price of oranges if a frost ruined much of the orange crop?

fers a severe winter and the frost ruins much of the state's orange crop, there will be fewer oranges. Consumers who place a higher value on the remaining supply of oranges will outbid those who place lower values on it, and the price of oranges will rise.

EXHIBIT 1	ECONOMISTS DO AGREE

Over 70 percent of economists agree that these statements are correct:

1. A ceiling on rents (rent control) reduces the quantity and quality of housing available (92.9% agree).
2. Tariffs and import quotas usually reduce general economic welfare (92.6% agree).
3. A minimum wage increases unemployment among the young and unskilled (78.9% agree).
4. Inflation is primarily a monetary phenomenon (70.1% agree).

Approximately 70 percent of economists agree that these statements are not accurate:

5. The cause of the rise in gasoline prices that occurred in the wake of the Iraqi invasion of Kuwait is the monopoly power of the large oil companies (69.3% agree).
6. Wage–price controls are a useful policy option in the control of inflation (73.9% agree).

SOURCE: Adapted from Richard M. Alston, J. R. Kearl, and Michael B. Vaughn, "Is There Consensus among Economists in the 1990s?" *American Economic Review,* May 1992, 203–209.

CONCEPT CHECK

1. Positive analysis is objective and value-free.
2. Normative analysis involves value judgments and opinions about the desirability of various actions.
3. Disagreement is common in most disciplines.
4. Most disagreement among economists stems from normative issues.

1. What is positive analysis? Must positive analysis be testable?
2. What is normative analysis? Is normative analysis testable?
3. Why is the positive–normative distinction important?
4. Why are there policy disagreements among economists?
5. Is the statement, "UFOs land in my back yard at least twice a week," a positive statement? Why or why not?
6. Is there any way to scientifically determine if the "rich" pay their "fair share" of taxes? Why or why not?

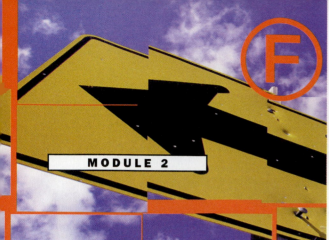

(F) Application: Scientists and Global Warming

How might disagreements in the scientific community affect the cost–benefit analysis of pollution regulation and subsequent governmental policy discussions?

Is global warming an inevitable catastrophe just waiting to happen? No one knows for sure. A 1989 *Time* magazine article stated, "The possible consequences [of global warming] are so scary that it is only prudent for governments to slow the build up of carbon dioxide through preventive measures." On the other hand, a 1994 *Time* magazine article titled "The Ice Man Cometh?" dismissed warnings of global warming as "apocalyptic" and readers were told to "start worrying about the next ice age instead."

Scientists have to sell their stories. So are we cooling down or warming up? The answer is that we have been warming up in this century. But there is ambiguity as to why we are warming up. Is it due to the build-up of greenhouse gases? And to what extent are humans responsible for global warming versus poorly understood natural processes? No one knows for sure. Surface temperature readings in the 1990s are the hottest on record. However, highly accurate satellite-based atmospheric temperature measurements report that the earth's atmosphere actually cooled by .13 degrees Celsius from 1979 to 1993. While the amount of global warming from 1881 to 1993 was 0.54 degrees Celsius, almost 70 percent of that increase occurred during the first half of this period, before the biggest build-up of greenhouse gases.

And we must consider the cost of choosing to control greenhouse gases now. Professor William Nordhaus of Yale University writes, "Given the high costs of controls [on greenhouse gases] . . . and the modest estimated impact of climate change along with other urgent concerns (nuclear proliferation, poverty, drug use, violence and civil wars), we might conclude that global warming should be demoted to a second-tier issue."

There are two important points here. First, while we should be concerned about the environment, we should also be equally concerned that every effort is made to produce objective science based on positive analysis rather than "political" science based on normative analysis. Second, as Professor Nordhaus states, life is about very tough choices, and good, positive analysis can help us make those choices better.

A final observation is that there are many different ways to achieve a given reduction in greenhouse gases by, say, the year 2050: We can clean up a lot now and a little later, or a lot later and a little now. Because the global circulation models will be far more accurate in a mere decade, some argue that it would be prudent to postpone very expensive controls until the seriousness of the problem can be better assessed.

Steve Sack, *Minneapolis Star Tribune*, 1997.

ONE STEP BEYOND

Do incentives matter? You bet! Need an incentive to check out your Workbook? Come on in and meet the Lowell family! You'll learn some important economic concepts—including incentives matter—simply by following them through their adventures and mishaps!

1. In the recent congressional debate about agricultural price supports, senators, congressmen, and experts made the following four statements. Which of these statements is a normative statement?

A. Price supports are important because America should preserve the small family farm.

B. Without price supports the price of wheat and corn will fall by over 20 percent.

C. The decline in commodity prices caused by the removal of price supports will result in fewer, larger farms.

D. The decline in commodity prices caused by the removal of price supports will reduce the number of tractors sold in the United States.

"If you use your Workbook and EconActive CD-ROM, you will get a better grade in economics." Is that a positive or a normative statement? To be sure, check out the exercises in your Workbook and then work the sample quizzes on the EconActive CD-ROM!

PHOTO CREDITS MODULE 2

Page **40:** top, © 1998 Don Couch Photography; bottom, © Mae Scanlan Photography; Page **41:** The Thinker, 1880, bronze, National Gallery of Art, Washington, D.C. Gift of Mrs. John W. Simpson; Page **42:** top, © PhotoDisc; DIL-BERT reprinted by permission of Universal Press Syndicate, Inc.; Page **43:** © O'Brien & Mayor Photography/FPG International; Page **44:** © PhotoDisc; Page **45:** © 1998 Don Couch Photography; Page **46:** top, © PhotoDisc; bottom, © 1998 Don Couch Photography; Page **47:** © 1998 FAR- WORKS, INC. Used by permission of UNIVERSAL PRESS SYNDICATE; Page **48:** left and right, Gaslight Archives, Commack, New York; Page **49:** left, © Ron Vesely Photography; right, From *The Wall Street Journal*. Reprinted by permission of Cartoon Feature Syndicate; Page **50:** top, © PhotoDisc; bottom, right, © Ron Vesely Photography; Page **51:** © Ria Novosti/Sovfoto/Eastfoto/PNI; Page **52:** © Charles Krupa/AP Wide World Photos; Page **53:** © N.R. Rowan/Index Stock Photography; Page **54:** © Robert Torrez/Tony Stone Images; Page **55:** © PhotoDisc; Page **56:** © Steve Sack/Minneapolis Star-Tribune.

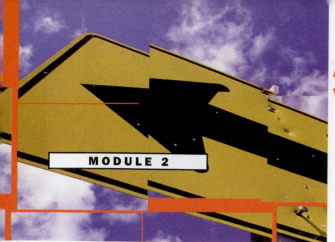

Appendix: Working with Graphs

WHY ARE GRAPHS SO IMPORTANT?

Sometimes the use of visual aids, such as graphs, greatly enhances our understanding of a theory. It is much the same as finding your way to a friend's house with the aid of a map rather than with detailed verbal or written instructions. Graphs are important tools for economists. They allow us to better understand the workings of the economy. To economists, a graph can be worth a thousand words. Graphs will be used throughout this text to enhance the understanding of important economic relationships. This appendix provides a guide on how to read and create your own graphs.

The most useful graph for our purposes is one that merely connects a vertical line (the Y-axis) with a horizontal line (the X-axis), as seen in Exhibit 1. The intersection of the two lines occurs at the origin, which is where both variables are equal to zero. In Exhibit 1, we see that the graph has four quadrants or "boxes." In this textbook we will be primarily concerned with the shaded box in the upper right-hand corner. You can see that this portion of the graph deals exclusively with positive numbers. Always keep in mind that moving to the right on the horizontal axis and up along the vertical axis each lead to higher values.

What Are Dependent and Independent Variables?

A **variable** is a quantity that can take on different numeric values. A **dependent variable** is one that *depends* on the independent variables. That is, the dependent variable value changes according to the values of the independent variables, while an **independent variable** is truly independent—on its own. An independent variable is not influenced by any other variable. The independent variable is determined outside the relationship in question—no matter what happens to the other variables in the equation. For example, imagine a two-variable world. The two variables are weight and food consumption. As food

EXHIBIT 1	PLOTTING A GRAPH

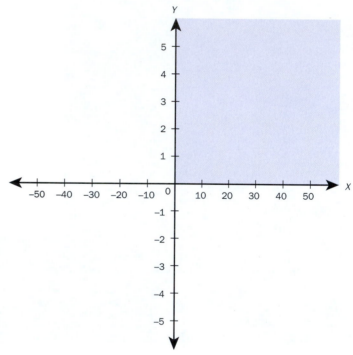

In the upper right-hand corner, we see that the graph includes a positive figure for the Y-axis and the X-axis. As we move to the right along the horizontal axis, the numerical values increase. As we move up along the vertical axis, the numerical values increase.

consumption (the independent variable) changes, weight (the dependent variable) changes, holding all other variables constant. In this example, we see that weight depends on how much food we eat. Theoretical relationships involving one dependent variable and one independent variable can be expressed in a simple two-dimensional graph.

USING GRAPHS AND CHARTS TO SHOW A SINGLE VARIABLE

Exhibit 2 presents three common types of graphs. The **pie chart** in Exhibit 2(a) shows where takeout food is taken. For example, we see that 53 percent of takeout food is taken home, 19 percent is eaten in the car, and 14 percent is taken to work. That is, each slice in the pie chart represents where the food is taken.

Exhibit 2(b) is a bar graph that shows the most popular tourist attractions in the United States. The height of the line represents the annual attendance at these popular tourist attractions. According to this graph, Disneyland was the most popular amusement/theme park in 1996.

EXHIBIT 2   PIE CHART, BAR GRAPH, AND TIME-SERIES GRAPH

a. Pie Chart
Where is take-out food taken?

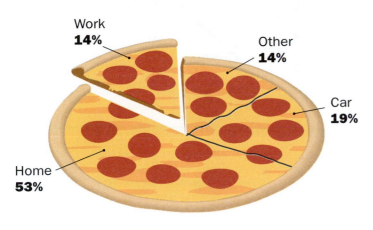

Work **14%**

Other **14%**

Car **19%**

Home **53%**

SOURCE: Beef Industry Council.

c. Time Series Graph
Prices and Inflation Ease, 1986–1997

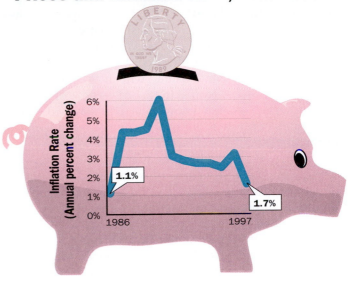

Inflation Rate (Annual percent change)

1.1%

1.7%

1986   1997

SOURCE: U.S. Department of Labor.

b. Bar Graph
Most popular Amusement/Theme Parks, by number of visitors, 1996

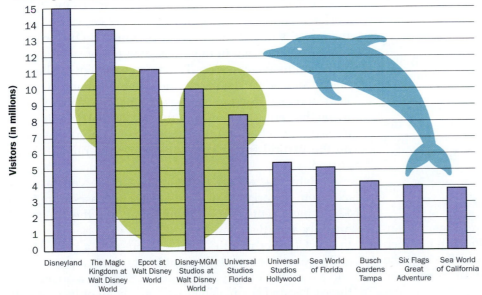

Visitors (in millions)

Disneyland | The Magic Kingdom at Walt Disney World | Epcot at Walt Disney World | Disney-MGM Studios at Walt Disney World | Universal Studios Florida | Universal Studios Hollywood | Sea World of Florida | Busch Gardens Tampa | Six Flags Great Adventure | Sea World of California

SOURCE: Amusement Business.

Exhibit 2(c) is a **time-series graph.** This type of graph shows changes over time. This is a visual tool that allows us to observe important trends over a certain period of time. In Exhibit 2(c) we see a graph that shows the percentage changes in inflation rates over time. The horizontal axis shows us the passage of time, and the vertical axis shows us the inflation growth, in percentage terms. From the graph we can see the trends in inflation from 1986 to 1997.

USING GRAPHS TO SHOW THE RELATIONSHIP BETWEEN TWO VARIABLES

While the graphs and chart in Exhibit 2 are important, they do not allow us to show the relationship between two variables. To more closely examine the structure of and functions of graphs, let us consider the story of Wanda Blade. Wanda is an avid inline skater who has aspirations of strutting her freestyle stuff at the Z Games next year. To get there, however, Wanda knows she will have to put in many hours of practice. But how many hours? In search of information about the practice habits of other skaters, Wanda logged onto the Internet at inline@rad.com, where she pulled up the results of a study conducted by ESPM 3 that indicated the score of each Z Games competitor and the amount of practice time per week spent by each skater. The results of this study (see Exhibit 3) indicated that skaters had to practice 10 hours per week to receive a score of 4.0, 20 hours per week to receive a score of 6.0, 30 hours per week to get a score of 8.0, and 40 hours per week to get a perfect score of 10. What does this information tell Wanda? By using a graph, Wanda can more clearly determine the relationships between practice time and overall score.

What Is a Positive Relationship?

The study that Wanda found on scores and practice times revealed what is called a **direct relationship,** often also called a **positive relationship.** A direct relationship means that the variables move in the same direction. That is, an increase in one variable (practice time) is accompanied by an increase in another variable (overall score), or a decrease in one variable (practice time) is accompanied by a decrease in another variable (overall score). In short, the variables move in the same direction.

What Is a Negative Relationship?

When two variables move in opposite directions, we say that there is an **inverse,** or **negative, relationship** between the two variables. That is, when one variable rises, the other variable falls, or when one variable decreases, the other variable increases.

| EXHIBIT 3 | A POSITIVE RELATIONSHIP |

Skater	Z Games Score	Practice Time per Week
A	4	10
B	6	20
C	8	30
D	10	40

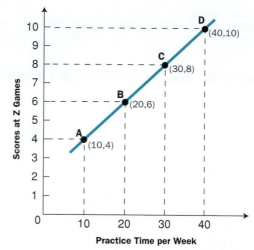

The inline skaters' practice times and scores in the competition are plotted on the graph. Each participant is represented by a point. The graph shows that those skaters who practiced the most scored the highest. This is called a positive, or direct, relationship.

THE GRAPH OF A DEMAND CURVE

Let us now examine the most important graphs in all of economics—the graph of a demand curve. In Exhibit 4, we see the demand curve for compact discs (CDs) for Roland Rocks. It shows the price of CDs on the vertical axis and the quantity of CDs purchased per month on the horizontal axis. Every point in the space shown represents a price and quantity combination. The downward-sloping line, labeled Demand Curve, shows the different combinations of price and quantity purchased. Note that the higher you go up on the vertical (price) axis, the smaller the quantity purchased on the horizontal axis and the lower you go down on the vertical (price axis) the greater the quantity purchased.

In Exhibit 4, we see that moving up the vertical price axis from the origin, the price of CDs increases from $5 to $25 in increments of $5. Moving out along the horizontal quantity axis, the quantity purchased increases from zero to five CDs per month. Point A represents a price of $25 and a quantity of one CD, point B represents a price of $20 and a quantity of two CDs, point C, $15 and a quantity of three CDs, and so on. When we connect all of these points we have what economists call a **curve.** As you can see, curves are sometimes drawn as straight lines for ease of illustration. Moving down along the curve, we see that as the price falls, the quantity that is purchased is greater; moving up the curve to higher prices, the quantity purchased is smaller. That is, when CDs become less expensive, Roland buys more CDs. When CDs become more expensive, Roland buys fewer CDs, perhaps choosing to go to the movies or buy a pizza instead.

rises, say he gets a raise at work, he is now able to buy more CDs than before at each possible price. As a result, the whole demand curve shifts outward to a new position that lies to the right of the old curve. That is, with the new income, Roland uses some of it to buy more CDs. This is seen in the graph in Exhibit 5(a). On the other hand, if Roland's income falls, say he quits his job to go back to school, he now has less income to buy CDs. This causes the whole demand curve to shift inward to a new position to the left of the old curve. This is seen in the graph in Exhibit 5(b).

EXHIBIT 4	A NEGATIVE RELATIONSHIP

Combination	Price of CDs	Quantity of CDs Purchased
A	$25	1
B	20	2
C	15	3
D	10	4
E	5	5

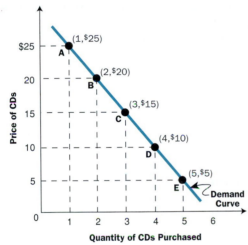

The downward slope of the curve means that price and quantity purchased are inversely, or negatively, related: When one increases, the other decreases. That is, moving down along the demand curve from point A to point E, we see that as price falls, the quantity purchased increases. Moving up along the demand curve from point E to point A, we see that as the price increases, the quantity purchased falls.

EXHIBIT 5	SHIFTING A CURVE

a. Demand Curve with Higher Income

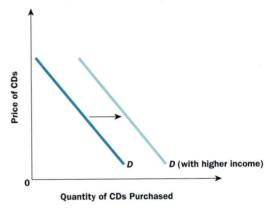

b. Demand Curve with Lower Income

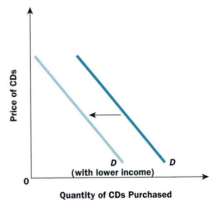

USING GRAPHS TO SHOW THE RELATIONSHIP BETWEEN THREE VARIABLES

Although only two variables are shown on the axes, graphs can be used to show the relationship between *three* variables. For example, say we add a third variable—income—to our earlier example. Our three variables are now income, price, and quantity purchased. If Roland's income

What Is the Difference between a Movement and a Shift in the Curve?

It is important to remember the difference between a movement up and down along a curve and a shift in the whole curve. A change in one of the variables on the graph, like price or quantity purchased will cause a movement along the curve, say, from point A to point B as shown in Exhibit 6. A change in one of the variables not shown, like income in our example, will cause the whole curve to shift, like the change from D_0 to D_1 in Exhibit 6.

EXHIBIT 6 | **SHIFTS VERSUS MOVEMENTS**

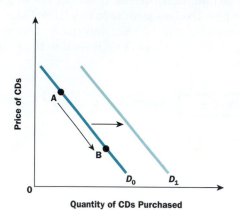

Quantity of CDs Purchased

WHAT IS A SLOPE?

In economics, we sometimes refer to the steepness of the lines or curves on graphs as the slope. A slope can be either positive (upward sloping) or negative (downward sloping). A curve that is **downward sloping** represents an inverse, or negative, relationship between the two variables

and slants downward from left to right, as seen in Exhibit 7(a). A curve that is **upward sloping** represents a direct, or positive relationship, between the two variables and slants upward from right to left, as seen in Exhibit 7(b).

How Do We Measure the Slope of a Linear Curve?

A straight line curve is called a linear curve. The slope of a linear curve between two points measures the relative rates of change of two variables. Specifically, the slope of a linear curve can be defined as the ratio of the change in the Y value to the change in the X value. The slope can also be expressed as the ratio of the rise to the run, where the rise is the change in the Y variable (along the vertical axis) and the run is the change in the X variable (along the horizontal axis).

$$\text{Slope} = \frac{\text{RISE}}{\text{RUN}} = \frac{\text{Change in the } Y \text{ variable (vertical axis)}}{\text{Change in the } X \text{ variable (horizontal axis)}}$$

In Exhibit 8, we show two linear curves, one with a positive slope and one with a negative slope. In Exhibit 8(a), the slope of the positively sloped linear curve from point A to B is 1/2, because the rise is 1 (from 2 to 3) and the run is 2 (from 1 to 3). In Exhibit 8(b), the negatively sloped linear curve has a slope of –4—the "rise" is –8 (a fall of 8 from 10 to 2) and a run of 2 (from 7 to 9), which gives us a slope of –4 (–8 ÷ 2). Note the appropriate signs on the slopes: There is a minus sign on the negatively sloped line and a plus sign on the positively sloped line.

EXHIBIT 7 | **DOWNWARD- AND UPWARD-SLOPING LINEAR CURVES**

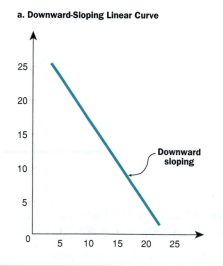

a. Downward-Sloping Linear Curve

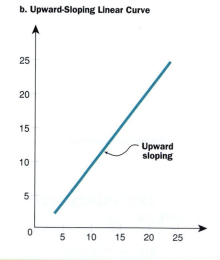

b. Upward-Sloping Linear Curve

| EXHIBIT 8 | **SLOPES OF POSITIVE AND NEGATIVE LINEAR CURVES** |

a. Positive Slope

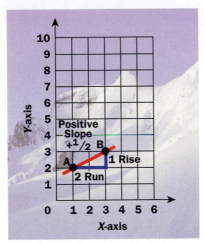

b. Negative Slope

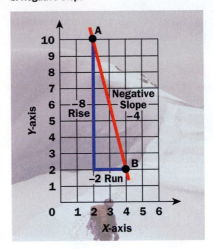

How Do We Find the Slope of a Nonlinear Curve?

In Exhibit 9, we show the slope of a nonlinear curve. A nonlinear curve is a line that actually curves. Here the slope varies from point to point along the curve. However, we can find the slope of this curve at any given point by drawing a straight line tangent to that point on the curve. A tangency is when a straight line just touches the curve without actually crossing it. At point A, we see that the slope of the positively sloped line that is tangent to the curve has a +1 slope—the line rises one unit and runs one unit. At point B, the line is horizontal, so it has zero slope. At point C, we see a slope of –2, because the negatively sloped line has a rise of –2 units (a fall of two units) for every one unit run.

Remember that failure to understand graphs are the reason that many students have problems with economics, so make sure that you understand this material before going on to Module 3.

| EXHIBIT 9 | **THE SLOPE OF A NONLINEAR CURVE** |

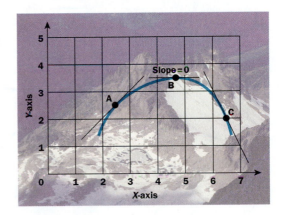

Scarcity and the Economizing Problem

A. The Factors of Production
What are the factors of production?

B. The Production Possibilities Curve
Why is the production possibilities curve useful?

C. Production Decisions
What and how much should we produce?

D. Production Methods
How will we produce those goods and services?

E. Distribution of Output
Who will get the goods and services we produce?

F. Efficiency in Production
How can we use our scarce resources efficiently?

G. Production and Growth
What do we have to sacrifice today to achieve greater economic growth?

H. Application: Tourism versus Ecosystems
Can we have more tourism and a better environment at the same time?

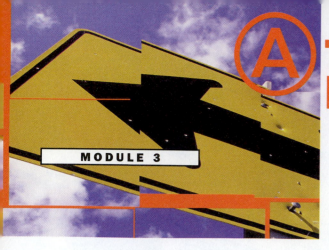

A The Factors of Production

■ What are the four factors of production?
■ What is labor?
■ What is land?
■ What is capital?
■ What is entrepreneurship?

WHAT ARE THE FOUR FACTORS OF PRODUCTION?

The three kinds of **resources—land, labor,** and **capital**—are each in limited supply and must be used in any productive activity. They are the "inputs" that result in "outputs" of final goods and services in the economy. The fourth factor of production, **entrepreneurship,** is the decision-making input that is concerned with the application of these resources and with identifying new possibilities, new products, and new methods of production.

You might want to use the word *CELL* to help you remember the four factors of production: *C*, capital; *E*, entrepreneurship; *L*, land; and *L*, labor.

What Is Labor?

The resource called **labor** includes the total of both physical and mental effort expended by people in the economy. In economics, we are concerned with both the quantity and the quality of labor. Increases in the quantity of labor, relative to the population, means more workers and fewer dependents. Increases in the quality of labor increases workers' productivity. Both factors can lead to greater economic growth.

What Is Land?

Economists stretch the term land to include all natural resources coming from the earth. Trees, animals, water, minerals and so on are all considered to be "land" for our purposes, along with the physical space normally thought

Everything you see here—water, trees, rocks, air, and, of course, land—is land to an economist.

of as land. Suppose you are making a table. You will need wood, metal, glass, plastic, stone, fiberglass, or some combination of these and possibly other materials. As a producer, you must choose which specific materials to use. In a market economy, you will see that it is largely prices (which reflect relative scarcity) that influence this decision, but under any system, the relative scarcity or availability of various materials will have a bearing on making production decisions.

What Is Capital?

Human-made resources that are used to produce final goods are called **capital goods.** Office buildings, tools, machines, and factories are all considered capital goods. Fishing nets are also capital goods, because they are made for the purpose of "producing" the final good—fish. When we invest in factories, machines, research and development, or education, we increase the potential to create more goods and services in the future.

When thinking about capital, most of us tend to think first of money. However, when considering capital in economics, it is important not to confuse capital goods with money capital. **Money capital** is not regarded as a distinct factor of production or as a good to be consumed. Rather, it is regarded as an instrument of exchange—a means by which other commodities are acquired. Money is essential for the efficient exchange of goods among households, business firms, and other economic decision-making units, but it may be best thought of as the "oil" that allows production and consumption to run smoothly.

What Is an Entrepreneur?

Someone has to make tough and risky decisions about how to combine land, labor, and capital together, which goods or services to produce, how many to produce, and so on. This decision maker is often called an **entrepreneur.** The management skills and innovative talents of entrepreneurs are crucial in expanding an economy's ability to produce goods over time.

Entrepreneurs are always looking for new ways to improve production techniques or to create new products. They are driven by the lure of a positive incentive—profits. It is this opportunity to make a profit that leads entrepreneurs to take risks. However, entrepreneurs do not have to be a Bill Gates (Microsoft) or a Henry Ford (Ford Motor Company). In some sense, we are all entrepreneurs when we try new products or when we find better ways to manage our households or our study time. Rather than money, then, our profits might take the form of greater enjoyment, additional time for recreation, or better grades.

Because a factory is built to produce other goods, it is considered to be a capital good.

BILL GATES, THE ENTREPRENEUR

When Bill Gates was in the sixth grade, his parents decided he needed counseling. He was at war with his mother, Mary, an outgoing woman who harbored the belief that he should do what she told him. She would call him to dinner from his basement bedroom, which she had given up trying to make him clean, and he wouldn't respond. "What are you doing?" she once demanded over the intercom. "I'm thinking," he shouted back. "You're thinking?" "Yes, Mom, I'm thinking," he said fiercely. "Have you ever tried thinking?"

The psychologist they sent him to "was a really cool guy," Gates recalls. "He gave me books to read after each session, Freud stuff, and I really got into psychology theory." After a year of sessions and a battery of tests, the counselor reached his conclusion. "You're going to lose," he told Mary. "You had better just adjust to it because there's no use trying to beat him." Mary was strong-willed and intelligent herself, her husband recalls, "but she came around to accepting that it was futile trying to compete with him."

A lot of computer companies have concluded the same. In the 21 years since he dropped out of Harvard to start Microsoft, William Henry Gates, III, 41, has thrashed competitors in the world of desktop operat-

ing systems and application software. Now he is attempting the audacious feat of expanding Microsoft from a software company into a media and content company.

In the process he has amassed a fortune . . . . The 88 percent rise in Microsoft stock in 1996 meant he made on paper more than $10.9 billion, or about $30 million a day. That makes him the world's richest person, by far. But he's more than that. He has become the Edison and Ford of our age. A technologist turned entrepreneur, he embodies the digital era.

His success stems from his personality: an awesome and at times frightening blend of brilliance, drive, competitiveness, and personal intensity . . . he has "incredible processing power" and "unlimited bandwidth," an agility at "parallel processing" and "multitasking." Watch him at his desk, and you see what they mean. He works on two computers, one with four frames that sequence data streaming in from the Internet, the other handling the hundreds of e-mail messages and memos that extend his mind into a network. He can be so rigorous as he processes data that one can imagine his mind may indeed be digital: no sloppy emotions or analog fuzziness, just trillions of binary impulses coolly converting input into correct answers.

Bill Gates receives profits for his entrepreneurial efforts.

SOURCE: "In Search of the Real Bill Gates," *Time*, 149, no. 2, January 13, 1997.

CONCEPT CHECK

1. Capital, entrepreneurship, land, and labor (CELL) are the four factors of production.
2. Labor is the physical and mental effort expended in production.
3. Land includes all of our natural resources.
4. Capital consists of all the human-made resources that are used to produce final goods.
5. An entrepreneur is the decision maker that combines the capital, land, and labor into production.

---

1. What are factors of production?
2. What do economists mean by land? Labor? Capital? Entrepreneurship?
3. What is the difference between capital goods and money capital?
4. Why do you think economists often refer to training that increases the quality of workers' skills as "adding to human capital"?
5. What are some of the ways that students act as entrepreneurs as they seek higher grades?

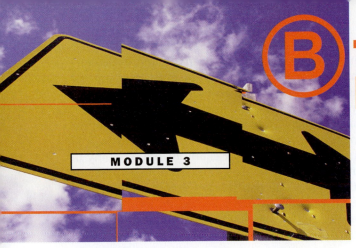

B The Production Possibilities Curve

- What is a production possibilities curve?
- What are consumption goods?
- What are investment goods?
- What is the law of increasing opportunity costs?

WHAT IS A PRODUCTION POSSIBILITIES CURVE?

The problem of deciding what to produce and in what quantities is sometimes illustrated visually by the use of a simple graph called a **production possibilities curve** (Exhibit 1). The production possibilities curve represents the potential total output combinations of any two goods for an economy. That is, it illustrates an economy's potential for allocating its limited resources to producing various combinations of goods. If an economy is operating on the production possibilities curve, then that economy is oper-

ating at full capacity, given the inputs and technology available to the economy.

How Do We Show Inefficiency on the Production Possibilities Curve?

If it is not operating at full capacity, the economy is operating inefficiently. As a result, actual output is less than potential output. If this occurs, the economy is operating inside the production possibilities curve. And operating inside the production possibilities curve reflects inefficiency in the economy. The concept of inefficiency will be covered in greater detail in Concept F of this Module.

EXHIBIT 1	A PRODUCTION POSSIBILITIES CURVE

Combination	Fishing Nets	Fish
A	50	0
B	40	350
C	30	600
D	20	800
E	10	900
F	0	950

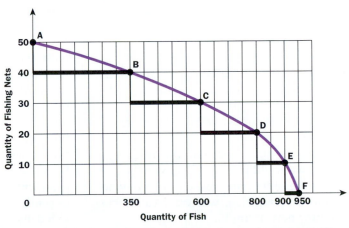

The production possibilities curve represents the potential amounts of two products that can be produced with given resources. It also illustrates the opportunity cost of producing more of a product. For example, if we increase fishing net output from 10 to 20 units (moving from point E to point D), we must produce 100 fewer units of fish (800 instead of 900). The opportunity cost of the 10 additional nets is therefore 100 units of fish. We can see that, moving up the curve from F, an additional 10 units of fishing nets costs society more and more fish—the law of increasing opportunity cost. The increasing opportunity cost is illustrated by the bold horizontal lines.

WHAT ARE CONSUMPTION GOODS AND INVESTMENT GOODS?

To more clearly illustrate the production possibilities curve, we will use an example involving an island economy that produces just two goods, fish and fishing nets. The fact that we have many goods in the real world makes actual decision making more complicated, but it does not alter the basic principles being illustrated. In this example, you can think of the fish as being symbolic of all the goods we consume that bring us immediate satisfaction. These goods are called **consumption goods.** Similarly, think of the fishing nets as being symbolic of all of the goods that give little immediate pleasure but that help increase the output of goods and services in future time periods, thus providing us with satisfaction at a later date. We call these **investment goods.**

Fish are a consumption good; fishing nets are investment goods.

Each point on the production possibilities curve shown in Exhibit 1 represents the potential amounts of fish and fishing nets that can be produced in a given time period, given the quantity and quality of resources available in the economy to use for production.

Note in Exhibit 1 that if we devoted all of our resources to making fishing nets, we could produce 50 new nets, but no fish (point A). If, on the other hand, we chose to devote all of our resources to catching fish, we could catch 950 fish, but produce no new nets (point F).

In reality, we would probably not choose either of these extreme production possibilities. Why? A nation that produced only nets (investment goods) would quickly starve to death (ignoring, for the time being, trade possibilities with other countries). On the other hand, if a nation devoted all of its resources to making consumption goods, such as fish, it would soon find its ability to produce deteriorating, as older resources (such as machines or, in this case, fishing nets) wear out. Thus, even economies that just want to maintain their current output must use some of their resources to replace some of their stock of output-creating investment goods, like fishing nets.

Therefore, nations would rarely opt for production possibility A or production possibility F, preferring instead to produce a mixture of goods. For example, the economy in question might produce 40 nets and 350 fish (point B), or perhaps 30 nets and 600 fish (point C). Still other combinations, such as point D, are possible, as long as all of the economy's resources are being used efficiently in production.

WHAT IS THE COST OF A FISHING NET?

The true cost of a fishing net in this economy is revealed by the production possibilities curve. By moving along the curve, the cost (really opportunity cost) of an additional fishing net is the number of fish that must be foregone as the limited resources are shifted from producing fish to producing fishing nets. For example, suppose the economy has been operating at point C, making 20 nets and catching 800 fish annually. Suppose now that people decide they want to produce 10 more fishing nets. To do this, they must reduce fish output to 600, a decrease of 200. Thus, the opportunity cost of those 10 additional fishing nets is the 200 fish that have to be given up as workers, raw materials, and so on are diverted from fishing to the production of 10 additional nets. In making the decision about whether to shift its resources, this society must somehow decide if the benefits of the 10 added fishing nets exceed the opportunity cost (200 fish) of having those fishing nets.

WHAT DOES A BOWED PRODUCTION POSSIBILITY CURVE MEAN?

Note that the production possibility curve in Exhibit 1 is not a straight line. It is concave from below (that is, bowed outward from the origin). Looking at the figure, you can see that at very low net output, a small increase in the number of nets produced will lead to only a small reduction in fish output. For example, increasing fishing net output from 0 to 10, or 10 units (moving from point F to point E on the curve), requires the use of resources capable of producing 50 fish. This means that for each net added between 0 and 10, an average of 5 fish are given up (50 divided by 10). When many nets are already being made, however, many more fish must be given up when switching additional resources from fish to fishing net production. Moving from point B to point A, for example, a reduction in fish output of 350 (from 350 to 0) releases resources to produce 10 more nets (the output of nets rises from 40 to 50). At this point, then, the average cost of each additional fishing net obtained, then, is 35 units of fish (350 divided by 10), considerably more than the 5 fish required in the earlier scenario. This difference shows us that opportunity costs have not remained constant, but have risen, as more fishing nets are produced. It is this increasing opportunity cost, then, that results in the bowed production possibilities curve.

Why Is There an Increasing Opportunity Cost?

A basic reason for the **increasing opportunity cost** of additional fishing net output as more nets are produced is that some resources cannot be easily adapted from their current uses to alternative uses. For example, some resources used in catching fish are difficult or impossible to use in the manufacture of fishing nets (e.g., fishing boats). At low levels of current fishing net output, rather large increases in output are obtained by switching easily adaptable resources, such as poor fishermen, from fishing to making nets. Soon these resources are exhausted and resources and workers that are less well suited or appropriate for net manufacture (or are better adapted to fishing) must be released from fishing in order to increase fishing net output. For example, a skilled fisherman may be an expert at catching fish but a very bad net maker, because he lacks the training and skills necessary in that occupation. So, using the skilled fisherman to make nets results in a relatively greater opportunity cost (that is, more fish lost) than using the poor fisherman to make nets. Hence, the production of additional fishing nets becomes increasingly costly as more nets are produced.

TUNE UP

THE PRODUCTION POSSIBILITIES CURVE

Q: Imagine that you are the overseer on a small island that only produces two goods, cattle and wheat. About a quarter of the land is not fertile enough for growing wheat, so cattle graze on it. What would happen if you tried to produce more and more wheat, extending your planting even to the less-fertile soil?

Will the costs of growing wheat increase as you continue to grow more and more wheat on this island?

A: This is the law of increasing opportunity costs in action. As we planted more and more of our acreage in wheat, we would move into some of the rocky, less-fertile land and, consequently, wheat yields on the additional acreage would fall. If we tried to plant the entire island with wheat, we would find that some of the rocky less-fertile acreage would yield virtually no extra wheat. It would, however, have been great for cattle grazing—a large loss. Thus, the opportunity cost of using that marginal land for wheat rather than cattle grazing would be very high. The law of increasing opportunity cost occurs because resources are not homogeneous (identical) and are not equally adaptable for producing cattle and wheat; some acres are more suitable for cattle grazing, while others are more suitable for wheat growing. This is seen in Exhibit 2, where the horizontal lines represent the opportunity cost of growing more wheat in terms of cattle production sacrificed. You can see that as wheat production increases, the opportunity costs in terms of lost cattle production rises.

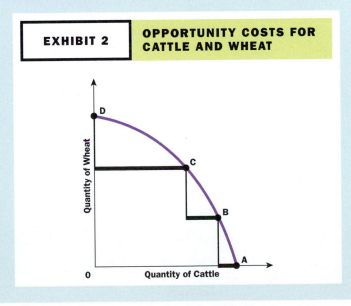

EXHIBIT 2   **OPPORTUNITY COSTS FOR CATTLE AND WHEAT**

1. The production possibilities curve represents the potential total output combinations of two goods available to a society.
2. If the economy is operating within the production possibilities curve, the economy is operating inefficiently; this means that actual output is less than potential output.
3. Goods that we consume and give us immediate satisfaction are called consumption goods; goods that give us little immediate pleasure but help increase output in future time periods are called investment goods.

4. A bowed production possibility curve means that the opportunity costs of producing additional units of a good rise as society produces more of that good (the law of increasing opportunity costs).

1. What does a production possibilities curve illustrate?
2. What distinguishes consumption goods and investment goods?
3. How are opportunity costs shown by the production possibilities curve?
4. Why do the opportunity costs of added production increase with output?
5. How does the production possibilities curve illustrate increasing opportunity costs?

6. If people reduced their saving (thus reducing the funds available for investment), what would that do to society's production possibilities curve over time?
7. If Robin's son, Crusoe, could produce 20 fishing nets in a day or catch 60 fish in a day, while Robin could produce only 10 fishing nets a day or catch 20 fish a day, who would you pick to begin making fishing nets first? Why?

Production Decisions

- What goods and services will be produced?
- What is a command economy?
- What is decentralized decision making?
- What is consumer sovereignty?

WHAT ECONOMIC QUESTIONS DO ALL SOCIETIES FACE?

Because of scarcity, certain economic questions must be answered regardless of the level of affluence of the society or its political structure. In the remainder of this Module, we will consider five fundamental questions that inevitably must be faced: (1) What and how much to produce? (2) How will we produce these goods and services? (3) Who will get the goods and services we produce? (4) How can we use our scarce resources efficiently? and (5) Will current sacrifices necessary for more rapid economic growth be worth the gains that growth will offer future generations? These questions are unavoidable in a world of scarcity.

What and How Much Should We Produce?

Because our wants exceed the amount of goods and services that can be produced from our limited resources, a decision must be made about which wants should have

How do we decide which colors and options to include with these cars?

priority over others. Should we produce lots of cars and few school buildings, or relatively few cars and more school buildings? Once we have decided how many cars to produce, we must also decide how many of them should be equipped with automatic rather than manual transmissions. How many should be painted red? Black? Forest green? How many should be sports cars, and how many should be four-wheel-drive sport utility vehicles? Because we have so many wants, answering these questions is not at all simple.

HOW DO DIFFERENT TYPES OF ECONOMIC SYSTEMS ANSWER THESE QUESTIONS?

Economies are organized in different ways to answer the question of what and how much to produce. The dispute over the best way to answer the what and how much to produce question has inflamed passions for centuries. Should decisions be made centrally by a planning board, as in North Korea, Cuba, or China? Sometimes these highly centralized economic systems are referred to as **command economies.** Under this type of regime, decisions about how many tractors or automobiles to produce are largely determined by a government official or committee associated with the central planning organization. That same group decides on the number and size of school buildings, refrigerators, shoes, and so on. Note that decisions are not made by "organizations" but rather by individuals within them, and the incentives those individuals face will impact their decisions regardless of the economic system.

Other countries, including the United States, much of Europe, and, increasingly, Asia and elsewhere, have largely adopted a decentralized decision-making process, with literally millions of individual producers and consumers of goods and services determining what goods, and how many of them, will be produced. A country that uses such a decentralized decision-making process to determine what is to be produced is often referred to as a **market economy.** Actually, no nation has a pure market economy. Most countries, including the United States, can

The degree of government involvement in the economy varies widely in different countries, but over the past 75 years in nearly all industrial countries, government involvement (shown here as the level of government spending) has expanded.

Entire courses in economics are devoted to the alternative methods of organizing economies to deal with scarcity (called *comparative economic systems*). The bulk of this book is taken up with the analysis of how such decisions are made in the mixed market economy. However, you should remember that the decision of what to produce inevitably must be made because of scarcity, regardless of whether that decision is centralized or decentralized, or whether the means of production is privately or publicly owned.

SOURCE: *The Economist*, September 20, 1997.

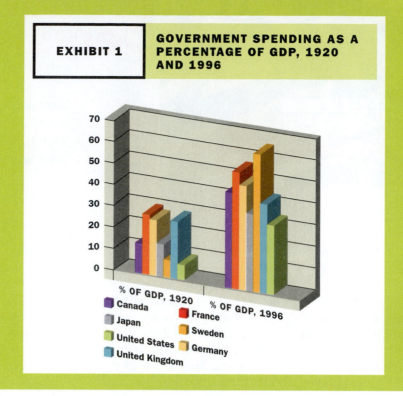

EXHIBIT 1

GOVERNMENT SPENDING AS A PERCENTAGE OF GDP, 1920 AND 1996

be said to have **mixed economies.** In such economies, some production decisions are made centrally by the government, while other decisions are made in a decentralized fashion through the interaction of individual producers and purchasers who are sometimes combined, for reasons which will become clear later, into groups of individuals such as corporations, unions, foundations, and the like.

HOW ARE PRODUCTION DECISIONS MADE IN MARKET ECONOMIES?

You already know that individuals play a major role in the decision-making processes of market economies. But how do individuals control the production decisions in these economies? The answer is that people "vote" in economic affairs with their dollars (or pounds or francs). This concept is called **consumer sovereignty** (the consumer is "king"). Television, VCRs, cellular telephones, pagers, camcorders, and computers, for example, became part of our lives because consumers "voted" hundreds of dollars apiece on these goods. As they bought more color TVs, consumers "voted" fewer dollars on black-and-white TVs. Similarly, record albums gave way to tapes and CDs as consumers voted for these items with their dollars. Consumer sovereignty, then, explains how individual consumers in market economies determine what and how much is to be produced.

Who decided that consumers would use CDs rather than record players?

TUNE UP

DID THE MARKET FAIL?

Q: Adam was a college graduate with a double major in economics and art. A few years ago, Adam decided that he wanted to pursue a vocation that utilized both of his talents. In response, he shut himself up in his studio and created a watercolor collection, "Graphs of Famous Recessions." With high hopes, Adam put his collection on display for buyers. After several years of displaying his econ-art, however, the only one interested in the collection was his eight-year-old sister, who wanted the picture frames for her room. Recognizing that Adam was having trouble pursuing his chosen occupation, Adam's friend Karl told him that the market had failed. What do you think? Is Karl right?

A: No. Markets provide important signals, and the signal being sent in this situation is that Adam should look for some other means of support—something that society values. Remember the function of consumer sovereignty in the marketplace. Clearly, consumers were not voting for Adam's art.

"We feel he's either going to be an artist or an economist."

CONCEPT CHECK

1. Every economy has to decide what and how much to produce.
2. In a command economy the what and how much decision is largely determined by the government.
3. In a decentralized market economy millions of buyers and sellers determine what and how much to produce.

---

1. Why does scarcity force us to decide what to produce?
2. How is a command economy different from a market economy?
3. How does consumer sovereignty determine production decisions in a market economy?
4. Do you think that what and how much an economy produces depends on who will get the goods and services produced in that economy? Why or why not?
5. Why do consumers have to "vote" for a product with their dollars for it to be a success?

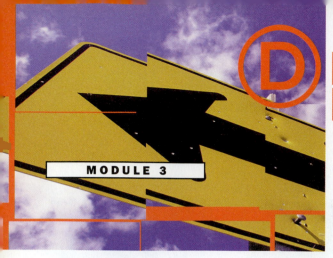

Ⓓ Production Methods

- How do we produce the goods and services we want?
- What is a capital-intensive production method?
- What is a labor-intensive production method?

HOW DO WE PRODUCE GOODS AND SERVICES?

All economies, regardless of their political structure, must decide how to produce the goods and services that they want—because of scarcity. Goods and services can generally be produced in several ways. For example, a ditch can be dug by many workers using their hands, by a few workers with shovels, or by one person with a backhoe. A decision must be made as to which method is most appropriate. The larger the quantity of the good and the more elaborate the form of capital (remember, goods like shov-

els or large earthmoving machines that enhance the production of other goods and services are called capital), the more labor that is saved and is thus made available for other uses. From the example, you might be tempted to conclude that it is desirable to use the biggest, most elaborate form of capital. But would you really want to plant your spring flowers with huge earthmoving machinery? The most capital-intensive method of production (that is, the method with a high capital-to-labor input ratio) may not always be the best. The best method is the least-cost method.

WHAT IS THE "BEST" FORM OF PRODUCTION?

The best or "optimal" form of production will usually vary from one economy to the next. For example, earthmoving machinery is used in digging large ditches in the United States and Europe, while in less-developed countries, such as India, China, or Pakistan, shovels are often used. Similarly, when a person in the United States cuts the grass, he or she may use his or her own labor and a power lawn mower, whereas in a poorer country, a hand mower would probably be used. In a still poorer country, grass might well be cut with an even simpler tool, such as a scythe, or it might not be cut at all. Why do these "optimal" forms of production vary so drastically? Compared to capital, labor is relatively cheap and plentiful in India but relatively scarce and expensive in the United States. In contrast, capital (machines and tools, mainly) is comparatively plentiful and cheap in the United States but scarcer and more costly in India. That is, in India, production would tend to be more **labor intensive,** or labor driven. In the United States, production would tend to be more **capital intensive,** or capital driven. Each nation tends to use the production processes that conserve its relatively scarce (and thus relatively more expensive) resources and use more of its relatively abundant resources.

"LEROY HAS FOUND A GREAT LABOR-SAVING DEVICE... IT'S CALLED 'TOMORROW.'"

LABOR-SAVING ANTI-THEFT DEVICES

LONDON, ENGLAND: Sainsbury's, one of the UK's big three supermarket chains, has started installing Checkpoint Systems' RF (radio frequency) anti-theft system on its high-value products. . . . Checkpoint's source tagging involves the insertion of a paper-thin RF label into products or packaging at the time of manufacture. This provides the retailer with items that require no further anti-theft tagging on the shop floor— so saving time and money, the company claims. It [the RF system] also, officials claim, offers an even greater deterrent to theft, as no one, not even staff, is aware of which products are tagged, or where the tag is hidden.

SOURCE: Newsbytes News Network: http://www.newsbytes.com. September 8, 1997. Copyright 1997, Newsbytes News Network

CONSIDER THIS:
This is an example of substituting labor-saving technology for expensive human monitoring. If the price is right, capital will be substituted for labor.

CONCEPT CHECK

1. The best form of production is the one that conserves the relative scarce resources and uses more of the abundant resource.
2. When capital is relatively scarce and labor plentiful, production tends to be labor intensive.
3. When capital is relatively abundant and labor relatively scarce, production tends to be capital intensive.

1. Why must we choose among multiple ways of producing the goods and services we want?
2. Why might production be labor intensive in one economy, but be capital intensive in another?
3. If a tourist from the United States notices on an overseas trip that other countries don't produce crops "like they do back home," would he be right to conclude that farmers in the other country produce crops less efficiently than U.S. farmers?
4. Why are the golf tee areas on driving ranges in Japan often multileveled, while they are usually on a single level in the United States?

E Distribution of Output

- Who gets the final goods and services?
- What is the relationship between scarce resources and income?

HOW ARE GOODS AND SERVICES DISTRIBUTED?

In every society, some mechanism must exist to determine how goods and services are to be distributed among the population. Who gets what? Why do some people get to consume or use far more goods and services than others? This question of distribution is so important that wars and revolutions have been fought over it. Both the French and Russian Revolutions were concerned fundamentally with the distribution of goods and services. Even in societies where political questions are usually settled peacefully, the question of the distribution of income is an issue that always arouses strong emotional responses. As we shall see, in a market economy, with private ownership and control of the means of production, the amount of output one is able to obtain depends on one's income, which depends on the quantity and quality of the scarce resources that the individual controls. For example, Tiger Woods makes a lot of money because he has unique and marketable skills as a golfer. This may or may not be viewed as "fair," an issue we shall look at in detail later in the book.

WHY DO BIG-NAME STARS MAKE $15–20 MILLION A FILM?

Some actors and actresses reap incredibly high salaries for their appearances in movies. Why? The reason that these actors and actresses are being paid such a large amount of money is because they control scarce resources—their talent and name recognition. In essence, what the studios are betting on is that the contribution of these stars to sales will more than offset the costs of their services. That is, they expect that by employing one of these actors or actresses, rather than a less-well-known actor or actress, they will reap greater profits. In addition, if others were not competing for their unique talents, stars would not be stars.

Why do Hollywood stars get paid so much for a film?

CONCEPT CHECK

1. In a market economy, the amount of output one is able to obtain depends on one's income.

2. The amount of one's income depends on the quantity and the quality of the scarce resources that the individual controls.

1. In a market economy, what determines "who gets what"?

2. In what way does scarcity determine income?

(F) Efficiency in Production

- What are unemployed resources?
- What are underemployed resources?
- What is efficiency?

ARE WE USING OUR RESOURCES EFFICIENTLY?

While the questions of deciding what, how, and for whom to produce are vital, they are not the only concerns that societies have. Most modern economies have resources that are idle, at least for some period of time. If those resources were *not* idle, people would have more scarce goods and services available for their use.

If those who, for whatever reason, are unable to employ their resources in the manner they wish, we have a serious problem. For example, consider the unemployed coal miner who is unable to find work at a "reasonable" wage, or those unemployed in depressed times when plants are

already operating below capacity. Clearly, the resources of these individuals are not being used efficiently.

WHAT ARE UNEMPLOYED AND UNDEREMPLOYED RESOURCES?

The fact that plants can operate below capacity suggests that it is not just labor resources that should be most effectively used. Rather, all resources entering into production must be used effectively. However, for several reasons, social concern focuses on labor. First, labor costs are the largest share of production costs. Also, **unemployed** or **underemployed laborers** (whose resources are not being used to their full potential) may have mouths to feed at home, while an unemployed machine does not (although the owner of the unemployed machine may). Finally, in terms of equity, most owners of nonlabor inputs, like capital and land, tend to be richer than those owning only their own labor. For all of these reasons, attention has focused on the unemployment of labor.

MATCHING RESOURCES TO BEST USE IS NOT ALWAYS EASY

The problem of matching resources, especially labor, with the many potentially valuable uses for them is a real problem in every society. Simplistic solutions to this problem abound. For example, a simple way to reduce unemployment would be to make it a criminal offense to be unemployed! Such a solution, however, would not relieve the underlying problem of attempting to match the resources available to the uses best suited to them. The problem of underutilized resources can be illustrated by the production possibilities curve introduced earlier. Consider Exhibit 1, which reproduces the production possibilities curve used earlier (p. 69). With resources fully employed, this economy could produce a variety of combinations of fishing nets and fish, including points C (30 fishing nets, 600 fish) and D (20 fishing nets, 800 fish).

If this coal miner loses his job, will he be able to find work?

EXHIBIT 1 | PRODUCTION POSSIBILITIES WITH UNEMPLOYED RESOURCES

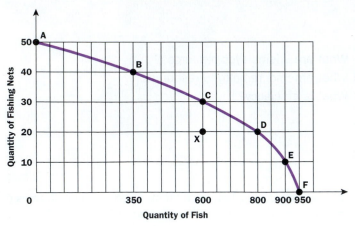

At point X, resources are unemployed or underemployed, so it is possible to increase both fish and fishing net production without incurring any opportunity costs.

WHY IS AN EFFICIENT USE OF RESOURCES IMPORTANT TO ME?

Suppose some resources are unemployed or are not being put to their best uses. The economy would then be operating at a point, such as X, inside the production possibilities curve. At point X, 20 fishing nets and 600 fish are being produced. By putting unemployed resources to work or by putting already employed resources to better uses, we could expand the output of fishing nets by 10 (moving to point C) without giving up any fish. Alternatively, we could boost fish output by 200 fish (moving to point D) without reducing fishing net output. We could even get more of both fish and fishing nets moving to a point on the curve between C and D. Increasing or improving the utilization of resources, then, can lead to greater output of all goods. That is why economists, and you too, have an interest in the efficient use of all of society's resources: There can be more of everything we care about for all of us as a result. Thus, **efficiency** requires society to use its resources to the fullest extent—getting the most from our scarce resources.

CONCEPT CHECK

1. Unemployed and underemployed resources mean that the economy is not working to its full potential.
2. Operating inside the production possibilities curve is an inefficient use of society's resources.
3. Efficiency requires society to use its resources to the fullest extent.

1. Why are we concerned with unemployed or underemployed resources in a society?
2. What do we mean by efficiency, and how is it related to underemployment of resources?
3. How are efficiency and inefficiency illustrated with a production possibilities curve?
4. Will a country that makes being unemployed illegal be more productive than one that does not? Why or why not?
5. If a 68-year-old worker in the United States chooses not to work at all, does that mean that the United States is functioning inside its production possibilities curve? Why or why not?

G Production and Growth

MODULE 3

- How much should we sacrifice today to get more in the future?
- How do we show economic growth on the production possibilities curve?

HOW MUCH ARE WE WILLING TO GIVE UP TODAY TO GET MORE TOMORROW?

Another question facing all economies is the extent to which the current sacrifices necessary for more rapid economic growth will pay dividends in the future. Are the sacrifices you are making really worth it? These growth questions can be crucial to a country's well-being. How have some nations, such as Hong Kong, been able to rapidly expand their output of goods and services over time, while others, such as many African nations, have apparently been unable to increase their standards of living at all? What are the costs and benefits to society of more rapid, as opposed to slower, growth in output? What is the best, or "optimal," rate of growth?

GLOBAL WATCH

FIVE RICHEST AND FIVE POOREST NATIONS IN OUTPUT PER PERSON

The rate of economic growth differs among economies. If they could fast forward past the process of growth to the final result, most people would find faster growth to their liking. Few would prefer the real per-person output of $450 per year in Ethiopia to the $20,000 to $25,000 per person, per year available in countries as diverse as Switzerland and the United States.

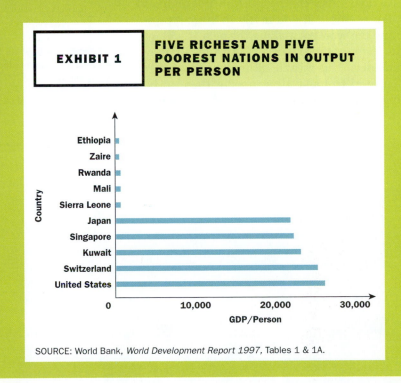

EXHIBIT 1

FIVE RICHEST AND FIVE POOREST NATIONS IN OUTPUT PER PERSON

SOURCE: World Bank, *World Development Report 1997*, Tables 1 & 1A.

Clearly, the optimal rate of growth will vary depending on the resources available in the economy. The primary point is that, regardless of the rate, sacrifices must be made for growth to occur.

HOW DO SACRIFICES LEAD TO GROWTH?

Specifically, to generate economic growth, a society must produce fewer consumer goods—like video games, stereos, cars, and so on—in the present and produce more capital goods. They must, then, sacrifice some consumption of consumer goods in the present in order to experience growth in the future. Why? Investing in capital goods like computers, and other new technological equipment, as well as investing in **human capital** by upgrading skills and knowledge, will shift out the economy's production possibilities over time. This will increase the future production capacity of the economy. That is, the economy that invests more now (consumes less now) will be able to produce, and therefore consume, more in the future.

This idea can be clearly illustrated by using the production possibilities curve (Exhibit 2). In terms of the production possibilities curve, economic growth means an outward shift in the "menu" of possible bundles of output. With growth comes the possibility to have more of both goods than were previously available. Suppose we were producing at point C (30 nets, 600 fish) on our original production possibilities curve. Additional resources and new methods of using them (technological progress) can lead to new production possibilities creating the potential for more of all goods (or more of some with no less of others). These increases would push the production possibilities curve outward. For example, if you invest in human capital, such as training the workers making the nets, it will increase the productivity of those workers. As a result, they will produce more nets. This means, ultimately, that fewer resources will be used to make nets, freeing them to be used for catching fish—resulting in a greater number of fish. Notice that, at point Z on the new curve, it is possible to produce 35 fishing nets and 750 fish, more of both goods than were previously produced, at point C.

GROWTH DOESN'T ELIMINATE SCARCITY

With all of this discussion of growth, it is important to remember that growth, or increases in a society's output, does not make scarcity disappear. Even when output has grown more rapidly than population so that people are made better off, they still face trade-offs: At any point along the production possibilities curve, in order to get more of one thing, you must give up something else. There are no free lunches *on* the production possibilities curve.

EXHIBIT 2	ECONOMIC GROWTH AND PRODUCTION POSSIBILITIES

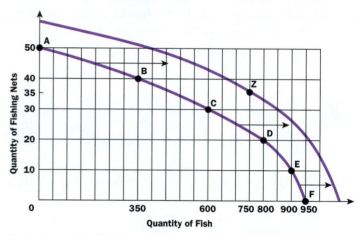

Economic growth shifts the production possibilities curve outward, allowing increased output of both fish and fishing nets (compare point Z with point C).

TUNE UP

PRODUCTION POSSIBILITIES CURVE

Q: The production possibilities curve shown in Exhibit 3 illustrates the choices faced by an economy that makes military goods and consumer goods. How are the economic concepts of scarcity, choice, opportunity costs, efficiency, and economic growth illustrated in this production possibilities curve framework?

A: In Exhibit 3 we can show scarcity, because resource combinations outside the production possibilities curve, like point D, are unattainable without economic growth. If the economy is operating efficiently, we are somewhere on the production possibilities curve, like point B or point C. However, if the economy is operating inefficiently, we are operating inside the production possibilities curve, like point A. We can also see in this graph that to get more military goods you must give up consumer goods—that is, there is an opportunity cost. Finally, we see that over time, with economic growth, the whole production possibilities curve can shift outward.

EXHIBIT 3	**PRODUCTION POSSIBILITIES CURVE**

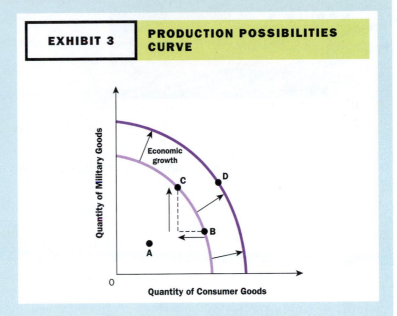

CONCEPT CHECK

1. Economies must decide how much current consumption they are willing to sacrifice for greater growth in the future.
2. Economic growth is represented by an outward shift of the production possibilities curve.
3. Economic growth increases the possibility of producing more of all goods.
4. Despite economic growth, scarcity inevitably remains a fact of life.

1. What is the essential question behind issues of economic growth?
2. What is the connection between sacrifices and economic growth?
3. How is economic growth shown in terms of production possibilities curves?
4. Why doesn't economic growth eliminate scarcity?
5. What would happen to the production possibilities curve in an economy where a new innovation greatly increased its ability to catch fish but did not change its ability to make fishing nets?

Application: Tourism versus Ecosystems

Is it possible to have more goods and services and a cleaner environment? Consider that question as you read the article below.

Canada's main transcontinental railway and transcontinental highway roll side-by-side down the length of Banff's main valley. On the busiest weekends, the road is clotted with cars, RVs, and tour buses, and a brown haze of exhaust fumes veils the celebrated vistas. Within the park lie three ski resorts and the town of Banff—home to 7,000 permanent residents. On the typical summer day, the townies may see 25,000 tourists streaming through their streets.

One local businessman and town council member remarked, "Environmentalists love to talk gloom and doom—but all you have to do is drive five miles out of town and you're in the middle of miles and miles of nothing but nature. You get tired of looking at all these big bare mountains; what's wrong with putting a restaurant or a little chalet up there to make it nicer for the people who come here?"

One thing that is wrong with it, according to a biologist who has studied wildlife throughout the Rocky Mountains, is that the human presence in Banff is wreaking havoc on the area's fragile makeup. "I'd say the park is in very, very poor condition compared with what is was 10 years ago, 20 years ago, 30 years ago," declared the biologist. "There's been a major decline in most of our large predators—black bears, grizzlies, wolverines, lynx, cougars. Such species are one of our best indicators of overall ecological health, and the way things are going, most of these animals will not survive here."

SOURCE: Adapted from "Rocky Times in Banff," *National Geographic,* July 1995.

Can Banff have more tourism *and* a better environment?

The principal point of this article is that choices have costs. In order to totally preserve the ecosystem of Banff, it would mean fewer tourists and commercial ventures. In this case, society must make a value judgment. If Banff is overdeveloped what will be the cost to future generations who will not be able to appreciate the visual splendors of this special "hamlet" nestled in the Canadian Rockies? On the other hand, how can you possibly accommodate the growing numbers of daily visitors without building additional restaurants, motels, and so on? Society must choose. This is demonstrated in the production possibilities curve in Exhibit 1. Society can choose point A (high

EXHIBIT 1 — PRODUCTION POSSIBILITIES CURVE

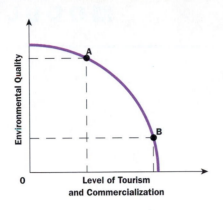

environmental quality but lower tourism *or* point B (more tourism and commercialization at the expense of the ecosystem), but society must choose. It involves a trade-off, and in this case Canada must choose between tourism and ecosystems.

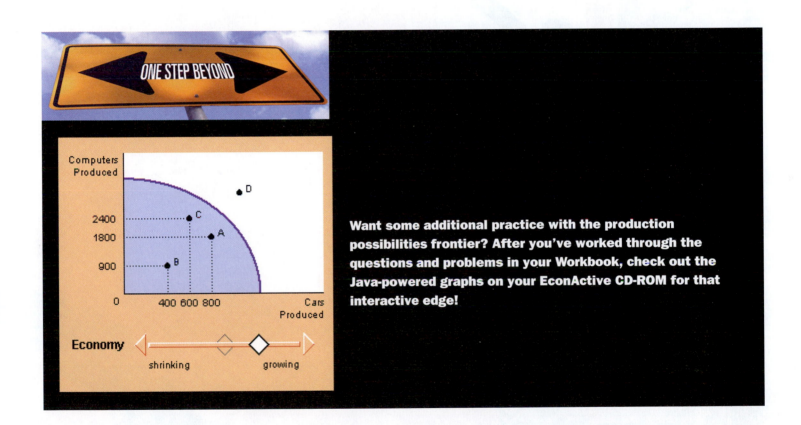

Want some additional practice with the production possibilities frontier? After you've worked through the questions and problems in your Workbook, check out the Java-powered graphs on your EconActive CD-ROM for that interactive edge!

PHOTO CREDITS MODULE 3

Page **66:** © Carr Clifton/Minden Pictures; Page **67:** © Larry Lee/Westlight Photography; Page **68:** Photo courtesy of Microsoft Corporation; Page **70:** © Hans Wiesenhofer/West Stock Photography; Page **73:** © PhotoDisc; Page **74:** bottom left, © 1998 Don Couch Photography; bottom right, © 1998 Don Couch Photography; Page **75:** © Chicago Tribune; Page **76:** Reprinted with special permission of King Features Syndicate; Page **77:** Checkpoint Systems; Page **78:** © Lennox McLendon/Associated Press; Page **79:** © Kozlowski Productions/FPG International; Page **84:** © Miles Ertman/Masterfile

Supply and Demand

A. Markets
What is a market?

B. Money and Relative Prices
Why are relative prices so important?

C. The Law of Demand
What is the difference between needs and wants?

D. The Demand Curve
Why is the demand curve negatively sloped?

E. Shifts in the Demand Curve
What are the major variables that determine the position
of the demand curve?

F. The Law of Supply
Why is the supply curve positively sloped?

G. Shifts in the Supply Curve
What are the major variables that determine the position
of the supply curve?

H. Application: A Shift in the Demand for Cuban Cigars
Which variables have impacted the demand curve for Cuban cigars?

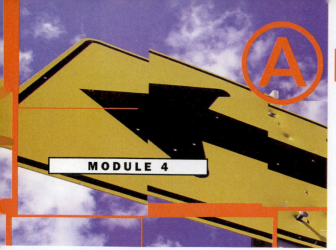

Ⓐ Markets

- Is a market just a geographic location?
- What are transaction costs?
- Why is it so difficult to define a market?

Is this a market?

Is this a market?

WHAT IS A MARKET?

Although we usually think of a **market** as a place where some sort of exchange occurs, a market is not really a place at all. A market is "a set of rules or an arrangement for the negotiation of exchange between buyers and sellers." You can think of a market as any situation where buyers, sellers, and middlepersons are in sufficiently close contact with one another to carry on exchange under a set of rules or customs. This means that supermarkets, the New York Stock Exchange, drug stores, roadside stands, garage sales, and restaurants are all markets.

The roles of buyers and sellers are undoubtedly familiar to you, but what is a middleperson? A middleperson is an individual who brings buyers and sellers together. For example, a realtor is a middleperson who exchanges information between buyers and sellers in the real estate market. Middlepersons help to reduce the **transaction costs**—the costs of making exchanges or transactions in a market.

WHY IS IT SO HARD TO *PRECISELY* DEFINE A MARKET?

Every market is different. That is, the conditions under which the exchange between buyers and sellers takes place can vary. These differences make it hard to precisely

Is this a market?

Is this a market?

define a market. After all, an incredible variety of exchange arrangements exists in the real world—organized securities markets, wholesale auction markets, foreign exchange markets, real estate markets, labor markets, and so forth.

The problem of defining a market is further compounded by goods being priced and traded in various ways at various locations by various kinds of buyers and sellers. For some goods, such as concrete, markets are numerous and more or less geographically isolated. Because transportation costs are so high relative to selling prices that the good will not be shipped any substantial distance, buyers are usually in contact only with local producers. Price and output are thus determined in a number of small

markets. In other industries, markets are national or even global. Automobile manufacturers, for example, sell to dealers throughout the world and determine prices and output largely on the basis of considerations relating to the domestic and global economies. Despite their differences, however, all of these situations are illustrations of markets in action.

Markets are not even defined by any moment in time: Goods can trade across space and time. For example, there are futures markets where buyers and sellers can trade bales of cotton that do not even exist yet. The important point is not what a market looks like, but what it does—it facilitates trade.

CONCEPT CHECK

1. Markets consist of buyers, sellers, and middle-persons making exchanges with one another.
2. Transaction costs are the costs of making exchanges in a market.

3. Markets can be regional, national, or global.

1. What are transaction costs?
2. Why is it hard to precisely define a market?
3. Why do you get your produce at a supermarket rather than directly from farmers?

4. Why do the prices people pay for similar items at garage sales vary more than the prices they pay for similar items in a department store?

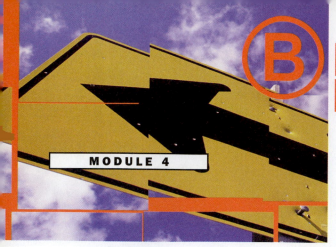

(B) Money and Relative Prices

- What is a money price?
- What is a relative price?

WHAT IS A MONEY PRICE?

Over the past 50 years, few goods have fallen in **money price**—that is, the price that you or I would pay in dollars and cents. The money price is sometimes called the absolute or nominal price, expressed in dollars of current purchasing power. There have been a few well-known examples of falling money prices—personal calculators, cellular telephones, video recorders, home computers, and so on—but the evidence indicates that *most* prices have risen in money terms.

Does the money price of most goods fall?

IN THE NEWS

LUNDBERG SURVEY SAYS GASOLINE PRICES HIT HISTORIC LOW IN 1998

According to a March 1998 survey, the average annual cost of gasoline to consumers in 1998 (in inflation-adjusted 1998 dollars) was the lowest since 1920, the beginning of recorded pump prices.

Prices have fallen despite rising taxes and more money spent to make environmentally cleaner gasoline by the oil industry. The reasons for the lower gasoline prices are: lower crude oil prices, improved technology in refining, distribution, and marketing, and most recently, the price wars among refiners and distributors.

The average retail price for all grades of gasoline was $1.09 per gallon in March of 1998. That's $1.18 less than it was in 1981, when pump prices reached an all-time high of $2.27 per gallon.

SOURCE: Cable News Network, Inc. (http://cnn.com/US/9803/08/briefs.pm/gas.prices/index.html), March 1998.

CONSIDER THIS:
Gasoline prices, when measured against the average price of all goods and services (that is, relative to the price of other goods and services), reached an all-time low in 1998, even though the money price of gasoline in the 1960s was far lower, at only 30 to 40 cents per gallon.

WHAT IS THE DIFFERENCE BETWEEN MONEY PRICES AND RELATIVE PRICES?

Money prices themselves are of little importance to most economic decisions in a world where virtually all prices are changing. It is **relative price,** the price of one good relative to others, that is crucial. If the price of movies rises relative to all other goods, we would predict that fewer people would go to the movies, *ceteris paribus.* They would look for alternative forms of entertainment, such as bowling, the video arcade, or watching television, or they might just go to the movies less frequently.

If the price of movies rises relative to other types of entertainment, will fewer people go to the movies?

T U N E   U P

TOOLING UP: RELATIVE PRICES

Q: Mary Witt-Children, a former economics major, has a theory about couples who eat out at restaurants. Her theory is as follows: When compared with childless couples, couples with young children, when dining *without* their kids, are more likely to eat out at an expensive restaurant than at an inexpensive restaurant, *ceteris paribus.* Do you think Mary is on to something?

A: The key to this question is relative prices. Add a $20 babysitting charge to the cost of an inexpensive meal and to an expensive meal:

When couples with children go out to eat without their kids, will they be more likely to go to an expensive or inexpensive restaurant, *ceteris paribus*?

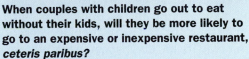

	Inexpensive Meal	Expensive Meal
Babysitting	$20	$ 20
Meal for two	20	80
Total	$40	$100

As you can see from the table, the babysitter's cost doubles the price of the inexpensive meal from $20 to $40, a 100 percent increase ($20/$20 = 100 percent). By comparison, the cost of a babysitter only increases the total price of the expensive meal from $80 to $100, a 25 percent increase ($20/$80 = 25 percent). Thus, for couples with children, the relative price of an expensive meal as compared to that of an inexpensive meal is lower. So for those couples with small children, we would predict a greater proportion of dinners out to be at expensive restaurants, *ceteris paribus.*

CONCEPT CHECK

1. The money price is what one pays in terms of dollars and cents.
2. The relative price is the price of one good relative to another.
3. Over time, money prices have risen for most goods.

---

1. How are money prices and relative prices different?
2. Why are economists so concerned about relative prices?
3. The money price of most goods has risen over time. What does that mean?
4. If Motel 6 began by charging $6 per night for a room but now charges $36 per night, what would have to be true for the relative price of its motel rooms to have fallen in that period?

© The Law of Demand

- What is the law of demand?
- Why do we say demand reflects willingness to pay?
- What is the difference between *needs* and *wants*?

WHAT IS THE LAW OF DEMAND?

Some laws are made to protect us, like "no speeding" or "no driving after drinking," while other laws are "natural" laws that are observed as behavior in various physical and social settings. One such natural law is the **law of demand,** which relates the price of a good to the quantity of that good demanded. According to the law of demand, the quantity of a good or service demanded varies inversely with its price, *ceteris paribus*. More directly, the law of demand says that, other things being equal, when the price (P) of a good or service falls, the quantity demanded (Q_d) increases, and conversely, if the price of a good or service rises, the quantity demanded decreases.

$$P \uparrow \Rightarrow Q_d \downarrow \quad \text{and} \quad P \downarrow \Rightarrow Q_d \uparrow$$

In the law of demand, price represents the sacrifice that a buyer must make in order to obtain a good. If obtaining a good required greater sacrifice than before, would you want as much of it? The relationship described by the law of demand is an **inverse,** or **negative, relationship,** because the variables move in opposite directions.

What can be done to alter reckless driving behavior?

DOES THE LAW OF DEMAND MAKE SENSE?

Stop reading for a second and try to think of a contradiction to the law of de-

If your house had been on the market for a year and you could not sell it at the current price, would you raise the price or lower it?

mand. Can you think of an item for which you would rather pay more than less? Have you ever heard anyone on a television or radio advertisement boasting that they have the highest prices in town? Just imagine the owner of a car dealership saying: "If you can find prices higher anywhere, bring in the receipt and we will match it. We won't be beat!"

If you had any product for sale and could not sell it, would you raise the price or lower it? You get the point. If you raise the price, you will sell less, *ceteris paribus* (that is, holding other variables such as income and taste constant). If you lower the price, you will sell more, holding everything else constant. Or if the opportunity cost of robbing a bank rises for any reason—say, because of a greater probability of being caught, of being convicted, or of receiving a stiffer sentence—we would expect fewer robberies. This is the law of demand, too, because we expect less of certain activities if the costs or prices of those activities rise.

WILL A CHANGE IN THE PRICE (OR COST) CHANGE DRIVING BEHAVIOR?

Malibu Canyon is a winding, two-lane road, where one driver can legally pass another in only a few places. What would we expect most drivers to do if the local judge declared that anyone crossing the solid, double-yellow lines would have to pay a $10,000 fine? Or what if the fatality statistics for the year were posted at the entrance of the canyon? Would this alter some drivers' "desire" to speed?

At some price, even the thrill-seekers would slow down, and each of the above circumstances should reduce the demand for speed (so, incidentally, would bad brakes, bald tires, and poor visibility). On the other hand, compulsory seat belts and airbags (side, front, and back) might cause drivers to drive faster. That is, making the car safer (or less safe) changes the ultimate cost to the driver and may alter his or her risk behavior.

IS DEMAND A WILLINGNESS TO PAY?

Demand is more than an imaginary desirability notion. For example, if you were to say, "I really would like a new Porsche," this statement, to be a true demand, must imply a willingness to pay for the Porsche. In every instance, one must be willing to give up other goods or services in order to get a desired good. For example, say you go to Tower Records and state that, at $15, you want one Smashing Pumpkins compact disc. The money measure here is merely a convenience. What you are really saying is that you are willing to give up $15 of anything else you might have purchased to get the CD. The concept of demand, then, really involves comparing goods with goods, not goods with money. It represents a willingness to pay (give up other goods) to get additional amounts of the good under consideration.

WHY IS THERE A NEGATIVE RELATIONSHIP BETWEEN PRICE AND QUANTITY DEMANDED?

As we mentioned earlier, the law of demand describes a negative relationship between price and quantity demanded. When price goes up, the quantity demanded goes down, and vice versa. But why is this so? The primary reason for this inverse relationship is the **substitution effect**. At higher prices, buyers increasingly substitute other goods for the good that now has a higher relative price. For example, if the price of orange juice increases, some consumers may substitute out of orange juice into other juices, such as apple or tomato juice, or perhaps water, milk, or coffee. This is what economists call the substitution effect of a price change. Of course, if the relative price of orange juice fell, then consumers would substitute out of other products and increase their quantity of orange juice demanded, because the lower relative price now makes it a more attractive purchase. The

primary reason for the inverse relationship between price and quantity demanded is the substitution effect.

WHAT IS THE DIFFERENCE BETWEEN *NEEDS* AND *WANTS*?

The law of demand puts the concept of basic human "needs," at least as an analytical tool, to rest. **Needs** are those things that you must have at any price. That is, there are no substitutes. There are usually plenty of substitutes for any good available, some better than others. The law of demand, with its inverse relationship between price and quantity demanded, implies that even so-called needs are more or less urgent, depending on the circumstances (opportunity costs). Whenever you hear somebody say, "I need a new car," "I need a new stereo," or "I need new clothes," always be sure to ask: What does the person really mean? At what price does that person "need" the good?

Do you *need* a new stereo or do you *want* a new stereo at the current price? Would you still "need" a new stereo if a new one cost $15,000?

For example, the person who claims that he or she needs a new car must sacrifice the items that could have been purchased if he or she did not purchase the car—perhaps jet skis, a stereo, clothes, and so on. In addition, there are many substitutes for cars, including motorcycles, buses, car pools, hitchhiking, or moving closer to work. In Module 1, we discussed the rule of rational choice, which must be applied here: Do the expected marginal benefits from purchasing a new car exceed the expected marginal costs? That is the relevant question. To answer that question wisely, we must realize that there are substitutes for just about everything and that decisions require choices, which always imply costs. Hence, we must weigh the benefits against the costs even for so-called needs.

GOODYEAR BEGINS SEARCH FOR HIGHWAY HEROES

Akron, OH—Each year, nominations for the Goodyear National Highway Hero roll in from motorists, fellow truck drivers, law enforcement officials, and trucking company representatives across the country. Previous years' nominees have demonstrated a wide range of heroics—from a driver who snatched a child out of a swirling tornado's path to a driver who posts pictures of missing children on the sides of his rig.

SOURCE: PR Newswire and The Goodyear Tire & Rubber Company, September 8, 1997.

CONSIDER THIS:
Some people will help others even when the costs are high. The truck driver who pulled the child out of the way of the swirling tornado wanted to save a stranger's life even when the cost to him, the possibility that he might lose his own life, was high. Since most people wouldn't risk their own life to save a stranger's, it demonstrates that benefits and costs are subjective.

Why would a truck driver risk his own life to pull an endangered child from the path of a tornado? Given the alternative, the death of a child, he was willing to risk his own life.

DO WE *NEED* MORE FREEWAYS?

Commuters are constantly complaining about how long it takes to drive to work. Do we *need* more freeways?

Perhaps many commuters would like to see more taxpayer dollars going toward freeways instead of museums, schools, or parks. Remember, the concept of need implies some type of urgency and conveys the message: "I will give up anything to get it." The real question is: At what price do we want more freeways? Would we need more freeways if the price of downtown parking was $1,000 a day? Probably not. Try to train yourself to think that we want different amounts of goods and services at different opportunity costs, and that costs are more than just dollars and cents. For example, a person who normally does not speed while driving may do so if the relevant benefit of speed rises—for example, if he is late for his final exam or wedding, or if she is on her way to the hospital to deliver her baby.

Would we "need" new freeways if parking was $1,000 a day?

SHOULD THERE BE EXPRESS LANES FOR URGENT NEEDS AT THE SUPERMARKET?

Occasionally, we encounter huge lines at all the open check-out counters in our local supermarkets. Perhaps we should have an express lane for people who have urgent needs. What do you think of this idea?

This idea would probably fail because a lot of people would develop what they felt were urgent needs if the "urgent need" line was much shorter than the other lines. It would be inevitable that the system would fall apart. In fact, it would be fun to guess what might be defined as an urgent need. It might include: "I am really in a hurry because I have to get home to clean up my apartment" or "I need to get back to the dorm to type my overdue term paper." Many people would perceive their needs as more urgent than other people's urgent needs. This is a reason that the concept of needs falls apart as a means of explaining behavior. It is impossible to make the concept of need useful when it is so hard to define or compare among people.

WHAT DO WE NEED? DOES IT DEPEND ON WHAT WE HAVE TO GIVE UP?

Water, air, and food are all items necessary to keep us alive. However, in the extreme, we may not even need these items. Imagine a hypothetical situation in which your car breaks down in the middle of the desert and there is no one within 100 miles. No one knows where you are. You and your eight-year-old daughter have no food or water, and you don't own a cellular telephone. Your only option is walking to find help. After 50 miles, you come across one bottle of water—enough for one of you to survive. You need water, but do you need water at the cost of your daughter's life? Perhaps you do not even "need" your life if you have to give up something more valuable to you— your daughter's life. While this is an extreme example, it emphasizes the point that a need implies *at any cost* and also illustrates that costs and benefits vary with different individuals and situations.

Similarly, most would not consider taking the life of another, but under certain circumstances—self-defense in a life or death situation, war, or even disconnecting the life-support system of a terminally ill loved one—some might. While any of these circumstances may alter the decisions of some individuals, they may not have impact on others. Costs and benefits are subjective.

Need water?

CONCEPT CHECK

1. The law of demand states that when the price of a good falls (rises), the quantity demanded rises (falls), *ceteris paribus*.
2. Demand is a willingness to pay for what you want.
3. The term *needs* implies that there are no substitutes.
4. Because there are substitutes for most goods, economists use the term *wants* rather than *needs*.

---

1. What is an inverse, or negative, relationship?
2. How do lower prices change buyers' incentives?
3. How do higher prices change buyers' incentives?
4. How does demand represent willingness to pay?
5. Why do economists prefer talking about wants and desires rather than needs?
6. If even a minor cheating infraction was punished by expulsion, what would happen to the extent of cheating on campus?
7. Assume that we "need" water, food, clothing, and shelter to survive. Why is talking about these as needs not very helpful in analyzing choices that must be made among them?

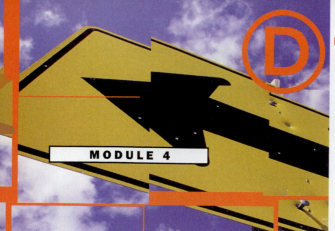

D The Demand Curve

- What is an individual demand schedule?
- What is an individual demand curve?
- What is a market demand schedule?
- What is a market demand curve?

WHAT IS AN INDIVIDUAL DEMAND SCHEDULE?

The **individual demand schedule** of an individual buyer for a product reveals the different amounts of that product the person would be willing to buy at various possible prices in a particular time interval. For example, Bob, a college student, enjoys drinking coffee. How many pounds of coffee will Bob be willing to buy at various prices during the year? At a price of $3 a pound, Bob buys 15 pounds of coffee over the course of a year. If the price is higher, at $4 per pound, he might only buy 10 pounds; if it is lower, say $1 per pound, he might buy 25 pounds of coffee during the year. Bob's demand for coffee for the year is summarized in the demand schedule in Exhibit 1. Bob might not be consciously aware of the amounts that he would purchase at prices other than the prevailing one. But that does not alter the fact that he has a schedule, in the sense that he would have bought various other amounts had other prices prevailed. It must be emphasized that the schedule is a list of alternative possibilities. At any one time, only one of the prices will prevail, and thus a certain quantity will be purchased.

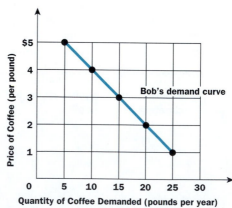

WHAT IS AN INDIVIDUAL DEMAND CURVE?

By plotting the different prices and corresponding quantities demanded from Bob's demand schedule in Exhibit 1 and then connecting them, we can create an **individual demand curve** for Bob (Exhibit 2). From the curve, we can see that when the price is higher, Bob demands fewer pounds of coffee, and when the price is lower, he demands more pounds of coffee. The curve is merely an aid for understanding, summarizing compactly the information in the demand schedule. For any price, the curve reveals the quantity of coffee Bob would purchase.

EXHIBIT 2	BOB'S DEMAND CURVE FOR COFFEE

The dots represent various quantities of coffee that Bob would be willing to buy at different prices in a given time period. The demand curve is formed by connecting the dots representing these price–quantity demanded pairs.

EXHIBIT 1	BOB'S DEMAND SCHEDULE FOR COFFEE

Price (per pound)	Quantity Demanded (pounds per year)
$5	5
4	10
3	15
2	20
1	25

IS THERE A DEMAND CURVE FOR ROADKILL?

SARA CORBETT

"You can pan-fry it, grill it, or put it in chili," reports Elizabeth Hatch of West Danville, Vermont. "And it makes the best lasagne you ever ate." At the Elks Lodge in Montpelier, chef Norm Champagne prepares it *au poivre*, deglazing the pan with brandy. "Folks who think it's weird don't bother to come around," he says.

Clear your plate for a helping of roadkill. Partly in response to a shorter moose-hunting season, Vermonters have found a way to get their fill of the knob-kneed beast: Follow the squealing tires. Under a program sanctioned by the state, a game warden will be dispatched any time a moose is reported killed by a passing vehicle. The carcass is winched onto a truck, driven to a butcher, and packaged into five-pound parcels. The meat then makes its way to dining room tables, according to a lengthy waiting list. The price per pound: $1.25. "It's the only way to get the stuff anymore," says game warden Evan Eastman. Regarding splattered moose's effect on the palate, opinions vary. "A leaner rendering of beef," says one fan. "A less stringy version of horse meat," claims another. A more reluctant connoisseur puts it this way: "Needs garlic."

SOURCE: *Outside*, June 1995, p. 32.

WHAT IS A MARKET DEMAND CURVE?

Although we introduced this concept in terms of the individual, economists usually speak of the demand curve in terms of large groups of people—a whole nation, a community, or a trading area. As you know, every single individual has his or her demand curve for every product. The horizontal summing of the demand curves of many individuals is called the **market demand curve**.

Suppose the consumer group is comprised of Homer, Marge, and the rest of their small community, Springfield, and that the product is still coffee. The effect of price on the quantity of coffee demanded by Marge, Homer, and the rest of Springfield is given in the demand schedule and demand curves shown in Exhibit 3. Homer would be willing to buy 20 pounds of coffee per year at a price of $4 per pound, and 25 pounds per year at $3 per pound. Marge would be willing to buy 10 pounds per year at $4, and 15 pounds per year at $3. The rest of Springfield would be willing to buy 2,970 pounds at $4, and 4,960 pounds at $3. The market demand curve is simply the (horizontal) sum of the quantities Homer, Marge, and the rest of Springfield

---

EXHIBIT 3	CHEATING A MARKET DEMAND CURVE

a. Creating a Market Demand Schedule for Coffee

	Quantity Demanded (pounds per year)							
Price (per pound)	Homer	+	Marge	+	Rest of Springfield	=	Market Demand
$4	20	+	10	+	2,970	=	3,000
$3	25	+	15	+	4,960	=	5,000

b. Creating a Market Demand Curve for Coffee

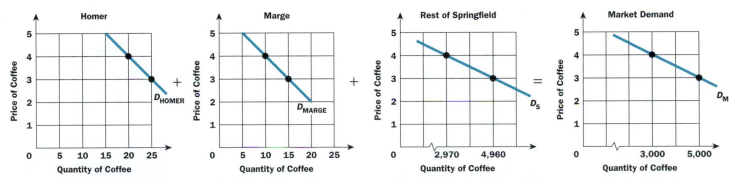

---

demand at each price. That is, at $4, the quantity demanded in the market would be 3,000 pounds of coffee (20 + 10 + 2,970 = 3,000), and at $3, the quantity demanded in the market would be 5,000 pounds of coffee (25 + 15 + 4,960 = 5,000).

In Exhibit 4, we offer a more complete set of prices and quantities from the market demand for coffee during the year. Remember, the market demand curve shows the amounts that all the buyers in the market would be willing to buy at various prices. For example, if the price of coffee is $2 per pound, consumers in the market would collectively be willing to buy 8,000 pounds per week. At $1 per pound, the amount demanded would be 12,000 pounds per week.

DON'T FORGET ABOUT RELATIVE PRICES!

Suppose you were exploring the inflation that prevailed in the United States during the 1960s and 1970s. You found that from 1960 to 1973, the price of gasoline at the pump rose markedly, but the quantities of gasoline demanded did not fall. Is this a flaw in the law of demand?

No. While it is true that gasoline prices in dollars rose significantly over this period, so did just about everything else—including wages. As it turns out, the relative price of gasoline, the price of gasoline as compared to that of other goods, did not change much over this period. Thus, we would not expect this to cause a fall in the quantity demanded (holding other things constant, especially income). That is, because the *relative* price did not rise, we would not expect a fall in gasoline consumption as a result.

EXHIBIT 4 | **A MARKET DEMAND CURVE**

a. Market Demand Schedule for Coffee

Price (per pound)	Total Quantity Demanded (pounds per year)
$5	1,000
4	3,000
3	5,000
2	8,000
1	12,000

b. Market Demand Curve for Coffee

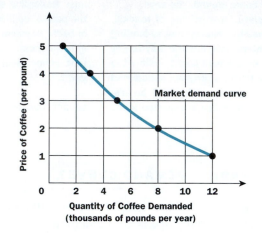

CONCEPT CHECK

1. An individual demand curve is a graphical representation of the different amounts of a good a person would be willing to buy at various prices.

2. The market demand curve shows the amount of a good that all the buyers in the market would be willing to buy at various prices.

1. What is an individual demand schedule?
2. What difference is there between an individual demand curve and a market demand curve?

3. Why does the amount of dating on campus tend to decline just before and during final exams?

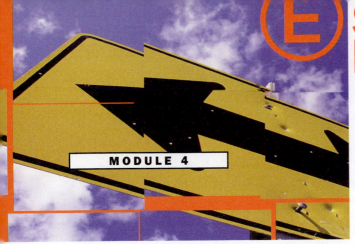

E Shifts in the Demand Curve

■ What is the difference between a change in demand and a change in quantity demanded?
■ What are substitutes and complements?
■ What are normal and inferior goods?
■ How does the number of buyers affect the demand curve?
■ How do changes in taste affect the demand curve?
■ How do changing expectations affect the demand curve?

WHAT IS THE DIFFERENCE BETWEEN A CHANGE IN DEMAND AND A CHANGE IN QUANTITY DEMANDED?

Economists think consumers are influenced by the prices of goods when they make their purchasing decisions. At lower prices, people prefer to buy more of a good than at higher prices, holding other factors constant. Why? Primarily, it is because goods are substitutes in various degrees for one another. A rise in the price of one good results in less of it, and more of other now relatively more attractive alternative goods, being bought. For example, an increase in the price of coffee might tempt some buyers to switch from buying coffee to buying tea or soft drinks. Understanding this relationship between price and how much consumers are willing to purchase is so important that economists make a clear distinction between it and the various other factors that can influence consumer behavior. A change in a good's own price is said to lead to a **change in quantity demanded.** That is, it "moves you along" a given demand curve. In contrast, a change in one of the other five factors that can influence consumer behavior—the prices of closely related goods, the incomes of demanders, number of demanders, tastes of demanders, and expectations of demanders—is said to lead to a **change in demand.** That is, a change in one of these factors shifts the entire demand curve. An increase in demand shifts the demand curve to the right; a decrease in demand shifts the demand curve to the left, as seen in Exhibit 1.

Remember that the law of demand expresses a relationship that is expected to hold when the *ceteris paribus* assumptions are met. If all these other factors are held constant, quantity demanded varies inversely with price (that is, if the price rises, the quantity demanded falls, and if the price falls, the quantity demanded rises). The *ceteris paribus* assumption allows us to isolate the effect of the price of a good on the quantity of that good that is demanded from other possible determinants. While this distinction may seem confusing to you at first, it will become clearer as we discuss in greater detail the five variables that lead to a change in demand.

| EXHIBIT 1 | DEMAND SHIFTS |

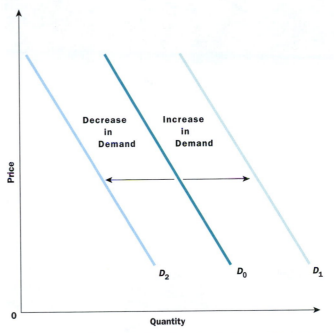

An increase in demand shifts the demand curve to the right. A decrease in demand shifts the demand curve to the left.

WHAT IS PYNTE?

The variables that shift the demand curve can be recalled using a memory device: PYNTE (the Old English spelling of *pint*). PYNTE stands for: P, prices of closely related goods; Y, incomes of demanders; N, number of demanders; T, tastes of demanders; and E, expectations of demanders. All of these variables are capable of shifting the demand curve to the right or left. We will now look more closely at each of these variables.

THE PRICES OF OTHER CLOSELY RELATED GOODS (*P*)

Each good and service has its own-price. But what does **own-price** mean? If Coca Cola sells a two-liter plastic bottle for $1, then $1 is said to be the own-price. Own-price,

The price of the item in question is its own-price.

then, is just the price of the item or service in question. Consumers are influenced by the own-price of a good or service in deciding how much of that good or service they want to buy. That relationship is summarized in the law of demand. However, consumers are also influenced by the prices of other goods and services—substitute goods and complementary goods.

Substitute Goods

Suppose you go into a store to buy RC Cola and you observe that Pepsi is on sale for half its usual price. Is it possible that you might decide to buy Pepsi instead of RC Cola? Economists argue that this is the case, and empirical tests have confirmed that persons are responsive to both own-prices and the prices of other goods. Note that, in this example, Pepsi is said to be a substitute for RC Cola. We can call it a **substitute good.** Generally speaking, the closer one good is as a substitute for a second good, the greater the impact that a change in the price of the first good will have on the willingness of consumers to buy the second. Thus, if the price of paper towels goes up, the impact on my decision to purchase RC Cola is likely to be negligible because my demand for cola is probably not closely related to how many paper towels I use. A fall in the price of a substitute good will, other things being equal, reduce demand for the good in question (a leftward shift); conversely, an increase in the price of a substitute will increase demand for the good in question (a rightward shift). If the price of apples rises, you are more likely to demand more oranges at the prevailing price for oranges, assuming you view these goods as substitutes. You should remember, however, that what are substitute goods for one person may not be so for another person, because personal tastes differ.

Good and Poor Substitutes

There are good substitutes and poor substitutes. For most people, good substitutes include butter and margarine, and Coca-Cola and Pepsi. Poor substitutes might include

IN THE NEWS

CAN A WIENER BECOME A POORER SUBSTITUTE FOR HAMBURGER?

Ashland, OR—The Oscar Mayer "Wiener-mobile" has been dogged along its cross-country tour this summer by a protesting pig—or rather a protester in a pig get-up—courtesy of the animal rights group People for the Ethical Treatment of Animals (PETA).

"Kids would lose their lunch if they knew what actually went into a wiener," says PETA President Ingrid Newkirk.

SOURCE: "Animal Activists Get Violent," *The Christian Science Monitor*, August 29, 1997.

CONSIDER THIS:
If many parents and their kids were influenced dramatically by this message from PETA, hot dogs would no longer be considered a close substitute for hamburgers by those families. As a result, we would predict that many would no longer increase their demand for hot dogs in response to an increase in the price of hamburgers.

If hot dogs and hamburgers are substitutes, what would happen to the demand for hot dogs if the price of hamburgers increased?

TUNE UP

SUBSTITUTE GOODS

Q: Suppose that you and your roommate are each partial to your own brand of soft drink. However, when the price of your brand, Sprite, increases, you decide to give your roommate's brand, 7-Up, a try. What would we call these two goods? Can you describe the change you would expect to see in the demand curve for 7-Up as the price for your soda, Sprite, increases?

A: If the price of one good increases and, as a result, an individual buys more of another good, the two related goods are substitutes. That is, buying more of one reduces purchases of the other. In Exhibit 2(a), we see that as the price of Sprite increased—a movement up along your demand curve for it—you increased your demand for 7-Up, resulting in a shift in the demand for 7-Up (Exhibit 2(b)). However, if you hated your roommate's brand of soft drink, then it might not matter if she were giving it away, but that is highly unlikely. The substitution effect varies among individuals, but in the aggregate, we can recognize substitutes fairly well. For example, if the price of gasoline increased significantly relative to other goods, we would predict that more people would car pool, buy cars that were more fuel efficient, use mass transit more often, shop less frequently, and so on, because each of these is a substitute for gasoline for some people.

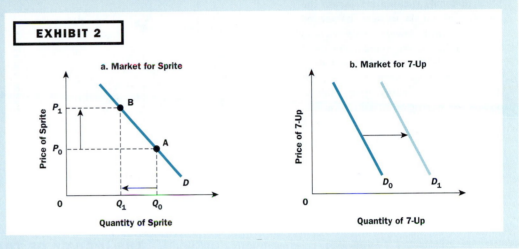

EXHIBIT 2

a. Market for Sprite

b. Market for 7-Up

economic textbooks and T-shirts, or hammers and shoes. Between these extremes, the quality of substitutes may be less clear. Consider, for example, children and pets. If the cost of raising children rises relative to other things, what will happen to the demand for pets? For some people—those who see a pet as an adequate substitute for a child—it would increase (shift to the right). These are a few examples of good and bad substitutes, keeping in mind that the degree of substitutability varies with different individuals.

Complementary Goods

Economists recognize that individuals are influenced not only by the prices of substitute goods but also by the prices of **complementary goods.** Complementary goods are things that "go together," often consumed and used simultaneously, such as skis and bindings, or hot dogs and mustard. For example, if the price of motorcycles rises sharply, other things equal, the demand for the complementary motorcycle helmets will fall. Why is this? As the price of motorcycles rises, *ceteris paribus*, fewer motorcycles are sold (a change in the quantity of motorcycles demanded, not in motorcycle demand!). Thus, people will also demand fewer motorcycle helmets at prevailing prices (a

change in demand for motorcycle helmets, not in the quantity demanded!). Likewise, a decrease in the price of stereo equipment probably will lead to an increase in the demand (a rightward shift) for compact discs and tapes, because falling stereo prices should, other things equal, lead to greater sales of stereo equipment (an increase in quantity demanded) and an increase in demand for

"Come on. If you sell beer, you must sell peanuts."

COMPLEMENTARY GOODS

Q: As he looked over the rackets hanging on the wall of the local sports shop, Clay Kort, an aspiring young tennis player, noticed that the price of the rackets was much higher (due to cost increases) than last month. Clay predicted that this increase in the relative price of tennis rackets would probably lead to a reduced demand for tennis balls. Do you agree with Clay?

A: Clay realized that there would be fewer tennis players on the courts if tennis rackets increased in price. In Exhibit 3(a) we see that as the price of tennis rackets increases, the quantity of tennis rackets demanded falls. And with fewer tennis rackets being purchased, we would also expect people to decrease their demand (a leftward shift) for tennis balls (Exhibit 3(b)). There are many other athletic equipment examples of complements: skis and bindings, golf clubs and golf balls, bows and arrows, and so on.

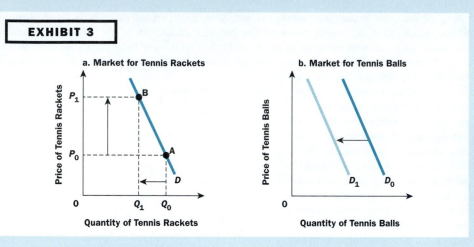

EXHIBIT 3

a. Market for Tennis Rackets

b. Market for Tennis Balls

---

complements like compact discs and tapes that are played on the stereo equipment. To summarize: An increase in the price of a complementary good will reduce demand for the product in question; a decrease in the price of a complementary good will increase demand for the product in question.

If the price of motorcycles rises, what do you think will happen to motorcycle helmet demand, *ceteris paribus*?

THE INCOME OF THE CONSUMER (*Y*)

Economists have observed that the consumption of goods and services is generally positively related to the income available to consumers. (Note: Economists often use the symbol Y to denote *income* because, in the discussion of macroeconomics, the letter I is used to denote *investment*.) Empirical studies support the notion that as individuals receive more income they tend to increase their purchases of most goods and services. For example, at your present level of income, the quantity of Porsche or Mercedes-Benz cars you demand at prevailing prices is probably zero. You tell yourself that you cannot afford such a luxury car. The opportunity cost is too great. If you were to buy a new Porsche, you simply could not live in the quality of housing that you deem appropriate, you could not obtain the amount of other consumer goods that you would like, and you would be forced to drastically curtail your travel below your usual levels.

On the other hand, if your income were to suddenly increase substantially (say, for instance, you won your state Lotto), then the opportunity cost of that new Porsche might not seem that prohibitive any longer. Remember, the price of the Porsche is still equal to the goods that you have to give up to buy it. However, you are now richer and you can buy more of all goods and services than before the

NORMAL AND INFERIOR GOODS

Q: Chester Drawer owns a furniture shop. With the recent boom in the economy (higher average income per person and fewer people unemployed), can Chester expect to sell more furniture?

A: Yes. In general, furniture is considered a normal good, so a rise in income will increase the demand for furniture (Exhibit 4(a)). However, if Chester sells unfinished, used, or lower-quality furniture, the demand for his products may fall, as higher incomes allow customers to buy furniture that is finished, new, or is of higher quality. Chester's furniture would then be an inferior good (Exhibit 4(b)).

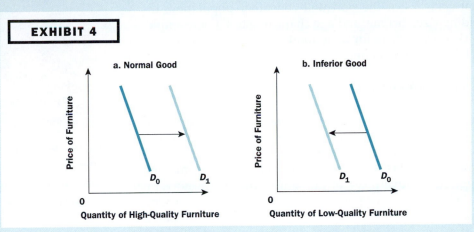

EXHIBIT 4

a. Normal Good — Price of Furniture / Quantity of High-Quality Furniture, D_0 to D_1

b. Inferior Good — Price of Furniture / Quantity of Low-Quality Furniture, D_1 to D_0

Lotto drawing. Thus, the cost of the car to you, in terms of the value to you of other items foregone, is now less than before, increasing the likelihood that you will buy it. Other things held equal, rising income usually leads to an increase in the demand for goods (a shift of the demand curve to the right), and decreasing income usually leads to a decrease in the demand for goods (a shift of the demand curve to the left).

Normal and Inferior Goods

Where higher incomes lead to a greater demand for the good, the good is called a **normal good.** However, there are some goods for which rising income leads to reduced demand. These are called **inferior goods.** For example, inferior goods for most people might include do-it-yourself haircuts, used cars, clothes from thrift shops, mail-order dentures, mini-mart burritos, store-brand products, and so on. Suppose most individuals prefer steak to hamburger, but usually buy hamburger because it is cheaper. Hamburger, then, is considered to be inferior to steak. As incomes rise, many persons may switch from buying hamburger to buying steak. Thus, the demand for hamburger may actually fall as incomes rise over this range. However, the concept of inferior versus normal goods differs among groups. Hamburger may be an inferior good in some countries, but not in others. In poorer countries where hamburger is still something of a luxury food, increased incomes may lead to greater demand for ham-

If people consume fewer fast-food meals when they become wealthier, what kind of good is a fast-food meal?

burger (and perhaps less demand for beans or rice). Whether goods are normal or inferior, the point here is that increasing income influences demand—usually positively, but sometimes negatively.

NUMBER OF BUYERS (N)

The demand for a good or service will vary with the size of the potential consumer population. The demand for wheat, for example, rises as population increases, because the added population wants to consume some wheat-derived products, like bread or cereal. Marketing experts, who closely follow the patterns of consumer behavior with regards to a particular good or service, are usually vitally concerned with the "demographics" of the product—the vital statistics of the potential consumer population, including size, income, and age characteristics. For example, market researchers for baby food companies keep a close watch on the birth rate.

TASTE CHANGES (T)

The demand for a good or service may increase or decrease suddenly with changes in fashions or fads. These non-price, non-income-related causes of changes in demand are said to be due to "taste changes." These taste changes may be triggered by advertising or promotion, by a news story, by the behavior of some popular public figure, and so on. One area in which taste changes are noticeable is in apparel. Shirt lapels, coat lapels, and ties change frequently. Recently, we have seen a resurgence in miniskirts as "the thing" to wear. But overall, in the last 10 years, skirts of all types suffered a decline in demand, as women began wearing pants in unprecedented numbers. Casual clothes in general have grown in popularity for both men and women.

Changes in preferences naturally lead to shifts in demand. Much of the predictive power of economic theory, however, stems from the assumption that tastes are relatively stable, at least over a substantial period of time. Tastes *do* change, though. A person may grow tired of one type of recreation or peanut butter and try another type. Changes in occupation, number of dependents, state of health, and age also tend to alter preferences. The birth of a baby may cause a family to spend less on recreation and more on food and clothing. Illness increases the demand for medicine and lessens purchases of other goods. A cold winter increases the demand for fuel. Changes in customs and traditions also affect preferences, and the development of new products draws consumer preferences away from other goods. Compact discs have replaced record albums, just as inline skates have replaced traditional roller skates.

What happens to the demand for baby products when birth rates increase?

EXPECTATIONS ABOUT THE FUTURE (*E*)

Sometimes the demand for a good or service in a given time period will dramatically increase or decrease because consumers expect the good to change in price or availability at some future date. When the Korean War broke out in the summer of 1950, car sales boomed because consumers were fearful that automobile production would be stopped, just as it had a few years earlier at the beginning of World War II. Individuals moved up the date of their new car purchases to avoid not being able to get one for several years.

T U N E   U P

EXPECTATIONS OF HIGHER PRICES

Q: Say it was just announced that next year there will be a 15 percent luxury tax charged on all purchases of new recreational vehicles (RVs). How would this impact current demand?

A: If potential buyers expect the future price of recreational vehicles to rise, you can bet that current sales will rise, holding gasoline prices and other important variables constant. In Exhibit 5, we see that the current demand curve for recreational vehicles will shift to the right as a result of the higher anticipated prices of new recreational vehicles.

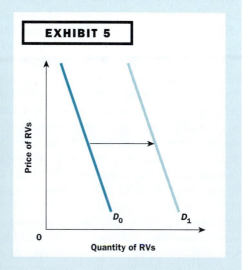

EXHIBIT 5

As it turned out, automobile production was not discontinued during the Korean War—but what was important in terms of demand was what people *expected* to happen, rather than what actually happened.

Fairly often, prospective changes in tax laws lead to changes in consumer behavior. For example, if people expect the relative price of automobiles to rise in three months because of a new tax on cars or the addition of newly mandated expensive anti-pollution equipment (which may, from the individual's perspective, have high costs relative to benefits), the demand for cars during the next three months will be enhanced, and car dealers will advertise, "Buy your car now before the price increase." Other examples, such as waiting to buy a home computer (because price reductions on electronic goods now may lead to expectations of further price reductions), are also common.

CHANGES IN DEMAND VERSUS CHANGES IN QUANTITY DEMANDED—REVISITED

Economists put particular emphasis on the impact of a change in the price of the good in question (own-price) on consumer behavior. We are interested in distinguishing between consumer behavior related to the price of a good itself (movement *along* a demand curve) from such behavior related to other things (shifts *of* the demand curve).

As indicated earlier, the expression we use to describe the effect of price changes of a good on its own sales is different from the expression we use to describe the impact any of the other factors (PYNTE) on a consumer's willingness to purchase that good. If the own-price of a good changes, we say that this leads to a *"change in quantity demanded."* If one of the five other factors influencing consumer behavior changes, we say that this leads to a *"change in demand."* Use the expression, "There was an increase in the quantity demanded," when the price of the good itself fell, or "There was a decrease in the quantity demanded" when the price of the good itself increased. Use the expression, "The demand for the good changes," when the factor influencing behavior was something (PYNTE) other than a change in own-price. The effects of some of the determinants that cause a change in demand (shifters) are reviewed in Exhibit 6.

| EXHIBIT 6 | POSSIBLE DEMAND SHIFTERS |

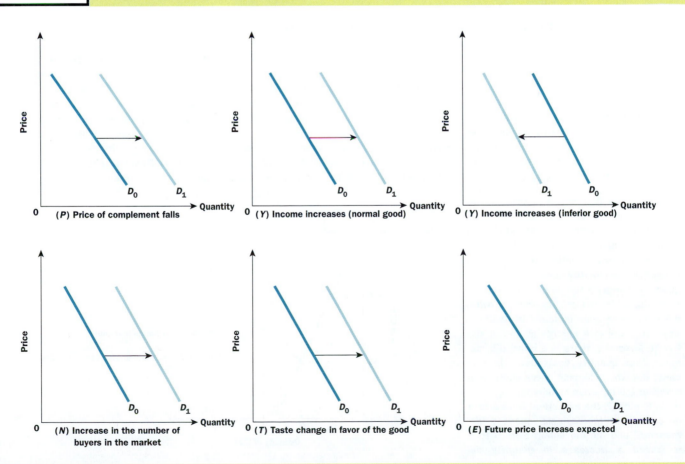

WHAT IS A TAMAGOTCHI?

Appealing virtual reality creatures, Tamagotchi ("tom-ah-got-chee") were first discovered in Japan. Tamagotchi hatch from tiny eggs after traveling millions of light years through cyberspace. With proper care and feeding (accomplished by pushing buttons on the egg), Tamagotchi quickly grow into adorable virtual reality pets in a wide variety of shapes and personalities.

Enormously popular in Japan, Tamagotchi have been adopted by children, teens, and adults of both sexes. Although there have been unsubstantiated reports of Tamagotchi sightings over Hawaii, the main flock is not expected to arrive in the United States until this summer.

SOURCE: www.bandai.com. September 15, 1997.

CONSIDER THIS: The Tamagotchi did hit the United States in the summer of 1997, and as predicted, the demand was strong. The subsequent popularity of the toy pushed the demand curve for Tamagotchi to the right.

TUNE UP

CHANGES IN DEMAND VERSUS CHANGES IN QUANTITY DEMANDED

Q: Roxanne Rolls has a vast collection of compact discs. Demonstrate graphically the two following scenarios: (1) Roxanne buys more CDs because the price of CDs has fallen; and (2) Roxanne buys more CDs because her grandparents just told her that they are going to give her an extra $500 a month while she is going to college.

A: In the first scenario there is an own-price change, so there is a change in the quantity demanded (i.e., a movement along the demand curve). Movement along a demand curve shows a change in the quantity demanded due to a good's own-price changing. In the second scenario, when the grandparents provide the gift, there is an increase in demand. Anytime there is a change in one of the PYNTE variables, there is a change in demand (not quantity demanded). In this case, the whole demand curve shifts as a result of the increase in income.

In Exhibit 7, the movement from A to B is called an *increase in quantity demanded,* and the movement from B to A is called a *decrease in quantity de-*manded. Economists use the phrase "increase or decrease in quantity demanded" to describe movements along a given demand curve. However, the change from A to C is called an *increase in demand,* and the change from C to A is called a *decrease in demand.* The phrase "increase or decrease in demand" is reserved for a shift in the whole curve. So if Roxanne buys more CDs because the price fell, we say there was an increase in quantity demanded. However, if she buys more CDs even at the current price, say $15, we say there is an increase in demand. In this case, the increase in income was responsible for the increase in demand, as Roxanne chose to spend some of her new income on CDs.

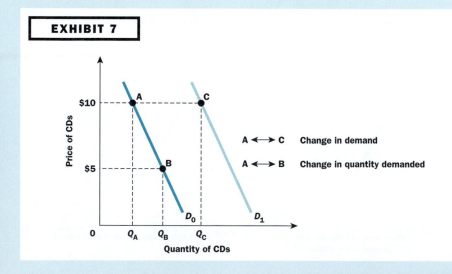

EXHIBIT 7

A ⟷ C   Change in demand

A ⟷ B   Change in quantity demanded

1. A change in the quantity demanded describes a movement along a given demand curve.
2. A change in demand shifts the entire demand curve. An increase in demand shifts the demand curve to the right; a decrease shifts it to the left.
3. A change in the price of a substitute or complement shifts the demand curve for the good in question.
4. Changes in income cause demand curve shifts.
5. The position of the demand curve will vary according to the number of consumers in the market.
6. Taste changes will shift the demand curve.
7. Changes in expected relative prices can shift the current demand curve.

---

1. What is the difference between a change in demand and a change in quantity demanded?
2. If the price of zucchini increases and it causes the demand for yellow squash to rise, what do we call the relationship between zucchini and yellow squash?
3. If incomes rise and, as a result, demand for jet skis increases, how do we describe that good?
4. How do expectations about the future influence the demand curve?
5. Would a change in the price of ice cream cause a change in the demand for ice cream? Why or why not?
6. Would a change in the price of ice cream likely cause a change in the demand for frozen yogurt, a substitute?
7. If plane travel is a normal good and bus travel is an inferior good, what will happen to the demand curves for plane and bus travel if people's incomes increase?

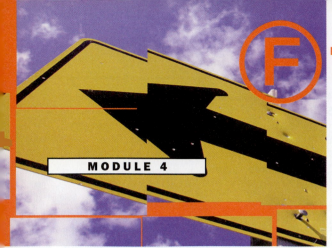

(F) The Law of Supply

MODULE 4

- What is the law of supply?
- What is an individual supply curve?
- What is a market supply curve?

WHAT IS THE LAW OF SUPPLY?

The market's answer to the fundamental question, "What do we produce, and in what quantities?" depends on the interaction of buyers and sellers. Demand is only half the story. The willingness and ability of suppliers to provide the good are equally important factors that must be weighed by decision makers in all societies. As in the case of demand, several factors are important to suppliers. One important factor, again, is the own-price of the good. While behavior will vary among individual suppliers, economists expect that other things being equal, the quantity supplied will vary directly with the price of the good. This relationship is called the **law of supply.** Following the law of supply, the higher the price of the good (P), the greater the quantity supplied (Q_s), and the lower the price of the good, the smaller the quantity supplied.

$$P\uparrow \Rightarrow Q_s\uparrow \quad \text{and} \quad P\downarrow \Rightarrow Q_s\downarrow$$

The relationship described by the law of supply is a direct, or positive, relationship, because the variables move in the same direction.

WHY IS THERE A POSITIVE RELATIONSHIP BETWEEN PRICE AND QUANTITY SUPPLIED?

Firms supplying goods and services want to increase their profits, and the higher the price per unit, the greater the profitability generated by supplying more of that good. For example, if you were a coffee grower, wouldn't you much rather be paid $5 a pound than $1 a pound?

There is another reason that supply curves are upward sloping. The law of increasing opportunity costs demonstrated that when we hold technology and input prices constant, increased opportunity costs will be required to produce additional units of a good. That is, when we produce more of anything, we use the most-efficient resources (those with the lowest opportunity cost) first and then draw on less-efficient resources (those with higher opportunity cost) only if still more of the good in question is to

If it costs more to increase oil production from a field, then oil prices would have to rise in order for producers to increase their output.

be produced. So, if costs are rising for producers as they produce more units, they must receive a higher price to compensate them for their higher costs. In short, increasing production costs means that suppliers will require higher prices to induce them to increase their output.

WHAT IS AN INDIVIDUAL SUPPLY CURVE?

To illustrate the concept of an individual supply curve, let's return to our coffee example, but this time we are referring to the amount of coffee that an individual supplier, John Valdez, is willing to supply in one year. The law of supply can be illustrated, like the law of demand, by a table or graph. John's supply schedule for coffee is shown in Exhibit 1(a). The price–quantity supplied combinations

EXHIBIT 1 | AN INDIVIDUAL SUPPLY CURVE

a. John's Supply Schedule for Coffee

Price (per pound)	Quantity Supplied (pounds per year)
$5	80
4	70
3	50
2	30
1	10

b. John's Supply Curve for Coffee

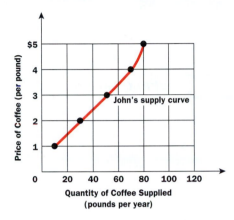

EXHIBIT 2 | A MARKET SUPPLY CURVE

a. Market Supply Schedule for Coffee

Price	John	x	Quantity Supplied (pounds per year) Other Producers	=	Market Supply
$5	80	×	100	=	8,000
4	70	×	100	=	7,000
3	50	×	100	=	5,000
2	30	×	100	=	3,000
1	10	×	100	=	1,000

b. Market Supply Curve for Coffee

The dots on this graph indicate different quantities of coffee that producers would be willing to supply at various prices. The line connecting those combinations is the market supply curve.

were then plotted and joined to create the individual supply curve shown in Exhibit 1(b). Note that the **individual supply curve** is upward sloping as you move from left to right. At higher prices, it will be more attractive to increase production. Existing firms, or growers, will produce more at higher prices than at lower prices.

WHAT IS A MARKET SUPPLY CURVE?

The **market supply curve** may be thought of as the horizontal summation of the supply curves for individual

forms. For simplicity, let's assume that there are 100 coffee producers (including John) and that all of them have the same supply curves as John. The market supply schedule, which reflects the total quantity supplied at each price by the 100 coffee producers, is shown in Exhibit 2(a). Exhibit 2(b) illustrates the resulting market supply curve for this group of coffee producers.

CONCEPT CHECK

1. The law of supply states that the higher (lower) the price of the good, the greater (smaller) the quantity supplied.
2. There is a positive relationship between price and quantity supplied because profit opportunities are greater at higher prices and because the higher production costs of increased output means that suppliers will require higher prices.
3. The market supply curve is a graphical representation of the amount of goods and services that suppliers are willing to supply at various prices.

1. What is a direct, or positive, relationship?
2. What are the two reasons why a supply curve is positively sloped?
3. What is the difference between an individual supply curve and a market supply curve?

4. When we say that the supply curve for economics tutoring services is upward sloping, what relationship does that statement represent?

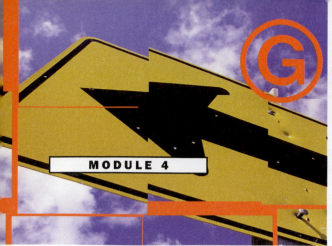

G Shifts in the Supply Curve

- What is the difference between a change in supply and a change in quantity supplied?
- What are the major supply shifters?

WHAT IS THE DIFFERENCE BETWEEN A CHANGE IN QUANTITY SUPPLIED VERSUS A CHANGE IN SUPPLY?

Changes in the price of a good lead to **changes in quantity supplied** by suppliers, just as changes in the price of a good lead to changes in quantity demanded by buyers. Similarly, a **change in supply,** whether an increase or a decrease, will occur for reasons other than changes in the price of the product itself, just as changes in demand are due to factors (PYNTE) other than the price of the good. In other words, a change in the own-price of a good, leading to a change in quantity supplied, is shown as a movement along a given supply curve. A change in any other factor that can affect supplier behavior (supplier input prices; prices of related goods; expectations; number of suppliers; and technology, taxes, tampering, and temperature), leading to a change in supply, results in a shift in the entire supply curve. An increase in supply shifts the supply curve to the right; a decrease in supply shifts the supply curve to the left, as seen in Exhibit 1.

WHAT IS SPENT?

We now have another memory device, SPENT, to aid in our understanding of the supply shifters. SPENT stands for: S, supplier input prices; P, prices of related goods; E, expectations; N, number of suppliers; and T, technology, taxes, tampering, and temperature. We will now look at each of these determinants of supply—factors that determine the position of the supply curve—in greater depth.

SUPPLIER INPUT PRICES (S)

Suppliers are strongly influenced by the costs of inputs used in the production process. Other things equal, the supply of a good at any given price will decline if labor or other input costs increase. This will cause the supply curve to shift to the left. Higher labor, materials, energy, or other

EXHIBIT 1   SUPPLY SHIFTS

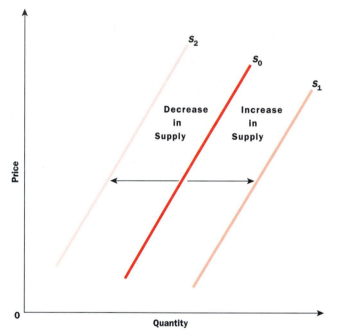

An increase in supply shifts the supply curve to the right. A decrease in supply shifts the supply curve to the left.

costs increase the cost of production, reducing the per-unit profit potential at existing prices. If input prices fall, the supply curve will shift to the right—more will be supplied at each and every price.

PRICE OF CLOSELY RELATED GOODS (P)

Let's say you own your own farm, on which you plant cotton and barley. Then, the price of barley falls and farmers reduce the quantity supplied of barley, as seen in Exhibit 3(a). What effect would the lower price of barley have on your cotton production? Easy—it would increase the

SUPPLIERS' INPUT PRICES

Q: The price of fertilizer has doubled in the last year. Do you think the rising price of fertilizer will have any effect on the supply of food at the market?

A: This is an example of an increase in suppliers' input prices, which will cause the supply curve for farmers to shift to the left. While there may be no immediate effect on the price of food already on store shelves (the change in fertilizer costs does not affect that), this new higher price of fertilizer increases the costs of farm production. At the original price, less will be supplied. In Exhibit 2, we can see that the higher fertilizer prices have caused the supply curve for food to shift to the left.

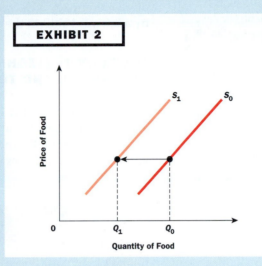

EXHIBIT 2

What will happen to the farmers' costs of production if fertilizer prices rise?

---

supply of cotton. You would want to produce relatively less of the crop that had fallen in price (barley) and relatively more of the now more attractive other crop (cotton). This example demonstrates why the price of related goods is important as a supply shifter as well as a demand shifter. Producers tend to substitute the production of more-profitable goods for that of less-profitable goods. This is desirable from society's perspective as well, because more-profitable goods tend to be those considered more valuable by society, while less-profitable goods are usually considered less valuable. Hence, the lower price in the

barley market has caused an increase in supply (a rightward shift) in the cotton market, as seen in Exhibit 3(b). We call these two goods **substitutes in production.**

If a farmer is growing both corn and wheat on his field and the price of wheat falls, will the farmer increase his supply of corn, *ceteris paribus?*

EXHIBIT 3   **SUBSTITUTES IN PRODUCTION**

a. Market for Barley

b. Market for Cotton

TUNE UP

EXPECTATIONS CAN SHIFT SUPPLY

Q: Jed just moved from Tennessee to Beverly Hills. He was shooting at a possum in his backyard, when he discovered a black liquid oozing out of the ground—oil. If Jed expects the future relative price of oil to be much higher next year because of tensions in the Middle East, will he put his oil on the market this year?

A: No. People aren't always right, but they do respond to their expectations—their guesses of what the future will bring. If Jed expects the price to be much higher next year, he will attempt to keep his supply of new-found oil until next year. If, on the other hand, Jed expects prices to be lower next year, he will supply the oil now.

EXPECTATIONS (*E*)

A third factor shifting supply is the suppliers' expectations. If producers expect a higher price in the future, they will supply less now than they otherwise would have, preferring to wait and sell when their goods will be more valuable. Similarly, if they expect prices to fall in the future, they will supply more now rather than wait until their goods are expected to be worth less. By moving goods to the time periods when they are most highly valued, this activity, sometimes called speculation, tends to reduce sharp price fluctuations that would otherwise occur and to smooth the consumption of goods over time (reducing "feast or famine" situations).

A major disaster like a flood or a hurricane can reduce the supply of crops.

NUMBER OF SUPPLIERS (*N*)

We are normally interested in market demands and supplies (because they together determine prices and quantities) rather than in the behavior of individual consumers and firms. As we discussed earlier, the supply curves of individual suppliers can be summed horizontally to create a market supply curve. An increase in the number of suppliers leads to an increase in supply, denoted by a rightward shift in the supply curve. An exodus of suppliers has the opposite impact, a decrease in supply, which is indicated by a leftward shift in the supply curve.

THE FOUR Ts (TECHNOLOGY, TAXES, TAMPERING, AND TEMPERATURE) (*T*)

Most of us think of prices as constantly rising, given the existence of inflation, but in fact, decreases in costs often occur because of technological progress, and such advances can lower prices. Human creativity works to find

TUNE UP

TAXES AND REGULATION AS SUPPLY SHIFTERS

Q: How do taxes and regulations deter producers from supplying larger quantities of certain goods?

A: Taxes and regulations both shift the supply curve to the left, as seen in Exhibit 4. These variables increase the costs of production, *ceteris paribus*, although the degree to which producers are deterred will vary with the regulatory rule and/or the tax selected.

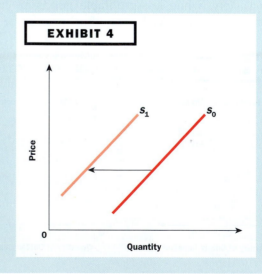

EXHIBIT 4

new ways to produce goods and services using fewer or less-costly inputs of labor, natural resources, or capital. In recent years, despite generally rising prices, the prices of electronic equipment such as computers, cellular telephones, and VCRs have fallen dramatically. At any given price in the 1990s, suppliers were willing to provide many more (of a given quality of) computers than in the 1970s, simply because technology had dramatically reduced the cost of providing them. Graphically, the increase in supply is indicated by a shift to the right in the supply curve.

Supply may also change because of changes in the legal and regulatory environment in which firms operate. Government regulations can influence the costs of production to the firm, leading to cost-induced supply changes similar to those just discussed. For example, if new safety or antipollution requirements increase labor and capital costs, the increased cost will result, other things equal, in a decrease in supply, shifting the supply curve to the left, or up. An increase in a government-imposed minimum wage may

Technological advances can lower the costs of production, *ceteris paribus.*

SUPPLY SHIFTERS IN THE OIL INDUSTRY

CRUDE OIL SAVINGS PASSED ON TO CONSUMERS: While crude oil prices go up and down over the short term, the long-term trend since the early 1980s has been toward more abundant, less-expensive supplies. Crude oil costs have declined from $1.41 per gallon in 1981 to 41 cents per gallon in 1995 (in inflation-adjusted 1995 dollars). These savings are reflected in the pump price of gasoline.

NEW TECHNOLOGIES CUT COSTS: By utilizing improved new technologies, the oil industry's downstream sector—which handles the manufacturing, marketing, and distribution of gasoline—has been able to cut costs significantly, and pass savings on to consumers at the pump. In 1981, downstream costs contributed 58.4 cents to the price of a gallon of gasoline. In 1995, these costs amounted to less than 37.1 cents per gallon.

A number of new technologies contributed to these savings, including: Longhaul pipelines, which have increasingly replaced less-efficient truck and barge transport of crude oil and petroleum products; newer, more efficient tankers with high-speed loading and unloading capabilities; pay-at-the-pump equipment and other labor-saving devices at service stations; new

computer-based inventory management techniques which allow companies to track their supplies more efficiently, assuring that most inventory is en route to users in tankers and in pipelines, rather than sitting idle in costly storage facilities; computerized processing that allows refiners to tailor their operations to obtain the optimum mix of products. Refiners are also now able to produce gasoline and other light fuels from grades of crude oil that, with older technology, were generally useful only for production of heavy boiler fuels and asphalt—products that aren't in high demand like unleaded gasoline.

TAXES: A GROWING PORTION OF PURCHASE PRICE: Gasoline prices declined in 1995 even though gasoline taxes were increasing. In that year, gasoline taxes became the single largest component in the cost of gasoline, more than either crude oil or marketing, refining, and distribution. They comprised 42.4 cents of the pump price of every gallon of gasoline, including 18.4 cents a gallon in federal taxes, 22 cents a gallon in weighted average state taxes, and an estimated 2 cents per gallon in average local taxes. In 1981, when prices reached an all-time high, taxes were just 27.7 cents per gallon in 1995 inflation-adjusted terms.

CLEAN AIR PROGRESS WITH LOWER PUMP PRICES: The falling costs of producing gasoline have occurred despite the requirements to make new, cleaner-burning fuels. In all, several billions of dollars have been spent on such new products and processes.

CONSIDER THIS:
Here we see some important shifters of the supply curve. Crude oil prices are supplier input prices (S); if they fall, we know the supply curve shifts to the right, *ceteris paribus*. Technology, taxes, and tampering are part of the four Ts. Remember, technology lowers costs of production and would tend to shift the supply curve to the right, *ceteris paribus*. On the other hand, tampering and taxes would tend to raise the costs of production, shifting the supply curve to the left, *ceteris paribus*.

Note: The study was prepared by API's Policy Analysis and Strategic Planning Department.
SOURCE: http://www.api.org/news/prices95.htm. September 15, 1997.

have a similar effect by raising labor costs and decreasing supply in markets where many low-wage workers are employed. Certain types of taxes can also alter the costs of production borne by the supplier, causing the supply curve to shift to the left at each price.

Government regulations (tampering) sometimes result in drastic supply curve shifts, such as when the production of a product is essentially prohibited for reasons of safety or environmental concerns. For example, the regulations placed on the production of some pesticides led some producers to stop making the product, shifting the supply curve far to the left.

In addition, temperature (more generally speaking, weather) can certainly affect the supply of certain commodities, particularly agricultural products and transportation services. A drought or freezing temperatures will almost certainly cause the supply curves for many crops to shift to the left.

CHANGE IN SUPPLY VERSUS CHANGE IN QUANTITY SUPPLIED—REVISITED

The SPENT mnemonic describes the five major reasons, other than own-price, why sellers might be willing to supply different amounts of goods and services. If the own-price of a good changes, we say this leads to a *change in the quantity supplied*. If one of the SPENT factors influences the seller's behavior, we say this leads to a *change in supply*. For example, if production costs rise because of a wage increase or higher fuel costs, then other things remaining constant, we would expect a decrease in supply—that is, a leftward shift in the supply curve. Alternatively, if some variable, like lower input prices, causes the costs of production to fall, the supply curve will shift to the right. Exhibit 5 illustrates the effect of some of the determinants that cause shifts in the supply curve.

EXHIBIT 5   **POSSIBLE SUPPLY SHIFTERS**

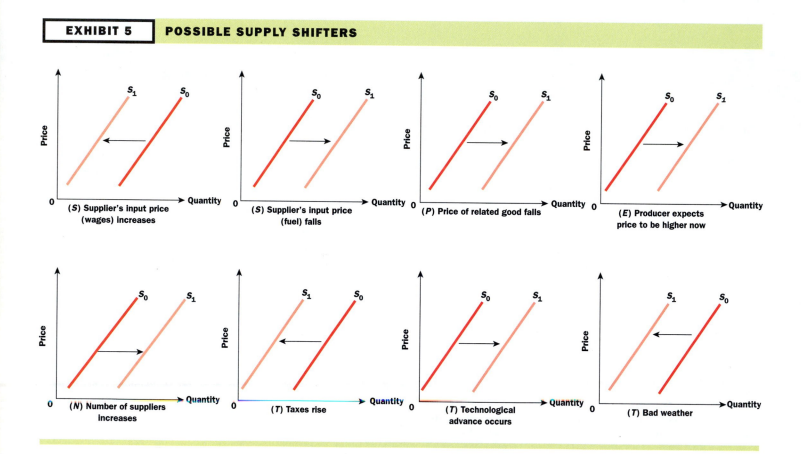

T U N E   U P

CHANGE IN SUPPLY VERSUS
CHANGE IN QUANTITY SUPPLIED

Q: Terry Cloth is a cotton farmer. Demonstrate graphically the two following scenarios: (1) the price of cotton has risen; and (2) good weather has caused an unusually abundant cotton harvest.

A: In the first scenario, there is an own-price change, so there is a change in quantity supplied (i.e., a movement along the supply curve). In the second scenario, the good weather causes the supply curve for cotton to shift to the right. This is called a change in supply (not quantity supplied). A shift in the whole supply curve is caused by one of the SPENT variables, not by a change in the good's own-price.

As shown in Exhibit 6, the movement from A to B is called an increase in quantity supplied, and the movement from B to A is called a decrease in quantity supplied. However, the change from B to C is called an increase in supply and the movement from C to B is called a decrease in supply.

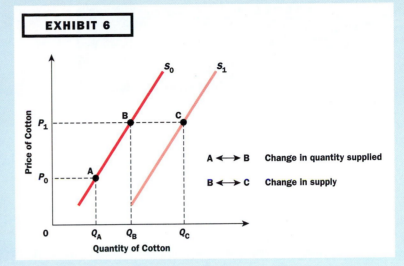

EXHIBIT 6

A ⟷ B   Change in quantity supplied

B ⟷ C   Change in supply

CONCEPT CHECK

1. A movement along a given supply curve caused by a change in the good's own-price is called a change in quantity supplied.
2. A shift of the entire supply curve is called a change in supply.
3. An increase in supply shifts the supply curve to the right; a decrease shifts it to the left.
4. Suppliers' input prices, the price of related goods, expectations, the number of suppliers, taxes, technology, regulations (tampering), and weather can all lead to changes in supply.

---

1. What is the difference between a change in supply and a change in quantity supplied?
2. What causes a movement along a supply curve?
3. What causes a shift in the entire supply curve?
4. If a seller expects the price of a good to rise in the near future, how will that affect his current supply curve?
5. Would a change in the price of wheat change the supply of wheat? Would it change the supply of corn, if wheat and corn can be grown on the same type of land?
6. If a guitar manufacturer had to increase its wages in order to keep its workers, what would happen to the supply of guitars as a result?
7. What happens to the supply of baby-sitting services in an area when many teenagers get their driver's licenses at about the same time?

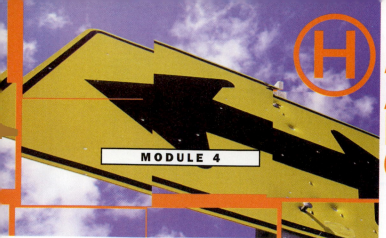

(H) Application: A Shift in the Demand for Cuban Cigars

What demand factors (PYNTE) have led to an increase in the demand for cigars? Do you think the "forbidden fruit" factor has shifted the demand curve?

WHERE THERE'S SMOKE: DEMAND FOR CIGARS FUELS SMUGGLING OF CUBAN CONTRABAND

ANNE-MARIE O'CONNOR

SAN DIEGO—The sweetest forbidden fruit at the border nowadays is not white, powdery, or from Colombia.

And it may not seem like the biggest threat to the Western world. But U.S. Customs Service officials are all fired up about a recent surge of the smuggling of Cuban cigars into San Diego.

In recent weeks, there have been back-to-back record seizures at the San Diego border, netting a cache of nearly 5,000 cigars with an estimated value of $283,500 on the black market, San Diego customs spokeswoman Bobbie Cassidy said.

The August seizures put San Diego squarely on the map of the Cuban contraband cigar trail, an exploding black market fueled by the yuppie cigar craze and a worldwide dictate that Cuba makes the champagne of *puros*.

"It's big money," said Rudy Camacho, top U.S. Customs administrator in San Diego. "It's a new smuggling trend, and it's indicative of the demand the American consumer has out there."

Nationwide, seizures of Cuban cigars have increased sixfold in the past three years, to more than $1.1 million worth in fiscal 1996, according to the Customs Service.

That's a leap from $318,401 in 1995 and a mere $142,014 in 1994, according to the service, which officials say reflects an increase in black market prices for the cigars as well as in seizures.

"It's the forbidden fruit factor," said Mike Sheehan, spokesman for customs in Miami, where Cuban cigars have become a status symbol for the terminally hip of South Beach.

"The fact that it's illegal and difficult to obtain makes it all the more desirable." . . . At the heart of Cuban cigar fever is the trendiness of cigars. In the past few years, cigars have become favored accessories for the likes of Demi Moore and Arnold Schwarzenegger. They have inspired the glossy specialty magazine *Cigar Aficionado*, whose cover has featured everyone from supermodel Claudia Schiffer to Castro, the man who made Cuban cigars emblematic.

Los Angeles Times, September 7, 1997, p. A30.

The popularity of cigars has increased nationwide over the past few years. With that, the demand for cigars, including the prized Cuban-made brands, has increased dramatically. This article identifies two possible reasons for this increase in demand for Cuban cigars: (1) trendiness, and (2) the forbidden fruit factor.

The first reason, trendiness, points to one of the PYNTE shifters, changes in taste (*T*). As we discussed in this Module, changes in preferences naturally lead to shifts in demand. Such is the case with Cuban cigars, which have become a popular status symbol in high-society circles.

The second reason, the forbidden fruit factor, provides a less satisfactory explanation of this change in demand. It has been illegal to import Cuban cigars since the 1960s, so why would the forbidden fruit factor suddenly become a significant factor? In short, then, the major cause for the increase in the demand for Cuban cigars is a change in tastes, which has pushed the demand curve for this contraband good to the right.

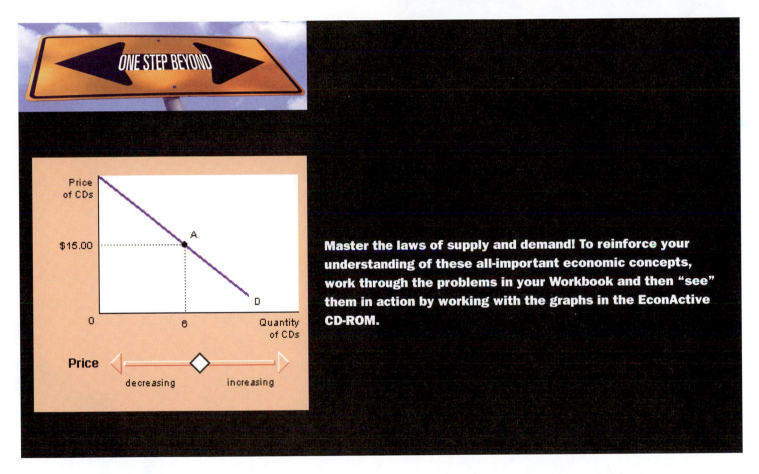

Master the laws of supply and demand! To reinforce your understanding of these all-important economic concepts, work through the problems in your Workbook and then "see" them in action by working with the graphs in the EconActive CD-ROM.

PHOTO CREDITS MODULE 4

Page **88**: left, © T/Maker Company; right, Used with permission of the New York Stock Exchange; Page **89**: left, © Robert Sexton; right, © Robert Sexton; Page **90**: © 1998 Don Couch Photography; Page **91**: top, © 1998 Don Couch Photography; bottom, © Robert Sexton; Page **92**: left, © Index Stock Photography; right, © Index Stock Photography; Page **93**: © 1998 Don Couch Photography; Page **94**: top, © Ted S. Warren/Austin American-Statesman/SYGMA; bottom, 1998 Don Couch Photography; Page **95**: © T/Maker Company; Page **96**: PhotoDisc; Page **97**: © PhotoDisc; Page **100**: top, © 1998 Don Couch Photography; bottom, Harcourt Brace Photo; Page **101**: Charles Barsotti © 1998 from The New Yorker Collection. All Rights Reserved. Page **102**: © 1998 Don Couch Photography; Page **103**: © 1998 Don Couch Photography; Page **104**: Harcourt Brace Photo; Page **106**: © 1998 Don Couch Photography; Page **108**: © 1998 Digital Stock; Page **111**: top, © 1998 PhotoDisc; bottom, © 1998 PhotoDisc; Page **112**: © Les Stone/SYGMA; Page **113**: © Alan Levenson/Tony Stone; Page **117**: © Los Angeles Times photo by Kevin P. Casey

Markets in Motion

A. Market Equilibrium Price and Quantity
Why is the concept of market equilibrium such a valuable tool?

B. Changes in Equilibrium Price and Quantity
What happens to equilibrium price and quantity when we shift the supply or demand curve?

C. Shifting Supply and Demand Together
What happens when supply and demand both shift?

D. Temporary Disequilibrium
What happens when companies do not correctly anticipate the demand for their products?

E. Price Controls
What are price ceilings and price floors?

F. Application: Supply and Demand in the Market for Super Bowl Tickets
How does the market for Super Bowl tickets work?

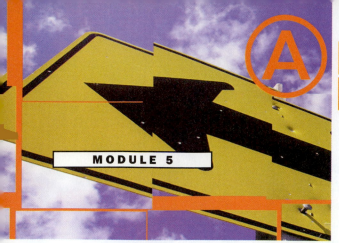

Ⓐ Market Equilibrium Price and Quantity

- What is the equilibrium price?
- What is the equilibrium quantity?
- What is a shortage?
- What is a surplus?

BRINGING SUPPLY AND DEMAND TOGETHER

Enough has been said for now about demand and supply separately. Bearing in mind our discussion of the "fuzzy" nature of many real-world markets, we now bring supply and demand together. How do supply and demand operate together to answer the first fundamental question facing all societies: What will be produced and in what quantities?

WHAT IS THE EQUILIBRIUM PRICE AND QUANTITY?

The market solution to this basic question is quite simple: Production and exchange will be determined by the price at which the quantity demanded equals the quantity supplied. This price is said to be an **equilibrium price,** and the quantity associated with this price is said to be an **equilibrium quantity,** because they are a price and a quantity that tend not to change. The result is stable if there are no unsettling forces at work to change either the quantity sold in the

market or the price at which it is sold. Only a change in one of the **determinants of demand** (PYNTE) or supply (SPENT) will alter the situation and lead to a change in quantity or price, or both. As long as these determinants remain unchanged, price and quantity will tend to remain at their equilibrium levels.

WHAT ARE SHORTAGES AND SURPLUSES?

The equilibrium market solution is best understood with the help of a simple graph. Let's return to the coffee example we used in our earlier discussions of supply and demand. Exhibit 1 combines the market demand curve for coffee with the market supply curve. At $3 per pound, buyers are willing to buy 5,000 pounds of coffee and sellers are willing to supply 5,000 pounds of coffee. Neither may be "happy" about the price, because the buyer would like a lower price and the seller would like a higher price. But both buyers and sellers are able to carry out their purchase and sales plans at that $3 price. However, at any

---

EXHIBIT 1   **A HYPOTHETICAL MARKET SUPPLY AND DEMAND SCHEDULE FOR COFFEE**

Price	Quantity Supplied	Quantity Demanded	Difference	State of Market
$5	8,000	1,000	7,000	Surplus
4	7,000	3,000	4,000	Surplus
3	5,000	5,000	0	Equilibrium
2	3,000	8,000	−5,000	Shortage
1	1,000	12,000	−11,000	Shortage

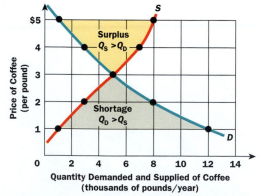

The equilibrium is $3 per pound and 5,000 pounds of coffee, where quantity demanded and quantity supplied are equal. At higher prices, quantity supplied exceeds quantity demanded, resulting in a surplus. Below $3, quantity demanded exceeds quantity supplied, leading to a shortage.

---

other price, either suppliers or demanders would be unable to trade as much as they would like at that price. As you can see on the graph, at $4 per pound, the quantity of coffee demanded would be 3,000 pounds but the quantity supplied would be 7,000 pounds. At that price, a **surplus** or excess quantity supplied would exist. That is, growers would be willing to sell more coffee than demanders would be willing to buy. To cut growing inventories, frustrated suppliers would cut their price and cut back on production. And as prices fall, consumers will buy more, ultimately eliminating the unsold surplus, at the equilibrium.

What would happen if the price of coffee was cut to $1 per pound? The yearly quantity demanded of 12,000 pounds would be greater than the 1,000 pounds that pro-ducers would be willing to supply at that low price. So, at $1 per pound, a **shortage** or excess quantity demanded would exist. Because of the coffee shortage, frustrated buyers would be forced to compete for the existing supply, bidding up the price. The rising price would have two effects: (1) producers would be willing to increase the quantity supplied; and (2) the higher price would decrease the quantity demanded. Together, these two effects would ultimately eliminate the shortage, at the equilibrium.

Again, only at $3 does neither a shortage nor a surplus exist. Thus, $3 is an equilibrium price, a steady price that will remain until the good's demand or supply curve is shifted by some consideration other than the price of coffee.

TUNE UP

SHORTAGES

Q: Imagine that you own a butcher shop. Recently, you have noticed that at about noon, you run out of your daily supply of chicken. Puzzling over your predicament, you hypothesize that you are charging less than the equilibrium price for your chicken. Should you raise the price of your chicken? Explain using a simple graph.

A: If the price you are charging is below the equilibrium price (P_E), then you can draw a horizontal line from that price straight across Exhibit 2 and see where it intersects the supply and demand curves. The point where this horizontal line intersects the demand curve indicates how much chicken consumers are willing to buy at that below-equilibrium price (P_{BE}). Likewise, the intersection of this horizontal line with the supply curve indicates how much chicken producers are willing to supply at P_{BE}. From this, it is clear that a shortage (or excess quantity demanded) exists, because consumers want more chicken (Q_D) than producers are willing to supply (Q_S) at this relatively low price. This excess quantity demanded will result in competition among buyers that will push prices up and eliminate the shortage. That is, it would make sense to raise your price on the chicken. As price moves towards the equilibrium price, consumers are willing to purchase less (some will substitute fish, steak, and ground round), and producers will have an incentive to supply more chicken. Excess quantity demanded, or a shortage, results from a price below the equilibrium price.

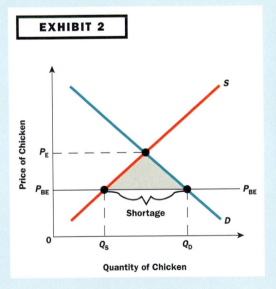

EXHIBIT 2

Price of Chicken / Quantity of Chicken / S / D / P_E / P_{BE} / Shortage / Q_S / Q_D

What is truly amazing is the fact that producers respond to the rather complex wants of the population without having tremendous shortages or surpluses, and the fact that in a "free market" we cannot point to any single individual or agency that makes the decision of what to pro-duce. We often say the decision is made by "the market" or "market forces," but this is of little help in pinpointing the name and place of the decision maker. In fact, no single person makes decisions about the quantity and quality of televisions, cars, beds, or any other goods or services consumed in the American economy. Literally millions of people, both producers and consumers, participate in the decision-making process. To paraphrase a statement made popular by the first great modern economist, Adam Smith, it is as if an *invisible hand* works to coordinate the efforts of millions of diverse participants in the complex process of producing and distributing goods and services.

HOW ARE MARKETS LIKE NON–RUSH-HOUR TRAFFIC?

Consumers and drivers are both motivated by self-interest. Just as there are many different consumers in the marketplace, there are many different types of drivers, with different preferences and attitudes towards risk. Despite these differences, we see that the social interaction on highways is quite amazing. No one is there to direct the actions of drivers, yet when drivers see that one lane is moving faster than others, a few drivers will switch lanes until the flow of traffic is approximately equal in all lanes. Such marginal adjustments are critical to the unregulated coordination process in the marketplace as well as on the highway.

How are markets and uncongested freeways similar?

TUNE UP

SHORTAGES AND SURPLUSES

Q: Plans are being made for the Concert of the Millennium. It is going to be a three-hour, one-time-only concert with no taping and no satellite feeds. All of the performers will make a brief appearance before returning to their point of origin. The artists will be playing some of their all time favorite hits: Kurt Cobain ("Smells like Teen Spirit"), Bob Marley ("I Shot the Sheriff"), Richie Valens ("La Bamba"), Jim Morrison ("Light My Fire"), Jimi Hendrix ("Purple Haze"), John Lennon ("Imagine"), Tupac Shakur ("Dear Mama"), Elvis ("Hound Dog"), Janis Joplin ("Just a Little Piece of my Heart"), Jerry Garcia ("Keep On Truckin"), Buddy Holly ("Everyday"), John Denver ("Rocky Mountain High"), and Frank Sinatra ("My Way"). The site is still undecided, but the promoters are considering Angel Stadium in California or Sun Devil Stadium in Arizona.

Hints: What will the supply curve look like if the stadium has a total capacity of 70,000 seats? Will changing the price alter the supply curve for this event? What would demand for the concert relative to the supply likely be at $1? at $100,000? at $1 million?

A: Of course, we can only speculate on consumer response to this bizarre hypothetical concert scenario. However, we can still make conjectures and have a little fun. Exhibit 3 shows the demand and supply curves for this scenario. At $1 per ticket, we would expect millions to show up for the concert, far more than the 70,000 available seats. Clearly, a serious shortage would appear at that price. At $1 million, the concert promoters might only fill a few hundred seats—a surplus. We could only guess what the equilibrium price might be for this rather unique concert.

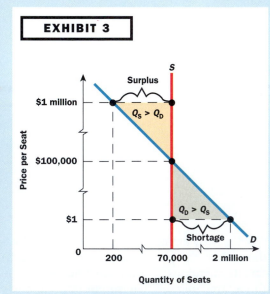

EXHIBIT 3

1. The intersection of the supply and demand curve determines the equilibrium price and quantity exchanged in a market.
2. If the price is set above the equilibrium price, there will be a surplus or excess quantity supplied.
3. If the price is set below equilibrium price, there will be a shortage or excess quantity demanded.
4. Shortages and surpluses set in motion forces that tend to move the market toward the equilibrium price and quantity unless otherwise prevented.

1. How does the intersection of supply and demand indicate the equilibrium price and quantity in a market?
2. What can cause a change in the supply and demand equilibrium?
3. What must be true about the price charged for there to be a shortage?
4. What must be true about the price charged for there to be a surplus?
5. Why do market forces tend to eliminate both shortages and surpluses?
6. Why do economists refer to the "invisible hand" of the market?
7. If tea prices were above their equilibrium level, what force would tend to push tea prices down? If tea prices were below their equilibrium level, what force would tend to push tea prices up?
8. Why does the time you spend in supermarket checkout lines tend to be about the same, regardless of which line you are in?

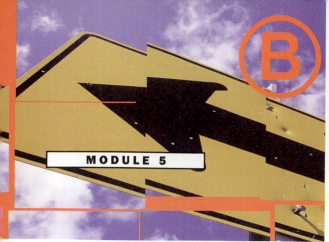

B Changes in Equilibrium Price and Quantity

- What happens to equilibrium price and quantity when we shift the demand curve?
- What happens to equilibrium price and quantity when we shift the supply curve?

As we discussed in Module 4, demand curves can shift when any of the PYNTE (but not the price of the good itself) factors change, and supply curves can shift when any of the SPENT factors change (but not the price of the good itself). These changes (shifts) in the demand and supply curves will lead to changes in the equilibrium price and equilibrium quantity.

HOW DOES A CHANGE IN DEMAND AFFECT EQUILIBRIUM PRICE AND QUANTITY?

A shift in the demand curve—caused by a change in (P) the price of a related good, (Y) income, (N) the number of buyers, (T) tastes, or (E) expectations—results in a change in both equilibrium price and equilibrium quantity. But how and why does this happen? This intersection can be most clearly explained through the use of an example.

The demand for restaurant meals in the little town of Diner is clearly affected by changes in consumer incomes. The willingness of consumers to pay for restaurant meals is illustrated in Exhibit 1, where line D_0 reflects current demand. Suppose, then, that incomes rise and that

Will higher incomes increase the demand for restaurant meals?

| EXHIBIT 1 | AN INCREASE IN DEMAND |

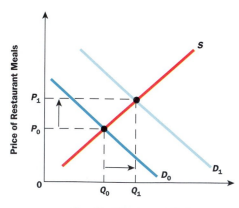

An increase in demand shifts the demand curve to the right, resulting in a new higher equilibrium price (P_1) and equilibrium quantity (Q_1).

consumers, now more affluent, increase their demand for restaurant meals. This means that, at any given price, the demand for these meals will be greater than before. The demand curve shifts to the right to represent this change in consumers' willingness to pay for restaurant meals. The new demand curve, D_1, in Exhibit 1 illustrates the resulting demand curve after this increase in income. Assume, for the moment, that the supply curve remains unchanged in this scenario; that is, assume that a rise in general income levels does not directly influence the ability or desire to produce and supply additional restaurant meals. As you can see, this increase in demand results in a higher equilibrium price (from P_0 to P_1) and an increase in the equilibrium quantity (from Q_0 to Q_1). If, in this same scenario, incomes were to fall rather than rise, both the equilibrium quantity and the equilibrium price would decrease as a result.

HOW DOES A CHANGE IN SUPPLY AFFECT EQUILIBRIUM PRICE AND QUANTITY?

Like a shift in demand, a shift in the supply curve will also influence both equilibrium price and equilibrium quantity, assuming that demand for the product has not changed. Recall from Module 4, each of the factors in SPENT—(S) suppliers' input prices, (P) the price of related goods, (E) expectations, (N) the number of sellers, and (T) technology, taxes, temperature, and tampering—can shift the supply curve. Consider the market for calculators, for example. In the late 1970s, technological breakthroughs led to lower input prices and an increase in the number of suppliers in the calculator market as established firms increased production and new firms entered the industry. These developments subsequently led to an increase in supply. In Exhibit 2, this increase in supply is

indicated in the rightward shift from S_0 to S_1. At P_0, consumers would not buy Q_1 calculators. Only at a lower price will consumers be willing to buy this larger supply of calculators. As you can see, the increase in the supply of calculators resulted in a lower equilibrium price (from P_0 to P_1) and a higher equilibrium quantity (from Q_0 to Q_1).

Again, in the same scenario, if the supply of calculators decreased rather than increased, perhaps because of an expensive labor settlement, the reverse would be true. An expensive labor settlement would effectively increase the input costs in the calculator market, shifting the supply curve to the left. This decrease in supply would then drive the equilibrium price up and force the equilibrium quantity down.

EXHIBIT 2	AN INCREASE IN SUPPLY

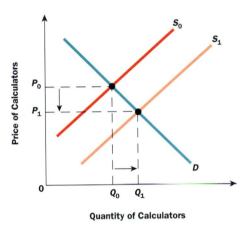

Quantity of Calculators

An increase in the supply curve, *ceteris paribus*, causes the equilibrium price to fall (from P_0 to P_1) and the equilibrium quantity to rise (from Q_0 to Q_1).

COFFEE, COCOA PRICES RISE ON EL NIÑO CONCERNS

LONDON (Reuters)—Coffee and cocoa prices have risen sharply in the past few weeks, as concern that a developing El Niño weather pattern could hit harvests has lured buyers to the market.

CONSIDER THIS:

In the summer of 1997 many buyers expected coffee and cocoa harvests to be lower in 1998 as a result of El Niño. As a result, they increased their current demand for coffee and cocoa. As shown in Exhibit 3, this change in consumers' expectations has resulted in an increase in demand—a shift in the demand curve from D_0 to D_1. This shift has resulted in a higher equilibrium price for coffee (from P_0 to P_1) and a higher equilibrium quantity (from Q_0 to Q_1).

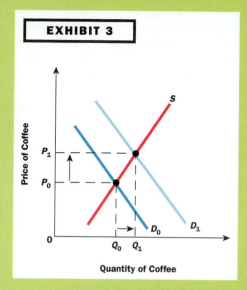

EXHIBIT 3

SOURCE: August 28, 1997, Reuters America Inc. http://www.newspage.com/NEWSPAGE/info/d18. . . ic.pre/public/B.d0828140.400.drt77100.htm.

If, due to changing expectations, consumers buy more coffee this year, what would you expect to happen to the price?

TUNE UP

THE IMPACT OF A CHANGE IN DEMAND ON EQUILIBRIUM PRICE AND QUANTITY

Q: Why are gasoline prices higher in the summer than in the winter?

A: More people travel during the summer months than during the winter months. Therefore, the demand for gasoline increases during the summer. The greater demand for gasoline during the summer sends prices upward, *ceteris paribus.* As shown in Exhibit 4, the rightward shift of the demand curve results in an increase in both equilibrium price and quantity.

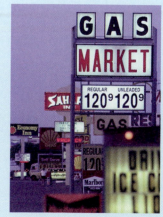

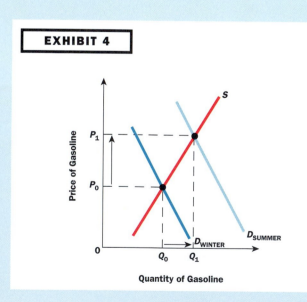

EXHIBIT 4

TUNE UP

THE IMPACT OF A CHANGE IN SUPPLY ON EQUILIBRIUM PRICE AND QUANTITY

Q: Why are strawberries more expensive in winter than in summer?

A: Assuming that consumers' tastes and income are fairly constant throughout the year, the answer lies on the supply side of the market. The supply of strawberries is lower during the winter, because strawberries are out of season. As shown in Exhibit 5, this decrease in supply shifts the supply curve to the left, resulting in a higher equilibrium price (from P_0 to P_1) and a lower equilibrium quantity (from Q_0 to Q_1).

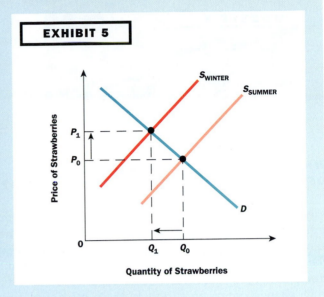

EXHIBIT 5

CONCEPT CHECK

1. Changes in demand and supply will cause a change in the equilibrium price and/or quantity.

2. Changes in supply will cause a change in the equilibrium price and/or quantity.

---

1. When demand increases, does that create a shortage or a surplus at the original price?
2. What happens to equilibrium price and quantity as a result of a demand increase?
3. When supply increases, does that create a shortage or a surplus at the original price?

4. What happens to equilibrium price and quantity as a result of a supply increase?
5. Why do heating-oil prices tend to be higher in the winter?
6. Why are evening and weekend long-distance calls cheaper than weekday long-distance calls?

Shifting Supply and Demand Together

MODULE 5

- What happens when both supply and demand shift in the same time period?
- What is an indeterminate solution?

WHAT HAPPENS IF BOTH SUPPLY AND DEMAND SHIFT IN THE SAME TIME PERIOD?

We have discussed that as part of the continual adjustment process that occurs in the marketplace, supply and demand can each shift in response to many different factors, with the market then adjusting toward the new equilibrium. We have, so far, only considered what happens when just one such change occurs at a time. In these cases, we learned that the results of these adjustments in supply and demand on the equilibrium price and quantity are predictable. However, very often, supply and demand will both shift *in the same time period*. That is, supply and demand will shift simultaneously in response to both PYNTE and SPENT factors. Can we predict what will happen to equilibrium prices and equilibrium quantities in these situations?

As you will see, when supply and demand move at the same time, we can predict the change in one variable (price or quantity), but we are unable to predict the direction of

effect on the other variable with any certainty. This change in the second variable, then, is said to be **indeterminate,** because it cannot be determined without additional information about the size of the relative shifts in supply and demand. This concept will become more clear to you as we work through the following example.

Simultaneous Supply Increase with Demand Decrease

When considering this scenario, it might help you to break it down into its individual parts. As you learned in the last Concept, an increase in supply (a rightward shift in the supply curve) results in a decrease in the equilibrium price and an increase in the equilibrium quantity. A decrease in demand (a leftward movement of the demand curve), on the other hand, results in a decrease in both the equilibrium price and the equilibrium quantity. These shifts are shown in Exhibit 1(a). Taken together, then, these changes

---

| **EXHIBIT 1** | **SHIFTS IN SUPPLY AND DEMAND** |

a. A Little Increase in Supply and a Big Decrease in Demand

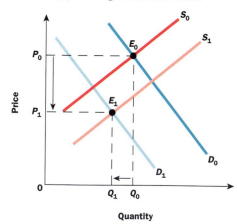

If the decrease in demand (leftward shift) is greater than the increase in supply (rightward shift), the equilibrium quantity will fall.

b. A Big Increase in Supply and a Little Decrease in Demand

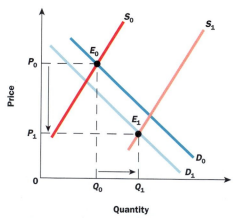

If the increase in supply (rightward shift) is greater than the decrease in supply (leftward shift), the equilibrium quantity will rise.

will clearly result in a decrease in the equilibrium price, because both the increase in supply and the decrease in demand work to push this price down. This drop in equilibrium price is shown in the movement from E_0 to E_1.

The effect of these changes on equilibrium price is clear, but how does the equilibrium quantity change? The impact on equilibrium quantity is indeterminate, because the increase in supply increases the equilibrium quantity and the decrease in demand decreases it. In this scenario, the change in the equilibrium quantity will vary depending on the relative changes in supply and demand. If, as shown in Exhibit 1(a), the decrease in demand is greater than the increase in supply, the equilibrium quantity will decrease. If, however, as shown in Exhibit 1(b), the increase in supply is greater than the decrease in demand, the equilibrium quantity will increase.

Demand and Supply Simultaneously Increase or Decrease

It is also possible that both demand and supply will increase (or decrease). This has, for example, been the case with VCRs. As a result of technological breakthroughs and lower input costs, the supply curve for VCRs shifted to the right. That is, at any given price, more VCRs were offered than before. But with rising income and an increasing number of buyers in the market, the demand for VCRs increased as well. As shown in Exhibit 2, both the increased demand and increased supply functioned to increase the equilibrium quantity—more VCRs were sold. The equilibrium price could have either gone up (because of increased demand) or down (because of increased supply), depending on the relative sizes of the demand and supply shifts. Price is, in this case, the indeterminate variable. However, in the case of the VCRs, we know that the supply curve shifted more than the demand curve, so that the effect of increased supply pushing prices down outweighed the effect of increased demand pushing prices up. As a result, the equilibrium price of VCRs has dropped (from P_0 to P_1) over time.

EXHIBIT 2 — **AN INCREASE IN THE DEMAND AND SUPPLY OF VCRS**

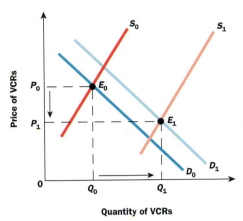

Quantity of VCRs

The increase in supply and demand caused in increase in the equilibrium quantity. Price is the indeterminate variable. Because the supply curve shifted more than the demand curve, the price fell.

THE COMBINATIONS OF SUPPLY AND DEMAND SHIFTS

The eight possible changes in demand and/or supply are presented in Exhibit 3, along with the resulting changes in equilibrium quantity and equilibrium price. While memorizing such a table is one way of "learning" the impact of the various possible changes in demand and supply, you will find it more profitable to draw a little graph, such as shown in Exhibit 4, whenever a situation of changing demand and/or supply arises, remembering that an increase in either demand or supply means a rightward shift in the curve, while a decrease in either means a leftward shift. Remember that where both demand and supply change, one of the two equilibrium values, price or quantity, will change in an indeterminate manner (can increase or decrease).

EXHIBIT 3 — **THE EFFECT OF CHANGING DEMAND AND/OR SUPPLY**

If Demand	and Supply	then Equilibrium Quantity	and Equilibrium Price
1. Increases	Stays unchanged	Increases	Increases
2. Decreases	Stays unchanged	Decreases	Decreases
3. Stays unchanged	Increases	Increases	Decreases
4. Stays unchanged	Decreases	Decreases	Increases
5. Increases	Increases	Increases	Indeterminate*
6. Decreases	Decreases	Decreases	Indeterminate*
7. Increases	Decreases	Indeterminate*	Increases
8. Decreases	Increases	Indeterminate*	Decreases

*May increase, decrease, or remain the same, depending on the size of the change in demand relative to the change in supply.

EXHIBIT 4 — THE COMBINATIONS OF SUPPLY AND DEMAND SHIFTS

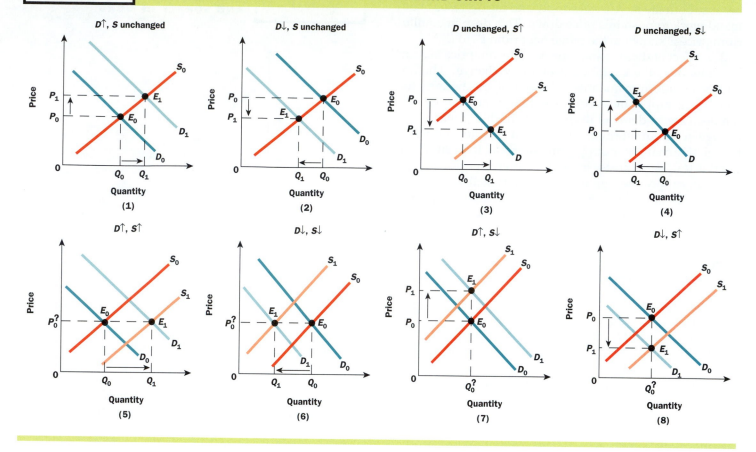

$D\uparrow$, S unchanged (1)
$D\downarrow$, S unchanged (2)
D unchanged, $S\uparrow$ (3)
D unchanged, $S\downarrow$ (4)

$D\uparrow$, $S\uparrow$ (5)
$D\downarrow$, $S\downarrow$ (6)
$D\uparrow$, $S\downarrow$ (7)
$D\downarrow$, $S\uparrow$ (8)

TUNE UP

SHIFTS IN BOTH SUPPLY AND DEMAND

Q: As a result of fiber optic technology, the production costs for long-distance calls have fallen. Graph this phenomenon, assuming for the moment that demand remains stable. What happened to the equilibrium price and quantity? What happens if there is a simultaneous increase in demand because of a rise in income?

A: Lower costs of production shift the supply curve to the right. With this increase in supply, the price of long-distance phone calls falls and the quantity demanded (and exchanged, in equilibrium) rises. This change is shown in Exhibit 5(a), with the movement from E_0 to E_1. If there is a simultaneous increase in demand, equilibrium quantity rises further, but the impact on equilibrium price now becomes indeterminate—that is, we need to know the magnitude of the increase in demand compared to the magnitude of the increase in supply to determine whether the price will rise or fall. This situation is shown in Exhibit 5(b).

EXHIBIT 5

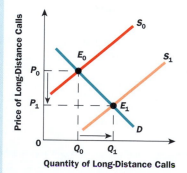

a. Increase in Supply

b. Simultaneous Increase in Supply and Demand

KIDNEYS FOR SALE?

A Chinese newspaper published in New York advertises "kidney transplant in mainland China. Don't miss the opportunity."

House lawmakers have demanded an investigation into an *ABCNEWS Prime Time Live* report that organs from executed Chinese prisoners are being sold on the international black market. Rep. Frank Wolf, R-Va., said there is "strong evidence that federal and state laws have been broken." "We're talking about real men and women being killed for someone who can pay for parts of their bodies," said Rep. Linda Smith, R-Wash.

Chinese Embassy spokesman Yu Shuning said the allegations of organ sales were "sheer fabrication," noting that the sale of human organs is prohibited in China.

Working undercover, ABC News correspondent Brian Ross responded to an advertisement in a New York-based Chinese language newspaper offering a kidney transplant in China and visited the doctor who told him about the grisly process.

"The doctor told us he had hospitals for transplants using prisoners' kidneys," said Ross. "Dr. Zhou Wei Zhang, who worked at one of the hospitals, told us the kidneys are actually removed in the field, moments after prisoners are shot. The total price— $30,000." But on a hidden ABC News camera, the doctor asks for part of the $30,000 payment in advance.

Apple Yoonuch, a woman from Bangkok, Thailand, said she underwent a transplant at the Nanfung Military Hospital in China, Ross reported. "Third of January, the doctor called me that there will be an execution," Yoonuch said. "It means that prisoners, some prisoners, are going to be shot dead. So I have to come over and prepare myself to get the operation, kidney operation." An embassy statement said the organs of executed criminals are used in transplants rarely and only with the consent of the prisoners or their families.

An official with the International Transplantation Society said the practice is barbaric and "makes me cringe." "The consent issue as far as I'm concerned is a bogus issue," said Dr. Ronald Guttman. "It's a justification for what they're doing." *Prime Time Live* also aired videotape made by the Chinese military showing guards making sure an executioner's gun is placed at the back of a condemned person's head. This is done to protect the organs from damage during the execution, and to ensure the organs are as fresh as possible when extracted.

http://abcnews.com/sections/world/china1015/index.html (October 22, 1997).

> **CONSIDER THIS:**
> If, in fact, this report is accurate (the Chinese deny the allegations), then we might ask these questions: Do supply and demand work better when markets are tempered by shared moral beliefs? Does unconstrained self-interest sometimes result in behavior that most would find unacceptable?

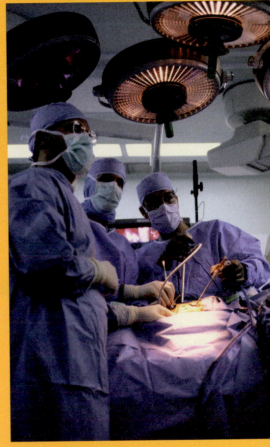

Do markets always lead to ethical outcomes?

Frank and Ernest

© 1997 Thaves/Reprinted with permission. Newspaper dist. by NEA, Inc.

Why is the market price higher for a wise man than for wise guys?

CONCEPT CHECK

1. Supply and demand curves can each shift simultaneously in response to changes in both SPENT and PYNTE factors.

2. When there are simultaneous shifts in both supply and demand curves, we will be able to determine one, but not both, of the variables. Either the equilibrium price or the equilibrium quantity will be indeterminate, without more information.

1. What would have to be true for both supply and demand to shift in the same time period?
2. How do we "add up" the effects of simultaneous changes in both supply and demand on equilibrium prices and quantities?
3. When both supply and demand shift, what added information do we need to know in order to determine in which direction the indeterminate variable changes?

4. If both buyers and sellers of coffee expect coffee prices to rise in the near future, what will happen to coffee prices and sales today?
5. If demand for peanut butter increases and supply decreases, what will happen to equilibrium price and quantity?

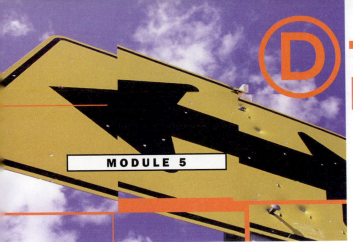

D Temporary Disequilibrium

- What is anticipated demand?
- Can anticipated demand be less than the actual demand?

REACHING EQUILIBRIUM: DO YOU REMEMBER CABBAGE PATCH DOLLS?

In 1983, Coleco, a major American toy company, started importing from China a handmade creation called "Cabbage Patch Dolls." The dolls took America by storm, and as the fad grew, newspapers were filled with accounts of otherwise dignified grandmothers fighting with one another, trying to get a store's last Cabbage Patch doll for their grandchildren.

WHY WERE SHOPPERS FIGHTING IN THE AISLES?

While Coleco showed great perceptiveness in coming up with the Cabbage Patch idea, it also initially goofed. It significantly underpriced the dolls, given their popularity, thereby reducing their revenues and profits compared to what they could have been, and causing all sorts of frustration among Cabbage Patch fans. Coleco, in short, inaccurately guessed the location of the demand curve. A firm selling a product typically sells it to a store and suggests a retail price. That initial price represents the firm's best guess as to where the demand and supply curves will intersect, if the good has many close competitors. Typically, the firm knows the supply curve pretty well, because it is determined by what the firm must pay to acquire various quantities of inputs, particularly wages. But businesses have to guess at the public reaction to the product; often that guessing is aided by market research, which provides information on consumer tastes and preferences.

Consider Exhibit 1. In a given period in late 1983, Coleco might have guessed that the demand curve for Cabbage Patch Dolls looked like the lower of the two demand curves ($D_{ANTICIPATED}$), suggesting that a price of $20 would have "cleared the market"—that is, would result in neither a shortage nor a surplus.

In fact, as the dolls caught on, demand was much greater than anticipated, say, that represented by the top demand curve (D_{ACTUAL}) in Exhibit 1. By pricing the product at $20, enormous shortages were created (shown as AB in Exhibit 1), and the firm was losing lots of potential revenue. Coleco could have charged $35 and even sold a few more dolls (upward sloping supply curve), making far greater profits.

What happens when you don't accurately anticipate consumer demand?

HOW DID THE MARKET RESOLVE THE DISEQUILIBRIUM?

Clearly, the initial Cabbage Patch situation, shown in Exhibit 1, was a disequilibrium condition. As we have learned, however, disequilibrium is a temporary condition, because market forces will intervene and move the market back towards equilibrium. In this case, the excess quantity demanded at $20 was a signal to the marketplace; the participants, acting in their own self-interest, responded to bring the market back to equilibrium.

In the case of the Cabbage Patch Dolls, an alerted Coleco quickly raised its price to reduce the disequilibrium. Following the law of supply, it makes sense for the company to want to increase output, and Coleco did, in this case, by having its Chinese suppliers increase deliveries (at increased costs, reflecting the greater costs of more hurried production rates). The combination of a higher price for the Coleco dolls, plus the increase in the supply of Cabbage Patch-like substitutes, largely eliminated the market shortage within months.

In time, the Cabbage Patch fad wore down, causing the demand curve to shift to the left (that is, at any price, de-

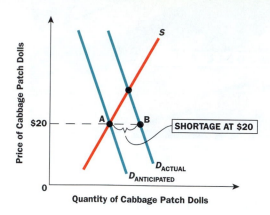

EXHIBIT 1 — **THE CABBAGE PATCH DOLL SHORTAGE**

mand was less than before). This caused both prices and sales to fall. The Cabbage Patch story had come full circle—market adjustments had reallocated resources successfully to deal with even such a fickle fad.

Sometimes anticipated demand may not be the same as actual demand.

1. Sometimes anticipated demand is different than actual demand.

2. While disequilibrium is possible, the period spent in disequilibrium tends to be very short for most goods and services, because a disequilibrium sets up profit incentives to move the market toward equilibrium prices.

1. What happens in a market when demand is greater than anticipated?

2. How do market adjustments resolve the temporary disequilibrium that results when demand is incorrectly estimated?

3. If the maker of Beanie Babies found that its inventories were plummeting, what kind of temporary disequilibrium would that indicate?

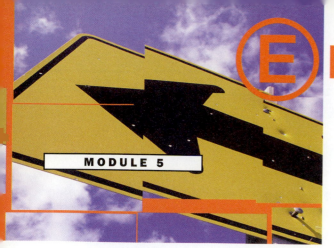

(E) Price Controls

MODULE 5

- What are price controls?
- What are price ceilings?
- What are price floors?

WHAT ARE PRICE CONTROLS?

While nonequilibrium prices can crop up in the private sector, reflecting uncertainty, they seldom last for long. Governments, however, often impose nonequilibrium prices for significant time periods. **Price controls** involve the use of the power of the state to establish prices different from the equilibrium prices that would otherwise prevail. The motivations for price controls vary with the market under consideration: a maximum, or **ceiling,** price is often set for goods deemed "important," like housing, or a minimum, or **floor,** may be set on wages because wages are the primary source of income for most people.

Price controls are not always implemented by the federal government. Local governments (and, more rarely, private companies) can and do impose local price controls. One fairly well-known example is rent controls. The inflation of the late 1970s meant rapidly rising rents, and some communities, such as Santa Monica, California, decided to do something about it. In response, they limited how much landlords could charge for rental housing.

PRICE CEILINGS: RENT CONTROL

Rent control experiences can be found in many cities across the country. San Francisco, Berkeley, and New York City all have had some form of rent control. While the rules may vary from city to city and over time, generally the price (or rent) of an apartment remains fixed over the tenure of an occupant, except for allowable annual increases tied to the cost of living or some other price index. When an occupant moves out, the owner can usually, but not always, raise the rent to a near-market level for the next occupant. The controlled rents for existing occupants, however, are generally well below-market rental rates.

Results of Rent Controls

First, persons living in rent controlled apartments have a good deal, one that they would lose by moving as their family circumstances or income change. Tenants thus are reluctant to give up their governmentally granted right to a below-market rent apartment. Second, because the rents received by landlords are constrained and below market levels, the rate of return (roughly, the profit) on housing investments falls compared to that on other forms of real estate not subject to rent controls, like office rents or mortgage payments on condominiums. Hence, the incentive to construct new housing is reduced. Where rent controls are truly effective, there is generally little new construction going on and a shortage of apartments that persists and grows over time.

Third, since landlords are limited in what rent they can charge, there is little incentive to improve or upgrade

The effect of rent controls is shortages.

apartments, say, by putting in new kitchen appliances or new carpeting, in order to get more rent. In fact, there is some incentive to avoid routine maintenance, thereby lowering the cost of apartment ownership to a figure approximating the controlled rental price, although the quality of the housing stock will deteriorate over time.

A fourth impact of rent controls is that they promote housing discrimination. Where rent controls do not exist, a prejudiced landlord might willingly rent to someone he believes is undesirable, simply because the undesirable family is the only one willing to pay the requested rent (and the landlord is not willing to lower the rent substantially to get a desirable family, since this could translate into the loss of thousands of dollars in income). With rent controls, there are likely to be many families wanting to rent the controlled apartment, some desirable and some undesirable, as seen by the landlord, simply because the rent is at a below-equilibrium price. The landlord can indulge in his "taste" for discrimination without any additional financial loss beyond that required by the controls.

Consequently, he or she will be more likely to choose to rent to a desirable family, perhaps a family without children or pets, rather than an undesirable one, perhaps one with lower income and so a greater risk of non-payment.

Exhibit 1 shows the impact of rent control. If the price ceiling is set below the market price, the quantity demanded will increase to Q_D from Q^* and the quantity supplied will fall to Q_S from Q^*. The rent control policy will therefore create a shortage, the difference between Q_S and Q_D.

PRICE FLOORS: THE MINIMUM WAGE

Suppose the government decided to increase the **minimum wage rate** for workers. The argument for doing so is simple: Existing minimum wages do not allow for a very high standard of living, and a higher minimum wage will allow workers (those continuing to work, and maintaining their hours worked, anyway!) to live better than before. Ever since 1938, when the first minimum wage was established (at 25 cents per hour), the federal government has, by legislation, made it illegal to pay most workers an amount below the current legislated minimum wage.

The quantity of labor demanded, as for other goods, varies inversely with its price, because at a lower price or wage, employers find it more profitable to hire more workers. Likewise, the supply of labor varies directly with price; at higher wages, more persons have an incentive to work (and the existing workers have an incentive to work longer hours).

If the government raises the minimum wage, the quantity of labor supplied to the market grows, because more are willing to work at a higher wage rate. However, the quantity of labor demanded falls because some employers would find it unprofitable to hire low-skilled workers at the higher wage rate. Examine Exhibit 2. At $5.15 an hour, there may be a gap between the quantity of labor demanded and the quantity supplied, AB; this represents willing workers who will be unable to find jobs. However, if the wage were increased by government mandate to $10, the gap between quantity demanded and quantity

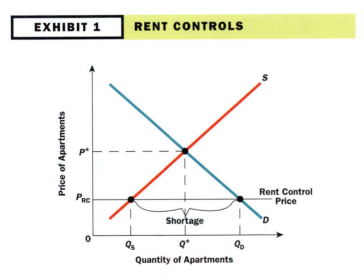

| EXHIBIT 1 | RENT CONTROLS |

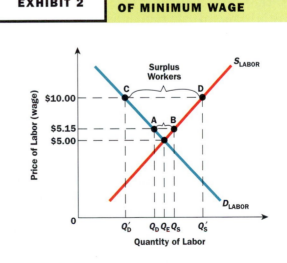

| EXHIBIT 2 | THE UNEMPLOYMENT EFFECTS OF MINIMUM WAGE |

What do you think would happen to the number of unskilled workers getting jobs if we raised the minimum wage to $50 an hour? How many more people would be sitting here?

supplied, CD, would be much larger. An increase in the minimum wage would, therefore, create additional unemployment.

The additional unemployment created by higher minimum wages is not evenly distributed among various racial, demographic, and educational groups in our population. An increase in the minimum wage will not have any important impact, for example, on the unemployment rate for physicians, all of whom earn far more than $10 an hour. Rather, the impact falls mainly on the least-experienced, least-skilled persons, holding the lowest-paying jobs. A large proportion of these jobs are held by teenagers. Those who continue to hold jobs after the minimum wage is increased gain substantially, and thereby are vociferous supporters of efforts to increase the minimum. Yet another group of persons suffers tremendously more from the higher minimum wage—they lose their jobs or are unable to get them in the first place (for new labor market entrants) and suffer a decline in earnings, not a gain. Others would be frustrated when they unsuccessfully attempted to get a job at $10 an hour. Although studies disagree somewhat on the precise magnitudes, they largely agree that minimum wage laws do create some unemployment, and that the unemployment is concentrated among teenagers, blacks, and other minorities. Minimum wage laws are one reason that black and teenage unemployment rates are at least twice as high as unemployment for white adults.

The above analysis does not "prove" minimum wage laws are "bad" and should be abolished. To begin with, there is the empirical question of how much unemploy-

ment is caused by increases in minimum wages. Secondly, the cost of higher unemployment might be viewed by some as a reasonable price to pay for assuring that those with jobs get a "decent" wage. The analysis does point out, however, that there is a cost to having minimum wages, and the burden of increases in the minimum wages falls not only on employers and purchasers of products made more costly by the minimum wage but also on poor, low-income Americans who become unemployed when such increases occur.

1. Price controls involve government mandates to keep prices above or below the market-determined equilibrium price.
2. Price ceilings are government-imposed maximum prices.
3. If price ceilings are set below the equilibrium price, shortages will result.
4. Price floors are government-imposed minimum prices.
5. If price floors are set above the equilibrium price, surpluses will result.

1. How is rent control an example of a price ceiling?
2. What predictable effects result from price ceilings like rent control?
3. How is the minimum wage law an example of a price floor?
4. What predictable effects result from price floors like the minimum wage?
5. What may happen to the amount of discrimination against groups such as families with children, pet owners, smokers, or students when rent control is imposed?
6. Why does rent control often lead to condominium conversions?

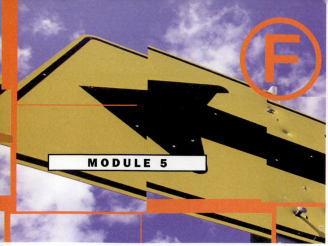

Ⓕ Application: Supply and Demand in the Market for Super Bowl Tickets

Why does ticket scalping occur? What role do ticket scalpers play in the market for Super Bowl tickets?

JUST THE TICKET FOR SUPER BOWL FANS

STEPHEN HAPPEL AND MARIANNE M. JENNINGS

TEMPE, Ariz.—You can't help but admire the power and influence of the Super Bowl. What else can close down Miami's freeways for hours on a Sunday afternoon for a parade of VIP limos? What else can cause a sacred Indian burial ground to be plowed up, without resistance, for a glitzy football theme park lasting just one week? Stronger than a sovereign nation, the National Football League rules in most situations. But the free market is the one force that eludes the NFL offense, despite its determined efforts.

The Super Bowl is a high-demand, limited-supply event. This year, in Tempe, there are some 80,000 seats for the 30th playing of football's crowning moment. The NFL has done such a good marketing job that half of the United States wants to attend. Yet, the league has no intention of allowing them in. Market control is the NFL goal.

For the first 29 Super Bowls, ticket prices for all stadium seats were the same regardless of location. So much for the market! This year's game has differential prices ($200, $250, and $350), "to more adequately reflect differences in seat quality," a league spokesman says. But with present market prices ranging from $1,000 to $3,000, the NFL has not priced to what the market will bear.

Even with the NFL in charge, scalping is inevitable. So many want seats, and some who receive official tickets are willing to sell them. Each year hundreds of ticket scalpers from across the United States descend on the host city a week before the game to trade from temporary command posts in motel rooms. Scalpers always appear at the stadium even when the probability of arrest is high.

Rather than ramming ahead into the force of the market, the NFL should try a reverse. Scalpers should be allowed to operate license-free at one location on game day. Phoenix pioneered such an ordinance for the 1995 NBA All-Star Game, and as we outlined on this page last year, the results have overwhelmingly benefited the customers. Search costs are minimized. Prices are lower. The nuisance effects of congested street corners, aggressive sellers and fights are gone. Counterfeit tickets are almost nonexistent. The common area will simply make shopping easier for those rabid fans who are willing to pay what it takes to achieve a once-in-a-lifetime dream.

The NFL, alas, has no plans for a reverse. League rules prohibit anyone affiliated with the NFL from scalping Super Bowl tickets. Also, the host city is required to have an antiscalping ordinance enforced at the event.

The Super Bowl's status as the top sporting event in the United States means that the vast majority of tickets never reach the open market. Yet the human spirit coupled with market forces still emerges as fans and scalpers search for each other. Just outside the stadium, within the shadow of the mighty NFL, they will meet. Neither ordinances nor screening can stop them. Even the NFL can't sack the laws of supply and demand.

Mr. Happel is a professor of economics and associate dean at the College of Business at Arizona State University, where Ms. Jennings is a professor of legal and ethical studies. George Alper, a Tempe ticket trader, contributed to this article.

SOURCE: Stephen Happel and Marianne Jennings, "Just the Ticket for Super Bowl Fans," *The Wall Street Journal,* January 25, 1996.

According to Happel and Jennings, for the first 29 years of the Super Bowl, the NFL did not differentiate their prices on the basis of seating—all seats regardless of location fetched the same price. Finally, in 1996, the NFL decided they should set their prices to reflect seat quality, so they did: $200, $250 and $350. Even at these new higher prices the NFL faced a situation of excess quantity demanded, or a shortage. As a result of the shortage, the ticket scalpers were getting anywhere from $1,000 to $3,000 per ticket—5 to 10 times the ticket price.

Would there be ticket scalping if the tickets were selling for $3,000 to $4,000 a piece? Maybe for the very best seats but, at that price, there would certainly be less work for scalpers. But when tickets are priced well below equilibrium, there is an important function for scalpers. Their objective is profit, no doubt, but they also provide an important function for society—they try to get tickets in the hands of people who value the tickets the most. The profits of buying from someone who values the tickets less and selling to those who value it more brings scalpers in from all over the United States—"even when the probability of arrest is high." As Happel and Jennings so aptly state, "Even the NFL can't sack the laws of supply and demand."

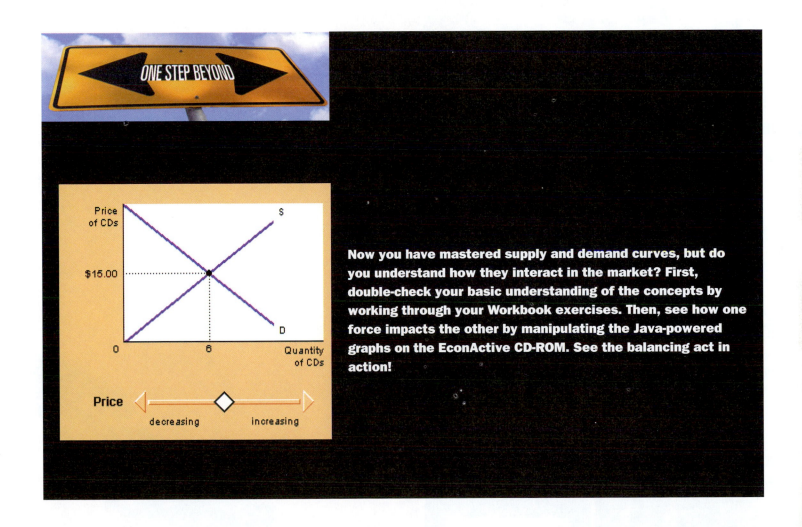

ONE STEP BEYOND

Now you have mastered supply and demand curves, but do you understand how they interact in the market? First, double-check your basic understanding of the concepts by working through your Workbook exercises. Then, see how one force impacts the other by manipulating the Java-powered graphs on the EconActive CD-ROM. See the balancing act in action!

PHOTO CREDITS MODULE 5

Page **122:** © T/Maker Company; Page **124:** © A. Bolesta/ H. Armstrong Roberts; Page **126:** top, AP Photo/Cor El Espectador; bottom, © PhotoDisc; Page **131:** © PhotoDisc; Page **132:** © 1997 Thaves/Reprinted with permission; Page **133:** © Lawrence Manning/Westlight; Page **134:** © Wiley Miller/The Washington Post Writers Group; Page **136:** © 1998 Don Couch Photography; Page **138:** top, © 1998 Don Couch Photography; bottom, © The Buffalo News. Reprinted with permission of UNIVERSAL PRESS SYNDICATE. All rights reserved; Page **140:** © Ron Vesely Photography.

Government and the Economy

A. Government and Property Rights
Should government protect
property rights?

B. Government and Externalities
Should government intervene to correct externalities?

C. Government and Public Goods
Should government provide public goods and services?

D. Government and Information Costs
Should government provide information to consumers?

E. Other Government Functions
How does government try to prevent insufficient competition
and achieve its macroeconomic goals?

F. Government and Income Distribution
Should government work to create more equality in income distribution?

G. Public Choice
Is politics influenced by self-interest?

H. Spending and Taxation
How do we pay for government?

I. Application: Revving Up the Helmet Law Debate
Can a balance of the freedom of the rider and the freedom
of the taxpayer be found?

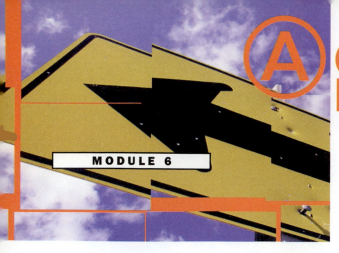

A Government and Property Rights

- What are property rights?
- How does government protect rights?
- What is the right of eminent domain?

GOVERNMENT INTERVENTION: HOW MUCH IS TOO MUCH?

For centuries, political scientists and economists have argued about the role of government in society. When is government intervention good or bad? Is there too much government involvement or too little? In Module 1, we touched on two primary justifications given for government intervention in the market system—market failure and externalities.

In this Module, we will address seven arguments for government intervention: (1) enforcement of property rights, (2) externalities, (3) provision of public goods, (4) information costs, (5) imperfect competition in markets, (6) macroeconomic goals, and (7) income distribution. In these discussions, we provide arguments both for and against this intervention in an attempt to help you understand the appropriate role of government in a market economy. The first point of contention, property rights, is discussed below.

WHY ARE PROPERTY RIGHTS SO IMPORTANT?

As we discussed in Module 1, property rights give individuals the power to use, sell, rent, dispose of, or enhance the value of the resources they own. The government defines and protects property rights through the legal system and police protection. By defining and enforcing these rights, the government actually provides incentives or disincentives for certain economic activities. On a basic level, if use of your own resources is protected, then it is clearly in your best interest to put those resources to their highest valued use. Otherwise, the value of those resources will be diminished to some degree and you will be less well off than you could have been. In this way, then, property rights are vital to the proper functioning of the market system, because they act as incentives that encourage all participants to use their resources efficiently.

When cattle ranchers are responsible for their cattle damage, they will act to reduce that damage. This might mean fencing their property.

CAN GOVERNMENT ASSUME OWNERSHIP OF PRIVATE PROPERTY?

However, while few would argue against the enforcement of property rights in general, some do point out that the government may wish to reduce the rights of private individuals to utilize their own resources in some instances. Thus, we have zoning laws that prohibit a person from building a factory or erecting a big billboard in predominantly residential areas. Owners of stores in some states are prohibited from operating on Sunday because of "blue" laws, and utility companies and local governments often have easement rights that allow them to construct water and sewer lines across private property. Indeed, through the ancient right of **eminent domain**, governments can assume ownership of private property if compensation is made to the original owners. If the government did not have this right, an individual property owner could block the construction of a new highway or hold out for a very high price. We often face such property rights issues.

CONCEPT CHECK

1. Property rights give individuals the power to use, sell, rent, dispose of, or enhance the value of their resources.
2. By defining and enforcing property rights, government provides incentives and disincentives for certain economic activities.
3. The right of eminent domain allows government to assume ownership of private property if it compensates the owner.

1. What are the arguments for government intervention in the economy?
2. How is government enforcement of property rights necessary to a market economy?
3. How does the government right of eminent domain affect property rights?
4. Would many bicycles be produced in a country where a person maintained his ownership of a bicycle only as long as he was sitting on it? Why?
5. How do laws against selling stolen property make private property rights more secure?

(B) Government and Externalities

- What is a negative externality?
- How are negative externalities internalized?
- What is a positive externality?
- How are positive externalities internalized?

The forces represented by supply and demand perform an extremely complicated and valuable function. However, these market forces do not always produce the "right" amount of all goods and services. That is, sometimes the market system fails to produce efficient outcomes because of side effects economists call externalities. An **externality** is said to occur whenever there are physical impacts (benefits or costs) of an activity on individuals not directly involved in the activity. If the impact on the outside party is negative, it is called a **negative externality;** if the impact is positive, it is called a **positive externality.**

WHAT ARE NEGATIVE EXTERNALITIES?

The classic example of a negative externality is pollution from an air-polluting factory. If the firm uses clean air in production and returns dirty air to the atmosphere, it has created a negative externality. The polluted air has "spilled over" to outside parties. Now people in the neighboring communities may experience higher incidences of disease, dirtier houses, and other property damage. Such damages are real costs, but because no one owns the air, the firm does not have to pay for its use. This is unlike the other resources the firm uses in production. A steel mill has to pay for its other inputs, like labor, capital, energy, and raw materials, because it must compensate the owners of those inputs for their use. If a firm can avoid paying the cost it imposes on others—the external costs—it has lowered its own costs of production, but not the true cost to society.

Examples of negative externalities are numerous: the roommate that plays his stereo too loud at 2:00 in the morning, the neighbor's dog that barks all night long or leaves "messages" on your front lawn, the gardener that runs his leaf blower on full power at 7:00 A.M. on a Saturday.

Graphing External Costs

In Exhibit 1, we see the market for steel. We also notice that at each level of output, the first supply curve, S_0, is lower

The government can intervene and help eliminate or minimize negative externalities such as pollution.

than the second, S_1. The reason for this is simple: S_0 only includes the private costs to the firm—the capital, entrepreneurship, land, and labor for which it must pay. However, S_1 includes all of those costs plus the external costs that production imposes on others. That is, if the firm could somehow be required to compensate those damaged, it would increase the cost of production for the firm and cause a leftward shift in the supply curve. In Exhibit 1, we see that if the government stepped in and made the firm pay for the external costs, then the output of steel would fall to Q_1, and the price would rise to P_1. However, if the government does not step in, the real price from society's standpoint is higher than P_1, at P_2. While the buyers of steel may only be paying P_0, there are also the implicit costs incurred by the bystanders who are suffering from the ill effects of the pollution. These costs are measured by the difference between P_0 and P_2. If the suppliers of steel are not aware of or not responsible for the external costs, they will tend to produce too much from society's standpoint. The efficiency loss from this overproduction is represented by the shaded area in Exhibit 1.

Regulation

Alternatively, the government might simply prohibit certain types of activities causing pollution, or might force firms to clean up their emissions. The purchase and use of new pollution-control devices can also increase the cost of production and shift the supply curve to the left, from S_0 to S_1.

EXHIBIT 1	NEGATIVE EXTERNALITIES

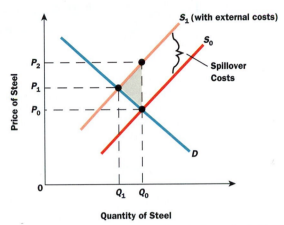

The supply curve S_1 includes the costs of production reflected by the private supply curve S_0, plus the external costs (such as pollution). Market production is greater and market price is lower than is socially desirable when externalities are not internalized. The shaded area designates the efficiency loss from overproduction.

RUBES

How to tell when water pollution
has reached unacceptably high levels

WHAT CAN THE GOVERNMENT DO TO CORRECT FOR A NEGATIVE EXTERNALITY?

The government can intervene in market decisions in an attempt to take account of these negative externalities. It may do this by estimating the amount of those external costs and then taxing the manufacturer by that amount, forcing the manufacturer to internalize (bear) the costs.

Pollution Taxes

Pollution taxes are designed to internalize negative externalities. If government could impose a pollution tax or an effluent fee equal to the exact size of the external cost, then the firm would produce at the socially desired level of output, Q_1. That is, the tax would shift the supply curve for steel up to S_1 and would provide an incentive for the firm to produce at the efficient level of output. An additional feature of this approach is that tax revenues would be generated that could be used to compensate those that had suffered damages from the pollution, or that could be used (or returned to taxpayers) in some other productive way.

WHAT ARE POSITIVE EXTERNALITIES?

For some goods, the individual consumer does not receive all of the benefits. This is not the case for, say, a hamburger; if you buy it, you get all of its benefits. However, consider education, well-kept home exteriors, beautiful art, or even praying mantises and ladybugs as alternatives to pesticides. Certainly, when you "buy" an education, you receive many of its benefits: greater future income, more choice of future occupations, and the consumption value of knowing more about life as a result of classroom (and extracurricular) learning. These benefits, however, great as they may be, are not all of the benefits associated with your education. You may be less likely to be unemployed or commit crimes, or you may end up curing cancer or solving some other social problem of importance. These nontrivial benefits are the *positive* external consumption benefits of education.

Why does the government subsidize and produce so much education? Presumably because the private market

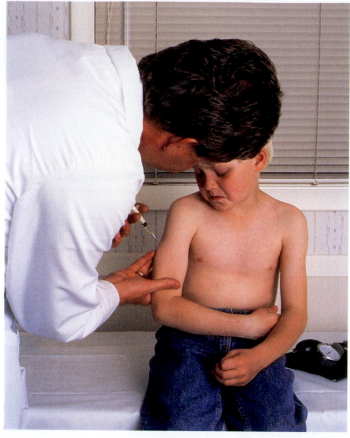

Governments provide some services because of the positive externalities.

does not provide enough. It is argued that the education of a person benefits not only that person, but all of society, because a more informed citizenry can make more intelligent collective decisions that benefit everyone. Another example: Why do public health departments sometimes offer "free" inoculations against certain communicable diseases, such as influenza? Partly because, by protecting one group of citizens, everyone gets some protection; if the first citizen does not get the disease, it prevents that person from passing it on to others. Many governmental efforts in the field of health and education are justified on the basis of perceived positive externalities. Of course, because positive externalities are often difficult to measure, it is hard to empirically demonstrate whether many governmental health and educational programs achieve their intended purpose.

Graphing External Benefits

Let's take the case of a new vaccine against the common cold. The market for the vaccine is shown in Exhibit 2. The demand curve D_0 represents the prices and quantities that buyers would be willing to pay to reduce their probability of catching the common cold. The supply curve shows the amounts that suppliers would offer for sale at different prices. However, at the equilibrium output, we are far

| EXHIBIT 2 | POSITIVE EXTERNALITIES |

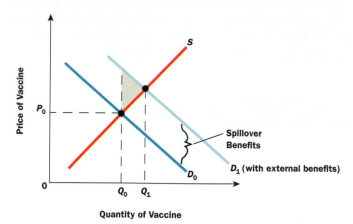

The private demand curve plus external benefits constitutes the social demand curve, D_1. The market output falls short of the socially optimal output, Q_1, and the market underproduces the good. The shaded area indicates the associated efficiency loss.

short of the desirable level of output for these vaccination shots. Why? The reason is that many people benefit from the vaccines. Those who do not have to pay for the vaccines are now less likely to be infected because others took the vaccine. If we could add the benefits that are derived by nonpaying consumers, the demand curve would shift to the right, from D_0 to D_1. The greater level of output, Q_1, that would result if D_1 were the observed demand reflects the total benefits and the desirable output level. However, because producers are unable to collect payments from all of those who are benefiting from the good or service, the market has a tendency to underproduce. In this case, the market is not producing enough vaccinations from society's standpoint. The efficiency loss associated with underproduction is represented by the shaded area in Exhibit 2.

WHAT CAN THE GOVERNMENT DO TO CORRECT FOR POSITIVE EXTERNALITIES?

How could society correct for this market failure? Two particular methods of achieving the higher preferred output are subsidies and regulations.

Subsidies

Government could either give refunds to individuals who receive an inoculation or they could provide an incentive for businesses to give their employees "free" inoculations at the office. Public schools receive huge subsidies from the government—of course, you pay for some of it as a taxpayer. If the subsidy was exactly equal to external benefits of inoculation, the demand curve would shift from D_0 to D_1, resulting in an efficient level of output, Q_1.

Regulation

The government could also pass a regulation requiring each person to get an inoculation shot. This would also shift the demand curve to the right toward the efficient level of output.

In summary, when there are positive externalities, the private market supplies too little of the good in question (such as education or inoculations for communicable diseases). When there are negative externalities, the market supplies too much. In either case, buyers and sellers are receiving the wrong signals. The producers and consumers are not doing what they do because they are evil; rather, both the well-intentioned and the ill-intentioned behave according to the incentives they face. The free market, then, works fine in providing most goods, but it functions less well without regulations, taxes, and subsidies in providing others.

NON-GOVERNMENT SOLUTIONS TO EXTERNALITIES

Sometimes the externality problems can be handled by individuals without the intervention of government. For example, moral and social codes may prevent some people from littering, driving gas-guzzling cars, or using gas-powered mowers and log burning fireplaces. In short, people may decide to take steps on their own to minimize negative externalities. For example, many environmental groups receive money from private sources to handle problems associated with negative externalities. These benefactors are acting on their own to reduce negative externalities. The same self-regulation also applies to positive externalities. For example, philanthropists frequently donate money to public and private schools. In part, this must be because they view the positive externalities from education as a good buy for their charitable dollars.

Some may switch from gas mowers and trimmers to battery-powered equipment to minimize negative externalities.

CONCEPT CHECK

1. If a market activity has a negative physical impact on an outside party, that side effect is called a negative externality.
2. The government can use pollution taxes or other forms of regulation to correct the overallocation problem associated with negative externalities.

3. If a market activity has a positive physical impact on an outside party, that side effect is called a positive externality.
4. The government can provide subsidies or other forms of regulation to correct the underallocation problem associated with positive externalities.

1. Why are externalities also called spillover effects?
2. How are externalities related to property rights?
3. How do external costs affect the price and output of a polluting activity?
4. How can the government intervene to force producers to internalize external costs?
5. How does internalizing the external costs improve efficiency?

6. How do external benefits affect the output of an activity that causes them?
7. How can the government intervene to force external benefits to be internalized?
8. Why do most cities have more stringent noise laws for the early morning and late evening hours than for during the day?

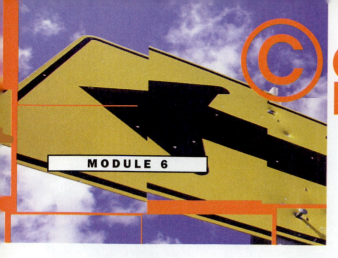

©

Government and Public Goods

- What are public goods?
- What is the free rider problem?
- Why does the government provide public goods?

WHAT IS A PUBLIC GOOD?

Externalities are not the only culprit behind resource mis-allocations. Another source of market failure is what economists call **public goods.** As used by economists, this term refers not to how particular goods are purchased—by a government agency rather than some private economic agent—but to the properties that characterize them. A private good such as a hamburger has two critical properties in the present context. First, if you buy it, it is yours—nobody else can have it (unless you let them, in which case you no longer have it). This property is referred to as **excludability.** Second, the user of a private good receives *all* the benefits of its consumption. Consumption of a private good is therefore **rivalrous.**

Unlike private goods, the consumption of public goods is both nonexcludable and nonrivalrous. One example of a public good is national defense. Whatever the level of national defense, we all benefit from it (consumption is nonrivalrous). That is, once the military has its defense in place, everyone is protected simultaneously. In addition, it is prohibitively costly to exclude anyone from consuming

national defense. For example, if you lived at 16 Main Street and you weren't willing to pay to be protected, it would be too costly to exclude you. That is, it is too difficult to exclude anyone from consuming a public good (consumption is nonexcludable).

WHAT IS A FREE RIDER?

Public goods are closely related to externalities and to something called the **free rider problem.** Suppose the quality of the air where you live is undesirable, so you clean it up. Perhaps you reduce your own pollution by substituting a cleaner wood-burning stove for a highly polluting one, or even by placing a huge filter upwind of your home. Because air quality is largely a public good, you know that others will benefit. It might well be advantageous from society's perspective for the air to be cleaned up in this way, but what incentive do your neighbors have to pay for the benefits they will receive?

The answer, of course, is very little. They know that if you choose to clean up the air, they cannot be prevented from receiving the benefits. They also know, individually, that not one of them would honestly be willing to pay enough to affect your decision. In other words, they may attempt to become what are known as "free riders." Because you do not receive compensation for the benefits accruing to them, you will not clean up and will pollute more than you would otherwise.

Now suppose a "Save the Whales" group came to your neighborhood collecting funds with which to lobby for protection of the blue whales (whose existence is a public good according to the definition). You may have a genuine interest in the whale's continued existence, but what incentives to contribute do you face? Suppose the whale's survival is actually worth $100 to you. If the 100 million households in the United States each made a similar contribution, this would add up to about $10 billion. You might write a check for $100. Or you might reason as follows: "If I give $100, there is no guarantee that the whale gets saved, because my contribution is negligible relative to the

Government provides important public goods, such as national defense.

No one has property rights over blue whales, so who has an incentive to protect this valuable asset?

is human values that matter and that some environmental degradation may be optimal: When the benefits of producing a polluting good are greater than the full social costs, there are no "environmental problems," in the sense that efforts to improve the environment further would make us worse off.

On both the supply and the demand side, it is clear that we are likely to get too little of public goods without some intervention—indeed, we generally get zero! On the supply side, nonexcludability precludes charging consumers for benefits received. As a result, producers are not able to cover their costs of producing public goods from revenues. On the demand side, individual consumers have an incentive to be free riders, further reducing the likelihood that goods having benefits greater than costs will be produced. Public goods, then, are not profitable to produce.

As a result of the nonexclusion provision of public goods, the free rider problem prevents the private market from supplying the efficient amount of the public goods. The government may be able to step in to overcome the free rider problem. For example, if national defense has total benefits that are greater than total costs, the government can provide defense and have all taxpayers pay for it. Without the government supplying national defense, some households may choose not to pay for it knowing that it is too difficult to keep them from receiving the benefits of protection.

amount required to convene conferences, pass legislation, buy up existing boats, and so on. Furthermore, if I don't give $100, the whale may get saved anyhow, and I'll continue to receive the benefits of its existence plus the benefits of the $100." Taking the latter course represents a rational attempt to become a free rider. The rub is that if everyone attempts to take a free ride, the ride will not exist.

PROPERTY RIGHTS AND FREE RIDES

It is easy to see how property rights figure into this discussion of the free rider problem by pursuing the previous examples. If air quality were like land quality, where rights of ownership and use were easy to prescribe and enforce, each "owner" of air would have an incentive to protect the value of his or her asset just as people paint their homes, rotate their crops, and take similar actions to maintain the value of other assets. The nature of air, however, precludes this—it is difficult to own.

For example, why are blue whales, condors, and bighorn sheep endangered when cows, chickens, and ordinary sheep are not? The property rights associated with cows and similar animals give their owners the incentive to care for them. Nobody owns whales (or acts as if they did); hence, whale users are not charged a price to reflect the scarcity of whales, as they would be if cows were scarce. An ironic conclusion emerges: It is often believed that the price system of capitalist economies is responsible for our environmental woes, when in fact the opposite is true. The problem is a lack of prices (charging a zero price for the use of socially scarce air or wildlife). Where prices work properly, we do not have environmental problems.

There is, however, a qualification to this assertion that there would be no environmental problems if the price system worked properly. The assertion takes, as seems appropriate to economists, negative externalities to be synonymous with environmental problems. This means that it

WHEN ARE PUBLIC GOODS NOT GOOD?

Arguments surrounding the government provision of public goods often involve the contention that production of many public goods represent an inefficient use of resources. But how? When evaluating the desire for a public good, the government cannot accurately assess the desires of market participants. In its assessment of the desire for a public good, the government must, just like other suppliers of goods, complete a benefit–cost analysis that weighs the benefits of providing the good against the cost that must be incurred to provide that good.

Consider the case of a new highway. Before it builds the highway, the appropriate government agency will undertake a benefit–cost analysis of the situation. In this case, it must evaluate consumers' willingness to pay for the highway against the costs that will be incurred for construction and maintenance. However, those individuals that want the highway have an incentive to exaggerate their desire for it. At the same time, individuals who will be displaced or otherwise harmed by the highway have an incentive to exaggerate the harm that will be done to them. Together, these elements make it difficult for the government to accurately assess need. Ultimately, their evaluations are reduced to educated guesses about the net impact, weighing both positive and negative effects, of the highway on all parties concerned.

1. A public good is both nonrival in consumption (one person's usage of it does not diminish another's ability to use it) and nonexclusive (no one can be excluded from using it).

2. A free rider is someone who attempts to enjoy the benefits of a good without paying for it.

3. The government provides public goods because the free rider problem results in underproduction of these goods in the marketplace.

1. How are public goods different from private goods?
2. Why does the free rider problem arise in the case of public goods?
3. How does the free rider problem relate to property rights?
4. In what way can government provision of public goods solve the free rider problem?

5. Why is it difficult for the government to determine the proper amount of a public good to produce?
6. How does a TV broadcast have characteristics of a public good?
7. Can lighthouse services be privately provided if all of the boats using the services of a lighthouse are heading for the port nearest that lighthouse? Why or why not?

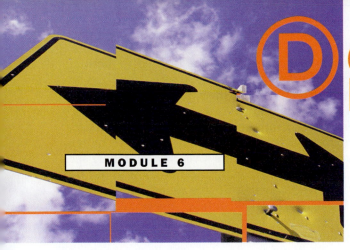

D Government and Information Costs

- What are information costs?
- How does the government disseminate information?
- Should the government be in the information business?

WHAT ARE INFORMATION COSTS?

It is assumed that persons buying or selling goods in the marketplace are acting in a manner that maximizes their satisfaction, or utility. For consumers to do this, however, they must have accurate information about the quality and characteristics of the goods and services in question.

Information can be treated like most other scarce goods: It is desirable and limited, and people are willing to pay a positive price to obtain it. In short, people are willing to pay a certain cost to obtain information. Just as in any other cost-benefit evaluation, however, individuals will stop searching for information when the cost of obtaining that additional information outweighs the benefit they expect to gain from it. This is why consumers are willing to spend more time researching before a car purchase than before buying toothpaste. Unlike the toothpaste purchase, the consequence of making a mistake when buying a car is significant, so the cost of gathering information is relatively small compared to the benefit that can be gained.

However, when information costs to consumers are greater than the perceived benefits, consumers will make less-informed decisions. As the late Nobel Laureate George Stigler pointed out years ago, "It is perfectly rational for people to make 'poor' decisions if the cost of information necessary to make good decisions exceeds the benefits." For example, consider the case of Pete Moss, an average consumer who desires to buy a lawn edger. Pete finds two virtually identical edgers, each costing $250. Because (as far as he knows) the cost to him ($250) is identical regardless of his purchase choice, Pete buys the first edger. Unbeknown to Pete, however, the blade on that edger is made of lower-quality materials, increasing the likelihood of accidents and product failure. Because he lacked the appropriate information, Pete made a poorer decision than he might have.

HOW DOES THE GOVERNMENT DISSEMINATE INFORMATION?

Much legislation passed at the federal as well as the state and local levels in the past 50 years seems directed towards reducing information costs and keeping consumers from making dangerous or worthless purchases. The U.S. Department of Agriculture inspects meat and rates its quality, giving consumers some information about meat quality. The inspection of scales used in markets is carried out by state and local governments to protect customers from misinformation. The Securities and Exchange Commission attempts to protect investors from unwitting losses by requiring sellers of securities to provide certain forms of information, to have training, and so forth. Another well-established form of consumer protection is **occupational licensing** laws for professions. Occupational licenses are now required to practice medicine, law, plumbing, marriage counseling, and so on.

Proponents of these laws argue that they assure consumers that certain minimal quality standards will be met, thus reducing private information costs. If a doctor has a license, which can be obtained by passing a licensing exam, presumably he or she has had reasonably good training in medicine. In recent years, consumer groups have pushed for new forms of protection in the form of information, such as warning labels on products that contain possible cancer-causing agents, "truth in lending" laws requiring interest rates and other loan terms to be stated clearly and honestly, laws forcing tire manufacturers to grade their tires according to uniform federal standards, and so on.

Sometimes the government provides warning labels on products to inform consumers.

Sometimes, rather than providing consumers with information about potentially injurious products and letting them make their own purchase decisions, the government simply bans the product. Examples include bans on the sale of certain insecticides and, more recently, the decision to take certain diet drugs off the market.

Sometimes governments ban certain products.

Governmental information services are not limited to purchasers of goods and services, but also extend to suppliers. For decades, the federal government has provided information to farmers on how to produce various types of agricultural products, via a system of county extension agents. Government has also mandated that producers reveal information like miles per gallon in city and highway driving on new cars or energy usage on electric appliances. Likewise it provides added information on weather conditions, prices, projected supplies, and so on. Also, suppliers of labor services—workers—are provided labor market information through state employment bureaus.

WHAT ARE THE OBJECTIONS TO GOVERNMENT INFORMATION SERVICES?

Few will quarrel with the objective of reducing information costs to consumers and suppliers, permitting more intelligent market decisions and leading to greater satisfaction. However, one can still oppose certain types of governmental action in this area on the grounds that the costs of providing the information are too high, that the government is disseminating inaccurate or misleading information, or that special-interest groups have managed to manipulate the regulation to their own advantage, which may not be in the public interest.

For example, occupational licensing laws supposedly protect misinformed consumers from getting shoddy services, but these laws may also restrict competition, reducing the supply of workers providing these services and leading to higher prices. For example, each plumber can

gain thousands of dollars in income by sharply limiting the number of competing plumbers, so some plumbers are willing to pay money and use their time to insure that occupational licensing of plumbers serves to restrict the supply of plumbers and thus competition. As a consequence of the restrictive licensing, hundreds of thousands of customers may pay $40 or $50 more a year for plumbing services, but these consumers either do not know about the effects of these restrictions or do not regard that potential cost to be big enough to make a fuss, so a small pressure group of plumbers could continue to control the licensing board. While it does not always work this way, it is possible that occupational licensing may do as much harm as good.

Likewise, Sam Peltzman has argued that the Food and Drug Administration, in its attempts to prevent drugs from going on sale when we are not certain as to their safety, has saddled pharmaceutical firms with so much higher information costs in the form of testing of new drugs that the companies have markedly reduced the amount of new life-saving drugs coming on the market. In its attempt to be sure that drugs are 100 percent safe, the FDA forces companies to spend millions of dollars on extremely elaborate testing, even where the drug has clear medical benefits and only a remote possibility of harm. On balance, the FDA *may* actually be raising the death and illness rate, not lowering it, because in its effort to keep bad drugs off the market, it also keeps good drugs off the market that may save thousands of lives.

Also, there can be much disagreement as to the methods the government uses to change consumer behavior for the

What do you think would happen to taxi fares if licenses were not required?

good. For example, years ago, the government decided to warn people of the dangers of cigarette smoking by requiring labeling information on cigarettes. Some would argue, however, that if cigarette smoking is truly as dangerous as alleged, the use of cigarettes should be banned. Taking another philosophical approach, some would condemn the prohibition of, say, cigarettes, arguing "Let adults decide for themselves if they wish to incur the health risks associated with tobacco consumption, as long as they do not impose harm on others." The "do at your own risk" group believes that government activity should be confined, at most, to providing individuals information and allowing them to make their own decisions.

Government-provided information, then, can be a good and efficient mechanism for reducing market failure from information costs. On the other hand, excessive governmental information policies can actually worsen the allocation of resources when the information provided is costly, relatively useless, and/or creates other market imperfections, such as a monopoly due to licensing.

THE WALL STREET JOURNAL

"But the government won't let me market it until I figure out a way to attach a warning label."

IN THE NEWS

RUDOLPH THE RED-TAPED REINDEER

It's a good thing Santa Claus lives and works at the North Pole rather than in the United States. If he had his shop in this country, Santa would have to function under so many laws and regulations that the federal government would likely close him down, leaving millions of boys and girls disappointed on Christmas morning.

Just consider some of the government agencies that could threaten Santa's work:

1. *The Fish and Wildlife Service.* Santa's sleigh is pulled by reindeer. But while reindeer are not an endangered species, flying reindeer are quite rare, and there is only one red-nosed reindeer known to exist. So under the Endangered Species Act, Dancer and Prancer might be allowed to continue working, but Rudolph would have to be placed in a safe habitat.

2. *The Occupational Safety and Health Administration.* It is not at all clear that Santa's workshop would pass federal OSHA standards for workplace safety. Does Santa have too many elves packed into a small room? Are there an adequate number of fire extinguishers and fire escapes?

3. *The Equal Employment Opportunity Commission.* It is clear that Santa hires a large number of vertically challenged people—elves. But all of these elves appear to be white males, which leaves the suspicion that Santa is in violation of the Civil Rights Act.

4. *The Federal Aviation Administration.* Santa's flying sleigh would need to be equipped with seat belts to be used on take-offs and landings. Since he flies over water, his sleigh would need a life preserver. The sleigh would also need the proper lighting—a real problem since Rudolph's nose is red, which would normally indicate the rear of the flying object rather than the front.

5. *The Commerce Department.* Santa is involved in the transport of consumable goods, which means he would be subject to certain weight restrictions and proper placarding of his sleigh if any hazardous materials were on board. Furthermore, regulations limit the number of hours a person can operate a vehicle transporting goods. After 10 hours behind the reins, Santa would probably have to take an 8-hour break, impeding his ability to finish his worldwide job on Christmas Eve.

6. *The National Labor Relations Board.* Is Santa using cheap elf labor, or is he paying his elves at least minimum wage? Is he giving them a lunch break? Paying overtime? Providing elf health insurance? A retirement plan?

All of these issues are important, yet Santa is avoiding them by doing business at the North Pole. Which raises another vital concern: By "dumping" toys in the United States at below-market prices (to wit, free), Santa is subjecting U.S. toy manufacturers and dealers to unfair competition and putting countless Americans out of work.

There's only one solution: Washington should impose stiff tariffs on goods imported from the North Pole, lifting them only when Santa ends his unfair trade practices and brings his operation up to American health and safety standards.

SOURCE: Merrill Matthews, Jr., *The Wall Street Journal,* December 24, 1997, Section A10.

CONSIDER THIS: Sometimes too much regulation can be burdensome to any economy.

1. Individuals will search for additional information as long as the marginal benefit gained from that information is greater than the marginal cost of obtaining it.
2. The government can reduce information costs to consumers and producers, permitting them to make better decisions.

3. Government information policies can be costly if the information provided is inaccurate, misleading, or relatively useless, or results in other market imperfections.

---

1. How long should you continue to seek more information before making a decision?
2. What is the rationale for government provision of information?
3. What are the objections to government provision of information?
4. Why do consumers spend more time researching a home purchase than an electric can opener purchase?

5. If someone argues that we need occupational licensing of gardeners to guarantee that misinformed consumers don't get shoddy service, is that person more likely to be a (highly trained) gardener or a homeowner who uses a gardening service? Why?

E Other Government Functions

- How does government discourage insufficient competition?
- What are the primary macroeconomic goals of government?
- How does government attempt to reach these goals?

INSUFFICIENT COMPETITION IN MARKETS

Another justification given for government intervention is to correct cases of insufficient competition that arise in the marketplace. As we discussed in Module 1, **monopoly,** or one-supplier, situations result in higher prices and lower quantities traded than might otherwise be supported by the market. When such conditions of restricted competition arise, the communication system of the marketplace is disrupted, causing the market to function inefficiently, to the detriment of consumers. For this reason, since the 1880s, the federal government has engaged in antitrust activities designed to encourage competition and discourage monopoly conditions. Specifically, the Antitrust Division of the Department of Justice and the Federal Trade Commission attempt to increase competition by attacking monopolistic practices.

MACROECONOMIC GOALS: FULL EMPLOYMENT, PRICE STABILITY, AND ECONOMIC GROWTH

The market mechanism does not assure fulfillment of some economic goals, most notably full employment but also stable prices and a high rate of economic growth. In the past 50 years, many have come to feel that governments can intervene in the economy to increase employment, stabilize prices, and/or bring about a greater growth in output over time. In particular, the objective of full employment has been used to justify government interventions. The apparent failure of the "self-correcting" market economy during the Great Depression led to a call for governmental involvement through spending and taxation programs designed to increase output and reduce unemployment.

Unemployment

During the 1930s, the unemployment rate rose to more than 20 percent of the labor force, and among some groups, notably female and minority workers, unemployment rates were even higher. For example, 75 percent of the black women of Detroit in early 1931 who wanted to work were unable to find a job. The concern over unemployment manifested itself in the passage of legislation committing the nation to a goal of full employment consistent with price stability, the Employment Act of 1946. Government policies, like taxes, and government spending can stimulate the economy when we are at less than full employment.

Massive unemployment in the Great Depression prompted passage of the Employment Act of 1946.

Inflation

An increase in the overall price level increases burdens on people with fixed incomes, particularly when the inflation is not anticipated. As we discussed in Module 1, inflation leads to market uncertainties and inefficiencies. In addition, incomes may be redistributed by changing prices, leading to a distribution that may conflict with national policy objectives. Again, policies of altering tax levels, government spending, and bank behavior have been used to deal with the problem of rising prices.

Economic Growth

Other goals, such as increasing the rate of economic growth over time, also sometimes command governmental attention, not only in the United States but also in many other countries of the world. In the United States, the question of the long-term performance of the economy has figured in most presidential campaigns and has influenced many public policy decisions.

There is much debate as to how successful economic intervention by the government has been in achieving these goals. Some economists believe that intervention is counterproductive. There is even greater disagreement among economists and policymakers over which goal to emphasize: What is the greater evil, unemployment or inflation?

CONCEPT CHECK

1. Government encourages competition and discourages monopoly, or one-supplier conditions, through its antitrust activities.
2. Many economists believe that lower taxes and government spending can promote employment when the economy is not operating close to full capacity.
3. With appropriate levels of taxation and government spending, coupled with sound banking policies, the government can help to keep inflation in check.

---

1. Why would the government want to prevent market conditions of insufficient competition?
2. What are the macroeconomic goals of government intervention in the economy?
3. What government policy changes might be effective in increasing employment in recessions?
4. What government policy changes might be effective in controlling inflation?

- What tools does government use to redistribute income?
- What are subsidies?
- What are transfer payments?

DOES THE MARKET DISTRIBUTE INCOME FAIRLY?

Not only does the market determine what goods are going to be produced, and in what quantities, but it also determines, through the interaction of demand and supply for productive resources, the distribution of output among members of society. It is the opinion of some that the market distribution of income produces disparities that violate a common sense of equity or fairness. For example, in the 1920s, the wealthiest 1 percent of income recipients received some 15 percent of the nation's income, and the top 5 percent received 30 percent, while the poorest 20 percent received only about 5 percent. Given these conditions, it is not surprising that many believed that community welfare could be increased by taking some income from the very rich and distributing it to the poor or even to the middle class.

There are three major ways that government redistributes income: taxes, subsidies, and transfer payments. We will now examine each of these methods in turn.

Taxes

In addition to being one of the primary ways that the government finances its activities, taxes are an important tool for redistributing income. Specifically, one type of tax, a progressive tax, is designed to take a larger percentage of higher incomes as compared to lower incomes. In this way, progressive taxes help to reduce income disparities. The federal income tax is an example of a progressive tax. The progressive tax and other types of taxes will be discussed in greater detail later in this Module.

Taxes are one way to attempt to change the distribution of income.

Government Subsidies

A second way that governments can help the less affluent is by the use of governmental revenues to provide low-cost public services. Inexpensive public housing, subsidized public transport, and even public parks

are services that probably serve the poor to a greater extent than the rich. "Free" public education is viewed by many as an equalizing force in that it opens opportunities for children of less prosperous members of society to obtain the skills necessary for employment that could improve their economic status.

Transfer Payments

A third means by which income redistribution can be carried out by government is through direct transfer payments. Transfer payments are income payments made by the government to the poor and aged for which no goods or services are exchanged. Transfer payments to individuals are a very rapidly growing form of governmental activity, now involving more public expenditure than for such traditional government programs as national defense or education. Between 1965 and 1995, federally funded transfer payments to individuals went from less than 6 percent of total output to roughly 15 percent of total output.

Public assistance programs, such as food stamps, Medicaid, and welfare payments, for example, are designed to raise the living standards of the poor. Social Security programs provide incomes to older persons who have little ability, or perhaps desire, to obtain work-related income. Social Security accounts for nearly half of all transfer payments. This includes retirement pensions, as well as survivor and disability benefits. Benefits for the unemployed in the form of unemployment compensation are also an important form of transfer payments. A rapidly growing form of transfer payment is in the area of health care, mostly as a consequence of the Medicare program for the elderly and the Medicaid program for the poor.

In a sense, many transfer payments are simply deferred compensation to employees, where certain job-related payments are not made until the individual retires, resigns, or is laid off. Social Security, other retirement programs for government workers, veteran's benefits, and unemployment compensation are examples. Recipients "earned" these payments by work done and taxes paid in

an earlier period. Still, some economists, particularly those with a conservative bent, worry about the impact on work incentives of transferring a growing proportion of income from the working to the nonworking population. Whether there is any validity to these concerns is an empirical question, one that has received increasing attention as transfer payments have grown. Many would support such payments, of course, even if they had some negative impact on the willingness of productive persons to work, as serving useful social purposes.

WHAT IS THE IMPACT OF GOVERNMENT ON THE DISTRIBUTION OF INCOME?

This is not an easy question to answer authoritatively, but it would appear to be in the direction of equalizing the distribution somewhat. While the tax system may be roughly "neutral," government expenditures go to lower- and middle-income classes far more than to upper-income groups (as measured as a proportion of income of those groups). During the first great expansion in government activity in the 1930s and 1940s, when progressive income taxation was first vigorously used and Social Security was inaugurated, income distribution in the United States moved sharply in the direction of equality. By one measure, the share of total income received by the top 5 percent of income recipients fell from 26 percent in 1929 to 17 percent in 1947. Since 1947, there is some dispute as to how much income inequality has been reduced; some argue that it has changed "very little," while others say it has increased. This issue will be explored in more detail later in this book. It is highly likely, however, that the impact of the expansion of government activity has been to reduce inequality at least somewhat from what it otherwise would have been.

Have government programs designed to reduce inequality worked?

ARE THERE OBJECTIONS TO THIS GOVERNMENT INTERVENTION?

As with other aspects of government intervention, the equity argument can generate some sharp disagreements. What is "fair" for one person may seem highly "unfair" to someone else. While one person may find it terribly unfair for some individuals to earn many times the amount that other individuals who work equally hard earn, another person may find it highly unfair to ask one group, the rela-tively rich, to pay a much higher proportion of their income in taxes than another group. Disputes over governmental income distribution policies have been important in domestic political campaigns in recent years; income distribution, indeed, has been the major economic issue in most of the great political upheavals of the past few centuries. Thus, politicians are constantly debating the fairness of the tax system, calling for reform of the welfare system, debating the merits of food stamps and public housing, and so on.

CONCEPT CHECK

1. The government redistributes income through taxes, subsidies, and transfer payments.
2. Government subsidizes some public services, such as housing and transportation, to help the less fortunate.
3. Transfer payments, such as food stamps and Medicaid, are income payments made by the government to the poor and aged for which no goods or services are exchanged.

---

1. What is the basic argument in favor of government redistribution of income?
2. What are the objections to government intervention intended to redistribute income?
3. How does the government use taxes, subsidies, and transfer payments to redistribute income toward lower-income groups?
4. If a government wanted to make the distribution of income more equal, would it be more effective to impose a tax on luxury cars or on food?

G Public Choice

- What is public choice theory?
- What is rational ignorance?
- Why do special-interest groups arise?

As we have discussed in this Module, when the market fails, as in the externality or the public good case, it may be necessary for government to intervene and make public choices. However, according to Buchanan and Tullock, government actions in response to externalities may make matters worse.[1] That is, just because markets have failed to generate efficient results doesn't necessarily mean that government can do a better job. One explanation for this is presented in *public choice theory*.

WHAT IS PUBLIC CHOICE THEORY?

Public choice theory is the application of economic principles to politics. Public choice economists believe that government actions are an outgrowth of individual behavior. Specifically, they assume that the behavior of individuals in politics, like those in the marketplace, will be influenced by self-interest. Bureaucrats, politicians, and voters make choices that they believe will yield them expected marginal benefits that are greater than their expected marginal costs. There are, of course, differences between the private sector and the public sector in the "rules of the game." But the self-interest assumption is central to the analysis of behavior in both arenas.

IS SCARCITY ALIVE AND WELL IN THE PUBLIC SECTOR?

The self-interest assumption is not the only similarity between the market and public sectors. For example, scarcity is present in the public sector as well as the private sector. Public schools and public libraries come at the expense of something else. Competition is also present in the public sector, as different government agencies compete for government funds, and lobbyists compete with each other to get through favored legislation.

Are politicians' actions driven by self-interest?

IS INFORMATION MORE COSTLY IN THE POLITICAL ARENA?

While there are similarities between market choice and political choice, there are also differences. For instance, the amount of information that is necessary to make an

---

[1] See James M. Buchanan and Gordon Tullock, *The Calculus of Consent* (Chicago: The University of Chicago Press, 1962).

efficient decision is much greater in political markets than private markets. In a private market, about the only information that a potential buyer needs to know is how much he or she is willing to pay for the good and how much the seller is willing to accept for the good. The market price informs the buyer how much is necessary to entice the seller to supply the good. Only one question remains: Is the good worth more to the consumer than he or she is willing to pay? If so, the consumer will purchase the good; if not, the consumer will not purchase the good.

Information is much more difficult to obtain when a political good is being considered. The problem is that political decisions usually affect a lot of people. For example, if voters decide to increase national defense, everyone will receive more and pay higher taxes for the additional national defense. However, for such a political decision to result in an efficient result, it will require that we have information on *everyone's preferences,* not just those of an individual buyer and an individual seller.

WHAT IS AN INDIVIDUAL-CONSUMPTION-PAYMENT LINK?

In private markets, when a shopper goes to the supermarket to purchase groceries, the shopping cart is filled with many different goods that the consumer presumably wants and is willing to pay for; this reflects the **individual-consumption-payment link.** The link breaks down when there is an assortment of political goods that have been decided on by majority rule. These political goods might include such items as additional national defense, additional money for the space program, new museums, new public schools, increased foreign aid, and so on. While an individual might be willing to pay for some of those goods, it is unlikely that he or she will want to consume or pay for all of them that have been placed in the political shopping cart. However, if the majority has decided that these political goods are important, the individual will have to purchase the goods through higher taxes, whether he or she values the goods or not.

VOTER APATHY AND SPECIAL-INTEREST GROUPS

Representative democracy has been a successful mechanism for making social choices in many countries. But there are some important differences in the way it is ideally supposed to work and how it actually does work.

One of the keys to an efficiently working democracy is a concerned and informed electorate. Everyone is supposed to take time to study the issues and candidates and then carefully weigh the relevant information before deciding how to vote. Although an informed citizenry is desirable from a social point of view, it is not clear that individuals will find it personally desirable to become politically informed.

Is this person picking the items she wants? Do taxpayers always pay for what they want?

What Are the Costs of Being Politically Informed?

Obtaining detailed information about issues and candidates is costly. Many issues are very complicated, and a great deal of technical knowledge and information is necessary to make an informed judgment on them. To find out what candidates are really going to do requires a lot more than listening to their campaign slogans. It requires studying their past voting records, reading a great deal that has been written either by or about them, and asking them questions at public meetings. Taking the time and trouble to do these things—and more—is the cost that each eligible voter has to pay personally for the benefits of being politically informed.

What Are the Benefits of Being Politically Informed?

Basically, there are two benefits of being politically informed. Some people simply enjoy being informed. These people will be willing to make an effort to acquire some information on public issues just for the sake of knowledge. The other benefit from being informed has nothing to do with satisfying intellectual curiosity. By being politically informed, individuals may be knowledgeable to influence social decisions in directions that will yield them greater benefits. Unfortunately, this does little to motivate most people to become informed, because it isn't much of a benefit. The probability of one person's vote having any effect on an election is practically zero. With many thousands often voting in local elections and millions voting in state and national elections, each citizen is safe in assuming that his or her vote really won't change the outcome.

What Is Rational Ignorance?

So, for most people, the costs of becoming politically informed are substantial, while the benefits are negligible. As a result, most people limit their quest for political information to listening to the radio on the way to work, conversations with friends, casual reading, and other things they normally do anyway. Even though most people in society might be better off if everyone became more informed, it isn't worth the cost for most individuals to make an effort to become informed themselves. As a result, these individuals assume a state of **rational ignorance.**

There are obvious advantages to be realized if the public became more politically aware. Unfortunately, there doesn't seem to be any easy or desirable way of overcoming the problem of rational ignorance. Perhaps the government could require everyone to become politically well informed. However, if the government did that, how would they determine when an individual is adequately informed? Unfortunately, most of us find a close correlation between how much others agree with us and how well informed we think they are. Hence, pushing very far in the direction of having the government require and test political awareness might lead to abuses that could more than offset the benefits of having a more informed society. According to public choice economists, political apathy is not the result of moral decay or lack of patriotism in our society. It's simply the result of individuals acting rationally ignorant.

What Are Special-Interest Groups?

This does not mean that public choice economists think that everyone is politically apathetic or rationally ignorant. This obviously is not the case. Many have a large stake in being politically informed on particular issues. For example,

T U N E   U P

RATIONAL IGNORANCE

Q: With only two out of three eligible voters registered, the "motor voter" bill has recently been passed, which will use the Department of Motor Vehicles to increase voter registration. If voter registration is done in conjunction with drivers' licenses, it is estimated that 91 percent of the eligible voters will then be registered to vote. Will this resolve the problem of rational ignorance?

A: Not according to public choice economists. They believe reasons for "voter apathy" have little to do with the number of voters registered and everything to do with individual incentives. That is, no matter how many voters are registered, individuals will still weigh the benefits and costs of acquiring additional information before voting.

"I think voter apathy is terrible...everybody should turn out and vote for either what's-his-name or you-know-who."

Why is voter turnout frequently so low?

cost will be spread over such a large number of taxpayers that the amount any one person will have to pay is negligible. There isn't much motivation for an individual citizen to spend time and effort to resist an interest group, even if it were guaranteed that this resistance would be effective.

With Special-Interest, A Few Gain at the Expense of Many

When a special-interest issue comes up that benefits the few at the expense of the many, it is likely that elected representatives will be solicited by special-interest groups. Because the special-interest activity will likely impose only small costs on each individual taxpayer, those paying the bill may know little or nothing about it. That is, if each representative believes that a favorable vote will be recognized and appreciated by those in favor of it and will go virtually unnoticed by those paying the bill, then he or she might be willing to support the special-interest group. Because getting reelected and receiving financial support are obviously important to elected representatives, special-interest groups will be effective at influencing their voting behavior. The other side of the coin is that it is difficult to reduce the size of government programs once they are in place. Government programs that arise because of the influence of special interests will generally be perpetuated by the influence of those same special interests. The elimination of such a program will deny a few significant benefits, while saving each general taxpayer but a few dollars in taxes. This might explain why it is so difficult politically to reduce government spending, even if the majority of the voters favored such a reduction in general. When people argue for cutting government spending, they invariably have in mind government programs other than the ones that benefit them. So any attempt to reduce government spending by isolating one program at a time generally meets strong resistance from those benefiting from the program under review and receives little support from the millions of taxpayers who will save but a few dollars each if the program were eliminated.

individuals may have a strong motivation to organize a political pressure group. As a group, these individuals are more likely to influence decision makers and have a far greater impact on the outcome of a social decision than they would with just their one vote. Also, members of these **special-interest groups** will find it easier to organize because of the commonality of their goals and purpose. And the smaller the group and the more specific their interest, the less costly it will become to organize and get everyone to contribute his or her share. Hence, it is not surprising that special-interest groups are often able to bring a great deal of political pressure to bear on certain public decisions.

What About Those Not in the Special-Interest Group?

Individuals who are not in the special-interest group will pay the bill if the special-interest group is successful. Why can't the majority of citizens effectively counter the political power of a minority group? The answer to this question lies in the fact that the majority makes up such a large group. If the special-interest group is successful in getting everyone else to pay for a project that benefits them, the

WHAT IS THE BEST WAY TO CONTROL GOVERNMENT?

According to public choice economists, the best hope for controlling government is by presenting a political package that calls for a simultaneous reduction in many programs. No special interest will be willing to sacrifice its program if it expects to be required to continue paying for the program of others. But if government has grown to the point where people feel that they are not getting their money's worth for the taxes they pay, then many groups will be willing to see their program reduced—if it means some savings on the taxes paid to support everyone else's programs.

WILD PITCH

ROGER G. NOLL

WASHINGTON—Even at a time when major league sports have become a cartoon of financial excess, the proposed new home for the Yankees is breathtaking in its audacity. Excluding land value, a multipurpose mausoleum on Manhattan's West Side would cost a billion dollars.

Independent studies of sports facilities invariably conclude that they provide no significant economic benefits. A sports team does increase overall income in a community slightly, but the increase never offsets the stadium's financing and operating costs. And because a team has relatively few (but very highly paid) employees, it usually causes overall employment in a city to fall because it can drive other entertainment businesses to cut back or close.

Stadiums are bad investments, which is why the teams themselves are never willing to pay for them. New York City would generate more cash by putting the money in a savings account.

Why do cities pour hundreds of millions into new stadiums? With intense competition for sports franchises, not even New York can keep a team without subsidizing it. New Jersey and New York have at various times fought over the Giants, Jets, Yankees, and Mets. The sad thing is that the states need not be competitors: Fans could easily support a third team in both football and baseball. But each league is a monopoly, doing what monopolists do best: making the product scarce to hike up the price.

There is a far cheaper way to keep the Yankees. Bribe them. A new stadium could give the Yankees an additional $10 million in profits each year. So instead of spending $80 million annually to finance and operate a new stadium, New York could just hand the Yankees $10 million. Or, even better, the city could pay $100,000 for each game won, with a million-dollar bonus for winning the pennant.

This plan would save the city money, improve the Yankee's bottom line and benefit fans, who would be less likely to have a team that collapsed in the stretch.

Roger G. Noll is a visiting fellow at the Brookings Institution.
SOURCE: *New York Times*, 4/11/96, p. A17.

CONSIDER THIS:
Many big cities have either built or are planning on building large sports arenas, largely at the taxpayers' expense. According to proponents, the new sports arenas will bring recognition and fame to the city, and this will benefit everyone who lives in the city because they will be living in a more prestigious community. Hence, everyone in the city should contribute to the sports arena, whether they go to the games or not.

This is a weak argument. The people who receive the primary benefits from a better sports arena are first, the owners, second, the players, and third, those who frequent it to watch ball games. Further, it's easy to prevent a fan from receiving this benefit if he or she doesn't pay at the gate. The assertion that everyone would benefit from the arena whether they go to the games or not has to be questioned. A sports arena will generate growth and congestion that many will find undesirable. To these people, being forced to pay for a big sports center makes no sense.

Perhaps some people who never go to a sporting event may feel a little bit better just knowing they can. This is what economists call *option demand*. But does this justify commandeering funds from everyone in the city to build a sports arena? What about fine restaurants? Certainly fine restaurants enhance the reputation of the city. Many people are happy to know that one is nearby, waiting to serve them, whether they visit it or not. But most people would find a proposal to publicly finance restaurants very farfetched. If desirable side effects justified government subsidies, well-kept yards, car washes, toothpaste, deodorants, and smiles would all qualify for a handout.

Regardless of the desirability of requiring the public to pay for certain things, it should be noted that special-interest groups expend a lot of effort to get subsidies for those things from which they receive enjoyment and profit. Many of these efforts have been successful; the sports arena example is only one of many. The more "cultured," and usually wealthier, members of many cities have managed to obtain government support for symphonies, operas, ballet, and the performing arts in general. The stated justification for requiring everyone to pay for entertainment that caters primarily to the tastes of the rich is similar to that given for subsidizing sports arenas. Supposedly, everyone in a community will benefit, even those who prefer to sit home with a can of beer and watch all-star wrestling on television.

CAN LESS BE MORE?

Public choice economists are convinced that we can get more from government only by having less government. They recognize that the advantage of government is found in its ability to establish a legal and economic environment that provides general opportunity for people to benefit from their own efforts through productive cooperation with others. But they also see the threat of government if its power is captured by organized special interests and used to advance narrow objectives by imposing costs on the general public. And if the government becomes a vehicle for promoting special interests, it fails in its primary responsibility of expanding opportunities for all. That is, instead of creating opportunities for people to benefit through productive cooperation with each other, government will have created the illusion that people can benefit at the expense of each other. Public choice economists are not callously indifferent to the social benefits that government can provide. In fact, the difference between public choice economists and those who see every social ill as justification for expanding government is not a difference in moral vision. Instead, it is a difference in their understanding of how government actually works. Public choice economists lean toward less government not because they want less from government, but because they believe that it is important to get more opportunities from its actions.

CONCEPT CHECK

1. Public choice theory is the theory that the behavior of individuals in politics, like that in the marketplace, is influenced by self-interest.
2. Rational ignorance is the condition in which voters tend to be relatively uninformed about political issues because of high information costs and low benefits of being politically informed.
3. A special-interest group is a political pressure group formed by individuals with a common political objective.
4. Special-interest groups are more likely to have an impact on the outcome of a social decision than their members would if they voted individually.

---

1. What principles does the public choice analysis of government behavior share with the economic analysis of market behavior?
2. Why is it rational to be relatively less informed about most political choices than about your own market choices?
3. Why can't the majority of citizens effectively counter the political power of special-interest groups?
4. According to public choice theorists, what is the primary advantage of government? What is the biggest threat from government?
5. Why are college students better informed about their own teachers' and schools' policies than about national education issues?
6. How can you be forced to pay for something you do not want to "buy" in the political sector? Is this sometimes good?
7. Why do you think news reporters are more informed than average citizens about public policy issues?

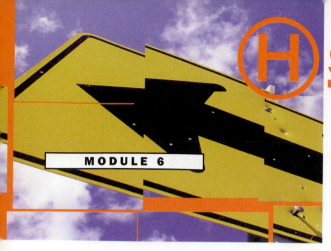

H Spending and Taxation

MODULE 6

- What has happened to the growth of government spending?
- How does government finance its spending?
- What are progressive and regressive taxes?

THE CHANGING ROLE OF GOVERNMENT

It is impossible to precisely measure the degree of governmental involvement in the economy with any single number. Nonetheless, patterns in the ratio of government spending to total output over time should tell us something about the changing governmental role, even if the figures for any specific point in time cannot indicate accurately the precise level of involvement.

Exhibit 1 shows the growth in total government spending in the United States as a percentage of output over time. The graph suggests that the growth of the government sector has indeed been substantial. Total government spending has grown from about 11 percent of output in 1929 to almost 35 percent today. A large part of the growth in the relative importance of government occurred between 1965 and 1980.

However, there has been a slower relative growth in government purchases, and indeed no growth in government purchases as a percentage of output since 1975. Then why has *total* government spending increased from 25 per-

| EXHIBIT 1 | GROWTH IN GOVERNMENT, 1913–1996 |

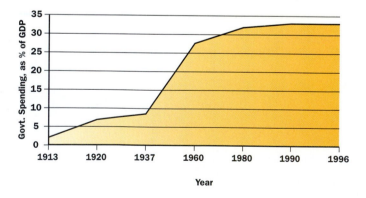

Year

SOURCE: *The Economist*, September 20, 1997.

cent of total output to almost 35 percent of total output? The answer is the increase in transfer payments for programs such as Social Security and welfare. Income transfer payments have risen from roughly 5 percent of total output in 1965 to 14 percent in 1997.

WHAT AREAS OF GOVERNMENTAL INVOLVEMENT IN THE ECONOMY HAVE GROWN?

Areas of government growth can be determined partly by looking at statistics of the types of government spending, although we would remind you again that the statistics fail to accurately reflect the growing impact of government regulation of the private sector's decision-making process. Exhibit 2 shows categories of government spending as a proportion of total spending.

During the 1920s, most government spending was for such traditional activities as highways, police and fire protection, and sanitation. Approximately one-fourth of governmental spending was for such social concerns as education, health, and public assistance. At that time, national defense accounted for a very small proportion of total spending. During the Great Depression of the 1930s, the welfare function became somewhat more important and other activities less important. During the 1940s, defense spending grew incredibly, accounting for more than three-quarters of the total spending by government in some years of World War II. While defense spending declined in relative importance after 1945, it grew again during the Korean War (1950–1953) and remained high during the Cold War of the 1950s. The share of government spending going for military purposes declined sharply after the mid-1950s, even with the Vietnam War of the 1960s. By the mid-1970s, less than 20 percent of total federal government spending was for defense. The big relative gainer in terms of spending has been for non-defense social concerns. The biggest single area of growth has come in social insurance, such as social security and other government pension programs. Spending in 1974 for social insurance was more than 10 times as great as in 1950. Other areas had rapid

| EXHIBIT 2 | GOVERNMENT EXPENDITURES |

a. Federal Expenditures, 1996

Social Security 23% | National Defense 17% | Income Security 14% | Health 8% | Medicare 12% | Net Interest on the National Debt 15% | Other 11%

b. State and Local Expenditures, 1993

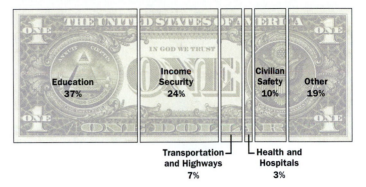

Education 37% | Income Security 24% | Transportation and Highways 7% | Health and Hospitals 3% | Civilian Safety 10% | Other 19%

spending growth as well. Educational expenditures, for example, tripled in the 1960s alone. By the mid-1970s, roughly half of government spending was for social concerns such as education, health, and public housing, for the first time in the nation's history. In the 1980s and 1990s, we have seen a continued increase in income transfer payments including Social Security, welfare, and unemployment compensation.

Exhibit 2(a) shows that 37 percent of federal government spending went to Social Security and **income security programs.** Another 20 percent was spent on **health care** and **Medicare** for the elderly. The rest of federal expenditures include national defense (17 percent), interest on the national debt (15 percent) and miscellaneous items such as foreign aid, education, agriculture, transportation and housing (11 percent).

Exhibit 2(b) shows that state and local spending is very different than federal spending. Education and public welfare account for roughly 60 percent of the state and local expenditures. Other areas of state and local spending include highways, housing, and police and fire protection.

HOW DOES GOVERNMENT GENERATE ITS REVENUE?

Governments have to pay their bills like any person or institution that spends money. But how do they obtain revenue? Two major avenues are open: taxation and borrowing. A third possibility, printing money for governmental use, is of lesser importance in most Western nations in recent decades. At this point, we will discuss the use of taxation as a revenue-generating mechanism.

TYPES OF TAXATION

In most years, a large majority of government activity is financed by taxation. What kinds of taxes are levied on the American population?

At the federal level, most taxes or levies are on income. Exhibit 3 shows that about 60 percent of tax revenues come in the form of income taxes on individuals and corporations, called **personal income taxes** and **corporate income taxes,** respectively. Most of the remaining revenues come from **payroll taxes,** which are levied on work related income—payrolls. These taxes are used to pay for Social Security and compulsory insurance plans like Medicare. This tax is split between employees and the employers. The Social Security share of federal taxes has steadily risen as the proportion of the population over 65 has grown and as Social Security benefits have been increased. Consequently, payroll taxes have risen significantly in recent years. In 1997, the employee and the employer were each required to pay 7.65 percent of the employee's income up to $65,400. In addition, employees and employers each must pay a 1.45 percent tax on all employee wages to pay for Medicare. Other taxes on items like gasoline, liquor, and tobacco products provide for a small proportion of government revenues, as do custom duties, estate and gift taxes, and some minor miscellaneous taxes and user charges. The United States federal government relies more heavily on income-based taxes than nearly any other government in the world. Most other governments rely more heavily on sales taxes, excise taxes, and custom duties.

Is an Excise Tax Fair?

Some consider an excise tax, a sales tax on individual products such as alcohol, tobacco, and gasoline, to be the least fair type of tax. This type of tax on specific items will impose a far greater burden, as a percentage of income, on the poor and middle class than on the wealthy, because low-income families pay a greater proportion of their income on these taxes than do high-income families.

In addition, excise taxes may lead to economic inefficiencies. By isolating a few products and subjecting them to discriminatory taxation, consumption taxes subject economic choices to political manipulation and lead to inefficiency.

| EXHIBIT 3 | TAX REVENUES |

a. Tax Revenues, Federal Government, 1997

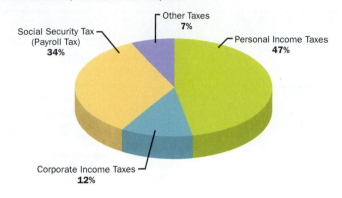

SOURCE: *Economic Report of the President, 1998.*

b. Tax Revenues, State and Local Governments, 1993

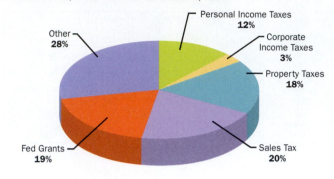

SOURCE: *Economic Report of the President, 1997, p. 397.*

What Is a Progressive Tax?

One impact of substantial taxes on income is that the effective "take home" income of Americans is significantly altered by the tax system. **Progressive taxes,** of which the federal income tax is one example, are designed so that those with higher incomes pay a greater proportion of their income in taxes. As we noted earlier in the Module, a progressive tax is one tool that the government can use to redistribute income. It should be noted, however, that certain types of income are excluded from income for taxation purposes. Much of this income is earned primarily by wealthy persons, such as interest on municipal bonds, although some of the excluded income is income in kind, such as foods stamps or other transfer income, that goes primarily to the poor.

What Is a Regressive Tax?

Payroll taxes, the second most important income source for the federal government, are actually **regressive;** that is, they take a greater proportion of the income of lower-income groups than higher-income groups. The reasons for this are simple. For example, Social Security and Medicare taxes are imposed as a fixed proportion (now 7.65 on employees and an equal amount on employers) of wage and salary income up to $62,700; beyond that income level, wages and salaries are only subject to the 1.45% Medicare tax. Also, wealthy persons have relatively more property income that is not subject to Social Security or Medicare taxes. Adding together individual income and Social Security taxes, the Federal tax system is probably only slightly progressive. The same would hold if other taxes are included.

HOW DO STATE AND LOCAL GOVERNMENT FINANCE ACTIVITIES?

Historically, the major source of state and local revenue has been property taxes. In recent decades, state and local governments have relied increasingly on sales and income taxes for revenues (see Exhibit 3b). Today, sales taxes account for roughly 20 percent of revenues, while personal and corporate income taxes account for 15 percent of revenues. Another 19 percent of state and local revenues come from the federal government in grants. The remaining share of revenues comes from license fees and user charges (e.g., payment for sewers, occupational license fees, tuition fees) and other taxes.

SHOULD WE HAVE A FLAT TAX?

Some politicians and individuals believe that we should scrap the current progressive income tax and replace it with a **flat tax.** A flat tax is designed so that everybody would be charged the same percentage of their income above some certain stipulated income level. How would a flat tax work? What do you think would be the advantages and disadvantages of a flat tax?

Actually, if the flat tax plan allowed individuals to deduct a standard allowance of, say, $20,000 from their wages, the tax would still be progressive. This is how it would work. If you were earning less than $20,000 a year, you would not have to pay any income taxes. However, if you earned $50,000 a year, and the flat tax rate was 15 percent, after subtracting your $20,000 allowance you would be paying taxes on $30,000. In this system, you would have

Used by permission of Chip Bok and Creators Syndicate.

CONTROVERSIAL TRANSIT BILL PASSES IN HOUSE

Ignoring objections from the White House and fiscal conservatives, the House voted 337 to 80 to pass a massive $217 billion transportation bill Wednesday evening.

The spending bill has been blasted by the Clinton administration as well as fiscal conservatives who call it a budget buster and "pork-barrel legislation" run amok. The Senate already has passed its own six-year, $214 billion plan. Both chambers are racing to finish legislation before supplemental money runs out May 1. The bill covers a virtual smorgasbord of programs that give nearly every congressional district a piece of federal largess to call its own. Besides the traditional funds for bridges and roads, the bill would build bike paths, buy clean-fuel buses, and study road congestion relief.

Fiscal conservatives criticized the bill for setting aside 5 percent of the money, more than $9 billion, for 1,463 projects that indi-vidual lawmakers requested for their districts. Republicans were given 55 percent of the money and Democrats 45 percent, and the complaint, strongly denied by the bill's backers, was that pork barrel politicking decided who got what. "I think it's doubtful that well over 1,400 projects are deserving of federal attention," said Rep. Porter Goss, R-Fla., noting that the last six-year program enacted in 1991 had only 539 such projects.

The proposed projects include a $100,000 rail-highway feasibility study in Muncie, Indiana, a $4.5 million pedestrian and bicycle path in New London, Connecticut, and a $97 million widening of the I-40 cross-town bridge in Oklahoma City. Watchdog groups, like Citizens Against Government Waste, pointed to a $12 million allocation for an Appalachian Transportation Institute and $3 million for a television documentary on highways as prime examples of the bill's excesses.

SOURCE: ABCNEWS.com. The Associated Press and Reuters contributed to this report. Also see: http://www.abcnews.com/sections/us/congresswatchindex/congresswatchindex.html

CONSIDER THIS:
Is Congress slipping back to its old spending habits? The President has blasted the legislation because it is full of pork. According to John Kasich, the House Budget Chairman, "Pigs get fat and hogs get slaughtered. This bill is a hog." While the house bill will probably not be approved in this form, it does demonstrate that pork is still alive and well in America.

A GLOBAL COMPARISON OF TAXATION

CONSIDER THIS:
Taxpayers in other parts of the developed world have a heavier per capita tax burden than those in the United States.

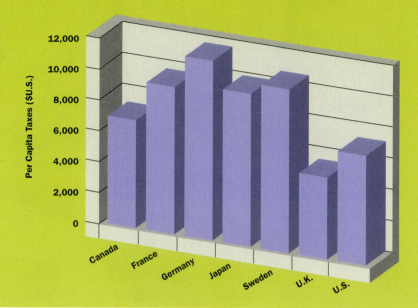

to pay $4,500 in taxes (.15 X $30,000) and your average tax rate would be 6 percent ($3,000/$50,000 = .09). Now, say you made a $100,000 a year. After taking your $20,000 allowance, you would have to pay a 15 percent tax on $80,000, and you would owe the government $12,000. Notice, however, that your average tax rate would be higher: 12 percent ($12,000/$100,000 = 12%) as opposed to 9 percent. So if the flat tax system allows individual taxpayers to take a standard allowance, like most flat tax proposals, then the tax is actually progressive. That is, lower- and middle-income families will pay, on average, a smaller average tax rate, even though everyone has the same tax rate over the stipulated allowance.

The advantages of the flat tax are that all of the traditional exemptions, like entertainment deductions, mortgage interest deductions, business travel expenses, and charitable contribution deductions, would be out the door, along with the possibilities of abuses and misrepresentations that go with tax deductions. Taxpayers could fill out tax returns like they did in the old days, in a space about the size of a postcard. Advocates argue that the government could collect the same amount of tax revenues, but the tax would be much more efficient, as many productive resources would be released from looking for tax loopholes to doing something productive from society's standpoint. In fact, according to the Internal Revenue Service, the federal government has long collected roughly the same revenues, despite changing top marginal tax rates, which have gone from a high of 91 percent in 1960–1965 to a low of 28 percent in 1988–1990.

Of course, some versions of the flat tax will hurt certain groups. Not surprisingly, realtors and homeowners, who like the mortgage interest deductions, and tax accountants, who make billions every year preparing tax returns, will not be supportive of a flat tax with no deductions. And, of course, many legitimate questions would inevitably arise, such as: What would happen to the size of charitable contributions if the charitable contribution deductions was eliminated? And how much will the housing sector be hurt if the mortgage interest deduction was eliminated or phased out? In addition, the critics of the flat tax believe that the tax is not progressive enough to eliminate the inequities in income and are skeptical of the tax-revenue-raising capabilities of a flat tax.

1. Income transfer payments have risen sharply since 1965.
2. Over a third of federal spending goes towards pensions and income security programs.
3. A progressive tax takes a greater proportion of the income of higher-income groups than of lower-income groups.
4. A regressive tax takes a greater proportion of the income of lower-income groups than of higher-income groups.

---

1. What accounts for most of the growth of government spending as a share of total output since 1965?
2. What options are available for a government to finance its spending?
3. What is the difference between a progressive tax and a regressive tax?
4. What are some advantages and disadvantages of a flat tax? Would it be progressive?

APPLICATION: Revving up the Helmet Law Debate

Should the government intervene and require motorcycle helmets? How does the debate illustrate the effects of a negative externality? Why are taxpayers concerned? Can you think of a compromise that would make motorcyclists and taxpayers who pay for uninsured motorcycle drivers happy? In other words, how might the externality be internalized to the satisfaction of all parties?

NOTES AND QUOTES FROM THE PREZ, MAY 1997

By the time you read this the Colorado Legislature will have concluded another session. No helmet law bill was introduced in Colorado, Utah, or Wyoming this year. It may be because we have won in these states so many times people are starting to get the message, or it could be that we have worked hard to get those pro-helmet law jerks out of office . . .

Due to at least some of the above listed reasons Arkansas, Guam, and Texas have repealed their helmet laws for adults. Arkansas has a helmet law for those under 21, Guam has a helmet law for those under 18, and Texas apparently has a helmet law for those under 18.

Texas had a problem in their House. It seems someone wanted the law to be for those under 21 and mandatory rider education, with the funds to come out of the general fund. Fortunately, the House sponsor adopted the Senate version in its entirety. The trend by some people to try for an under 21 repeal does not set well with many Legislators, not because they are for helmet laws, but because 18 year olds are adults. It is unfortunate that many so called rights groups are too willing to compromise someone else's freedom, health, and lives.

SOURCE: http://usff.com/RFJ/RFJhome.html.

Many states have now passed mandatory motorcycle helmet laws. And proponents have lauded them as huge successes. But despite this seemingly convincing "proof" of the law's success, opponents remain unconvinced. They have argued that requiring state-approved helmets would have only a minor effect in reducing head injuries and the resulting fatalities, largely because they do little good in most accidents, which occur at more than 20 m.p.h., and may even cause accidents by impairing peripheral vision and hearing.

However, the biggest unresolved objection of the helmet law opponents has never been the issue of safety, but rather the loss of personal freedom involved. They believe that they have the right to choose not to wear a helmet, even given higher risks. After all, each of us sacrifices some safety for thrills, convenience, and savings. For example, heavier cars are generally safer than compact cars, but many people find the savings from driving a small car worth the safety sacrificed. And don't we sacrifice some safety for thrills when we ski, snowboard, hang glide, or skateboard?

Even if one concedes that wearing a helmet does decrease the chance of head injuries, why do some motorcyclists choose not to wear them? Motorcyclists revel in the thrill and sense of freedom they experience. Wearing a bulky motorcycle helmet greatly reduces the quality of this experience for many, and they claim to be willing to pay the price, in terms of reduced safety, for the enjoyment of riding without a helmet.

Helmet law supporters argue that requiring all motorcycle riders to wear helmets would save taxpayers millions of dollars a year, primarily in health care costs.

Ironically, beneath the rhetoric, both opponents and proponents of mandatory helmet laws are seeking freedom. Opponents want the freedom to ride as they wish, even though costs are currently imposed on others in the process. Proponents are arguing for freedom from having to pay the bills for those injured because they chose not to wear a helmet.

Given that under our present health care system, taxpayers assume responsibility for medical care beyond that paid for by insurance, the central problem is really that the freedom to ride without a helmet violates the freedom of taxpayers from footing others' bills. Mandating helmets appears to many as a reasonable compromise, if states are to continue to pick up this tab. However, why must there be such a compromise? Let the riders absorb that cost through mandatory liability insurance. Then riders would not have to sacrifice their freedom, but neither would taxpayers.

Mandatory personal injury insurance, with sufficient coverage, could easily be included as part of motorcycle registration or licensing. Assuming such a law was actually enforced, unlike so many mandatory automobile insurance laws, motorcyclists would finally be required to bear the true costs of not wearing helmets (although insurance companies would have to be allowed to differentiate between helmeted and helmet-less riders in setting their rates). The outcome of such an approach would be far superior to the current compromise. As opposed to mandating helmets, which restricts one type of freedom to enhance another, requiring insurance would allow motorcyclists to maintain their freedom of choice, while giving taxpayers freedom from paying injured motorcyclists' health care tab.

Whether you think its involvement is too much, too little, or just about right, government clearly has a significant impact on the market system. Through the cyberproblems on your EconActive CD-ROM, you can access current information sources on the World Wide Web that will help you to examine specific areas of government intervention, such as transfer payments like Social Security.

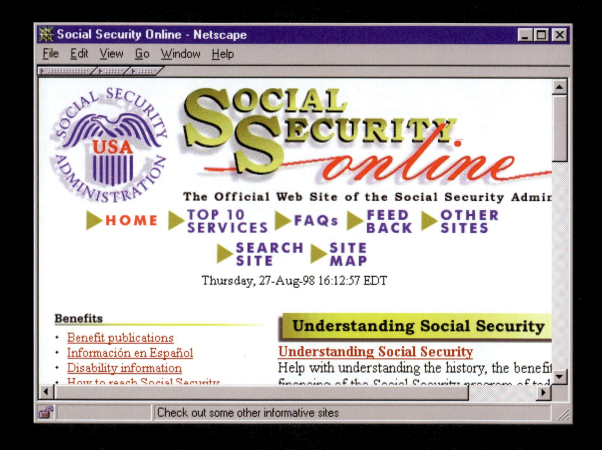

PHOTO CREDITS MODULE 6

Page **144:** © PhotoDisc; Page **146:** © Frans Lanting/Minden Pictures; Page **147:** Reprinted courtesy of Leigh Rubin and Creators Syndicate; Page **148:** © S. Feld/H. Armstrong Roberts; Page **149:** © Robert Sexton; Page **150:** © George Hall/Check Six/PNI; Page **151:** © Tom Bean/Corbis Images; Page **153:** © 1998 Don Couch Photography; Page **154:** left, © Galen Rowell/Corbis Images; right, © Kunio Owaki/The Stock Market; Page **155:** From The Wall Street Journal. Reprinted by permission of Cartoon Features Syndicate; Page **157:** © American Stock/Archive Photos; Page **159:** U.S. Treasury Department; Page **160:** left, © 1998 Don Couch Photography; right, © 1998 Don Couch Photography; Page **162:** © Lisa Quinones/Black Star/PNI; Page **163:** © PhotoDisc; Page **164:** © Wayne Stayskal. Reprinted by permission; Page **165:** © D. Logan/H. Armstrong Roberts; Page **171:** By permission of Chip Bok and Creators Syndicate; Page **174:** Courtesy of Riders for Justice.

Consumer Choice and Elasticities

A. Consumer Behavior
What is utility?

B. The Consumer's Choice
How do consumers maximize their satisfaction?

C. Consumer Surplus
What is consumer surplus?

D. Price Elasticity of Demand
What is price elasticity of demand?

E. Total Revenue and Price Elasticity of Demand
What is the relationship between price, total revenue, and the price elasticity of demand?

F. Other Types of Elasticities
How are other types of elasticities useful?

G. APPLICATION: Condoms and Elasticities
If sexual activity becomes less risky, is it possible there will be more sexually transmitted diseases?

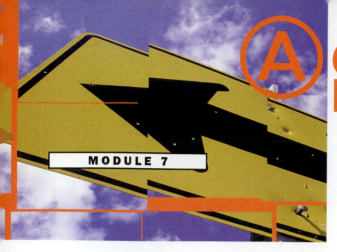

A Consumer Behavior

MODULE 7

- What is utility?
- Can we make interpersonal utility comparisons?
- What is the law of diminishing marginal utility?

THE RULE OF RATIONAL CHOICE REVISITED

Individuals do not just follow simple patterns of behavior. They take action in response to recognized opportunities to advance their goals. This assumption that individuals act to advance their goals—known as the rule of rational choice—merely implies that whatever individuals do is done with a purpose. In economics we assume that each individual seeks to maximize his or her own well-being or satisfaction.

WHAT IS UTILITY?

In an attempt to more clearly define the relationship between consumer choice and resource allocation, economists developed the concept of **utility** to allow them to study the relative levels of satisfaction that consumers get from the consumption of goods and services. Suppose we could measure something called a **util**, the equivalent to one unit of satisfaction. Economists could then indicate relative levels of consumer satisfaction that result from alternative choices. A first cup of coffee, for example, might generate 150 utils of satisfaction for Rich Brew, a java junkie, while a first cup of tea might only generate 20 utils of satisfaction, because Rich prefers coffee to tea.

Inherently, utility varies from individual to individual depending on specific preferences. For example, John might get 50 utils of satisfaction from eating his first piece of apple pie, while Sandy may only derive 4 utils of satisfaction from her first piece of apple pie.

UTILITY IS A PERSONAL MATTER!

Economists recognize that it is not really possible to make **interpersonal utility comparisons.** That is, they know that it is impossible to compare the relative satisfactions of different persons. The relative satisfactions gained by two people drinking cups of coffee, for example, simply cannot be measured in comparable terms. Likewise, while it might be tempting to believe that a poorer person would derive greater utility from finding a $100 bill than a richer

Who enjoys their coffee more? We can guess, but are we sure?

person, the temptation should be resisted. We simply cannot prove it. The poorer person may be "monetarily" poor because money and material things are not important to him, and the rich person may have become richer because of his lust for the things money can buy.

WHAT ARE TOTAL UTILITY AND MARGINAL UTILITY?

Economists consider two different dimensions of utility: total utility and marginal utility. **Total utility** is the total amount of satisfaction derived from the consumption of a certain number of units of a good or service. In comparison, **marginal utility** is the additional satisfaction generated by the last unit of a good that is consumed. In other words, marginal utility measures the increase in satisfaction derived from the last unit of a good that has been consumed, beyond the amount of satisfaction that has been generated by the consumption of previous units of the good in a particular time period. For example, eating 4 pieces of pizza in an evening might generate 36 utils of satisfaction. The first 3 slices of pizza might generate 35 utils, while the last slice generates only 1 util. In this case, the total utility of eating 4 slices of pizza is 36 utils, and the marginal utility of the fourth slice is 1 util. Notice in Exhibit 1(a) how marginal utility falls as consumption increases, while in Exhibit 1(b), total utility increases as consumption increases (there is more total utility after the fourth slice of pizza than after the third).

| **EXHIBIT 1** | **TOTAL AND MARGINAL UTILITY** |

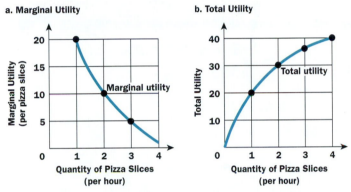

As you can see in (a), marginal utility decreases as consumption increases. As you eat more pizza, your satisfaction from each additional slice diminishes. In (b), the total utility from each slice of pizza increases as consumption increases.

WHY DOES MARGINAL UTILITY DIMINISH?

Although economists believe that total utility increases with additional consumption, they also argue that the incremental satisfaction—the marginal utility—that results from the consumption of additional units tends to decline as consumption increases. In other words, each successive unit of a good that is consumed generates less satisfaction than did the previous unit. This concept is traditionally referred to as the **law of diminishing marginal utility.** This is shown graphically in Exhibit 1(a), where the marginal utility curve has a negative slope.

It follows from the law of diminishing marginal utility that as a person uses more and more units of a good to satisfy a given want, the intensity of the want, and the utility derived from further satisfying that want, diminishes. For example, as you eat 10 pieces of pepperoni pizza in a 30-minute setting, your desire for another piece of pepperoni pizza, and thus the satisfaction you get from satisfying that

"It's been fun, Dave, but I think we're entering the diminished marginal utility phase of our relationship."

© Robert Mankoff from the Cartoon Bank, Inc.

Will the last piece of pizza you eat in a brief time period yield the same satisfaction as the first piece?

desire, diminishes with each slice that is eaten. Think about it: If you are starving, your desire for that first piece of pizza will be great, but as you eat, you gradually become more and more full, reducing your desire for yet another piece.

TUNE UP

MARGINAL UTILITY

Q: Why do most individuals take only one newspaper from covered, coin-operated newspaper racks when it would be so easy to take more? Do you think potato chips, candy, or sodas could be profitably sold in the same kind of dispenser? Why or why not?

A: While ethical considerations keep some people from taking additional papers, the law of diminishing marginal utility is also at work here. The second newspaper adds practically zero utility to most individuals on most days, so there is typically no incentive to take more than one. The exception to this case might be on Sundays, when supermarket coupons are present. In that instance, while the marginal utility is still lower for the second paper than the first, the marginal utility of the second paper may be large enough to tempt some individuals to take additional copies.

On the other hand, if you put your money in the vending machine and had access to many bags of potato chips, candy bars, or sodas, the temptation to take more than one might be too great for some. After all, the potato chip bags will still be good tomorrow; yesterday's news gets stale quickly. Therefore, vending machines with foods and drinks only dispense one item at a time, because it is likely that, for most people, the marginal utility gained from another unit of food or drink is higher than that for a second newspaper.

Why are newspaper racks different from vending machines?

CONCEPT CHECK

1. Utility is the level of satisfaction an individual receives from consumption of a good or service.
2. Economists recognize that it is not possible to make interpersonal utility comparisons.
3. Total utility is the amount of satisfaction derived from all units of goods and services consumed. Total utility increases as consumption increases.
4. Marginal utility is the change in utility from consuming an additional good or service.
5. According to the law of diminishing marginal utility, as a person consumes additional units of a given good, marginal utility declines.

---

1. How do economists define utility?
2. Why can't interpersonal utility comparisons be made?
3. What is the relationship between total utility and marginal utility?
4. Why could you say that Rich, who is a millionaire, gets less marginal utility from a second piece of pizza than from the first piece, but you couldn't say whether he got more or less marginal utility from a second piece of pizza than Les, who has a very low income?

5. How would it be possible for someone to get negative marginal utility from consuming an additional piece of pizza for dinner?
6. Are you likely to get as much marginal utility from your last piece of chicken at an all-you-can-eat restaurant as a restaurant where you pay $2 per piece of chicken?

The Consumer's Choice

■ How do consumers maximize satisfaction?
■ What is the connection between the law of demand and the law of diminishing marginal utility?

WHAT IS THE "BEST" DECISION FOR CONSUMERS?

We have established the fact that marginal utility diminishes as additional units of a good are acquired. But what significance does this have for consumers? Remember, consumers try to add to their own total utility, so when the marginal utility generated by the purchase of additional units of one good drops too low, it can become rational for the consumer to purchase other goods rather than to purchase more of the first good. In other words, a rational consumer will avoid making purchases of any one good beyond the point at which other goods will yield greater satisfaction for the amount spent.

Marginal utility, then, is an important concept in understanding and predicting consumer behavior, especially when combined with information about prices. By comparing the marginal utilities generated by units of the goods that he or she desires as well as their prices, a rational consumer seeks the combination of goods that maximizes his or her satisfaction. When the optimum, utility-maximizing level of each good has been purchased, the consumer is said to have reached the point of **consumer equilibrium.**

HOW IS CONSUMER EQUILIBRIUM ACHIEVED?

In order to reach consumer equilibrium, consumers must allocate their income in such a way that the marginal utility per dollar's worth of any good is the same for every good. That is, the "bang per buck" is equal for all goods at consumer equilibrium. When this goal is realized, one dollar's worth of gasoline will yield the same marginal utility as one dollar's worth of additional bread or apples or movie tickets or soap. This concept will become clearer to you as we work through an example illustrating the forces that are present when you are not at equilibrium.

Given a fixed budget, if the marginal utilities per dollar spent on additional units of two goods are not the same, the consumer can increase total satisfaction by buying more of one good and less of the other. For example, assume that the price of a loaf of bread is $1, the price of a bag of apples is $1, the marginal utility of one dollar's worth of apples is 1, and the marginal utility of a dollar's worth of bread is 5. In this situation, the consumer's total satisfaction can be increased by buying more bread and fewer apples, because bread is currently giving you greater satisfaction (5 utils versus 1 util) per dollar than apples. By buying more bread, though, you alter the marginal utility of both bread and apples. Consider what would happen if, next week, you buy one more loaf of bread and one less bag of apples. Because you are consuming more of it now, the marginal utility for bread will fall, say to 4. On the other hand, the marginal utility for apples will rise, perhaps to 2, because you now have fewer apples.

A comparison of the marginal utilities for these goods in week 2 versus week 1 would look something like this:

Week One	Week Two
$MU_{bread}/\$1 > MU_{apples}/\$1$	$MU_{bread}/\$1 = MU_{apples}/\$1$
$5/\$1 > 1/\$1$	$4/\$1 > 2/\$1$

Notice that, although the marginal utilities of bread and apples are now closer, they are still not equal. Because of this, it is still in the consumer's interest to purchase an additional loaf of bread rather than the last bag of apples. By buying yet another loaf of bread, the consumer once again pushes further down his marginal utility curve for bread, and as a result, the marginal utility for bread falls. With that, the relative value of apples to the consumer increases again, changing the ratio of marginal utility to dollar spent for both goods in the following manner:

Week Three
$MU_{bread}/\$1 = MU_{apples}/\$1$
$3/\$1 = 3/\$1$

What this example shows is that, to achieve maximum satisfaction—consumer equilibrium—consumers have to

If you are currently deriving more satisfaction per dollar from bread than apples, how will you spend your next dollar?

allocate income in such a way that the ratio of the marginal utility to the price of the goods is equal for all goods purchased. In other words, in a state of consumer equilibrium,

$$MU_1/P_1 = MU_2/P_2 = MU_3/P_3 = \ldots MU_N/P_N$$

In this state, each good will provide the consumer the same level of marginal utility per dollar spent.

WHAT IS THE CONNECTION BETWEEN THE LAW OF DEMAND AND THE LAW OF DIMINISHING MARGINAL UTILITY?

The law of demand states that when the price of a good is reduced, the quantity of that good demanded will increase. But why is this the case? By examining the law of diminishing marginal utility in action, we can determine

the basis for this relationship between price and quantity demanded. Indeed, the demand curve merely translates marginal utility into dollar terms.

For example, consider the case in which you are in consumer equilibrium when the price of a personal size pizza is at $4 and the price of a hamburger is $1. Let us say, that, in equilibrium, the marginal utility on the last pizza consumed is 40 utils and the marginal utility on the last hamburger is 10 utils. So in consumer equilibrium:

$$MU_{pizza} (40)/\$4 = MU_{hamburger} (10)/\$1 = 10 \text{ utils per dollar}$$

Now suppose the price of the personal size pizza falls to $2, *ceteris paribus*. Now, instead of the *MU/P* ratio of the pizza being 10 utils per dollar, it is now 20 (40 utils/2). This implies, *ceteris paribus,* that you would now buy more pizza at the lower price because you are getting relatively more satisfaction for each dollar you spend on pizza.

We're Tossin' You a Great Offer!

FREE MEDIUM DOMINO'S PIZZA
Buy a Large One-Topping Pizza at Menu Price, Get a Medium One-Topping Pizza Free.
©1998 Domino's Pizza, Inc. Coupon not valid with any other offer. Offer valid with coupon only. Valid at participating stores only. Prices may vary. Customer pays sales tax where applicable. Our drivers carry less than $20. Cash value 1/20¢. Limit one coupon per household. Offer good for delivery and carry-out. Offer expires December 31, 1998. Coupon distributed by General Mills, Inc., Minneapolis, MN 55440. Coupon issued by Domino's Pizza, Inc., Ann Arbor, MI 48106.

FREE MEDIUM DOMINO'S PIZZA
When You Buy One Large Pizza.

Delivering a Million Smiles a Day.™

For the Domino's location nearest you, consult your yellow pages or our web site at www.dominos.com

MU_{pizza} (40)/$2 > $MU_{hamburger}$ (10)/$1

In other words, because the price of the personal size pizza fell, the consumer is now willing to purchase more pizza.

If the marginal utility of pizza per dollar is now higher than the marginal utility of hamburger per dollar because the price of pizza fell, would you buy more pizza?

CONCEPT CHECK

1. In order to maximize consumer satisfaction, income must be allocated so that the ratio of the marginal utility to the price is the same for all goods purchased.

2. If the marginal utility per dollar of additional units is not the same, a person can increase total satisfaction by buying more of some goods and less of others.

1. What do economists mean by consumer equilibrium?
2. How could a consumer raise his total utility if the ratio of his marginal utility to the price for good A was greater than that for good B?
3. What must be true about the ratio of marginal utility to price for each good consumed in consumer equilibrium?
4. How does the law of demand reflect the law of diminishing marginal utility?
5. Why doesn't consumer equilibrium imply that the ratio of total utility per dollar is the same for different goods?

6. Why does the principle of consumer equilibrium imply that people would tend to buy more apples when the price of apples is reduced?
7. If the price of walnuts is $6 per pound and the price of peanuts is $2 per pound, if a person gets 20 units of added utility from eating the last pound of peanuts he consumes, how many units of added utility would that person have to get from eating the last pound of walnuts in order to be in consumer equilibrium?

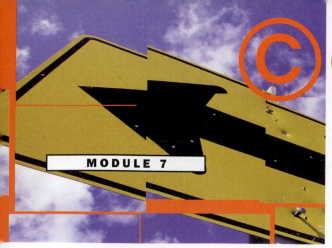

© Consumer Surplus

- Is what you are required to pay for a good the same thing as what you are willing to pay for that good?
- What is consumer surplus?
- What is the diamond–water paradox?

WHAT IS CONSUMER SURPLUS?

What a consumer is *required* to pay for a good is usually less than what she is *willing* to pay. For example, say the price of a glass of iced tea is $1. If a consumer did not place a value of at least $1 on that glass of iced tea, she would not purchase it. On the other hand, if someone was willing to pay $2 for the glass of iced tea but was only required to pay a market price of $1, then she would receive the difference as a surplus of $1. This monetary difference between what the consumer is willing to pay and what the consumer is required to pay is called **consumer surplus.** In Exhibit 1, this is shown as the area under the demand curve and above the market price (area a). Areas a and b together represent total willingness-to-pay for Q units of the good, while area b is the amount the consumer is required to pay for that quantity ($P \times Q$). The difference is consumer surplus, the shaded area, a.

DO EARLIER UNITS OF A GOOD YIELD GREATER SATISFACTION?

Suppose it is a very hot day and iced tea is going for $1 per glass, but the consumer is willing to pay $4 for the first

| EXHIBIT 1 | CONSUMER SURPLUS |

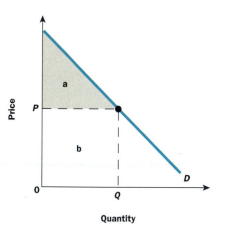

Do you think people get consumer surplus from garage door openers? Might it be even greater in areas where it rains and snows a lot?

glass, $2 for the second glass, and $0.50 for the third glass, reflecting the law of demand. How much consumer surplus will this individual receive? First, it is important to note the general fact that if the consumer is a buyer of several units of a good, the earlier units will have greater marginal value and therefore create more consumer surplus, because marginal willingness to pay falls as greater quantities are consumed in any period. This is demonstrated by the consumer's willingness to pay $4 and $2 successively for the first two glasses of iced tea. Thus, the consumer will receive $3 of consumer surplus for the first glass ($4 – $1) and $1 of consumer surplus for the second glass ($2 – $1), for a total of $4, as seen in Exhibit 2. He will not be willing to consume the third glass, because it would reduce his consumer surplus.

EXHIBIT 2	CONSUMER SURPLUS FOR ICED TEA

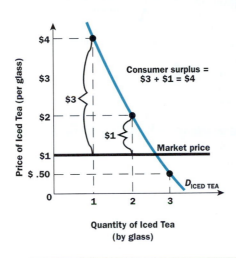

Imagine it is 115 degrees in the shade. Do you think you would get more consumer surplus from your first glass of iced tea than you would from a fifth glass?

TUNE UP

CONSUMER SURPLUS

"Nothing is more useful than water: but it will not purchase scarce anything. . . . A diamond, on the contrary, has scarce value in use; but a very great quantity of other goods may frequently be had in exchange for it."

—Adam Smith, *Wealth of Nations*, 1776

Q: Use the concept of consumer surplus to evaluate the social value of water versus diamonds.

A: This classic water–diamond paradox demonstrates an apparent inconsistency between market value and use value. Market value—the value of the last, or marginal unit traded—depends on both supply and demand. Thus, the limited supply of diamonds generates a high price while an abundant supply of water results in a low price. The net benefits to society from diamonds and water—the difference between their total values and their total costs—however, are better represented by consumer surplus. Exhibit 3 shows that the consumer surplus for water, shown as the shaded region in Exhibit 3(b), far surpasses the consumer surplus for diamonds, shown as the shaded region in Exhibit 3(a). In other words, value-in-use of water (consumer's total willingness to pay) is very large in comparison with what consumers have to pay. Indeed, the demand curve may never intersect the vertical axis even if water prices keep rising because it is necessary for life at low quantities. This difference is smaller in the case of diamonds, where the consumer surplus is relatively small.

Why is water, which is so critical to life, less "valuable" than diamonds?

EXHIBIT 3

a. Consumer Surplus from Diamonds

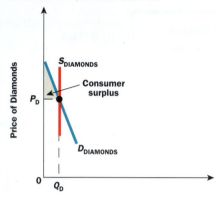

b. Consumer Surplus from Water

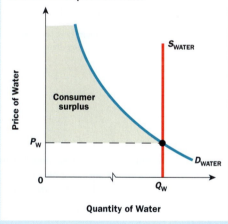

DOES A PRICE CHANGE CAUSE A CHANGE IN CONSUMER SURPLUS?

A change in price will cause consumer surplus to change. Imagine the case in which your favorite beverage fell in price. Wouldn't you feel better off? A lower price will increase your consumer surplus for each of the units you were already consuming, and will also increase consumer surplus from increased purchases at the lower price. Conversely, an increase in price will lower the amount of consumer surplus.

Exhibit 4 shows the gain in consumer surplus associated with a technological advance that shifts the supply curve to the right. As a result, equilibrium price falls (from P_0 to P_1) and quantity rises (from Q_0 to Q_1). Consumer surplus then increases from area P_0AB to area P_1AC, or a gain in consumer surplus of P_0BCP_1.

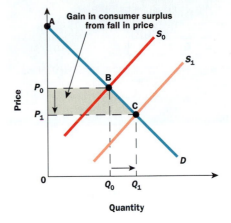

1. The difference between how much a consumer is willing to pay and how much a consumer has to pay is called consumer surplus.

2. A lower price will increase consumer surplus; a higher price will decrease consumer surplus.

---

1. What is consumer surplus?
2. Why do the first units consumed at a given price add more consumer surplus than the last units consumed?
3. Why does a decrease in a good's price increase the consumer surplus from consumption of that good?

4. Why might the consumer surplus from purchases of mink coats, which are very expensive, be less than the consumer surplus from purchases of far less-expensive leather coats?

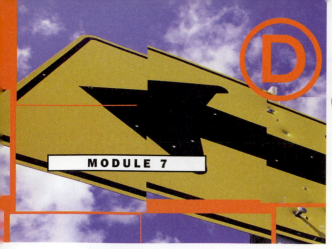

Price Elasticity of Demand

- Why are price elasticities of demand important?
- How do we measure consumers' responses to price changes?
- What determines the price elasticity of demand?

WHY ARE PRICE ELASTICITIES OF DEMAND IMPORTANT?

In learning and applying the law of demand, we have established the basic fact that quantity demanded changes inversely with changes in price, *ceteris paribus*. But how much does quantity demanded change? The extent to which quantity demanded is impacted by a change in price is very important to understand for many economic issues. That is, what the price elasticity of demand is designed to answer is how responsive quantity demanded is to changes in price.

For example, a bus company might want to know whether doubling its fares to $2 will reduce ridership by a little or a lot in percentage terms. Likewise, a sportswear company might want to know how much the sales of its basketball shoe would be impacted by a 20 percent reduction in price. Government officials and business forecasters are also interested in estimating the magnitude of these

If bus fares double, will ridership fall a little or a lot?

effects because they will greatly impact future investment decisions.

WHAT IS THE PRICE ELASTICITY OF DEMAND?

In order to get information on the responsiveness of quantity demanded to a change in price, we use the concept of **price elasticity of demand.** The price elasticity of demand measures how responsive consumer behavior (quantity demanded) is due to an incentive (price) change. More specifically, price elasticity is defined as the percentage change in quantity demanded divided by the percentage change in price:

$$\text{Price elasticity of demand } (E_d) = \frac{\text{Percentage change in quantity demanded}}{\text{Percentage change in price}}$$

Note that, following the law of demand, there is an inverse relationship between price and quantity demanded. For this reason, price elasticity of demand is, in theory, always negative. In practice, however, this quantity is always expressed in absolute value terms, as a positive number, for simplicity.

HOW DO YOU CALCULATE THE PRICE ELASTICITY OF DEMAND?

To get a clear picture of exactly how the price elasticity of demand is calculated, consider the case for the compact disc market. Say the price of compact discs increases from $19 to $21. If we take an average between the old price, $19, and the new price, $21, we can calculate an average price of $20. As result of the increase in price of CDs, Exhibit 1 shows that the quantity demanded has fallen from 82 million CDs to 78 million CDs per year. If we take an average between the old quantity demanded, 82 million, and the new quantity demanded, 78 million, we have an average quantity demanded of 80 million CDs per year. That is, the $2 increase in price of CDs has led to a 4 million reduction in quantity demanded. How can we figure out the price elasticity of demand?

The first thing you might ask is, Why are we using the average price and average quantity? The answer is that if we did not use the average amounts, we would come up with different values for the elasticity of demand depending on whether we moved up or down the demand curve. To avoid this confusion, economists often use this average technique. Specifically, we are actually calculating the elasticity at a midpoint between the old and new prices and quantities.

First, we must calculate the percent change in price. To find the percentage change in price, we take the change in price (ΔP) and divide it by the average price (P_{ave}). (Note: the Greek letter delta, Δ, means *change in*.)

Percentage change in price = $\Delta P / P_{ave}$

In our CD example, the original price was $19, and the new price is $21. The change in price (ΔP) is $2, and the average price (P_{ave}) is $20. The percentage change in price can then be calculated as follows:

Percentage change in price = $\$2/\$20 = 1/10 = .10 = 10\%$

Next we must calculate the percentage change in quantity demanded. To find the percentage change in quantity demanded, we take the change in quantity demanded (ΔQ_d) and divide it by the average quantity demanded ($Q_{d\,ave}$).

Percentage change in quantity demanded = $\Delta Q_d / Q_{d\,ave}$

In our CD example, the original quantity demanded was 82 million, and the new quantity demanded is 78 million. The change in quantity demanded (ΔQ_d) is 4 million, and the average quantity demanded ($Q_{d\,ave}$) is 80 million. The percentage change in quantity demanded can then be calculated as follows:

Percentage change in quantity demanded =
4 million/80 million = $1/20$ = .05 = 5%

Because the price elasticity of demand is equal to the percentage change in quantity demanded divided by the percentage change in price, the price elasticity of demand for CDs between point A and point B can be shown as follows:

$$E_d = \frac{\text{Percentage change in quantity demanded}}{\text{Percentage change in price}}$$

$$= \frac{\Delta Q_d / Q_{d\,ave}}{P / P_{ave}} = \frac{4 \text{ million}/80 \text{ million}}{\$2/\$20} = \frac{1/20}{2/20} = .5$$

IS THE DEMAND CURVE RELATIVELY ELASTIC OR RELATIVELY INELASTIC?

While it is important to learn how to calculate an elasticity, it is equally if not more important to understand the basic intuition behind elasticities. This can be easily understood

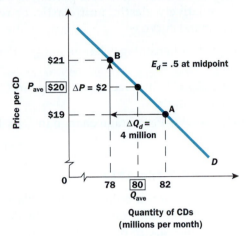

EXHIBIT 1   **CALCULATING THE PRICE ELASTICITY OF DEMAND**

The price elasticity of demand is found with the formula:

$$\frac{\Delta Q_d / Q_{d\,ave}}{\Delta P / P_{ave}}$$

by focusing on the percentage changes in quantity demanded and price.

Think of elasticity as an elastic rubber band. If the quantity demanded (or length) is very responsive to even a small change in price (or pressure), we call it elastic. On the other hand, if even a huge change in price (or pressure) results in only a small change in quantity demanded (or length), then the demand is said to be inelastic. Let's throw some percentages in. If a 10 percent increase in the price leads to a 50 percent reduction in the quantity demanded, we say that demand is **elastic** because the quantity demanded is very sensitive to the price change.

$$E_d = \frac{\%\Delta Q_d}{\%\Delta P} = \frac{50 \text{ percent}}{10 \text{ percent}} = 5$$

Demand is relatively elastic in this case, because a 10 percent change in price led to a larger (50 percent) change in quantity demanded.

Alternatively, if a 10 percent increase in the price leads to a 1 percent reduction in quantity demanded, we say that demand is relatively **inelastic** because the quantity demanded did not respond much to the price reduction.

$$E_d = \frac{\%\Delta Q_d}{\%\Delta P} = \frac{1 \text{ percent}}{10 \text{ percent}} = .10$$

Demand is relatively inelastic in this case, because a 10 percent change in price led to a smaller (1 percent) change in quantity demanded.

WHAT ARE THE RANGES OF ELASTICITY?

Economists refer to a variety of demand curves based on their elasticity. A demand curve or a portion of a demand curve can be **relatively elastic, unit elastic,** or **relatively inelastic.** A demand curve is:

Elastic ($E_d > 1$) if Percentage change in Q_d > Percentage change in P

Unit elastic ($E_d = 1$) if Percentage change in Q_d = Percentage change in P

Inelastic ($E_d < 1$) if Percentage change in Q_d < Percentage change in P

Elastic Demand Segments

Elastic demand segments are those with an elasticity that is numerically greater than one ($E_d > 1$). In this case, a small percentage increase in price, say 10 percent, leads to a larger percentage change in quantity demanded, say 20 percent, as seen in Exhibit 2(a). If the curve was perfectly elastic, a small percentage increase in price would cause the quantity demanded to fall dramatically to zero. For example, say there are two side-by-side roadside fruit stands selling the same quality of oranges. If one stand has lower prices, then the higher-priced fruit stand would soon be selling no oranges. In Exhibit 2(b), a perfectly elastic demand curve (horizontal) is illustrated. Economists define the elasticity of demand in this case as infinity, because the quantity demanded is infinitely responsive to even a very small percentage change in price.

Inelastic Demand Segments

Inelastic demand segments are those with elasticity less than one ($E_d < 1$). In this case, a larger percentage (10 percent) change in price is accompanied with a smaller (5 percent) reduction in quantity demanded, as seen in Exhibit 3(a). If the demand curve is perfectly inelastic, the quantity demanded is the same regardless of the price, as illustrated in Exhibit 3(b).

Unit Elastic Demand Segments

Goods for which E_d equals one ($E_d = 1$) are said to be unit elastic. In this case, the percentage change in quantity demanded is the same as the percentage change in price that caused it. For example, a 10 percent increase in price will lead to a 10 percent reduction in quantity demanded. This is illustrated in Exhibit 4.

HOW CAN SLOPE INDICATE RELATIVE PRICE ELASTICITY OF DEMAND?

The slopes of demand curves can also be used to indicate their relative demand elasticities at a given point. In Exhibit 5, D_0 is steeper than D_1. D_0 is also relatively inelastic compared to D_1 at that point. To show this we can measure the relative responsiveness of quantity demanded to an identical price change for the two demand curves. In Exhibit 5, we see that when the price changes, quantity demanded ($Q_0 - Q_2$) is much more responsive on the flatter, more elastic demand curve, D_1. On the steeper, more

---

EXHIBIT 2	ELASTIC DEMAND

a. Relatively Elastic Demand ($E_d > 1$)

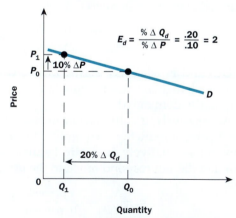

$$E_d = \frac{\% \, \Delta \, Q_d}{\% \, \Delta \, P} = \frac{.20}{.10} = 2$$

A small percentage change in price leads to a larger percentage change in quantity demanded.

b. Perfectly Elastic Demand ($E_d = \infty$)

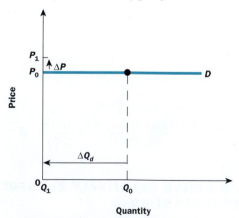

A small percentage change in price will change quantity demanded by an infinite amount.

EXHIBIT 3   INELASTIC DEMAND

a. Relatively Inelastic Demand ($E_d < 1$)

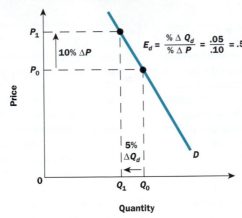

$$E_d = \frac{\% \Delta Q_d}{\% \Delta P} = \frac{.05}{.10} = .5$$

A change in price leads to a smaller percentage change in quantity demanded.

b. Perfectly Inelastic Demand ($E_d = 0$)

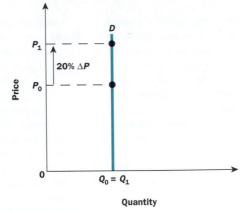

The quantity demanded does not change regardless of the percentage change in price.

EXHIBIT 4   UNIT ELASTIC DEMAND

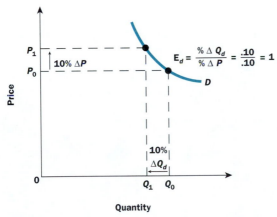

$$E_d = \frac{\% \Delta Q_d}{\% \Delta P} = \frac{.10}{.10} = 1$$

The percentage change in quantity demanded is the same as the percentage change in price that caused it ($E_d = 1$).

EXHIBIT 5   SLOPE AND RELATIVE ELASTICITY

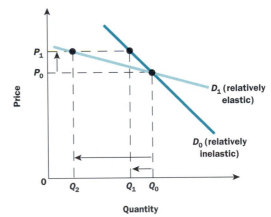

When a demand curve is relatively steep, such as D_0 in this graph, its price elasticity of demand is relatively inelastic. When a demand curve is relatively flat, such as D_1, its price elasticity of demand is relatively elastic.

inelastic D_0, quantity demanded ($Q_0 - Q_1$) changes only slightly when the price changes. In sum, we can say that when a demand curve is relatively steep, *ceteris paribus*, its price elasticity of demand is relatively low (more inelastic), and when the demand curve is relatively flat, its price elasticity of demand is relatively high (more elastic).

WHAT INFLUENCES THE PRICE. ELASTICITY OF DEMAND?

As you have learned, the elasticity of demand for a specific good refers to movements along its demand curve as its price changes. A lower price will increase quantity

CLINTON TARGETS TEEN SMOKING

ASSOCIATED PRESS

WASHINGTON—President Clinton consigned the landmark $368 billion tobacco deal to limbo yesterday, calling instead for legislation raising cigarette prices by up to $1.50 per pack and for harsher penalties on tobacco firms that market to teens. "Reducing teen smoking has always been America's bottom line. It must be the industry's bottom line," Mr. Clinton said.

He also asked Congress to pass legislation that sets targets to cut teen smoking by 30 percent in five years, 50 percent in seven years and 60 percent in a decade. Penalties for missing those targets, including the $1.50 price hike, which would phase in over a decade, should not be capped or tax-deductible as a business expense, he said.

Under the negotiated deal, industry fines would have been capped at $2 billion. Ending three months of divisive internal debate among administration officials, Clinton said he is not out to punish cigarette makers. "It is not about how much money we can extract from the tobacco industry. It's about fulfilling our duties as parents and responsible adults to protect our children," he said.

Papers accompanying the announcement cited estimates that a 10 percent increase in cigarette prices will lead to a 7 percent drop in youth smoking.

SOURCE: Associated Press and *Christian Science Monitor,* September 18, 1997.

ANALYSIS:
According to this article, a 10 percent increase in the price of cigarettes will lead to a 7 percent reduction in youth smoking. In this price range, however, demand is still relatively inelastic at $-.7$. Of course, proponents of higher taxes to discourage underage smoking would like to see a more elastic demand, where a 10 percent increase in the price of cigarettes would lead to a more than 10 percent reduction in quantity demanded.

demanded, and a higher price will reduce quantity demanded. But what factors will influence the magnitude of the change in quantity demanded in response to a price change? That is, what will make the demand curve relatively more elastic (where Q_d is responsive to price changes), and what will make the demand curve relatively less elastic (where Q_d is less responsive to price changes)?

For the most part, the price elasticity of demand depends on the following factors: (1) the ease of substitutability between goods, (2) the proportion of income spent on the good, and (3) the amount of time that has elapsed since the price change.

Number of Close Substitutes

The larger the number of close substitutes, the greater the elasticity. If the price of a good increases, the consumers may select a now relatively lower-priced substitute instead. For example, the elasticity of demand for a Ford, Toyota, or a Honda is more elastic than the demand for a car, because there are more and better substitutes for a certain type of car than for a car itself. There are many other examples where the ease of substitution will make the demand relatively more elastic for most individuals such as butter and margarine, one soft drink as opposed to another, and different brands of cold medications or gasoline.

The demand for many types of emergency medical care is relatively inelastic, because there are very few good substitutes when you "really need" a physician.

The fewer the number of close substitutes, the less elastic the demand curve. For example, there are some goods and services that have few good close substitutes: insulin for diabetics, cigarettes for chain smokers, heroin for an addict, or emergency medical care for someone with appendicitis or a broken leg.

EARTH'S BIGGEST BOOKSTORE

Welcome to Earth's Biggest Bookstore. You've just entered an amazing world of books. Whether you know the title you're looking for or you're in need of inspiration, you're sure to find it here. Know what you want?

Amazon.com has the books you're looking for—at savings of up to 40 percent. We're called Earth's Biggest Bookstore because we offer 2.5 million titles—more than 14 times as many as the largest chain superstores. Whether you're shopping for a bestseller or a book on a highly specialized subject, we've got what you're looking for.

CONSIDER THIS:
While you might be able to buy books from Amazon.com at a lower price than at many other bookstores, it is likely that, even here, you will pay a lot more for a hardcover book than a paperback book. Why? While a hardcover book is only slightly more expensive to publish, the real reason for the price differential between hardcover and softcover books is the price elasticity of demand. Some people are willing to pay a higher price to be among the first to read a book or see a movie; their demand curve is relatively inelastic. Other individuals have a more elastic demand curve for these goods and are willing to wait for the book to come out in paperback or the movie to reach the video store. Other customers, like libraries, find that paperbacks are not durable enough to be good substitutes for hardbacks. Sellers are able to profit from this difference in elasticities of demand by charging more to those who are more willing to pay and charging a lower price to those who are less willing to pay.

Proportion of Income Spent on the Good

The smaller the proportion of income spent on a good, the lower its elasticity of demand. If the amount spent on a good relative to income is small, then the impact of a change in its price on one's budget will also be small. As a result, consumers will respond less to price changes for these goods than for similar percentage changes in large-ticket items, where a price change could have a potentially large impact on the consumer's budget. For example, a 50 percent increase in the price of salt will have a much smaller impact on consumers' behavior than a similar percentage increase in the price of a new automobile. Similarly, a 50 percent increase in the cost of private university tuition will have a greater impact on students' and parents' budgets than a 50 percent increase in textbook prices.

Time

The more time that people have to adapt to a new price change, the greater the elasticity of demand. Immediately after a price change, consumers my be unable to locate very good alternatives or easily change their consumption patterns. But the more time that passes, the more time consumers have to find or develop suitable substitutes and to

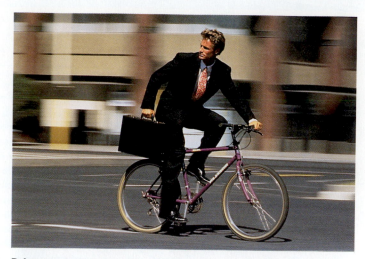

Drivers may not respond immediately to an increase in gas prices, perhaps believing it to be temporary. However, if the price persists over a longer period, we would expect people to drive less, buy more fuel-efficient cars, move closer to work, or even bike to work.

plan and implement changes in their patterns of consumption. Hence, the short-run demand curve is generally less elastic than the long-run demand curve.

CONCEPT CHECK

1. Price elasticity of demand measures the percentage change in quantity demanded divided by the percentage change in price.
2. If the demand for a good is relatively elastic in the relevant range, quantity demanded it is very responsive to a price change. If the demand for a good is relatively inelastic, quantity demanded is not very responsive to a price change.

3. When demand curve is relatively steep, demand is relatively inelastic; when the demand curve is relatively flat, demand is relatively elastic.
4. The elasticity of demand depends on: (1) the number of close substitutes, (2) the proportion of income spent on the good, and (3) the amount of time that buyers have to respond to a price change.

---

1. What question is the price elasticity of demand designed to answer?
2. How is the price elasticity of demand calculated?
3. What is the difference between a relatively elastic demand curve and a relatively inelastic demand curve?
4. What is the relationship between the price elasticity of demand and the slope at a given point on a demand curve?
5. What factors tend to make demand curves more elastic?

6. Why would a tax on a particular brand of cigarettes be less effective at reducing smoking than a tax on all brands of cigarettes?
7. Why is the elasticity of demand for products at a 24-hour convenience store likely to be lower at 2 A.M. than at 2 P.M.?
8. Why is the elasticity of demand for turkeys likely to be lower, but the elasticity of demand for turkeys at a *particular* store likely to be greater, at Thanksgiving than at other times of the year?

Total Revenue and Price Elasticity of Demand

- What is total revenue?
- What is the relationship between total revenue and the price elasticity of demand?
- Does the price elasticity of demand vary along a linear demand curve?

HOW DOES THE PRICE ELASTICITY OF DEMAND IMPACT TOTAL REVENUE?

The price elasticity of demand for a good also has implications for **total revenue,** the revenue generated from the sale of a good at different points on a demand curve. Total revenue (TR) is simply the price of the good (P) times the quantity of the good sold (Q): $TR = P \times Q$. In Exhibit 1, we see that when the demand is relatively elastic ($E_d > 1$), total revenues will rise as the price declines, because the percentage increase in the quantity demanded is greater than the percent reduction in price. For example, if the price of a good is cut in half (say from $10 to $5) and the quantity demanded more than doubles (say from 40 to 100), total revenue will rise from $400 ($10 × 40 = $400) to $500 ($5 × 100 = $500). Equivalently, if the price rises from $5 to $10 and the quantity demanded falls from 100 to 40 units, then total revenue falls from $500 to $400. As this example illustrates, if the demand curve is relatively elastic, total revenue varies inversely with a price change.

You can see from the following what happens to total revenue when demand is elastic. (Note: The price and quantity arrows represent percentage changes.)

Demand Curve Relatively Elastic

$$\downarrow TR = \uparrow P \times \downarrow Q$$

or

$$\uparrow TR = \downarrow P \times \uparrow Q$$

On the other hand, if demand for a good is relatively inelastic ($E_d < 1$), the total revenue will be lower at lower prices than at higher prices, because a given price reduction will be accompanied by a proportionately smaller increase in quantity demanded. For example, as seen in Exhibit 2, if the price of a good is cut, say from $10 to $5, and the quantity demanded less than doubles—say it increases from 30 to 40—total revenue will fall from $300 ($10 × 30 = $300) to $200 ($5 × 40 = $200). Equivalently, if

EXHIBIT 1   ELASTIC DEMAND AND TOTAL REVENUE

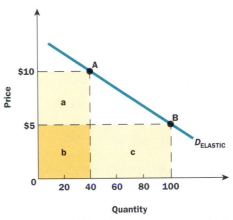

At point A, total revenue is $400 ($10 × 40), or area a + b. At point B, the total revenue is $500 ($5 × 100), or area b + c. Total revenue has increased by $100. We can also see in the graph that total revenue has increased because the area b + c is greater than area a + b, or c > a.

the price increases from $5 to $10 and the quantity demanded falls from 40 to 30, total revenue will increase from $200 to $300. To summarize, then, if the demand curve is inelastic, total revenue will vary directly with a price change.

Demand Curve Relatively Inelastic

$$\uparrow TR = \uparrow P \times \downarrow Q$$

or

$$\downarrow TR = \downarrow P \times \uparrow Q$$

In this case, the "net" effect on total revenue is reversed but easy to see. (Again, price and quantity arrows represent percentage changes.)

EXHIBIT 2 | INELASTIC DEMAND AND TOTAL REVENUE

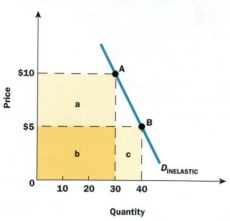

At point A, total revenue is $300 ($10 × 30), or area a + b. At point B, the total revenue is $200 ($5 × 40), or area b + c. Total revenue has fallen by $100. We can also see in the graph that total revenue has decreased because area a + b is greater than area b + c, or a > c.

WHY DOES PRICE ELASTICITY CHANGE ALONG A LINEAR DEMAND CURVE?

As we have already shown (pp. 192–193), the slopes of demand curves can be used to estimate their *relative* elasticities of demand: The steeper one demand curve is relative to another, the more inelastic it is relative to the other. However, beyond the extreme cases of perfectly elastic and perfectly inelastic curves, great care must be taken when trying to estimate the degree of elasticity of one demand curve from its slope. In fact, as we shall see, a straight-line demand curve with a constant slope will change elasticity continuously as you move up or down it.

We can easily demonstrate that the elasticity of demand varies along a linear demand curve by using what we already know about the interrelationship between price and total revenue. Exhibit 4 shows a linear (constant slope) demand curve. In Exhibit 4(a), we see that when the price falls on the upper half of the demand curve from P_0 to P_1, and quantity demanded increases from Q_0 to Q_1, total revenue increases. That is, the new area of total revenue (area b + c) is larger than the old area of total revenue (area a + b).

TUNE UP

ELASTICITIES AND TOTAL REVENUE

Q: Is a poor wheat harvest bad for all farmers? (Hint: Assume that demand for wheat is relatively inelastic.)

A: Without a simultaneous reduction in demand, a reduction in supply results in higher prices. With that, if demand for the wheat is inelastic over the pertinent portion of the demand curve, the price increase will cause farmers' total revenues to rise. As shown in Exhibit 3(a), if demand for the crop is relatively inelastic, an increase in price would cause farmers to lose the revenue indicated by area c. They would, however, experience an increase in revenue equal to area a, resulting in an overall increase in total revenue equal to area a – c. Clearly, if some farmers lose their entire crop because of, say, bad weather, they are worse off; but *collectively* farmers can profit from events that reduce crop size—and they do, because the demand for most agricultural products is relatively inelastic. Interestingly, if all farmers were hurt equally, say, losing one-third of their crop, each farmer would be better off. Of course, consumers would be worse off because the price of agricultural products would be higher. If, however, the demand for a crop was relatively elastic, a reduction in its supply will lead to lower total revenues, as shown in Exhibit 3(b). In this case, farmers' total revenue will fall by an amount equal to the area a – c.

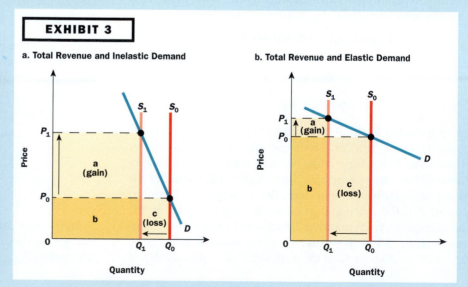

It is also true that if price increased in this region (from P_1 to P_0), total revenue would fall, because b + c is greater than a + b. In this region of the demand curve, then, there is a negative relationship between price and total revenue. As we discussed earlier, this is a characteristic of an elastic demand curve ($E_d > 1$).

Exhibit 4(b) illustrates what happens to total revenue on the lower half of the same demand curve. When the price falls from P_2 to P_3 and the quantity demanded increases from Q_2 to Q_3, total revenue actually decreases, because the new area of total revenue (area e + f) is less than the old

area of total revenue (area d + e). Likewise, it is clear that an increase in price from P_3 to P_2 would increase total revenue. In this case, there is a positive relationship between price and total revenue, which, as we discussed, is characteristic of an inelastic demand curve ($E_d < 1$). Together, parts (a) and (b) of Exhibit 4 illustrate that, although the slope remains constant, the elasticity of a linear demand curve changes along the length of the curve—from relatively elastic at higher price ranges to relatively inelastic at lower price ranges.

| EXHIBIT 4 | PRICE ELASTICITY ALONG A LINEAR DEMAND CURVE |

a. Relatively Elastic Segment

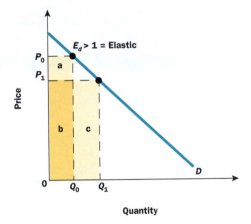

b. Relatively Inelastic Segment

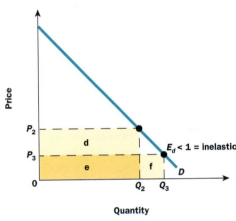

The slope is constant along a linear demand curve, but the elasticity varies. Moving down along the demand curve, the elasticity is relatively elastic at higher prices and relatively inelastic at lower prices.

CONCEPT CHECK

1. Total revenue is the price of the good times the quantity sold ($TR = P \times Q$).
2. If demand is relatively elastic ($E_d > 1$), total revenue will vary inversely with a change in price.
3. If demand is relatively inelastic ($E_d < 1$), total revenue will vary in the same direction as a change in price.
4. A linear demand curve is more elastic at higher price ranges and more inelastic at lower price ranges.

1. Why does total revenue vary inversely with price if demand is relatively elastic?
2. Why does total revenue vary in the same direction as price if demand is relatively inelastic?
3. Why is a linear demand curve more elastic at higher price ranges than at lower price ranges?
4. If demand for some good was perfectly inelastic, how would total revenue from its sales change as its price changed?
5. Assume that both you and Art, your partner in a picture-framing business, want to increase your firm's total revenue. You argue that in order to achieve this goal, you should lower your prices; Art, on the other hand, thinks that you should raise your prices. What assumptions are each of you making about your firm's elasticity of demand?

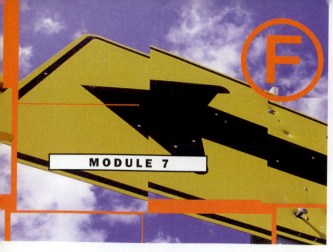

(F) Other Types of Elasticities

- What is the cross price elasticity of demand?
- What is the income elasticity of demand?
- What is the price elasticity of supply?
- What is the relationship between elasticities and tax burdens?

WHAT IS THE CROSS PRICE ELASTICITY OF DEMAND?

The price of a good is not the only factor that affects the quantity consumers will purchase. Sometimes, the quantity of one good demanded is affected by the price of a related good. For example, if the price of potato chips falls, what is the impact, if any, on the quantity of soda demanded? Or if the price of soda increases, to what degree will Kool-Aid sales be affected? The **cross price elasticity of demand** measures both the direction and magnitude of the impact that a price change for one good will have on the quantity of another good demanded at a given price. The cross price elasticity of demand indicates not only the degree of the connection between the two variables but also whether the goods in question are substitutes or complements for one another.

How Do I Calculate the Cross Price Elasticity of Demand?

Specifically, the cross price elasticity of demand is defined as the percentage change in the quantity demanded of one good at a given price divided by the percentage change in price of another good, or

$$\text{Cross price elasticity of demand} = \frac{\text{Percentage change in the quantity demanded of one good at a given price}}{\text{Percentage change in the price of another good}}$$

For example, let's calculate the cross price elasticity of demand between soda and Kool-Aid, where a 10 percent increase in the price of soda results in a 20 percent increase in the quantity of Kool-Aid demanded. In this case, the cross elasticity of demand would be +2 (+20 percent ÷ +10 percent = +2). Consumers responded to the soda price increase by buying less soda (moving along the demand curve for soda) and increasing the quantity demanded of Kool-Aid at every price (shifting the demand curve for Kool-Aid). In general, if the cross elasticity is positive, we can conclude that the two goods are substitutes, because

If a 10 percent increase in the price of soda leads to a 20 percent increase in the quantity of Kool-Aid demanded, what can we say about these two goods?

the price of one good and the demand for the other move in the same direction.

As another example, let's calculate the cross elasticity of demand between potato chips and soda, where a 10 percent decrease in the price of potato chips results in a 30 percent increase in the quantity of soda demanded. In this case, the cross elasticity of demand is −3 (+30 percent ÷ −10 percent = −3). The demand for chips increases as a result of the price decrease, as consumers then purchase additional soda to wash down those extra bags of salty chips. Potato chips and soda, then, are complements. In general, if the cross elasticity is negative, we can conclude that the two goods are complements, because the price of one good and the demand for the other move in opposite directions.

THE INCOME ELASTICITY OF DEMAND

While the most widely employed demand relationship is that relating price and quantity demanded, it is also sometimes useful to be able to relate quantity demanded to income. The **income elasticity of demand** is a measure of the relationship between a relative change in income and the consequent relative change in quantity demanded, *ceteris paribus*. The income elasticity of demand coefficient not only expresses the degree of the connection between the two variables, but it also indicates whether the good in question is normal or inferior.

How Do I Calculate the Income Elasticity of Demand?

The income elasticity of demand is defined as the percentage change in the quantity demanded divided by the percentage change in income, or

$$\text{Income elasticity of demand} = \frac{\text{Percentage change in the quantity demanded}}{\text{Percentage change in income}}$$

For example, let's calculate the income elasticity of demand for lobster, where a 10 percent increase in income results in a 15 percent increase in the quantity of lobster demanded at a given price. In this case, the income elasticity of demand is +1.5 (+15 percent ÷ +10 percent = +1.5). Lobster, then, is a normal good, because an increase in income results in an increase in demand at each price. In general, if the income elasticity is positive, then the good in question is a normal good, because income and demand move in the same direction.

In comparison, let's calculate the income elasticity of demand for beans, where a 10 percent increase in income results in a 15 percent decrease in the demand for beans at

While buying used books can be fun, used books for most people probably have a negative income elasticity. So are used books normal or inferior goods to most people?

each price. In this case, the income elasticity of demand is –1.5 (–15 percent ÷ +10 percent = –1.5 percent). In this example, then, beans are an inferior good, because an increase in income results in a decrease in the purchase of beans at a given price. If the income elasticity is negative, then the good in question is an inferior good, because the change in income and the change in demand move in opposite directions.

WHAT IS THE PRICE OF ELASTICITY OF SUPPLY?

According to the law of supply, there is a positive relationship between price and quantity supplied, *ceteris paribus*. But by how much does quantity supplied change as price changes? It is often helpful to know the degree to which a change in price changes the quantity supplied. The **price elasticity of supply** measures how responsive the quantity sellers are willing to sell is to changes in the price. In other words, it measures the relative change in the quantity supplied that results from a change in price.

How Do I Calculate the Price Elasticity of Supply?

The price elasticity of supply (E_s) is defined as the percentage change in the quantity supplied divided by the percentage change in price, or

$$E_s = \frac{\text{Percentage change in the quantity supplied}}{\text{Percentage change in price}}$$

The price elasticity of supply is calculated in much the same manner as the price elasticity of demand. Consider, for example, the case in which it is determined that a 10 percent increase in the price of artichokes results in a 25 percent increase in the quantity of artichokes supplied after, say, a few harvest seasons. In this case, the price elasticity is 2.5 (+10 percent ÷ +25 percent = 2.5). This coefficient indicates that each 1 percent increase in the price of artichokes induces a 2.5 percent increase in the quantity of artichokes supplied.

What Are the Ranges of the Price Elasticity of Supply?

Economists delineate several ranges of the price elasticity of supply. As with the elasticity of demand, these ranges center around whether the elasticity coefficient is greater than or less than one. Goods with a supply elasticity that is greater than one ($E_s > 1$) are said to be relatively elastic in supply. With that, a 1 percent change in price will result in a greater than 1 percent change in quantity supplied. In our earlier example, artichokes were elastic in supply, because a 1 percent price increase resulted in a 2.5 percent increase in quantity supplied. An example of a relatively elastic supply curve is shown in Exhibit 1(a).

| EXHIBIT 1 | THE PRICE ELASTICITY OF SUPPLY |

a. Relatively Elastic Supply ($E_s > 1$)

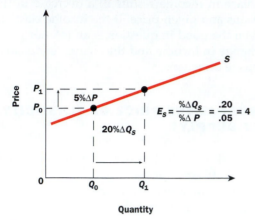

$$E_s = \frac{\%\Delta Q_S}{\%\Delta P} = \frac{.20}{.05} = 4$$

A change in price leads to a larger percentage change in quantity supplied.

b. Relatively Inelastic Supply ($E_s < 1$)

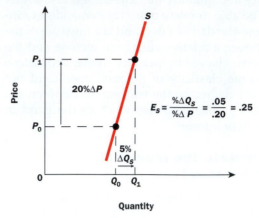

$$E_s = \frac{\%\Delta Q_S}{\%\Delta P} = \frac{.05}{.20} = .25$$

A change in price leads to a smaller percentage change in quantity supplied.

c. Perfectly Inelastic Supply ($E_s = 0$)

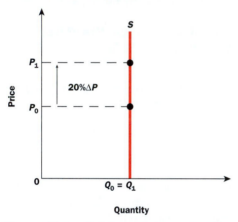

The quantity supplied does not change regardless of the change in price.

d. Perfectly Elastic Supply ($E_s = \infty$)

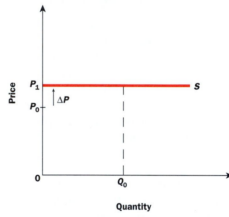

Even a small percentage change in price will change quantity supplied by an infinite amount.

Goods with a supply elasticity that is less than one ($E_s < 1$) are said to be relatively inelastic in supply. This means that a 1 percent change in the price of these goods will induce a proportionately smaller change in the quantity supplied. This situation is shown in the supply curve in Exhibit 1(b).

Finally, there are two extreme cases of price elasticity of supply: perfectly inelastic supply and perfectly elastic supply. In a condition of perfectly inelastic supply, an increase in price will not change the quantity supplied. For example, in a sports arena in the short run (that is, in a period too brief to adjust the structure) the number of seats available will be almost fixed, say 20,000 seats. Additional portable seats might be available, but for the most part, even if there is a higher price, there will only be 20,000 seats available. We say that the elasticity of supply is zero, which describes a perfectly inelastic supply curve. Famous paintings, like Van Gogh's "Starry Night," provide another example; there is only one original in existence, and therefore only one can be supplied, regardless of price. An example of this condition is shown in Exhibit 1(c).

In a condition of perfectly elastic supply, nothing will be supplied at any price up to a certain level, but at some higher price, sellers would be willing to supply whatever quantity buyers wished to buy. At the other extreme is a perfectly elastic supply curve where the elasticity equals infinity. In this case, if the price is below the market price, say, $5, the quantity supplied will fall to zero, as seen in Exhibit 1(d). But at $5, sellers will sell all that buyers wish to buy. However, the more realistic cases fall somewhere between the two extremes.

How Does Time Impact Supply Elasticities?

Time is usually critical in supply elasticities, because it is more costly for producers to bring forth and release resources in a shorter period of time. For example, the higher wheat prices may cause farmers to grow more wheat, but big changes cannot occur until the next growing season. That is, immediately after harvest season, the supply of wheat is relatively inelastic, but over a longer period that extends over the next growing period, the supply curve becomes much more elastic. Hence, supply tends to be more elastic in the long run than the short run, as shown in Exhibit 2.

EXHIBIT 2	SHORT-RUN AND LONG-RUN SUPPLY CURVES

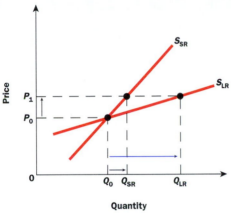

For most goods, supply is more elastic in the long run than in the short run. For example, if price increases, firms have an incentive to produce more but are constrained by the size of their plant. In the long run, they can increase their capacity and produce more.

Immediately after harvest season is over, the supply of pumpkins is inelastic.

COMBINING SUPPLY AND DEMAND ELASTICITIES: WHO PAYS THE TAX?

The relative elasticity of supply and demand determines the distribution of the tax burden for a good. As we shall see, if demand has a lower elasticity than supply in the relevant tax region, the largest portion of the tax is paid by the consumer. However, if demand is relatively more elastic than supply in the relevant tax region, the largest portion of the tax is paid by the producer.

In Exhibit 3, we see that when the 50 cent tax is imposed on a good, the supply curve shifts vertically by the amount of the tax (just as if an input price rose 50 cents). In the case where demand is relatively less elastic than supply in the relevant region, almost the whole tax is passed on to the consumer, *ceteris paribus*. For example, in Exhibit 3(a), the supply curve is relatively more elastic than the demand curve. In response to the tax, the consumer pays $1.40 per unit, 40 cents more than the consumer paid before the tax increase. The producer, however, receives 90 cents per unit, which is 10 cents less than he or she received before the tax. In Exhibit 3(b), demand is relatively more elastic than the supply in the relevant region. Here, we see that the greater burden of the same 50 cent tax falls on the producer, *ceteris paribus*. That is, the producer is now responsible for 40 cents of the tax, while the consumer only pays 10 cents. In general, then, the tax burden falls on the side of the market that is less elastic. Note that who actually pays the tax at the time of the purchase has nothing to do with who incurs the ultimate burden of the taxation—that depends on the relative elasticity.

Who do you think will bear the greatest burden of taxes imposed on these goods, consumers or producers?

EXHIBIT 3	ELASTICITY AND THE BURDEN OF TAXATION

a. Demand Is Relatively Less Elastic than Supply

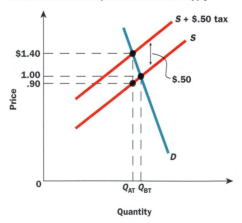

b. Demand Is Relatively More Elastic than Supply

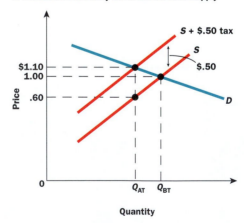

When demand is less elastic (or more inelastic) than supply, the tax burden falls primarily on consumers, as shown in Exhibit 3 (a). When demand is more elastic than supply, as shown in Exhibit 3 (b), the tax burden falls primarily on producers.

DRUGS ACROSS THE BORDER

"They are just limited by their imagination," said a U.S. official who closely monitors Mexican trafficking groups. "Money is no obstacle at all." Trafficking schemes run the gamut from the mundane to the Byzantine. In recent years, drug mafias have bought 727-style planes and built a fleet of two-man submarines to move drugs to the United States. They have secreted loads in propane tanks and containers of hazardous materials, in small cans of tuna fish and five-gallon drums of jalapeño peppers. One trafficking group fashioned a special mold that was used successfully to ship cocaine from Mexico through the United States and into Canada completely sealed inside the walls of porcelain toilets.

The groups are using satellite-linked navigation and positioning aids to coordinate airplane drops to boats waiting in the Caribbean and to trucks in the Arizona and Texas deserts. They are using small planes equipped with ordinary car radar detectors to probe radar coverage along the border, then slipping other drug-laden aircraft through the gaps before U.S. officials can react. They are racing hauls of drugs up the coast in 22-foot-long powerboats with massive engines, digging holes in the Gulf beaches of Texas and burying their loads like hidden treasure for pickup at a later date.

Among the more ambitious drug-smuggling methods in recent years was the construction of tunnels under the border at Douglas, Arizona, and Otay Mesa, California, . . . used to smuggle tons of cocaine into the United States until it was shut down following a tip from an informant.

SOURCE: © Copyright 1997, The Washington Post Company.

John Ward Anderson and William Branigin, "Border Plagued by Drug Traffickers," Post Foreign Service, November 2, 1997, Page A01.

COMMENT:

The United States spends billions of dollars a year to halt the importation of illegal drugs across the border. Although these efforts are clearly targeted at suppliers, who really pays the price for these greater enforcement efforts? The government crackdown has increased the probability of apprehension and conviction for drug smugglers. That increase in risk for suppliers increases their cost of doing business. This would shift the supply curve for smuggled drugs to the left, as seen in Exhibit 4. For most drug users—addicts, in particular—the price of drugs like cocaine and heroin lies in the highly inelastic region of the demand curve. Because the demand for drugs is inelastic in this region, the seller would be able to shift most of this cost onto the consumer (think of it like the tax shift discussed earlier). That is, enforcement efforts increase the price of illegal drugs, but only a small reduction in quantity demanded results from this price increase. Increased enforcement efforts may have unintended consequences due to the fact that buyers bear the burden of this price increase. These tighter smuggling controls may, in fact, result in higher levels of burglary, muggings, and white-collar crime, as cash-strapped buyers search for alternative ways of funding their increasingly expensive habit.

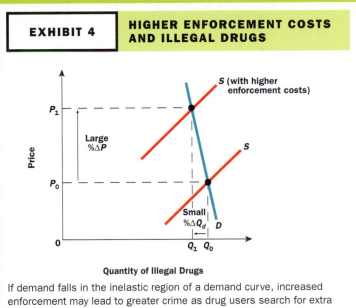

EXHIBIT 4 — **HIGHER ENFORCEMENT COSTS AND ILLEGAL DRUGS**

If demand falls in the inelastic region of a demand curve, increased enforcement may lead to greater crime as drug users search for extra cash to fund their habits.

1. The cross elasticity of demand is the percentage change in the quantity demanded of one good at a given price divided by the percentage change in price of another good.
2. If the sign on the cross elasticity is positive, the two goods are substitutes; if it is negative, the two goods are complements.
3. The income elasticity of demand is the percentage change in quantity demanded divided by the percentage change in income.

4. If the income elasticity is positive, then the good is a normal good; if it is negative, the good is an inferior good.
5. The price elasticity of supply measures the relative change in the quantity supplied that results from a change in price.

---

1. How does the cross elasticity of demand tell you whether two goods are substitutes? Complements?
2. How does the income elasticity of demand tell you whether a good is normal? Inferior?
3. What does it mean to say that the elasticity of supply for one good is greater than that for another?
4. How do the relative elasticities of supply and demand determine who bears the greater burden of a tax?
5. If the cross elasticity of demand between potato chips and popcorn was positive and very large, would popcorn makers benefit from a tax imposed on potato chips?

6. As people's incomes rise, why will they spend an increasing portion of their incomes on goods with income elasticities greater than one (CDs) and a decreasing portion of their incomes on goods with income elasticities less than one (food)?
7. If people spent three times as much on restaurant meals and four times as much on CDs as their incomes doubled, would restaurant meals or CDs have a greater income elasticity of demand?

G Application: Condoms and Elasticities

Does condom use reduce the health risks from sexual encounters? The answer seems obvious. However, it isn't as obvious as it appears. The answer depends on elasticity. What if the elasticity of demand for sexual activities is greater than one? What if it is less than one?

Sexually transmitted diseases (STDs) are among the easiest of diseases to prevent. Despite this basic fact, STDs are on the rise. Syphilis and gonorrhea are increasing in disadvantaged communities and acquired immunodeficiency syndrome (AIDS) is becoming prevalent in these areas. Herpes, genital warts (which can lead to cancer of the cervix), and chlamydia (which can make women infertile) are turning up in middle-class whites. Most efforts to control the AIDS epidemic have focused on education. Lectures, ads, and even a program in New York high schools that hands out free condoms have been offered. Despite efforts to educate people on how to prevent AIDS, many people still continue to practice unsafe sex. In a survey of California college students, they found that "less than 20 percent of the currently sexually active women and men reported using condoms 75 percent of the time or more . . ."

SOURCE: "Safer Sex," *Newsweek*, 118, 24 (December 9, 1991), pp. 52–56.

Does condom use reduce the health risks from sexual activity?

This application is not intended to offend anyone; however, scientists must objectively study pressing social issues like the rise in unwed mothers and sexually transmitted diseases (STDs). This means that scientists sometimes tread on controversial ground. Here, we do not endorse any particular view, but illustrate how we can use the tools of elasticity to shed light on an important social issue.

As we found out in Module 1, there is no such thing as a free lunch. There is also no such thing as free love, particularly when it involves sexual activity. Like every other ac-

tivity, engaging in sex involves costs. One of the most significant of those costs is the risk of contracting a serious or even fatal disease, such as AIDS. To an economist, this suggests that the amount of sexual activity demanded will be influenced by the risk of that activity.

There is a demand curve for sexual activity that, like any other demand curve, is downward sloping. People will demand more the lower the cost per unit. In the case of the demand curve for sexual activity, it is possible to measure the cost in terms of risk rather than dollars. Such a demand curve would show that if the risk per sexual encounter is reduced, the number of sexual encounters will increase, as seen in Exhibit 1.

While it is difficult to know the precise shape of the demand curve for sexual activity, such knowledge would be useful when considering the controversy over condom availability. Those who favor making condoms more readily available might argue it would make sex safer by encouraging condom use. Those who oppose a policy of readily available condoms argue that such a policy would cause an increase in sexual promiscuity by making it less costly.

Both sides in this argument make valid points. Greater availability of condoms would certainly reduce the health risk per sexual encounter. But reducing the health risk per sexual encounter will surely increase the number of such encounters. The important question is: By how much?

The answer to the "how much" question depends on the "elasticity" of the demand for sexual activity, which, in this context, is the percentage increase in the number of sexual encounters that will result from a 1 percent reduction in the risk per encounter.

If the value of the demand for sexual activity is relatively inelastic ($E_d < 1$), then increasing the availability of condoms (and thus reducing the "cost" of sexual activity) will only lead to slightly more sexually activity. For each 1 percent reduction in the risk of contracting a disease from each instance of sexual intercourse, there will be less than a 1 percent increase in the instances of intercourse. So when the demand for sexual activity is inelastic, lowering the risk of sexual activity will only increase sexual activity slightly as seen in Exhibit 1(a); and the net effect will be a reduction in the number of individuals who will contract AIDS or other sexually transmitted diseases. The slight increase in sexual activity will be more than offset by the increased safety from condom use so on net, people would get fewer cases of STDs.

But if the elasticity of demand for sexual activity is greater than one, then a policy that lowers the average per-unit risk of sexual intercourse might increase the number of cases of AIDS and other sexually transmitted diseases. That is, if the demand for sexual activity is elastic, then the reduced risk per episode from engaging in sexual intercourse will result in a larger than proportional increase in the amount of intercourse in which individuals engage as seen in Exhibit 1(b). If the lowered risk leads to far more sexual activity and more sexual partners, then it is possible that the occurrence rate of STDs might rise as the risk falls, because condoms are not perfect protection from STDs.

What is the real "risk" elasticity of the demand for sexual activity? That's an empirical question, one that could only be answered by estimating the demand curve for sexual activity with respect to risk. While we can speculate about the risk elasticity, it's unlikely that anyone will produce a convincing estimate anytime soon. And even if we knew what the elasticity was, that would not, by itself, resolve the condom controversy.

The fact remains that an important issue in this controversy concerns demand elasticity. Economic theory can't tell us what the elasticity is. But as is often the case with public policy questions, economic theory can raise considerations that might be otherwise overlooked, such as the possibility that making sexual activity safer, theoretically, could increase the incidence of STDs such as AIDS.

| EXHIBIT 1 | RISK AND SEXUAL ENCOUNTERS |

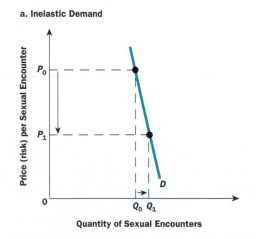

a. Inelastic Demand

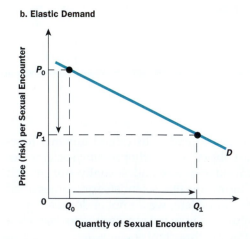

b. Elastic Demand

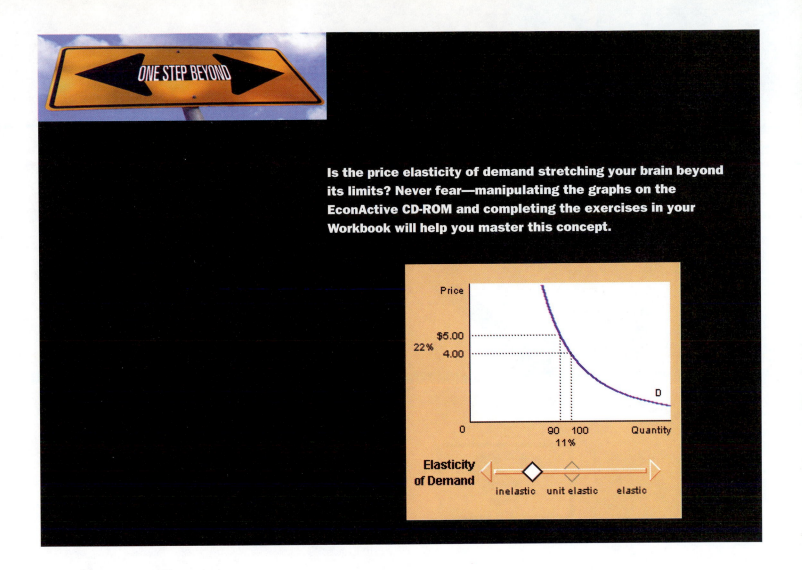

ONE STEP BEYOND

Is the price elasticity of demand stretching your brain beyond its limits? Never fear—manipulating the graphs on the EconActive CD-ROM and completing the exercises in your Workbook will help you master this concept.

PHOTO CREDITS MODULE 7

Page **180:** © 1998 Don Couch Photography; Page **181:** top, © 1998 Robert Mankoff, from Cartoonbank.com. All Rights Reserved; bottom, © PhotoDisc; Page **182:** © 1998 Don Couch Photography; Page **184:** left, a. © 1998 Don Couch Photography, b. © PhotoDisc; Page **185:** Domino's Pizza; Page **186:** © 1998 Don Couch Photography; Page **187:** © 1998 Don Couch Photography; Page **188:** © PhotoDisc; Page **190:** © 1998 Don Couch Photography; Page **194:** bottom, © Richard Pasley/Stock, Boston/PNI; Page **195:** Courtesy of Amazon.com; Page **196:** © E. Gebhardt/Mauritius/H. Armstrong Roberts; Page **200:** N/A; Page **201:** © 1998 Don Couch Photography; Page **203:** © PhotoDisc; Page **204:** © 1998 Don Couch Photography; Page **207:** N/A

Production and Costs

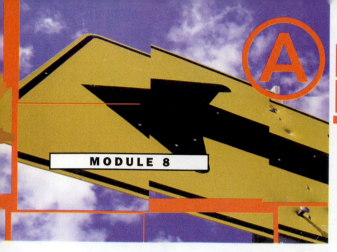

Ⓐ Profits: Total Revenues Minus Total Costs

- What are explicit and implicit costs?
- What is profit?
- What are accounting profits?
- What are economic profits?
- Do firms really maximize profits?

Economists generally assume that the ultimate goal of the firm is to maximize profits. In other words, firms try to maximize the difference between what they give up for their inputs—their total costs—and the amount they receive for their goods and services—their total revenue. Total revenue, then, is the amount that a firm receives for selling its goods or services. But what exactly makes up a firm's total costs? Total cost consists of two elements: explicit costs and implicit costs.

WHAT ARE EXPLICIT COSTS?

Most costs that we encounter are **explicit costs.** That is, they are highly visible, are readily measured by the money spent on the resources used, and are often contractural in nature. For example, the labor costs of businesses are for the most part highly explicit in nature—wages have to be paid and "on the books" or workers will not provide their services. Other examples of explicit costs include payments for raw materials, fuel, transportation, utilities, advertising, interest on borrowed capital, rent on land and capital equipment leased, and so on.

WHAT ARE IMPLICIT COSTS?

Implicit costs do not represent an outlay of money or a contractural obligation, but they are still very real. For example, whenever an investment is made, opportunities are foregone to invest elsewhere, and this lost opportunity is an implicit cost that economists include in the total costs of firms, even though no money is expended. A typical farmer or small business owner may also perform work without receiving formal wages. But the value of the alternative earnings foregone represents an implicit opportunity cost to the firm. Such implicit opportunity costs must also be included whenever resources owned by the firm—say, land or equipment—are employed without explicit payment for their use. Because these resources could have been used by other firms, what they could have earned elsewhere is an implicit cost to the firm.

As the owner of his own shop, what implicit and explicit costs might this barber incur?

WHAT ARE PROFITS?

Once we understand the concepts of revenues and costs, we can look more closely at the concept of profits. As we noted earlier, **profits** are the difference between the total revenues (TR) of a firm and its total costs (TC). For example, if a firm's total revenues are $8,000 in a given time

TUNE UP

EXPLICIT AND IMPLICIT COSTS

Q: Hugh Jenterprise owns a company whose office is located in a growing urban area. Can Hugh's company be protected from rising rents by purchasing its building outright rather than continuing to rent its office spaces?

A: Hugh's company cannot avoid implicit costs. If the company owned the building and rents increased, so would the opportunity cost of owning the building. That is, by occupying the building, Hugh's company is giving up the new higher rents it could receive from renters.

Can you protect yourself from higher rents if you own your own building?

period and its total costs in that period are $7,400, profits are $600 ($8,000 – $7,400). Profits can be negative as well as positive; a negative profit is called a loss. If over the year a firm has total revenue of $50,000 and total costs of $60,000, it has profits of –$10,000; we usually say that "the firm lost $10,000 last year."

Like revenues and costs, profits refer to flows over time. When we say that a firm earned $5 million in profits, we must clarify the time period in which the profits were earned—a week, month, year, and so on. Generally, large businesses report their profits on a quarterly basis, in three-month periods.

ARE ACCOUNTING PROFITS THE SAME AS ECONOMIC PROFITS?

A firm can make a profit in the sense that the total cash revenues that it receives exceed the total money costs that it incurs in the process of doing business. We call these **accounting profits**—profits as accountants record them based on actual cash receipts (revenues) and actual expenditures of cash (explicit costs). In other words, accounting profits do not include implicit costs.

Economists prefer an alternative way of measuring profits; they are interested in what are known as **economic profits.** In their calculation of the costs of a firm, economists include the opportunity cost of the resources that the firm uses—the implicit costs—as well as the explicit costs when calculating the total costs of the firm. Using this criteria, any positive economic profits suggest that a firm is successful, because they indicate that the firm is deriving a return on its resources beyond what they could earn if they were invested elsewhere.

Summing up, measured in terms of accounting profits, like those reported in real-world financial statements, a

Date	Item	Jrnl. Ref.	Debit	Credit	Balance
					Account No.

Accounting profits do not include implicit costs.

EXHIBIT 1   ACCOUNTING PROFITS VERSUS ECONOMIC PROFITS

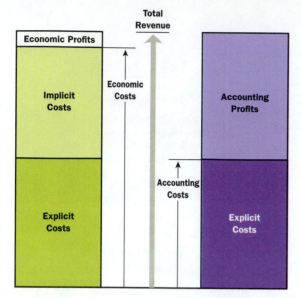

Economic profits equal total revenue minus economic costs (explicit plus implicit costs). Accounting profits equal total revenue minus accounting costs (explicit costs).

firm must earn a positive rate of return—positive profits or total revenues that exceed explicit costs. In terms of economic profits, any positive profits signal an above-normal rate of return; that is, the firm is more than covering both its explicit costs and implicit costs. The difference between accounting profits and economic profits is illustrated in Exhibit 1.

DO FIRMS STRICTLY MAXIMIZE THEIR PROFITS?

Up to this point, we have assumed that business firms seek to maximize a stream of total profits over a period of time. However, a careful examination of this assumption suggests that certain modifications are necessary.

TUNE UP

ACCOUNTING PROFITS AND ECONOMIC PROFITS

Q: Emily, an energetic 10-year-old, set up a lemonade stand in front of her house. One Saturday, she sold 50 cups of lemonade at 50 cents apiece to her friends, who were hot and thirsty from playing. These sales generated $25 in total revenues for Emily. Emily was pleased, because she knew that her total costs—lemonade mix, cups, and so on— were only $5. As she was closing up shop for the day, her neighbor, an accountant, stopped by to say hello. Emily told him about her successful day. He said, "What a great job! You made a $20 profit!" Excited, Emily rushed into the house to tell her mother, an economist, the great news. Will Emily's mother agree with the accountant's calculation of Emily's profits? If not, why not?

A: No, Emily's mother will not agree with the accountant, because he forgot to include the implicit costs when calculating Emily's profits. That is, he neglected to take into account what Emily could have been doing with her time if she had not been selling lemonade. For example, she could have been playing with her friends, cleaning her room, or perhaps helping her friends make money at their garage sale. These lost opportunities are implicit costs that should be included in the calculation of Emily's profits.

Firms do not strictly maximize their profits by the day or the week. If that were the case, they might choose not to lubricate their machinery or they might sell inferior products to their customers—not worrying about repeat business. While this would surely lower the firm's costs in the immediate period, it would be detrimental to future business. So we assume that firms try to maximize the value of a stream of future profits—that is, profits over a longer period of time.

If a company was strictly maximizing profits by the day, it might not even lubricate this machine.

1. Total cost consists of explicit costs and implicit costs.
2. Explicit costs are measured by the money spent on resources.
3. Implicit costs are the opportunity costs incurred by a firm.
4. Profits are the difference between the total revenues of a firm and its total costs.
5. Accounting profits are based on actual cash receipts and actual expenditures of cash.
6. Economic profits occur when the firm is covering both its explicit and implicit costs.
7. Firms try to maximize the value of a stream of future profits.

1. What is the difference between explicit costs and implicit costs?
2. Are both explicit costs and implicit costs relevant in making economic decisions?
3. How do we measure profits?
4. What is the difference between economic profits and accounting profits?
5. If you turn down a job offer of $45,000 per year to work for yourself, what is the opportunity cost of working for yourself?
6. What happens to the cost of growing strawberries on your own land if a housing developer offers you three times what you thought your land was worth?
7. As a farmer, you work for yourself, using your own tractor, equipment, and farm structures, and you cultivate your own land. Why might it be difficult to calculate your profits from farming?

The Production Function

- What is a production function?
- What is the law of diminishing marginal product?

WHAT IS A PRODUCTION FUNCTION?

There is a specific relationship between a firm's inputs and its output. A **production function** describes the maximum amount of a product that a firm can produce with each combination of inputs, using existing technology. Of course, there are many combinations of inputs or factors of production that could be used to produce a given level of output, but for the purposes of this discussion, we are

going to focus on two particularly important inputs—labor and capital. That is, we want to know how much output we can produce using various amounts of these two inputs.

Holding technology constant, we may assume that an increase in the combination of labor and capital will, at least up to some limit, increase output. The proportions in which various factor inputs can be combined to produce a given quantity of output are normally variable. That is, one material can be substituted for another in the production of houses or automobiles; capital equipment may be substituted for labor in the production of wheat or oriental rugs, and so on.

WHAT IS TOTAL PRODUCT?

Suppose that Moe's Bagel Shop has just one input that is variable, labor, while the size of the bagel shop is fixed in the short run. What will happen to **total product** (*TP*), the total amount of output (bagels) generated by Moe's shop as we increase the level of the variable input (labor)? Common sense suggests that total product will start at a low level and increase—perhaps rapidly at first, and then more slowly—as the amount of the variable input increases. It will continue to increase until the quantity of the variable input (labor) becomes so large in relation to the quantity of other inputs—like the size of the bagel shop—that further increases in output become more and more difficult or even impossible. In the second column of Exhibit 1, we see that as we increase the number of workers in Moe's Bagel Shop, Moe is able to produce more bagels. The addition of the first worker results in a total output of 10 bagels per hour. When Moe adds a second worker, bagel output climbs to 24, an increase of 14 bagels per hour. Total product continues to increase even with the sixth worker hired, but you can see that it has slowed considerably, with the sixth worker only increasing total product by one bagel per hour. Beyond this point, additional workers may even result in a decline in total bagel output as workers bump into each other in the small bagel shop. This outcome is

Capital equipment can be substituted for labor.

EXHIBIT 1	MOE'S PRODUCTION FUNCTION WITH ONE VARIABLE, LABOR

Variable Input Labor (Workers)	Total Output (Bagels per hour) Q	Marginal Product of Labor (Bagels per hour) $\Delta Q/\Delta V$
0	0	
		10
1	10	
		14
2	24	
		12
3	36	
		10
4	46	
		4
5	50	
		1
6	51	

evident both in the table in Exhibit 1, as well as in the total product curve shown in Exhibit 2(a).

As another example, consider your grade point average this term as the output and your average weekly input of study hours as the variable input. Depending on your intelligence, the quality of your personal and college libraries, your computer equipment the competence of your teachers, the personality of your roommate, and other factors which are fixed for this term, the curve relating your input to your output may be relatively steep or relatively flat, but its general shape will in all probability be as illustrated in Exhibit 2(a). That is, the initial hours will probably generate greater payoffs than the last few hours.

WHAT IS MARGINAL PRODUCT?

The **marginal product** (*MP*) of any single input is defined as the change in total product resulting from a small change in the amount of input used. This concept is shown in the final column in Exhibit 1, and it is illustrated by the marginal product curve, *MP*, in Exhibit 2(b). As you can see in Exhibit 2(b), the *MP* curve first rises and then falls. The initial rise in the marginal product is the result of more effective use of fixed inputs (the bagel shop) as the number of workers increases (due to specialization and division of labor). For example, a conveyor belt (fixed input) is of little value with a single worker (variable input). As additional

EXHIBIT 2	TOTAL PRODUCT AND MARGINAL PRODUCT

a. Total Product

b. Marginal Product

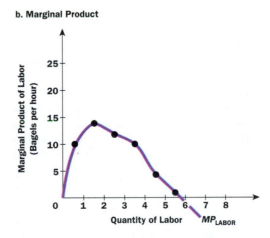

If we continue to add more workers to this one jack hammer, will we continue to get more output from each additional worker?

this discussion is that production functions conform to the same general pattern as that shown by Moe's Bagel Shop, shown in the third column of Exhibit 1 and illustrated in Exhibit 2(b).

In the third column of Exhibit 1, we see that as we increase the number of workers in Moe's Bagel Shop, Moe is able to produce more bagels. The first worker is able to produce 10 bagels per hour. When Moe adds a second worker, total bagel output climbs to 24, an increase of 14 bagels per hour. However, when Moe hires a third worker, bagel output still increases, but a third worker's marginal production (12 bagels per hour) is less than that of the second worker. In fact, the marginal product continues to drop as more and more workers are added to the bagel shop. This is the law of diminishing marginal product at work. Note that it is not because the third worker is not as "good" as the second that marginal product fell. Even with identical workers, crowding causes marginal output to eventually fall.

A firm never *knowingly* allows itself to reach the point where the marginal product becomes negative, the situation in which the use of additional variable input units actually reduces total product. In such a situation, there are so many units of the variable input—inputs with positive opportunity costs—that efficient use of the fixed input units is impaired. For example, too many workers in a store make it difficult for customers to shop; too many workers in a factory get in one another's way. In such a situation, *reducing* the number of workers might actually *increase* total product.

workers are added to an assembly line, marginal product rises. But why does marginal product then fall? The answer is the law of diminishing marginal product, which stems from the crowding of the fixed imput.

WHAT IS THE LAW OF DIMINISHING MARGINAL PRODUCT?

The **law of diminishing marginal product** runs as follows: As the amount of a variable input is increased, the amount of other (fixed) inputs being held constant, a point ultimately will be reached beyond which marginal product will decline. For example, even a genius can only learn so much in a day. The empirical validity of this proposition can be supported with endless expressions, such as, "too many cooks spoil the broth" or "you can't grow the entire world's food supply in a single flower pot." The point of

If you add more seeds to this pot, will you continue to get more flowers?

1. The production function describes the maximum amount of a product that a firm can produce with any combination of inputs, using existing technology.

2. The law of diminishing marginal product states that as the amount of a variable input is increased, the amount of other (fixed) inputs being held constant, a point ultimately will be reached beyond which marginal product will decline.

1. What is the difference between fixed and variable inputs?
2. Why do we call the long run a planning horizon?
3. Why are all inputs variable in the long run?
4. What relationship does a production function represent?
5. What is the law of diminishing marginal product? What causes it?
6. Why is entering an industry a long-run decision, while once you have entered the industry, you operate in the short run?

7. Say that your firm's total product curve includes the following data: 1 worker can produce 8 units of output; 2, 20 units; 3, 34 units; 4, 50 units; 5, 60 units; 6, 70 units; 7, 76 units; 8, 78 units; and 9, 77 units.
   a) What is the marginal product of the seventh worker?
   b) When does the law of diminishing product set in?
   c) Under these conditions, would you ever choose to employ nine workers?

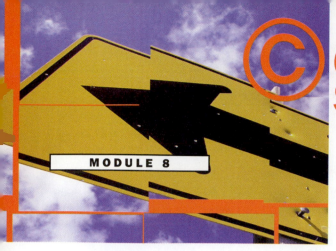

Costs in the Short Run

- What are fixed costs?
- What are variable costs?
- What are average fixed, average variable, and average total costs?
- What are marginal costs?

In the last Concept we learned about the relationship between a firm's inputs and its level of output. But that is only one part of the discussion; we must also consider how much it will cost the firm to use each of these inputs in production. In this section, we will examine the short-run costs of the firm—what they are and how they vary with the output levels that are produced. The short-run total costs of a business fall into two distinct categories: fixed costs and variable costs.

WHAT ARE FIXED COSTS?

Fixed costs are expenses that a firm has that exist at a level independent of the level of output. They are costs that exist because of past decisions committing the firm to some expenses that are not related to the level of output. What are good examples of fixed costs? The rent on buildings or equipment is usually fixed at least for some period of time; if the firm produces lots of output or little output, the rent stays the same. Other fixed costs typically include insurance, property taxes, and interest payments on debt used to finance capital equipment. While most labor costs are not fixed, occasionally some are. For example, an important managerial employee may have a five-year contract guaranteeing payment under any set of circumstances; that sort of contract may be viewed as a fixed expense. Most labor costs, however, are directly related to output levels and, thus, are not fixed.

WHAT ARE VARIABLE COSTS?

Costs that are not fixed are called **variable costs.** Variable costs change as the level of output changes. Most labor costs tend to be variable in nature. As output expands, more workers must be hired and wage payments increase. As output declines, workers are laid off and overtime payments are reduced, so the firm has some reduction in its labor costs. Besides labor, raw material costs are variable in nature, as is the cost of power used to run machinery.

Is dough at a pizza parlor a fixed or variable cost?

While we are often interested in the total amount of costs incurred by business enterprises, sometimes we find it convenient to discuss these costs on a per-unit-of-output basis. For example, if Pizza Shack Company has $1,600 in fixed costs and $2,400 in variable costs, its total costs are $4,000. If it produces 800 pizzas in the time period in question, its total costs per unit of output equal $5 ($4,000 total costs divided by 800 units of output). We call this per-unit cost the **average total cost,** or *ATC*. Likewise, we might talk about the fixed costs per unit of output, or **average fixed costs.** In the case of Pizza Shack, the average fixed costs, or *AFC*, would equal $2 ($1,600 in fixed costs divided by 800 units of output). Similarly, we can speak of per-unit variable costs, or **average variable costs,** abbreviated as *AVC*. In this example, the average variable costs would equal $3 ($2,400 divided by 800 units of output).

TUNE UP

AVERAGE TOTAL COSTS

Q: Mark Key is the only cashier at the new movie complex. Will the movie complex experience declining average total costs when there are more customers?

A: Sure. Extreme examples such as this can be found in certain service industries. For example, one airport shuttle van and one driver are required whether two passengers or ten are carried in a van; and as the number of passengers increases, those costs per passenger fall. Similarly, a movie complex must have at least one cashier on duty while it is open, regardless of the number of customers.

How many bus drivers will you likely need whether the bus is full or almost empty?

WHAT ARE MARGINAL COSTS?

To this point, eight different cost concepts have been introduced: implicit costs, explicit costs, total costs, fixed costs, variable costs, average total costs, average fixed costs, and average variable costs. All of these concepts are relevant to a discussion of firm behavior and profitability. The most important single cost concept, however, has yet to be mentioned: marginal cost. **Marginal costs** are the change in total costs associated with a change in output by one unit. Put a bit differently, marginal costs, abbreviated as *MC*, are the costs of producing one more unit of output. As such, marginal costs are really just a very useful way to view variable costs—costs that vary as output varies. Marginal costs represent the added labor, raw materials, and miscellaneous expenses that are incurred in making an additional unit of output. Marginal costs are the additional, or incremental, costs associated with the "last" unit of output produced.

To clarify why marginal costs are so important, recall that, in deciding how much of any activity to do, the rational individual compares the added benefits *(MB)* with the added costs *(MC)*. If the marginal benefits of production exceed the marginal costs of production, the firm owner will want to produce more because profit increases. If marginal costs exceed marginal benefits, the firm will want to produce less to increase profit. Hence, it is critical to understand the nature of marginal costs.

TUNE UP

MARGINAL COSTS

Q: On average, say that the cost of producing a barrel of oil to an oil producer has been $10 a barrel and the oil producer can sell that oil to a distributor for $13 a barrel. On average, this seems like a profitable business. Should the oil producer expand production given this profitability?

A: Not necessarily. Remember, it is marginal costs that are critical. The next barrel of oil might cost $20 because the well may be drying up or the company might have to drill deeper to get additional oil. And the marginal cost of the additional barrels of oil may be greater than the market price and, thus, no longer profitable.

What will be the marginal cost of the next barrel of oil? Will it be the same as the average cost?

HOW ARE THESE COSTS RELATED?

Exhibit 1 summarizes the definitions of the seven different short-run cost concepts introduced in this Module. To further clarify these concepts and to illustrate the relationships between them, we will now return to our discussion of the costs faced by Pizza Shack.

Exhibit 2 presents the costs incurred by Pizza Shack at various levels of output. Note that the fixed costs are the same at all output levels and that at very low output levels (four or fewer units in the example), fixed costs are the dominate portion of total costs. At high output levels (eight or more units in the example), fixed costs become quite small relative to variable costs. As the firm increases its output, it spreads its fixed costs across more units; as a result, average fixed costs decline continuously.

It is often easier to understand the cost concepts by examining graphs that show the levels of the various costs at different output levels. The graph in Exhibit 3 shows the first three cost concepts: fixed, variable, and total costs. A

EXHIBIT 1	A SUMMARY OF THE SHORT-RUN COST CONCEPTS

Concept	Abbreviation	Definition
Total costs	TC	The total expenses of doing business (implicit plus explicit costs).
Fixed costs	FC	Costs that are the same at all output levels (e.g., taxes, rent).
Variable costs	VC	Costs that vary with the level of output (e.g., labor, raw material expenses).
Average total costs	ATC	TC per unit of output; TC divided by output (TC/Q).
Average fixed costs	AFC	FC per unit of output; FC divided by output (FC/Q).
Average variable costs	AVC	VC per unit of output; VC divided by output (VC/Q).
Marginal costs	MC	The added cost of producing one more unit in output; change in TC associated with one more unit of output.

EXHIBIT 2	COST CALCULATIONS FOR PIZZA SHACK COMPANY

Hourly Output (Q)	Fixed Costs (FC)	Variable Costs (VC)	Total Costs (TC)	Average Fixed Costs (AFC)	Average Variable Costs (AVC)	Average Total Costs (ATC)	Marginal Costs (MC)
0	$40	$ 0	$ 40				
							$10.00
1	40	10	50	$40.00	$10.00	$50.00	
							8.00
2	40	18	58	20.00	9.00	29.00	
							7.00
3	40	25	65	13.33	8.33	21.66	
							10.00
4	40	35	75	10.00	8.75	18.75	
							12.00
5	40	47	87	8.00	9.40	17.40	
							13.00
6	40	60	100	6.67	10.00	16.67	
							15.00
7	40	75	115	5.71	10.71	16.42	
							20.00
8	40	95	135	5.00	11.88	16.88	
							25.00
9	40	120	160	4.44	13.33	17.77	
							30.00
10	40	150	190	4.00	15.00	19.00	

fixed cost curve is always a horizontal line because, by definition, fixed costs are the same at all output levels. The total cost (TC) curve is the summation of the variable cost (VC) and fixed cost (FC) curves. Because the fixed cost curve is horizontal, the total cost curve lies above the variable cost curve by a fixed (vertical) amount.

Exhibit 4 shows fixed, variable, and total costs on a per-unit, or average, basis and also graphs the associated mar-ginal costs. In this Exhibit, note how the average fixed cost (AFC) curve constantly declines, approaching but never reaching zero. Also observe how the marginal cost (MC) curve crosses the average variable cost (AVC) and average total cost (ATC) curves at their lowest points. At higher output levels, high marginal costs pull up the average variable cost and average total cost curves, while at low output levels, low marginal costs pull the curves down.

EXHIBIT 3	TOTAL AND FIXED COSTS

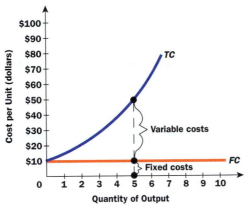

A fixed cost (FC) curve is, by definition, a horizontal line. The total cost (TC) curve is the vertical summation of the variable cost (VC) and fixed cost (FC) curves.

EXHIBIT 4	FOUR COST CONCEPTS

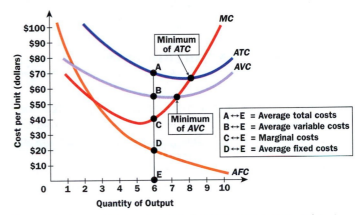

The marginal cost (MC) curve always intersects the average total cost (ATC) and average variable cost (AVC) curves at those curves' minimum points. Average fixed cost (AFC) curves always decline and approach but never reach zero. The ATC curve is the vertical summation of the AFC and AVC curves; it reaches its minimum (lowest unit cost) point at a higher output than the minimum point of the AVC curve.

CONCEPT CHECK

1. Fixed costs are expenses that stay constant regardless of the level of output.
2. Variable costs are costs that are not fixed. Variable costs change as the level of output changes.
3. Average total costs are total costs divided by output.
4. Average fixed costs are fixed costs divided by output.
5. Average variable costs are variable costs divided by output.
6. Marginal cost is the added cost of producing one more unit of output; it is the change in total cost associated with one more unit of output. It is this cost that is relevant to decisions to produce more or less.

---

1. What is the difference between fixed costs and variable costs?
2. How are average fixed cost, average variable cost, and average total cost calculated?
3. Why is marginal cost the relevant cost to consider when one is deciding whether to produce more or less of a product?
4. If the average variable cost curve was constant over some range of output, why would the average total cost be falling over that range of output?
5. If your season batting average going into a game was .300 (3 hits per 10 at bats) and you got 2 hits in 5 at bats during the game, would your season batting average rise or fall as a result?
6. As a movie exhibitor, you can choose between paying a flat fee of $5,000 to show a movie for a week or paying a fee of $2 per customer. Will your choice affect your fixed and variable costs? How?
7. If your university pays lecture note takers $20 per hour to take notes in your economics class, and then sells subscriptions for $15 per student, is the cost of the lecture note taker a fixed or variable cost of selling an additional subscription?

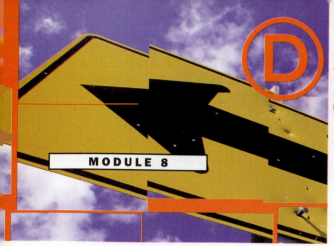

D Short-Run Costs and Diminishing Marginal Product

- What is the relationship between marginal costs and diminishing marginal product?
- Why is the average total cost curve U-shaped?
- When marginal cost is greater than average cost, what happens to the average?

WHAT IS THE RELATIONSHIP BETWEEN MARGINAL COSTS AND MARGINAL PRODUCT?

The behavior of marginal costs bears a definite relationship to marginal product (*MP*). Say, for example, that the variable input is labor. Initially, as we add more workers, the marginal product of labor tends to rise. When the marginal product of labor is rising, marginal costs are falling, because each additional worker adds more to the total product than the previous worker. Thus, the increase in total cost resulting from the production of another unit of output—the marginal cost—falls. However, when marginal product of labor is declining, marginal costs are rising because additional workers are adding less to total output. In sum, if an additional worker's marginal product is lower (higher) than that of previous workers, marginal costs increase (decrease), as seen in Exhibit 1. In area a of the two graphs in Exhibit 1, we see that as marginal product rises, marginal costs fall; in area b, we see that as marginal product falls, marginal costs rise.

WHY DOES THE AVERAGE TOTAL COST CURVE FALL AS OUTPUT EXPANDS?

The average total cost (*ATC*) curves introduced to this point have been roughly U-shaped. That is, the average cost per unit declined as output expanded, but then started increasing again as output expanded still further beyond a certain point. But why does the *ATC* curve have this particular shape?

In the short run, the firm can vary its use of labor and raw material inputs but not its capital, which takes time to acquire or construct. Capital is a fixed cost for such a short-run period. As output expands, average fixed costs per unit fall rapidly at first, as fixed costs are spread out over more units of output. This is a primary reason that the average total costs per unit decline at low levels of output.

| EXHIBIT 1 | MARGINAL PRODUCT AND MARGINAL COST |

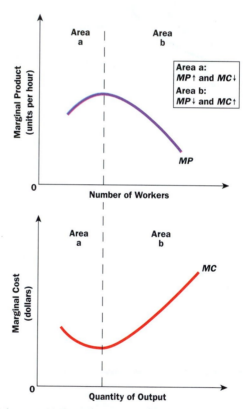

There is an inverse relationship between marginal product (*MP*) and marginal costs (*MC*). When marginal product is rising, marginal costs must fall, and when marginal product falls, marginal costs must rise.

If the next worker's marginal product is less than that of previous workers, marginal costs will rise.

WHY DOES THE AVERAGE TOTAL COST CURVE EVENTUALLY RISE AS OUTPUT GROWS LARGER?

The average total cost curve rises at high levels of output because of the law of diminishing marginal product. For example, as more and more workers are put to work on a fixed quantity of machines, the result may be crowded working conditions and perhaps increasing maintenance costs as equipment is used more intensively or older, less-efficient machinery is called upon to handle the greater output. That is, diminishing marginal product causes the marginal costs to increase, eventually pulling up average total costs and average variable costs in the process.

As more and more workers are added to the plant, diminishing marginal product eventually sets in, causing first the marginal cost curve to rise and, later, the average total cost curve and average variable cost curve to rise.

WHAT IS THE RELATIONSHIP BETWEEN MARGINAL COSTS AND THE AVERAGE TOTAL COSTS?

Certain relationships exist between marginal costs and average total costs. When average total costs are falling, marginal costs must be less than average total costs; and when average total costs are rising, marginal costs are greater than average total costs. Marginal costs are equal to average total costs at the lowest point of the *ATC* curve, as seen in Exhibit 2. This is the lowest point of the **efficient scale** because it is the output level that minimizes the firm's average total costs. In area a of Exhibit 2, marginal costs are less than average total costs, and the averages are falling. In area b of the curves, marginal costs are greater than average total costs, and the averages are rising. The same relationship holds for the marginal cost curve and the average variable cost curve.

This relationship between the marginal and the average is simply a matter of arithmetic; when a number (the marginal cost) being added into a series is smaller than the previous average of the series, the new average will be lower than the previous one. Likewise, when the marginal number is larger than the average, the average will rise. For example, if you have taken two economics exams and received a 90 percent on your first exam and 80 percent on your second exam, you have an 85 percent average. If after some serious studying, you get a 100 percent on the third exam (the marginal exam), what happens to your average? It rises to 90 percent; because the marginal is greater than the average, it "pulls" the average up. However, if the score on your third (marginal) exam is lower, a 70 percent, your average will fall to 80 percent because the marginal is below the average.

EXHIBIT 2	MARGINAL COSTS AND AVERAGE TOTAL COSTS

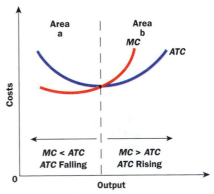

The marginal cost curve crosses the average total cost curve at its minimum point.

TUNE UP

RELATING MARGINAL AND AVERAGE TOTAL COSTS

Q: If a small horse-racing jockey decided to join your economics principles class of 25 students, what would happen to the *average* height of the class?

A: The *marginal* addition, the jockey, would presumably be smaller than the *average* person in the class, so the *average* height in the class would fall. Now, if the star 7-foot center on the basketball team joined your class, the *average* height would rise, as the newer marginal member would be presumably taller than the average person. In sum, if the margin is greater (less) than the average, the average will rise (fall).

If Shaquille O'Neal joined your small class, what would happen to the average class height?

IN THE NEWS

CALIFORNIA'S THREE STRIKES LAW

Reg Tavernetti punched out his own mother. Arthur Charles Gonzalez bit off a portion of his girlfriend's face. Herbert Harry Mahaffey raped his 14-year-old daughter. Alexander Komarenko, with $100 in his pocket, broke into a store and stole a barbecued beef sandwich and a few Lotto tickets. David Juarez stole the fetal heart monitor from his neighborhood health clinic. And Felipe Ornelas lit up his crack pipe on the street, in front of a passing patrol officer. From the pathological to the pathetic, more than 1,400 criminals have been sentenced to life in prison during the first two years of the state's "three strikes and you're out" law, setting off an ongoing debate in the criminal justice community about whom the statute is targeting.

Decreasing crime rates and the exodus of hundreds of parolees from the state provide evidence that the law well may be acting as a deterrent to crime, at least with some classes of criminals. But there is no conclusive proof of the law's deterrent effect, and some leading social scientists as well as some youth workers and criminal defense lawyers contend the law is having no impact whatsoever. . . . In the vast majority of the cases, regardless of the third strike, the law is snaring long-term habitual offenders with multiple felony convictions, the kind who prosecutor after prosecutor says is "doing life on the installment plan" anyway.

SOURCE: Andy Furillo, "Most Offenders Have Long Criminal Histories," *The Sacramento Bee*, March 31, 1996.

CONSIDER THIS:
While California's three strikes law is certainly controversial, it does have an interesting twist that is related to marginal costs. Specifically, the three strikes law has unintended consequences because of the marginal costs associated with being caught and convicted for the third criminal offense. It is the third offense, no matter what it is, violent or nonviolent, that will put the convicted two-striker away for 25 years to life. Because the marginal costs of the third crime is so high, two-strikers might take extreme actions to avoid being caught—perhaps even murdering a witness or a police officer to go undetected. The Fresno Police Department reported a 48 percent increase in assaults on police officers after the passage of the three strikes law. In addition, the number of high-speed chases has increased. There is even the possibility that prisons may become less safe, because three-strikers will not be paroled for good behavior. This puts prison staffs and fellow prisoners at higher risk. In short, we see that under the three strikes law, the marginal costs of a third conviction are much higher than for the second.

1. If marginal product is rising, marginal cost must be decreasing.
2. If marginal product is falling, marginal cost must be increasing.
3. Average total costs decline as output expands, but then increase again as output expands still further beyond a certain point.
4. When marginal costs are less than average total costs, average total costs must be falling.
5. When marginal costs are greater than average total costs, average total costs must be rising.

---

1. What is the primary reason that average total cost falls as output expands over low output ranges?
2. Why does average total cost rise at some point as output expands further?
3. When marginal cost is not equal to average total cost, why does average total cost change in the direction of marginal cost?
4. Why does the law of diminishing marginal productivity imply the law of increasing costs?
5. What is likely to happen to your marginal costs when adding output requires working beyond an eight-hour day, if workers must be paid time-and-a-half wages beyond an eight-hour day?
6. A one-day ticket to visit the Screaming Coasters theme park costs $36, but you can also get a two-consecutive-day ticket for $40. What is the average cost per day for the two-day ticket? What is the marginal cost of the second consecutive day?

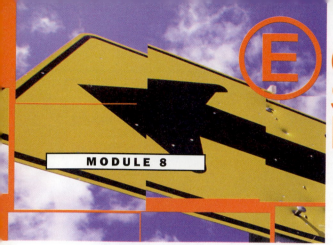

E Cost Curves: Short Run versus Long Run

- What are economies of scale?
- What are diseconomies of scale?
- What are constant returns to scale?

WHY ARE LONG-RUN COST CURVES DIFFERENT THAN SHORT-RUN COST CURVES?

Over long enough periods of time, firms can vary all of their productive inputs. Time provides an opportunity to substitute lower-cost capital, like larger plants or newer, more-sophisticated equipment, for more-expensive labor inputs. For example, if a company has to pay many workers overtime wages in order to get expanded output in the short run, it may opt to invest in new, highly automated machinery that reduces expensive labor costs in the long run. With that, the effects of diminishing returns can be reduced if not eliminated, because the law of diminishing returns assumes that one input of production, like the firm's plant size, is fixed.

The fact that the cause of diminishing returns—fixed inputs in the short run—can be altered in the long run implies that a firm's average total cost curve will tend to be flatter, more horizontal, and less U-shaped in the long run than in the short run. In Exhibit 1, we see that the long-run average total cost curve (*LRATC*) lies equal to or below the short-run average total cost curves (*SRATC*). In the long run, costs are lower, because firms have greater flexibility in changing those inputs that are fixed in the short run. For example, in Exhibit 1, if we wanted to expand output in the medium plant size from q_0 to q_1, short-run average total costs rise from C_0 to C_1, but the long-run average total costs remain constant in this region. That is, a move from point A to point B with a given plant size costs more than a move from point A to point C when the plant size can also be altered.

Even allowing for substitution among the factors of production, however, costs will not be the same per unit of output at all output levels. At extremely low output, there may be no technique available that will allow per-unit costs to be as low as at larger output where fixed costs can

Larger plants may be built in the long run.

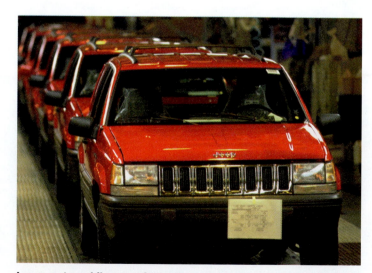

Large automobile manufacturers can produce at lower average total costs as a result of economies of scale considerations.

be spread out. Similarly, at huge outputs, it may be that the organizational and administrative costs of running a large firm start growing faster than output itself. In the long run, firms will gravitate to the output where per-unit costs are lowest, because, other things equal, lower per-unit costs mean bigger per-unit profits.

WHAT ARE ECONOMIES OF SCALE?

By examining the long-run average total cost curve for a firm, we can see three possible production patterns. In Exhibit 1, we see that extremely small firms experience **economies of scale,** falling per-unit costs as output expands. These firms, then, are functioning inefficiently from a long-run perspective. The efficient scale plant is one in which the economies of scale are exhausted and the long-run average total costs are minimized. Similarly, firms that expand beyond a certain point encounter **diseconomies of scale;** that is, they incur rising per-unit costs as their output grows. In more intermediate output ranges, firms of varying sizes can compete on a roughly equal basis as far as costs are concerned, because they all exhibit approximately **constant returns to scale.** That is, their per-unit costs remain stable as output grows.

| EXHIBIT 1 | SHORT- AND LONG-RUN AVERAGE TOTAL COSTS |

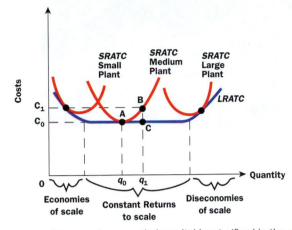

In the long run, firms can increase their capital inputs (fixed in the short run) as well as their inputs that are variable in the short run, in some cases lowering average costs per unit and overcoming the cost-increasing effects of the law of diminishing returns. The curve is thus less U-shaped than short-run average total cost curves. Still, at very low output levels, some reduction of average costs per unit are obtainable by expanding output and productive capacity; in those output ranges, economies of scale exist. At high output ranges, average costs per unit may start rising if the firm enters an output range characterized by diseconomies of scale.

CONCEPT CHECK

1. At low output levels, some firms will experience economies of scale, where their per-unit costs decrease as output increases when all inputs can be varied; these firms are operating inefficiently from a long-run perspective.
2. Firms that expand all inputs beyond a certain point will encounter diseconomies of scale, incurring rising per-unit costs as output grows in the long run.
3. In more intermediate output ranges, firms exhibit roughly constant returns to scale; in this range, their per-unit costs remain stable as output increases.

---

1. Why is the law of diminishing returns a short-run, rather than a long-run, concept?
2. What are economies of scale, diseconomies of scale, and constant returns to scale?
3. How might cooking for a family dinner be subject to falling average total cost in the short run as the size of the family grows?
4. How might a university cafeteria cooking for 400 students rather than 4 be subject to economies of scale in the long run?

(F) APPLICATION: Cineplexes and Economies of Scale

Why are cineplexes replacing single-screen theaters? Are there economies of scale in producing this service? If so, how do you think a firm can cut its costs per unit because of its size?

COMPANIES TO FORM WORLD'S LARGEST MOVIE-THEATER FIRM
NEW LOEWS CINEPLEX ENTERTAINMENT WOULD OWN MORE THAN 460 MULTIPLEXES

PETER ALAN HARPER

NEW YORK—Sony Corp. of America and Cineplex Odeon announced Tuesday they are merging their theater businesses to form the world's largest movie theater company with more than 2,600 screens in North America. The combined company would be named Loews Cineplex Entertainment and would have more than 460 theater complexes. The merger involves Cineplex Odeon and the Loews Theatres Exhibition Group, which consists of Sony/Loews Theatres and its joint ventures with Star Theatres and Magic Johnson Theatres.

SOURCE: Peter Alan Harper, *Corpus Christi Caller-Times,* October 1, 1997.

The reason we have seen the multiplex movement, and mergers for that matter, is that firms believe that, through these efforts, they can consolidate their costs and gain greater economies of scale. That is, by having several screens in one complex, the company can cut down on advertising and employee costs as well as rent. For example, it would be less expensive to have eight screens in one building with one concession area than eight separate theaters, each with one screen and a concession area. This situation is illustrated in Exhibit 1.

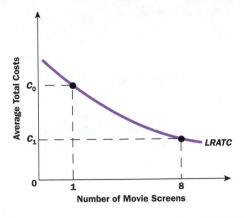

| EXHIBIT 1 | MULTIPLEXES AND ECONOMIES OF SCALE |

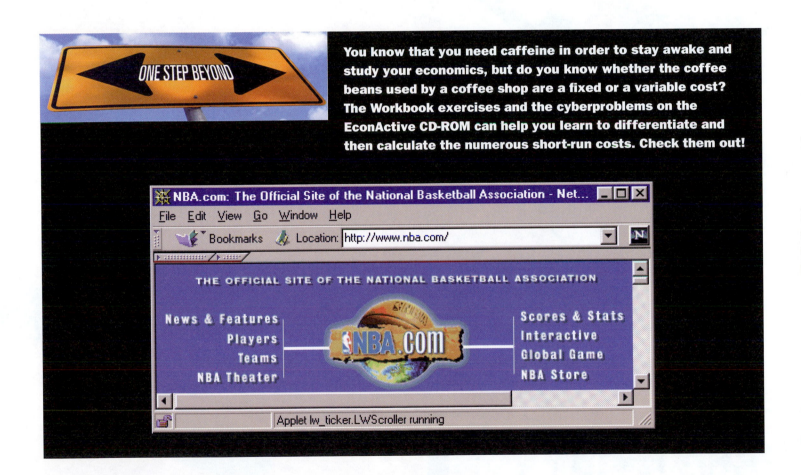

ONE STEP BEYOND

You know that you need caffeine in order to stay awake and study your economics, but do you know whether the coffee beans used by a coffee shop are a fixed or a variable cost? The Workbook exercises and the cyberproblems on the EconActive CD-ROM can help you learn to differentiate and then calculate the numerous short-run costs. Check them out!

PHOTO CREDITS MODULE 8

Page **212:** © PhotoDisc; Page **213:** © T/Maker Company; Page **215:** © Charles Feil/Stock Boston/PNI; Page **216:** © 1998 Don Couch Photography; Page **218:** top, © Photo-Disc, bottom, © Robert Sexton; Page **220:** © 1998 Don Couch Photography; Page **221:** top, © 1998 Don Couch Photography, bottom, © Bill Ross/Westlight Photography; Page **225:** bottom, © Tomas Muscionico/Contact Press Images/PNI, top, © 1998 Don Couch Photography; Page **226:** © Brian Spurlock/Spurlock Photography; Page **228:** left, © Lynn Johnson/Black Star/PNI, right, © Bob Sacha/Aurora/PNI; Page **230:** © 1998 Don Couch Photography

Perfect Competition

A. A Perfectly Competitive Market
What are the characteristics of perfect competition?

B. An Individual Seller's Demand Curve
Why can't an individual seller charge more than the market price?

C. Profit Maximization
What is the profit-maximizing output level for a perfectly competitive firm?

D. Short-Run Profits and Losses
How can you determine if a perfectly competitive firm is generating a short-run profit or loss?

E. Long-Run Equilibrium
What is the long-run response to economic profits in perfect competition?

F. Long-Run Industry Supply
What are constant- and increasing-cost industries?

G. Application: Cybergambling
Will cybergambling cut into market profits?

A Perfectly Competitive Market

■ What is a price taker?
■ What are barriers to entry?

WHAT IS PERFECT COMPETITION?

The determination of prices and outputs of goods and services is affected by the type of market in which they are bought and sold. For example, the price and output will obviously be different if the entire supply is controlled by one firm, such as DeBeers' control of diamonds, than if it is provided by a large number of small sellers, like roadside fruit stands.

This Module examines **perfect competition,** a market structure characterized by (1) many buyers and sellers, (2) a homogenous product and (3) easy market entry and exit. Next, we will examine these characteristics in greater detail.

WHAT ARE THE CHARACTERISTICS OF A PERFECTLY COMPETITIVE MARKET?

Many Buyers and Many Sellers

Perfect competition requires the presence of many buyers and sellers. Because there are so many buyers and sellers, they each regard price as something over which they have little control. For all practical purposes, they simply ignore any influence their actions might have on price. For example, because there are so many buyers, no single buyer of apples can appreciably influence the market price because each buyer purchases only a small portion of the total amount traded. Likewise, because there are so many sellers, no single apple seller is large enough to appreciably influence the market price for apples, because he sells only a small portion of the total amount traded. Furthermore, each apple seller can sell all he wants at the going market price. He wouldn't charge less because he can sell all he wants at the going market price. He would not be able to charge more, because his buyers could buy the same quality apples from others willing to sell at the going market price.

This is why perfectly competitive firms are called **price takers.** That is, they must take the price given by the mar-
ket, because their influence on price is insignificant. If the price of apples in the apple market is $2 a pound, then individual apple farmers will receive $2 per pound for their apples. We will see how this works in more detail in Concept B.

Homogeneous Product

Firms in perfect competition sell a **homogeneous** or **standardized product.** For example, in the wheat market, it is not possible to determine any significant and consistent qualitative differences in the wheat produced by different farmers. Wheat produced by Farmer Jones looks, feels, smells, and tastes like that produced by Farmer Smith. In short, a bushel of wheat is a bushel of wheat.

Can the owner charge a noticeably higher price for the same quality of fruit and stay in business?

Why is wheat considered a homogeneous good?

Easy Entry and Exit

Product markets characterized by perfect competition have no significant **barriers to entry or exit.** This means that it is fairly easy for entrepreneurs to become suppliers of the product or, if they are already producers, to stop supplying the product. "Fairly easy" does not mean that any person on the street can instantly enter the business, but rather that the financial, legal, educational, and other barriers to entering the business are modest, so that large numbers of people can overcome the barriers and enter the

business if they so desire in any given time period. For example, opening up your own fruit stand would be far easier than starting up your own automobile or aircraft company. As a result of this easy market entry and exit, perfectly competitive markets generally consist of a large number of small suppliers.

One barrier to effective entry into a business activity is ignorance. People will not enter a business activity if they have insufficient information about the potential rate of return on invested capital. If the actual rate of return on invested capital using accounting profits is 15 percent, but those outside the industry believe that the rate of return is less than 10 percent, resources will not flow into the industry to the same extent as they would if people were correctly informed. Thus, information costs have to be low (strictly speaking, zero) for competition to be truly "perfect" in nature.

A perfectly competitive market is approximated most closely in highly organized markets for securities and agricultural commodities, such as the New York Stock Exchange or the Chicago Board of Trade. Wheat, corn, soybeans, cotton, and many other agricultural products are sold in perfectly competitive markets.

To summarize, in a perfectly competitive market, market prices are treated as known and given to the many buyers and many sellers, who are assumed to be perfectly

TUNE UP

THE PERFECTLY COMPETITIVE MARKET

Q: Why are stock and securities markets and agricultural markets good examples of a perfectly competitive market structure?

A: In these markets, a large number of investors (buyers and sellers) trade with relatively low information costs, because the goods in question are standardized (e.g., grade A winter wheat or McDonald's shares) and information about stock prices and companies' profit and loss statements are readily available. This information is quickly incorporated into the price of the stock, rendering old information (often only as old as a few minutes) useless to those who want to "beat the market." For example, if a news story breaks on an infestation of the cotton crop, the price of cotton futures will rise immediately, and only those that speculated before the news or had inside information will make profits. Thus, prices move rapidly in response to news, and it is difficult for any individual to make unusually large profits when information about products and prices flows so freely. As evidence of this, even the most successful analysts on Wall Street have only a slightly better than average record over the long haul.

Perfect competition is also approximated in some markets other than product markets. For example, the market for some unskilled forms of labor, such as farm workers, may be close to perfectly competitive. For true perfect competition to exist, however, there must be lots of both buyers and sellers of the good or service, no one of which is large enough to influence the market demand or supply curves appreciably.

At the Chicago Board of Trade, prices get set by thousands of buyers interacting with sellers—supply and demand.

informed about the tastes and technology, and the output of each seller is said to be identical or homogeneous. Moreover, in perfectly competitive markets, because of the ease of entry and exit, buyers and sellers are assumed to be perfectly mobile, assuring they can act on market information when it is in their interests to do so. While these assumptions may seem a bit unrealistic, it is important to note that studying the model of perfect competition is useful because there are many markets that resemble perfect competition.

CONCEPT CHECK

1. Firms in perfectly competitive markets sell virtually identical products. They are called homogeneous goods.
2. Because there are so many buyers and so many sellers, neither have any control over price in perfect competition. They must take the going price and are called price takers.
3. Perfectly competitive markets have no significant barriers to entry. That is, the barriers are significantly modest so that many sellers can enter or exit the industry.

---

1. Why do perfectly competitive markets involve homogeneous goods?
2. Why does the absence of significant barriers to entry tend to result in a large number of suppliers?
3. Why does the fact that perfectly competitive firms are "small" relative to the market make them price takers?
4. Why is the market for used furniture unlikely to be perfectly competitive?

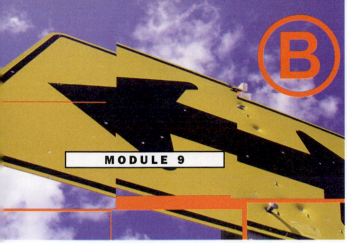

(B) An Individual Seller's Demand Curve

- Why won't an individual seller raise or lower his price?
- Can an individual seller sell all she wants at the market price?
- Will the position of an individual seller's demand curve change when market price changes?

WHAT DOES AN INDIVIDUAL SELLER'S DEMAND CURVE LOOK LIKE?

As we discussed in Concept A, perfectly competitive firms are price takers; that is, they must sell at the market-determined price. An individual wheat farmer knows that he cannot dispose of his wheat at any figure higher than the current market price; if he attempts to charge a higher price, potential buyers would simply make their purchases from other wheat farmers. And he certainly would not knowingly charge a lower price, because he could sell all he wants at the market price.

Likewise, in a perfectly competitive market, an individual seller can change his output and it will not alter the market price. This is possible because of the large number of sellers that are selling identical (homogeneous) products. Each producer provides such a small fraction of the total supply that a change in the amount he or she offers does not have a noticeable effect on market price. In a perfectly competitive market, then, an individual firm can sell as much as it wishes to place on the market at the prevailing price. In other words, the demand, as seen by the seller, is perfectly elastic. For example, the wheat farmer assumes that he can dispose of his entire crop at the market price, for he knows that any change he makes in the amount he offers for sale will have no appreciable effect on the market price.

With these two characteristics in mind, it is easy to construct the demand curve for an individual seller in a perfectly competitive market. Remember, he won't charge more than the market price because no one will buy it, and he won't charge less because he can sell all he wants at the market price. Thus, the farmer's demand curve appears to be horizontal over the entire range of output that he or she could possibly produce. If the prevailing market price of the product is $5, the farmer's demand curve will be represented graphically by a horizontal line at the market price of $5, as shown in Exhibit 1(a).

Does the individual lettuce producer take the market-determined price for lettuce?

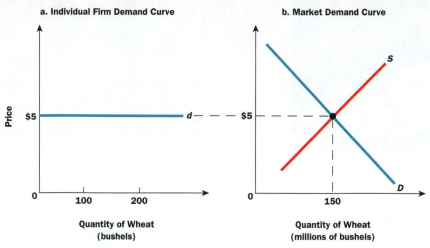

a. Individual Firm Demand Curve

b. Market Demand Curve

At the market price for wheat, $5, the individual farmer can sell all the wheat he wishes. Because each producer provides only a small fraction of industry output, any additional output will have an insignificant impact on market price. The firm's demand curve is, therefore, assumed to be perfectly elastic at the market price.

TUNE UP

CHARACTERISTICS OF A PERFECTLY COMPETITIVE MARKET

Q: Artie Choke wants to sell his bountiful artichoke crop. Despite the fact that his fellow artichoke growers are selling their crops for $1 per artichoke, Artie insists that his artichokes are superior (but they aren't), so he marks them for sale at $2 per artichoke. What is the likely outcome of Artie's pricing strategy? Explain your answer using the characteristics of a perfectly competitive market, including a graph of the individual seller's demand curve for this artichoke market.

A: Advertising does little good in this market, because we assume that all products are homogeneous and that the buyers and sellers know this. If Artie's artichokes are the same as others, he will lose all of his customers by trying to sell his artichokes at $2. As seen in Exhibit 2, at $2 no one will demand any of Artie's artichokes, because everyone can buy the same quality artichokes at the market price, $1.

| EXHIBIT 2 |

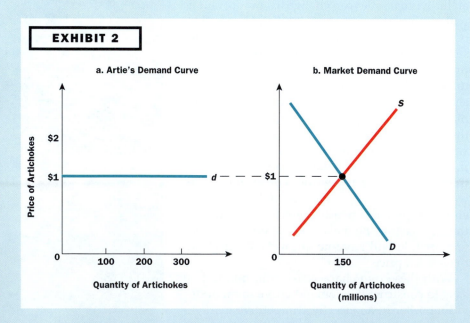

a. Artie's Demand Curve

b. Market Demand Curve

HOW DOES A CHANGE IN MARKET PRICE IMPACT THE FIRM'S DEMAND CURVE?

To say that producers under perfect competition regard price as a given is not to say that price is constant. The *position* of the firm's demand curve varies with every change in the market price, as seen in Exhibit 3. We see that when the market price increases (Exhibit 3(a)), the price-taking firm will receive a higher price for all of its output. When the market price decreases, as shown in Exhibit 3(b), the price-taking firm will receive a lower price for all of its output.

In effect, sellers are provided with current information about market demand and supply conditions as a result of price changes. It is an essential aspect of the perfectly competitive model that sellers respond to the signals provided by such price movements. That is to say, sellers must alter their behavior over time in the light of actual experience, revising their production decisions to reflect changes in market price. In this respect, the perfectly competitive model is very straightforward; unlike other models of firm behavior, it does not assume any knowledge on the part of individual buyers and sellers about market demand and supply—they only have to know the price of the good they sell.

EXHIBIT 3	MARKET PRICES AND THE POSITION OF A FIRM'S DEMAND CURVE

a. Impact of an Increase in Market Price

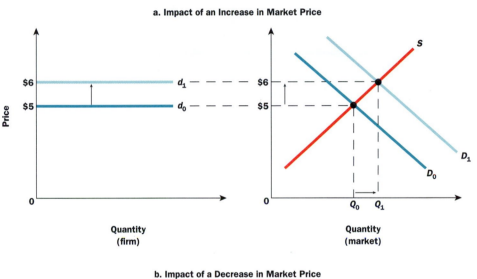

b. Impact of a Decrease in Market Price

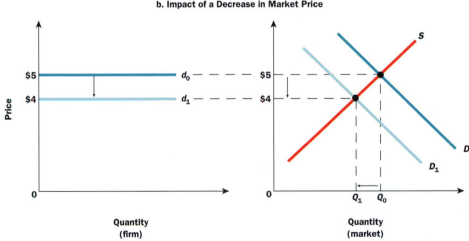

The position of the firm's demand curve will vary with every change in the market price.

CONCEPT CHECK

1. An individual seller won't sell at a higher price than the going price because buyers can purchase the same good from someone else at the going price.
2. Individual sellers won't sell for less than the going price because they are so small relative to the market they can sell all they want at the going price.

3. The position of the individual firm's demand curve varies directly with the market price.

---

1. Why would a perfectly competitive firm not try to raise or lower its price?
2. Why can we represent the demand curve of a perfectly competitive firm as perfectly elastic (horizontal) at the market price?

3. How does an individual perfectly competitive firm's demand curve change when the market price changes?
4. If the marginal costs facing every producer of a product shifted up, would the position of the perfectly competitive firm's demand curve be likely to change as a result?

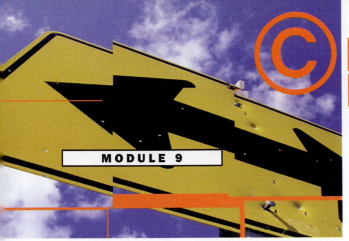

Profit Maximization

- What is total revenue?
- What is average revenue?
- What is marginal revenue?
- Why does the firm maximize profits where marginal revenue equals marginal costs?

REVENUES IN A PERFECTLY COMPETITIVE MARKET

The objective of the firm is to maximize profits. To maximize profits the firm wants to produce the amount that maximizes the difference between its total revenues and total costs. In this Concept, we will examine the different ways to look at revenue in a perfectly competitive market: total revenue, average revenue, and marginal revenue.

WHAT IS TOTAL REVENUE?

Total revenue (TR) is the revenue that the firm receives from the sale of its products. Total revenue from a product equals the price of the good (P) times the quantity (q) of units sold ($TR = P \times q$). For example, if a farmer sells 10 bushels of wheat a day for $5 a bushel, his total revenue is $50 ($5 × 10 bushels). (Note: We will use the small letter q to denote the single firm's output and reserve the large Q for the output of the entire market. For example, q would be used to represent the output of one lettuce grower, while Q would be used to represent the output of all lettuce growers in the lettuce market.)

WHAT ARE AVERAGE REVENUE AND MARGINAL REVENUE?

Average revenue (AR) equals total revenue divided by the number of units sold of the product (TR/q, or $(P \times q)/q$). For example, if the farmer sells 10 bushels at $5 a bushel, total revenue is $50 and average revenue is $5 ($50/10 bushels = $5 per bushel). So, *in perfect competition, average revenue is equal to price of the good.*

Marginal revenue (MR) is the additional revenue derived from the production of one more unit of the good. In other words, marginal revenue represents the increase in total revenue that results from the sale of one more unit. In a perfectly competitive market, because additional units of output can be sold without reducing the price of the product, marginal revenue is constant at all outputs and equal to average revenue. For example, if the price of wheat per bushel is $5, the marginal revenue is $5. Because total revenue is equal to price multiplied by quantity ($TR = P \times q$), as we add one additional unit of output, total revenue will always increase by the amount of the product price, $5. Marginal revenue facing a perfectly competitive firm is equal to the price of the good.

| EXHIBIT 1 | REVENUES FOR A PERFECTLY COMPETITIVE FIRM |

Quantity (q)	Price (P)	Total Revenue (TR = P × q)	Average Revenue (AR = TR/q)	Marginal Revenue (MR = ΔTR/Δq)
1	$5	$ 5	$5	
				$5
2	5	10	$5	
				$5
3	5	15	$5	
				$5
4	5	20	$5	
				$5
5	5	25	$5	

In perfect competition, then, we know that marginal revenue, average revenue, and price are all equal:

$$P = MR = AR$$

These relationships are clearly illustrated in the calculations presented in Exhibit 1.

HOW DO FIRMS MAXIMIZE PROFITS?

Now that we have discussed both the firm's costs curves (Module 8) and the firm's revenues, we are ready to see how a firm maximizes its profits. A firm's profits equal its total revenues minus its total costs. But at what output level will a firm produce and sell in order to maximize profits? There are two methods for identifying this output, the marginal approach and the total cost–total revenue approach. In all types of market environments, firms will maximize profits at that output that maximizes the difference between total revenue and total costs, which is at the same output level where marginal revenue equals marginal costs.

WHAT IS THE MARGINAL APPROACH?

The importance of equating marginal revenue and marginal costs is seen in the graph of Farmer John's wheat production shown in Exhibit 2. As John expands output beyond zero bushels of wheat up to q^*, the marginal revenue derived from the expanded output exceeds the marginal cost of that output, so the expansion of output creates positive profits. This profit is shown as the left-most shaded section in Exhibit 2. As long as marginal revenues exceed marginal costs, profits continue to grow. At output q^*, marginal costs equal marginal revenues. Further expansion of output beyond q^* will decrease profits because the marginal costs of production will then exceed marginal revenues. Only at output q^*, where marginal revenues equal marginal costs, are profits maximized. Thus, following the marginal approach, John's profit-maximizing position is four bushels of wheat.

We can also use the marginal approach to find Farmer John's profit-maximizing position from the data in Exhibit 3. In the table in Exhibit 3, columns 5 and 6 show the marginal revenue and marginal costs, respectively. We see that output levels of one and two bushels produce outputs that have marginal revenues that exceed marginal costs—John certainly wants to produce those units and more. That is, as long as marginal revenue exceeds marginal costs, producing and selling those units add more to revenues than to costs; in other words, they add to profits. However, once he expands production beyond four units of output, John's marginal costs are greater than his marginal revenues, and as a result, his profits begin to fall. Clearly, Farmer John should not produce beyond four bushels of wheat.

EXHIBIT 2	FIRM OUTPUT IN PERFECT COMPETITION

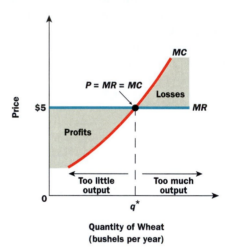

At any output below q^* the marginal revenue (MR) from expanding output exceeds the added costs (MC) of that output, so Farmer John expands output. Beyond q^*, marginal costs exceed marginal revenue, so output expansion is unprofitable. Profit is maximized at q^*. Because the price of the good, $5, is the same as marginal revenue, Farmer John simply finds that output where the marginal costs of production equal the price of the good.

WHAT IS THE TOTAL COST–TOTAL REVENUE APPROACH?

Let us take another look at profit maximization using the table in Exhibit 3. Comparing columns 2 and 3, the calculations of total revenues and total costs, respectively, we see that Farmer John maximizes his profits at output levels of three or four bushels, where he will make profits of $4. In column 4, profits, you can see that there is no higher level of profit at any of the other output levels.

| EXHIBIT 3 | COST AND REVENUE CALCULATIONS FOR A PERFECTLY COMPETITIVE FIRM |

Quantity (1)	Total Revenue (2)	Total Cost (3)	Profit (TR − TC) (4)	Marginal Revenue ($\Delta TR/\Delta q$) (5)	Marginal Cost ($\Delta TC/\Delta q$) (6)
0	$ 0	$ 2	$–2		
				$5	$2
1	5	4	1		
				5	3
2	10	7	3		
				5	4
3	15	11	4		
				5	5
4	20	16	4		
				5	6
5	25	22	3		

CONCEPT CHECK

1. Total revenue is price times the quantity sold ($TR = P \times q$).
2. Average revenue is total revenue divided by the quantity sold ($AR = TR/q = P$).
3. Marginal revenue is the change in total revenue from the sale of an additional unit of output ($MR = \Delta TR/\Delta q$).

4. Firms maximize total profits at the profit-maximizing output, q^*, where $MR = MC$. At outputs less than q^* ($MR > MC$), the firm can increase profit by expanding output. At outputs greater than q^* ($MR < MC$), the firm can reduce output and increase profits.

1. How is total revenue calculated?
2. How is average revenue derived from total revenue?
3. How is marginal revenue derived from total revenue?
4. Why is marginal revenue equal to price for a perfectly competitive firm?

5. Why must a perfectly competitive firm's marginal cost curve be rising at its profit-maximizing level of output?

D Short-Run Profits and Losses

- How do we determine if a firm is generating an economic profit?
- How do we determine if there is a loss?
- How do we determine if a firm is making zero economic profits?
- Why doesn't a firm produce when price is below average variable costs?

In the previous Concept, we discussed two methods of determining the profit-maximizing output level for a perfectly competitive firm. However, producing at this profit-maximizing level does not mean that a firm is actually generating profits; it merely means that a firm is maximizing its profit opportunity at a given price level. How do we know if a firm is actually making profits, is generating losses, or is merely breaking even?

THE THREE-STEP METHOD

What Is the Three-Step Method?

Determining whether a firm is generating economic profits, economic losses, or zero economic profits at the profit-maximizing level of output, q^* can be done in three easy steps. First, we will walk through these steps, and then we will apply the method to four different situations for a hypothetical firm in the short run.

1. Find where marginal revenues equal marginal costs and proceed straight down to the horizontal quantity axis to find q^*, the profit-maximizing output level.

2. At q^*, go straight up to the demand curve to find the market price, P^*. Once you have identified P^* and q^*, you can find total revenue at the profit-maximizing output level, because $TR = P \times q$.

3. The last step is to find total costs. Again, go straight up from q^* to the average total cost *(ATC)* curve; this will give you the average total cost *per unit*. If we multiply average total costs by the output level, we can find the total costs ($TC = ATC \times q$).

If total revenue is greater than total costs at q^*, the firm is generating economic profits. And if total revenue is less than total costs at q^*, the firm is generating economic losses. Remember, the cost curves include implicit and explicit costs—that is, we are covering the opportunity costs of our resources. So even if there are zero economic profits, no tears should be shed, because the firm is covering both its implicit costs and explicit costs. Because firms are also

covering their implicit costs, or what they could be producing with these resources in another endeavor, economists sometimes call this zero economic profit a normal rate of return. That is, the owners are doing as well as they could elsewhere, in that they are getting the normal rate of return on the capital they invested in the firm.

The Three-Step Method in Action

In Exhibit 1, there are three different short-run equilibrium positions; in each case, the firm is producing at a level where marginal revenue equals marginal costs. Each of these alternatives shows that the firm is maximizing profits or minimizing losses in the short run.

Assume that there are three alternative prices—$6, $5, and $4—for a firm with given costs. In Exhibit 1(a), the firm receives $6 per unit at an equilibrium level of output ($MR = MC$) of 120 units. Total revenue ($P \times q^*$) is $6 × 120, or $720. The average total costs at 120 units of output is $5, and the total cost ($ATC \times q^*$) is $600. Following the three-step method, we can calculate that this firm is earning short-run economic profits of $120.

In Exhibit 1(b), the market price has fallen to $4 per unit. At the equilibrium level of output, the firm is now producing 80 units of output at an average total cost of $5 per unit. The total revenue is now $320 ($4 × 80), and the total costs are $400 ($5 × 80). We can see that the firm is now incurring economic losses of $80.

In Exhibit 1(c), the firm is earning zero economic profits, or a normal rate of return. The market price is $4.90, and the average total cost is $4.90 per unit for 100 units of output. In this case, economic profits are zero, because total revenue, $490, minus total cost, $490, is equal to zero. This firm is just covering all its costs, both implicit and explicit.

EVALUATING ECONOMIC LOSSES IN THE SHORT RUN

A firm generating an economic loss faces a tough choice: Should it continue to produce or shut-down its operation? To make this decision, we need to add another variable to

EXHIBIT 1   SHORT-RUN PROFITS, LOSSES, AND BREAKING EVEN

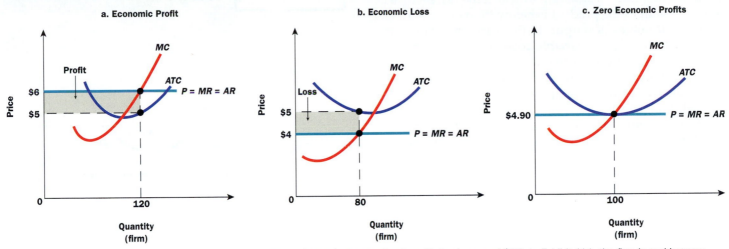

In Exhibit 1(a), the firm is earning short-run economic profits of $120; in (b), the firm is suffering losses of $80. In Exhibit 1(c), the firm is making zero economic profits, with the price just equal to the average total cost in the short run.

our discussion of economic profits and losses: average variable costs. Variable costs are those costs that vary with output, such as wages, raw material, transportation, and electricity. If a firm cannot generate enough revenues to cover its variable costs, then it will have larger losses if it operates than if it shuts down (losses in that case = fixed costs). That is, the average, or per-unit, revenue must cover the average variable costs generated by that production or firms are better off jumping to zero production. As we noted earlier, in perfect competition, average revenue equals price. Thus, a firm will not produce at all unless the price or average revenue it can obtain is equal to or greater than its average variable costs.

Operating at a Loss

At price levels greater than or equal to average variable costs, a firm may continue to operate in the short run even if average total costs—variable and fixed costs—are not completely covered. That is, the firm may continue to operate even though it is experiencing an economic loss. Why? Because fixed costs continue whether the firm produces or not, it is better to earn enough to cover a portion of these costs rather than earn nothing at all.

In Exhibit 2, price is less than average total costs but more than average variable costs. In this case, the firm produces in the short run, but at a loss. To shut down would make this firm worse off, because it can cover at least *some* of its fixed costs with the excess of revenue over its variable costs.

EXHIBIT 2   SHORT-RUN LOSSES: PRICE ABOVE *AVC* BUT BELOW *ATC*

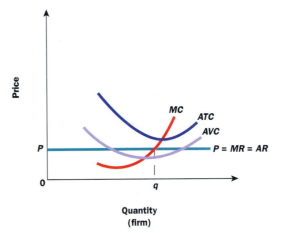

In this case, the firm operates in the short run but incurs a loss because average total cost exceeds price, or average revenue. Nevertheless, price is greater than average variable costs, and revenues cover variable costs and partially defray fixed costs. This firm will still leave the industry in the long run unless prices are expected to rise in the near future.

The Decision to Shut Down

Exhibit 3 illustrates a situation in which the price a firm is able to obtain for its product is below its average variable costs at all ranges of output. In this case, the firm is unable to cover even its variable costs in the short run, so since it is losing even more than the fixed costs it would lose if it shut down, it is most logical for the firm to cease operations. A perfectly competitive firm owner must ask himself whether he can cover all his variable costs. That is, if the revenue from operating at low demand periods does not even cover the variable costs, the owner will shut down.

| EXHIBIT 3 | SHORT-RUN LOSSES: PRICE BELOW *AVC* |

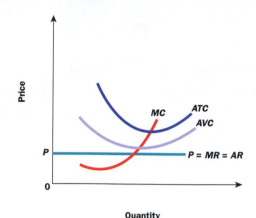

Because its average variable costs exceed price at all levels of output, this firm would cut its losses by discontinuing production.

TUNE UP

EVALUATING SHORT-RUN ECONOMIC LOSSES

Q: Rose Budd is one of many florists in a medium-sized urban area. That is, we assume that she works in a market similar to a perfectly competitive market and operates, of course, in the short run. Rose's cost and revenue information is provided in the table below. Based on this information, what should Rose do in the short run, and why?

EXHIBIT 4	ROSE'S DAILY REVENUE AND COST SCHEDULE

Total Revenue	$2,000
Total Costs	2,500
Variable Costs	1,500
Fixed Costs	1,000

If the florist cannot cover her fixed costs, will she continue to operate?

A: Fixed costs are unavoidable unless the firm goes out of business. Rose really has two decisions in the short run—either to operate or to shut down temporarily. Say Rose makes $2,000 a day in total revenues but her daily costs (fixed and variable) are $2,500. She has to pay her workers, pay for the fresh flowers, and pay for the fuel used by the drivers in picking up and delivering the flowers. She must also pay the electricity bill to heat her shop and keep her refrigerators going to protect her fresh flowers. That is, every day, poor Rose is losing $500, but she still might want to operate the shop despite the loss. Why? Rose's average variable costs (flowers, transportation fuel, daily wage earners, and so on) cost her $1,500 a day, and her fixed costs (insurance, property taxes, rent for the building, and refrigerator payments) are $1,000 a day. Now, if Rose does not operate, she will save on her average variable costs—$1,500 a day—but she will be out the $2,000 a day she makes in revenues from selling her flowers. So every day she operates, she is better off than if she had not operated at all. That is, if the firm can cover average variable costs, it is better off operating than not operating. Suppose Rose's *AVC* was $2,100 a day. Then Rose should not operate, because every day she does, she is $100 worse off than if she shut down altogether.

Why does Rose even bother operating if she is making a loss? Perhaps the economy is in a recession and the demand for flowers is temporarily down, but with Valentine's Day right around the corner, Rose thinks things will pick up. If Rose is right and demand picks up, her prices and marginal revenue will rise and she may then have a chance to make short-run economic profits.

1. The profit-maximizing output level is found by equating $MR = MC$ at $q*$. If at that output the firm's price is greater than its average total costs, it is making an economic profit.
2. If at the profit-maximizing output level, $q*$, the price is less than the average total cost, the firm is incurring an economic loss.
3. If the profit-maximizing output level, $q*$, the price is equal to average total cost, the firm is making zero economic profits; that is, the firm is covering both its implicit and explicit costs.
4. If the price falls below average variable cost, the firm is better off shutting down than operating in the short run.

---

1. How is the profit-maximizing output quantity determined?
2. How do we determine total revenue and total cost for the profit-maximizing output quantity?
3. If a profit-maximizing, perfectly competitive firm is earning a profit because total revenue exceeds total cost, why must the market price exceed average cost?
4. If a profit-maximizing, perfectly competitive firm is earning a loss because total revenue is less than total cost, why must the market price be less than average cost?
5. If a profit-maximizing, perfectly competitive firm is earning zero economic profits because total revenue equals total cost, why must the market price be equal to the average cost for that level of output?
6. Why would a profit-maximizing, perfectly competitive firm shut down rather than operate if price was less than its average variable costs?
7. Why would a profit-maximizing, perfectly competitive firm continue to operate for a period of time if price was greater than average variable cost but less than average total cost?

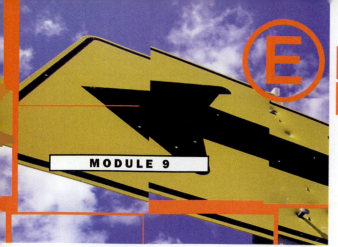

(E) Long-Run Equilibrium

■ If there are profits being earned in an industry, will this encourage the entry of new firms?

■ Why do perfectly competitive firms make zero economic profits in the long run?

WHY DO PROFITS DISAPPEAR IN THE LONG RUN IN A PERFECTLY COMPETITIVE MARKET?

If farmers are able to make economic profits producing wheat, what will their response be in the long run? Farmers will increase the resources that they devote to the lucrative business of producing wheat. Say Farmer John is making an economic profit (he is earning an above-normal rate of return) producing wheat. To make even more profits, he may take land out of producing other crops and plant more wheat. Other farmers or people who are holding land for speculative purposes might also decide to plant wheat on their land.

As the word gets out that wheat production is proving profitable, there will be a supply response—the market supply curve will shift to the right as more firms enter the industry (Exhibit 1(a)). With this shift, the quantity of wheat supplied at any given price is greater than before. It may take a year or even longer, of course, for the complete supply response to take place, simply because it takes some time for information to spread on profit opportunities, and still more time to plant, grow, and harvest the wheat. Note that the impact of increasing supply, other things equal, is to reduce the equilibrium price of wheat. Suppose that, as a result of the supply response, the price of wheat falls from P_0 to P_1.

The impact of the change in the market price of wheat, over which John has absolutely no control, is very simple. If his costs have not changed, he will move from making a profit ($P_0 > ATC$) to breaking even ($P_1 = ATC$), as seen in Exhibit 1(b). In long-run equilibrium, perfectly competitive firms make zero economic profits. Remember, zero

EXHIBIT 1   PROFITS FOR A COMPETITIVE FIRM

a. Shift in Market Supply

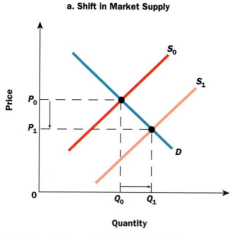

b. Impact on Individual Firm

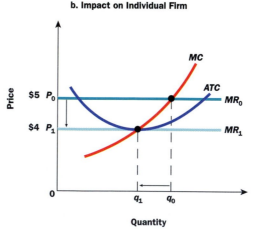

As the industry-determined price of wheat falls, Farmer John's marginal revenue curve shifts downward from MR_0 to MR_1. A new profit-maximizing ($MC = MR$) point is reached at q_1. When the price is P_0, Farmer John is making a profit because $P_0 > ATC$, but when the market supply increases, causing the market price to fall to P_1, Farmer John's profits disappear because $P_1 = ATC$.

EXHIBIT 2	THE LONG-RUN COMPETITIVE EQUILIBRIUM

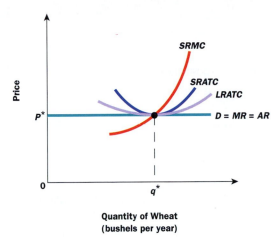

**Quantity of Wheat
(bushels per year)**

In the long run in perfect competition, a stable situation or equilibrium is achieved when economic profits are zero. In this case, at the profit-maximizing point where *MC = MR*, short-run and long-run average total costs are equal. Industrywide supply (or demand) shifts would change prices and average revenues and wipe out any losses or profits that develop in the short run, leading to the situation depicted above.

economic profits means that the firm is actually earning a normal return on the use of its capital. Zero economic profits is an equilibrium or stable situation because any posi-

tive economic (above-normal) profits signal resources into the industry, beating down prices and thus revenues to the firm; any economic losses signal resources to leave the industry, leading to supply reductions that lead to increased prices and higher firm revenues. Only at zero economic profits is there no tendency for firms to either enter or leave the industry.

ZERO ECONOMIC PROFITS IN THE LONG RUN

The long-run competitive equilibrium for a perfectly competitive firm is graphically illustrated in Exhibit 2. At the equilibrium point (where *MC = MR*), short-run and long-run average total costs are also equal. The average total cost curves touch the marginal cost and marginal revenue (demand) curves at the equilibrium output point. Because the marginal revenue curve is also the average revenue curve, average revenues and average total costs are equal at the equilibrium point. The long-run equilibrium in perfect competition depicted in Exhibit 2 has an interesting feature. Note that the equilibrium output occurs at the lowest point on the average total cost curve. As you may recall, this occurs because the marginal cost curve must intersect the average total cost curve at the latter curve's lowest point. Hence, the equilibrium condition in the long run in perfect competition is for firms to produce at that output that minimizes average total costs. At this long-run equilibrium, new firms have no incentive to enter the market and existing firms have no incentive to exit the market.

CONCEPT CHECK

1. Economic profits will encourage entry of new firms, which will shift the market supply curve to the right.
2. Any positive economic profits signal resources into the industry, driving down prices and revenues to the firm.
3. Any economic losses signal resources to leave the industry, leading to supply reduction, higher prices, and increased revenues.
4. Only at zero economic profits is there no tendency for firms to either enter or exit the industry.

---

1. Why do firms enter profitable industries?
2. Why does entry eliminate positive economic profits in a perfectly competitive industry?
3. Why do firms exit unprofitable industries?
4. Why does exit eliminate economic losses in a perfectly competitive industry?

5. Why is a situation of zero economic profits a stable long-run equilibrium situation for a perfectly competitive industry?
6. Say that there are a large number of small producers in an industry but very large barriers to entry to new firms. After a large, permanent increase in industry demand, would producers in the industry again earn zero economic profits in long-run equilibrium?

(F) Long-Run Industry Supply

- What are constant-cost industries?
- What are increasing-cost industries?

The preceding sections have considered the costs of an individual perfectly competitive firm as it varies output, on the assumptions that prices paid for inputs (costs) are given. When the output of an entire industry changes, the likelihood is greater of changes occurring in costs. We will look at two possible industry cost conditions—constant and increasing.

WHAT IS A CONSTANT-COST INDUSTRY?

Constant-cost conditions, in which the cost curves of the firms are not affected by changes in the output of the entire industry, will occur when the industry does not use inputs in sufficient quantities for their prices or efficiency to be affected by changes in the output of the industry.

As explained in Module 8, once long-run adjustments are complete, by necessity each firm operates at the point of lowest long-run average total costs, because supply shifts with entry and exit eliminate profits. Therefore, each firm supplies the market the quantity of output that it can produce at the lowest possible long-run average total cost.

In Exhibit 1, we can see the impact of an unexpected increase in market demand. Suppose that recent reports show that Vitamin Q can lower cholesterol, lower blood pressure, and significantly reduce the risk of all cancers. The increase in market demand for Vitamin Q leads to a price increase from P_0 to P_1, as the firm increases output from q_0 to q_1, and vitamin industry output increases from Q_0 to Q_1 as seen in Exhibit 1(b). The increase in demand generates a higher price and positive profits for existing firms in the short run. The existence of economic profits will attract new firms into the industry, causing the short-run supply curve to shift from SRS_0 to SRS_1 and lowering price until excess profits are zero. This shift results in a new equilibrium point C in Exhibit 1(c). Because the industry is one of constant costs, industry expansion does not alter firms' cost curves, and the industry long-run supply curve is horizontal. That is, the long-run equilibrium price is at the same level that prevailed before demand increased; the only long-run effect of the increase in demand is an increase in industry output, as more firms enter that are just like existing firms as Exhibit 1(c) indicates. However, the long-run supply curve does not have to be horizontal, as we will see in the next section.

WHAT IS AN INCREASING-COST INDUSTRY?

In an **increasing-cost industry,** the cost curves of the individual firms rise as the total output of the industry increases. Increases in input prices (upward shifts in cost curves) occur as larger quantities of factors are employed in the industry. When an industry utilizes a large portion of an input whose total supply is not huge, input prices will rise when the industry uses more of the input.

Increasing cost conditions are typical of "extractive" industries, such as agriculture, fishing, mining, and lumbering, which utilize large portions of the total supply of specialized natural resources such as land or mineral deposits. As the output of such an industry expands, the increased demand for the resources raises the prices that must be paid for their use. Because additional resources of given quality cannot be produced, greater supplies can be obtained (if at all) only by luring them away from other industries, or by using lower-quality (and less-productive, thus higher-cost) resources.

Wheat production is a typical example of an increasing-cost industry. As the output of wheat increases, the demand for land suitable for the production of wheat rises, and thus the price paid for the use of land of any given quality increases.

Whether the industry is one of constant cost or increasing cost, the basic point is the same. The long-run supply is usually more elastic than the short-run supply because in the long run, firms can enter and exit the industry.

If there was a construction boom in a fully employed economy, would it be more costly to get additional resources like workers and raw materials?

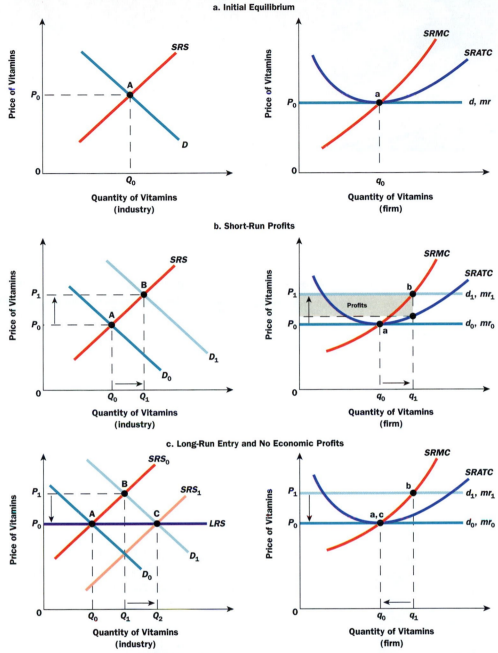

a. Initial Equilibrium

b. Short-Run Profits

c. Long-Run Entry and No Economic Profits

An unexpected increase in market demand for Vitamin Q leads to an increase in the market price in (b). The new market price leads to positive profits for existing firms, which attracts new firms into the industry, shifting market supply from SRS_0 to SRS_1 in (c). This increased short-run industry supply curve intersects D_1 at point C. Each firm (of a new larger number of firms) is again producing at q_0 and earning zero economic profit.

CONCEPT CHECK

1. In constant-cost industries, the cost curves of the firm are not affected by changes in the output of the entire industry. Such industries must be very small demanders of resources in the market.

2. In an increasing-cost industry, the cost curves of the individual firms rise as total output increases. This case is the most typical.

1. What must be true about input costs as industry output expands for a constant-cost industry?

2. What must be true about input costs as industry output expands for an increasing-cost industry?

3. What would be the long-run equilibrium result of an increase in demand in a constant-cost industry?

4. What would be the long-run equilibrium result of an increase in demand in an increasing-cost industry?

(G) Application: Cybergambling

Has Internet betting cut into casino profits?

Gambling on the Internet is currently a $2 billion business worldwide that could double by the year 2000, estimates Kevin Mercuri from the Interactive Services Association, a trade group. But cybergambling is still a penny-ante game compared to $586 billion America's bettors plunked down last year, American Gaming Association figures show. Not many of the cyber casinos and online bookies are based in the United States, though many have offices here.

Kathleen Shippers of the American Gaming Association said the casino operators oppose Internet gambling because there's no way to regulate it, ensure that winners get paid, or protect consumers from a business that closes up overnight.

In another story, a Columbia University economics major stands accused of taking part in an illegal extracurricular activity. Prosecutors said he was among 16 people in a $10 million sports gambling ring.

The 20-year-old college student was accused of being one of the network's runners—a person who collects bets and distributes winnings. He allegedly worked out of his Zeta Beta Tau fraternity house room, taking bets from as many as 30 students at the Ivy League school.

SOURCES: "Some in Congress Want to Outlaw Gambling Online," abcnews.com; Bruce Melzer, "Law Seeks to Curb Internet Gambling," abcnews.com, April 6, 1998; "Bye Bye Cyber Bookie?" abcnews.com; and Donna de la Cruz, "Columbia Student to $10 Million Gambling Ring Saturday," February 7, 1998, The Associated Press.

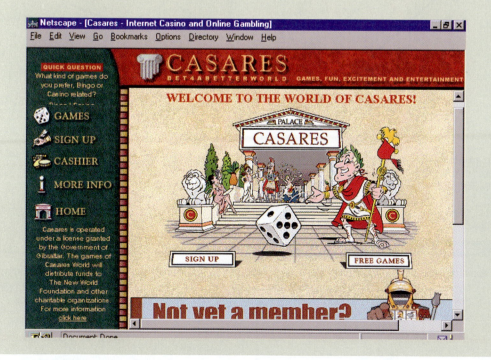

In reality, very few markets fit all the criteria of a perfectly competitive market—large number of buyers and sellers, homogeneous goods, free entry, and perfect information. Agriculture markets probably come the closest, but still many agricultural markets have some form of market imperfections. However, just because the industry may not fully satisfy all of the conditions of perfect competition, the model is not rendered useless.

Consider the gaming market, for example. It certainly cannot be considered a precise example of the perfectly competitive market. However, the model can still be useful, especially when considering the many buyers and sellers and the entry and exit aspect of the market. To a lesser extent they are all selling pretty much the same product—of course, gambling comes with more bells and whistles in Las Vegas.

The profits that were once almost exclusively Nevada's in the 1960s and 1970s now are divvied up by many more sellers: Atlantic City casinos, legal lottos, casinos on Native American reservations, river boat and cruise ship gambling, and Internet betting. Add to that the thousands of bookies all over the country, some illegally placing the bets themselves and others using messengers in legal sites like Las Vegas or Atlantic City. The point is this: What once was dominated by a few is now shared by many, with the profits being shared by many new competitors that have provided viable substitutes.

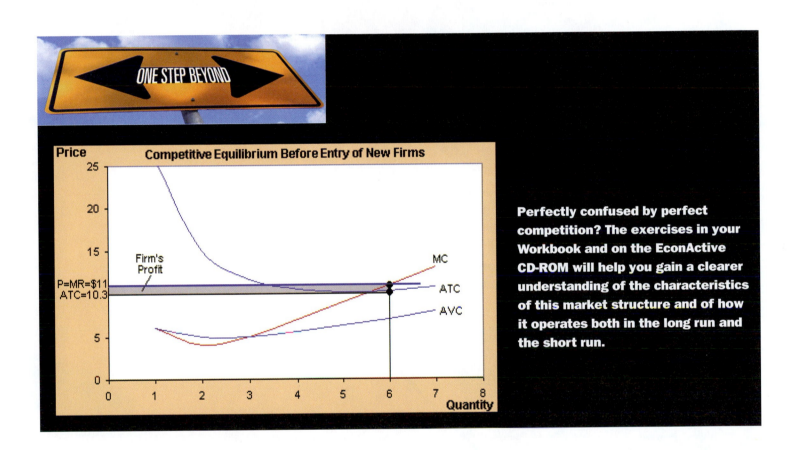

Perfectly confused by perfect competition? The exercises in your Workbook and on the EconActive CD-ROM will help you gain a clearer understanding of the characteristics of this market structure and of how it operates both in the long run and the short run.

PHOTO CREDITS MODULE 9

Page **234:** © Richard Pasley/Stock, Boston/PNI; Page **235:** bottom, Photo courtesy of the Chicago Board of Trade; top, © Barry L. Runk/Grant Heilman Photography; Page **237:** © Dagmar Fabricius; Taylor/Stock, Boston/PNI; Page **246:** © PhotoDisc; Page **250:** © Guy Motil/Westlight; Page **252:** Courtesy of Casares.com

Monopoly

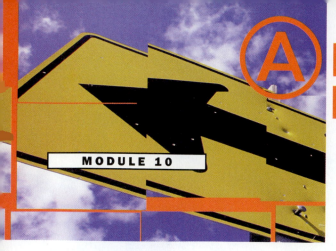

A Monopoly: The Price Maker

MODULE 10

- What is a monopoly?
- How is monopoly different from perfect competition?
- What is the monopolist's demand curve?

WHAT IS A MONOPOLY?

Perfect competition is at one end of the continuum of market environments, while on the other end is monopoly. A true or pure **monopoly** exists where there is only one seller of a product for which no close substitute is available. The firm and "the industry" are one and the same. Consequently, the firm sets the price of the good, because the firm faces the industry demand curve and can pick the most profitable point on that demand curve. Monopolists are price makers (rather than takers) who try to pick the price that will maximize their profits. For a monopoly to persist and be a stable continuing market structure, it must be virtually impossible for other firms to overcome barriers to entry. There might be either enormous financial obstacles, legal barriers, or a lack of access to critical inputs. In the case of legal barriers, the government might franchise only one firm to operate an industry, or a patent right might effectively close out competition.

Monopoly is more than a game.

WHY IS A PURE MONOPOLY A RARITY?

Few goods and services truly have only one producer. One might think of a small community with a single bank, a single newspaper, or even a single grocery store. Even in these situations, however, most people can bank out of town, use a substitute financial institution, buy out-of-town newspapers or watch TV, go to a nearby town to buy groceries, and so on. Near-monopoly conditions may exist, but absolute total monopoly is rather unusual.

One area where there is typically only one producer of goods and services within a market area is public utilities. There is usually only one natural gas provider in any given market and one seller of water. Moreover, governments themselves provide many services for which they are often the sole providers—garbage collection, sewer services, educational services, fire and police protection, and military protection. Most of these situations resemble a pure monopoly. Again, however, for most of the above cited goods and services, substitute goods and services are available. The person heating his or her home with natural gas can switch to electric heat (or vice versa). In some areas, one can even substitute home-collected rain water or well water for the water provided by the local water company.

While the purist might correctly deny the existence of monopoly, the number of situations where monopoly conditions are fairly closely approximated are sufficiently numerous to make the study of monopoly more than a theoretical abstraction; moreover, the study of monopoly is useful in clarifying certain desirable aspects of perfect competition.

THE MONOPOLIST'S DEMAND, MARGINAL REVENUE, AND TOTAL REVENUE CURVES

In monopoly, the market demand curve may be regarded as the demand curve for the firm's product because the monopoly firm *is* the market for that particular product. The demand curve indicates the quantities that the firm can sell at various possible prices. In Exhibit 1, we see the monopolist's demand and marginal revenue curves.

| EXHIBIT 1 | DEMAND AND MARGINAL REVENUE FOR A MONOPOLIST |

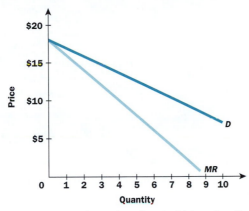

The market demand curve shows the price at which each unit of output can be sold. Price exceeds marginal revenue because selling additional units of output requires lowering the price on all preceding units that could have been sold at higher prices.

| EXHIBIT 2 | DAILY QUANTITY OF MYSTIC COATS DEMANDED |

Price per Mystic Coat	Daily Quantity of Mystic Coats Demanded	Total Revenues per Day	Marginal Revenue per Day
$500	1	$500	
			$300
400	2	800	
			100
300	3	900	
			0
225	4	900	
			−25
175	5	875	
			−65
135	6	810	

In monopoly, we see that the demand curve for the firm's product declines as additional units are placed on the market—the demand curve is downward sloping. In monopoly, because the firm controls the whole market, it has the ability to alter how much it supplies to the market. That is, if the monopolist reduces output, the price will rise; and if the monopolist expands output, the price will fall.

Recall that in perfect competition, because there are many buyers and sellers of homogeneous goods (resulting in a perfectly elastic demand curve), the individual seller can sell all he or she wants at the market price along a horizontal demand curve.

In Exhibit 1, we see that the marginal revenue curve for a monopolist lies below the demand curve and declines at a more rapid rate than the demand curve. Why is this the case? Each additional unit sold adds less to total revenue than the price received for it, because the firm has to lower the price on *all* units to sell additional units. For example, to sell eight units instead of seven, say a firm must lower the price on all goods sold from $10 to $9; thus, while the eighth unit sells for $9, it adds only $2 to total revenue. That is, total revenue at 7 units is $70 ($10 × 7 = $70), and at 8 units it is $72 ($9 × 8 = $72). The marginal revenue, the additional revenue from selling one more unit of output, is $2. Thus, marginal revenue ($2) is below price ($9). This is true for any negatively sloped demand curve: If the price is declining as more is sold, marginal revenue must be below price.

As another example, let us now consider the case of the Mystic Apparel Company (MAC). Suppose MAC has a monopoly on a coat that conforms to all weather conditions and that has a secret patented lining that makes the

wearer feel good whenever he or she is wearing the coat. When the company cuts the price of its product, the volume sold increases, perhaps rather substantially, because the demand for coats is elastic with respect to price, at least in some price range. The table in Exhibit 2 offers some mythical but plausible figures for the number of coats MAC could sell daily at various prices.

Even if this coat had a secret patented lining, you could sell more by lowering the price, resulting in a downward-sloping demand curve.

This discussion assumes, of course, that all customers pay the same price for coats. This is usually a fairly realistic assumption, because the monopolist lacks sufficient information to allow him or her to charge the ardent coat users more than the customer who can take or leave Mystic coats, depending on the price. The monopolist simply does not know who the diehard Mystic coat lovers are.

When MAC sets its price at $500, it only sells one coat a day. Suppose it cuts the price to $400, and as a consequence, sales increase to two coats per day. Does the company receive $400 in additional, or marginal, revenue because it is selling two coats instead of one? No! MAC's marginal revenue is only $300, which is less than the price of the coat ($400). Why? When the firm cuts the price in order to induce the second daily customer to buy a coat, it now gains only $400 from the first customer even though he or she is willing to pay $500. That is, because both customers are now paying $400, the company is receiving $400 more from customer two, but it is now earning $100 less from customer one. Remember, the first customer was willing to pay $500 for the coat. Thus, in order to get revenue from marginal customers who want Mystic coats but only at lower prices, the firm has to sacrifice some revenue by offering coats to some ardent customers at a price *less* than they were willing to pay.

In order to induce a third daily customer to purchase a coat, MAC finds that it has to cut its prices to $300. In doing so, it gains $300 in revenue from the new, third customer, but it loses $200 in revenue because each of the first two customers are now paying $100 less than previously.

Do department stores generally charge different prices to different people?

The net gain in revenue is $100 ($300 − $200), well below the price of the coat ($300).

Finally, in order to get a fourth customer, MAC has to cut the price to $225. The firm finds that in doing so, it gains no additional revenue, because the new revenue received from the fourth customer is exactly offset by losses in revenues from the first three customers, who pay less than previously for the product. Expanding sales beyond four coats a day is possible only by cutting prices so substantially that the firm actually would find its total revenues declining; that is, the marginal revenue is negative.

TUNE UP

DEMAND AND MARGINAL REVENUE

Q: Using the concepts of total revenue and marginal revenue, show why marginal revenue is less than price in a monopoly situation. For example, assume that the price of the product falls from $5 to $4 and the quantity demanded changes from 1 unit to 2 units. Will the marginal revenue be less than the price?

Price	Quantity	Total Revenue	Marginal Revenue
$5	1	$5	
			$3
$4	2	$8	

A: Yes, we see that the marginal revenue is $3, which is less than the price ($4). The key is seen in Exhibit 3 below: To sell another unit, we have to lower the price on both units. That is, the seller doesn't receive $5 from unit 1, but rather, receives $1 less than before—$4. However, the seller does receive an extra $4 in revenue from the sale of the second unit. The result is a marginal gain of $3 in revenue.

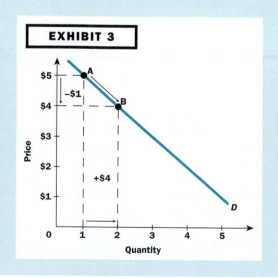

EXHIBIT 3

MONOPOLISTS ALWAYS OPERATE ON THE ELASTIC PORTION OF THE DEMAND CURVE

Recall from Module 8 that if a firm cuts a price and total revenues expand, demand is elastic with respect to price. The percent growth in quantity demanded is greater than the percent reduction in price. The monopolist, like other firms, wants to produce where some additional, or marginal, revenue is being obtained. The monopolist therefore always produces at an output where marginal revenue is positive, meaning that it always produces where the demand is elastic.

CONCEPT CHECK

1. A pure monopoly exists where there is only one seller of a product for which no close substitute is available.
2. Barriers to entry tend to be very high in monopoly.
3. Pure monopolies are rare because there are few goods and services where only one producer exists.
4. The monopolist's demand curve is downward sloping because it is the market demand curve. To produce and sell another unit of output, the firm must lower its price on all units. As a result, the marginal revenue curve lies below the demand curve.

1. Why are the industry and firm demand curves the same for a monopoly?
2. Why is a monopoly a price maker but a perfectly competitive firm a price taker?
3. Why is monopoly as a stable market structure dependent on the existence of barriers to entry?
4. Why is a pure monopoly a rarity?
5. Why is marginal revenue less than price for a profit-maximizing monopolist?
6. Why does the marginal revenue curve decline at a more rapid rate than the linear demand curve from which it derives?
7. Why does a monopolist always operate on the elastic portion of its demand curve?
8. If a monopolist had zero production costs, would it operate at a point where its demand curve was relatively elastic?

B The Monopolist's Equilibrium

- How does the monopolist decide what output to produce?
- How does the monopolist decide what price to charge?
- How do we know if the monopolist is making a profit?
- How do we know if the monopolist is incurring a loss?

HOW DOES A MONOPOLIST DETERMINE ITS PROFIT-MAXIMIZING OUTPUT?

The monopolist's decision of what level of output to produce depends on more than the marginal revenue derived at various outputs, of course. The firm faces production costs, and the monopolist, like the perfect competitor, will maximize profits at that output where $MC = MR$. This point is demonstrated graphically in Exhibit 1.

As you can see in Exhibit 1, at output levels less than Q^*, the marginal revenue from more production exceeds the marginal cost of that production, so it is profitable for the monopolist to expand output. Profits continue to grow (or losses shrink) until output Q^* is reached. Beyond that output, the marginal cost of production exceeds the marginal

| EXHIBIT 1 | EQUILIBRIUM OUTPUT AND PRICE FOR A PURE MONOPOLIST |

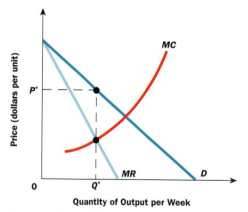

The monopolist maximizes profits at that quantity where $MC = MR$, at Q^*. Rather than charging a price equal to marginal cost or marginal revenue at their intersection, however, the monopolist charges the price that customers are willing to pay for that quantity as indicated on the demand curve at P^*.

The only musical instrument store in a small town may have a monopoly. Will the owner expand services if she perceives her marginal revenues to be greater than her marginal costs?

revenue from production, so profits decline. Therefore, the equilibrium output is Q^*. At this output, marginal costs and marginal revenues are equal.

HOW DOES A MONOPOLIST DETERMINE PRICE?

The point where marginal costs equal marginal revenues determines the equilibrium output level for a monopolist. This output level, in turn, determines the price that a monopolist will charge for that output. To find this price, extend a vertical line from Q^*, the equilibrium output, up to the demand curve. This intersection indicates the price, P^*, that consumers are willing to pay for quantity Q^*. This, then, is the price that a monopolist will charge.

PROFITS FOR A MONOPOLIST

Exhibit 1 does not show what profits, if any, the monopolist is actually making. This is rectified in Exhibit 2, which shows the equilibrium position of a monopolist, this time adding an average total cost (ATC) curve. As we just discussed, the firm produces where MC = MR, or output Q*. At output Q* and price P*, the firm's total revenue is equal to P*AQ*0, which is P* times Q*. At output Q*, the firm's total cost is CBQ*0, which is ATC times Q*. In Exhibit 2, we see that total revenue are greater than total costs so the firm has a profit of area P*ABC.

In perfect competition, profits in an economic sense will persist only in the short run, because in the long run, new firms will enter the industry, increasing industry supply and thus driving down the price of the good. With this, profits are eliminated. In monopoly, however, profits are not eliminated, because one of the conditions for monopoly is that barriers to entry exist. Other firms cannot enter, so economic profits persist.

EXHIBIT 2 — A MONOPOLIST'S PROFITS

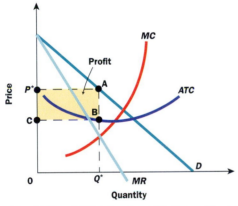

The intersection of MR and MC determines Q*, the profit-maximizing level of output. The demand curve shows the price that can be charged for Q*. Total profits equal the area P*ABC—the difference between total revenues (P*AQ*0) and total costs (CBQ*0).

LOSSES FOR A MONOPOLIST

It is easy to imagine a monopolist ripping off consumers by charging exorbitant prices and capturing huge profits. However, there are also many companies with monopoly power that have gone out of business. Imagine that you received a patent on a bad idea like running shoes with a built-in umbrella, or that you had the sole rights to turn an economics textbook into a screen play for a motion picture. While you may be the sole supplier of a product, that does not guarantee that consumers will demand your

product. There may be no close substitue for your product, but there is always competition for the consumer dollar—other goods may provide greater satisfaction. Exhibit 3 illustrates loss in a monopoly situation. In this graph, notice that the demand curve is well below the average cost curve. In this case, the monopolist will incur a loss because there is insufficient demand to cover average total costs at any price and output combination along the demand curve. At Q*, total costs, CAQ*0, are greater than total revenues, P*BQ*0, so the firm incurs a loss of CABP* in Exhibit 3.

A patent may make you the sole supplier, but it does not guarantee monopoly profits. What if you had a patent on a bad idea like a roof ejection seat for a helicopter?

EXHIBIT 3 — A MONOPOLIST'S LOSSES

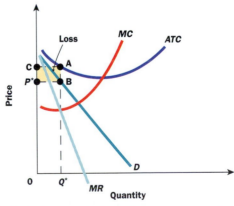

Total losses equal the area CABP*—the difference between total costs (CAQ*0) and total revenues (P*BQ*0).

1. The monopolist, like the perfect competitor, maximizes profits at that output where marginal revenue equals marginal cost.
2. The monopolist sets the price according to the demand for the product at the profit-maximizing output.
3. Monopoly profits can be found by comparing price per unit and average total cost per unit at $Q*$. If $P > ATC$, there are economic profits. If $P < ATC$, there are economic losses.
4. Monopolists' profits can last into the long run, because in monopoly, there are barriers to entry.

---

1. What is a monopolist's principle for choosing the profit-maximizing output?
2. How do you find the profit-maximizing price for a monopolist?
3. For a monopolist making positive economic profits, what must be true about the relationship between price and average total cost?
4. For a monopolist making negative economic profits, what must be true about the relationship between price and average total cost?
5. Why, unlike perfectly competitive firms, can a monopolist continue to earn positive economic profits over time?

Arguments Against and For Monopoly

- How does monopoly lead to inefficiencies?
- What is the welfare loss in monopoly?
- Does monopoly retard innovation?
- Can economies of scale lead to an argument for monopoly?
- What is a natural monopoly?

THE CASE AGAINST MONOPOLIES

Monopoly Promotes Inefficiency

Monopoly is often considered to be bad. But what is the basis in economic theory for concerns about the establishment of monopoly power? There are two main objections to monopoly. First, on equity grounds, many people feel that it is not "fair" for monopoly owners to get very rich from persistent profits when they work no harder than other firms. This is a normative issue about which people could disagree. A second objection—that monopolies result in market inefficiencies—is more important to economists (and others). The major objection to monopoly is that it leads to a lower output and to higher prices than would exist under perfect competition. To demonstrate why this is so, return to Exhibit 1. In monopoly, the firm produces output Q_M and charges a price of P_M. Suppose, however, that we had perfect competition and that the industry was characterized by many small firms that could

---

EXHIBIT 1	PERFECT COMPETITION VERSUS MONOPOLY

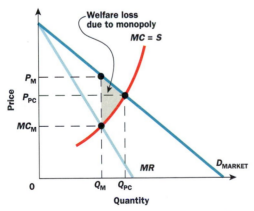

Compared with perfect competition, the monopolist's equilibrium price is higher, P_M, and its equilibrium output is lower, Q_M. Also notice that P_M is greater than MC_M, which means the value of the last unit produced by the monopolist (P_M) is greater than the cost (MC_M), so from society's point of view the monopolist is producing too little output.

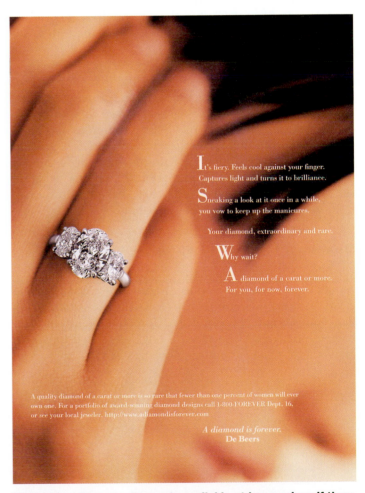

It's fiery. Feels cool against your finger. Captures light and turns it to brilliance.

Sneaking a look at it once in a while, you vow to keep up the manicures.

Your diamond, extraordinary and rare.

Why wait?

A diamond of a carat or more. For you, for now, forever.

A quality diamond of a carat or more is so rare that fewer than one percent of women will ever own one. For a portfolio of award-winning diamond designs call 1-800-FOREVER Dept. 16, or see your local jeweler. http://www.adiamondisforever.com

A diamond is forever.
De Beers

Would there be more diamonds available at lower prices if there were more competitors in the diamond business?

---

produce output with the same efficiency (at the same cost) as one large firm. Then the marginal cost curve shown in Exhibit 1 could be the sum of the individual marginal cost curves of the individual firms, and the upward portion of that curve might be considered the industry supply curve.

Equilibrium price and quantity would be determined where the marginal cost (or supply) curve intersects with the demand curve, at output Q_{PC} and price P_{PC}. Thus, the competitive equilibrium solution provides for more output and lower prices than the solution prevailing in monopoly. This provides the major efficiency objection to monopoly: Monopolists charge higher prices and produce less output. This may also be viewed as "unfair," in that consumers are burdened more than under the alternative competitive arrangement.

Welfare Loss in Monopoly

In addition to the monopolist producing lower levels of output at higher prices, notice that the monopolist produces at an output where the price (P_M) is greater than the marginal cost (MC_M). Because $P > MC$, it means that the value to society from the last unit produced is greater than its costs (MC_M). That is, the monopoly is *not* producing enough of the good from society's perspective. We call the shaded area in Exhibit 1, the welfare loss due to monopoly.

The actual amount of the welfare loss in monopoly is of considerable debate among economists. Estimates vary between one-tenth of 1 percent to 6 percent of national income. The variation depends on the researchers' estimates of elasticity of demand, whether firm or industry data was used, whether adjustments for profits were made (for the inclusion of royalties and intangibles), and last, whether the researcher included some proxy for scarce resources used in attempting to create a monopoly.

Monopoly Results in a Concentration of Economic Power

Monopoly means that a concentration of economic power exists because the monopolist controls significant quantities of inputs and outputs. Some think that bigness itself is bad in a democratic society for reasons related to equity, justice, and quality, economic efficiency aside.

Monopoly power may not last forever. What did trucks, cars, and planes do to the so-called railroad "monopoly"?

Monopoly Retards Innovation

It is also argued that a lack of competition tends to retard technological advance. The monopolist becomes comfortable, reaping his monopolistic profits, so he does not work hard at product improvement, technical advances designed to promote efficiency, and so forth. The American railroad is sometimes cited as an example of this situation. Early in this century, railroads had a strong amount of monopoly power, but they did not spend much on research or development; they did not aggressively try to improve rail transport. As a consequence, technical advances in other transport modes—like cars, trucks, and airplanes—led to a loss of monopoly power, as transportation substitutes came into existence.

However, the notion that monopoly retards all innovation can be disputed. Many near-monopolists are, in fact, important innovators. AT&T's Bell Laboratories is renowned for important technological advances (e.g., transistors, laser technology). Companies like Microsoft, International Business Machines (IBM), Polaroid, and Xerox have all, at one time or another, had very strong market positions, in some instances approaching monopoly secured by patent protection. They were also important innovators. Indeed, innovation helps firms initially obtain a degree of monopoly status, as patents can give a monopoly new products and/or cost-saving technology. Even the monopolist wants more profits, and any innovation that lowers costs or expands revenues creates profits for the monopolist. In addition, because patents expire in 17 years, a monopolist may be expected to innovate in order to obtain additional patents and preserve its monopoly power. Therefore, the incentive to innovate may well exist in monopolistic market structures.

THE CASE FOR MONOPOLIES

The Impact of Economies of Scale

The theoretical analysis presented to this point clearly suggests that monopolies are economically inefficient—and in most peoples' minds, inequitable—with one of the primary arguments against monopolies being that they result in higher prices and lower output than would be the case in a perfectly competitive environment. It should be noted, however, that the notion that monopoly will lead to higher prices and reduced output rests on the assumption that the monopolist has no inherent efficiencies that relate to size.

In Exhibit 2, there are economies of scale, so that large firms are more efficient than smaller ones. In this situation, it is likely that, given demand conditions, the market will accommodate only one large, low-cost firm. In this case, it does not follow that prohibiting monopoly would necessarily lead to higher output and lower prices. The marginal costs of many small producers at any given total output could be so much higher than the marginal costs of the monopolist that it is conceivable that the supply and demand curves could intersect at higher prices and lower output in competition than in monopoly.

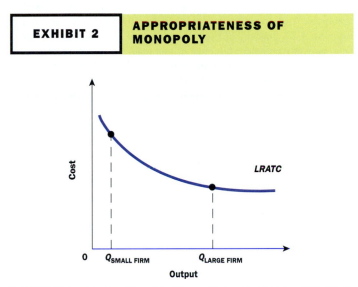

| EXHIBIT 2 | APPROPRIATENESS OF MONOPOLY |

In Exhibit 2, economies of scale exist, creating a situation in which small firms are inherently inefficient. A case can be made for a regulated monopoly under these conditions.

IS MICROSOFT A MONOPOLY?

Imagine a world with a computer in every home. All running on the same software, all hooked up to a television and the Internet so that users can enjoy both interactive entertainment and one-stop shopping.

Now imagine that all users have personal computing accounts, which allows them to make any purchase through their Internet television. One company monitors every account, the same company that owns the technology. For every purchase made, that company gets a commercial transaction fee. Microsoft could be that company.

Bill Gates' Microsoft made $9.6 billion last year. The company currently owns an estimated 85 percent of the operating system market worldwide. Success of this magnitude brings not only admiration, but legal inquiries. The U.S. Justice Department, the European Union, and consumer advocate Ralph Nader are all looking into Microsoft's alleged anti-competitive business practices.

On Monday, the Justice Department sought to impose an unprecedented $1 million-a-day fine on the software giant for failing to end its anti-competitive licensing practices. The department claims that Microsoft's requirement that personal computer manufacturers license and distribute its Internet Explorer Web browser violates a previous arrangement with the Justice Department in which Microsoft agreed not to force manufacturers to "bundle" its operating system.

Nader, for one, believes that this kind of strategy, indeed Microsoft itself, poses a grave danger to technological innovation and to the company's economic health. The longtime champion of consumers plans to explore the company's practices in a conference in Washington next month.

Nader's conference will address whether Microsoft, through monopolistic practices, has caused a slowing in technological innovation; whether the company engages in predatory pricing as a prelude to raising prices; and whether control of so many lines of commerce by one company is, as Nader puts it simply, "not good."

Critics argue that by giving away products like Internet Explorer for free, Microsoft is engaging in predatory pricing. It can gain market share and then raise prices. The planned integration of Internet Explorer into the Windows 98 operating system would further eliminate the need for separate and competitive software, such as Netscape Navigator.

Microsoft has also entered new markets such as Internet-based car sales, real-estate listings, banking transactions, and even stock trading. "When you move from conduit to content, as Microsoft is doing—into publishing, into cable, encyclopedias, etc.," says Nader, "you get another abuse of concentrated power. We've always believed the conduit should be separate from content."

[Microsoft spokesman Mark] Murray believes Microsoft's actions are simply good business. "Anybody that stops innovating is going to be roadkill on the information highway," he says, quoting a phrase often used at Microsoft.

Who's right? That may be decided in court.

CONSIDER THIS:
Are consumers necessarily worse off as a result of a few powerful computer companies that dominate the industry? There may be economies of scale in production and technology. Furthermore, the monopoly might well be short-lived. And are the barriers to entry in the computer industry insurmountable? The history of the computer industry has several success stories of individuals with great ideas that have successfully broken into the industry. In addition, Microsoft and Intel are at least partially responsible for making computer power what it is today. A Pentium II Intel computer with Microsoft 95, available for roughly $2,000, could not be matched in performance 10 years ago at almost any price.

However, it is important to remember that if the computer market was more competitive, prices might have gone down even faster and the quality of the products might be even higher. For example, look what happened to long-distance rates when Sprint and MCI entered the long-distance telephone market. And just because prices are falling now, will they continue to fall if markets do not become more competitive in the future?

SOURCE: Joe Feese, ABCNEWS.com. December 12, 1997.

http://www.abcnews.com/sections/tech/DailyNews/microsoft1021.html

What Is a Natural Monopoly?

The situation in which one large firm can provide a good or service at a lower cost than two or more smaller firms is called a **natural monopoly.** The economies of scale depicted in Exhibit 2 is a situation conducive to the formation of a natural monopoly. As previously indicated, public utilities such as water and electric power companies are examples of natural monopolies.

Sometimes a single firm, with economies of scale, can provide a good or service to the market at a lower cost than can multiple firms. This is the case with many public utilities, such as electricity.

CONCEPT CHECK

1. Monopoly results in smaller output and a higher price than would be the case under perfect competition.
2. The monopolist produces at an output where $P > MC$. This means the value to society of the last unit produced is greater than its cost. In other words, the monopoly is not producing enough output from society's standpoint.
3. Monopoly may lead to greater concentration of economic power and could retard innovation.
4. A natural monopoly occurs when one firm can provide the good or service at a lower cost than two or more smaller firms. Under these conditions, a number of small firms may be less efficient than one large firm, particularly if the latter is regulated.

1. Why does the reduced output under monopoly cause inefficiency?
2. Does monopoly power retard innovation?
3. What does the welfare cost of monopoly represent? How is it measured?
4. How can economies of scale lead to monopoly? How can it result in monopoly increasing rather than decreasing market output relative to the competitive market structure?
5. Can monopoly be the result of a new innovation that leaves consumers better off than before?

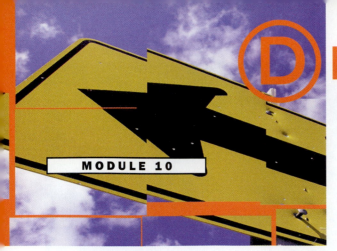

ⒹMonopoly Policy

- What is antitrust policy?
- What is regulation?
- What is average cost pricing?

Because monopolies pose certain problems with respect to efficiency, equity, and power, the public, through its governments, must decide how to deal with the phenomenon. Three major approaches to dealing with the monopoly problem are commonly used: antitrust policies, regulation, and public ownership. We will discuss the first two of these approaches here; the topic of government-run monopolies is covered in the next Concept. It should be pointed out that in these discussions, the word "monopoly" is sometimes used in a loose, general sense to refer to imperfectly competitive markets, not just to "pure" monopoly.

ANTITRUST POLICIES

Perhaps the most obvious way to deal with monopoly is to make monopoly illegal. The government can bring civil lawsuits or even criminal actions against business people or corporations engaged in monopolistic practices. By imposing monetary and nonmonetary costs on monopolists (the fear of lawsuits or even jail sentences), antitrust policies reduce the profitability of monopoly.

Keeping Firms From Getting Too Big

For example, antitrust efforts in the 1960s and 1970s turned increasingly against conglomerate-type mergers, where firms acquired firms producing goods in other industries. More traditional-type antitrust suits against firms with dominant market positions within a single industry also continued, however, perhaps most notably in a monumental suit brought against International Business Machines (IBM) that alleged that IBM had a near-monopoly role in the computer business. More recently, Netscape has claimed that the same monopoly power exists with Microsoft.

Promoting More Price Competition

Many professional associations have restricted the promotion of price competition by prohibiting advertising among their members. Recently, both the FTC and the Jus-

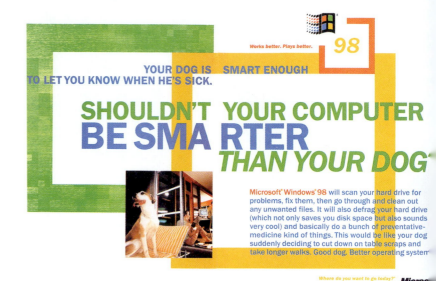

Is Microsoft too big? Netscape thinks so.

tice Department have successfully attacked these types of restrictions on price competition on the grounds that they violate the antitrust laws. They have been spurred on in their efforts by consumer groups who have noticed that prices tend to be much lower where price competition is allowed to flourish. Thus, optometrists were prodded to advertise the price of eyeglasses; pharmacists, the price of commonly prescribed drugs; and even lawyers, the price of a simple divorce. Even Ivy League schools have been charged with violating antitrust regulations; they have been charged with illegally colluding to fix the price of scholarships. Ivy League schools wanted to make sure they did not get into a "scholarship war," so the participating schools collectively met and fixed scholarship packages so students would pick their schools on the basis of academic quality, not the size of scholarship package. These activities guaranteed that any student applying to more than one of these schools would receive the same financial package.

Do Ivy League schools collude to fix prices?

HAVE ANTITRUST POLICIES BEEN SUCCESSFUL?

The success of antitrust policies can be debated. Surely very few giant monopolies have been disbanded as a consequence of antitrust policies. Studies have shown that there was little change in the degree of monopoly/oligopoly power in the first 100 years or so of U.S. antitrust legislation. Manufacturing, as a whole, has actually become more concentrated; that is, there are now fewer firms in the industry. However, the service and banking industries have become less concentrated. On the other hand, the relevant question is, "What would have been the degree of monopoly power if antitrust legislation had not existed?" On that score, it is very likely that at least some anticompetitive practices have been prevented simply by the existence of laws prohibiting monopoly-like practices. While the laws have probably been enforced in an imperfect fashion, on balance, they have probably successfully impeded monopoly influences to some degree.

GOVERNMENT REGULATION

Government regulation as an alternative approach to dealing with monopolies has received greater acceptance in the United States. Privately owned monopolies are allowed to operate, but they are regulated by a government agency that restricts the pricing and possibly other practices of the monopolist. The goal is to achieve the efficiency of large-scale, privately owned operations without permitting the high monopoly prices that can promote inefficiency and also inequity. Public utilities are a major example of regulated monopolies in United States with natural monopolies, such as electric power and water. That is, natural monopolies occur when one large firm can produce as much output as many smaller firms at a lower average cost per unit.

The basic dilemma that regulators often face in attempting to fix maximum prices can be rather easily illustrated. Consider Exhibit 1. Without regulation, say the profit-maximizing monopolist operates at point A, at output Q_M and price P_M. At that output, the price exceeds the average total cost, so monopoly profits exist. However, the monopolist is producing relatively little output and is charging a relatively high price, and it is producing at a point where price is above marginal cost. This is not the best point from society's perspective.

Allocative Efficiency

From society's point of view, what would be the best price and output position? **Allocative efficiency** occurs where the price of the good is equal to the marginal cost of producing it ($P = MC$). This is because the equilibrium price represents the marginal value of output. The marginal cost represents society's opportunity costs in making the good as opposed to something else. Where price equals marginal cost, society is matching marginal value and marginal cost; this is seen at point C in Exhibit 1.

EXHIBIT 1	**MARGINAL COST PRICING VERSUS AVERAGE COST PRICING**

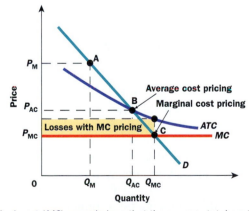

The marginal cost (*MC*) curve is less that the average total cost curve (*ATC*) for a natural monopolist as the average cost falls. If the monopolist is unregulated, it could produce a relatively small level of output, Q_M, at a relatively high price, P_M. If regulators require the natural monopolist to use marginal cost pricing, the monopoly will lose money, because P_{MC} is less than average total costs. Average cost pricing (at point B) would permit firms to make a normal rate of return, where $P_{AC} = ATC$.

Can the Regulated Monopolist Operate at *P = MC*?

Natural monopolies, like public utilities, have economies of scale (note that average total costs fall in Exhibit 1), because they have enormous fixed capital costs that have to be spread out over a large output volume in order to reduce average total costs. Unfortunately, at the point where $P = MC$, indicated at point C on Exhibit 1 by the intersection of the demand and marginal cost curves, average total costs are greater than price as denoted by the demand curve. The so-called optimal output, then, is an output that produces losses for the producer. Any regulated business that produced for long at this "optimal" output would go bankrupt; it would be impossible to attract new capital to the industry.

Therefore, the "optimal" output from a welfare perspective really is not viable because losses are incurred. The regulators cannot force firms to price their product at P_{MC} and to sell Q_{MC} output, because the firm would go out of business. Indeed, in the long run, the industry's capital would deteriorate as investors failed to replace old capital when it became worn out or obsolete. If the monopolist's unregulated output at point A is not optimal from society's standpoint, and the short-run optimal output at point C is not feasible from the monopolist's standpoint, where should the regulated monopolist be allowed to operate?

The Compromise: A Fair Return

A compromise between the two positions is found at point B on Exhibit 1, output Q_{AC}, which is somewhere between the excessively low output and high prices of an unregulated monopoly and the excessively large output and low prices achieved when prices are equated with marginal cost pricing. At point B, price equals average total costs. The monopolist is permitted to price the product where economic profits are zero, meaning that a normal return is being permitted in an accounting sense. This is also the return on capital investment realized by firms in perfect competition. This compromise is called **average cost pricing**.

In the real world, regulators often permit utilities to receive a "fair and reasonable" return that is a rough approximation to that suggested by point B. Point B would seem "fair" in that the monopolist is receiving rewards equal to those that a perfect competitor would ordinarily receive— no more and no less. Remember, however, that what is fair to one person may not seem fair to another; fairness requires the making of a value judgment. Point B permits more output at a significantly lower per-unit price than would occur if the monopolist were unregulated, point A, even though output is still somewhat less and price somewhat more than that suggested by point C, the social optimum, or best position.

DIFFICULTIES IN IMPLEMENTING A FAIR PRICE

Accurate Calculations of Costs

The actual implementation of a rate (price) that permits a "fair and reasonable" return is more difficult than the analysis suggests. The calculations of costs and values are very difficult. In reality, the firm may not know exactly what its demand and cost curves look like. This forces regulatory agencies to use profits, another somewhat ambiguous target, as a guide. If profits are "too high," lower the price, and if profits are too low, raise the price.

No Incentives to Keep Costs Down

Another problem is that average cost pricing gives the monopolists no incentive to reduce costs. That is, if the firm's costs rise from ATC_0 to ATC_1 in Exhibit 2, the price will rise from P_0 to P_1. And if costs fall, the firm's price will fall. In either scenario, the firm will still be earning a normal rate of return. This is equivalent to saying that if the regulatory agency sets the price at any point where the ATC curve intersects the demand curve, the firm will earn a normal rate of return. So why keep costs down? Let your employees fly first class and dine in the finest restaurants. While you are at it, why not buy concert tickets and season tickets to sporting events? Regulators have tackled this problem by allowing the regulated firm to keep some of the profits that come from lower costs; that is, they do not adhere strictly to average cost pricing.

Employees might get to enjoy their favorite game in an expensive sky box if regulated firms have no incentives to keep costs down.

Special Interest

Also, in the real world, consumer groups are constantly battling for lower rates, while the utilities themselves are lobbying for higher rates so that they can approach the monopoly profits indicated by point A on Exhibit 1. Decisions are not always made in a calm, objective, dispassionate atmosphere free of outside involvement. It is precisely the political economy of rate setting that disturbs some critics of this approach of dealing with the monopoly problem. For example, it is possible that a rate-making commissioner could become friendly with a utility company believing that he can obtain a nice job after his tenure as a regulator is over. The temptation is great for the commissioners to be generous to the utilities. On the other hand, there may be a tendency for regulators to bow to pressure from consumer groups. A politician who wants to win votes can almost always succeed by attacking utility rates and promising rate "reform" (lower rates). If zealous rate regulators listen too closely to the consumer groups and push rates down to a level indicated by point C in Exhibit 1, the industry might be too unstable to attract capital for expansion.

| EXHIBIT 2 | CHANGES IN AVERAGE COSTS |

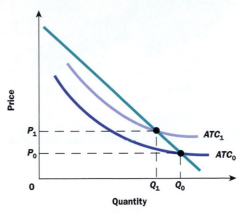

An increase in average total costs leads to a higher price and lower output ($P_1 Q_1$); lower average total costs leads to a lower price and greater output ($P_0 Q_0$). However, both situations lead to a normal rate of return. Because the regulated firm has little incentive to minimize costs, average total costs would have a tendency to rise.

CONCEPT CHECK

1. Antitrust policies can reduce the profitability of a monopoly and push production closer to the social optimum.
2. Privately owned monopolies may be allowed to operate but can be regulated by a government agency.
3. Average cost pricing sets price equal to average total cost, where the demand curve intersects average total costs.

---

1. What alternative ways of dealing with the monopoly problem are commonly used?
2. How do antitrust laws promote more price competition?
3. What price and output are ideal for allocative efficiency for a regulated natural monopolist? Why is an unregulated natural monopolist unlikely to pick this solution?
4. What is average cost pricing? How is it different from marginal cost pricing?
5. What are some difficulties encountered when regulators try to implement average cost pricing on natural monopolies?
6. Why might a job with a regulated natural monopolist that is allowed to earn a "fair and reasonable" return tend to have more perks (non-cash forms of compensation) than a comparable job in a non-regulated firm?

(E) Government Monopoly

- What are some examples of a government-run monopoly?
- What is the rationale for government monopoly?
- What is the rationale against government monopoly?
- Why is it important that the government provide patents and copyrights?

The third way that government addresses the problem of monopolies is to establish public ownership of the monopoly. That is, the government itself becomes a monopolistic provider of the good or service. In this Concept, we will discuss three government-run monopolies: the postal service, patents, and government licenses.

THE POSTAL SERVICE

Probably the oldest and best-known government monopoly in the United States is the United States Postal Service. Essentially, by law the government prohibits private companies from engaging in the business of delivering first-class letters (alternative suppliers are not allowed to use your mailbox). Virtually every nation in the world has a governmental postal monopoly, and most also extend the monopoly to telephone and other forms of communication (and many also cover most forms of transportation, including the railroads and airlines).

What Is the Rationale for the Government Postal Monopoly?

The historical rationale for the government postal monopoly begins with the proposition that it is inherently inefficient to have more than one firm providing postal service. One mail carrier with 30 pounds of letters can cover a route with little more effort than three competing firms, each with their own carriers covering the same residential area, each carrying 10 pounds or so of mail. In addition, given this "natural monopoly" aspect of postal services (meaning that average costs decline over the range of demand if a single firm is providing the service), a privately owned firm providing those postal services could exact enormous economic profits from providing postal services, and barriers to entry would prevent the market from increasing the supply of these services and lowering the price. It is better to have government provide the service and charge a low price that does not allow the greedy private entrepreneur who gets in first to earn huge profits by charging high prices. It is also argued that a company controlling mail services has enormous control over communications. The possibility exists that these private interests will use the power associated with mail delivery in a mischievous manner (e.g., opening and reading sensitive letters) that is clearly not in the public interest.

Finally, as a matter of public policy, we might wish to subsidize some forms of mail service on the grounds that the communication thereby encouraged serves the national interest in ways beyond the narrow interest of those participating in that communication. In other words, there are positive externalities, or social benefits, that accrue to individuals not directly part of mail service that need to be captured. Thus, newspaper publishers often get low mail-service rates, based on the idea that an informed public is vital to the smooth functioning of democracy (currently, however, most newspaper publishers would argue they are paying high prices for mail services).

Does the post office have a natural monopoly?

What Are the Arguments Against the Government Postal Monopoly?

On the other hand, there are good arguments against the government postal monopoly, and they have grown more compelling in recent years. First of all, it is doubtful that even decades ago, mail service was truly a natural monopoly. For example, several newspapers and dairies (milk used to be delivered to the door) would deliver their goods along the same route in a seemingly efficient fashion. More importantly, a monopolist, and particularly a government monopolist, has relatively little incentive to become more efficient. There are no bonuses or stock options for managers who make a profit by cutting costs; and there is little impetus to improve service, because the fear of losing business to competition is minimal. It is not surprising, then, that there is a strong general feeling that United States Postal Service in the 1990s is little speedier or more reliable than it was 50 years before airplanes speeded delivery and before modern mail-sorting equipment was available. In addition, there are scholarly studies that suggest that postal employees are better paid but less productive than comparable private-sector employees (e.g., those of United Parcel Service) who are subject to competitive pressures.

Moreover, technology has removed much of the "monopoly" nature of mail service. Whereas 100 years ago there was no long-distance telephone service, and even 60 years ago the cost of a transcontinental phone call was perhaps 200 times the cost of a letter, today a short coast-to-coast phone call may cost only three times the cost of a letter. Electronic mail (E-mail) is increasingly common, providing written communication over long distances instantly at near zero marginal cost; and a host of private letter services like Federal Express provide fast delivery of valuable written materials. In no sense does the United States Postal Service have a true monopoly on communication services, reducing the force of the argument for maintaining the monopoly on ordinary first-class mail service.

PATENTS AND COPYRIGHTS

One form of monopoly power conferred by governments is provided by patents and copyrights. A patent puts the government's police power behind the patent holder's right to make a product for a period of time (17 years) without anyone else being able to make an identical product. As Exhibit 1 suggests, this gives the supplier at least temporary monopoly power over that good or service. This allows the firm with the patent to price its product well above marginal costs, at P_M. When patents expire, the price of the patented good or service usually falls substantially with the entry of competing firms. The price will fall towards the perfectly competitive price P_{PC} and the output will increase towards $Q_{NO\ PATENT}$.

EXHIBIT 1	IMPACT OF PATENT PROTECTION ON EQUILIBRIUM PRICE AND QUANTITY

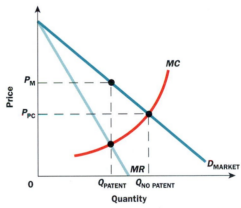

Patent power allows the firm to charge the higher monopoly price, P_M, which is well above the marginal cost of producing that good. However, when the patent runs out, the price falls to a position closer to the perfectly competitive price, P_{PC}.

Why does the government give inventors this limited monopoly power, raising the prices of pharmaceutical drugs and other "vital" goods? The rationale is simple. Without patents, there would be little incentive for inventors to incur millions of dollars in research and development expenses to create new products (e.g., life-saving drugs) if others can then copy the idea and manufacture the products without incurring these research expenses. Similarly, copyrights stimulate creative activity of other

What has happened in recent years to diminish the United States Postal Service's monopoly powers?

kinds, giving writers the incentive to write books that earn royalties and are not merely copied freely. Similarly, the enormous number of computer programs written for home computers reflects the fact that program writers receive royalties from the sale of each copy sold; that is, why they and the firms they work for vehemently oppose unauthorized copying of their work.

Without patents, would some life-saving drugs have been invented?

GOVERNMENT LICENSES

In order to engage in some activities, an individual or firm must obtain a license from a governmental authority. For example, nearly every city licenses its taxicabs. The argument for this is that license fees provide the government resources to police taxicabs, keeping unscrupulous drivers out of business—including those who rob passengers, ones who take their customers to their location by a circuitous route to increase the fare, and those who drive unsafe vehicles (or safe vehicles unsafely).

Licenses Are Barriers to Entry

Like some other types of consumer protection, governmental licensing has its drawbacks as well as advantages. License fees are a barrier to entry, reducing the supply of providers of the service and raising the price towards the monopoly price, shown as P_M in Exhibit 2. In some jurisdictions, notably New York City, cab drivers have managed to convince the regulators to limit the number of licenses, allowing those with licenses (called medallions in New York) to charge more than otherwise. Under current laws, unlicensed cab drivers are arrested for engaging in illegal activity. This allows cab drivers to charge a higher price because the law prohibits competition from new drivers entering the business. Without licensing, the pool of cabs would greatly expand, and as a result, the fares would fall towards a perfectly competitive price (P_{PC}) and the number of riders would increase towards Q_{PC}, as shown in Exhibit 2.

EXHIBIT 2	RESTRICTIVE LICENSING ON TAXICAB FARES

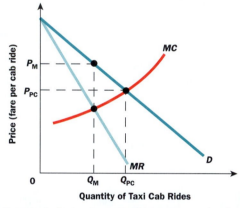

Licensing allows taxicabs to charge the higher monopoly price, P_M, which is well above the marginal cost of producing a taxicab ride. Without licensing, the pool of cabs would be greater and fares would be closer to P_{PC}.

CONCEPT CHECK

1. Government-run monopolies include postal services, patents, and licensing.
2. Arguments for a government-run monopoly include natural monopolies and possible positive externalities.
3. Many are skeptical of the arguments favoring government monopoly.
4. Patents and copyrights give inventors incentives to take risks and to produce more innovative products.

---

1. What is the argument most commonly made in favor of government monopoly?
2. What arguments are commonly made against government monopoly?
3. What is the argument in favor of the government enforcing patents and copyrights?
4. How can government licensing act as a barrier to entry?
5. How can government licensing result in higher prices than would otherwise be the case?

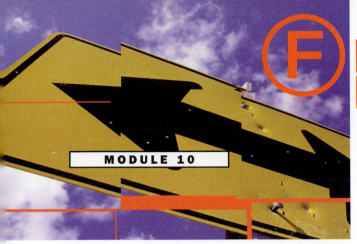

F Price Discrimination

- What is price discrimination?
- Why does price discrimination exist?
- Does price discrimination work when reselling is easy?

WHAT IS PRICE DISCRIMINATION?

Sometimes, producers will charge different customers different prices for the same good or service when the cost of providing that good or service does not differ among the customers. This is called **price discrimination**. For example, kids go the movies for less than adults; senior citizens get discounts on hotels, restaurants, museums, and zoos; most vacation travelers fly between places for less than business travelers; some patients of a doctor may pay more for treatment than others because of their income or insurance coverage; and so on.

Note that price discrimination is possible only with monopoly or where members of a small group of firms (oligopolists, to be considered later) follow identical pricing

Some patients of a doctor may pay more for the treatment than others on the basis of their income or insurance coverage.

policies. When there are a number of competing firms, discrimination is impossible because competitors will undercut the high prices charged by others to those they discriminate against.

WHY DOES PRICE DISCRIMINATION EXIST?

Price discrimination results from the profit-maximization motive. In our graphical analysis of monopoly, we suggested that there was a demand curve for the product and a corresponding marginal revenue curve. Sometimes, however, different groups of people have different demand curves and therefore react differently to price changes. A producer can make more money by charging those different buyers different prices. For example, if the price of a movie is increased from $5 to $8, many kids who would attend at $5 may have to stay home at $8, as they (and perhaps their parents) balk at paying the higher prices. The impact on attendance of raising prices may be less, however, for adults, who have higher incomes in the first place and for whom the ticket price may represent a smaller part of the expenses of an evening out.

Thus, there is a different demand curve for those under, say, 16, as opposed to those who are older. Specifically, the elasticity of demand with respect to price is greater for children than for adults. This means that there is a different marginal revenue curve for children than for adults. The profit-maximizing movie theater owner will price where marginal costs equal marginal revenue for each group. As you can see in Exhibit 1(b), the demand curve for kids is rather elastic, perhaps not too different than the perfectly elastic demand curve of perfect competition, where marginal revenue is equal to price. The adult demand curve, shown in Exhibit 1(a), is more downward sloping at any given price and quantity (relatively inelastic), meaning the marginal revenue curve lies well below the demand curve at most output levels. Thus, the price charged adults is way above the point where marginal revenue equals marginal costs, whereas for kids, the price is not as much above the point where marginal revenue equals marginal costs.

EXHIBIT 1   **PRICE DISCRIMINATION IN MOVIE TICKET PRICES**

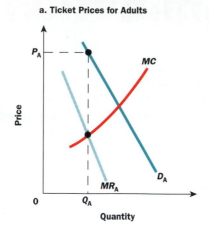

a. Ticket Prices for Adults

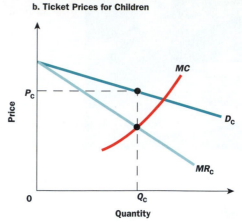

b. Ticket Prices for Children

If the movie theaters in the area have some monopoly power and if children have a lower willingness to pay than adults, then movie theaters can increase profits by price discriminating.

TUNE UP

PRICE DISCRIMINATION

Q: Landon Disembark enjoys traveling, but he hates to pay full price for his airline tickets. He wants to know why airlines require Saturday night stay-overs on their super-saver flights. Can you tell him?

A: This airline policy allows the airlines to discriminate against business travelers, who usually travel on the weekdays and are not as willing to spend their weekends away from home, family, or their favorite golf course. Thus, the business traveler has a more inelastic demand curve for flights (fewer substitutes). And if the airlines cut prices for these clients their revenues will fall. However, the personal traveler (perhaps a vacationer) is operating on a much more elastic demand curve. For these travelers, there are many substitutes, such as other modes of transportation, different times, and so on. Thus, the airlines can clearly make more money by separating the market according to each group's elasticity of demand rather than charging all users the same price.

Why do airlines make travelers stay overnight on the weekend to get the great rates?

RESALE PREVENTION: THE KEY TO PRICE DISCRIMINATION

For price discrimination to work, the person buying the product at a discount from the highest charged price must have difficulty in reselling the product to customers being charged more. Otherwise, those getting the item cheaply would want to buy extra amounts of the product at the discounted price (increasing demand and thus the profit-maximizing price for the discounted product) and sell them at a profit to others, reducing the number of customers available to the firm to sell at the higher price (thus reducing demand and lowering the profit-maximizing price for that group). Price differentials between groups will erode if reselling is easy. Usually, price discrimination is limited to services and to some goods where it is inherently difficult to resell or where the producer can effectively prevent resale. For example, the movie theater operator can simply refuse to admit adults who show a child's admission ticket, and airlines can put restrictions on a ticket indicating the conditions under which it may be used by passengers.

TUNE UP

PRICE DISCRIMINATION

MANUFACTURER'S COUPON / EXPIRES 9/26/98

SAVE 50¢ on MOP & GLO® Floor Shine Product

Q: Tara Longaline loves to go through the Sunday paper and cut out supermarket coupons. How do you think Tara's coupon-clipping habits apply to the concept of price discrimination?

A: Often, the key to price discrimination is observing the difference in demand curves for different customers. For example, Tara, who spends an hour looking through the Sunday paper for coupons, will probably have a relatively more elastic demand curve than, say, a busy and wealthy physician or executive.

QUANTITY DISCOUNTS

Another form of price discrimination occurs when customers buy in large quantities. This is often the case with public utilities and wholesalers, but even stores will sell a six-pack of soda for less than six single cans. For example, the local bagel shop might sell you a baker's dozen, where you may get 13 bagels for the price of 12. This type of price discrimination allows the producer to charge a higher price for the first unit than for, say, the 20th unit. If the monopolists charged the same price for all of the units that they charged for the 20th unit, then consumers would have a lot more consumer surplus. That is, instead of charging the lower price for all the units, this form of price discrimination allows the producer to extract some consumer surplus.

CONCEPT CHECK

1. Price discrimination occurs when producers charge different prices for the same good or service when no cost differences exist.
2. Price discrimination occurs because producers can make profits by charging different prices, if demand differs among buyers.
3. Price discrimination would not work well if the person buying the product could easily resell the product to another customer at a higher, profitable price.

---

1. How do we define price discrimination?
2. Why does price discrimination arise from the profit-maximization motive?
3. What principle will a profit-maximizing monopolist use in trying to price discriminate among different groups of customers?
4. Why will a price-discriminating monopolist charge a higher price to relatively inelastic demanders than to relatively elastic demanders?
5. Why is preventing resale the key to successful price discrimination?
6. Why is it generally easier to price discriminate for services than for goods?

ⓖ Application: Let's Play Monopoly

Is a true monopoly hard to find? There are substitutes for just about everything. Admittedly, some substitutes are better than others. However, there are some situations that come close to a monopoly. In this article you will see some of the candidates.

THE FIRST ANNUAL CONTEST FOR BEST MONOPOLY IN AMERICA

It's time for the first annual contest to choose the best operating monopoly in America. The finalists, selected by a panel of Harvard economists, are as follows:

1. The U.S. Postal Service
2. OPEC
3. Almost any cable TV company
4. The Ivy League universities (for administering financial aid to students)
5. The NCAA (for administering payments to student-athletes)

The U.S. Postal Service claims to be the longest-running monopoly in America and has the distinction of having its control over first-class mail prescribed (perhaps) by the U.S. Constitution. The monopoly has preserved large flows of revenues and high wage rates despite studies that show that private companies could carry the mail more efficiently at substantially reduced cost. On the other hand, the position of the service has been eroded by successful competition on package delivery, the entry of express delivery services, and, potentially most damaging, the entry of introduction of fax machines and e-mail. Thus, despite past glories, it is hard to be sanguine about the long-term prospects of the post office as a flourishing monopoly.

OPEC (the Organization of Petroleum Exporting Countries) was impressive in generating billions of dollars for its members from 1973 to the early 1980s. To understand the functioning of this cartel, it is important to sort out the good guys from the bad guys. The good

103RD MEETING OF THE CONFERENCE
ORGANIZATION OF THE PETROLEUM EXPORTING COUNTRIES (OPEC)

The Dharmawangsa, 26 November - 1 December 1997
JAKARTA, INDONESIA

guys, like Saudi Arabia and Kuwait, are the ones that have typically held oil production below capacity and thereby kept prices above the competitive level. The bad guys, like Libya and Iraq (when Iraq was allowed to produce oil), are the ones that have produced as much as they could and thereby kept prices low. The good guys were responsible for the vast expansion of oil revenues during the blissful period after 1973. (Hence, these producers were responsible for the considerable difficulties endured by oil consumers.) But, unfortunately, these countries could not keep the other OPEC members in line and were also unable to exclude new producers or prevent conservation by consumers. Thus, oil prices plummeted in 1986, and only the start of the Persian Gulf crisis in summer 1990 could get prices temporarily back to a responsible level. In any event, it is unclear that OPEC qualifies for the contest: it is not really American, and its members would probably be arrested for price fixing if they ever held an official meeting in America.

Most cable TV companies have government-issued licenses that keep competitors out. Thus, this business supports the hypothesis that private monopolies are not sustainable for long unless they have the weight of government behind them. The rapid escalation of prices and the limitations on services seem, however, to be getting customers and their congressional representatives progressively more annoyed. Thus, it would not be surprising if legislative action leads soon to a deterioration of the cable companies' monopoly power. It may even happen that consumers will be able to choose among cable companies in the same way that they choose currently among long-distance telephone carriers. The growing market for satellite dishes is also a concern. How will the struggling cable providers maintain a respectable cartel in this environment? This fear about the future diminishes the claim of this otherwise worthy contestant for the first annual prize.

Officials of Ivy League universities have been able to meet in semipublic forums to set rules that determine prices of admission (tuition less financial aid) as a func-

tion of applicant characteristics, especially financial resources. In some cases, the schools pooled information to agree in advance on the right price to charge to a specific customer. Airlines and other industries that wish to price discriminate can only dream about this kind of set-up. Moreover, the universities have more or less successfully applied a high moral tone to the process: rich applicants—especially smart rich applicants—are charged more than the competitive price for schooling in order to subsidize the education of the smart poor. (It may be desirable public policy to subsidize the smart poor, but it is unclear why this subsidy should come from the smart rich rather than from taxpayers in general.) The universities' enviable cartel position was damaged by the unenlightened Department of Justice, which argued that the price-setting meetings were a violation of antitrust laws. Since most of the universities involved agreed to stop these practices, it may be that future prices for private higher education will come closer to being competitively determined. It seems that this prospect has already motivated some distinguished universities to declare themselves as being in financial difficulty.

The final contestant, the NCAA (National Collegiate Athletic Association), has been highly successful in holding down "salaries" paid to college athletes. It would be one thing merely to collude to determine price ceilings (for example, to restrict payments so that they not exceed tuition plus room and board and some minor additional amounts), but the NCAA has also managed to monopolize all the moral arguments. Consider a poor ghetto resident who can play basketball well but not well enough to make it to the NBA (National Basketball Association). If there were no NCAA, this player might be able legitimately to accumulate a significant amount of cash during a four-year career. But the NCAA ensures that the player will remain poor after four years and, moreover, has convinced most observers that it would be morally wrong for the college to pay the player a
continued

competitively determined wage for his or her services. For many economists, this interference with competition—in a setting that has no obvious reasons for market failure—is itself morally repugnant. But the outrage is compounded here because the transfer is from poor ghetto residents to rich colleges. Compare the situation of contestant number 4, the Ivy League universities, in which the transfer from rich to poor students can readily be supported on Robin Hood grounds. The NCAA has the much more difficult task of defending a policy that prevents many poor individuals from earning money. Incredibly, this defense has been so successful that it has even allowed the organization to maintain the moral high ground. When the NCAA maintains its cartel by punishing schools that violate the rules (by paying too much), almost no one doubts that the evil entities are the schools or persons who paid the athletes rather than the cartel enforcers who prevented the athletes from getting paid. Given this extraordinary balancing act, the decision of the panelists was straightforward: the NCAA is the clear and deserving winner of the first annual prize for Best Monopoly in America.

SOURCE: Robert Barro, *The Wall Street Journal*, August 27, 1991, p. A12.

We see in this rather lengthy article that a true monopolist is very hard to find. Over time, monopoly power seems to fade. We have seen the stagecoach lose its monopoly power to the railroad, only to lose its monopoly power to trucks and cars. In other words, monopoly power is one of degree, and it is very difficult to hold monopoly power for a long period of time because there are substitutes for most goods and services.

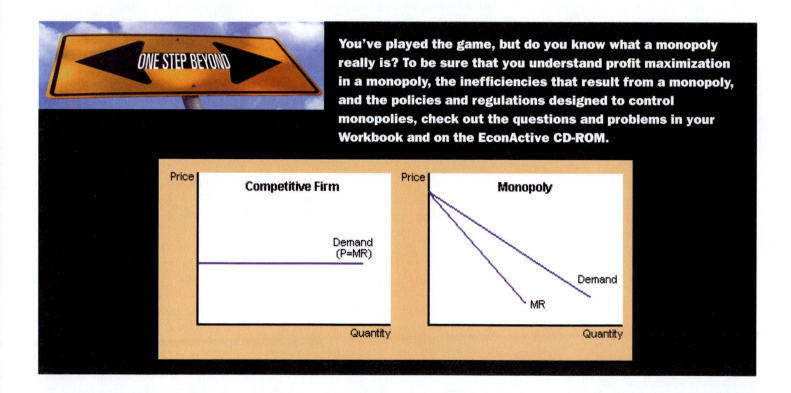

ONE STEP BEYOND

You've played the game, but do you know what a monopoly really is? To be sure that you understand profit maximization in a monopoly, the inefficiencies that result from a monopoly, and the policies and regulations designed to control monopolies, check out the questions and problems in your Workbook and on the EconActive CD-ROM.

PHOTO CREDITS MODULE 10

Page **256:** © 1998 Don Couch Photography; Page **257:** © 1998 Don Couch Photography; Page **258:** © 1998 Don Couch Photography; Page **260:** © 1998 Don Couch Photography; Page **261:** © Timothy O'Keefe/Bruce Coleman/PNI; Page **263:** DeBeers, Inc.; Page **264:** © Dean Abramson/ Stock, Boston/PNI; Page **266:** © Don Wright. Reprinted by permission; Page **267:** © PhotoDisc; Page **268:** Microsoft Corporation; Page **269:** © David Burnett/Contact Press Images/PNI; Page **270:** © Ron Vesely Photography; Page **272:** © Lawrence Migdale/Stock, Boston/PNI; Page **273:** © Bill Gallery/Stock, Boston/PNI; Page **274:** © Digital Stock; Page **275:** © Jeff Kaufman/FPG International; Page **276:** © Dennis Junor/Photo Network/PNI; Page **278:** top, © Brian Spurlock/Spurlock Photography; bottom, © Costa Manos/Magnum Photos/PNI; Page **279:** left, © Liane Enkelis/Stock, Boston/PNI; right, AP Photo/Charles Dharapak

Monopolistic Competition

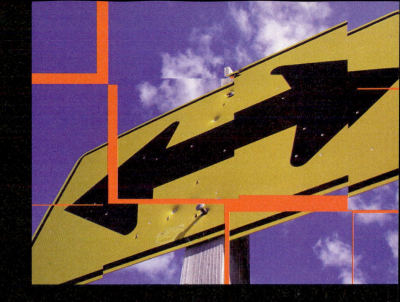

A. Monopolistic Competition
What are the distinguishing
characteristics of monopolistic
competition?

B. Price and Output Determination in Monopolistic Competition
How are equilibrium price and output determined
in monopolistic competition?

C. Monopolistic Competition versus Perfect Competition
What are the similarities and differences between monopolistic
competition and perfect competition?

D. Advertising
Is advertising a waste of society's resources?

E. Application: New Balance Carves Out a Niche
How does New Balance differentiate its product?

A Monopolistic Competition

- What is monopolistic competition?
- What is product differentiation?
- What is the shape of the demand curve for a monopolistic competitive firm?

The range of potential practical applications of monopoly and perfect competition analysis is very broad. In reality, many goods and services will be traded in markets that contain elements of both monopoly and perfect competition. Theories of monopolistic competition, which we will cover here, and oligopoly, which we shall consider in Module 12, are designed to deal with markets that lie between the extreme cases of perfect competition and monopoly.

WHAT IS MONOPOLISTIC COMPETITION?

Monopolistic competition is a market structure that allows many producers of somewhat different products to compete with one another. For example, a restaurant is a monopoly in the sense that it has a unique name, menu, quality of service, location, and so on, but it also has many competitors—others selling prepared meals. That is, monopolistic competition has features common to both monopoly and perfect competition even though that might sound like an oxymoron—like jumbo shrimp. Like monopoly, individual sellers believe that they have some market power; but unlike monopoly, there are many close substitutes coming from other monopolistically competitive firms. Firms in monopolistically competitive markets recognize the existence of competitors as a group, imposing a limit on the prices they can charge and still selling a particular level of output, but they do not consider competitors as rivals who are watching them closely (e.g., restaurants in a medium-sized city). Because of the relatively free entry of new firms, the long-run price and output behavior and zero long-run economic profits of monopolistic competition are similar to that of perfect competition. However, the monopolistically competitive firm produces a product that is different (that is, differentiated rather than homogeneous) from others, which leads to some degree of monopoly power. In a sense, each seller in a market of monopolistic competition may be regarded as a "monopolist"

of his own particular brand of the commodity, but unlike a firm in the monopoly model, there is competition by many firms selling similar (but not identical) brands. For example, a buyer in a city of moderate size in the market for books, CDs, toothpastes, furniture, shampoo, video rentals, restaurants, eyeglasses, running shoes, and music lessons has many competing sellers from which to choose.

WHAT ARE THE THREE BASIC CHARACTERISTICS OF MONOPOLISTIC COMPETITION?

The theory of monopolistic competition is based on three characteristics: (1) product differentiation, (2) many sellers, and (3) free entry.

What Is Product Differentiation?

One characteristic of monopolistic competition is **product differentiation**. Product differentiation is the accentuation of unique product qualities—real or perceived—to develop a specific product identity. The significant feature of differentiation is the belief on the part of the buyers that the products of the various sellers are not the same, whether the products are actually physically different or not. An example of a product of which the various brands are very similar or identical but buyers may believe them to be different is aspirin or some brands of over-the-counter cold medicines. Product differentiation leads to preferences among buyers to deal with particular sellers or to purchase the products of particular sellers.

Physical differences Physical differences constitute a primary source of product differentiation. For example, brands of ice cream, beer, or colas (such as Pepsi versus Coca-Cola) differ significantly in taste to many buyers. Also, there are physical differences among various makes of cars, which lead some buyers to prefer one make over another.

Which is a homogeneous good and which is a differentiated good?

IS A BEER A BEER?

To show that some differentiation is perceived rather than real, blind taste tests on beer were conducted on 250 participants. Four cans of identical beer with different labels were presented to the subjects as four different brands of beer. In the end, all of the subjects believed that the brands of beer were different and that they could tell the difference between them. Another interesting result came out of the taste tests—most of the participants commented that at least one of the beers was unfit for human consumption.

SOURCE: R. Ackoff and J. Emshoff, *Sloan Management Review*, Spring 1976, p. 12.

CONSIDER THIS:
Product differentiation, whether perceived or real, can be effective.

Some buyers view these two different types of ice cream as being very different.

Some people will write with any pen, while others will only use expensive ones.

Prestige Prestige considerations also differentiate products to a significant degree. Many persons prefer to be seen using the currently popular brand, while others prefer the "off" brand. Prestige considerations are particularly important with gifts—Cuban cigars, Montblanc pens, caviar, Godiva chocolates, fine wines and champagnes, BMWs, and so on.

Location Location is a major differentiating factor in retailing. Shoppers are not willing to travel long distances to purchase items that are minor in the overall expenditure pattern, which is one reason for the large number of convenience stores and service station mini-marts. Because most buyers realize that there is no significant difference among brands of gasoline, their choice of gasoline might be influenced by the location of a gas station.

Service Service considerations are likewise significant for product differentiation. Speedy and friendly service or lenient "return" policies are important to many people. Likewise, speed and quality of service may significantly influence a person's choice of restaurants.

What Is the Impact of Many Sellers?

When many firms compete for the same customers, any particular firm has little control or interest over what other firms do. That is, a fast-food restaurant may charge a higher or lower price or improve service without a retaliatory move on the part of a competing fast-food restaurant, because the effort necessary to learn about such changes may have marginal costs that are greater than the marginal benefits—you are busy "doing your thing."

What Is the Significance of Free Entry?

Entry in monopolistic competition is relatively unrestricted in the sense that new firms may easily start the production of close substitutes for existing products, like restaurants, styling salons, barber shops, and many forms of retail activity. Because of relatively free entry, economic profits tend to be eliminated in the long run, as was the case in perfect competition.

Some shop here because they can order their groceries by phone, fax, or computer and then have them delivered to their home.

STORES CRACK DOWN ON RETURN POLICIES

Retailers are reaching to the point of no return. Why? Take the Best Buy customer who recently demanded a refund on a hand-held video recorder that he insisted was defective. When the stores repair technicians played back the tape inside, they found the camera had done its job: First was the splashy shot as the camera tumbled into a swimming pool. Then underwater footage as it sank to the bottom. That was where the recording stopped. . . .

Best Buy has quit taking back goods from customers who don't have a sales receipt. No exceptions. If customers want to bring back an already opened laptop computer or a video camera, they must now pay Best Buy a "restocking fee" equal to 15 percent of the purchase price.

Wal-Mart Stores Inc. of Bentonville, Arkansas, has abandoned its open-ended return offer and set a 90-day limit for most items. The new policy is designed to combat customers who take their sweet time returning merchandise, such as the shopper who several years ago received a refund for a battered thermos. The store later learned from the manufacturer that the thermos had been purchased in the 1950s, before Wal-Mart opened.

Catalog clothier L.L. Bean Inc., which for years didn't question customers about returns, has decided to crack down. That, a spokeswoman for the Freeport, Maine company says, is because some shoppers were returning goods they had purchased at garage sales. One even tried to return worn clothes dug out of a closet of a relative who died.

SOURCE: "Without a Receipt You May Get Stuck," *Wall Street Journal*, November 18, 1996, p. 1.

CONSIDER THIS:
If most stores start applying tougher standards for returned goods, is it possible that a store that keeps a liberal return policy might benefit? It might be one way for a store to differentiate its product from those of its competitors.

We guarantee everything but the weather.

For a wide variety of gear and clothing that looks good, feels great, and is always 100% guaranteed, there's only one place to turn. The new L.L. Bean Fall catalog.

Call for your FREE Fall catalog. 1-800-394-5046.

Or shop on-line at www.llbean.com

CONCEPT CHECK

1. The theory of monopolistic competition is based on three primary characteristics: product differentiation, many sellers, and free entry.

2. There are many sources of product differentiation, including physical differences, prestige, location, and service.

---

1. How is monopolistic competition a mixture of monopoly and perfect competition?
2. Why is product differentiation necessary for monopolistic competition?
3. What are some common forms of product differentiation?
4. Why are many sellers necessary for monopolistic competition?

5. Why is free entry necessary for monopolistic competition?
6. List three ways that a grocery store might differentiate itself from its competitors.
7. What might make you choose one gas station over another?

(B) Price and Output Determination in Monopolistic Competition

■ How is short-run equilibrium determined?
■ How is long-run equilibrium determined?

HOW IS SHORT-RUN EQUILIBRIUM DETERMINED?

Because monopolistically competitive sellers are price makers (like monopolists) rather than price takers, they do not regard price as a given by market conditions like perfectly competitive firms. Because each firm sells a slightly different product, the firm's demand curve is downward sloping but quite flat because of many close substitutes. In perfect competition, the demand curve was horizontal because each firm, of a great many sellers, sold the same homogeneous product. Given the position of an individual firm's demand curve, we can determine short-run equilibrium output and price using a method similar to that used to determine monopoly output and price.

The cost and revenue curves of a typical seller are shown in Exhibit 1; the intersection of the marginal revenue and marginal cost curves indicates that the short-run equilibrium output will be q^*. Now, by observing how much will be demanded at that output level, we find our equilibrium price, P^*. In Exhibit 1(a), we see that the firm is making short-run economic profits because P^* is greater than average total costs at q^*. In Exhibit 1(b), at q^*, price is below average total cost, so the firm is minimizing its economic loss. Other than the shape of the demand curve, this is no different than the monopolist's determination of price and output in the short run.

| EXHIBIT 1 | SHORT-RUN EQUILIBRIUM IN MONOPOLISTIC COMPETITION |

a. Determining Profits

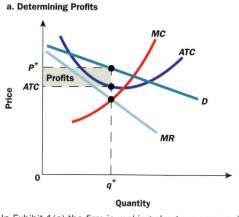

b. Determining Losses

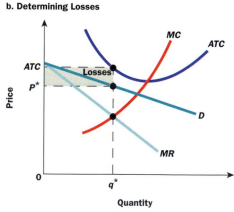

In Exhibit 1(a) the firm is making short-run economic profits because $P > ATC$. In Exhibit 1(b) the firm is incurring a short-run economic loss because $P < ATC$.

"GIVEN THE DOWNWARD SLOPE OF OUR DEMAND CURVE, AND THE EASE WITH WHICH OTHER FIRMS CAN ENTER THE INDUSTRY, WE CAN STRENGTHEN OUR PROFIT POSITION ONLY BY EQUATING MARGINAL COST AND MARGINAL REVENUE. ORDER MORE JELLY BEANS."

HOW IS LONG-RUN EQUILIBRIUM DETERMINED?

The short-run equilibrium situation, whether involving profits or losses, will probably not last long, because there

is entry and exit in the long run. If market entry and exit are sufficiently free, new firms will enter when there are economic profits, and some firms will exit when there are economic losses.

What Happens to Economic Profits When There Is Entry?

In Exhibit 2(a), we see the market impact as new firms enter to take advantage of the economic profits. As a result of this influx, there are now more sellers of similar products. This means that each new firm will cut into the demand of the existing firms. That is, the demand curve for each of the existing firms will fall. We see this in Exhibit 2(a) when demand shifts leftward from D_{SR} to D_{LR}. This decline in demand continues to occur until the long-run average total cost (LRATC) curve becomes tangent with the demand curve, and economic profits are reduced to zero.

What Happens to Losses When Some Firms Exit?

When firms are making economic losses, some firms will exit the industry. As some firms exit, there are now fewer firms in the market. This increases the demand for the remaining firms' product, shifting their demand curves to the right, from D_{SR} to D_{LR} as seen in Exhibit 2(b). The higher demand results in smaller losses for the existing firms until all losses finally disappear where the LRATC curve is tangent to the demand curve.

| EXHIBIT 2 | MARKET ENTRY AND EXIT IN THE LONG RUN |

a. Firms Enter the Market

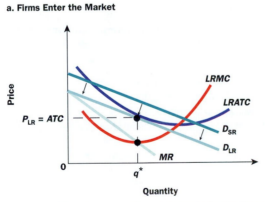

b. Firms Exit the Market

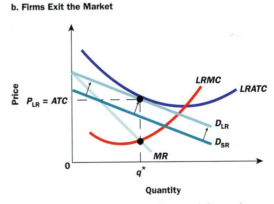

Excess profits attract new firms into the industry. As a result, the firm's share of the market declines and demand shifts down. Profits are eliminated when $P_{LR} = LRATC$; that is, when the LRATC curve is tangent to D_{LR}.

ACHIEVING LONG-RUN EQUILIBRIUM

In short, long-run equilibrium will occur when demand is equal to average total costs for each firm at a level of output at which each firm's demand curve is just tangent to its *LRATC* curve. The point of tangency will always occur at the same level of output as that at which marginal cost is equal to marginal revenue, as seen in Exhibit 3. At this equilibrium point, there are zero economic profits and there are no incentives for firms to either enter or exit the industry.

CAN FIRMS GUARD AGAINST FREE ENTRY AND STILL MAKE ECONOMIC PROFITS?

Complete adjustment toward equality of price with average cost may be checked by the strength of reputation (a "differentiation") built up by established firms. Those firms that are particularly successful in their advertising campaigns may create such strong consumer preferences that newcomers—even though they are able to enter the industry freely and cover their own costs—will not take sufficient business away from the well-established firms to eliminate their excess profits. Thus, a restaurant that has been particularly successful in promoting customer goodwill may continue to earn economic profits long after the

EXHIBIT 3

LONG-RUN EQUILIBRIUM FOR A MONOPOLISTICALLY COMPETITIVE FIRM

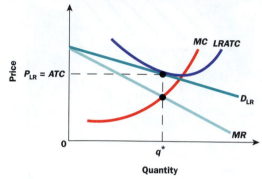

Long-run equilibrium occurs at q^*, where $D = LRATC$ and $MR = MC$.

entry of new firms has brought about equality of price and average cost, or even losses, for the others. In these instances, adjustments toward a final equilibrium situation involving equality of price and average cost do not proceed with the certainty that is illustrated by the model of monopolistic competition.

TUNE UP

LONG-RUN EQUILIBRIUM

Q: Cassie Blanca is a movie buff who loves old Humphrey Bogart films. She's thinking about getting together with several friends to buy a movie theater that would show all of the old classic films. Cassie is convinced that because everyone loves classic movies, their theater will be fantastically successful, making her and her friends all very rich. Is Cassie right?

A: Possibly. But even if she is right, once other entrepreneurs see large potential profits from investing in old classic films, the economic profit will be gradually eliminated. So if Ms. Blanca and her friends do exceptionally well in their venture, there will always be the threat of new entrants, and that threat is greater when entry is easy and economic profits are high. So, even if their theater is successful, their profits will decline in the long run—but it may still be worth doing, because recall that even at zero economic profits, the firm is covering explicit and implicit costs.

BURGER KING'S LEFT-HANDED HAMBURGER

CONSIDER THIS:
If sellers can differentiate their products, they may continue to make economic profits after entry. Effective advertising may be one way to keep loyal customers and appeal to new ones. Burger King apparently had thousands of customers requesting their left-handed Whopper, even though it was just an April Fool's joke.

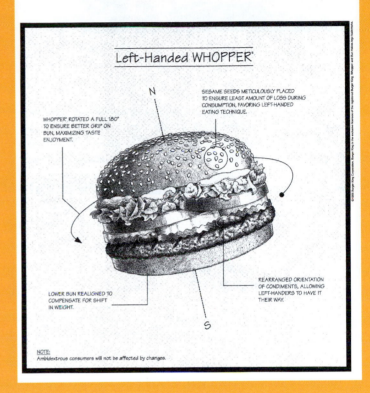

Burger King® introduces the left-handed Whopper.®

Finally, after years of neglect, left-handed eaters will no longer need to conform to traditional right-handed eating methods when enjoying America's favorite burger.

CONCEPT CHECK

1. A monopolistic competitive firm is making short-run economic profits when the equilibrium price is greater than average total costs at the equilibrium output; when equilibrium price is below average total cost at the equilibrium output, the firm is minimizing its economic loss.

2. In the long run, equilibrium price equals average total costs. With that, economic profits are zero, so there are no incentives for firms to either enter or exit the industry.

1. How is the short-run profit-maximizing policy of a monopolistically competitive firm like that of a monopoly?
2. How is the choice of whether to operate or shut down in the short run the same for a monopolistic competitor as for either a monopoly or a perfectly competitive firm?
3. How is the long-run equilibrium of monopolistic competition like that of perfect competition?

4. How is the long-run equilibrium of monopolistic competition different from that of perfect competition?
5. If Frank's hot dog stand was very profitable when he first opened, why should he expect those profits to fall over time?
6. Why do you think there are some restaurants that are highly profitable while other restaurants in the same general area are going out of business?

Monopolistic Competition versus Perfect Competition

- What are the differences and similarities between monopolistic competition and perfect competition?
- What is excess capacity?
- What is allocative efficiency?

We have seen that both monopolistic competition and perfect competition have many buyers and sellers and relatively free entry. However, product differentiation allows a monopolistic competitor the ability to have some influence over price. Consequently, a monopolistically competitive firm has a downward-sloping demand curve, but because of the large number of good substitutes for its product, it tends to be much more elastic than the demand curve for a monopolist.

WHAT IS THE SIGNIFICANCE OF EXCESS CAPACITY?

Because of the downward slope of the demand curve, its point of tangency with the *LRATC* curve *will not* and *cannot* be at the lowest level of average cost. What does this mean? It means that even when long-run adjustments are complete, firms will not be operating at a level that permits the lowest average cost of production—the *efficient scale* of the firm. The existing plant, even though optimal for the equilibrium volume of output, will not be used to capacity; that is, **excess capacity** will exist at that level of output. Unlike a perfectly competitive firm, a monopolistically competitive firm could increase output and lower its average total costs, as seen in Exhibit 1(a). However, any attempt to increase output to attain lower average cost would be unprofitable, because the price reduction necessary to sell the greater output would cause marginal revenue to fall below the marginal cost of the increased output. As you can see in Exhibit 1(a), to the right of q^*, marginal cost is greater than marginal revenue. Consequently, in monopolistic competition, there is a tendency toward too many firms in the industry, each producing a volume of output less than that which would allow lowest cost. The term economists use for this is that the firm is failing to reach **productive efficiency.** For example, there may be too many grocery stores and too many service stations, in the sense that if the total volume of business were concentrated in a smaller number of sellers, average cost, and thus price, could in principle be less.

WHAT IS ALLOCATIVE EFFICIENCY?

Productive inefficiency is not the only problem with a monopolistically competitive firm. Exhibit 1(a) shows that the firm is also not operating where the price is equal to marginal costs. In the monopolistic competitive model, at the intersection of the *MC* and *MR* curves (q^*), we can clearly see that price is greater than marginal cost. This means that society is willing to pay more for the product (the price, P^*) than it costs society to produce it. In this case, the firm is failing to reach allocative efficiency, where price equals marginal cost. In short, this means that the firm is underallocating resources—too many firms are producing, each at output levels that are less than full capacity. Note that in Exhibit 1(b), the perfectly competitive firm has reached both productive efficiency ($P = ATC$ at the minimum point on the *LRATC* curve) and allocative efficiency ($P = MC$). However, it is clear that these drawbacks in the monopolistically competitive market would be far greater in monopoly, where the demand curve is relatively inelastic (steeper).

Furthermore, in defense of monopolistic competition, the higher average costs and the slightly higher price and lower output may just be the price we pay for differentiated products—variety. That is, just because we have not met the conditions for productive and allocative efficiency, it is difficult to say whether society is better off or not. Imagine a world where everyone wore the same drab clothes, drove the same boring cars, and lived in identical houses. In other words, most individuals are willing to pay for a little variety even if it costs somewhat more.

WHAT ARE THE REAL COSTS OF MONOPOLISTIC COMPETITION?

We have just argued that perfect competition meets the test of allocative and productive efficiency and monopolistic competition does not. So can we "fix" monopolistic competition to look more like an efficient, perfectly competitive firm? One remedy might entail using government

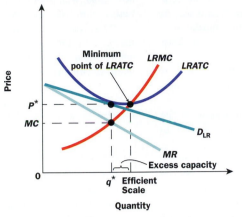

a. A Monopolistically Competitive Firm

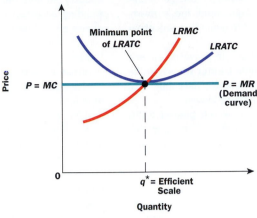

b. A Perfectly Competitive Firm

Comparing the differences between perfect competition and monopolistic competition, we see that the monopolistically competitive firm fails to meet both productive efficiency, minimizing costs in the long run, and allocative efficiency, producing output where $P = MC$.

regulation, as in the case of a natural monopoly. However, this process would be costly, because a monopolistically competitive firm makes no economic profits in the long run. Therefore, asking monopolistically competitive firms to equate price and marginal costs would lead to economic losses, because long-run average total costs would be greater than price at $P = MC$. Consequently, the government would have to subsidize the firm. It might be easier to live with the inefficiencies in monopolistically competitive markets rather than the difficulties in regulating and the cost of subsidizing them.

We argued that the monopolistically competitive firm does not operate at the minimum point of the *LRATC* curve and the perfectly competitive firm does. However, is this a fair comparison? In monopolistic competition there are differentiated goods and services, and in perfect competition there are not. In other words, the excess capacity that exists in monopolistic competition is the price we pay for product differentiation. Have you ever thought about the many restaurants, movies, and gasoline stations that have "excess capacity"? Can you imagine a world where all firms were working at full capacity? After all, choice is a good, and most of us value some choice dearly. Thus, excess capacity is the price we pay for differentiated goods, and many of us are willing to pay this price.

ARE THE DIFFERENCES BETWEEN MONOPOLISTIC COMPETITION AND PERFECT COMPETITION EXAGGERATED?

The significance of the difference between the relationship of long-run marginal cost to price in monopolistic competition and in perfect competition can easily be exaggerated. As long as preferences for various brands are not extremely strong, the demand for the products of firms will be highly elastic. Accordingly, the points of tangency with the *LRATC* curves are not likely to be far above the point of lowest cost, and excess capacity will be small, as

How much do you value variety in clothing?

REI: TRY IT, YOU'LL LIKE IT

Pull into the parking garage under Recreational Equipment Inc.'s downtown store and it looks like any other parking garage.

But when you ride the elevator up and open the door, you don't enter the store. Instead, you're back outside, listening to a waterfall and the rustle of leaves.

. . . The company, which posted $536 million in sales last year, is a cooperative where customers become members for a one-time fee.

. . . The Seattle store has become a leading tourist attraction, rivaling the Space Needle and Pike Place Market for the number of annual visitors. It was two years in the design and construction. The result is a superstore that takes the current trend among retailers to entertain customers to another level. The design, layout, and features of the store serve to not just enthrall shoppers, but educate them.

. . . REI is about outdoor, muscle-powered sports—climbing, hiking, skiing, paddling and bicycling. REI created an open space in the front of the store, with trees and indigenous Washington foliage, and a waterfall that captures rainwater from the roof. Cutting through the trees is a 417-foot gravel path for customers to try out mountain bikes.

. . . From the hallway one can enter the store or stop at the flagship's trademark—a 65-foot climbing pinnacle encased in glass and lighted at night.

When the store first opened, customers would rush in and sign their names on a list to climb the pinnacle while testing rock-climbing equipment. They received beepers that would buzz them wherever they were in the store to let them know it was their turn to climb. Initial waits were a couple of hours, but that has shortened in the 20 months the store has been open.

For REI to remain a healthy retailer—it's the 14th largest sports goods retailer in the country—it must also increase membership. Building an urban superstore is one way to excite city slickers to the great outdoors.

. . . Test a waterproof coat in the Gore-Tex rain room.

Want a water purifier? Head to the fountain display where various types are assembled for testing.

Like a certain tent? Find a spot on the floor in the tent area and see how easy or difficult it is to pitch it.

Looking for a pair of heavy-duty hiking boots? Try one on and walk up and down the footwear test trail on the second floor. It has a gravel slope and logged steps so you can see how the boot feels going up hill and downhill.

. . . Granted, trying out a product may make a customer decide the product is not what he or she needs. But more often than not, they will make a purchase they are happy with, [REI spokesman] Collins said.

"They are not going to get six miles away from their car—down a trail somewhere—and decide 'this is not the product I wanted," he said.

SOURCE: Dina Bunn, "The Outside Story," *Rocky Mountain News,* May 17, 1998, pp. 1G, 12G.

CONSIDER THIS:
REI is trying to increase the demand for its products, as well as change the elasticity, through the use of its unique interactive facilities. If it is successful, the result could be an increase in demand and a demand curve that is relatively more inelastic.

REI, which sells outdoor athletic gear, differentiates its product by allowing customers to try out the equipment before they buy it.

decline more than the amount of the per-unit costs of advertising. In other words, average total costs in some situations actually decline after extensive advertising is begun. This can happen because advertising may allow firms to operate closer to the point of minimum cost on their *LRATC* curve. Therefore, it is possible that the decline in production costs (through specialization and division of labor in the short run and/or scale economies in the long run) exceeds the added advertising cost, per unit of output, allowing the firm to sell its product at a lower price—like Toys R Us versus a smaller, owner-operated toy store (see Exhibit 2). Unless advertising significantly increases total demand for the product, other firms may be forced out of business, and sales will then be concentrated in the hands of a smaller number of firms.

Firms in monopolistic competition are not likely to experience substantial cost reductions as output increases. Therefore, they probably will not be able to offset advertising costs with lower production costs, particularly if advertising costs are high. Even if advertising does add to total cost, however, it is true that advertising conveys information. Through advertising, the customer becomes aware of options that he or she has in terms of product choice. Advertising helps the customer arrive at a choice of product that best meets his or her needs, and it also informs the price-conscious customer about the cost of the product. In this way, advertising lowers information costs. That is one reason that the Federal Trade Commission opposes bans on advertising.

TUNE UP

ADVERTISING

Q: Polly Ester manages a clothing shop in Chicago. Polly knows that advertising can be expensive, and she is trying to decide if the benefits are worth the costs she would incur in advertising her store. How would you advise Polly?

A: In order for Polly's shop to compete with many other shops, she must advertise to demonstrate that her clothing store is not just there, but is different. Remember, monopolistically competitive firms are different from competitive firms because of their ability, to some extent, to set prices. If Polly can convince her customers that her product is better than her competitors, she may be able to influence the shape and position of the demand curve for the products she sells and potentially reap higher profits as a result of her advertising efforts.

EXHIBIT 2	ADVERTISING AND ECONOMIES OF SCALE

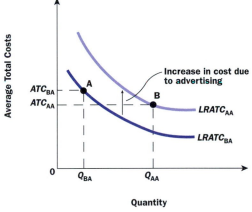

The long-run average total cost before advertising is shown as $LRATC_{BA}$. After advertising, the curve shifts to $LRATC_{AA}$. If the increase in demand resulting from advertising is significant, economies of scale from higher output levels may offset the advertising costs, allowing the firm to sell its product at a lower price.

What If Advertising Increases Competition?

However, if advertising reduces information costs, this leads to some interesting economic implications. For example, say that, as a result of advertising, we now know about more products that may be substitutes for the products we have been buying for years. That is, the more goods that are advertised, the more consumers are aware about different "substitute" products; consequently, this leads to increasingly competitive markets. Studies in the eyeglass, toy, and drug industries have shown that advertising has increased competition and led to lower prices in these markets.

1. With advertising, a firm hopes it can alter the elasticity of the demand for its product, making it more inelastic, and cause an increase in demand that will enhance profits.

2. To some, advertising manipulates consumer tastes and creates "needs" for trivial products. However, if one believes that people act rationally, this argument loses much of its force.

3. Where substantial economies of scale exist, it is possible that average production costs will decline more than the amount of the per-unit costs of advertising in the long run. Even in the short run, specialization and division of labor may cause advertising to decrease average costs.

4. By making consumers aware of different "substitute" products, advertising may lead to more competitive markets and lower consumer prices.

---

1. How can advertising make a firm's demand curve more inelastic?

2. What are the arguments made against private sector advertising?

3. What are the arguments made for private-sector advertising?

4. Can advertising actually result in lower costs? How?

5. Why is advertising more important for the success of chains such as Toys R Us and Office Depot than for the corner barber shop?

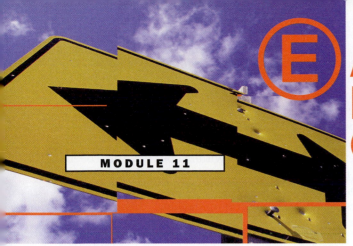

Application: New Balance Carves Out a Niche

Instead of paying big-time athletes huge advertising endorsements, what has New Balance's strategy been to market its product? How has New Balance differentiated its product from the others? In the athletic shoe market, do you think advertising is more effective on older adults or youths and teenagers?

SNEAKER COMPANY TAGS OUT-OF-BREATH BABY BOOMERS

JOSEPH PEREIRA

BOSTON—New Balance, Inc. has been spending a scant $4 million a year to advertise its athletic shoes. Its best-known endorser is a marathoner named Mark Coogan, who placed 41st in the last Olympics. Its logo is a prosaic NB.

And its shoes are jumping off retailers' shelves.

While Nike, Inc. and other sneaker makers struggle to eke out gains in shoe sales, New Balance is riding a boom—specifically, the baby boom. Using a flashless formula that includes moderate prices, links to podiatrists, and an expansive range of widths tailored to an aging population's expanding heft, the company gobbled up market share last year while recording a 16 percent gain in sales to $560 million.

It's a triumph of demographics over razzle-dazzle. While industry leaders like Nike, Reebok International Ltd., and Fila Holdings SpA jump through expensive hoops to court youngsters, New Balance is quietly tracking America's changing population. U.S. Census figures show that while the number of 20- to 34-year-olds in the country has declined by 5.3 million in the past seven years, the population of 35- to 59-year-olds has jumped by 16.5 million.

Although a youngster tends to buy more sneakers than a middle-ager, New Balance's older-age niche has some potent marketing virtues. Customers are less fickle, so the company doesn't worry as much about fashion swings.

"You won't find a poster of Michael Jordan hanging in the bedroom of a New Balance customer," says Jim Davis, New Balance's president and chief executive. The $4 million the company spends on advertising and promotions is less than 1 percent of Nike's $750 million or Reebok's $425 million.

Another tactic: While most companies offer shoes in two widths—medium and wide—New Balance offers consumers five choices, ranging from a narrow AA to an expansive EEEE. About 20 percent to 30 percent of the population has narrower, or wider, than average feet, and retailers say that they sell more EE and EEEE New Balances than any other widths offered under the brand.

SOURCE: Joseph Pereira, "Sneaker Company Tags Out-of-Breath Baby Boomers," *The Wall Street Journal*, January 1998, pp. B14, B21.

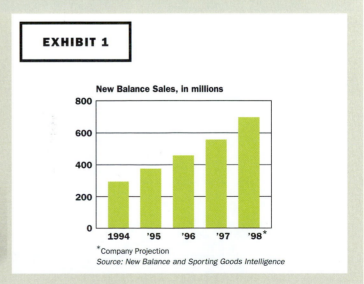

EXHIBIT 1

New Balance Sales, in millions

(Bar chart showing sales: 1994 ≈ 300, '95 ≈ 375, '96 ≈ 460, '97 ≈ 560, '98* ≈ 700)

*Company Projection
Source: New Balance and Sporting Goods Intelligence

In this article, we see that New Balance is spending a lot less money than its competitors—like Nike, Reebok, and Fila—on the advertising of athletic shoes. Instead of targeting the youth market, New Balance has decided to cater to the "baby boomers."

While this portion of the market is smaller, the strategy to target older customers has several benefits. Older customers seem to be less concerned if a prominent athlete is wearing their shoe. This saves millions of dollars in advertising endorsements. In addition, older customers are less concerned about new models. This allows retail stores to hold on to their inventories for longer periods of time before heavily discounting the discontinued models to free up shelf space.

New Balance has also differentiated its product by offering their shoes in a number of different widths. Because 20 to 30 percent of the population has narrower or wider than average feet, this has been a particularly important part of New Balance sales. The wider shoes have also been a favorite for podiatrists because it makes it easier to insert arch supports or other types of foot support devices. With podiatrists recommending New Balance, this has also helped New Balance sales over the years.

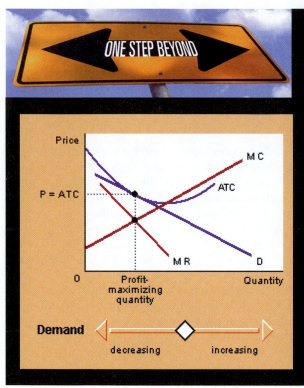

ONE STEP BEYOND

Studying late? Need a snack? Is your favorite late-night pizza parlor a monopolistically competitive firm? Use the Workbook problems and the Java-powered graphs on the EconActive CD-ROM to check your recall of the characteristics of a monopolistically competitive firm and your understanding of how those firms achieve equilibrium in the short run and long run.

PHOTO CREDITS MODULE 11

Page **285:** top left, © PhotoDisc; top right, © 1998 Don Couch Photography; bottom, © 1998 Don Couch Photography; Page **286:** top left, © 1998 Don Couch Photography; top right, © 1998 Don Couch Photography; bottom, Courtesy of Peapod, Inc.; Page **287:** L.L. Bean; Page **289:** © 1998 Sidney Harris; Page **291:** Burger King Corporation; Page **293:** © Digital Stock; Page **294:** left and right, © Benjamin Benschneider/1996, Seattle Times; Page **299:** © 1998 Don Couch Photography.

Oligopoly

A. Oligopoly
What are the distinguishing
characteristics of oligopoly?

B. Collusion and Cartels
What is collusion?

C. Oligopoly in the Long Run
Can market entry be deterred in the long run?

D. Game Theory and Strategic Behavior
How does game theory enlighten our understanding of the
strategic behavior of oligopolists?

E. Application: The OPEC Cartel
How has OPEC impacted the oil market?

Ⓐ Oligopoly

- What is oligopoly?
- What is mutual interdependence?
- Are economies of scale a major barrier to entry?

WHAT IS OLIGOPOLY?

Oligopolies exist, by definition, where relatively few firms control all or most of the production and sale of a product ("oligopoly" = few sellers). The products may be homogeneous or differentiated, but the barriers to entry are often very high, which makes it very difficult for firms to enter into the industry. Consequently, long-run economic profits may be earned by firms in the industry. Examples of oligopoly markets include commercial airlines, oil, automobiles, steel, breakfast cereals, computers, cigarettes, tobacco, and sports drinks. In all of these instances, the market is dominated by a few or several big companies, although they may have many different brands (e.g., General Motors, General Foods).

Sometimes oligopolies are local or regional in character, because high transportation costs or other considerations keep markets from being truly national or international in scope. For example, the top four newspapers in the United States have less than 10 percent of total U.S. newspaper circulation, but within their respective markets they are very strong. The *Los Angeles Times*, for example, has a large majority of readership in Los Angeles and the immediate surrounding areas, but it controls only a very small percent of the nation's total. Only a few daily newspapers, such as *The Wall Street Journal, USA Today*, and *The New York Times*, have a readership that is truly well dispersed throughout the country.

WHAT IS MUTUAL INTERDEPENDENCE?

Oligopoly is characterized by **mutual interdependence** among firms; that is, each firm shapes its policy with an eye to the policies of competing firms. Oligopolists must strategize, much like good chess or bridge players who are constantly observing and anticipating the moves of their

How many companies are in this market?

How is oligopoly like a game of chess?

rivals. Oligopoly is likely to occur whenever the number of firms in an industry is so small that any change in output or price by one firm appreciably impacts the sales of competing firms. In this situation, it is almost inevitable that competitors will respond directly to these actions in determining their own policy.

WHY DO OLIGOPOLIES EXIST?

Primarily, oligopoly is a result of the relationship between technological conditions of production and potential sales volumes. For many products, a reasonably low cost of production cannot be obtained unless a firm is producing a large fraction of the market output. In other words, substantial economies of scale are present in oligopoly markets. Automobile and steel production are classic examples of this. Because of legal concerns like patents, large start-up costs, and the presence of pronounced economies of scale, the barriers to entry are quite high in oligopoly.

HOW ARE ECONOMIES OF SCALE A BARRIER TO ENTRY?

Economies of large-scale production make operation on a small scale during the early years of a new firm extremely unprofitable. A firm cannot build up a large market overnight; in the interim, average total cost is so high that losses are heavy. Recognition of this fact discourages new firms from entering the market, as seen in Exhibit 1. In this graph, we see that if an automobile company produces quantity Q_1 rather than Q_0, they will be able to produce cars at a significantly lower cost. If the average total cost to a potential entrant is equivalent to point A on the $LRATC$ curve and the price of automobiles is less than P_0, then a new firm would be deterred from entering the industry.

EQUILIBRIUM PRICE AND QUANTITY IN OLIGOPOLY

It is difficult to predict how firms will react when there is mutual interdependence. No firm knows what its demand curve looks like with any degree of certainty and therefore has a very limited knowledge of its marginal revenue curve. In order to know anything about its demand curve, the firm must know how other firms will react to its prices and other policies. Thus, in the absence of additional assumptions, equating marginal revenue and expected marginal cost is regulated to guesswork. Thus, it is difficult for an oligopolist to determine its profit-maximizing price and output.

Do you think economies of scale are important in this industry? Unlike home-cooked meals, there are very few "home made" cars.

| EXHIBIT 1 | ECONOMIES OF SCALE AS A BARRIER TO ENTRY |

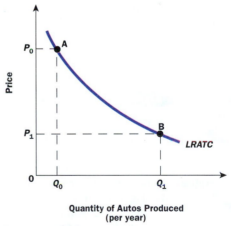

Economies of large-scale production make operation on a small scale more costly, *ceteris paribus*.

BEER WARS

REKHA BALU

A costly second front has opened in the Beer Wars: price.

A summer ritual in the beer business, discounting has in the past two years become a marketing tool for all seasons. That's great news for cost-conscious beer drinkers, of course, who are seeing 30-packs of popular brands in some markets priced as low as $7.99. For the brewers, however, kicking the year-round discounting habit could be difficult. And it is already cutting into industry profits.

Anheuser-Busch Cos. and Miller Brewing Co. have always slugged it out with advertising and promotions, spending hundreds of millions of dollars a year to boost their brands.

Talking frogs and skimpily clad young women, however, haven't been able to revive Americans' interest in beer drinking. Per capita annual beer consumption has fallen since its 1981 peak of 24.6 gallons or about 262 12-ounce cans for every man, woman, and child to 22.1 gallons in 1996. During those years, health awareness has cut into all kinds of booze consumption, rendering alcoholic beverages a mature business in which the best chance for growth is to take market share from a competitor.

Miller, a unit of Philip Morris Cos., and a distant No. 2 in beer to Anheuser, started a price war in early 1997 and was initially successful. . . . Anheuser didn't immediately follow, and Miller was able to seize almost two full points of market share, jumping from 20.6 percent of industry sales in the fourth quarter of 1996 to 22.4 percent in the second quarter of 1997. Anheuser's share fell during that same period to 43.8 percent from 46.6 percent, according to Beer Marketer's Insights Inc., a Nanuet, New York, consultant.

The move appears to have caught Anheuser off guard. . . But the Big Bud doesn't sleep for long. Anheuser responded with its own price cuts and quickly grabbed back lost sales; its market share soared to 47.5 percent for the fourth quarter of 1997, and Miller's was back to 20.9 percent. "It's tough with pricing to maintain an offensive advantage because the competition will follow," says Scott Bussen, a Miller spokesman.

TO SOME, PRICE DOESN'T MATTER: The discounting has taken its toll on brewer profits. Anheuser's revenue per 31-gallon barrel fell to $90.58 in 1997 from $91.12 the prior year. Miller's revenue per barrel fell to $78.19 from $80.79 in 1996, according to Beer Marketer's Insights. Anheuser's revenue per barrel for the first quarter of 1998 was 2 percent lower than a year earlier, according to the company.

ANHEUSER TRIES TO CUT BACK: At the same time, both major brewers are spending more on advertising and promotion this year, which raises costs and further pinches profit margins. "They're spending more and charging less, which leads to shrinking margins," says Tom Pirko, a consultant at Bevmark LLC.

FEW GAINS: Despite cutting prices, Miller has lost sales while Coors has gained by avoiding the price war.

	% Change in Volume	% Change in Price
Anheuser-Busch	+4%	−1%
Miller	−1	−2
Coors	+2	+1

SOURCE: Rekha Balu, "Big Brewers Find Price War Seems to Have No End" *The Wall Street Journal*, Industry Focus, July 2, 1998, p. B6.

CONSIDER THIS:
This rivalry shows the mutual interdependence characteristic of oligopoly markets. If Miller cuts prices, will Anheuser-Busch follow? How about Coors and others?

CONCEPT CHECK

1. Oligopolies exist where relatively few firms control all or most of the production and sale of a product. The products may be homogeneous or differentiated, but the barriers to entry are often very high and, consequently, there may be long-run economic profits.
2. Oligopoly is characterized by mutual interdependence among firms, with each firm shaping its policy with an eye to the policies of competing firms.
3. Economies of large-scale production make operation on a small scale extremely unprofitable. Recognition of this feature discourages new firms from entering the market.
4. Because the pricing decision of one firm influences the demand curve of competing firms in oligopoly, the oligopolist faces considerable uncertainty as to the location and shape of its demand and marginal revenue curves. Thus, it is difficult for an oligopolist to determine its profit-maximizing price and output.

---

1. Why is oligopoly characterized by mutual interdependence?
2. Why do economies of scale result in few sellers in oligopoly models?
3. How do economies of scale result in barriers to entry in oligopoly models?
4. Why does an oligopolist have a difficult time in finding its profit-maximizing price and output?
5. Why would an automobile manufacturer be more likely to be an oligopolist than your corner baker?

B Collusion and Cartels

- What is a price leader?
- Why do firms collude?
- What is joint profit maximization?
- Why does collusion break down?
- What is cost-plus pricing?

UNCERTAINTY AND PRICING DECISIONS

The uncertainties of pricing decisions are substantial in oligopoly. The implications of misjudging the behavior of competitors could prove to be disastrous. An executive who makes the wrong pricing move might force the firm to lose sales or, at a minimum, be forced to back down in an embarrassing fashion from an announced price increase. Because of this uncertainty, some believe that oligopolists change their prices less frequently than perfect competitors, whose prices may change almost continuously. The empirical evidence, however, does not clearly indicate that prices are in fact always "sticky" in oligopoly situations.

WHAT IS A PRICE LEADER AND A PRICE FOLLOWER?

Over time, an implied understanding may develop in an oligopoly market that a large firm is the **price leader,** sending a signal to competitors, perhaps through a press release, that they have increased their prices. Competitors that go along with the pricing decisions of the price leader are called **price followers.** However, in reality, in most industries it is doubtful that a single firm always serves as the initiator of price changes. Still, the pricing decisions of a giant firm are probably far more influential on industry trends than the actions of a small company. For example, General Motors was an important price leader in the automotive industry in the 1970s, Chase Manhattan has been a price leader (more precisely, an interest rate leader), and Kellogg is a price leader in the breakfast food industry.

WHY COLLUDE?

It is true that firms might tend to go along with price increases of competitors, the more certain they will be of having relatively inelastic demand curves (since the closest substitutes have also risen in price), meaning that they

What is a price leader?

have the potential of charging prices well above their marginal costs, producing greater monopoly profits. Because the actions and profits of oligopolists are so dominated by this mutual interdependence, the temptation is great for firms to collude—to get together and agree to act jointly in pricing and other matters. Collusion reduces uncertainty and increases the potential for monopoly profits. That is, firms might know that a price increase would enhance profits. From society's point of view, however, collusion has the same disadvantages monopoly does; namely, it creates a situation in which goods very likely become overpriced and underproduced, with consumers losing out from a misallocation of resources.

IS COLLUSION LIKE A MONOPOLY?

A truly collusive oligopoly that involves all firms in an industry could act as the equivalent of one large firm with several "plants" from the standpoint of pricing and output decisions. Acting in this matter, the economic effect of the collusive oligopolist is exactly the same as a monopolist; a single demand curve exists for the group of companies, which, after they determine the profit-maximization price, can agree on the output to be offered for sale by each firm in the group. Agreements between firms on sale, pricing, and other decisions are usually referred to as cartel agreements. The **cartel** is the collection of firms making the agreement.

WHAT IS JOINT PROFIT MAXIMIZATION?

Cartels may lead to what economists call **joint profit maximization.** Joint profit maximization requires the determination of price on the basis of the marginal revenue function derived from the total (or market) demand schedule for the product and the marginal cost schedules of the various firms, as shown in Exhibit 1. With outright agreements—necessarily secret because of antitrust laws (in the United States, at least)—firms that make up the market will attempt to estimate demand and cost schedules, and will set optimum price and output levels accordingly. If prices are set by one firm and followed by all others, the price setter will act on the basis of total cost schedules rather than its own situation, and other firms will abide by the decision. When collusive action is absent, maximum joint profits can be obtained only if each firm, acting independently, correctly estimates the price that is optimal from the standpoint of the group.

Equilibrium price and quantity for a collusive oligopoly, like those of a monopoly, are determined according to the intersection of the marginal revenue curve derived from the market demand curve and the horizontal sum of the short-run marginal cost curves for the oligopolists. As shown in Exhibit 1, the resulting equilibrium quantity is Q^*, and the equilibrium price is P^*. Collusion facilitates joint profit maximization for the oligopoly. Like monopoly, if the oligopoly is maintained in the long run, it charges a

higher price, produces less output, and fails to maximize social welfare, relative to perfect competition.

The manner in which total profits are shared among firms in the industry depends in part upon the relative costs and sales of the various firms. Firms with low costs and large supply capabilities will obtain the largest profits because they have great bargaining power. Sales, in turn, may depend in large measure upon consumer preferences for various brands if there is product differentiation. With outright collusion, firms may agree upon market shares and the division of profits. The division of total profits will depend upon the relative bargaining strength of the firms, influenced by relative financial strength, ability to inflict damage (through price wars) on other firms if an agreement is not reached, ability to withstand similar action on the part of other firms, relative costs, consumer preferences, and bargaining skills.

WHY ARE MOST COLLUSIVE OLIGOPOLIES SHORT-LIVED?

Collusive oligopolies are potentially highly profitable for participants but detrimental for society. Fortunately, most strong collusive oligopolies are rather short-lived for two reasons. First, in the United States and in some other nations, collusive oligopolies are strictly illegal under antitrust laws. On several occasions, firms convicted of illegal price-fixing agreements have been heavily fined and publicly embarrassed (although usually, but not always, the business executives running the corporations have avoided jail sentences). Therefore, there are possible costs both to executives and their corporations from engaging in illegal behavior.

Second, for collusion to work, firms must agree to restrict output to a level that will support the profit-maximization price. At that price, firms can earn above-normal accounting profits, or positive economic profits. Yet there is a great temptation for firms to cheat on the agreement of the collusive oligopoly, and because collusive agreements are illegal, the other parties have no way to punish the offender.

Suppose a cartel is formed that sells oil for $30 a barrel, well above the marginal cost of $6 (assuming for simplicity that marginal cost is constant for successive barrels). One firm that sells 50,000 barrels a day now may secretly cut the price to $29.50 and increase its sales to 100,000. By doing so, the firm can get some $450,000 in additional revenues (total revenues rise from $1,500,000 to $2,950,000) but incur only $300,000 in marginal costs ($6 per barrel of oil × 50,000 more barrels of oil per day), for an increase in profits of $1,150,000. The cheater is clearly undercutting the collusive agreement. However, if all of the cartel participants engage in such tactics, the real prevailing price will fall well below the price fixed by the colluders, as industry supply grows beyond the agreed-upon levels, causing the gains from collusion to erode.

EXHIBIT 1	COLLUSION IN OLIGOPOLY

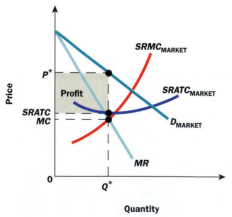

In collusive oligopoly, the producers would restrict joint output to Q^*, setting their price at P^*. The price and output situation is identical to monopoly. The members of the collusive oligopoly would share the profits in the shaded area.

THE CRASH OF AN AIRLINE COLLUSION

Mr. Crandall: I think it's dumb as @#$% for !@#$%* sake, all right to sit here and pound the @#$% out of each other and neither one of us making a #!@!$&* dime. I mean, you know, @!#$, what the @#$!, is the point of it.

Mr. Putnam: Do you have a suggestion for me?

Mr. Crandall: Yes, I have a suggestion for you. Raise your @#$&!$% fares 20 percent. I'll raise mine the next morning . . . You'll make more money and I will, too.

Mr. Putnam: We can't talk about pricing!

Mr. Crandall: Oh @#$% we can talk about any @#$%&*# thing we want to talk about.

SOURCE: "American Air Accused of Bid to Fix Prices," *The Wall Street Journal,* February 24, 1983, pp. 2, 23.

COMMENT:
At the time of this conversation, Crandall was the president of American Airlines and Putnam was the president of Braniff Airlines. According to the Sherman Antitrust Act, it is illegal for corporate leaders to talk with their competitors about and propose price fixing. Putnam turned the tapes over to the Justice Department. After the Justice Department reviewed the tapes of this conversation, they ruled that attempts to fix prices could potentially monopolize the airline industry. American Airlines promised they would not engage in this type of activity again.

CONCEPT CHECK

1. A price leader sends a signal to competing firms about a price change. Competitors that go along with the pricing decisions of the price leader are known as price followers.
2. The mutual interdependence of oligopolists tempts them to collude in order to reduce uncertainty and increase the potential for monopoly profits.
3. Joint profit maximization requires the determination of price on the basis of the market demand for the product and the marginal costs of the various firms.
4. There are two primary reasons that most strong collusive oligopolies are rather short-lived: (1) Collusive oligopolies are strictly illegal under U.S. antitrust laws, and (2) there is a great temptation for firms to cheat on the agreement of the collusive oligopoly.

---

1. How does having a price leader reduce pricing uncertainty in oligopolistic industries?
2. How is a collusion or a cartel like a monopoly?
3. Why are collusive agreements typically unstable and short-lived?
4. Why is the temptation to collude greater when the industry's demand curve is relatively more inelastic?

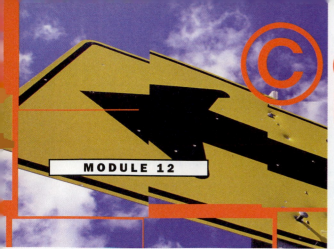

Oligopoly in the Long Run

■ What happens to the profits of oligopolists if entry is easy?
■ How can existing firms deter potential entrants?

WHAT HAPPENS IN THE LONG RUN IF ENTRY IS EASY?

Mutual interdependence is, in itself, no guarantee of economic profits, even if the firms in the industry succeed in maximizing joint profits. The extent to which economic profits disappear depends on the ease with which new firms can enter the industry. When entry is easy, newcomers are attracted by excess profits. New firms may break down existing price agreements by cutting prices in an attempt to establish themselves in the industry. In response, older firms may reduce prices to avoid excessive sales losses, and as a result, the general level of prices will begin to approach average total cost.

HOW DO OLIGOPOLISTS DETER MARKET ENTRY?

If most firms reach a scale of plant and firm size great enough to allow lowest cost operation, their long-run positions will be similar to that shown in Exhibit 2. To simplify, we have drawn *LRMC* and *LRATC* constant. The equilibrium, or profit-maximizing price, in an established

---

TUNE UP

MUTUAL INTERDEPENDENCE IN OLIGOPOLY

Q: Suppose that Firm A is a member of a naive oligopoly, meaning that neither Firm A nor its competitors recognize the mutual interdependence that exists between them. Firm A decides to lower its price in order to capture a greater market share. What will happen to profits in this market in the long run?

A: If an oligopolist believes that its rivals will not respond to pricing policies, it will expect to capture market share by reducing price. In response, rivals will cut prices as well, and if they do not understand the mutual interdependence among firms, they will attempt to *undercut* prices, as shown in Exhibit 1 in the movement from P_1 to P_2, and so on. This exchange would result in a price war, which could continue until economic profits were zero and price equaled average cost. Alternatively, it could even proceed until one of the firms reached its average variable cost shutdown point.

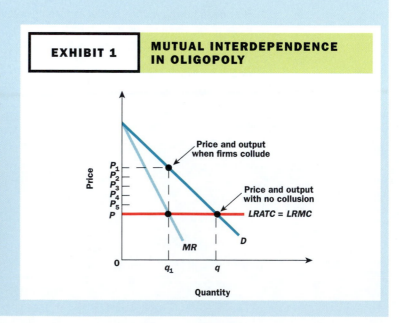

EXHIBIT 1 — MUTUAL INTERDEPENDENCE IN OLIGOPOLY

---

oligopoly is represented by P^*. Typically, the rate of profit in these industries is high, which would encourage entry. But empirical research indicates that oligopolists often initiate pricing policies that reduce the entry incentive for new firms. Established firms may deliberately hold prices below the maximum-profit point at P^*, charging a price of, say, P_1. This lower-than-profit-maximizing price may discourage newcomers from entering. Because new firms would likely have higher costs than existing firms, the lower price may not be high enough to cover their costs. However, once the threat of entry subsides, the market price may return to the profit-maximizing price, P^*.

Oligopolists may initiate pricing policies that reduce the entry incentive for new firms.

| EXHIBIT 2 | LONG-RUN EQUILIBRIUM AND DETERRING ENTRY |

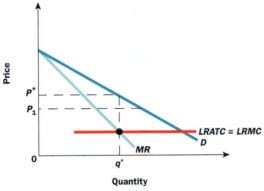

With barriers to entry, oligopolists may earn excess profits in the long run. Theoretically, profit maximization occurs at P^* and q^* in the short run. Empirical work, however, suggests that oligopolists often actually charge a lower price than the short-run profit-maximizing price (such as P_1). This strategy discourages entry because newcomers may have costs higher than P_1.

CONCEPT CHECK

1. When market entry is easy, newcomers are attracted by excess profits. They may break down existing price agreements, causing older firms to reduce their prices and, ultimately, drive the general level of prices toward average total cost.

2. Firms in an oligopoly may deliberately hold prices below the short-run profit-maximizing point in order to discourage newcomers from entering the market.

1. What impact does easy entry have on the profitability of oligopolies?
2. Why are barriers to entry necessary for successful, ongoing collusion?
3. Why might oligopolists charge less than their short-run profit-maximizing price when threatened by entry?

4. A group of colluding oligopolists incur costs of $10 per unit, and their profit-maximizing price is $15. If they know that potential market entrants could produce at a cost of $12 per unit, what price are the colluders likely to charge?

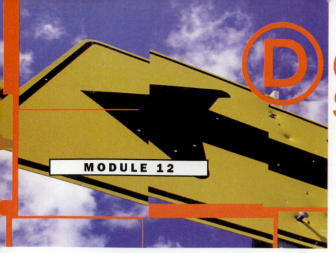

Game Theory and Strategic Behavior

- What is game theory?
- What are cooperative and noncooperative games?
- What is a dominant strategy?
- What is a Nash equilibrium?

WHAT ARE SOME STRATEGIES FOR NONCOLLUSIVE OLIGOPOLIES?

In some respects, noncollusive oligopoly resembles a military campaign or a poker game. Firms take certain actions not because they are necessarily advantageous in themselves but because they improve the position of the oligopolist relative to its competitors and may ultimately improve its financial position. For example, a firm may deliberately cut prices, sacrificing profits either to drive competitors out of business or to discourage them from undertaking actions contrary to the interests of other firms.

WHAT IS GAME THEORY?

Some economists have suggested that the entire approach to oligopoly equilibrium price and output should be recast. They replace the analysis that assumes that firms attempt to maximize profits with one that examines firm behavior in terms of a strategic game. This point of view, called **game theory,** stresses the tendency of various parties in such circumstances to act in such a way as to minimize damage from opponents. With this approach, there is a set of alternative actions (with respect to price and output levels, for example); the action that would be taken in a particular case depends on the specific policies followed by each firm. The firm may try to figure out its competitors' most likely countermoves to its own policies and then formulate alternative defense measures.

WHAT ARE COOPERATIVE AND NONCOOPERATIVE GAMES?

Games, in interactions between oligopolists, can either be cooperative or noncooperative. An example of a **cooperative game** would be two firms that decide to collude in order to improve their profit-maximization position. However, as we discussed earlier, enforcement costs are usually too high to keep all firms from cheating on collusive agreements. Consequently, most games are **noncooperative games,** in which each firm sets its own price without consulting other firms. The primary difference between cooperative and noncooperative games is the contract. For example, players in a cooperative game can talk and set binding contracts, while those in noncooperative games are assumed to act independently, with no communication and no binding contracts. Because antitrust laws forbid firms to collude, we will assume that most strategic behavior in the marketplace is noncooperative.

THE PRISONERS' DILEMMA

A firm's decision makers must map out a pricing strategy based on a wide range of information. They must also decide whether or not their strategy will be effective and whether it will be affected by competitors' actions. A strategy that will be optimal regardless of the opponents' actions is called a **dominant strategy.** A famous game that has a dominant strategy and demonstrates the basic problem confronting noncolluding oligopolists is known as the **prisoners' dilemma.**

Imagine that there is a bank robbery and two suspects are caught. The suspects are placed in separate cells in the county jail and are not allowed to talk with each other. There are four possible results in this situation: both prisoners confess, neither confesses, Prisoner A confesses but Prisoner B doesn't, and Prisoner B confesses but Prisoner A doesn't. In Exhibit 1, we see the **payoff matrix,** which summarizes the possible outcomes from the various strategies. Looking at the payoff matrix, we can see that if each prisoner confesses to the crime each will serve two years in jail. However, if neither confesses, each prisoner may only get one year because of insufficient evidence. Now, if Prisoner A confesses and Prisoner B does not, Prisoner A gets six months (because of his cooperation with the authorities and his evidence) and Prisoner B gets six years. Alternatively, if Prisoner B confesses and Prisoner A does not, Prisoner B gets six months and Prisoner A gets six years.

Module 12 **312** Oligopoly

Should he confess or remain silent?

<table>
<tr><td rowspan="2">EXHIBIT 1</td><td colspan="2">THE PRISONERS' DILEMMA PAYOFF MATRIX</td></tr>
</table>

		Prisoner B	
		Confesses	**Doesn't Confess**
Prisoner A	**Confesses**	2 years (A) 2 years (B)	6 months (A) 6 years (B)
	Doesn't Confess	6 years (A) 6 months (B)	1 year (A) 1 year (B)

PROFITS UNDER DIFFERENT PRICING STRATEGIES

To demonstrate how the prisoners' dilemma can shed light on oligopoly theory, let us consider the pricing strategy of two firms. In Exhibit 2, we present the payoff matrix—the possible profits that each firm would earn under different pricing strategies. Assume that each firm has total production costs of $1 per unit. When both firms set their price at $10 and each sells 1,000 units per week, then each earns a profit of $9,000 a week. If each firm sets its price at $9, each sells 1,100 units per week, for a profit of $8,800 [($9 − $1) × 1,100]. However, what if one firm charges $10 and the other firm charges $9? The low-price firm increases its profits through additional sales. It now sells, say, 1,500 units for a profit of $12,000, while the high-price firm sells only 600 units per week for a profit of $5,400.

When the two firms each charge $9 per unit, they are said to have reached a **Nash equilibrium.** At a Nash equilibrium, each firm is said to be doing as well as it can *given the actions of its competitor.* For example, if each firm believes the other is going to charge $9, then the best strategy for both firms is to charge $9. In this scenario, if Firm A charges $9, the worse possible outcome is a profit of $8,800. However, if Firm A prices at $10 and Firm B prices at $9, Firm A will have a profit of only $5,400. Hence, the choice that minimizes the risk of the worst scenario is $9. The same is true for Firm B; it, too, minimizes the risk of the worst scenario by choosing to price at the Nash equilibrium, $9. In this case the Nash equilibrium is also the dominant strategy. The Nash equilibrium takes on particular importance because it is a self-enforcing equilibrium. That is, once this equilibrium is established, there is no incentive for either firm to move.

In sum, we see that if the two firms were to collude and set their price at $10, it will be in their best interest. However, each firm has a strong incentive to lower its price to $9 if this pricing strategy goes undetected by its competitor. However, if both firms defect by lowering their prices from the joint-profit-maximization level, both will be worse off than if they had colluded, but at least each will have minimized its potential loss if it cannot trust its competitor. This is the oligopolist's dilemma.

As you can see, then, the prisoners have a dilemma. What should they do?

Looking at the payoff matrix, we can see that if Prisoner A confesses, it is in the best interest for Prisoner B to confess. If Prisoner A confesses, he will get either two years or six months depending on what B does. But Prisoner B knows the temptation to confess facing Prisoner A, so confessing is also the best strategy for Prisoner B. This would mean a lighter sentence for Prisoner B—two years rather than six years.

It is clear that both would be better off confessing *if* they knew for sure that the other was going to remain silent, because that would lead to a six-month sentence for each. But in each case, can the prisoner take the chance that his co-conspirator will not talk? The dominant strategy, while it may not lead to the best outcome, is to confess. That is, the prisoners know that confessing is the way to make the best of a bad situation. No matter what his counterpart does, the maximum sentence will be two years for each, and each feels there is a possibility he will be out in six months.

Firms in oligopoly often behave like the prisoners in the prisoners' dilemma, carefully anticipating the moves of their rivals in an uncertain environment. For example, should a firm cut its prices and try to gain more sales by luring customers away from its competitors? What if the firm keeps its price stable and competitors lower theirs? Or what if the firm and its competitors all lower their prices? What if all of the firms decide to raise their prices? Each of these situations will have vastly different implications for an oligopolist, so it must carefully watch and anticipate the moves of its competitors.

| EXHIBIT 2 | THE PROFIT PAYOFF MATRIX |

		Firm B's Pricing Strategy	
		Charge $10	Charge $9
Firm A's Pricing Strategy	Charge $10	$9,000 (Firm A) $9,000 (Firm B)	$5,400 (Firm A) $12,000 (Firm B)
	Charge $9	$12,000 (Firm A) $5,400 (Firm B)	$8,800 (Firm A) $8,800 (Firm B)

ADVERTISING

Advertising can lead to a situation like the prisoners' dilemma. For example, perhaps the decision makers of a large firm are deciding whether or not to launch an advertising campaign against a rival firm. According to the payoff matrix in Exhibit 3, if neither company advertises, the two companies split the market, each making $100 million in profits. They also split the market if they both advertise, but their profits are, on net, smaller, at $75 million, because they would both incur advertising costs that are greater than any gains in additional revenues from advertising. However, if one advertises and the other does not, the company that advertises takes customers away from the rival. Profits for the company that advertises would be $125 million, and profits for the company that does not advertise would be $50 million.

The dominant strategy—the optimal strategy regardless of the rival's actions—is to advertise. In this game, both firms will choose to advertise, even though both would be better off if no one advertised. But one company can't take a chance and not advertise, because if its competitor then elects to advertise, the competitor could have a very big year, primarily at the expense of the firm that doesn't advertise.

REVIEWING THE MARKET STRUCTURES

We have now studied four different market structures in which firms operate: perfect competition, monopoly, monopolistic competition, and oligopoly. Each structure or environment has certain key characteristics that distinguish it from the other structures, although in practice it is sometimes difficult to decide precisely which structure a given firm or industry most appropriately fits, because the dividing line between the structures is not always crystal clear.

Is this advertising approach too risky? Will it increase profits? Will it cause rivals to retaliate? Perhaps some will view it as distasteful and not react.

| EXHIBIT 3 | ADVERTISING |

		Firm B's Decision	
		Firm B Advertises	Firm B Doesn't Advertise
Firm A's Decision	Firm A Advertises	$75 million (A) $75 million (B)	$125 million (A) $50 million (B)
	Firm A Doesn't Advertise	$125 million (A) $50 million (B)	$100 million (A) $100 million (B)

| EXHIBIT 4 | CHARACTERISTICS OF THE FOUR MAJOR MARKET STRUCTURES |

Characteristic	Perfect Competition	Monopoly	Monopolistic Competition	Oligopoly
Number of firms	Very many	One	Many	A few
Firm role in determining price	No role; price taker	Major role; price maker	Some role	Some role
Close substitutes available	Perfect substitutes	No	Yes	Usually but not always
Barriers to entry or exit from industry	No substantial ones	Extremely great	Minor barriers	Considerable barriers
Type of product	Homogeneous	Homogeneous	Differentiated	Homogeneous or differentiated
Key characteristic	Firms are price takers	Only one firm	Product differentiation	Mutual interdependence

CONCEPT CHECK

1. Game theory stresses the tendency of various parties to minimize damage from opponents. A firm may try to figure out its competitors' most likely countermoves to its own policies and then formulate alternative defense measures.
2. Players in cooperative games can talk and set binding contracts, while those in noncooperative games are assumed to act independently with no communications and no binding contracts.
3. The prisoners' dilemma is an example of a noncooperative game.
4. A dominant strategy is optimal regardless of the opponents' actions.
5. At a Nash equilibrium each player is said to be doing as well as it can given the actions of its competitor.

1. How is noncollusive oligopoly like a military campaign or a poker game?
2. What is the difference between cooperative and noncooperative games?
3. How does the prisoners' dilemma illustrate a dominant strategy for noncolluding oligopolists?
4. What is a Nash equilibrium?
5. In the prisoners' dilemma, if each prisoner believed that the other prisoner would deny the crime, would each choose to deny the crime?
6. Suppose Pepsi is considering an ad campaign aimed at rival Coca-Cola. What is the dominant strategy if the payoff matrix is similar to the one shown in Exhibit 3?
7. Suppose your professor announces that each student in your large lecture class who receives the highest score (no matter how high or how low) on a take-home exam will get an A in the course. She points out that if the entire class colludes, everyone will get the same score. Is it likely that everyone in the class will get an A?

E Application: The OPEC Cartel

The OPEC cartel—which includes Saudi Arabia, Iran, Venezuela, Iraq, Kuwait, Qatar, Nigeria, the United Arab Emirates, Indonesia, Algeria, and Libya—supplies almost 40 percent of the world's oil. What does this article suggest is happening to the power of the OPEC cartel? What impact do you think an increase in production will have on supply? When the cartel was effective, how did they keep their prices up? Were there (and are there) incentives to cheat on production quotas? What factors do you think are responsible for the cartel becoming less effective since the early 1980s?

OPEC ACCORD TO LIFT CAP ON OUTPUT MAY CUT PRICES
RISE OF 2.5 MILLION BARRELS OF OIL A DAY IS MORE THAN ANALYSTS EXPECTED

PETER FRITSCH

JAKARTA—An Organization of Petroleum Exporting Countries agreement over the weekend to raise its production cap for the first time in four years will likely lead to more oil on world markets and potentially lower energy prices.

While OPEC's action was widely expected, observers were surprised at the size of the increase: 2.5 million barrels a day above OPEC's current production ceiling of 25 million barrels a day. The increase is a signal that the 11-nation group believes world demand will continue to grow despite a raft of bearish short-term fundamentals and an expected economic slowdown in Asia.

Saudi Arabia had argued for the 2.5 million barrel-a-day increase, seeking to legitimize its own rising production. But other members—notably Iran, Libya and Indonesia—lobbied for a smaller rise for fear of spooking oil markets and sending prices lower. Unlike Saudi Arabia, those nations have little to gain from a quota increase since they are widely believed to be pumping all the oil they can.

News that the Saudi agenda had won the day touched off speculation that the group's true objective is to push prices lower in order to discourage non-OPEC producers from bringing new, high-cost oil fields on line. In theory, that would allow OPEC to make up in market share what it loses to lower prices.

The irony of OPEC's latest quota reshuffle is that widespread quota cheating has pushed the organization's current production to nearly 28 million barrels a day—already above the new limit. And while OPEC members agreed for the record to adhere to their respective quotas, that is unlikely to happen.

SOURCE: Peter Fritsch, "OPEC Accord to Lift Cap on Output May Cut Prices," *The Wall Street Journal*, December 1, 1997, pp. A3–A4.

Why do cartels break down?

The most spectacular successful example of a collusive oligopoly being able to earn monopoly-type profits is the cartel of the Organization of Petroleum Exporting Countries (OPEC), which, although organized in 1960, only began acting as a successful collusive oligopoly in 1973.

OPEC began acting as a cartel in 1973, in part because of political concern over U.S. support for Israel. For two decades prior to 1973, the price of crude oil had hovered around $2 a barrel. In 1973, OPEC members agreed to quadruple oil prices in nine months; later price increases pushed the cost of a barrel of oil to over $20. Prices then stabilized, falling in real terms (adjusted for inflation) between 1973 and 1978, as the profit-maximizing price was sought and politics remained relatively calm. By the early 1980s, however, prices were approaching $40 per barrel. The relative impact of the OPEC cartel on the supply and price of oil is illustrated in Exhibit 1.

The OPEC nations were successful with their pricing policies between 1973 and the early 1980s for several reasons. First, the worldwide demand for petroleum was highly inelastic with respect to price in the short run. Second, OPEC's share of total world oil output had steadily increased, from around 20 percent of total world output in the early 1940s to about 70 percent by 1973, when OPEC became an effective cartel. Third, the price elasticity of supply of petroleum from OPEC's competitors was low in the short run: Ability to increase production from existing wells is limited, and it takes time to drill new ones.

More recently, OPEC oil prices have hovered around $20, because of increases in non-OPEC production and the

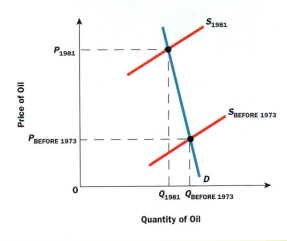

| EXHIBIT 1 | THE IMPACT OF THE OPEC CARTEL |

uncertain willingness of key suppliers (such as Saudi Arabia) to restrict supply. Moreover, at the higher prices of the 1970s, long-run substitution possibilities caused oil consumption to fall almost 5 percent per year, with conservation and alternative energy easing the demand for OPEC oil. After adjusting for inflation, today, oil prices are roughly the same as they were before OPEC formed. The cartel has lost its clout!

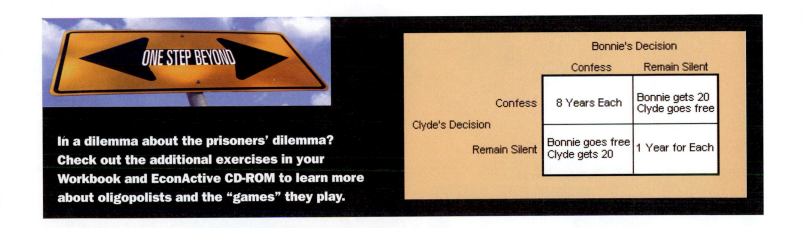

In a dilemma about the prisoners' dilemma? Check out the additional exercises in your Workbook and EconActive CD-ROM to learn more about oligopolists and the "games" they play.

PHOTO CREDITS MODULE 12

Page **304**: left, © 1998 Don Couch Photography; right, © David Sacks/FPG International; Page **305**: © Jim Stratford/Black Star/PNI; Page **307**: © C. Zlotnick; S. Seitz/ Woodfin, Camp & Associates/PNI; Page **309**: Photo courtesy of American Airlines; Page **311**: © PhotoDisc; Page **313**: © John Running/Stock, Boston/PNI; Page **314**: Domecq Importers, Inc.; Page **316**: AP Photo/Muchtar Zakaria

Supply and Demand in Input Markets

A. Input Markets
How do supply and demand determine price and quantities in input markets?

B. Supply and Demand in the Labor Market
What determines the slopes of the demand and supply curves for labor?

C. Labor Market Equilibrium
How is equilibrium determined in the labor market?

D. Labor Unions
What impact do labor unions have on labor markets?

E. Labor Productivity and Wages
What impact does labor productivity have on living standards?

F. Land and Capital
How are rental prices determined?

G. Application: Immigration
Do immigrants necessarily take jobs from domestic workers?

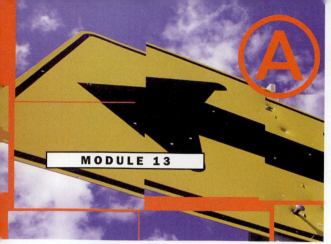

Ⓐ Input Markets

- How is income distributed among workers, land owners, and the owners of capital?
- How does utility maximization relate to the owners of productive resources?
- What is derived demand?

MARKETS FOR THE FACTORS OF PRODUCTION

Approximately 75 percent of national income goes to laborers for their services. But how are salary levels among those individuals determined? After laborers take their share, the remaining 25 percent of national income is compensation received by the owners of land and capital and the entrepreneurs who employ those resources to produce valued goods and services. How can we explain the variations in these forms of income, such as rents on houses, offices, or factories, or interest on borrowed money?

For example, most highly successful music stars earn incomes that are 5 to 25 times as great as the average physician, who in turn earns twice as much as the average college professor. Why is this the case? There is certainly no law that requires rock stars to make more than doctors or college professors.

In Module 3, we discussed the factors of production—the inputs that are used to produce output. The three major productive resources, labor, land, and capital, are typically combined in production by the entrepreneur. For example, a farmer might use workers (labor) and heavy equipment like tractors (capital) to harvest the crops in his field (land). As for other goods, the price and quantity of each of these factors of production is determined by the intersection of their market supply and demand curves.

WHAT IS THE PRICE OF A PRODUCTIVE FACTOR?

Remember that the wages paid by an employer is the "income" from labor service to the worker. Likewise, the rent from land is the cost of land to the tenant farmer but is the income to the landowner. The buyer's cost is the seller's income.

DETERMINING THE PRICE OF A PRODUCTIVE FACTOR: DERIVED DEMAND

There is one difference between output (goods and services) markets and input markets. In input or factor markets, the demand for an input is called a **derived demand.** That is, the demand is derived from consumers'

How are the price and quantity of each of the factors of production determined?

demand for the good or service. For example, the chef at a restaurant is paid, and her skills are in demand, because she produces what the customer wants—a meal; and a mechanic at an auto repair shop is paid because he produces what the customer wants—a repaired car. The "price" of a productive factor, then, is directly related to consumer demand for the final good or service.

Does the owner of this repair shop pay his mechanics because he likes them or because they produce what his customers want?

CONCEPT CHECK

1. The price and output in the markets for labor, land, and capital are determined by the intersection of the supply and demand curves.

2. In factor or input markets, demand is derived from consumers' demand for the good or service.

1. Why is the demand for productive inputs derived from the demand for the outputs those inputs produce?

2. Why is the demand for tractors and fertilizer derived from the demand for agricultural products?

Supply and Demand in the Labor Market

- What is the marginal revenue product for an input?
- What is the marginal resource cost of hiring another worker?
- Why is the demand curve for labor downward sloping?
- Why is the supply curve for labor upward sloping?

HOW IS THE DEMAND CURVE FOR LABOR DETERMINED?

Because firms are trying to maximize their profits, they try (by definition) to make the *difference* between revenue and cost as large as possible. The attractiveness of a resource, then, varies with what the resource can add to the revenues received by the firm relative to what it adds to costs. The demand for labor is determined by its **marginal revenue product (MRP),** which is the additional revenue that a firm obtains from one more unit of input. Why? Suppose a worker adds $500 per week to a firm's sales by his productivity; he produces 100 units that add $5 each to firm revenue. In order to determine if the worker adds to the firm's profits, we would need to calculate the marginal resource cost associated with the worker. The **marginal resource cost (MRC)** is the amount that an extra input adds to the firm's total costs. In this case, the marginal resource cost is the wage the employer has to pay to entice an extra worker. Assume that the marginal resource cost of the worker, the market wage, is $350 per worker. In our example, the firm would find its profits growing by adding one more worker, because the marginal benefit (MRP) associated with the worker, $500, would exceed the marginal cost (MRC) of the worker, $350. So, we can see that just by adding another worker to its labor force, the firm would increase its weekly profits by $150 ($500 − $350). Even if the market wage were $490 per week, the firm could slightly increase its profits by hiring the employee because the marginal revenue product, $500, is greater than the added labor cost, $490. At wage payments above $500, however, the firm would not be interested in the worker because the marginal resource cost would exceed the marginal revenue product, making additional hiring unprofitable.

CAUTION laser light

OPERATION OF LASERS REQUIRES USING COMMON SENSE. AS WITH OTHER BRIGHT LIGHTS, DO NOT STARE DIRECTLY INTO BEAM.

LASER ALIGNMENT, INC. GRAND RAPIDS, MICHIGAN 49506

NOT HIRING (CREW ALREADY HIRED)

Should another worker be hired?

WHY IS THE DEMAND CURVE FOR LABOR DOWNWARD SLOPING?

The demand curve for labor is downward sloping. This indicates that there is a negative relationship between wage and the quantity of labor demanded. Higher wages will decrease the quantity of labor demanded, while lower wages will increase the quantity of labor demanded. But why does this relationship exist?

The major reason for the downward-sloping demand curve for labor (illustrated in Exhibit 1), is the law of diminishing returns. Remember that the law of diminishing returns says that as increasing quantities of some variable input (say labor or capital) are added to fixed quantities of another input (say land), output will rise, but at some point it will increase by diminishing amounts.

Consider a farmer who owns a given amount of land. Suppose he is producing wheat, and the relationship between his output and his labor force requirements is that indicated in Exhibit 2. Output expands as more workers are hired to cultivate the land, but the growth in output steadily slows, meaning the added output associated with one more worker declines as more workers are added. For example, in Exhibit 2 when a third worker is hired, total wheat output increases from 5,500 bushels to 7,000 bushels, an increase of 1,500 bushels in terms of marginal product. However, when a fourth worker is added, total wheat output only increases from 7,000 bushels to 8,000 bushels, or an increase of 1,000 bushels in terms of marginal product. Note that the reason for this is *not* that the workers being added are steadily inferior in terms of ability or quality relative to the first workers.

EXHIBIT 2	DIMINISHING MARGINAL PRODUCTIVITY ON A HYPOTHETICAL FARM

Units of Labor Input (workers)	Total Wheat Output (bushels per year)	Marginal Product of Labor (bushels per year)
0		
		3,000
1	3,000	
		2,500
2	5,500	
		1,500
3	7,000	
		1,000
4	8,000	
		500
5	8,500	
		300
6	8,800	
		200
7	9,000	

Indeed, for simplicity, we assume that each worker has exactly the same skills and productive capacity. But as more workers are added, each additional worker has fewer of the fixed resources with which to work. The ratio of land to the number of workers, for example, falls. While a second worker might result in economies of specialization and division of labor with the first worker, the fourth or fifth worker might just cultivate the same land more intensively than before. The work of the fifth worker, then, might only slightly improve output. The **marginal product (MP)**—the number of physical units of added output from the addition of one additional unit of input—falls.

As we discussed earlier, the marginal revenue product (MRP) is the change in total revenue associated with an additional unit of input. The marginal revenue product is equal to the marginal product, the units of output added by a worker, multiplied by marginal revenue, in this case the price of the output (e.g., $10 per bushel of wheat).

$$MRP = MP \times P$$

(Note that, in this case, the price of the output, wheat, is the same at all outputs because the farmer is a price taker in a competitive market.)

The marginal revenue product of labor declines because of the diminishing marginal product of labor when additional workers are added. This is illustrated in Exhibit 3, which shows various output and revenue levels for a wheat farmer using different quantities of labor. We see in Exhibit 3 that the marginal product, or the added physical volume of output, declines as the number of workers grows because of diminishing marginal product. Thus, the fifth worker adds only 60 bushels of wheat per week, compared with 100 bushels for the first worker.

EXHIBIT 1	THE MARGINAL REVENUE PRODUCT OF LABOR

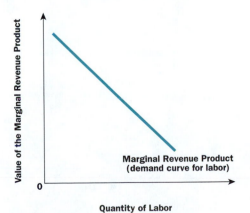

The value of the marginal revenue product of labor ($MP \times P$) shows how the marginal revenue product depends on the number of workers employed. The curve is downward sloping because of the diminishing marginal product of labor.

Quantity of Labor	Total Output (bushels per week)	Marginal Physical Product of Labor (bushels per week)	Product Price (dollars per bushel)	Marginal Revenue Product of Labor	Wage Rate (MRC) (dollars per week)	Marginal Profit (MRP-W)
0	0					
1	100	100	$10	$1,000	$550	$450
2	190	90	10	900	550	350
3	270	80	10	800	550	250
4	340	70	10	700	550	150
5	400	60	10	600	550	50
6	450	50	10	500	550	−50
7	490	40	10	400	550	−150
8	520	30	10	300	550	−250

HOW MANY WORKERS WILL AN EMPLOYER HIRE?

Profits are maximized if the firm hires only to the point where the wage equals the expected marginal revenue product; that is, the firm will hire up to the last unit of input for which the marginal revenue product is expected to exceed the wage. Because the demand curve for labor and the value of the marginal revenue product show the quantity of labor that a firm demands at a given wage in a competitive market, we say that the value of the marginal revenue product (MRP) is the same as the demand curve for labor for a competitive firm.

Using the data in Exhibit 3, if the market wage payment for a week is $550, it would pay the grower to employ five workers. The fifth worker's marginal revenue product ($600) exceeds the wage, so profits are increased $50 by adding the worker. Adding a sixth worker would be unprofitable, though, as that worker's marginal revenue product of $500 is less than the wage of $550. Hiring the sixth worker would reduce profits by $50.

But what if the market wage increases from $550 to $650? In this case, the hiring of the fifth worker becomes unprofitable, because the marginal resource cost, $650, is now greater than the marginal revenue product of $600. This relationship is the basis for the assertion made in earlier modules that raising wages, *ceteris paribus,* lowers the employment levels of individual firms.

Exhibit 4 shows the competitive equilibrium quantity, Q^*, and wage of labor, W^*. In a competitive labor market, many firms are competing for workers and no single firm

What is responsible for the declining output of successive workers when they are added to the field?

EXHIBIT 4 | THE DEMAND CURVE FOR LABOR

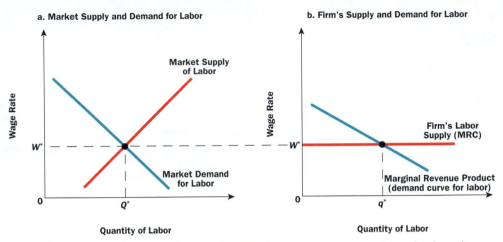

a. Market Supply and Demand for Labor

b. Firm's Supply and Demand for Labor

The firm's supply curve for labor is determined by the intersection of the market demand and supply curves for labor, shown in Exhibit 4(a). The firm's supply curve for labor is horizontal because it is such a small part of the total market that it can hire any number of potential workers at the market-determined wage; it is a price (wage) taker. In Exhibit 4(b) at employment levels less than $q*$, additional workers add profits. At employment levels beyond $q*$, additional workers are unprofitable; at $q*$, profits are maximized.

is big enough by itself to have any significant effect on the level of wages. The intersection of the market supply and demand curve for labor determines the equilibrium wage and employment level, as seen in Exhibit 4(a). Even if a firm hires a large number of workers, the wage rate will not change. The firm's supply of labor, then, is perfectly elastic at the prevailing wage rate. The ability to hire all you wish at the prevailing wage is analogous to perfect competition in output markets, where a firm could sell all it wanted at the going price.

When the firm hires fewer than $q*$ workers in Exhibit 4(b), the marginal revenue product exceeds the wage, so adding workers expands profits. With more than $q*$ workers, though, the "going wage" exceeds marginal revenue product, and hiring additional workers lowers profits. With $q*$ workers, profits are maximized.

When does adding more workers enhance profits?

TUNE UP

LABOR SUPPLY AND DEMAND

Q: Blaze N. Brite is a firefighter who realizes the city is in serious danger without his services. Therefore, Blaze thinks that all firefighters (because their job is so important) should make at least $100,000 a year, just like star football players. Do you think Blaze is too "fired up"?

A: If Blaze had read this Module, he would know that it is the marginal revenue product of an additional firefighter and the supply of firefighters that determines the market wage (regardless of the job's importance). Unfortunately for Blaze, a firefighter's marginal revenue product is likely to be below $100,000. Most people probably think that firefighters are more important than star football players, yet they make a lot less money. Of course, the reason for this is simple supply and demand. There are a lot of people that enjoy watching star football players and only a few individuals that have the skill to perform at that level. While there is also a large demand for firefighters, there is also a relatively large number of potential suppliers. As seen in Exhibit 5, this translates into a much lower wage for firefighters than star football players.

EXHIBIT 5

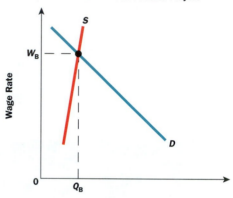

a. Labor Market for Star Football Players

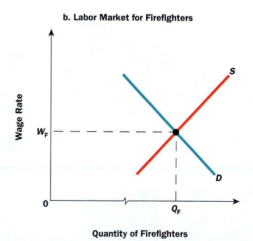

b. Labor Market for Firefighters

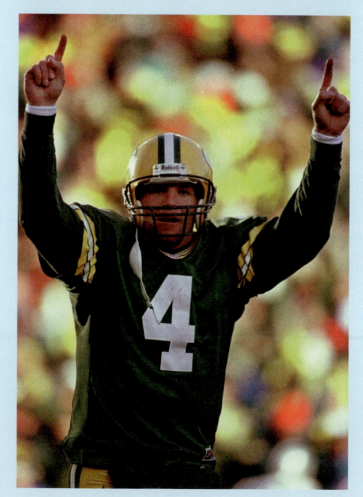

Why do star football players make more money than firefighters even though many people think firefighters are more important?

WHAT IS THE MARKET LABOR SUPPLY?

How much work effort will individuals collectively be willing and able to supply to the marketplace? This is the essence of the market labor supply. Just as was the case in our earlier discussions of the law of supply, there is a positive relationship between wage level and the quantity supplied of labor. Higher wages will increase the quantity of labor supplied; lower wages will reduce the quantity of labor supplied. This relationship is shown in the graph in Exhibit 6.

EXHIBIT 6 | **MARKET LABOR SUPPLY CURVE**

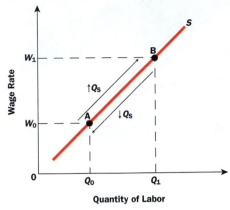

Higher wages will increase the quantity supplied of labor. Lower wages will decrease the quantity supplied of labor.

CONCEPT CHECK

1. The marginal revenue product of an input is the additional revenue that a firm obtains from utilizing one more unit of that input.
2. The marginal resource cost of an input is the amount that an extra unit of that input adds to the firm's total costs.
3. The demand curve for labor is downward sloping because of the law of diminishing returns. That is, if additional labor is added to a fixed quantity of land or capital equipment, output will increase, but eventually by smaller amounts.

---

1. Why is the marginal revenue product of labor the demand curve for labor?
2. Would a firm hire another worker if the marginal revenue product of labor exceeded the marginal factor cost of labor? Why or why not?
3. How does the law of diminishing returns imply that the marginal product of labor must eventually fall?
4. Why does the eventually falling marginal product of labor mean that the marginal revenue product of labor must also eventually fall?
5. Why is a firm hiring in a competitive labor market a price (wage) taker for a given quality of labor?
6. Why are wages in different fields not necessarily related to how important people think those jobs are?
7. Would the owner of University Pizza Parlor hire another worker for $60 per day if that worker added 40 pizzas a day and each pizza added $2 to University Pizza Parlor's revenues? Why or why not?

Labor Market Equilibrium

MODULE 13

- How are the equilibrium wage and employment determined in labor markets?
- What shifts the labor demand curve?
- What shifts the labor supply curve?

DETERMINING EQUILIBRIUM IN THE LABOR MARKET

The wage in the labor market is determined by the intersection of demand and supply. The equilibrium wage, W^*, and equilibrium employment level, Q^*, are found at that point where the quantity of labor demanded equals the quantity of labor supplied. This point is illustrated in Exhibit 1. At any wage higher than W^*, the quantity of labor supplied exceeds the quantity of labor demanded, resulting in a surplus of labor. In this situation, unemployed workers will be willing to undercut the established wage in order to get jobs, pushing the wage down and returning the market to equilibrium. Likewise, at a wage below the equilibrium level (W^*), quantity demanded would exceed quantity supplied, resulting in a labor shortage. In this situation, employers would be forced to offer higher wages in order to hire as many workers as they would like. Note that only at the equilibrium wage are both suppliers and demanders able to exchange the quantity of labor they desire.

EXHIBIT 1	SUPPLY AND DEMAND IN THE LABOR MARKET

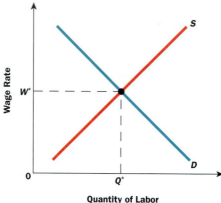

Quantity of Labor

Prices and quantities in the labor market are determined in the same way that prices and quantities of goods and services are determined: by the intersection of demand and supply. At wages above the equilibrium wage, W^*, quantity supplied exceeds quantity demanded, and potential workers will be willing to supply their labor services for an amount lower than the prevailing wage. At a wage lower than W^*, potential demanders will overcome the resulting shortage of labor by offering workers a wage greater than the prevailing wage. In this case, wages are pushed toward the equilibrium value.

T U N E   U P

LABOR MARKET EQUILIBRIUM

Q: Ed U. Cater is a dean at Middle State University. Dean Cater knows that in the private market, poets generally earn less than engineers; that is, the equilibrium wage for engineers is higher than that for poets. Suppose that all colleges and universities pay their professors according to their potential private market wage, except for Middle State University. The administration at Middle State believes that salaries should be equal across all disciplines, because their professors work equally hard and because all of the professors have similar degrees—Ph.D.s. As a result, Middle State opts to pay all of its professors a mid-range wage, W_{MS}. What do you think is likely to happen to the engineering and poetry programs at Middle State?

A: The market for poetry professors is illustrated in Exhibit 2(a), and the market for engineering professors is shown in Exhibit 2(b). Middle State pays all of its professors W_{MS} regardless of their field of specialization. We can see that this leads to a surplus of poetry professors and a shortage of engineering professors. If the administration refuses to adjust, we could predict that quality adjustments will occur, *ceteris paribus*. Middle State will be able to choose high-quality poetry professors, because it is paying a wage that is higher than the going wage rate for poets. However, it will also be forced to accept engineering professors that cannot find employment at the going wage rate for engineers. As a result, Middle State can be expected to develop a much stronger reputation in poetry than in engineering.

EXHIBIT 2

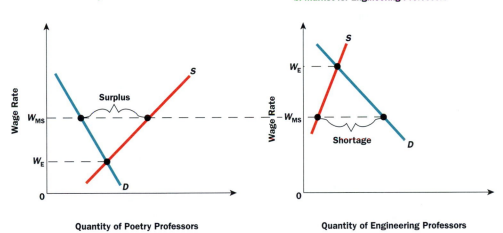

a. Market for Poetry Professors

b. Market for Engineering Professors

SHIFTS IN THE LABOR DEMAND CURVE

In Module 4, we demonstrated that the PYNTE factors can shift the demand curve for a product of service. In the case of an input such as labor, there are two important factors that can shift the demand curve. Shifts in the demand curve for labor may arise from increases in labor productivity due, for example, to technological advances, or changes in the price of the good, due, for example, to increased demand for the firm's product. The impact of these changes is highlighted in Exhibit 3.

Changes in Labor Productivity

Workers can increase productivity if they have more capital or land with which to work, if technological improvements occur, or if their "human capital" increases. This increase in productivity will increase the marginal product of the labor and shift the demand curve for labor to the right. However, if labor productivity falls, then marginal product will fall and the demand curve for labor will shift to the left. An increase in output per worker will raise the marginal product of labor, shifting the labor demand curve to the right from D_0 to D_1 in Exhibit 3.

Changes in the Demand for the Firm's Product

The greater the demand for the firm's product, the greater the firm's demand for labor or any other variable input (the "derived demand" discussed earlier). The reason for this is that the higher demand for the firm's product increases the firm's marginal revenue, which increases marginal revenue product. That is, the greater demand for the product will cause prices to rise, and the price of the product is part of the value of the labor to the firm ($MRP = MP \times P$). Of course, if demand for the firm's product falls, the labor demand curve will shift to the left as marginal revenue product falls.

EXHIBIT 3	SHIFTS IN THE LABOR DEMAND CURVE

a. Increase in Labor Demand

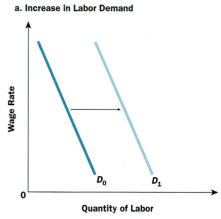

b. Decrease in Labor Demand

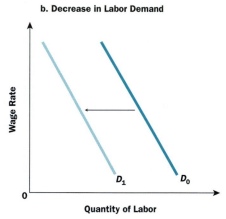

An increase in labor demand will shift the demand curve for labor to the right. A decrease in labor demand will shift the demand curve for labor to the left.

TUNE UP

CHANGES IN LABOR PRODUCTIVITY

Q: Suppose a state decides to train its resident workers in robotics at a local vocational-technical college. How would this training affect the demand for labor and the equilibrium employment rates in the state?

A: Vocational-technical training would increase the productivity of the labor available to manufacturing firms in the state. This education would increase the output per worker, resulting in a higher marginal product. Because *MRP* = *MP* × *P*, the greater marginal product would shift the labor demand curve to the right, as shown in Exhibit 4. As a result of this shift, the intersection of the labor demand curve and the labor supply curve occurs at greater employment level, ($q_1 > q_0$), so the equilibrium employment rate will be higher.

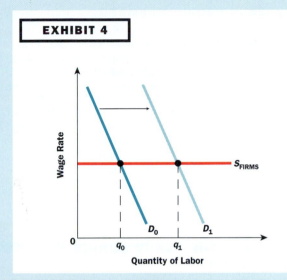

EXHIBIT 4

Will an increase in worker productivity shift the demand curve for labor to the right?

CHANGES IN PRODUCT DEMAND

Q: Mary Gold, a florist, always experiences a huge increase in sales during the week before Mother's Day. How does this affect her demand for labor?

A: The number of workers hired by the florist is determined by the equality of supply and demand for labor. Because demand for flowers picks up before Mother's Day, the price of flowers also increases. Because $MRP = MP \times P$, the increase in price also increases marginal revenue product, and the florist is willing to employ more workers because the demand curve for labor has shifted to the right, as seen in Exhibit 5.

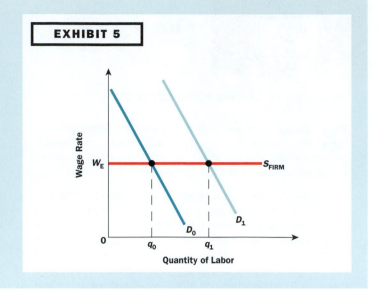

EXHIBIT 5

WHAT CAUSES THE LABOR SUPPLY CURVE TO SHIFT?

In Module 4, we learned that changes in the SPENT factors can shift the supply curve for goods and services to the right or left. Likewise, several factors can cause the labor supply curve to shift. These factors include immigration and population growth, the number of hours workers are willing to work at a given wage (worker tastes or preferences), nonwage income, and amenities. The impact of these factors on the labor supply curve is illustrated in Exhibit 6.

Immigration and Population Growth

If new workers enter the labor force, it will shift the labor supply curve to the right, as from S_0 to S_1 in Exhibit 6(a). Of course, if workers leave the country—and thus the labor force—or the relevant population declines, it will cause the supply curve to shift to the left, as shown in Exhibit 6(b).

Number of Hours People Are Willing to Work (Worker Preferences)

If people become willing to work more hours at a given wage (due to changes in worker tastes or preferences), the labor supply curve will shift to the right. This is shown in the movement from S_0 to S_1 in Exhibit 6(a). If they become willing to work fewer hours at a given wage, the labor supply curve will shift to the left, as shown in Exhibit 6(b).

Nonwage Income

Increases in income from other sources than employment can cause the labor supply curve to shift to the left. For example, if you just won $20 million in your state's Super Lotto, you might decide to take yourself out of the labor force. Likewise, a decrease in nonwage income might push a person back into the labor force, thus shifting the labor supply curve to the right.

Will an increase in nonwage income cause a decrease in the supply of labor?

EXHIBIT 6 | **SHIFTS IN THE LABOR SUPPLY CURVE**

a. Increase in Labor Supply

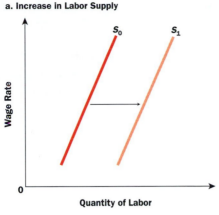

b. Decrease in Labor Supply

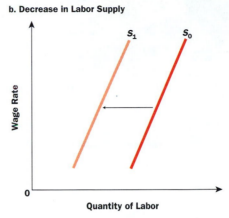

An increase in labor supply shifts the supply curve to the right, while a decrease in labor supply shifts the curve to the left.

Amenities

Amenities associated with a job or a location—like good fringe benefits, safe and friendly working conditions, a child-care center, and so on—will make for a more desirable work atmosphere, *ceteris paribus*. These amenities would cause an increase in the supply of labor, resulting in a rightward shift, such as from S_0 to S_1 in Exhibit 6(a). If job conditions deteriorate, it would lead to a reduction in the labor supply, shifting the labor supply curve to the left, as shown in Exhibit 6(b).

CONCEPT CHECK

1. Wages in the labor market are determined by the intersection of the labor demand curve and the labor supply curve.
2. The labor demand curve can shift if there is a change in productivity or a change in the demand for the final product.
3. The labor supply curve can shift if there are changes in immigration or population growth, workers' preferences, nonwage income, or amenities.

1. If wages were above their equilibrium level, why would they tend to fall toward the equilibrium level?
2. If wages were below their equilibrium level, why would they tend to rise toward the equilibrium level?
3. Why do increases in technology or increases in the amounts of capital or other complementary inputs increase the demand for labor?
4. Why can any of the PYNTE shifters of demand in output markets shift the demand for labor and other inputs used to produce that output in the same direction?
5. Explain why increases in immigration or population growth, increases in workers' willingness to work at a given wage, decreases in nonwage income, or increases in workplace amenities will increase the demand for labor.
6. What would happen to the supply of labor if non-wage incomes increased and workplace amenities also increased over the same time period?
7. If the private-market wage of engineers was greater than that of sociologists, what would happen if a university tried to pay all of its faculty the same salary?
8. If a competitive firm was paying $8 per hour (with no fringe benefits) to its employees, what would tend to happen to its equilibrium wage if the company began to give on-the-job training or free health insurance to its workers?

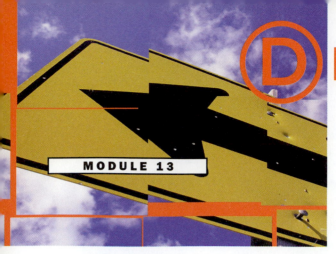

(D) Labor Unions

- Why do labor unions exist?
- What is the impact of unions on wages?
- Can unions increase productivity?

WHY ARE THERE LABOR UNIONS?

When economies begin to industrialize and urbanize, firms become larger and often the "boss" becomes more distant from the workers. In small shops or on farms, workers usually have a close relationship with an owner-employer, but in larger enterprises, the workers may only know a hired foreman or supervisor, and have no direct contact with either the owner or upper management. Workers realize that acting together, as a union of workers, gives them more collective bargaining power than acting individually. The two primary objectives of labor unions are to increase their members' wages and to improve working conditions.

WHERE ARE LABOR UNIONS FOUND?

The growth in union membership certainly has slowed since 1947, and relative to the labor force as a whole, membership has declined by a fairly significant amount, from a peak of 25.5 percent in 1953 to only about 15 percent today (and less than 10 percent of private-sector employment). The recent sluggish absolute growth (and relative decline) in labor union membership probably reflects, to a considerable extent, structural shifts in the occupations of American workers. Unions have traditionally found it difficult to organize workers in white-collar jobs, in the service industries, and in southern and western states. By contrast, blue-collar manufacturing positions in the North and East, especially in large firms, have been unionized to a considerable extent. One reason for this is that workers' tasks are typically standardized, making such workers better able to negotiate as a group. Yet in the past 30 years, manufacturing has moved increasingly to the South and West, and automation has led to a declining proportion of the work force in manufacturing pursuits. Many of the fastest-growing occupations are in the service industries, which are characterized by small firms where workers' tasks are far more varied, making it harder for workers to organize to negotiate as a group. In addition, holders of these jobs find unions less appealing, partly because they work more closely with management or owners.

Workers have more bargaining power if they act together, as a union.

Unionization efforts have been particularly successful in the public sector. In education, teachers organizations like the National Education Association (NEA) have converted from being primarily professional organizations concerned with improving education to being powerful labor unions. The NEA is now, by some measures, the most powerful union in the country.

HOW DO UNIONS IMPACT LABOR SUPPLY AND WAGES?

Labor unions influence the quantity of union labor hired and the wages at which they are hired primarily through their ability to alter the supply of labor services to employers from what would exist if workers acted independently. One way to do this, of course, is by raising barriers to entry into a given occupation. For example, by restricting membership, unions can reduce the quantity of labor supplied to industry employers from what it otherwise would be, and as a result, wages in that occupation would increase from W_0 to W_1, as shown in Exhibit 1(a). As you can see in the shift from Q_0 to Q_1 in Exhibit 1(a), while some union workers will now receive higher wages, others will become unemployed. Many economists believe that this is why wages are approximately 15 percent higher in union jobs, even when nonunion workers have comparable skills. Of course, some of these gains will be appropriated by the unions in the form of dues, initiation fees, and the like, so the workers themselves will benefit less.

WHY ARE THERE WAGE DIFFERENCES FOR SIMILARLY SKILLED WORKERS?

Suppose you had two labor sectors: the union sector and the nonunion sector. If unions are successful in obtaining higher wages either through bargaining, threatening to strike, or by restricting membership, wages will rise and employment will fall in the union sector, as seen in Exhibit 1(a). With a downward-sloping demand curve for labor, higher wages mean that less labor is demanded in the union sector. Those workers that are equally skilled but are unable to find union work will seek nonunion work, thus increasing supply in that sector and, in turn, lowering wages in the nonunion sector. This effect is shown in Exhibit 1(b). Thus, comparably skilled workers will experience higher wages in the union sector (W_1) than in the nonunion sector (W_2).

CAN UNIONS LEAD TO INCREASE IN PRODUCTIVITY?

Two Harvard economists, Richard Freeman and James Medoff, argue that unions might actually increase worker productivity by increasing marginal productivity. Their argument is that unions provide a collective voice that workers can use to communicate their discontents more effectively. This might lower the number of union workers that quit their jobs. Resignations can be particularly costly for firms, because they have often invested in

---

EXHIBIT 1 | **THE EFFECT OF UNIONS ON WAGES**

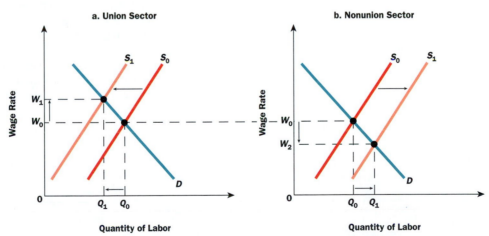

Through restrictive membership practices and other means, a union can reduce the labor supply in its industry, thereby increasing the wage rate they can earn (from W_0 to W_1) but reducing employment (from Q_0 to Q_1). However, as workers unable to get jobs in the union sector join the nonunion sector, the supply of labor in the nonunion sector increases (from Q_0 to Q_1), lowering wages in those industries (from W_0 to W_2).

UNION WAGE PREMIUMS IN SELECTED COUNTRIES

Country	Year	Estimated Difference between Union and Nonunion Wages (percent)
South Africa[a]	1985	10–24%
Mexico	1989	10
Malaysia	1988	15–20
Ghana	1992–1993	31
United States	1985–1987	20
United Kingdom	1985–1987	10
Germany	1985–1987	5

CONSIDER THIS:
Union wages are also higher than nonunion wages in other parts of the world.

a. Black unions only.
SOURCE: "Workers in an Integrating World," *World Report*, 1995, p. 81.

training and job-specific skills for their employees. In addition, by handling worker's grievances, unions may increase workers' motivation and morale. The combined impact of fewer resignations and improved morale could boost productivity.

However, this improvement in worker productivity in the labor sector should show up on the bottom line—the profit statement of the firm. While the evidence is still preliminary, it appears that unions tend to lower the profitability of firms, not raise it.

CONCEPT CHECK

1. Workers realize that acting together gives them collective bargaining power.
2. Labor unions try to increase their members' wages and improve their working conditions.
3. Through restrictive membership, a union can reduce the labor supply in the market for union workers, thus reducing employment and raising wages. This increases the supply of workers in the nonunion sector, shifting supply to the right and lowering wages for nonunion workers.

---

1. How can acting together as a group increase workers' bargaining power?
2. Why are service industries harder to unionize than manufacturing industries?
3. How do union restrictions on membership or other barriers to entry affect the wages of members?
4. What would increasing unionization do to the wages of those who were not in unions?
5. How can unions potentially increase worker productivity?
6. Why does data indicating that unionization tends to lower firm profits weaken the argument that the primary effect of unionization is increased worker productivity?

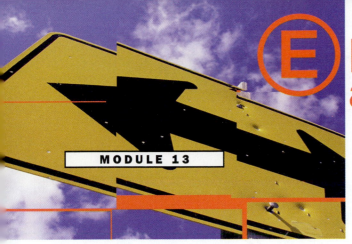

E Labor Productivity and Wages

MODULE 13

■ What causes real wages to rise and fall?
■ Why has there been a slowdown in labor productivity growth?

THE REAL WAGE SLOWDOWN

From the 1940s to the mid-1970s, the real wages (adjusted for inflation) of American workers rose an average of about 3 percent a year. The purchasing power of American labor accordingly increased greatly, bringing about profound changes in standards of living in the United States. Why did this increase in real wages occur? We return to economic theory for the answer: The demand for labor increased faster than the supply, reflecting a rising marginal productivity of labor. The rising labor productivity, in turn, reflects the fact that new, improved capital, new forms of technology, and better labor skills led to greater physical output per worker.

This is illustrated in Exhibit 1, which compares labor markets over time. Since 1950, the supply of most forms of labor has increased, reflecting both increasing population and the increasing number of women participating in the labor force. This increase in the labor supply has caused the labor supply curve to shift to the right. By itself, this factor would tend to lower wages. At the same time, however, additions to capital per worker, technological advances, and increased skill levels in the labor force have caused increases in marginal revenue product, leading to a rightward shift in the labor demand curve. In fact, if the demand effect exceeds the supply effect, real wages (and the equilibrium quantity of workers) will rise as they did

from 1950 to 1970; real earnings increased over 3 percent a year from 1950 to 1970. However, real wages only increased 1 percent a year from 1970 to 1997.

One must be careful of this data because some of this decline in real wages can be explained by increases in employee benefits (holiday pay, vacation and sick leave, insurance, and retirement). In many large firms, nonwage compensation is almost 30 percent of total compensation. In 1960, nonwage compensation was only 20 percent of total compensation. So part of the slowdown in wage growth is due to a growth in benefits.

The success of the three decades immediately following WWII has been followed by two and a half decades of moderate increases in labor productivity or output per worker (Exhibit 1). Since the 1970s, the average rate of growth in labor productivity has been roughly 1 percent. Why? There are several possible culprits. One is the slowdown in capital

EXHIBIT 1	GROWTH IN LABOR PRODUCTIVITY, 1950–1996

Average Annual Increases in Nonfarm Business Productivity

1950–1959	2.8%
1960–1969	2.8
1970–1979	1.9
1980–1989	1.1
1990–1996	0.9

SOURCE: *Los Angeles Daily News*, August 14, 1997, Section B, p. 1.

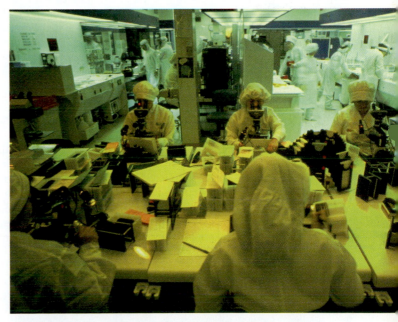

Has a slowdown in the growth in technology led to slower growth in labor productivity?

formation. Workers are generally more productive when they have more and better equipment. Second, total employment increased by 20 million in the 1970s. Many of these first-time baby-boom workers were unskilled and lacked any previous working experience. By adding many unskilled workers to the work force, it was inevitable that the economy would initially experience lower output per worker. Third, the economy is moving towards the service sector, where measured productivity tends to be lower (and measures of productivity less accurate). It is much more difficult to improve output per worker in the service industry (doctors, waiters, airline stewardesses, fast-food servers, and so on) than it is in manufacturing.

In Exhibit 2, we use supply and demand to highlight the changes in real wages over the period from 1950 to 1997. In the years from 1950 to 1970, the increases in capital per worker, technology, organizational improvements, and improved skill levels of workers all contributed to the increases in the demand for labor. In Exhibit 2, we see that in the 1950–1970 period, demand increased more rapidly than the supply of labor; as a result, real wages increased significantly. While there continues to be an increase in labor demand, there has been a much larger increase in the labor supply curve in the years from 1970 to 1997, as a result of population and labor force growth. This has resulted in a much smaller increase in real wages over the last 20 years. Consequently, there has been greater employment but only a slightly higher real wage.

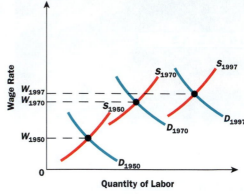

| EXHIBIT 2 | WAGES AND ECONOMIC GROWTH, 1950–1997 |

The increase in labor supply, by itself, would have lowered wages since 1950. This has been more than offset, however, by a large increase in labor demand, reflecting the rising productivity of labor. Rising labor productivity reflects the various factors contributing to economic growth, including capital formation, technological advances, and improvements in workers' skill levels. However, we see that in the 1970–1997 period, there was a large increase in labor supply coupled with a smaller increase in the demand for labor. The inevitable result was slower real wage growth over this period.

CONCEPT CHECK

1. Real wages are determined by the intersection of the labor demand and labor supply curves.
2. If the demand for labor rises more rapidly than the supply of labor, real wages will rise. If the supply of labor rises more rapidly than the demand for labor, real wages will fall.

3. Reasons for the slowdown in real wage growth since 1970 include the slowdown in new capital formation, the increase in labor supply, and the increase in employment in the service sector.
4. A larger supply of workers tends to lower real wages, *ceteris paribus*.

1. If labor demand rises faster than labor supply, what will happen to real wages?
2. What will either a slowdown in the growth rate of labor demand or an increase in the growth rate of labor supply do to the growth rate of real wages?
3. Say there are completely different "men's jobs" and "women's jobs." If the labor supply of women grows faster than the labor supply of men, what will happen to the average wage of a woman versus the average wage of a man?

4. If a large number of skilled workers retire at about the same time, what will happen to the wages of skilled workers, other things equal?

Ⓕ Land and Capital

- How is the rental price of capital determined?
- How is the rental price of land determined?

As we discussed earlier, the three productive factors are labor, capital, and land. Our discussion so far has focused on labor. Factor prices for land and capital are determined in the same way—supply and demand.

SUPPLY AND DEMAND IN THE CAPITAL MARKET

Resources like capital or land are "leased" or "rented," or as we more often put it, they are borrowed for some stipulated period of time. This cost is called the rental price of capital or land. For example, instead of talking about a particular type of labor, we might want to analyze the market for a certain type of machine that can be used in making running shoes. Following the law of demand, the lower the rental price of a shoe-making machine (which would lower the cost of making running shoes), the greater the quantity of shoe machines demanded. Following the law of supply, the greater the rental price of the machine, the more willing owners of shoe machines are to supply them to entrepreneurs.

Rather than renting a shoe machine, a shoemaker may borrow funds and buy his own machine. In this case, the manufacturer is borrowing funds for the purpose of acquiring capital. The price of the borrowed funds is usually called the **interest rate.** At lower interest rates, the cost of financing the purchase of the shoe machine is lower. If a machine costs $1,000 and the interest rate being charged is 10 percent, the interest cost of a shoe machine is $100 a year ($1,000 × .10); if the relevant interest rate is 8 percent, interest costs are only $80 a year ($100 × .08). At lower interest rates, then, capital costs are lower, and the quantity of funds demanded is greater. Likewise, the loaners of funds will derive greater income the greater the interest rate, so the benefits to them of making a loan increase as interest rates (the price of funds) rise. Thus, the quantity of funds supplied is positively related to interest rates.

The graph in Exhibit 1 is virtually the same whether we are renting the capital equipment or we are borrowing to pay for that capital. The intersection of the upward-sloping supply curve for capital and the downward-sloping demand curve for capital determines the rental price of capital. As in labor markets, the profit-maximizing competitive firm will continue to demand more capital as long as the marginal revenue product of that capital exceeds the rental price. The supply and demand in capital markets is seen in Exhibit 1.

EXHIBIT 1	THE SUPPLY AND DEMAND FOR CAPITAL GOODS

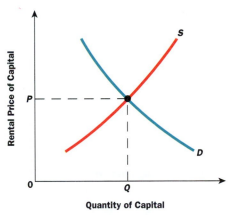

The demand curve for capital is downward sloping, reflecting the fact that as more capital is employed, the marginal revenue product of capital falls. The supply curve for capital is upward sloping, implying that owners of capital will be more willing to supply at higher rental prices. The rental price of capital is found at the intersection of the supply and demand curves.

THE SUPPLY AND DEMAND FOR LAND

The supply of some land and natural resources is sometimes fixed and not at all responsive to prices—that is, it is perfectly inelastic. For example, if you own 100 acres of land, the same 100 acres are available for use at any positive price. Hence, the supply curve for land resources is often perfectly inelastic (vertical) or nearly so, rather than positively sloped. Of course, at higher rent, owners may have an incentive to make improvements such as irrigating, draining, or clearing. Technically, then, the supply curve for land might be less than perfectly inelastic. The price of using land—its rental price—can nonetheless be determined by demand and supply considerations. Simply, changes in the demand for land will change the rental value. If the price of wheat rises, the marginal revenue product of wheat-producing land will also rise, inducing an increase in the demand for land. Given a fixed supply, this will lead to an increase in the rental price of land. That is, we would anticipate that rising wheat prices will be accompanied by a big jump in land prices, as seen in Exhibit 2.

In competitive land markets, the rental price for land will adjust to the point where the demand for and supply of land are equal, as seen in Exhibit 2. At this profit-maximizing level, the rental price of land will equal the marginal revenue product of land.

THE INTERDEPENDENCE OF INPUT MARKETS

For simplicity, we have treated the labor, capital, and land markets independently. In reality, these markets are interconnected. For example, if wages rise and the rental price of capital falls, machines might be used as a substitute for some workers.

If demand for a crop rises, what will happen to the price of land on which that crop is grown?

EXHIBIT 2 | **SUPPLY AND DEMAND IN THE LAND MARKET**

The supply and demand curves for land determine the amount paid to land owners.

1. The rental price of capital is determined by the intersection of the demand and supply curves for capital.
2. At the profit-maximizing level of capital, the rental price of capital will equal the marginal revenue product of capital.
3. The price of using land is called the rental price. The intersection of the supply and demand curves for land determines the rental price of land, the compensation to land owners.
4. At the profit-maximizing level, the rental price of land will equal the marginal revenue product of land.

---

1. Why is the demand curve for capital downward sloping?
2. Why is the supply curve for capital upward sloping?
3. Why does the price of agricultural land so closely reflect the prices of what is produced on the land?
4. If a new machine could earn a 12 percent rate of return in your firm, and you could borrow the funds to finance it at an interest rate of 15 percent per year, would you borrow the money to buy it? Why or why not?

G Application: Immigration

What impact does an increase in immigrants have on the supply curve for labor of their skill level? How will this impact wages for that skill level? Is it possible that these changes will also impact the demand for goods and services and therefore the demand for labor? How will these changes impact the supply of goods and services?

STEPPING THROUGH AMERICA'S GOLDEN DOOR

WILLIAM H. CARLILE

In a recent ceremony in Tucson, more than 1,000 people from around the globe took the oath that transformed them into U.S. citizens.

It was the city's largest such event to date, paralleling many similarly crowded initiations across the nation. Chicago recently held record-breaking, back-to-back ceremonies for 10,000 new Americans; in the New York area, roughly 6,000 immigrants become citizens every week, five times as many as a year ago.

As the United States prepares to celebrate the Fourth of July, it is clear the country continues to draw like a magnet those who seek a new and better life, often at considerable personal sacrifice. And on the surface, it has been a banner year for new citizens.

By October, officials expect roughly 1 million immigrants to have completed background checks, taken citizenship tests, and sworn loyalty to their new country—all as part of an effort to reduce a massive backlog generated by the immigration amnesty offered in 1986. . . .

Indeed, immigrants have borne the brunt of Americans' frustration in the face of economic uncertainty brought about by layoffs and downsizings. California put the issue front and center in 1994, when voters approved Proposition 187, which sought to eliminate social services, public schooling, and medical care for illegal immigrants. Many legal immigrants felt it created an atmosphere of hostility toward them.

Those opposed to curbs on immigration, meanwhile, argue that the system already is adequately controlled and regulated. There are fewer immigrants now than at the turn of the century: 720,000 in 1995, compared with 1.3 million in 1907. And according to the 1990 census, the number of foreign-born Americans was 7.9 percent of the population, lower than at most times since 1850. . . .

Since 1981, more than 13 million newcomers have arrived in the United States.

SOURCE: William H. Carlile, "Stepping through America's Golden Door," *The Christian Science Monitor*, July, 3, 1996, p.10.

One of the consistent criticisms of liberal immigration policies is that they take jobs away from U.S. workers. While an overwhelming number of people believe this, there is very little evidence that it is true.

The answer to this confusion may be couched in the laws of supply and demand. The conventional view is that the influx of immigrants increases the supply curve for labor, as seen in Exhibit 1(a). The increase in labor supply shifts the labor supply curve from S_0 to S_1; as a result, the wage falls from W_0 to W_1 and employment increases from Q_0 to Q_1. The only problem is that the number of jobs going to U.S. workers falls to Q_2. Why? This is the smaller number of U.S. workers that would be willing to work at the new lower wage. This quantity is found by the intersection of the pre-immigration labor supply curve, S_0, at the new wage, W_1.

However, a more careful analysis of the impact of immigration should incorporate the immigrants as consumers and savers, not just workers. That is, the new immigrants are also buying food, clothing, housing, transportation, and other goods. As a result of the increased demand for these products, there will be an increase in the demand for labor, as seen in Exhibit 1(b). Immigrants are also investing directly and saving some of their money in banks, where the money may be borrowed to build new factories and homes, creating still more jobs. If the immigrants' consumption and saving equal their earnings, then the increase in the demand for labor may equal the increase in the supply of labor. As a result, wages will rise from W_1 back to W_0 and employment will increase beyond Q_1 to Q_2.

EXHIBIT 1	IMPACT OF IMMIGRATION ON LABOR SUPPLY AND DEMAND

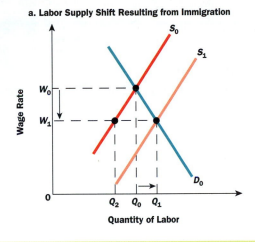

a. Labor Supply Shift Resulting from Immigration

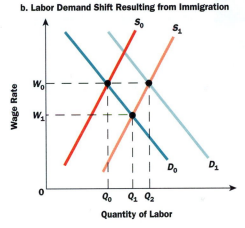

b. Labor Demand Shift Resulting from Immigration

ONE STEP BEYOND

Do you know how supply and demand in the labor market impact wages? You might not care right now, but you will certainly want to know before you enter your chosen profession! To check your understanding of the workings of this and other input markets, be sure to work the problems and exercises in the Workbook and on the EconActive CD-ROM.

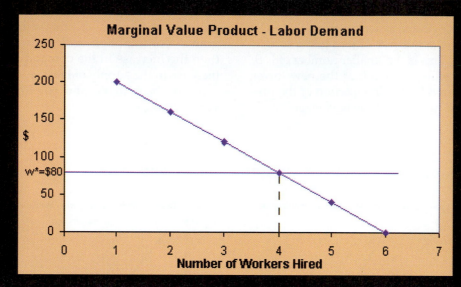

Marginal Value Product - Labor Demand

PHOTO CREDITS MODULE 13

Page 320: © PhotoDisc; Page 321: © Billy E. Barnes/Stock Boston/PNI; Page 322: © PhotoDisc; Page 324: © Digital Stock; Page 325: © PhotoDisc; Page 326: AP Photo/Morry Cash; Page 331: © David Simson/Stock, Boston/PNI; Page 332: AP Photo/Don Edgar; Page 334: AP Photo/Carlos Osorio; Page 337: © Dan McCoy/Rainbow/PNI; Page 340: © 1998 Don Couch Photography; Page 342: © Jim West/Impact Visuals/PNI

Income Distribution and Poverty

A. Income Distribution
How equal is the distribution
of income?

B. The Pros and Cons of Income Equality
What are the arguments for and against a more
equal distribution of income?

C. The Economics of Discrimination
What are the effects of discrimination?

D. Poverty
How do absolute measures of poverty differ from relative measures?

E. Application: Welfare Reform
How does the principle "incentives matter" relate to welfare reform?

(A) Income Distribution

- What has happened to the income distribution since 1935?
- Are the income distribution statistics accurate?
- How significant is income mobility?
- How much income inequality is there in other countries?

The ultimate purpose of producing goods and services is to satisfy the material wants of people. Up to this point, we have examined the process by which society decides which wants to satisfy in a world characterized by scarcity; we have examined the question of how goods are produced; and we have examined the question of how society can fully utilize its productive resources. We have not, however, looked carefully into the question of for whom society produces consumer goods and services. Why are some people able to consume much more than others?

THE RECORD SINCE 1935

Exhibit 1 illustrates the changing distribution of measured income in the United States since 1935. As you can see in this graph, the proportion of income received by the richest Americans (top 5 percent) declined sharply after 1935 but has been edging back up since the 1980s. The proportion received by the poorest Americans (the lowest 20 percent) has remained virtually unchanged since 1935. Most of the observed changes occurred between 1935 and 1950, probably reflecting the impact of the Great Depression and new government programs in the 1930s, as well as World War II. From 1950 to 1980, there was very little change in the overall distribution of income. Since the 1980s, there have been two significant changes: The lowest one-fifth of

families has seen their share of measured income fall from 5.2 to 4.2 percent of all income, and the top one-fifth of families has seen their share of measured income rise from 41.5 to 46.9 percent of all income.

ARE WE UNDERSTATING TRUE INEQUALITY?

Some observers have argued that the income distribution statistics cited above understate true inequality and, perhaps more important, mistake the direction American society is moving with respect to equality. Rather than slowly become more equal, these observers claim, inequality is probably growing, because the published data exclude much nonmonetary income and many privileges of the relatively well-to-do, privileges that have grown in recent years largely as a means of tax avoidance. For example, the corporate executive of today may eat elaborate expense account lunches, fly all over the world in private corporate

EXHIBIT 1			BEFORE-TAX INCOME SHARES			
Year	Lowest Fifth	Second Fifth	Third Fifth	Fourth Fifth	Highest Fifth	Highest 5%
1935	4.1%	9.2%	14.1%	20.9%	51.7%	26.5%
1950	4.5	12.0	17.4	23.4	42.7	17.3
1960	4.8	12.2	17.8	24.0	41.3	15.9
1970	5.2	12.2	17.6	23.8	40.9	15.6
1980	5.2	11.5	17.5	24.3	41.5	15.3
1990	4.6	10.8	16.6	23.8	44.3	17.4
1994	4.2	10.0	15.7	23.3	46.9	20.1

SOURCE: U.S. Department of Commerce

Do perks such as rides in a corporate jet show up in official measures of income?

jets, stay in lavish, company-owned condominiums, and so on. None of these things show in official measures of income for such executives, but in fact, they constitute a form of compensation that is real and relevant.

ARE WE OVERSTATING THE DISPARITY IN THE DISTRIBUTION OF INCOME?

While the growth of executive "perks" may be real, a number of other adjustments to the measured income distribution data would suggest that we might be overstating inequality. Differences in age, certain demographic factors, institutional factors, and government redistributive activities have all been identified as elements that influence income distribution data.

Differences in Age

The aggregate data cited fail to account for a rather sizable shift in the age distribution of the U.S. population, a shift that has tended, by itself, to increase the observed inequality in the distribution of income. At any moment in time, middle-age persons tend to have higher incomes than younger and older persons, because they are at an age when their productivity is at a peak and they are participating in the labor force to a greater extent than are very old or very young persons. Put differently, if every individual earned exactly the same total income over his or her lifetime, there would still be some observed inequality at any given moment in time, simply because people earn more in middle age.

Inequality resulting from this demographic difference overstates the true inequality in the lifetime earnings of people. A typical 50-year-old male earns nearly twice the income of a male in his early 20s and nearly one-third more than workers over 65. Since 1950, the proportion of

Typical middle-aged workers earn one-third more than workers over age 65.

TUNE UP

DEMOGRAPHIC FACTORS AND INCOME DISTRIBUTION

Q: Dee Vorce and Al E. Moenee recently separated. Dee knew that she would not be alone if she decided to file for divorce, because divorce rates have been climbing in recent years. What impact do you think higher divorce rates will have on income inequality?

A: As you would probably imagine, when one family with two incomes turns into two families with one income each, there will now be more families reporting and there will be less income per family, often causing one high income household to become two middle income households in the data. However, the most dramatic changes in the distribution of income may occur in so-called "traditional" households, consisting of one male breadwinner. Now, when the breakup occurs, the woman, who may have little previous job experience, is forced to look for her first job. And if she receives custody of the children, her search might be further limited to part-time jobs or low-paying jobs with flexible hours. Her new household income will undoubtedly be far lower, also increasing measured income disparities between families.

individuals that are either very young or very old has grown, meaning that in a relative sense, more people are in lower-income age groups.

Other Demographic Trends

Other demographic trends, like the increased number of divorced couples and the rise of two-income families (and DINKs—Double Income, No Kids), have also caused the measured distribution of income (which is measured in terms of household income) to appear more unequal. For example, in the 1950s, the overwhelming majority of families had single incomes. In the 1990s, a family that decides to have two bread winners instead of one might be making $70,000 or $80,000 a year instead of, say, $40,000 a year; thus, they would move into a higher-income quintile and create greater apparent income inequality. At the same time, divorces create two households instead of one, lowering income per household for divorced couples; thus, they move into lower-income quintiles, also creating greater apparent income inequality.

Government Activities

Other scholars have argued that the impact of increased government activity should be considered in evaluating the measured income distribution.[1] Government-imposed taxes burden different income groups in different ways. Also, government programs benefit some groups of income recipients more than others. For example, it has been argued that state-subsidized higher education has benefitted the higher- and middle-income groups more than the poor (because far more students from these income groups go to college), as have such things as government subsidies to airports and airlines, operas, and art museums. Some programs, though, clearly aid the poor more than the rich. Food stamps, school lunch programs, housing subsidies, Medicaid, and several other programs provide recipients with in-kind income—that is, income in a nonmonetary form. When these nonmonetary forms of income are included, many economists conclude that they have served to reduce levels of inequality significantly from the levels suggested by aggregate income statistics.

On balance, the evidence suggests that inequality of money income in the United States declined from 1935 to 1950, then remained rather stable until 1980. Since then, the distribution of income has become less equal. However, if we consider age distribution, institutional factors, and in-kind transfer programs, it is safe to say that the income distribution is considerably more equal than it appears in Exhibit 1.

---

[1] Edgar Browning, "The Trend Towards Equality in the Distribution of Income," *Southern Economic Journal*, July 1976, pp. 912–23; Frank Levy, *Dollars and Dreams* (New York: Norton, 1987), p. 195.

HOW MUCH MOVEMENT IS THERE ON THE ECONOMIC LADDER?

While the distribution of current income is an important piece of information, it is also critical to know how much movement goes on between different income levels. That is, are the people that make up the top income group or the bottom group always the same people? And which income groups are growing most rapidly? A study from the Urban Institute by Isabel Sawhill and Mark Condon found that during the periods from 1967 to 1976 and from 1977 to 1986, the average income in the families in the bottom 20 percent grew 12 to 15 times more rapidly than those in the top 20 percent. However, even more surprising, the Urban Institute study found that about half of the group that started in the bottom quintile moved up, some all the way to the top quintile, and about half of those who started at the top wound up in lower quintiles, with some moving all the way to the bottom. The study also indicated that slightly less than 70 percent of those in the middle quintiles moved up or down. Another study conducted by the Treasury Department confirmed the Sawhill and Condon results. The Treasury Department study found that between 1979 and 1988, over 85 percent of the taxpayers who were in the bottom quintile moved up, and 40 percent of this group moved into the top two quintiles. The study also found that less than 50 percent of those that started in the top 1 percent were able to maintain that position at the end of the period. That is, high-income and low-income earners will always be with us, but more than likely, they will be different people.

WHY DO SOME EARN MORE THAN OTHERS?

There are many reasons why some people make more income than others. Some reasons for differences in income include differences in skill, education, training, and preferences toward risk and leisure.

Skills and Human Capital

Some workers are just more productive than others and therefore earn higher wages. The greater productivity may be a result of innate skills or of improvements in human capital, such as training and education. Still others, like star athletes and rock stars, have specialized talents that are in huge demand, so they make more money than those with fewer skills or with skills that are in less demand.

Worker Preferences

Aside from skills, education, and training, people have different attitudes about and preferences regarding their work. Workaholics earn more than others with comparable skills because they work longer hours. Some earn more because they work more intensely than others. Still others may choose jobs that pay less but have more amenities—flexible hours, favorable job location, generous benefit programs, child care, and so on. And some may choose to work less and spend more time pursuing leisure activities, like traveling, watching television, or exercising. It is not for us to say that one preference is better than another but simply to recognize that these choices lead to differences in earnings.

Job Preferences

Finally, some of the differences in income are the result of the risks or undesirable features of some occupations. Police officers and firefighters are paid higher wages because of the dangers associated with their jobs. The same would be true for window washers on skyscrapers and painters on the Golden Gate bridge. Coal miners and garbage collectors are paid more than other workers with comparable skill levels because of the unpleasantness of the jobs. In short, some workers have higher earnings because they are compensated for the difficult, risky, or unappealing nature of their jobs.

INCOME DISTRIBUTION IN OTHER COUNTRIES

Is the United States a typical advanced industrial nation with respect to the distribution of income among its population? That is a difficult question to answer with absolute certainty, given international differences in defining income, difficulties in measuring the impact of taxes, the problem of nonmonetary payments, and so on. Despite these hurdles, international comparisons of income distribution have been made.

Exhibit 2, constructed with data from the World Bank, shows that income inequality is greater in the United States and United Kingdom than in Sweden and Japan. However, the table also shows that some of the greatest disparities in income are found in lower-income countries, such as India, China, and Brazil. If you look at income earned by the top 20 percent of "bread winners," it is obvious that many developed countries have more equal distributions of income than developing countries.

While income inequality within nations is often substantial, it is far less than income inequality among nations. A majority of income inequality on the planet Earth reflects differences in living standards among countries rather than disparities within nations. This is borne out by statistics.

Low-income countries such as Brazil have great disparities in income among their residents.

EXHIBIT 2	GLOBAL INCOME INEQUALITIES AS A PERCENT OF TOTAL NATIONAL INCOME				
Country	Lowest Fifth	Second Fifth	Third Fifth	Fourth Fifth	Highest Fifth
India	8.5%	12.1%	15.8%	21.1%	42.6%
China	5.5	9.8	14.9	22.3	47.5
Mexico	4.1	7.8	12.5	20.2	55.3
Brazil	2.1	4.9	8.9	16.8	67.5
Chile	3.5	6.6	10.9	18.1	61.0
United Kingdom	4.6	10.0	16.8	24.3	44.3
Canada	5.7	11.8	17.7	24.6	40.2
Sweden	8.0	13.2	17.4	24.5	36.9
France	5.6	11.8	17.2	23.5	41.9
United States	4.7	11.0	17.4	25.0	41.9
Japan	8.7	13.2	17.5	23.1	37.5

SOURCE: World Bank, *World Development Report 1997*, pp.223–224.

Note: The income inequality differences are approximations, because the data vary according to survey year and different methods are used for computing the distribution of income in different countries.

1. From 1935 to 1980, the distribution of income became more equal. However, since 1980, there has been increased inequality.
2. Nonmonetary income and privileges to the well-to-do may understate the disparity in income inequality, while demographics, institutional factors, and government programs may overstate the disparity in income inequality.

3. High-income and low-income earners will always be with us, but they will likely be different people.
4. Income inequality between nations is substantial.

---

1. Why might patterns in the measured income distribution give an incorrect impression?
2. Why might measured income shares understate the degree of income inequality?
3. Why might measured income shares overstate the degree of income inequality?
4. How does the fraction of the population that is middle aged, rather than young or old, affect measurements of income inequality?

5. How does the growth of both two-earner families and divorced couples increase measured income inequality?
6. Why is it important to take account of the substantial mobility of families within the income distribution over time when evaluating the degree of income inequality in the United States?

B The Pros and Cons of Income Equality

■ What is the case for income redistribution?
■ What is the case against income redistribution?

The emphasis to this point has been on describing the amount of income inequality present in the United States and the rest of the world. Little has been said about the impact that inequality has on human welfare. Because of the difficulty of measuring welfare or of comparing the welfare of one person with another, it is impossible to "prove" that a given income distribution is better than another.

At the same time, however, it is clear that political and social changes in the past century or two have generally worked to reduce income inequality. In some cases, revolutions have been fought with income redistribution as a paramount motive—such is the case with the Russian Revolution and probably the French Revolution, not to mention many more recent upheavals in less-developed countries. Why is it generally felt that justice, fairness, and happiness would all be improved by increasing the income of the poor relative to the well-to-do or rich?

THE CASE FOR INCOME REDISTRIBUTION

The economic theory that is supportive of policies of income redistribution is derived from the principle of diminishing marginal utility. According to this principle, increases in income generate less additional happiness (utility) at higher levels of income.

Consider Exhibit 1. Suppose a family with an income of $300,000 a year has $30,000 taken from it in the form of a tax on income. The family accordingly reduces its consumption spending, forcing it to cut out some spending on luxuries—perhaps taking less-expensive vacations, foregoing a vacation home, and so on. This lowers the family's daily utility, say from 27 utils to 25 utils. The marginal utility of the income given up is 2 utils (27 – 25). Now, suppose the income of some family making $10,000 a year is increased by the $30,000 taken from the first, well-to-do

EXHIBIT 1	DIMINISHING MARGINAL UTILITY OF INCOME

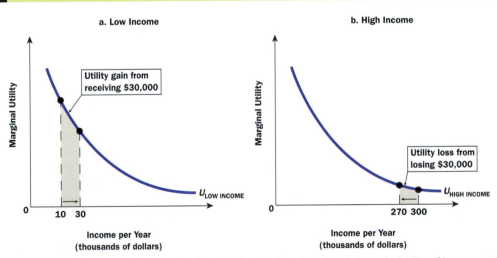

As income rises, the happiness associated with that income also rises, but the principle of diminishing marginal utility of income means it rises by diminishing amounts. The decrease in utility that results from taking some income from high-income groups may be less than the increase in utility generated by giving this income to low-income groups. Total utility in society would be enhanced by such redistribution if people have similar preferences for income. The exact utility–income relationship is impossible to state, however, because of our inability to measure utility or to make utility comparisons among individuals.

family. The poor family was formerly unable to purchase cars or appliances or take vacations. Now, their utility is very positively influenced by the transfer payment of $30,000, as it increases from 6 to 15 utils a week. The marginal utility to the poor family of the $30,000 in transfer payments is 9 utils (15 – 6). Using the Robin Hood approach—taking from the rich and giving to the poor—could possibly increase society's total utility in this case, because the rich family loses only two utils a week, while the poor family gains nine utils.

Did Robin Hood increase or decrease society's total utility?

Thus, there is a theoretical argument favoring income redistribution. Note, however, that the argument is based on the critical assumption that people are alike in how they experience diminishing marginal utility from increasing income, a proposition impossible to prove. Many people believe that it is a plausible assumption, but it is merely an assumption nonetheless. It is possible, however, that an entertainer making $20 million a year after taxes will lose little utility if his or her income is cut to $17 million, compared to the gains of the many poor families who could have their income doubled or tripled by receiving a portion of that income.

Polls of people have been taken from time to time asking: "Are you happy?" There is evidence from these polls that, at a moment in time within a country, happiness is positively correlated with income—rich people are generally happier than poor people. This does not necessarily support the existence of diminishing marginal utility, but it might be evidence used by those who argue that income ought to be redistributed simply on the grounds of economic justice and fairness. Many people are able to command high incomes simply because of some inherited physical or mental talents that they develop or because they were, in some other way, "lucky." Why should these persons be happier than others simply because of an accident? If you believe society should try to equalize happiness among its members, some income redistribution could be argued to make sense.

THE CASE AGAINST INCOME DISTRIBUTION

Even if one agreed that income redistribution from the rich to the poor would both tend to equalize happiness and, in the short run, increase the total utility received by the population, one might legitimately oppose some income redistribution on other grounds. If some income redistribution is good, why not go all the way and completely equalize everyone's income, taxing the rich extremely heavily and giving massive subsidies to the poor? Nearly everyone opposes that scenario; because our incomes would all be equal but much smaller, there would be little incentive to work or invest. Most of us believe, for efficiency and equity reasons, that there ought to be some limits on redistributive efforts. The principal disagreement is not over whether we should have some redistribution, but rather over at what point we should stop in our redistributive efforts. Some believe we should go further than we have, while others think we have already gone too far in attempts to alter the distribution of income in favor of the poor and less affluent.

"Fair" May or May Not Be Fair

What are the arguments against a radical redistribution of income that would eliminate virtually all inequality? The first argument is an equity one. Is it "fair" to take most of the income of hard-working, talented persons who earn high incomes, particularly when some of it is given to persons who perhaps are shiftless and lazy? Not all poor persons are automatically good and deserving, nor are all rich persons undeserving. Related to that, some income inequality would seem desirable, because consumption needs may well vary with family size, age of family members, and other factors (physical health, for example). Total equality of *family* income, for example, would penalize those who choose to have big families, while total equality in *individual* incomes would perhaps penalize those who choose to have small families or live alone.

Indeed, it is possible that the rich are rich largely because of their high marginal utility of income, while many poor may be poor because they care less about goods rela-

| EXHIBIT 2 | DIFFERENCES IN MARGINAL UTILITY OF INCOME |

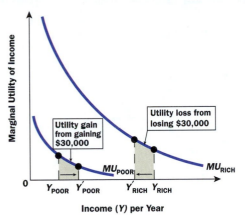

The rich may have a higher marginal utility of income. Therefore, transferring income from rich to poor could make society worse off.

| EXHIBIT 3 | THE LAFFER CURVE |

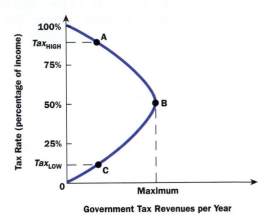

When tax rates are low, increasing the tax rates will increase government revenue. At very high rates, though, disincentive effects and increased tax evasion may actually reduce government revenue. Over this range of tax rates, lowering them can increase government tax revenue. A very high marginal tax rate on the rich, then, would not only reduce earned incomes, it would also lower tax revenues. Whether the tax rate–revenue relationship is similar to that depicted here, as Arthur Laffer suggests, is debatable.

tive to non-work activities. As you can see by comparing the shaded areas of Exhibit 2, if this is indeed the case, the rich lose more than the poor gain from the transfer of income. In this situation, then, transferring income from rich to poor actually makes society worse off!

The Impact on Economic Growth

A second argument against massive income redistribution is that it very likely would lower the rate of economic growth reducing future real income. Why? First, incentives to earn income are lowered. In Great Britain, the highest marginal income tax rate on some forms of income in the not-too-distant past was 98 percent. Why work hard to earn more income when little of it will be available to advance your interests? Rather than work harder to slightly increase after-tax income, the incentive for high-income earners would need to be significantly greater to make that additional work effort worthwhile. Similarly, attempts to make money by engaging in business ventures involving capital formation and risk are substantially eroded when the government confiscates nearly all of any rewards, but does not also subsidize financial losses if those ventures fail. Some people believe that excessive taxation of higher-income persons in some Western nations, including the United States, has greatly lowered the rate of capital formation and led to rates of economic growth that are lower than in countries where such high marginal rates of taxation do not exist.

The Laffer Curve

High tax rates could conceivably reduce work incentives to the point that government revenues are lower at high marginal rates of taxation than they would be at somewhat

lower rates. Economist Arthur Laffer has argued that point graphically in what has been called the Laffer Curve (Exhibit 3). At a marginal tax rate greater than that indicated by Tax$_{High}$ on Exhibit 3, revenues received by the government actually decline, reflecting both a reduction in work effort arising from the disincentive effect and, perhaps as

"I said no to drugs, but I couldn't say no to drug money."

How does the underground economy impact government revenues?

important, illegal shifts in transactions to the **underground economy,** meaning that people make cash and barter transactions that are very difficult for any tax collector to observe. If tax evasion becomes common, the equity and revenue-raising efficiency of the tax system suffers, as does general respect for the law.

The validity of the Laffer-curve argument has been questioned, and little reliable empirical evidence has been introduced to support the argument (especially given the difficulty of measuring the relevant marginal tax rates for different people). At the same time, most economists would agree that at some level of taxation, substantial disincentive effects develop. To the extent that this is the case, nations may face a trade-off. If they push vigorously to divide up the nation's income pie more equally among the population now, they may reduce the growth of that pie in later years. Is it more important to have economic equality now than to have more income for everyone, but with greater inequality, at a later date? Indeed, it is a distinct possibility that the poorest of the poor in a high-growth, high-inequality economy might be far better off in a few generations than the middle class would be in a low-growth but low-inequality economy.

Perhaps we operate on a curve such as that illustrated in Exhibit 4, which presents a possible relationship between income distribution and economic growth. Where income is very unequally distributed, a move to increase income equality through redistribution of income might be made without sacrificing very much economic growth; indeed, economic growth might actually increase as the redistribution to lower-income groups raises their productivity via improved health and education. In Exhibit 4, this is illustrated in the movement from point A to point B. At some point, however, increased redistribution of income from the rich to the poor might create increasing disincentive effects. Also, the rate of savings might decline, because the poor are often thought to save less of their incomes than the rich. This, in turn, would retard capital formation. As shown in the movement from point B to point C, then, further moves to bring about income equality are likely to reduce the rate of economic growth. Ultimately, the cost of more current income equality is less income growth.

| EXHIBIT 4 | **INCOME REDISTRIBUTION AND ECONOMIC GROWTH—A POSSIBLE RELATIONSHIP** |

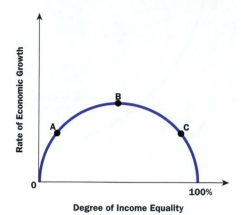

It is possible that redistributing income from rich to poor would stimulate aggregate demand to the extent that rising investment to serve the increasing demands of the poor would lead to an increase in long-run capital formation. Thus, a move from point A to point B could be growth stimulating. A move from point B to point C, however, would lead to a retardation in the growth rate, as high taxation of the rich would lead to reduced work effort and capital formation. Whether the curve is in fact shaped like that suggested above is conjectural, as is the point on the curve at which the United States is currently operating.

The actual relationship between income distribution and economic growth can be debated. The figure suggests that some income redistribution might be growth-inducing, but *massive* redistribution is almost certainly growth retarding. The real world growth–income distribution relationship might be different; the growth-reducing impact of income redistribution, for example, might set in only at an extremely high level of inequality. We still have much to learn about the distribution–growth relationship. Exhibit 4 is merely a representation of a possible relationship that shows the consequences arising from increasing the pursuit of income equality.

TUNE UP

INCOME REDISTRIBUTION

Q: If you grew up in a family with brothers and sisters, your parents probably tried very hard to make sure that everyone was treated equally. Why would most people be opposed to incorporating this approach on a societal level?

A: People would object to this practice because it would decrease the incentive to work hard or invest. No matter how hard you worked or how successfully you invested your money, it would all be taxed away. Over time, less work and less investment would turn the economic pie into a tart. In a family, equality works better for several reasons: (1) your parents are far more likely to care about you than government; (2) they know far more about you and what is good for you than government decision makers, so they can better achieve "fairness" of treatment; and (3) redistribution among children is a very different thing than redistribution among adults, who are presumed to be competent to make more choices that best further their interests.

CONCEPT CHECK

1. If the happiness or utility derived from additional income is subject to diminishing marginal utility, then it is possible that income taken from the very rich and given to the very poor might increase total utility.

2. Income redistribution may be unfair and lead to lower economic growth.

---

1. How is the principle of diminishing marginal utility used to justify income redistribution?
2. Why is the idea that redistributing income from rich to poor will increase society's utility not provable?
3. What are the fairness and incentive arguments against government redistribution of income?
4. How might lower tax rates sometimes increase both incomes and government tax revenues?

5. Why are there likely to be trade-offs between income redistribution and economic growth?
6. If high-income individuals must pay increased income-tax rates in order to provide subsidies for low-income individuals (and the subsidies are phased out as income increases), are the productive incentives of both high- and low-income individuals reduced? Why or why not?

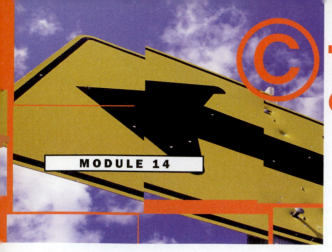

The Economics of Discrimination

- What is job-entry discrimination?
- What is wage discrimination?
- Do earnings differences reflect discrimination or differences in productivity?
- How can we remedy discrimination?

Sometimes workers may be denied employment on the basis of some biological feature, such as sex or race, without any regard to the productivity of the worker. On other occasions, women or black workers may be hired, but at wages below those offered to other employees who are no more productive. The situation where a worker is denied employment on the basis of some noneconomic factor, such as race, religion, sex, or ethnic origin, is called **job-entry discrimination**. The situation where workers are given employment at wages lower than that of other workers on some basis other than productivity differences is called **wage discrimination**.

JOB-ENTRY DISCRIMINATION

In a world where sex and race have absolutely no bearing whatsoever on the employment circumstances of persons (e.g., talent, education, willingness and ability to work, move, etc.), every occupation would, apart from random variations, have a work force with the same sex and race proportions as the population at large. Thus, 51 percent of employees in each occupation would be expected on average to be female, if women comprised 51 percent of the population, and approximately 12 percent or so would be blacks and other racial minorities, reflecting the proportion of nonwhites to the total population.

In fact, the proportion of women working (46 percent) is slightly less than the proportion of men. Likewise, the proportion of blacks in the work force is lower than would be expected given the general population percentages. Looking first at women, their failure to work in gainful employment as much as males might be viewed as a matter of choice; some women may prefer to be engaged in full-time household production rather than work outside the house. On the other hand, others argue that this attitude reflects ingrained sexism and that there is no inherent reason that the adult male member of the household should not stay at home with the kids as much as the female member. In any case, the proportion of women to men in the work force has dramat-

The number of women in the work force has increased dramatically since 1970.

ically increased over time—women were only 38 percent of the labor force in 1970 and now they are over 46 percent.

Moving along to specific occupations, it is clear that a higher proportion of white males have relatively high-paying jobs; the other side of the coin is that females and nonwhites have a relatively larger proportion of employees working in unskilled jobs with low pay and relatively little prestige.

WAGE DISCRIMINATION

A strong statistical correlation exists between lifetime earnings and years of schooling. High-school graduates earn roughly two-thirds of the salary of college graduates.

While a major reason women and nonwhites earn less than white males is that they occupy jobs that are lower paying, it is possible also that they earn less because of wage discrimination—being paid less for a job strictly because of their race or sex.

Clearly, women earn less than men within most occupational categories. As shown in Exhibit 1, in 1997, on average, women in managerial positions received about half the earnings of men. For college teachers, the median weekly earnings for men was $936, $107 more per week than that for women ($829). Overall, white women make 25 to 30 percent less than white males.

White males also typically earn 25 to 30 percent more than black males. The differential rates may not simply reflect racial prejudice on the part of employers, but the fact that blacks and women may have acquired fewer years of schooling, less training, and fewer years of experience. For example, almost 25 percent of whites have a college degree, but less than 14 percent of blacks have completed four years of college and less than 10 percent of Hispanics.

Also, while 26 percent of men have completed four years of college, less than 22 percent of women have completed college. Among females, black women earned 10 percent less than white women. Part of this wage differential can be explained by differences in educational attainment.

Education level has a great impact on earnings potential.

EXHIBIT 1	MEDIAN WEEKLY EARNINGS, FULL-TIME WORKERS IN SELECTED OCCUPATIONS BY SEX, 1997		

| | Earnings | | |
Occupational Group	Men	Women	Percentage Female
Lawyers	$1,269	$959	26.6
Physicians	1,220	946	26.2
Managers, marketing, advertising and public relations	1,059	736	34.6
Engineers	994	837	10.2
College professors	936	829	42.7
Computer system analysts	952	850	28.6
Accountants	791	590	56.6
Real estate sales	685	523	50.0
Insurance sales	755	493	42.8
Registered nurses	778	705	93.5
Mail carriers, postal	691	610	30.7
Teachers, elementary school	719	655	83.9
Police and detectives	628	547	17.4
Mechanics and repairers	581	489	3.7
Truck drivers	509	399	5.7
Secretaries and typists	NA	411	97.9
Bartenders	341	293	57.2
Waiters and waitresses	328	268	77.8
Janitors and cleaners	330	275	34.0
Maids and housemen	292	259	80.1
Farm workers	276	247	19.0

SOURCE: Bureau of Labor Statistics, *Employment and Earnings*, January 1998, pp. 209–213.

DISCRIMINATION OR DIFFERENCES IN PRODUCTIVITY?

Merely demonstrating that wages are lower for blacks and females does not in itself prove wage discrimination, although it is consistent with the notion that discrimination occurs. Likewise, just because there are fewer female lawyers than males is not proof that discrimination exists. However, if occupational and wage differentials are not caused by discrimination, what are the causes?

Several scholars have developed statistical models that argue that a great deal of the earnings differentials across the sexes and races can be explained by differences in productivity. In other words, employers hire and pay workers roughly an amount equal to their perceived contributions (marginal revenue product). Now, if it happens that the marginal revenue product of blacks and women is lower on average than that of white men, even within occupational groups, then one could argue that employers are not discriminating on the basis of race or sex, but rather on the basis of expected productivity. Assuming this is at least partly true, why might male white workers be more productive than other workers?

Productivity Differences: An Environmental Explanation

The first explanation is that various environmental factors have prevented blacks and women from gaining the training and skills necessary to achieve high productivity. In the past, blacks often received less schooling than whites, and the quality of that schooling has often been lower. Women, because they are far more likely to interrupt their careers to have and care for children, often have less work experience than their male counterparts. This, too, may lower their productivity relative to males. This environmental explanation of productivity differences does not rule out discrimination, but rather argues that past discrimination's perverse influences on the environment of women and nonwhites has caused them to have an inferior endowment of human capital now, even if present-day employers were color- and sex-blind in terms of paying workers.

WHY DO PEOPLE DISCRIMINATE?

Why would any employer want to discriminate against an employee on the basis of race or sex? At first, it might appear that discrimination is totally inconsistent with the economist's view of the rational utility-maximizing person. After all, if a firm really wants to maximize profits, it should minimize costs by hiring the best persons available per dollar of wage expenditure, regardless of the age, sex, race, or other attribute of the worker.

Reducing Information Costs

To some extent, discrimination may reflect information costs. Suppose an employer has previously hired 10 green workers and 10 blue workers for a certain type of work, and 8 of the green workers performed well while only two of the blue workers did (the poorer blue worker performance may have reflected poorer training and educational backgrounds). In this situation, the employer might prefer to hire a green employee for the next job opening, because past experience suggests that the probability is greater that the green worker will perform well. In this case, the color of the worker is used as a screening device, a means of narrowing the list of job candidates.

It costs money and time to evaluate the prospects of every applicant, and race is an imperfect but cheap way of doing some of the screening. The fact that using color of workers as a screening device discriminates against good blue workers is not a major concern to a profit-maximizing employer. The information cost reduction from hiring on the basis of color may exceed the perceived benefits from the identification of good blue workers.

Personal Preferences

Beyond this, though, it is a fact that some people prefer association with persons with certain racial and/or sexual attributes. These persons may have developed these preferences out of an ignorance that breeds bigotry and racism, but the preferences are nonetheless there. The utility gained from having the desired racial mix might exceed the loss in income from not having the best employees. A racially prejudiced person might prefer making $900,000 a year in profits from a business with an all-white labor force to making $1,000,000 with a racially mixed force. In the words of the pioneer in the economics of discrimination, Gary Becker, the person has acquired a "taste" for discrimination, just as one might acquire a taste for certain goods. That is, an employer may be willing to trade away some income in order to satisfy the taste for discrimination.

THE COSTS OF DISCRIMINATION

It is also true that in competitive industries, firms who discriminate may lose out ultimately to those firms that do not. The nondiscriminating firm can hire the unfavored but equally competent workers and have a cost advantage over employers who discriminate. This cost advantage may allow the nondiscriminating firm to undercut its discriminating competitors' prices and either force them out of business or make them change their hiring practices. That is, in the long run, competition has the potential to reduce discrimination.

REMEDYING DISCRIMINATION

The primary means used to address economic discrimination in the United States is affirmative action programs, in which employers are strongly encouraged to hire more minority group workers in occupations where those groups are now relatively under-represented. The second aspect of affirmative action is correcting wage and salary inequities. Beyond this, some of the possible environmental causes of productivity differences between racial and sex groups have been attacked, such as through compensatory education programs (e.g., Head Start), increased efforts to increase minority enrollments in colleges and universities, and so on. There is some evidence that these various efforts have met with some success, as the proportion of employees from minority groups in higher-paying occupations has increased in recent years, and blatant wage and salary discrimination has become less frequent. Still, the economic differences between different races and sexes are rather large.

Affirmative action job hiring programs are controversial. The establishment of what are, in effect, quotas on the hiring of minorities increases the probability that some persons will be hired on some basis other than productivity. While this may be desirable from the standpoint of equalizing opportunities between demographic groups, it also can serve to lower the output of society as a whole and profits to firms. Also, the "reverse discrimination" equity argument is raised. For example, with respect to productivity, a firm may be forced to hire a minority worker with a marginal revenue product of $80, instead of a white male whose marginal revenue product is $100. Society ultimately loses $20 in output (the difference in the value of marginal output). Moreover, if the firm that hires the minority worker has to pay the prevailing wage (say $90) to avoid wage discrimination charges, hiring that worker will lower profits. With that, the firm might decide to not hire anyone, knowing that affirmative action pressures prevent them from hiring the profitable white male (whose marginal revenue product exceeds the prevailing wage by $10) instead of the minority worker (whose hiring will reduce profits by $10).

Employer actions to protect profits, then, might negate some or all the expected gains from affirmative action programs. An alternative approach to one using implicit quotas would be to subsidize employers for hiring minority workers. Some would regard this approach as a gift or bail out for business enterprise more than a help to minorities, and thus oppose the approach. The subsidy approach would, however, provide employers with greater incentive to increase minority job opportunities.

Affirmative action programs are a controversial approach to remedying discrimination.

1. If a worker is denied employment on the basis of some noneconomic factor like race, religion, sex, or ethnic origin, it is called job-entry discrimination.
2. If workers are given employment at wages lower than that of other workers on some basis other than productivity differences, it is called wage discrimination.
3. If a firm really wants to maximize profits, it should minimize costs by hiring the best persons available per dollar of wage expenditure, regardless of the age, sex, race, or other attribute of the worker.

4. Discrimination may occur because of information costs or because some workers may prefer to associate with persons with certain racial and/or sexual attributes.
5. Remedies to discrimination might include affirmative action and education programs.

1. What is the difference between job-entry discrimination and wage discrimination?
2. Explain how earnings differences could reflect either discrimination or productivity differences.
3. What is the environmental explanation for differences in earnings across the sexes and races?
4. How do firms' incentives to maximize profits tend to reduce the extent of discrimination?
5. How can discrimination reflect imperfect information and the costs of acquiring more information about potential employees?

6. Say you now hire only purple workers. If purple workers strongly prefer to work with one another instead of with other groups, why might you prefer to hire a less-productive purple worker than a more-productive non-purple worker at the same wage?
7. Why would subsidizing employers for hiring minority workers give employers greater incentives to expand minority job opportunities than imposing implicit hiring quotas for minority workers?

(D) Poverty

- How do we define poverty?
- How many people live in poverty?
- What is relative income?

At several points in the previous discussion, the words "rich" and "poor" have been used without being defined. Of particular interest is the question of poverty. Our concern over income distribution largely arises because most people believe that those with low incomes have lower satisfaction than those with higher incomes. Thus, the "poor" people are those who, in a material sense, suffer relative to other persons. It is desirable, therefore, to define and measure the extent of poverty in the United States.

ABSOLUTE INCOME DEFINITION

One approach to defining poverty is to determine an absolute income level that is considered necessary to provide the basic necessities of life. A poverty rate would then be the proportion of persons who fail to earn that minimum income standard. With some modification, the official poverty rate today is based on such an absolute income standard. The income standard, set at roughly $15,000 for a family of four, varies with the size of the family (because, for example, a single person with $15,000 in income is much better off economically than a family of 10 with $20,000 in income). Also, of course, the minimum money income necessary to be above the poverty line has increased over time with inflation, as rising prices have eroded the purchasing power of the dollar.

According to the Department of Labor, the amount of poverty fell steadily in the 1960s, was steady in the 1970s, and rose during the recession in the early 1980s. The poverty rate then fell slightly during the rest of the 1980s and rose again during the recession of 1990–1991. As you would expect, when the economy is in a recession, unemployment rises and poverty tends to increase. Exhibit 1 provides some statistics on poverty in the United States, both overall and by age.

With a definition of poverty that is determined at some fixed, real income level (that is, an income that has been adjusted for inflation), poverty over time should decline and, indeed, largely disappear, because real incomes generally rise over time with economic growth. Unless lower income groups do not share at all in the rising incomes of the population, some reduction in poverty is inevitable. Thus, one cure for poverty, as defined by some absolute income or standard or living criterion, is economic growth. The greater the rate of economic growth, the more rapidly poverty will be eradicated.

Poverty is relative. $15,000 a year would go a long way in many developing countries.

AN ALTERNATIVE DEFINITION OF POVERTY

Many "poor" individuals in the United States, as defined using the official definition, would be considered well off, even "rich," in many less-developed countries. For example, $15,000 of income a year, while not much in the United States, would make you very rich in a country like Ethiopia. On the other hand, many Americans with incomes just above the poverty line as officially defined in the future would be considered "poor" a generation or two from now, even though their income will permit them to buy far more than what today are considered to be the necessities of life. Why?

To most persons, being "poor" means having less income and purchasing power than most other persons living in the same community or nation. A person is "poor" if his or her income is low relative to the incomes of most other persons in the same geographical area, and "rich"

if his or her income exceeds that of most other persons in the area. Poverty is therefore often thought of as a *relative income* concept, rather than being determined by some ability to buy some specific fixed basket of goods and services.

Alternative definitions of poverty have been suggested based on relative income measures. For instance, families that earn less than one-half the median (or middle) family income could be considered poor. Over time, as economic growth proceeds, the income necessary to avoid being considered poor by this measure increases. Using this definition, then, poverty cannot be eradicated by economic growth, but only by income redistribution. Even from an equity or fairness point of view, few persons favor total income equality, because income needs presumably vary with family size and possibly with the ages of the family members and the cost of living in different cities. Even some of the poor might not favor such policies of equality,

TUNE UP

POVERTY

Q: If the poverty level of income does not change, can poverty be eliminated over time?

A: With enough economic growth or sufficient redistribution (which may have a long-run effect on additional growth), poverty in an absolute sense could be eliminated—as long as the poverty level of income stays the same. However, if poverty is defined as a relative concept, then there will always be someone that is relatively poor.

EXHIBIT 1	FAMILIES BELOW POVERTY LEVEL IN THE UNITED STATES

a. Percentage of All Persons below Poverty Level

Year	Percentage Below Poverty Level
1947	32.0
1960	18.1
1970	10.1
1975	9.7
1980	10.3
1985	11.4
1990	10.7
1995	13.8

b. Poverty Rates by Age, 1965–1996

(graph: Under 18 years; 18 to 64 years; 65 years and over — vertical axis 0–40%, horizontal axis 1965–1996)

SOURCE: U.S. Bureau of Census, from *The Wall Street Journal Almanac*, 1998, p. 177.

because their kids would—in such a system—have less of a chance of "making good." It is clear, then, that "poverty" in a relative income sense will always be with us. We can perhaps reduce the consequences of being poor by policies that raise the incomes of lowest-income persons to levels closer to the median, but we cannot raise everyone's income to a level equal to or above that median; that is an economic impossibility.

CONCEPT CHECK

1. One method of defining poverty is to determine an absolute income level that is necessary to provide the basic necessities of life in minimum quantities. The poverty rate, then, would be the proportion of persons who fail to earn the minimum income standard.

2. An alternative definition of poverty is a relative income measure. For instance, families that earn less than one-half the median (or middle) family income are considered poor. Using this definition, poverty cannot be eradicated by economic growth, but only by income redistribution.

1. How are absolute and relative measures of poverty different?
2. Why could economic growth potentially eliminate absolute measures of poverty but not relative measures of poverty?

3. Some people have argued that poverty could be eliminated by "rich" countries. Can both absolute and relative poverty be eliminated by "rich" countries? Why or why not?

(E) Application: Welfare Reform

Will changing the incentive structure for welfare recipients reduce the number of applicants? Can a dependent welfare culture be changed overnight?

"WELFARE REFORM" BEGINS NOW

BUCK WOLF

At midnight Monday, Robin LeFlore's clock started ticking much louder. The 40-year-old mother of three boys has 24 months to find a job or lose her family's federal benefits, under new federal welfare rules that took effect today.

"My watch is now a time bomb, not a time piece," said LeFlore, who lives in Chicago. "It reminds me that a crisis is coming." A federal law takes effect Tuesday that will bring sweeping changes to the nation's welfare system, ending the government's six-decade guarantee of assistance to the neediest. The new system shifts responsibility for the poor to the states. No federal money can be spent on people who receive welfare benefits for more than two years or who have spent more than five years on the dole.

Nearly a year after President Clinton signed the law, most states have installed new welfare systems. Nearly all have stepped up work requirements for benefit recipients and refocused on getting people into jobs.

However, the states with the largest welfare populations . . . have yet to issue new rules.

Thanks in part to the booming economy, the number of Americans on welfare has already dropped dramatically. About 4 million families were on assistance in March, down 20 percent from the 1994 peak.

Although given unprecedented authority to design their plans, states do not differ radically in their approaches. Most hold to the traditional premise of welfare: a check to help families in need. Some states have created strong "work-first" programs that assume everyone can and should work immediately. Led by Wisconsin, they include Texas, Virginia, Mississippi, and Georgia. "Instead of saying, 'You're poor and you need help,' we look at what strengths you bring," said Michael Thurmond, who directs Georgia's program. "We try to build on those."

Arizona plans to convert all welfare offices into "empowerment centers," featuring job postings, computers for resumes, and telephones for interviews. All adults signing up for welfare will have to enter two-week classes, emphasizing work habits and attitude. Then they'll look for work.

The idea is to see who sinks and who swims before intervening with help for those who need it, said Gretchen Evans, who runs the Arizona work program. "It makes no difference if you have a GED or a diploma," she said.

In Iowa, those who want benefits must develop an individual plan, promising to take steps toward self-sufficiency in exchange for cash in the meantime, said Mary Jean Timp, spokeswoman for the welfare department. "It recognizes that the barriers are different for each person," she said. Only one state is changing that basic formula. In pioneering Wisconsin, there will be no more welfare—just help finding a job, and if necessary, a paycheck for showing up to perform community service.

SOURCE: Buck Wolf, ABCNEWS.com, July 2, 1997.
http://archive.abcnews.com/sections/us/welfare630/index.html

Certainly, trillions of dollars have flowed through government programs supposedly established to redistribute from the non-poor to the poor, but the poor did not structure these programs. The middle-class bureaucrats that run the programs; the consultants and academics who study them; and the doctors, farmers, and construction workers whose services are demanded by them are the ones who shape welfare programs and receive most of the benefits from them. Typically, less than 25 percent of federal spending earmarked for the poor actually goes to the poor.

The benefits the poor do receive have often been provided in such a way as to make the poor more, rather than less, dependent on public support. As a result, the poor may be worse off rather than better off in the long run. For example, previous programs discouraged the poor from entering the job market and encouraged poor husbands to abandon their families so that they would be entitled to more money.

Both Democrats and Republicans are beginning to recognize that the welfare industry as it is today might be perpetuating itself by undermining the economic incentives and the family structure that are so important if the poor are to develop the skills they need to move up the economic ladder. This is not to say that the poor would be better if welfare were suddenly eliminated. But having created a dependent welfare subculture of poor, it looks like the government is now taking steps to scale back existing programs while increasing incentives for productive work.

"Work-first" programs try to utilize the strengths of welfare recipients to help them become self-sufficient.

ONE STEP BEYOND

While on a student's budget, you may *feel* poor, but are you really? The problems and exercises in your Workbook can help you to distinguish some of the different ways that poverty is defined, and the cyberproblems on the EconActive CD-ROM will link you to current data on income, poverty, and other economic indicators in the United States, such as can be found on the Website of the U.S. Census Bureau.

PHOTO CREDITS MODULE 14

Page **348:** © Mike Fizer/Check Six/PNI; Page **349:** © Jack Kurtz/Impact Visuals/PNI; Page **351:** © Jose Azel/ Aurora/PNI; Page **354:** The Everett Collection; Page **355:** © The New Yorker Collection. 1994 Frank Cotham, from cartoonbank.com; Page **358:** © Adamsmith/FPG International; Page **359:** © PhotoDisc; Page **361:** AP Photo/Susan Ragan; Page **363:** © Peter Turnley/Black Star/PNI; Page **367:** AP Photo/Carl M. Gail, WNET

The Environment

A. Negative Externalities
What are private and social costs?

B. Public Policy and the Environment
What are some public policy solutions to externalities?

C. Property Rights
What is the Coase Theorem?

D. Application: California's Smoke-Free Bars
Who owns the rights to pollute the air in restaurants and bars?

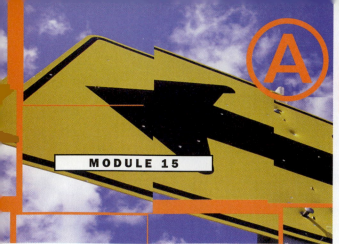

(A) Negative Externalities

■ What are social costs?
■ How are negative externalities internalized?

WHAT ARE SOCIAL COSTS?

As we learned in Module 6, whenever an economic activity has benefits or costs that are shared by persons other than the demanders or suppliers of a good or service, an externality is involved. If the activity imposes costs on persons other than the demanders or suppliers of a good or service, it is said to have **negative externalities.** Put another way, negative externalities exists any time the social costs of producing a good or service exceed the private costs. By **social costs** we refer to costs that accrue to the total population; private costs refer only to those costs incurred by the producer of the good or service.

NEGATIVE EXTERNALITIES AND POLLUTION

The classic example of a negative externality is pollution. When a steel mill puts soot and other forms of "crud" into the air as a by-product of making steel, it imposes costs on others not connected with buying or selling steel from the steel mill. The soot requires homeowners to paint their homes more often, entailing a cost. Studies show that respiratory diseases are greater in areas with high air pollution, imposing a substantial cost, often the shortening of life itself. In addition, the steel mill might discharge chemicals or overheated water into a stream, thus killing wildlife, ruining business for fishermen, spoiling recreational activities for the local population, and so on.

In deciding how much to produce, the steel makers are governed by demand and supply. They do not worry (unless forced to) about the external costs imposed on members of society that they do not have to pay, and in all likelihood, they would not even know the full extent of those costs.

Consider the hypothetical steel industry in Exhibit 1. It produces where demand and supply intersect, at output $Q_{PRIVATE}$ and $P_{PRIVATE}$. Let us assume that the marginal social cost of producing the product is indicated by the marginal social cost (*MSC*) curve, lying above the supply curve, which represents the industry's marginal private costs (*MPC*). The marginal social costs of production are higher at all output levels, as those costs include all of the industry's private costs plus the costs that spill over to other members of society from the pollution produced by the industry—that is, the external costs.

At output Q_{SOCIAL}, the marginal social costs to society equal the marginal social benefits (as indicated by the demand curve) from the sale of the last unit of steel. At that output, the price of steel is P_{SOCIAL}. If the firm were some-

| EXHIBIT 1 | THE EFFECT OF A NEGATIVE EXTERNALITY |

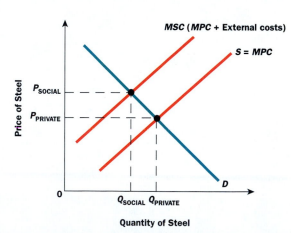

The industry would normally produce where demand equals supply (where supply is equal to the marginal private costs), at output $Q_{PRIVATE}$, charging price $P_{PRIVATE}$. If, however, the industry were forced to also pay those external costs incurred by others as a result of its activities, the industry would produce where demand equals marginal social costs, at output Q_{SOCIAL} and price P_{SOCIAL}. Where firms are *not* forced to pay for negative externalities, output tends to be larger and prices lower than the optimal output, where the marginal benefits to society (as measured by demand) equal the marginal costs to society.

If the government does not step in, can we presume that the company will clean this stream on its own?

how forced to compensate persons who incur the costs of its pollution, the firm would produce at output Q_{SOCIAL} and price steel at P_{SOCIAL}. In that case, we would say that the externalities were **internalized,** because each firm in the industry would now be paying the entire costs to society of making steel. When negative externalities are internalized, steel firms produce less output (Q_{SOCIAL} instead of $Q_{PRIVATE}$) and charge higher prices (P_{SOCIAL} instead of $P_{PRIVATE}$). Optimal output occurs where the marginal social costs are equal to the marginal social benefits. When the firms in the industry do not pay all of the social costs, and there is therefore too much output, there is also too much pollution, because the output of pollution is directly related to the output of the primary goods produced by the firm.

HOW ARE EXTERNALITIES MEASURED?

It is generally accepted that in the absence of intervention, the market mechanism will underproduce goods and services with positive externalities, such as education, and overproduce those with negative externalities, such as pollution. But the exact extent of these market misallocations is quite difficult to establish in the real world, because the divergence between social and private costs and

benefits is often difficult to measure. For example, exactly how much damage at the margin does an aluminum mill's air pollution do to non-consumers of the aluminum? No one really knows, because no market fully measures those costs. Indeed, the costs are partly **nonpecuniary,** meaning that no outlay of money occurs. While we pay dollars to see the doctor for respiratory ailments and pay dollars for paint to repair pollution-caused peeling, we do not make explicit money payments for the visual pollution and undesirable odors that the mill might produce as a by-product of making aluminum. Nonpecuniary costs are real costs and potentially have a monetary value that can be associated with them, but there are immense practical difficulties in assessing that value. While you might be able to decide how much you would be willing to pay to live in a pollution-free world, there is no mechanism at present for anyone to express the perceived monetary value of having clear air to breathe and smell. Even some pecuniary, or monetary, costs are difficult to truly measure: How much respiratory disease is caused by pollution and how much by other factors, like secondhand cigarette smoke? Continued progress by environmental economists in valuing these difficult damages is, however, being made.

TUNE UP

NEGATIVE EXTERNALITIES

Q: After months of looking at houses he could not afford, Roger Overanout recently bought a home near the airport. After living in his house for only a week, Roger was so fed up with the noise that he decided to organize a group of local homeowners in an effort to stop the noise pollution. Should Roger be compensated for bearing this negative externality?

A: Because few people want to live in noisy areas, housing prices and rents in those areas are lower, reflecting the cost of the noise in the area. As a result, fewer people competed with Roger for the purchase of his house relative to houses in quieter neighborhoods, so it is likely he did not pay as much as he might have in another area. Because Roger paid a lower price for living in a noisier area, he has already been compensated for the noise pollution.

If you buy a house next to an airport, should you be able to sue for the noise pollution?

IS IT A POSITIVE OR A NEGATIVE EXTERNALITY?

Sometimes, even the direction of the externality of an activity is debatable. One person's positive externality may be another person's negative externality. Should cellular phones be outlawed because of the distractions they may impose on drivers? Some would say "yes," because cell phones can distract drivers and lead to traffic accidents, certainly a negative externality. On the other hand, drivers with cellular phones might be able to report accidents, crimes, stranded motorists, or drunken or "road raging" drivers, certainly a form of a positive externality. Where an externality has such opposing effects on different people, it is difficult to reach a public policy that is agreed upon as being best.

Do cell phones result in a positive or a negative externality?

HOW RISKY IS IT TO TALK AND DRIVE?

The number of cell phones in the United States has exploded from 345,000 in 1985 to 50 million today. Cell phones and other wireless accessories distract drivers but much more research is needed to determine the size of the problem, a U.S. safety agency said today.

". . . it is clear that at this time there are insufficient data to indicate the magnitude of any safety-related problem associated with cellular telephone use while driving," the report said. A much publicized study issued last year said the risk of having a traffic accident while using a cellular phone was the same as driving drunk, a quadrupling of the accident risk.

But NHTSA said even the authors of that study of 699 Canadian drivers were aware of its limitations. For example, NHTSA said, emotional stress might lead to both increased cellular phone use and decreased driving ability, so individual calls might have nothing to do with the crash risk. NHTSA also noted the benefits of cellular phones to road safety, including faster notification of emergency services to vehicle accidents.

CONSIDER THIS:
Are cellular telephones a negative externality or a positive externality?

SOURCE: Reuters, 1998
http://www.abcnews.com/sections/living/car-phones0108/index.html

---

CONCEPT CHECK

1. Social costs are those that accrue to the total population; private costs refer to those costs incurred only by the producer of the good or service.
2. If the industry were somehow forced to compensate persons who incur the costs of pollution, we would say that the industry had internalized the externality.
3. When negative externalities are internalized, the industry produces less output at a higher price.
4. Optimal output occurs when marginal social benefits are equal to marginal social costs.

---

1. What is the difference between private and social costs?
2. Why do decision makers tend to ignore external costs?
3. How can internalizing the external costs of production move us closer to the efficient level of output?
4. Why is it particularly difficult to measure the value of external costs or benefits?

5. Say that the last ton of steel produced by Remington's Steel imposes three types of costs: labor costs of $25; additional equipment costs of $10; and the cost of additional "crud" dumped into the air of $15. What costs will Remington's Steel consider in deciding whether to produce another ton of steel?
6. Why can a homeowner make a better argument for compensation for noise pollution if a local airport was built after he moved in than if it was already there when he moved in? Would it matter whether or not he knew it was going to be built?

B Public Policy and the Environment

- What are compliance standards?
- What is the "best" level of pollution?
- What is a pollution tax?
- What are transferable pollution rights?

While measuring externalities, both negative and positive, is often nearly impossible, that does not necessarily mean that it is better to ignore the externality and allow the market solution to operate. As already explained, the market solution will almost certainly result in excessive output by polluters unless some intervention occurs. But what form should the intervention take?

WHAT ARE COMPLIANCE STANDARDS?

One approach to dealing with externalities is to require private enterprise to produce their output in a manner that would reduce the negative externality below the amount that would persist in the absence of regulation. For example, the Environmental Protection Agency, which was created by the Clean Air Act of 1970, was established to serve as a watchdog over the production of goods and services in areas where externalities, especially negative externalities, exist. The EPA's main duty is to enforce environmental standards.

Using the **compliance standards** approach, the EPA identifies and then enforces a standard equal to the maximum amount of pollution that firms can produce per unit of output per year. To be effective in pollution reduction, of course, these standards must result in less pollution than would exist in the absence of the compliance standards. The standards, then, force companies into finding less pollution-intensive ways of producing goods and services. Or in the case of consumer products that pollute—such as automobiles, for example—manufacturers have been forced to reduce the emissions from the products themselves.

Evidence exists that pollution has declined since 1970, although this does not prove exactly what the EPA's impact has been, as other things were also changing. For example, carbon monoxide emissions per mile of motor vehicle use has dropped by about 25 percent since 1970. Motor vehicles account for over one-half of air pollutants by weight, so the indicated decline is important. It would appear that the compliance standards approach to limiting key pollutants has led to some reduction in pollution levels from what would otherwise be the case. For example, in Exhibit 1, we see that the phasing out of leaded gasoline, which started in 1984, has had a dramatic impact on the levels of lead in our atmosphere. Also, important progress has been made in reducing the levels of carbon monoxide, sulphur dioxide, and nitrogen oxides.

The compliance standards approach, however, is not without its problems. Stating, as U.S. law has, that hydrocarbon emissions, which averaged 8.7 grams per mile in the early 1960s, must be no more than 0.41 grams per mile, helped lower the level of pollution. While the levels of hydrocarbons did drop dramatically—to around 0.75 in the mid-1980s—we were not able to reach the rigorous 0.41

Los Angeles has made important strides in cleaning up its environment.

standard set by the government. Some believe that the standards have been set at too strict a level so that the marginal social costs of eliminating the pollution might actually exceed the marginal social benefits. That is, they have charged that environmental regulators have too little regard for the costs of pollution control.

WHY IS A CLEAN ENVIRONMENT NOT FREE?

In many respects, a clean environment is no different from any other desirable good. In a world of scarcity, we can increase our consumption of clean environment only by giving up something else. The problem that we face is choosing the combination of goods that does most to enhance human well-being. Few people would enjoy a perfectly clean environment if they were cold, hungry, and generally destitute. On the other hand, an individual choking to death in smog is hardly to be envied, no matter how great his or her material wealth. Only by considering the additional cost as well as the additional benefit of increased consumption of all goods, including clean air and water, can decisions on the desirable combination of goods to consume be made properly.

WHAT ARE THE COSTS AND BENEFITS OF POLLUTION CONTROL?

It is possible, even probable, that pollution elimination, like nearly everything else, is subject to diminishing returns. A large amount of pollution can be eliminated fairly inexpensively initially, but getting rid of still more pollution may prove more costly. Likewise, it is also possible that the benefits from eliminating "crud" from the air might decline as more and more pollution is eliminated. For example, perhaps some pollution elimination initially would have a profound impact on health costs, home repair expenses, and so on, but as pollution levels fall, further elimination of pollutants brings fewer marginal benefits.

The cost–benefit trade-off discussed above is illustrated in Exhibit 2, which examines the marginal social benefits and marginal social costs associated with the elimination of air pollution. In the early 1960s, we had few regulations as a nation on pollution control, and as a result, private firms had little incentive to eliminate the problem. In the context of Exhibit 2, we may have spent $Q_{TOO\ LITTLE}$ on controls, meaning that the marginal social benefits of greater pollution control expenditures exceeded the marginal costs associated with having the controls. Investing more capital and labor to reduce pollution is efficient in such a situation.

Optimum pollution control occurs when Q^* of pollution is eliminated. Up to that point, the benefits from the elimination of pollution exceed the marginal costs, both pecuniary and nonpecuniary, of the pollution control. Overly stringent compliance levels force companies to control pollution to the level indicated by $Q_{TOO\ MUCH}$ in Exhibit 2, where the additional costs from the controls far outweigh the environmental benefits. It should be stated, however, that increased concerns about pollution have probably caused the marginal social benefit curve to shift to the right over time, increasing the optimal amount of pollution control. Because of measurement problems, however, it is difficult to state whether we are generally below, at, or above the optimal pollution level.

EXHIBIT 1	REDUCTIONS IN AIR POLLUTION LEVELS FROM 1978 TO 1990

Pollution Source	Reduction in Levels from 1978 to 1990 (percent change)
Sulphur dioxide	39%
Carbon monoxide	42
Nitrogen oxides	24
Lead	93*
Ozone	27

*Lead was phased out of gasoline beginning in 1984.

SOURCE: *Council on Environmental Quality*, 1991.

EXHIBIT 2	COSTS AND BENEFITS OF POLLUTION CONTROLS

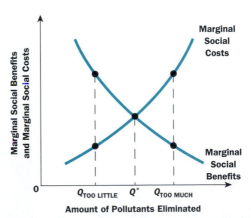

With the principles of diminishing marginal utility and increasing marginal cost at work, the marginal benefits of further expenditures on pollution control will, at some point, fall below the added costs to society imposed by still stricter controls. At output $Q_{TOO\ LITTLE}$, pollution control is inadequate; on the other hand, elimination of $Q_{TOO\ MUCH}$ pollution will entail costs that exceed the benefits. Only at Q^* is pollution-control expenditure at an optimum level. Of course, it is difficult in practice to know exactly the position and slope of these curves.

HOW MUCH POLLUTION?

It is practically impossible to get widespread agreement on what the appropriate level of pollution should be. Indeed, if we *did* have the appropriate level, about half of the people would think it too little and half would think it too much. People with different preferences and situations are simply going to have different ideas about the costs and benefits of pollution abatement. For example, consider a community that contains a college and an oil refinery, the latter emitting large quantities of nauseating and potentially noxious fumes into the atmosphere. Who do you think is most likely to participate in a protest favoring stringent pollution controls on the refinery: the college students or the townspeople? It is a safe bet that the answer is the college students. Why is this? One may think that college students are more aware of and sensitive to the environmental quality of the community. Maybe. But the long-term residents of the community, those who plan to stay there and raise their children there, are certainly at least as concerned about the air quality in their community. Indeed, they may well be more concerned about local pollution than the college students who, after all, will typically live in the community only until they graduate. The difference between the townspeople and the students is probably not found primarily in a difference in the desire for a clean environment. The difference is probably best explained by the fact that the cost of cleaning up the environment will fall almost entirely on the townspeople. It is their jobs, incomes, and retirement plans that will be jeopardized by strict pollution control requirements on the refinery. The students will not have to pay this cost, because their job prospects and current income will be quite independent of the profitability of the local refinery. Not surprisingly, then, it is the students who will be most eager to clean up the refinery, because they will reap many of the benefits and pay few of the costs. The townspeople will be a little less enthusiastic about environmental purity because they are likely to pay for much of it.

The point is not to decide which group is right or wrong. Both the students and the townspeople are quite rational, given the different situations they face. The purpose here is to emphasize that controversy is sure to arise when a community of people have to share a common, or public, good (or bad). Conflicts are inevitable because different people have different preferences and face different costs. This explains much of the controversy that surrounds environmental issues. If everyone could pay for and consume a preferred level of environmental quality, independent of the level paid for and consumed by others, controversy over environmental protection would largely disappear, in much the same way that individuals could choose either hamburgers or tofu burgers—each getting the private goods they want. But there is no way to completely avoid this type of controversy for public goods like air quality or national defense. It should be recognized, however, that one way people often moderate controversies of this type is by sorting themselves into relatively homogeneous groupings. Communities that contain people with similar backgrounds, preferences, and circumstances are more likely to avoid socially divisive controversies than are communities containing more diverse populations.

WHAT ARE POLLUTION TAXES?

Another means of solving the misallocation problem (relatively too many polluting goods) posed by the existence of externalities is for the government to create incentives for firms to internalize the external costs or benefits resulting from their activities. For example, returning to the case of pollution, suppose that the marginal private cost

Do pollution costs vary over location?

RELATIVE COSTS AND BENEFITS OF POLLUTION CONTROL

Q: Moe Knockside drives a large 1958 Cadillac Sedan De Ville that has no smog equipment and gets poor gas mileage. Moe lives in a sparsely populated area of Wyoming and this is where most of his driving takes place. Do you think Moe should be required to install the same smog equipment on his car as someone living in downtown Los Angeles or Denver with a similar vehicle?

A: The economic benefits of pollution control vary over location. In the wide-open, low population-density areas of Wyoming, the marginal benefit of pollution clean-up is lower than it would be in a large metropolitan area that already has a large amount of smog. Why? In Wyoming there is so much space and so few people that the marginal benefit of pollution abatement is quite low. This would certainly not be the case in Los Angeles, where the air is already more polluted by cars and factories. Because there are so many people affected and the air is already so saturated with pollutants, the marginal benefit of pollution elimination is much higher in Los Angeles than it would be in rural Wyoming. That is, if a uniform standard is applied regardless of location, then the car in Wyoming would be overcontrolled and the car in Los Angeles would be undercontrolled. Unfortunately, many of our environmental laws contain this "uniformity" flaw.

of making steel was $150 a ton. Suppose further that at the margin, each ton of steel added two tons of pollution to the environment that caused $20 in damages per ton. If the government were then to levy a **pollution tax** on the steel maker equal to $20 per ton, the manufacturer's marginal private cost would rise from $150 to $190; the $190 figure would then be equal to the true marginal social cost of making steel. The firm would accordingly alter its output and pricing decisions to take into account its higher marginal cost, leading ultimately to reduced output (and pollution) and higher prices. The firm also has an incentive to seek new, less pollution-intensive methods of making steel.

Using taxes to internalize external costs is very appealing because it allows the relatively efficient private sector to operate according to market forces in a manner that takes socially important spillover costs into account. A major objection to the use of such taxes and subsidies is that in most cases it is very difficult to measure externalities with any precision. Choosing a tax rate involves some guesswork, and poor guessing might lead to a solution

that is far from optimal. But it is likely to be better than ignoring the problem. In spite of the severe difficulties in measurement, however, many economists would like to see greater effort made to force internalization of externalities through taxes rather than using alternative approaches. Why? We know that firms will seek out the least-expensive (in terms of using society's scarce resources) approaches to clean up, because they want more profits. This is good for them and good for society, because we can have more of everything that way, including environmental quality.

WHAT ARE TRANSFERABLE POLLUTION RIGHTS?

Economists see an opportunity to control pollution through a government-enforced system of property rights. In this system, the government issues **transferable pollution rights** that give the holder the right to discharge a specified amount (smaller than the uncontrolled amount) of pollution into the air. In this plan, firms have an incentive to lower their levels of pollution because they can sell their permits if they go unused. Specifically, those firms that can lower their emissions at the lowest costs will do so and trade their pollution rights to firms that have high costs of reducing their pollution levels as easily. That is, each polluter—required to reduce pollution to the level allowed by the number of rights held or buy more—will be motivated to eliminate all pollution that is cheaper than the price of pollution rights. The crucial advantage to the pollution-rights approach comes from the fact that the rights are private property and can be sold.

It is worth emphasizing that this least-cost pattern of abatement does not require any information about the techniques of pollution abatement on the part of the government—more specifically, the Environmental Protection Agency (EPA). The EPA does not need to know the cheapest abatement strategy for each and every polluter. Faced with a positive price for pollution rights, each polluter has every motivation to discover the cheapest way to reduce pollution and to utilize it. Nor does the EPA need to know anything about the differences in abatement costs among polluters. Each polluter is motivated to reduce pollution as long as the cost of reducing one more unit is less than the price of pollution rights. The information and incentives generated by private ownership and market exchange of these pollution rights automatically leads to the desirable pattern of pollution abatement—namely, having those best at cleaning up doing all of the clean-up.

The pollution-rights approach also creates an incentive for polluters to develop improved pollution-abatement technologies. Our economic history is full of examples of technological development that has allowed more output to be produced with less land and labor. Conspicuously absent until recently have been technological developments

TUNE UP

POLLUTION TAXES

Q: Greg Garyus is in charge of designing a social policy relating to loud fraternity parties. Greg develops a plan to tax the fraternity a specific amount per party that would just compensate those damaged. His two-part plan is as follows: (1) loud rock music, beer-bash, dancing parties will now be subject to a large tax, and (2) quiet, classical music, wine and cheese, conversational parties will not be subject to tax. What impact would you expect this large tax to have on the number of beer bashes? the number of quiet parties?

A: The tax on beer bashes would most likely reduce the number of loud parties. As shown in Exhibit 3, the optimum allocation of beer-bash parties before the tax occurs at Q_{BT}. With the tax, beer bashes become relatively more expensive, and the new optimum occurs at Q_{AT}. If the relatively quiet, classical music parties are substitutes for rock and beer bashes, then the higher price for rock and beer parties caused by the tax will increase the demand for the more "elegant" parties.

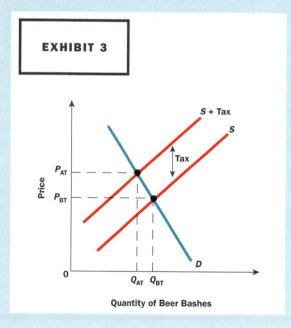

EXHIBIT 3

Would a large tax on loud fraternity parties solve the externality problem?

---

designed for output to be produced with less pollution. Market prices on land and labor have always provided a strong incentive to conserve these resources. The absence of prices for the use of our atmosphere and waterways, however, made it privately unprofitable to worry about conserving their use. Marketable pollution rights could remedy this neglect.

The prospect of buying and selling pollution permits would allow firms to move into an area that is already as polluted as allowed by EPA standards. Under the tradable

permits policy, the firm can set up operation by purchasing pollution permits from an existing polluter in the area. This type of exchange allows the greatest value to be generated with a given amount of pollution. It also encourages polluters to come up with cheaper ways of reducing pollution, because the firm that reduces pollution is able to sell its pollution credits to others, making pollution reduction profitable.

Although the pollution market is still in its infancy, and many legal considerations are yet to be resolved, some tradable exchanges have already taken place. Wisconsin Power and Light purchased the rights to generate 15,000 tons of sulfur dioxide from Duquesne Light Co., a Pittsburgh Pennsylvania utility company. The Times Mirror Company completed a $120 million expansion of its paper plant in the Portland, Oregon, area after purchasing the right to discharge an additional 150 tons of hydrocarbons annually from other polluters. Mobil Oil paid the city of Torrance, California, $3 million for rights to dump 900 pounds of reactive vapors daily.

IS THERE AN IDEAL POLLUTION-CONTROL POLICY?

What would be the objectives of an ideal pollution-control policy? First, and most obviously, we want pollution reduced to the efficient level, the level that maximizes the value of all of our resources. This would involve continuing to reduce pollution by one more unit only as long as the value of the improved environmental quality is greater than the value of ordinary goods that are sacrificed.

A second, related objective is to reduce pollution as cheaply as possible. There are two separate considerations here. If pollution is to be reduced as cheaply as possible, it is obvious that each pollution source has to abate at minimum cost. There are many ways to cut back on pollution, but not all are equally costly. But even if all polluters are abating as cheaply as possible, it does not necessarily mean that pollution overall is being reduced at least cost. The pattern of pollution abatement over all sources is of great importance here. Because some polluters will be more efficient at pollution reduction than others, the least-cost abatement pattern will require some polluters to clean up more than others. In general, the least-cost pattern of abatement involves finding the cost of reducing pollution by one more unit that is the same for all polluters. If this condition is not satisfied, the cost of achieving a given amount of overall abatement can be reduced by having the low-cost abater reduce pollution by an additional unit and the high-cost abater reduce pollution by one unit less. This type of adjustment will continue to reduce abatement costs, without increasing pollution, until reducing pollution by the additional unit costs everyone the same amount.

A third objective of a pollution-control policy is to establish incentives that will motivate advances in pollution-abatement technology. Over the long run, this may be an even more important objective than the first two. For example, the cost of controlling pollution can be significantly

A paper mill might purchase the rights to pollute more.

reduced over time, even if the second objective is not fully realized, if consistent advances are made in the technology of pollution control.

It should be clear that these three objectives, (1) achieving the efficient level of pollution, (2) achieving pollution reduction at least cost, and (3) motivating advances in abatement technology, may never be fully realized. This is particularly true of the first objective. By not being able to own and control identifiable and separate portions of the atmosphere, for example, no one is in a position to require that a price be paid in exchange for fouling his, and only his, clean air. Without such exchanges and prices, we have no way of knowing the value people place on clean air. And without this information, there is no way of determining the efficient level of air pollution. Likewise, private ownership of identifiable and separate portions of water in our lakes, rivers, and oceans is not possible, and thus there are no precise ways of determining the efficient level of water pollution. In the absence of market exchange, we have to rely on the political process to determine the efficient level of pollution. In a democratic political order, there is the presumption that the information provided by voting and lobbying will keep the political process at least somewhat responsive to the preferences of the citizens. To the extent that this presumption is justified, there is hope that political decision makers will arrive at a level of pollution that is not too far removed from the efficient level.

T U N E   U P

INCENTIVES AND POLLUTION

Q: Rex R. View was horrified with the number of abandoned automobiles in his community. He was trying to think of a solution for this form of visual pollution—perhaps something along the line of deposits on bottles. Can you help Rex with this idea? How would deposits on autos work? How would it affect the incentives of the litterer and the recoverer?

A: It is estimated that 15 percent of all automobiles in this country are abandoned at the end of their useful lives along streams, fields, highways, and streets. However, mandatory deposits would provide incentives for both recovery and against the littering of abandoned automobiles. That is, if the deposit is set sufficiently high, there will be less likelihood of people abandoning their auto because they will lose their deposit. On the other hand, if people do decide to abandon their auto, someone else has the incentive to tow it to a recycling center and receive the deposit. This is just another example of the essential economic reasoning—incentives matter.*

How can we internalize this externality?

*For more detail see D. Lee, P. Graves and R. Sexton, "Controlling the Abandonment of Automobiles: Mandatory Deposits Versus Fines," *Journal of Urban Economics* 31, no. 1 (January 1992).

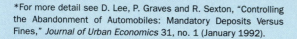
CONCEPT CHECK

1. Compliance standards force companies to find less pollution-intensive ways of producing goods and services.
2. Pollution taxes can be used to force firms to internalize externalities. This allows the relatively efficient private sector to operate according to market forces in a manner that takes socially important spillover costs into account.
3. Tradable pollution rights create incentives for the firms that are best at cleaning up to do the cleaning up.
4. The tradable pollution rights policy encourages polluters to come up with cheaper ways of reducing pollution, because the firm that reduces pollution is able to sell its remaining pollution credits to others.

---

1. How do compliance standards act to internalize external costs?
2. How does pollution control lead to both rising marginal costs and falling marginal benefits?
3. How is the optimal amount of pollution control determined, in principle? Why is it so difficult to achieve agreement on what that optimal level of pollution is?
4. How could transferable pollution rights lead to pollution being reduced at the lowest possible opportunity cost?

5. What are the objectives of an ideal pollution-control policy from the perspective of economists interested in resource allocation?
6. Why might an efficient pollution tax be lower in Fargo, North Dakota, than in Los Angeles, California?
7. If a firm can reduce its sulfur dioxide emissions for $30 per ton, but it owns tradable emissions permits that are selling for $40 per ton, what will the firm want to do if it is trying to maximize profits?

© Property Rights

- Why are property rights important?
- What is the Coase Theorem?

PROPERTY RIGHTS AND THE ENVIRONMENT

The existence of externalities and the efforts to deal with them in a manner that will enhance the social good can be looked at as largely being a question as to the nature of property rights. If the EPA limits the soot that a steel company emits from "its" smokestack, then the property rights of the steel company with respect to its smokestack have been altered or restricted. Similarly, zoning laws restrict how property owners can use their property. Sometimes, in order to deal with externalities, governments radically alter property rights arrangements.

Indeed, the entire matter of dealing with externalities ultimately evolves into a question of how property rights should be altered. If no externalities existed in the world, there would be relatively few reasons for prohibiting property owners from using their property in any manner they voluntarily chose. Ultimately, then, externalities involve an evaluation of the legal arrangements under which we operate our economy, and is thus one area where law and economics merge.

WHAT IS THE COASE THEOREM?

In a classic paper, Nobel laureate Ronald Coase observed that if the benefits are greater than the costs for some course of action (say, environmental cleanup), there must be potential transactions that can make some people better off without making anyone worse off. To appreciate this important insight, consider the following problem: A cattle rancher lives downstream from a paper mill. The paper mill dumps sulfurous compounds into the stream, which injures the rancher's cattle. If the rancher is not compensated, an externality exists. The question is: Why does the externality persist? Suppose the courts have established (perhaps because the paper mill was there first) that the property rights to use (or abuse) the stream reside with the mill. If the benefits of cleanup are greater than the costs, the rancher should be willing to pay the mill owner to stop polluting. Let's assume that the rancher's benefits from the cleanup (say $10,000) undertaken by the mill are greater than the cost (say $5,000). If the rancher were to offer $7,500 to the mill owner to undertake the cleanup activity, both the rancher and the mill owner would be better off than with continued pollution. If, on the other hand, the property rights to the use of the stream resided with the rancher, and there was a sufficiently high benefit to the mill owner from polluting the river, then it would be rational for the mill owner to pay the rancher to adjust his cattle raising activity up to the point where the marginal benefits to the mill owner of polluting equaled the marginal damages to the rancher from pollution.

Can ranchers and farmers get along?

TRANSACTION COSTS AND THE COASE THEOREM

The mill owner and rancher example hinges critically on low transaction costs. Transaction costs are the costs of negotiating and executing an exchange, excluding the cost of the good or service bought. For example, when buying a car, it is usually rational for the buyer to spend some time searching for the "right" car and negotiating a mutually agreeable price.

Suppose that instead of one rancher there were a thousand, and that instead of one mill owner, there were ten—but with the same total benefits and costs of cleanup. The desirable outcome—that the workings of voluntary exchange will eliminate the externality—would disappear. Not only would there be complicated issues of how to assign observed damages to specific mill owners, but each individual rancher might try to become a free rider. The $10,000 of benefits would now be only $10 per rancher, but the transactions costs of successfully dealing with the several polluters (either to bribe them or bring suit, depending on property rights assignment) would be far higher than that. Now imagine the complexities of more realistic cases: There are 12 million people within 60 miles of downtown Los Angeles. Each of them is damaged a little by each of a very large number of firms and other consumers (for example, automobile drivers) in Los Angeles.

It thus becomes apparent why the inefficiencies resulting from pollution control are not eliminated by private negotiations. First, there is ambiguity regarding property rights in air, water, and other environmental media. Firms that have historically polluted resent controls, giving up their rights to pollute only if bribed, yet consumers feel they have the right to breathe clean air and use clean bodies of water. These conflicting positions must be resolved in court, with the winner being, of course, made wealthier. Second, transaction costs increase greatly with the number of transactors, making it next to impossible for individual firms and citizens to negotiate private agreements. Finally, the properties of air or water quality (and similar public goods) are such that additional people can enjoy the benefits at no additional cost and cannot be excluded from doing so. Hence, in practice, private agreements are unlikely to solve many problems of market failure.

It is, however, an easy jump to the conclusion that governments should solve any problems that cannot be solved by private actions. No solution may be possible, or all solutions may involve costs that exceed benefits. In any event, the ideas developed in this Module should enable you to think critically about such problems and the difficulties in formulating appropriate policies.

CONCEPT CHECK

1. If no externalities existed in the world, there would be relatively few reasons to prohibit property owners from using their property in any manner they desired. Ultimately, then, externalities involve an evaluation of the legal arrangements in which we operate our economy.

2. The Coase Theorem states that where property rights are defined in a clear-cut fashion, externalities are internalized. This condition holds where information and transaction costs are close to zero.

1. Why can externalities be considered a property rights problem?
2. Why, according to the Coase Theorem, will externalities tend to be internalized when property rights are clearly defined and information and transaction costs are low?

3. How do transaction costs and the free rider problem limit the market's ability to efficiently solve externality problems?

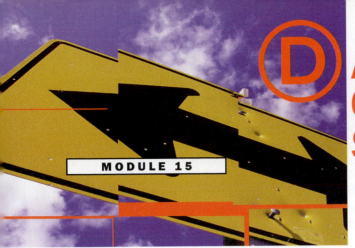

D Application: California's Smoke-Free Bars

Who has the right to the air—smokers or nonsmokers? Why are property rights important in understanding the pollution problem?

Who owns the right to the air?

LAW DESIGNED TO PROTECT HEALTH OF BAR EMPLOYEES

California banned smoking in most indoor workplaces in 1995, including the non-bar areas of restaurants. A temporary exemption for more than 35,000 bars, casinos, and bar-restaurants ended on January 1, 1998. The only exempt businesses now are casinos and bars on American Indian reservations and owner-operated businesses with no employees.

California is the first state to ban smoking in most bars and casinos. The ban isn't meant to criminalize smoking, state officials say, but to give employees a workplace free of secondhand smoke, which has been linked to lung cancer, respiratory problems, and other illnesses.

WHOM TO PUNISH: BAR OWNERS OR SMOKERS?

Bar owners breaking the law could be fined up to $100 for a first offense and up to $7,000 per violation for a se-

ries of offenses. The law also allows for fines against smokers, but just as enforcement is proving tricky, so is determining whom to punish. Some municipalities believe it's a labor law and therefore applies only to bar owners, not smokers themselves. So far, Los Angeles has received only a few complaints and no one has been fined.

As long as "no smoking" signs are posted and patrons are informed of the law, bar owners are off the hook, meaning their smoking customers are free to do as they please.

Correspondent Greg Lamotte contributed to this report. January 23, 1998, http://cnn.com/US/9801/23/smoking.ban/index.html

The classic dilemma in this situation is that smokers believe that it is their right to be able to dump their smoke into the air without added costs to them, because nobody really owns the air. On the other hand, nonsmokers believe they have the right to breathe fresh air. Who is right? The issue is one of property rights. If there were only a few individuals involved and therefore the cost of negotiating was relatively low, then it is possible that an exchange could take place that might make both parties better off. For example, if the property rights were assigned to smokers, then nonsmokers could bribe smokers for the right to clean air.

Boulder, Colorado, has taken an approach that allows for separation of use (like having smoking and nonsmoking cars on trains). This city requires bars, restaurants, and other public places to provide separately ventilated smoking areas or to go entirely smoke-free. Most establishments have provided such areas and find business booming, because both smokers and nonsmokers can enjoy the same businesses. Such separation-of-use policies have been shown to be effective in minimizing social strife. For example, policies of this sort have been used in the Ruhr Valley of Germany to help both water-using industries and water-using recreationists to be better off.

Are you positive that you understand externalities? Or does studying externalities put you in a negative frame of mind? To be sure that you understand these concepts and that you grasp the economic impact of pollution taxes and pollution rights, complete the exercises in the Workbook and answer the self-tests on the EconActive CD-ROM.

THE KYOTO PROTOCOL ON GLOBAL WARMING

After over ten years of research and heated debate, many of the world's prominent scientists, business people, and labor leaders recognize global warming as a real and serious problem. Global warming occurs when fossil fuels, coal and oil, are burned, generating carbon dioxide. The carbon dioxide gas traps the sun's heat, which raises the earth's temperature having far-reaching impacts. For example, a warmer climate will begin to melt glaciers, causing flooding in many areas. Warmer temperatures can encourage the spread of topical diseases by allowing microbes causing those diseases to thrive in nontropical areas. Climate changes may also have a devastating effect on agriculture, an industry which is already straining to provide enough food for the rapidly increasing world population.

In early December, 1997, delegates from 170 nations met in Kyoto, Japan, to address the problem of global warming. The conference soon turned into a battle between the industrialized nations, including the United States, Japan, and the 15 nations of the European Union, and the developing countries and China over who would do the

most to reduce the fossil fuel emissions. After lengthy negotiations, an agreement known as the Kyoto Protocol was reached. The United States agreed to reduce its fossil fuel emission to 7 percent below 1990 levels by the year 2012; Japan, 6 percent; and the European Union, 8 percent. The developing countries are not required to limit their emissions, but are encouraged to do so. The agreement also allows for emissions trading, whereby countries who reduce emissions by more than their target may sell some of their excess reductions to other countries who fall short of their target.

As critics of the treaty are quick to point out, the costs of reducing global warming can be substantial. Instead of burning increasing amounts of fossil fuels, the world's inhabitants must drastically improve fossil fuel efficiency and convert to alternative energy sources, such as solar, wind, electricity, nuclear, and natural gas. Many fear that the development and adoption of expensive energy saving technology will severely slow the growth of the economy. The immediate impact would include a decrease in employment in

the energy and automobile sectors of the economy, two major employers. Many businesses fear that the increase in costs would decrease profits and hamper their ability to compete with corporations in developing countries which are not required to limit their emissions. Advocates of the treaty maintain that these costs are much smaller than the immeasurable benefits to be gained from a cleaner environment and a stable climate, absolute necessities for the survival of the planet.

Questions:
1. Discuss the externalities resulting from the consumption of fossil fuels.
2. Why has market failure occurred in the case of global warming?
3. Explain how tradable pollution permits can aid in achieving economic efficiency.
4. What is the Coase Theorem? Do you think that the Coase Theorem is relevant in solving the problem of global warming? Why or why not?

SOURCES: Michael D. Lemonick, "Hot Air in Kyoto," *Time*, December, 8, 1997, pp. 79-80. Michael D. Lemonick, "Turning Down the Heat," *Time*, December, 22, 1997, pp. 23-27.

PHOTO CREDITS MODULE 15

Page **373:** © Kirk Condyles/Impact Visuals/PNI; Page **374:** top, Matt Lindsey/Nonstock/PNI; bottom, © T/Maker Company; Page **376:** © PhotoDisc; Page **378:** © Kurt Knudson/Southern Stock/PNI; Page **380:** The Everett Collection; Page **381:** © John M. Warden/Alaska Stock/PNI; Page **382:** © PhotoDisc; Page **383:** © PhotoDisc; Page **385:** © PhotoDisc.

Introduction to the Macroeconomy

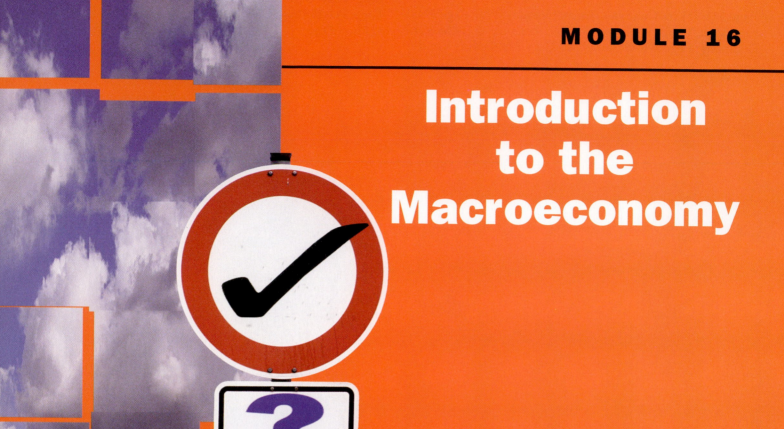

A. Macroeconomic Goals
What are the three major macroeconomic goals?

B. Employment and Unemployment
What is the unemployment rate?

C. Different Types of Unemployment
What are the different types of unemployment?

D. Inflation
Why is price level stability important?

E. Economic Growth
What are the benefits of economic growth?

F. Economic Fluctuations
What are economic fluctuations?

G. Application: Economic Freedom and Economic Growth
Does economic freedom guarantee economic growth?

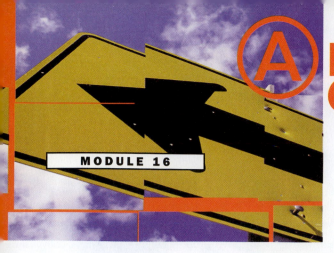

Ⓐ Macroeconomic Goals

■ What are the most important macroeconomic goals in the United States?

■ Are these goals universal?

■ How has the United States pursued these goals?

THREE MAJOR MACROECONOMIC GOALS

Nearly every society has been interested in three major macroeconomic goals: (1) maintaining employment of human resources at relatively high levels, meaning that jobs are relatively plentiful and financial suffering from lack of work and income is relatively uncommon; (2) maintaining prices at a relatively stable level so that consumers and producers can make better decisions; and (3) achieving a high rate of economic growth, meaning a growth in real per capita total output over time.

WHAT OTHER GOALS ARE IMPORTANT?

In addition to these primary goals, concern has been expressed at various times and places about other economic issues, some of which are essentially microeconomic in character. For example, concern about the "quality of life" has prompted some societies to try to reduce "bads" such as pollution and crime, and increase goods and services such as education and health services. Another goal has been "fairness" in the distribution of income or wealth. Still another goal present in many nations at one time or another has been becoming self-sufficient in the production of certain goods or services. For example, in the 1970s, the United States implemented policies that reduced U.S. reliance on other nations for supplies of oil, partly for reasons of national security.

HOW DO VALUE JUDGMENTS AFFECT ECONOMIC GOALS?

In stating that nations have economic goals, we must acknowledge that nations are made up of individuals. Individuals within a society may differ considerably in their evaluation of the relative importance of certain issues, or even whether certain "problems" are really problems after all. For example, economic growth, viewed positively by most persons, is not considered so favorably by others.

What are the major macroeconomic policy goals? Why are they important?

While some citizens may think the income distribution is just about right, others might think it provides insufficient incomes to the poorer members of society, while still others think it involves taking too much income from the relatively well-to-do and thereby reduces incentives to carry out productive income-producing activities.

ACKNOWLEDGING OUR GOALS: THE EMPLOYMENT ACT OF 1946

Many economic problems—particularly those involving unemployment, price instability, and economic stagnation—are pressing concerns for the U.S. government. In fact, it was the concern over both unemployment and price instability that led to the passage of the **Employment Act of 1946,** in which the United States committed itself to policies designed to reduce unemployment in a manner consistent with price stability. This was the first formal acknowledgment of these primary macroeconomic goals. Likewise, many forms of legislation have been adopted that are designed to increase the rate of economic growth.

CONCEPT CHECK

1. The most important macroeconomic goals are full employment, price stability, and economic growth.
2. Individuals each have their own reasons for valuing certain goals rather than others.
3. The United States showed its commitment to the major macroeconomic goals with the Employment Act of 1946.

1. What are the three major economic goals of most societies?

2. What is the Employment Act of 1946? Why was it significant?

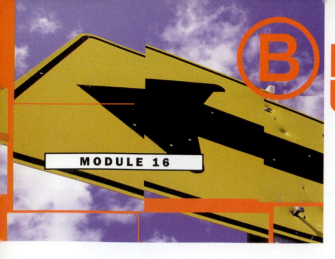

(B) Employment and Unemployment

- What are the consequences of unemployment?
- What is the unemployment rate?
- Does unemployment affect everyone equally?
- What causes unemployment?
- Is full employment desirable?

WHAT ARE THE CONSEQUENCES OF HIGH UNEMPLOYMENT?

Nearly everyone agrees that it is unfortunate when a person who wants a job cannot find one. A loss of a job can mean financial insecurity and a great deal of anxiety. High rates of unemployment in a society can lead to increased tensions and despair. A family without income from work undergoes great suffering, as its savings fade and it wonders where it is going to obtain the means to survive. Society loses some potential output of goods when some of its productive resources—human or non-human—remain idle, and potential consumption is also reduced. Clearly, then, there is a loss in efficiency when people willing to work and productive equipment remain idle. That is, other things equal, relatively high rates of unemployment are almost universally viewed as undesirable.

What are the costs to society of high unemployment?

WHAT IS THE UNEMPLOYMENT RATE?

When discussing unemployment, economists and politicians refer to the **unemployment rate.** In order to calculate the unemployment rate, you must first understand another important concept—the **labor force.** The labor force is the number of people over the age of 16 who are available for employment, regardless of whether or not they are currently employed, as seen in Exhibit 1. The civilian labor force figure excludes all those in the armed services and those in prison or mental hospitals. Those outside of the labor force also include homemakers, retirees, and full-time students. These groups are excluded from the labor force because they are not considered currently available for employment.

When we say that the unemployment rate is 5 percent, we mean that 5 percent of the population over the age of 16 who are willing and able to work are unable to obtain a job. The 5 percent means that 5 out of 100 people in the total labor force are unemployed. To calculate the unemployment rate, we simply divide the number of unemployed by the number in the labor force.

Unemployment rate = Number of unemployed/Labor force

In June 1998, the number of civilians unemployed in the United States was 6.2 million and the civilian labor force totalled 137.5 million. Using this data, we can calculate that the unemployment rate in June 1998 was 4.5 percent.

Unemployment rate = 6.2 million/137.5 million = .045 = 4.5 percent

WHAT WAS THE WORST CASE OF UNEMPLOYMENT IN THE UNITED STATES?

By far the worst employment downturn in U.S. history was the Great Depression, which began in late 1929 and continued until 1941. Unemployment fell from only 3.2 percent of the labor force in 1929 to more than 20 percent in the early 1930s, and double-digit unemployment

| EXHIBIT 1 | THE U.S. LABOR FORCE, 1997 |

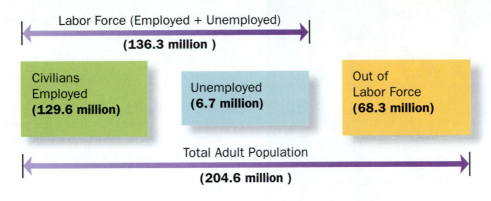

SOURCE: U.S. Department of Labor

persisted through 1941. The debilitating impact of having millions of productive persons out of work led Americans (and persons in other countries too) to say "Never again." Some economists would argue that modern macroeconomics, with its emphasis on the determinants of unemployment and its elimination, truly began in the 1930s.

ARE THERE SIGNIFICANT VARIATIONS IN THE UNEMPLOYMENT RATE?

Exhibit 2 shows the unemployment rates over the last 37 years. Unemployment since 1960 has ranged from a low of

3.5 percent in 1969 to a high of 9.7 percent in 1982, with the average rate over the entire period slightly exceeding 5.5 percent. Unemployment in the worst years is twice or more than what it is in good years. Before 1960, variations tended to be even more pronounced.

ARE UNEMPLOYMENT STATISTICS ACCURATE REFLECTIONS OF THE LABOR MARKET?

In periods of prolonged recession, some individuals think that the chances of landing a job are so bleak that they quit looking. These people are called "discouraged workers."

| EXHIBIT 2 | UNEMPLOYMENT RATES, 1960–1997 |

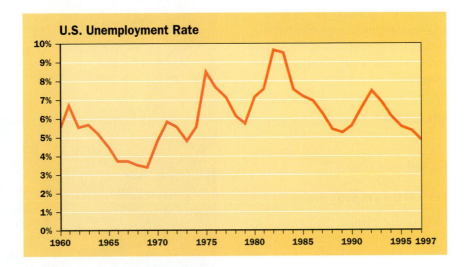

SOURCE: U.S. Bureau of Labor Statistics.

Are these jobs included in the official labor statistics?

Individuals who have not actively sought work for four weeks are not counted as unemployed; instead, they fall out of the labor force. Also, people looking for full-time work who grudgingly settle for a part-time job are counted as "fully" employed, yet they are only "partly" employed. However, at least partially balancing these two biases in government employment statistics is the number of people that are overemployed—that is, working overtime or extra jobs. Also, there are a number of jobs in the underground economy (drugs, prostitution, gambling, and so on) that are not reported at all. In addition, there may be many people that claim they are actually seeking work when, in fact, they may just be going through the motions so that they can continue to collect unemployment compensation or receive other government benefits.

WHO ARE THE UNEMPLOYED?

Unemployment usually varies greatly between different segments of the population and over time.

Education as a Factor in Unemployment

According to the Bureau of Labor Statistics, the unemployment rate among college graduates is significantly lower than for those without a high school diploma across sex and race. In January 1998, unemployment rates for individuals without a high school diploma was 8.4 percent, versus 2.0 percent for college graduates. Also, college graduates have lower unemployment rates than those

with some college education, but who have not completed a bachelor's degree (3.5 percent).

Age, Sex, and Race as Factors in Unemployment

The incidence of unemployment varies widely among the population. Unemployment tends to be greater among the very young, among blacks and other minorities, and among less-skilled workers. Adult female unemployment tends to be higher than adult male unemployment.

Considering the great variations in unemployment for different groups in the population, we calculate separate unemployment rates for groups classified by sex, age, race, family status, and type of occupation. Exhibit 3 shows unemployment rates for various groups for the year 1996. Note that the variation around the average unemployment rate for the total population of 5.4 percent was considerable. The unemployment rate for blacks and Hispanics averaged nearly twice the rate for whites, a phenomenon that has persisted throughout the post–World War II period. Unemployment among teenagers was much higher than even among blacks, at 16.7 percent. Some would regard teenage unemployment a lesser evil than unemployment among adults, because most teenagers have parents or guardians on whom they can rely for subsistence. On the other hand, some social scientists have observed a relationship between teenage unemployment, criminal activity, and social tensions.

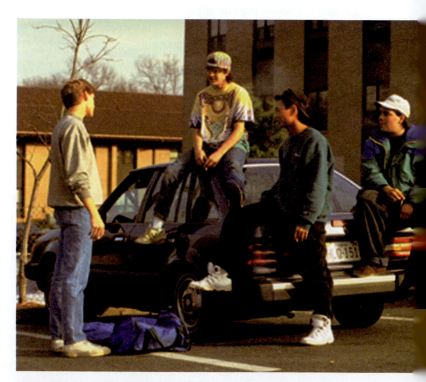

Teenagers have the highest rates of unemployment. Do you think it would be easier for them to find jobs if they had more experience and higher skill levels?

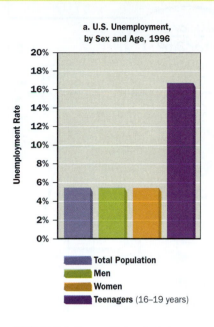

a. U.S. Unemployment, by Sex and Age, 1996

Legend:
- Total Population
- Men
- Women
- Teenagers (16–19 years)

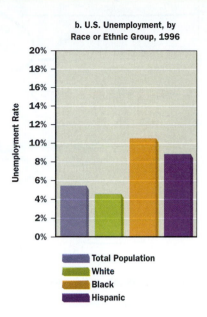

b. U.S. Unemployment, by Race or Ethnic Group, 1996

Legend:
- Total Population
- White
- Black
- Hispanic

SOURCE: U.S. Bureau of Labor Statistics.

REASONS FOR UNEMPLOYMENT

According to the Bureau of Labor Statistics, there are four main categories of unemployed workers: job losers (temporarily laid off or fired), job leavers (quit), re-entrants (worked before and now reentering labor force), and new entrants (entering the labor force for first time—primarily teenagers). It is a common misconception that most workers are unemployed because they have lost their jobs. While job losers may typically account for 50 to 60 percent of the unemployed, a sizeable fraction is due to job leavers, new entrants, and re-entrants, as seen in Exhibit 4.

| EXHIBIT 4 | REASONS FOR UNEMPLOYMENT |

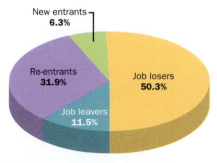

New entrants 6.3%
Re-entrants 31.9%
Job losers 50.3%
Job leavers 11.5%

Approximately 6.4 million people in the United States were unemployed in January 1998. Here is why they were unemployed, by reasons given.

SOURCE: U.S. Bureau of Labor Statistics, January 1998.

SHOULD THE GOVERNMENT ATTEMPT TO ACHIEVE FULL EMPLOYMENT?

Full employment is not necessarily a desirable goal. While unemployment is painful to those who have no source of income, reducing unemployment is not costless. In the short run, a reduction in unemployment may come at the expense of a higher rate of inflation, especially if the economy is close to full capacity, where resources are almost fully employed. Also, trying to match employees with jobs quickly may lead to significant inefficiencies because of mismatches between the worker's skill level and the level of skill required for a job. For example, the economy would be wasting a lot of resources subsidizing education if people with Ph.D.s in biochemistry were driving taxis or tending bar. That is, the skills of the employee may be higher than that necessary for the job, resulting in what economists call **underemployment.** Alternatively, employees may be placed in jobs beyond their abilities, which would also lead to inefficiencies.

HOW IMPORTANT IS THE AVERAGE DURATION OF UNEMPLOYMENT?

The *duration* of unemployment is equally as important as the amount of unemployment. The financial consequences of a head of household being unemployed four or five weeks are usually not extremely serious, particularly if the individual is covered by an unemployment compensation system. The impact becomes much more serious if a person

If he gets the job, will he be underemployed?

is unemployed for several months. Therefore, it is useful to look at the average duration of unemployment to discover what percent of the labor force is unemployed for more than a certain time period, say 15 weeks. Exhibit 5 presents data on the duration of unemployment in 1998. As you can see in this table, almost 45 percent of the unemployed were out of work less than five weeks, and only 15.2 percent of the total unemployed were out of work for more than six months. The duration of unemployment tends to be greater when the amount of unemployment is high, and smaller when the amount of unemployment is low. Unemployment of any duration, of course, means a potential loss of output. This loss of current output is permanent; it is not made up when unemployment starts falling again.

EXHIBIT 5	DURATION OF UNEMPLOYMENT, JANUARY 1998

Duration	Percent Unemployed
Less than 5 weeks	44.3%
5 to 14 weeks	28.8
15 to 26 weeks	11.7
27 weeks and over	15.2

SOURCE: U.S. Bureau of Labor Statistics.

1. The consequences of unemployment to society include a reduction in potential output and consumption—a decrease in efficiency.
2. The unemployment rate is found by dividing the number of people officially unemployed by the number in the labor force.
3. Unemployment rates are the highest for minorities, the young, and less-skilled workers.
4. There are four main categories of unemployed workers: job losers, job leavers, re-entrants, and new entrants.
5. The duration of unemployment tends to be greater (smaller) when the amount of unemployment is high (low).

---

1. What happens to the unemployment rate when the number of unemployed people increases, *ceteris paribus?* When the labor force grows, *ceteris paribus?*
2. How might the official unemployment rate understate the "true" degree of unemployment? How might it overstate it?
3. Why might the fraction of the unemployed who are job leavers be higher in a period of strong labor demand?
4. Suppose you live in a community of 100 people where no one was unwilling or unable to work. If 80 people are over 16 years old and 72 people are employed, what is the employment rate in that community?
5. What would happen to the unemployment rate if a substantial group of unemployed people started going to school full time? What would happen to the size of the labor force?
6. What happens to the unemployment rate when people become discouraged workers? Does anything happen to employment in this case?

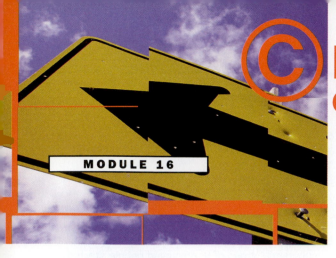

©Different Types of Unemployment

- What is frictional unemployment?
- What is structural unemployment?
- What is cyclical unemployment?
- What is seasonal unemployment?
- What is the natural rate of unemployment?

In examining the status of and changes in the unemployment rate, it is important to recognize that there are numerous types of unemployment. In this Concept, we will examine these different types of unemployment and evaluate the relative impact of each on the overall unemployment rate.

WHAT IS FRICTIONAL UNEMPLOYMENT?

Some unemployment results from persons being temporarily between jobs. For example, consider Bill Board, an advertising executive who was fired in Chicago on March 1 and is now actively looking for similar work in San Francisco. This is an example of **frictional unemployment.** Of course, all workers do not get fired from their jobs; some may voluntarily quit their jobs. In either case, frictional unemployment is short term and results from the normal turnover in the labor market, such as when people change from one job to another.

SHOULD WE WORRY ABOUT FRICTIONAL UNEMPLOYMENT?

Geographic and occupational mobility are considered to be good for the economy because they generally lead human resources to go from activities of relatively low productivity or value to areas of higher productivity, increasing output in society as well as the wage income of the mover. Hence, frictional unemployment, while not good in itself, is a by-product of a healthy phenomenon, and because it is often short-lived, it is therefore not generally viewed as a serious problem. While the amount of frictional unemployment varies somewhat over time, it is unusual for it to be much less than 2 percent of the labor force. Actually, frictional unemployment tends to be somewhat greater in periods of low unemployment, when job opportunities are plentiful. This high level of job opportunities stimulates mobility, which, in turn, creates some frictional unemployment.

Would there be less frictional unemployment if potential employers and prospective employees had better information about each other?

WHAT IS STRUCTURAL UNEMPLOYMENT?

A second type of unemployment is **structural unemployment.** Like frictional unemployment, structural unemployment is related to occupational movement or mobility, or, in this case, to a lack of mobility. Structural unemployment reflects the existence of persons who lack the necessary skills for jobs that are available. For example, if a machine operator in a manufacturing plant loses his job, he could still remain unemployed despite the existence of several openings for computer programmers in his community. The quantity of unemployed workers conceivably could equal the number of job vacancies, but the unemployment persists because of the unemployed's lack of skills. Given the existence of structural unemployment, it is wise to look at both unemployment and job vacancy statistics in assessing labor market conditions. Structural unemployment, like frictional unemployment, reflects the dynamic dimension of a changing economy. Over time, new jobs open up that require new skills, while old jobs that required different skills disappear. It is not surprising, then, that many persons advocate government-subsidized retraining programs as a means of reducing structural unemployment.

The dimensions of structural unemployment are debatable, in part because of the difficulty in precisely defining the term in an operational sense. Structural unemployment varies considerably—sometimes it is very low and at other times, like the 1970s and early 1980s, it is high. To some extent, in this latter period, jobs in the traditional sectors like autos and oil gave way to jobs in the computer and biotechnology sectors. Consequently, structural unemployment was higher.

What type of unemployment would occur if these coal miners lost their jobs as a result of a reduction in demand for coal and needed retraining to find other employment?

IMPERFECTIONS AND UNEMPLOYMENT

To a considerable extent, one can view both frictional and structural unemployment as phenomena resulting from imperfections in the labor market. For example, if individuals seeking jobs and employers seeking workers had better information about each other, the amount of frictional unemployment would be considerably lower. It takes time for suppliers of laborers to find the demanders of labor services, and it takes time and money for labor resources to acquire the necessary skills. But because information is not costless, and because job search also is costly, the bringing of demanders and suppliers of labor services together does not occur instantaneously.

WHAT IS CYCLICAL UNEMPLOYMENT?

In well over half of the years between 1960 and 1996, the unemployment rate exceeded 5.5 percent. Clearly, then, unemployment in many years is composed of more than just frictional and structural unemployment. In years of relatively high unemployment, some joblessness may result from an insufficient level of demand for goods and services. The demand for labor is derived from the demand for goods and services, so when the level of demand decreases, the demand for labor drops as well. We call this **cyclical unemployment.**

Most economists believe cyclical unemployment is the most volatile form of unemployment. Furthermore, many economists believe that insufficiency in aggregate demand explains most pronounced variations in the rate of unemployment over time.

CAN CYCLICAL UNEMPLOYMENT BE REDUCED?

Given its volatility and dimensions, governments, rightly or wrongly, have viewed unemployment resulting from inadequate demand to be especially correctable through government policies. Most of the attempts to solve the unemployment problem have placed an emphasis on increasing aggregate demand. Attempts to reduce frictional unemployment by providing better labor market information and to reduce structural unemployment through job retraining have also been made, but these efforts have received fewer resources and much less attention from policymakers.

T U N E   U P

CYCLICAL UNEMPLOYMENT

Q: Are layoffs more prevalent during a recession than a recovery? Do most resignations occur during a recovery?

A: Layoffs are more likely to occur during a recession. When times are bad, employers are often forced to let workers go. Resignations are relatively more prevalent during good economic times, because there are more job opportunities for those seeking new jobs.

WHAT IS SEASONAL UNEMPLOYMENT?

Some unemployment occurs because certain types of jobs are seasonal in nature. This type of unemployment is called **seasonal unemployment.** For example, a ski instructor in Aspen might become seasonally unemployed at the end of April when ski season is over. Or a roofer in Minnesota may become seasonally unemployed during the harsh winter months. Even a forest firefighter in a National Park might only be employed during the summer and fall, when forest fires peak. Occupations that experience either sharp seasonal shifts in demand or are subject to changing weather conditions may lead to seasonal unemployment.

What type of unemployment would occur if these firefighters lost their jobs at the end of the fire season?

WHAT ELSE CAN AFFECT THE UNEMPLOYMENT RATE?

It is likely that some unemployment reflects certain institutional aspects of the economy. For example, some unemployed persons may show little drive in seeking new employment, given the existence of unemployment com-

pensation. Unemployment compensation lowers the opportunity cost of being unemployed. Say a worker making $400 a week when employed receives $220 in compensation when unemployed; as a result, the cost of losing his job is not $400 a week in foregone income, but only $180. It has been estimated that the existence of unemployment compensation programs may raise overall unemployment rates by as much as 1 percent. Other studies have shown that in some cases, minimum-wage laws create an above-equilibrium price (wage) for labor, where the quantity of labor supplied exceeds the quantity demanded, meaning unemployment exists. Racial and sex discrimination may also cause some unemployment. Restrictive practices of labor unions (such as limiting membership into the union) may also contribute to some unemployment, as do laws restricting job entry (e.g., laws requiring a license to sell real estate or repair your toilet).

If unemployment compensation benefits increased, would this line be even longer?

DOES NEW TECHNOLOGY LEAD TO GREATER UNEMPLOYMENT?

Although many believe that technological advances inevitably result in the displacement of workers, this is not necessarily the case. If the new equipment is a substitute for labor, then it might displace workers. For example, many fast-food restaurants have substituted self-service beverage bars for workers. However, new capital equipment means that new workers will be needed to manufacture and repair the new equipment. The most famous example of this is the computer, which was supposed to displace thousands of workers. Instead, the computer generated a whole new growth industry that created jobs. The key point is that new inventions are generally cost saving, and these cost savings will generally generate higher incomes for producers and lower prices and better products for consumers, benefits that will ultimately result in the

Will new technology in one industry displace workers in the whole economy?

growth of other industries. The problem is that it is easy to just see the initial effect (displaced workers) of technological advances, without recognizing the implications of that invention throughout the whole economy over time.

WHAT IS THE NATURAL RATE OF UNEMPLOYMENT?

It is interesting to observe that over the period during which annual unemployment data are available, the median, or "typical," annual unemployment rate has been at or slightly above 5 percent. Some economists call this typical unemployment rate the **natural rate of unemploy-**

ment. When unemployment rises well above 5 percent, we have abnormally high unemployment; when it falls below 5 percent, we have abnormally low unemployment. The natural rate of unemployment of approximately 5 percent roughly equals the sum of frictional and structural unemployment when they are at a maximum. Thus, one can view unemployment rates below the natural rate as reflecting the existence of a below-average level of frictional and structural unemployment. When unemployment rises above the natural rate, however, it reflects the existence of cyclical unemployment.

WHAT EXACTLY IS FULL EMPLOYMENT?

There is some dispute over what constitutes full employment. Literal full employment (everyone who wants a job can have one without any need to spend time searching) is virtually impossible, given the existence of frictional and structural unemployment. During the 1960s, government economists and politicians generally suggested that full employment existed whenever the unemployment rate was 4 percent or less. In the early 1970s, economists generally accepted the notion that full employment should meaningfully be defined as being present when the unemployment rate was 5 percent or less. Because the actual rate of unemployment during the late 1970s and 1980s was substantial, economists claimed that the natural rate at that time might be as high as 6 or 7 percent. Today, however, economists, for the most part, have come back to accept a current range somewhere between 5.0 and 5.5 percent. The natural rate of unemployment may change over time as technological, demographic, institutional, and other conditions vary, ranging somewhere from 4.5 to 6 percent. In any case, for some economists, the operational definition of full employment is the elimination of cyclical unemployment.

GLOBAL WATCH

UNEMPLOYMENT AROUND THE GLOBE, 1996

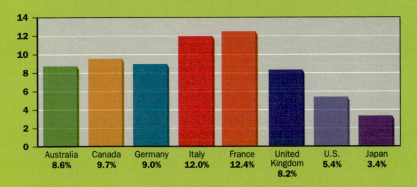

| Australia 8.6% | Canada 9.7% | Germany 9.0% | Italy 12.0% | France 12.4% | United Kingdom 8.2% | U.S. 5.4% | Japan 3.4% |

CONSIDER THIS:
Many developed countries had higher unemployment rates than the United States in 1996. Generous unemployment benefits and sluggish economic growth in European countries have helped cause higher unemployment rates than in the United States.

SOURCE: Organization for Economic Cooperation and Development, *Quarterly Labor Force Statistics.*

THE NEWS

A LIGHT THAT NEVER GOES OUT

(CNN)—Lighthouses have been called the most altruistic structures ever built. After almost 300 years of guiding ships along the U.S. coasts and Great Lakes, their usefulness is waning. But they have never lost their power to ignite poetry in those who visit them.

"Lighthouses are to America what castles are to Europe. They're among the oldest standing structures in (the U.S.)," says Tim Harrison, editor of the Maine-based *Lighthouse Digest.*

When the United States became a country, 12 lighthouses kept vigil over settled shores, according to Wayne Wheeler, founder of the U.S. Lighthouse Society. Over the years, he says more than 2,000 light stations were built. Today, the National Park Service estimates about 634 lighthouses remain, 405 of which are in service.

Automation has virtually eliminated the romantic tradition of lighthouse keepers—salty, solitary souls guiding ships safely through treacherous storms. And electronic pings are replacing the mournful drone of the foghorn calling sailors home.

SOURCE: CNN Interactive, Destinations, April 19, 1997. http:// cnn.com/TRAVEL/DESTINATIONS/9704/light houses.usa

CONSIDER THIS:
Just like elevator operators and service station attendants, now lighthouse keepers have given way to automation. In a world of scarcity, lighthouse keepers can now be employed producing something that is more valuable from society's perspective.

CONCEPT CHECK

1. The four types of unemployment are frictional unemployment, structural unemployment, cyclical unemployment, and seasonal unemployment.
2. Frictional unemployment results from the movement of persons from one job to another.
3. Structural unemployment results when people who are looking for jobs lack the required skills for the jobs that are available.
4. Cyclical unemployment is caused by an inadequate level of aggregate demand.
5. Imperfections in the labor market and institutional factors result in higher rates of unemployment.
6. When cyclical unemployment is almost completely eliminated, our economy is said to be operating at full employment.

1. Why do we want some frictional unemployment?
2. Why might a job retraining program be a more useful policy to address structural unemployment than to address frictional unemployment?
3. What is the traditional government policy "cure" for cyclical unemployment?
4. Does new technology increase unemployment?
5. What types of unemployment are present at full employment (at the natural rate of unemployment)?
6. Why might frictional unemployment be higher in a period of plentiful jobs (low unemployment)?
7. If the widespread introduction of the automobile caused a very productive maker of horse-drawn carriages to lose his job, would he be structurally or frictionally unemployed?
8. If a fall in demand for domestic cars causes auto workers to lose their jobs in Michigan, while there are plenty of jobs for lumberjacks in Montana, what kind of unemployment results?

Module 16   **402**   **Introduction to the Macroeconomy**

D Inflation

- Why is the overall price level important?
- How has the price level behaved this century?
- Who are the winners and losers during inflation?
- Can wage earners avoid the consequences of inflation?
- Why is it important to anticipate inflation correctly?

WHY IS PRICE LEVEL STABILITY A DESIRABLE GOAL?

Just as full employment brings about economic security of one kind, an overall stable price level increases another form of security. The **price level** is the average level of all prices in the economy. When the price level is rising, we have **inflation,** and when the price level is falling, we have **deflation.** In both inflation and deflation, a country's currency unit changes in purchasing power. Without price level stability, consumers and producers will experience more difficulty in coordinating their plans and decisions.

WHAT HAS HAPPENED TO THE PRICE LEVEL OVER THE YEARS?

Unanticipated and sharp changes in the price level are almost universally considered to be a "bad" thing that needs to be remedied by some policy. What is the historical record of changes in the overall price level in the United States? Exhibit 1 shows changes in the **Consumer Price Index,** the standard measure of inflation, from 1914 to 1996. For the typical college-age reader of this book, the average price level has more than doubled in his or her lifetime. Moreover, the same statement could have been made to readers of 20 years ago. Over the past 40 years, the average price level has roughly quintupled (risen fivefold). Can you believe that in 1940 stamps were three cents per letter, postcards were a penny, the median price of a house was $2,900, and the price of a new car was $650?

Compare, however, the price level in 1940 with that in 1800. Both consumer and wholesale prices in 1940 were actually lower than in 1800. Before 1940, inflation rates rose a great deal in wartime but tended to fall in peacetime, remaining roughly stable over long time periods. Since 1940, however, inflation rates have risen in peacetime as well as wartime.

EXHIBIT 1	THE PRICE LEVEL IN THE UNITED STATES, 1914–1996

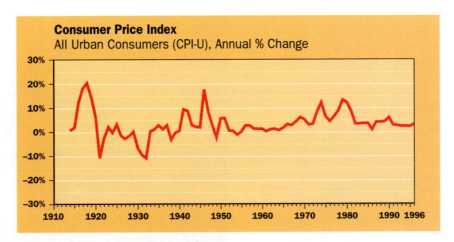

SOURCE: U.S. Bureau of Labor Statistics.

WHO LOSES WITH INFLATION?

Suppose you retire on a fixed pension of $2,000 per month. Over time, the $2,000 will buy less and less if prices generally rise. Your real income—your income adjusted to reflect changes in purchasing power—falls. Inflation lowers income in real terms for persons on fixed-dollar incomes. Creditors likewise can be hurt by inflation. If you loaned someone $1,000 in 1985 and were paid back $1,000 plus interest in 1995, the $1,000 in principal that was paid back actually is worth less in 1995 than it was in 1985 because inflation has eroded the purchasing power of the dollar. Thus, the real wealth of the creditor is eroded because of inflation. Another group that sometimes loses at least temporarily from inflation includes people whose incomes are tied to long-term contracts. If inflation begins shortly after a labor union signs a three-year wage agreement, it may completely eat up the wage gains provided by the contract. The same applies to businesses who agree to sell a quantity of something, say, coal, for a fixed price for a given number of years.

If some people lose because of changing prices, others must gain. The debtor pays back dollars worth less in purchasing power than those he borrowed. Corporations who can quickly raise the prices on their goods may have revenue gains greater than their increase in costs, providing additional profits. Wage earners sometimes lose from inflation.

If you borrowed money from a bank at 5 percent for 20 years and inflation averaged 10 percent over that period, who got the better end of the deal, you or the bank?

THE REDISTRIBUTION IMPACT OF INFLATION

A key point in our discussion of inflation is that it brings about changes in real incomes of persons, and these changes may be either desirable or undesirable. The redis-

T U N E   U P

INFLATION

Q: Di Gress, in her presentation to her Economics 101 class, stated that inflation meant that people have less money to spend, that there are less goods available, and that one must pay more money for goods they purchase. So far, what kind of a grade would you give Di?

A: Of the three statements Di made about inflation, only one is correct: With inflation, we must, on average, pay more money for the goods we purchase. Inflation does not necessarily mean we have fewer goods but rather that, on net, these goods have higher price tags. Inflation does not necessarily mean that people have less money to spend. Employees and unions will bargain for higher wages when there is inflation.

Does a higher price level mean lower living standards?

tributional impact of inflation is not the result of conscious public policy; it just happens. Moreover, inflation can raise one nation's price level relative to price levels in other countries, which can lead to difficulties in financing the purchase of foreign goods or to a decline in the value of the national currency relative to that of other countries. In its extreme form, inflation can lead to a complete erosion in faith in the value of the pieces of paper we commonly call money. In Germany after both World Wars, prices rose so fast that people in some cases finally refused to take paper money, insisting instead on payment in goods or metals whose prices tend to move predictably with inflation.

THE MENU AND SHOE LEATHER COSTS OF INFLATION

One cost of inflation is the cost that firms incur as a result of being forced to change their prices more frequently. For example, a restaurant may have to print new menus, or a department or mail-order store may have to print new catalogs to reflect changing prices. These costs are called **menu costs,** and they are the costs of changing posted prices. In some South American economies in the 1980s, inflation increased at over 300 percent per year, with prices changing on a daily, or even hourly, basis in some cases. Imagine how large the menu costs could be in an economy such as this!

Another cost of inflation is **shoe leather cost.** Shoe leather cost is the cost of going to and from the bank (and thus wearing out the leather on your shoes) to check on your assets. For example, higher inflation rates lead to higher nominal interest rates. The higher interest rate may induce more individuals to put money in the bank rather than allowing it to depreciate in their pockets.

NOMINAL VERSUS REAL INTEREST RATES

The interest rate is usually reported as the **nominal interest rate.** We determine the actual **real interest rate** by taking the nominal rate of interest and subtracting the inflation rate.

Real interest rate = Nominal interest rate − Inflation rate

For example, if the nominal interest rate was 5 percent and the inflation rate was 3 percent, then the real interest rate would be 2 percent.

WHAT IS ANTICIPATED INFLATION?

Most of the possible evils of inflation may not occur in periods of rising price levels. If people correctly anticipate inflation, they will behave in a manner that will largely protect them against loss. Consider the creditor who believes that it is likely that the price level will rise 6 percent a year, based on the immediate past experience. Would

that creditor lend money to someone at a 5 percent rate of interest? No. A 5 percent rate of interest means that a person borrowing $1,000 now will pay back $1,050 ($1,000 plus 5 percent of $1,000) one year from now. But if prices go up 6 percent, it will take $1,060 to buy what $1,000 does today ($1,060 is 6 percent more than $1,000). Thus, the person who lends at 5 percent will get paid back an amount ($1,050) that is less than the purchasing power of the original loan ($1,000) at the time it was made. The real interest rate, then, would actually be negative. Hence, to protect themselves, lenders will demand a rate of interest that is large enough to compensate for the deteriorating value of the dollar.

HOW DOES ANTICIPATED INFLATION AFFECT THE INTEREST RATE?

The economic theory behind the behavioral responses of creditors and debtors to anticipated inflation is straightforward and can be expressed in a simple diagram (Exhibit 2). An interest rate is, in effect, the price that one pays for the use of funds. Like other prices, interest rates are determined by the interaction of demand and supply forces. The lower the interest rate (price), the greater the quantity of funds people will demand, *ceteris paribus*; the higher the interest rate (price), the greater the quantity of loanable funds supplied by individuals and institutions like banks, *ceteris paribus*. Suppose that in an environment where prices are in general expected to remain stable in the near future, the demand for loanable funds is depicted by D_0 and the supply of such funds is indicated by S_0. In this

| EXHIBIT 2 | NOMINAL INTEREST RATES |

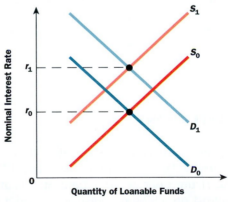

Nominal interest rates are determined by the intersection of the demand and supply curves for loanable funds. The lower the interest rate (price), the greater the quantity of loanable funds demanded, *ceteris paribus;* the higher the interest rate, the greater the quantity of loanable funds supplied by individuals and institutions like banks, *ceteris paribus.* Expected inflation shifts the supply curve left and the demand curve right, both of which tend to increase nominal (money) interest rates.

scenario, the equilibrium price, or interest rate, will be r_0, where the quantity demanded equals the quantity supplied.

When people start expecting future inflation, creditors such as banks will become less willing to lend funds at any given interest rate, because they fear they will be repaid in dollars of lesser value than those they loaned. This is depicted by a leftward shift in the supply curve of loanable funds (a decrease in supply) to S_1. Likewise, demanders of funds (borrowers) are more anxious to borrow, because they think they will pay their loans back in dollars of lesser purchasing power than the dollars they borrowed. Thus, the demand for funds increases from D_0 to D_1. Both the decrease in supply and the increase in demand push up the interest rate to a new equilibrium, r_1. Whether the equilibrium quantity of loanable funds will increase or decrease depends on the relative sizes of the shifts in the respective curves.

TUNE UP

ANTICIPATED INFLATION AND INTEREST RATES

Q: Carrie A. Loan has a 30-year, fixed-interest mortgage on her home, which she purchased six years ago. In the meantime, the inflation rate has fallen considerably and probably will not reach that higher level again. Is Carrie happy?

A: No. Carrie guessed incorrectly. If she stays with the initial loan, Carrie will be paying a higher interest rate to borrow money than others who have borrowed money more recently. Now, of course, Carrie could refinance to get a lower interest rate, but she would need to calculate how much she would save on her loan and compare it to the cost of refinancing to determine whether that would be worth doing.

DO CREDITORS ALWAYS LOSE DURING INFLATION?

Very often lenders are able to anticipate inflation with reasonable accuracy. For example, in the early 1960s, when prices were rising only about 1 percent a year, nominal rates of interest on a 90-day treasury bill ran a bit over 4 percent. Today, with prices rising around 2 percent a year,

the nominal interest rate is around 5.5 percent. The real interest rate received by the lender in both periods was between 3 and 4 percent (early 1960s: 4 percent nominal interest rate − 1 percent inflation = 3.0 percent real interest rate; 1998: 5.5 − 2 = 3.5). With inflation anticipated, new creditors did not lose, nor did debtors gain, from inflation. However, nominal interest rates and real interest rates do not always run together. For example, in periods of high unexpected inflation, the nominal interest rates can be very high while the real interest rates are low or even negative.

DO WAGE EARNERS ADJUST THEIR DEMANDS TO ACCOUNT FOR EXPECTED INFLATION?

Like creditors, wage earners, especially when organized by strong labor unions, adjust their wage demands to reflect the impact of inflation. In the mid-1990s, wage increases of slightly more than 4 percent a year were common. After allowing for inflation of slightly more than 3 percent a year, real wages rose about 1 percent. However, if expected inflation grew to 7 or 8 percent, wage demands would grow in response to the growing inflation rate; that is, money wages would rise to around 8 or 9 percent per year, again implying real wage increases of around 1 percent a year.

HOW CAN WE PROTECT OURSELVES FROM INFLATION?

Increasingly, groups try to protect themselves from inflation by using cost-of-living clauses in contracts. With these clauses, laborers automatically get wage increases that reflect rising prices. The same is true of many pensioners, including those on Social Security. Personal income taxes are also now indexed for inflation. Some economists have argued that we should go one step further and index everything, meaning that all contractual arrangements would be adjusted frequently to take account of changing prices. Such an arrangement might reduce the impact of inflation, but it would also entail additional contracting costs (and not every good—notably currency—can be indexed). An alternative approach has been to try to stop inflation through various policies relating to the amount of government spending, tax rates, or the amount of money created. **Wage and price controls**—legislation limiting wage and price increases—offer still another approach to the inflation problem. We will discuss this topic in greater detail later in the text.

AVERAGE ANNUAL INFLATION RATES, SELECTED COUNTRIES, 1996

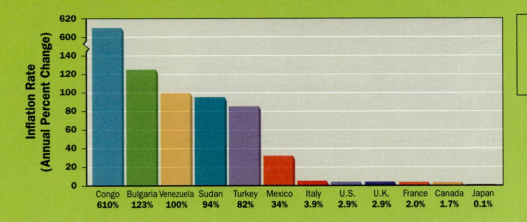

| Congo 610% | Bulgaria 123% | Venezuela 100% | Sudan 94% | Turkey 82% | Mexico 34% | Italy 3.9% | U.S. 2.9% | U.K. 2.9% | France 2.0% | Canada 1.7% | Japan 0.1% |

Inflation Rate (Annual Percent Change)

CONSIDER THIS:
Many countries around the world had a serious problem with inflation in 1996.

SOURCE: International Monetary Fund, 1997.

CONCEPT CHECK

1. Price stability provides security in the marketplace by ensuring constant purchasing power of a nation's currency.
2. Prior to 1940, prices tended to fall during peacetime, but since that time, they have been rising consistently each year, regardless of external factors.
3. Inflation generally hurts creditors and those on fixed incomes and pensions; debtors generally benefit from inflation.

4. The nominal interest rate is the actual amount of interest you pay. The real interest rate is the nominal rate minus the inflation rate.
5. Wage earners attempt to keep pace with inflation by demanding higher wages each year or by indexing their annual wage to inflation.

---

1. How does price level instability increase the difficulties buyers and sellers have in coordinating their plans?
2. What will happen to the nominal interest rate if the real interest rate rises, *ceteris paribus?* What if expected inflation increases, *ceteris paribus?*
3. Say you owe money to the River Bank. Will you gain or lose from an unanticipated decrease in inflation?
4. How does a variable interest rate loan "insure" the lender against unanticipated increases in inflation?

5. Why will neither creditors nor debtors lose from inflation if it is correctly anticipated?
6. How can inflation make people turn to exchange by barter?
7. What would happen in the loanable funds market if suppliers of loanable funds expect a substantial fall in inflation, while demanders of funds expect a substantial rise in inflation?

(E) Economic Growth

- What benefits does economic growth provide?
- How can a nation achieve economic growth?
- Is the economy of the United States growing?

WHY DO NATIONS WANT ECONOMIC GROWTH?

The desire to bring about long-term economic growth—an increase in the output of goods and services—has been expressed in nearly every economy. To be sure, there is not unanimous agreement that economic growth is desirable, as some writers have been outspoken about negative impacts of growth, such as increased environmental problems, growing inequalities, higher crime, a decline in moral standards, and so on. Still, economic growth is considered a "good" thing by most people, and in some countries it has been the primary concern of public policy. Economic growth, of course, enhances the potential amount of individual consumption; the greater the economic growth, the more goods we and our descendants have to consume in the future. In addition, economic growth increases a nation's potential military and political power, enhancing prestige and security.

WHICH COUNTRIES CAN ACHIEVE ECONOMIC GROWTH?

Economic growth is not something reserved exclusively for prosperous nations. Some relatively poor nations, like Chile and China, had growth rates during the 1990s that exceeded those of most European countries and the United States. Even India, with a per capita income level among the lowest in the world, achieved substantial annual growth during the 1990s. Economic growth varies widely between nations, even between these that presently have similar levels of per capita output.

HOW CAN A NATION IMPROVE ITS GROWTH RATE?

Nations engage in a variety of policies designed to increase their output over time. Some of these policies are designed to increase capital formation. The construction of tools and machinery today increases output in future time periods. Thus, it is not an accident that the nations with high investment and capital formation as a percent of gross domestic product (GDP) have had higher average annual growth rates. Nor is it an accident that the nations devoting the smallest proportion of their output to capital formation have had lower growth rates. Nations can encourage capital formation through such policies as favorable tax treatment of investment spending, using tax revenues to form capital, and through subsidies for capital-intensive forms of production. In centrally planned economies like Cuba or North Korea, the government simply emphasizes the production of capital goods at the expense of consumer goods.

Nations also attempt to increase their rate of per capita economic growth by increasing the output of the labor force by education, training programs, and improved health standards, or by using tariffs to protect native industries from foreign competition.

IS THE UNITED STATES ECONOMY STRUGGLING?

Despite faster growth rates in many other countries, the per capita GDP in the United States is still higher than that in any other nation. Exhibit 1 shows per capita U.S. output compared to other industrialized countries in 1995, using **purchasing power parity.** The use of purchasing power parity allows us to estimate the number of units of currency that are needed in one country to buy the same amount of goods and services that one unit of currency will buy in another country. We see from Exhibit 1 that the United States has the highest per capita GDP, followed by Switzerland, Luxembourg, Germany, Canada, Japan, and France. Exhibit 2 shows the growth rates for selected advanced economies from 1979 to 1998.

EXHIBIT 1	1995 PER CAPITA GDP IN SELECTED COUNTRIES USING PURCHASING POWER PARITY[1]

Country	Per Capita GDP (dollars)
Canada	$21,031
France	19,939
Germany	20,497
Italy	19,465
Japan	21,795
Norway	22,672
Sweden	18,673
Switzerland	24,809
United Kingdom	17,776
United States	26,438

[1]PPP shows how many units of currency are needed in one country to buy the same amount of goods and services that one unit of currency will buy in the other country.

SOURCE: Organization for Economic Cooperation and Development, Paris, France, *National Accounts, Main Aggregates*, vol. 1, annual; and "OECD Statistics GDP," published January 1997; http://www.oecd.org/std/gdp.htm

EXHIBIT 2	GROWTH IN REAL PER CAPITA GDP, SELECTED INDUSTRIAL COUNTRIES

	10-Year Averages	
	1980–1989	1990–1999
United States	1.8%	1.2%
Japan	3.1	1.5
Germany[1]	1.7	2.0
France	1.8	1.4
Italy	2.3	1.5
United Kingdom	2.2	1.4
Canada	1.7	0.7

[1]Data through 1991 apply to West Germany only.

SOURCE: International Monetary Fund, *World Economic Outlook,* May 1998.

CONCEPT CHECK

1. Economic growth increases the potential amount of individual consumption and enhances a nation's potential military and political power.
2. Nations can achieve economic growth by encouraging increases in investment, which increases capital formation, as well as through other, more controversial, methods.
3. While the United States economy has lagged behind many other nations in its per capita growth rate, it has the highest per capita GDP in the world.

1. In what way does the desire for economic growth arise from scarcity?
2. How does encouraging capital investment or educational training enhance economic growth?
3. Why do we use purchasing power parity to compare per capita GDP across countries?
4. If a country increased its rate of capital formation, what would happen to its current consumption possibilities? What would happen to its consumption possibilities 15 years from now?

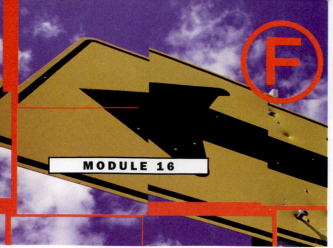

(F) Economic Fluctuations

- What are short-term economic fluctuations?
- What are the four stages of a business cycle?
- Is there a difference between a recession and a depression?
- Can an economy be in a recession while still growing?

ARE THERE SHORT-TERM FLUCTUATIONS IN ECONOMIC GROWTH?

The aggregate amount of economic activity in the United States and most other nations has increased markedly, even on a per capita basis, over time; there has been economic growth. There are short-term fluctuations in the level of economic activity, however. We sometimes call these short-term fluctuations **business cycles.** The distinction between long-term economic growth and short-term economic fluctuations is illustrated in Exhibit 1. Over a long period of time, the line representing economic activity slopes upwards, indicating increasing real output. Over short time periods, however, there are downward, as well as upward, output changes. Business cycles refer to the short-term ups and downs in economic activity, not to the long-term trend in output, which in modern times has been upward.

WHAT ARE THE PHASES OF A BUSINESS CYCLE?

A business cycle has four phases—expansion, peak, contraction, and trough—as illustrated in Exhibit 2. The period of expansion is when output is rising significantly. Usually during the expansion phase, unemployment is falling and both consumer and business confidence is high. Thus, investment is rising, as well as expenditures for expensive durable consumer goods, such as automobiles and household appliances. The peak is the point in time when the expansion comes to an end, when output is at the highest point in the cycle. The contraction is a period of falling real output, and is usually accompanied by rising unemployment and declining business and consumer confidence. Investment spending and expenditures on consumer durable goods fall sharply in a typical contraction.

EXHIBIT 1	BUSINESS CYCLES AND ECONOMIC GROWTH

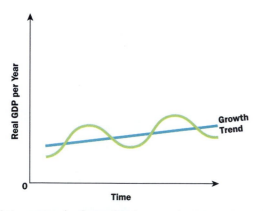

In a growing economy, business downturns are temporary reversals from a long-term trend of economic growth.

EXHIBIT 2	FOUR PHASES OF A BUSINESS CYCLE

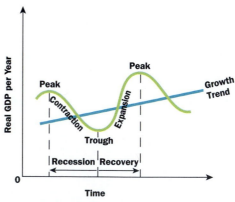

Business cycles have four phases: expansion, peak, contraction, and trough. The expansion phase usually is longer than the contraction, and in a growing economy, output (real GDP) will rise from one business cycle peak to the next.

The trough is the point in time when output stops declining; it is the moment when business activity is at its lowest point in the cycle. Unemployment is relatively high at the trough, although the actual maximum amount of unemployment may not occur exactly at the trough. Often, unemployment remains fairly high well into the expansion phase.

HOW LONG DOES A BUSINESS CYCLE LAST?

There is no uniformity to a business cycle's length. In both the 1980s and 1990s, one cycle lasted eight years—an unusually long period by historical standards. By contrast, two years would be a very short cycle. The contraction phase is one of recession, a decline in business activity. Severe recessions are called **depressions**. Likewise, a prolonged expansion in economic activity is sometimes called a **boom**. Exhibit 3 shows the record of American business cycles over recent times, in terms of deviations from its long-term trend in economic activity. Note in Exhibit 3 that contractions seem to be getting shorter over time.

CAN SEASONAL FLUCTUATIONS AFFECT ECONOMIC ACTIVITY?

While the determinants of cyclical fluctuations in the economy are the major thrust of the next several Modules, it should be mentioned that some fluctuation in economic activity reflects seasonal patterns. Business activity, whether measured by production or by the sale of goods, tends to be high in the two months before the winter holidays, and somewhat lower in summertime, when many families are on vacation. Within individual industries, of course, seasonal fluctuations in output often are extremely

Is there a correlation between the strength of the economy and an incumbent being reelected?

pronounced, agriculture being the best example. Often, key economic statistics, like unemployment rates, are seasonally adjusted, meaning the numbers are modified

| EXHIBIT 3 | A HISTORICAL RECORD OF U.S. BUSINESS CYCLES, 1928–1998 |

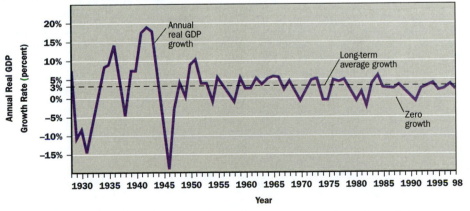

Since 1928, real GDP has increased, on average, 3 percent per year. However, we do see alternating swings from the average.

SOURCE: *Economic Report of the President*, 1998.

IS THE BUSINESS CYCLE GONE?

Boom times never last forever. A recession is inevitable. But experts say it will be short and mild—nothing like the Great Depression of the 1930s. "The old-fashioned business cycle, in its virulence, should be as gone as the old-fashioned diphtheria and pre-penicillin diseases are gone," maintains MIT economist Paul Samuelson.

Why? Because America has learned how to keep the economy growing with a balanced budget, low interest rates, and efficient companies—all making Main Street a prosperous place.

And what about Wall Street? It's been an incredible run by the bulls with three years in a row of huge gains averaging 27 percent a year. The question is, How long can it last? And will it all come crashing down?

Experts predict a big fall, of 20 percent to 25 percent, within the next two to three years, but then stocks will start up again, partly because of all the money being pumped in by young people like Brian O'Neal.

"Basically, everything I have saved up is riding on this market," says O'Neal. He's 26, and he's a new breed of investor—he trades on the Internet. O'Neal says he absolutely will not dump out when the markets take a tumble. "I feel like at this point, if I'm going to lose anything, I can take the losses," he says.

It is truly a Goldilocks economy: not too hot, not too cold, but just right, and it shows no sign of faltering.

SOURCE: http://www.msnbc.com/NEWS/150339.asp

CONSIDER THIS:
Many believe that the stability of the economy is shaped by government and its ability to counteract economic fluctuations—stimulating the economy with tax cuts, spending, easy money, and low interest rates when the economy is weak, and restraining it when it overheats. However, this is a difficult task. The first assumption is that economists know exactly where the economy is headed and, secondly, that will they apply the right amount of stimulus or impediment with their economic policies to promote long-term stable economic growth. Information about the economy will always be less than perfect. In fact, a standard joke in economics is that the purpose of economic forecasting is to make astrologists look respectable.

---

to take account of normal seasonal fluctuations. Thus, seasonally adjusted unemployment rates in summer months are below actual unemployment rates, because unemployment is normally high in summertime as a result of the inflow of school-age workers into the labor force.

HOW CAN POLITICS AFFECT THE ECONOMY?

Studies have shown there is a strong correlation between the performance of the economy and the fate of an incumbent's bid for reelection. In fact, the 1992 presidential election sheds light on this hypothesis. President Bush had lost his reelection bid shortly after the economy had struggled through the 1990–1991 recession. Some scholars have speculated that if the election had taken place a few months later when the economic data looked a lot stronger, President Bush would have been reelected.

If this correlation between the strength of the economy and a successful reelection bid does exist, then it would be in the best interest of the incumbent to do everything in his power to stimulate the economy in the period leading up to the election. This might take the form of trying to pressure the Federal Reserve System into lowering the interest rate or pressing Congress to cut taxes or increase government spending—anything that might generate more spending and thus greater employment. Of course, the negative side to all of this is that although the incumbent may get reelected, the economy may have been overstimulated, causing inflationary problems.

JAPANESE GOVERNMENT EXPECTS SLOW RECOVERY

TOKYO (AP)—The Japanese government now expects the troubled economy could take up to three years to recover instead of the two years it previously projected, a top official says.

In another burst of bad news, a research agency reported today that Japanese bankruptcies rose in September, pushing the debt left over from failed businesses for the month to more than $25 billion, a post-war high.

The comments by Chief Cabinet Secretary Hiromu Nonaka, reported today by Kyodo News agency, was the second time in recent days that a Japanese official has played down hopes for a quick end to Japan's deepest recession since World War II.

Last week, the government revised downward its economic forecast for the fiscal year ending March 31, predicting shrinkage of 1.8 percent instead of the previously forecast growth of 1.9 percent.

"We think the economy will recover in two or three years," Nonaka was quoted as saying to reporters. Until now, the government has said the recovery would take one or two years.

Copyright 1998 The Associated Press, October 14, 1998. http://cgi.newsweek.com/cgi-bin/nwframe?url=http://search.washingtonpost.com/wp-srv/WAPO/19981014/V000716-101498-idx.html

> **CONSIDER THIS:**
> For years the Japanese economy seemed as if it was immune to recession—but it finally hit and hit hard. It has been over 50 years since Japan has gone through a recession.

CONCEPT CHECK

1. Business cycles are short-term fluctuations in the amount of economic activity, relative to the long-term trend in output.
2. The four phases of a business cycle are expansion, peak, contraction, and trough.
3. Recessions occur during the contraction phase of a business cycle. Severe, long-term recessions are called depressions.
4. The economy often goes through short-term contractions even during a long-term growth trend.

---

1. Why would you expect unemployment to tend to fall during an economy's expansionary phase and to rise during a contractionary phase?
2. Why might a politician want to stimulate the economy prior to his or her reelection bid?
3. Why is the output of investment goods and durable consumer goods more sensitive to the business cycle than that of most goods?
4. Why might the unemployment rate fall after output starts recovering during the expansion phase of the business cycle?

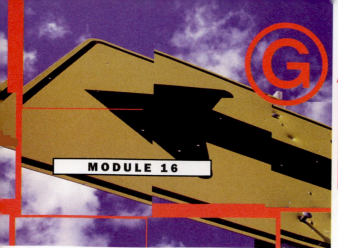

G Application: Economic Freedom and Economic Growth

What is economic freedom? Does economic freedom lead to greater economic growth?

ECONOMIC FREEDOM AND THE GROWTH OF EMERGING MARKETS

DOES ECONOMIC THEORY PROVIDE A PRECISE RECIPE FOR GROWTH? Probably not. But according to economists James Gwartney and Robert Lawson, it does reveal several of the important ingredients. Other things being constant, their research suggests that countries investing a larger share of their GDP (gross domestic product) will tend to grow more rapidly. Until the troubles hit Southeast Asia in early 1998, high investment rates had contributed to high levels of growth in several Asian countries, including Singapore, Malaysia, and South Korea. However, if investment is going to exert a strong impact on growth, it must be channeled into productive projects. As the experience of Eastern European countries and the former Soviet Union illustrates, high investment rates do not guarantee rapid growth and prosperity.

WHAT IS ECONOMIC FREEDOM? According to Gwartney and Lawson, a country's institutional arrangements and policies will also influence growth and the efficiency of resource use. The two researchers created a rating system based on economic freedom. Specifically, a country has a high level of economic freedom if it has the following characteristics: private ownership, a stable monetary environment, low taxes, and freedom of exchange. They used a rating system of economic freedom to determine the countries that improved the most as well as those that regressed the most during the 1975–1994 period.

WHAT HAPPENED TO THE COUNTRIES WHOSE ECONOMIC FREEDOM EXPANDED? The 12 countries with the largest increases in economic freedom achieved impressive growth rates during 1985–1994 (Exhibit 1). On average, the real per capita GDP of the nations in the most improved category grew at an annual rate of 4 percent between 1985 and 1994. At this rate, their real per capita income would double every 18 years.

WHAT HAPPENED TO THE COUNTRIES WHOSE ECONOMIC FREEDOM CONTRACTED? In the 11 countries for which the index of economic freedom fell the most, the level of real per capita GDP declined, on average, at an annual rate of 1.2 percent during 1985–1994 (Exhibit 2).

SOURCE: James Gwartney and Robert Lawson, *Economic Freedom of the World: 1975–1995*, Cato Institute, 1996. http://www.cipe.org/e20/gwa_E20.html

| EXHIBIT 1 | PERCENT CHANGE IN PER CAPITA GDP 1985–1994 IN COUNTRIES WITH LARGEST INCREASES IN FREEDOM RATINGS |

EXHIBIT 1	PERCENT CHANGE IN PER CAPITA GDP 1985–1994 IN COUNTRIES WITH LARGEST INCREASES IN FREEDOM RATINGS

EXHIBIT 2	PERCENT CHANGE IN PER CAPITA GDP 1985–1994 IN COUNTRIES WITH LARGEST DECLINES IN FREEDOM RATINGS

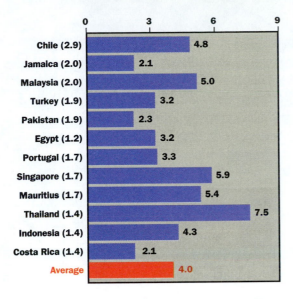

Exhibit 1 data:

Country	Percent Change
Chile (2.9)	4.8
Jamaica (2.0)	2.1
Malaysia (2.0)	5.0
Turkey (1.9)	3.2
Pakistan (1.9)	2.3
Egypt (1.2)	3.2
Portugal (1.7)	3.3
Singapore (1.7)	5.9
Mauritius (1.7)	5.4
Thailand (1.4)	7.5
Indonesia (1.4)	4.3
Costa Rica (1.4)	2.1
Average	4.0

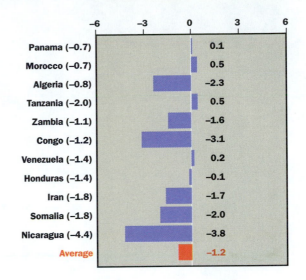

Exhibit 2 data:

Country	Percent Change
Panama (−0.7)	0.1
Morocco (−0.7)	0.5
Algeria (−0.8)	−2.3
Tanzania (−2.0)	0.5
Zambia (−1.1)	−1.6
Congo (−1.2)	−3.1
Venezuela (−1.4)	0.2
Honduras (−1.4)	−0.1
Iran (−1.8)	−1.7
Somalia (−1.8)	−2.0
Nicaragua (−4.4)	−3.8
Average	−1.2

Note: Changes in ratings, 1975–1990, are in parentheses.
SOURCE: James Gwartney and Robert Lawson, *Economic Freedom of the World 1975–1995*, Cato Institute, 1996.

Note: Changes in ratings, 1975–1990, are in parentheses.
SOURCE: James Gwartney and Robert Larson, *Economic Freedom of the World 1975–1995*, Cato Institute, 1996.

Along with high investment, Gwartney and Lawson have argued that countries need a high degree of economic freedom. Recall from Module 1 our discussion of the 10 powerful ideas in economics. Many of these ideas are scattered throughout the success stories of developed and developing countries. Specifically, most economists believe that greater growth can be achieved when government is enforcing property rights, supporting freer trade, and ensuring a stable monetary environment. Of course, all economies, developed and developing, have to deal with the issues of scarcity and choice. As individuals and nations seek to make themselves better off, they will choose to specialize and produce those goods and services they produce best or most efficiently. This, coupled with trade and a legal system that protects property rights, has historically led to greater economic growth and higher standards of living.

Changes in economic freedom between 1985 and 1994 resulted in an increase in the per capita GDP of Malaysia and a decrease in Nicaragua's per capita GDP during that same time period.

ONE STEP BEYOND

If you are a full-time student, are you part of the labor force? Are you unemployed? Not sure? Use the problems and questions in your Workbook to solidify your grasp on the three primary macroeconomic goals, and then click on the World Wide Web links on your EconActive CD-ROM to connect to current data and statistics on unemployment in the United States.

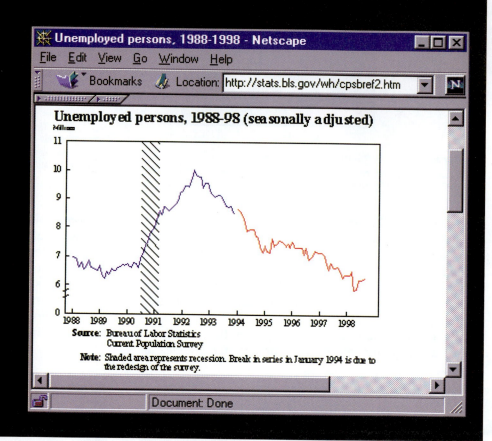

PHOTO CREDITS MODULE 16

Page **392:** © 1998 Don Couch Photography; Page **394:** top, © Richard Hutchings/Photo Edit/PNI; bottom, © Rob Crandall/Stock, Boston/PNI; Page **396:** © Dennis Pritchard. Reprinted by permission; Page **398:** © 1998 Don Couch Photography; Page **399:** © Phil Schofield/AllStock/PNI; Page **400:** left, © J.B. Diederich/Contact Press Images/PNI; right, © Lisa Quinones/Black Star/PNI; Page **401:** © Bob Sacha/Aurora/PNI; Page **402:** © F. Stuart Westmorland/AllStock/PNI; Page **404:** top, © John Coletti/Stock, Boston/PNI; bottom, © 1998 Don Couch Photography; Page **411:** © Dennis Brack/Black Star/PNI; Page **415:** left, © Paul Van Riel/Black Star/PNI; right, © Cindy Karp/Black Star/PNI.

Economic Growth

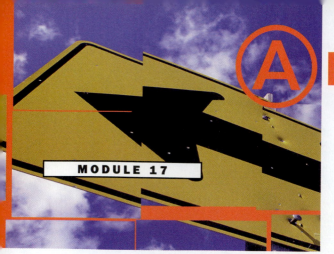

A Economic Growth

MODULE 17

- What is economic growth?
- How dramatic are the differences in economic growth between countries?

SHORT RUN VERSUS LONG RUN

John Maynard Keynes, one of the most influential economic thinkers of all times, once said that "in the long run we are all dead." The reason Keynes said this is that he was primarily concerned with explaining and reducing short-term fluctuations in the level of business activity. He wanted to smooth out the business cycle, largely because of the implications that cyclical fluctuations had for buyers and sellers in terms of unemployment and price instability. No one would deny that Keynes' concerns were important and legitimate.

At the same time, however, Keynes' flippant remark about the long run ignores the fact that human welfare is greatly influenced by long-term changes in a nation's capacity to produce goods and services. Emphasis on short-run economic fluctuations ignores the longer-term dynamic changes that affect output, leisure, real incomes, and life styles.

Putting it differently, it is unlikely that a nation that has cyclical stability (little troughs and peaks) but little long-term growth in output will be better off than a nation with greater instability but more long-term growth. Consider Exhibit 1. Is nation A (with much economic stability but little economic growth) better off than nation B (with much growth but little stability)? While this question probably cannot be definitively answered, many would argue that in the long run, economic growth is a crucial determinant of people's well-being. Therefore, we now turn to study the forces that permit long-term growth in output and production.

What are the determinants of long-run economic change in our ability to produce goods and services? What are some of the consequences of rapid economic change? Why are some nations rich while others are poor? Does growth in output improve our economic welfare? These are a few questions that we wish to explore.

HOW IS ECONOMIC GROWTH DEFINED?

Economic growth is usually measured by the annual percent change in real output of goods and services per capita (real GDP per capita). In Module 3, we introduced

the production possibilities curve. Along the production possibilities curve, the economy is producing at its potential output. How much the economy will produce at its potential output, sometimes called its natural level of output, depends on the quantity and quality of an economy's resources, including labor, capital (like factories, machinery, and tools), and natural resources (land, coal, timber, oil, iron, and so on). In addition, technology can increase

| **EXHIBIT 1** | **GROWTH VERSUS STABILITY** |

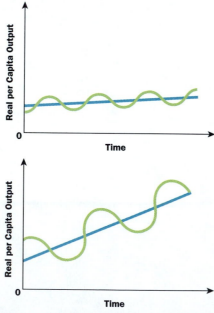

Nation A has little short-term economic instability and thus does not continually face great economic changes, and the uncertainties they cause; at the same time, however, output per capita grows little in the long term. Nation B, by contrast, has great instability, resulting in sharp variations in unemployment rates, and other economic circumstances, but is growing rapidly over long time horizons. We would typically like both growth and stability, so nations often attempt to implement stabilization policies in ways they hope will not retard long-term growth rates.

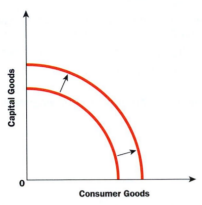

Increases in capital, land, labor, and entrepreneurial activity can expand the production possibilities curve.

the economy's production capabilities. As shown in Exhibit 2, improvements in and greater stocks of land, labor, capital, and entrepreneurial activity will shift out the production possibilities curve. Another way of saying that economic growth has shifted the production possibilities curve out is to say that it has increased potential output.

HOW MUCH VARIATION IN GDP IS THERE IN THE WORLD?

The "richest" or "most-developed" countries today have many times the market output of the "poorest" or "least-developed" countries (see Exhibit 3). Put differently, the most-developed countries produce and market more output in a day than the least-developed countries do in a year. The international differences in income, output, and wealth are indeed striking and have caused a great deal of friction between developed and less-developed countries. The United States and the nations of the European Union have had sizeable increases in real output over the past two centuries, but even in 1800 most of these nations were better off in terms of market output than such contemporary impoverished countries as Ethiopia, India, or Nepal.

EXHIBIT 3 — SELECTED ECONOMIES BY SIZE OF GDP

Country	GDP (billions of dollars)
United States	$7,100
Japan	4,964
Germany	2,252
France	1,451
United Kingdom	1,095
Italy	1,088
China	745
Brazil	580
Canada	574
Russia	332
India	320
Mexico	305
Hong Kong	142
Chile	59
Egypt	46
Cuba	14
Costa Rica	9
Kenya	8
Iceland	7

SOURCE: *World in Figures, 1998 edition* (New York: John Wiley & Sons, Inc., 1998), p. 22.

CONCEPT CHECK

1. Economic growth is usually measured by the annual percent change in real output of goods and services per capita.

2. Improvements in and greater stocks of land, labor, capital, and entrepreneurial activity will shift out the production possibilities curve.

1. Why does the production possibilities curve shift out with economic growth?
2. Even if "in the long run we are all dead," are you glad that earlier generations of Americans worked and invested for economic growth?

3. If long-run consequences were not important, would many students go to college or participate in internship programs without pay? Why or why not?
4. When the Dutch "created" new land with their system of dikes, what did it do to their production possibilities curve? Why?

B The Impact of Economic Growth

- What is the relationship between economic growth and other economic and social factors?
- How is urbanization affected by economic growth?
- How has industrialization been affected by economic growth?
- Why is the saving rate so important in economic growth?

WHAT IS THE IMPACT OF ECONOMIC GROWTH?

Economic growth means more than an increase in the real income (output) of the population. Changes in output are accompanied by a number of other important changes. The most comprehensive investigation of the relationship between economic growth and other economic and social factors was done by the late Nobel laureate Simon Kuznets, although others have made important contributions in Kuznets' tradition.

Before listing some of the observed relationships between economic growth and other variables, it is important to distinguish between cause and effect. Several things that increase in abundance with economic growth may be by-products or effects of growth, while other things may be causes. Wine consumption may be higher in developed than in less-developed countries. Does this mean that wine consumption causes growth by making people more productive, or that wine consumption is a result of that growth (with growth people have higher disposable incomes)? Showing that a statistical relationship exists, then, does not say anything about the direction of causation—that is, correlation does not prove causation.

Generally speaking, the greater the level of per capita real output (which reflects past economic growth),

1. the greater the proportion of the population living in urban areas;
2. the smaller the proportion of the labor force engaged in agricultural pursuits;
3. the greater the amount of specialization, trade, and economic interdependence, and the smaller the amount of self-sufficiency;
4. the greater the average educational attainment of the population and the lower the amount of illiteracy;
5. the lower the birth rate;
6. the lower the death rate;
7. the greater the amount of capital available per capita;
8. the greater the mobility of human and physical resources.

Note that the preceding list reflects relationships that generally, but do not always, hold. For example, New Zealand has a greater proportion of its population engaged in agriculture than many countries with lower per capita incomes. In other words, the correlation between the eight factors above and economic growth is not perfect.

This list does not include many other variables that are related to growth, but perhaps less conclusively. For example, does work effort rise or fall with economic growth? We might think that it falls, because rising incomes in many developed countries have resulted in shorter work weeks and longer vacations. On the other

Urbanization tends to rise with the level of per capita output.

hand, labor force participation by women typically rises with per capita incomes. Moreover, the move from farm to non-farm activities sometimes means an increase in hours worked given the seasonal nature of farm activity.

Some have also claimed that economic growth stimulates political freedom or democracy, but the correlation here is far from conclusive. While there are rich democratic societies and poor authoritarian ones, the opposite also holds. That is, some features of democracy, such as majority voting and special interest groups, may actually be growth retarding. For example, if the majority decides to vote in large land reforms and wealth transfers, this will lead to higher taxes and market distortions that will reduce incentives for work, investment, and ultimately economic growth. A decline in religious influences often accompanies economic growth, but again the correlation is not a perfect one.

HOW IS URBANIZATION AFFECTED BY ECONOMIC GROWTH?

Elaborating on the eight relationships suggested above, the majority of the population of most highly developed nations lives in urban areas. In 1790, when per capita income was only $400 or $500, only 5 percent of the American population lived in urban areas; now, three-fourths of the population is urbanized. Closely related to that, in 1790 some 80 percent of American workers were farmers, while less than 3 percent are today. Why? On the supply side, agricultural productivity has risen dramatically, meaning that a given farmer today is producing far more than his counterpart of two centuries ago. On the demand side, incomes have risen, but the population has chosen to spend a smaller proportion of its income on food. That is, as incomes rise, people increase their consumption of luxury goods (often manufactured in cities) relatively faster than their consumption of essential items like food.

HOW HAS INDUSTRIALIZATION BEEN AFFECTED BY ECONOMIC GROWTH?

The corollary to the decline in the relative importance of agriculture has been an increase in the relative importance of non-agricultural pursuits, especially manufacturing but also transportation, construction, and service industries (professional services, education, health care, recreation and tourism, etc.). As an illustration, in 1820 the United States had at least 10 times as many farmers as workers in manufacturing; a century later the number in manufacturing exceeded the number of farmers.

How did New Zealand and Denmark, which are primarily agricultural countries, experience high rates of economic growth?

Could an increase in manufacturing occur without improvement in agricultural productivity?

WHAT IS THE RELATIONSHIP BETWEEN ECONOMIC GROWTH AND LITERACY?

With economic growth, illiteracy falls and formal education grows. This is demonstrated in Exhibit 1, which shows the adult literacy rates and per capita output levels for various nations. The correlation between per capita output and the proportion of the population that is unable to read or write is striking. Improvements in literacy stimulate economic growth by reducing barriers to the flow of information; when information costs are high, out of ignorance many resources flow to or remain in uses that are rather unproductive. Moreover, education imparts skills that are directly useful in raising labor productivity, whether it is mathematics taught to a sales clerk, engineering techniques taught to a college graduate, or just good ideas that facilitate production and design.

Education may also, however, be a consequence of economic growth, because as incomes rise, people's tendency to consume education increases. People increasingly look to education for more than the acquisition of immediately applicable skills. Education becomes a consumption good as well as a means of investing in human capital.

| EXHIBIT 1 | LITERACY AND ECONOMIC DEVELOPMENT |

Country	Output Per Capita	Adult Literacy Rates
United States	$27,500	97%
Japan	21,300	99
Italy	18,700	97
Brazil	6,100	83
India	1,500	52
Haiti	1,000	45
Ethiopia	400	35

NOTE: The literacy rates are based on the ability to read and write at an elementary school level.

SOURCE: *The Wall Street Journal Almanac, 1998.*

HOW ARE BIRTH RATES AFFECTED BY ECONOMIC GROWTH?

The assertion that economic growth results in lower birth and death rates is supported by Exhibit 2. The poorer a nation, the higher the birth rate is likely to be. Thus, Ethiopia has nearly 45 babies born every year for every 1,000 persons, while the United States has one-third that number, 15. Why? To be sure, the answer is complex, and numerous cultural factors are involved (e.g., religious attitudes or traditional extended families). Still, the primary reason that birth rates in richer nations like the United States have fallen dramatically in the past two centuries is economic.

Countries with low incomes tend to be primarily agricultural; in these societies, children fairly quickly reach an age where they can "earn their own keep" (even though their "keep" may be relatively primitive by standards of developed nations). At the age of 8 or 10, a child in a rural area may be contributing more to the output of a farm than his maintenance costs; in a financial sense, then, this child is "profitable." By contrast, children living in developed countries are usually a substantial financial liability to their parents until the age of 18 or even 21 or 22 (or even longer), particularly given the tendency to attend school for longer periods of time. Moreover, in less-developed countries, the children usually care for their parents when they get old; having children is a means of getting the equivalent of social security and a pension. Children, in short, serve both as investment goods and consumer goods in poorer countries, while in more economically advanced nations, children are primarily consumer goods.

Is this one possible answer to economic growth in poorer countries?

EXHIBIT 2 — BIRTHS, DEATHS, AND ECONOMIC GROWTH

Nation	Output Per Capita	Birth Rate*	Death Rate*	Natural Population Increase*
United States	$27,500	15	9	6
Japan	21,300	10	8	2
Italy	18,700	10	10	0
Brazil	6,100	21	9	12
India	1,500	26	10	16
Haiti	1,000	39	16	23
Ethiopia	400	46	18	28

*Per 1,000 inhabitants living at the beginning of the year.
SOURCE: *The Wall Street Journal Almanac*, 1998.

HOW ARE DEATH RATES RELATED TO DIFFERENT LEVELS OF ECONOMIC DEVELOPMENT?

As you can see in Exhibit 2, death rates often fall fairly sharply early in the development process, as per capita output rises from, say, the $100 to $500 level to the $3,000 level. Nations place a high priority on using sufficient quantities of their increased resources to the task of reducing death rates. Health and sanitation get major attention after the elemental needs of nourishment and clothing are attended to in an adequate fashion. Therefore, in the early stages of development, the natural rate of population increase (births minus deaths) actually grows, as death rates fall faster than birth rates. As nations get still more developed (to perhaps $10,000 output per capita), natural population growth begins to fall, because death rates fall more slowly, while birth rates begin to decline dramatically.

SAVINGS RATES, INVESTMENT, CAPITAL STOCK, AND ECONOMIC GROWTH

One of the most important determinants of economic growth is the savings rate. In order to consume more in the future, we must save more now. Generally speaking, higher levels of savings will lead to higher rates of investment and capital formation and, therefore, to greater economic growth. Individuals can either consume or save their income. If individuals choose to consume all of their income, there will be nothing left for savings, which businesses could use for investment purposes to build new plants or replace worn-out or obsolete equipment. With little investment in capital stock, there will be lit-

tle economic growth. Capital can also increase as a result of capital injections from abroad (foreign direct investments), but the role of national saving rates in economic growth is of particular importance.

Exhibit 3 clearly shows that sustained rapid economic growth is associated with high rates of saving and investment around the world. However, investment alone does not guarantee economic growth. Economic growth hinges importantly on the quality and the type of investment as well as on investments in human capital and improvements in technology.

WHY DO RESOURCES BECOME MORE MOBILE WITH ECONOMIC DEVELOPMENT?

Mobility of resources—human and physical capital—tends to speed up somewhat with economic development, partly because movement and search costs decline. As transportation and communications improve in the course of economic growth, people become more aware of economic opportunities and can better afford to respond to them (given the decline in transport costs). Indeed, in the United States the extent of human migration has not increased too much over time, but the responsiveness of migrants to economic opportunities has grown significantly. The United States has received millions of immigrants, has had a massive internal geographic redistribution of the population as

EXHIBIT 3 — SAVING RATES AND GDP GROWTH DURING HIGH-GROWTH PERIODS IN SELECTED ECONOMIES

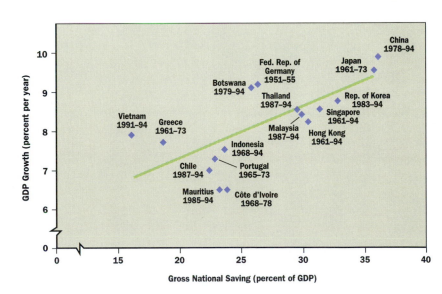

NOTE: Data are annual averages for the periods indicated.
SOURCE: World Bank, *World Development Report, 1996*, Oxford University Press, 1996.

a consequence of the Westward Movement, and has through migration also become a nation of urban dwellers rather than farmers. In a dynamic, growing economy, then, resources are constantly moving to opportunities that are perceived to be better.

WHAT IS THE RELATIONSHIP BETWEEN ECONOMIC GROWTH AND SELF-SUFFICIENCY?

The notion that with economic development people tend to work increasingly for other people rather than being self-employed is closely related to the growth in urbaniza-tion and the accompanying decline in the relative impor-tance of agriculture. Farmers tend to be self-employed; non-farmers usually are not. Even within manufacturing, however, the scale of operations tends to grow with devel-opment, meaning that workers are not only working for others, but they are less likely to even know who their boss really is. In 1860, the average American manufacturing firm employed fewer than 10 workers and only a handful of firms employed more than 1,000. By the 1990s however, almost half of the manufacturing firms employed 500 or more employees.

CONCEPT CHECK

1. Economic growth is usually defined as increases in the real income of the population. Economic devel-opment includes increasing affluence and other fun-damental changes in lifestyles and the social environment.

2. With economic growth tends to come urbanization, industrialization, greater specialization, rising liter-acy, falling birth and death rates, greater capital for-mation, and increased mobility.

3. Higher savings rates generally lead to greater in-vestment and capital formation, which lead to eco-nomic growth.

1. Why does knowing what factors are correlated with economic growth not tell us what causes economic growth?

2. How does increasing the capital stock lead to eco-nomic growth?

3. How do increases in savings affect long-run eco-nomic growth?

4. Why would you expect an inverse relationship be-tween self-sufficiency and real GDP per capita?

5. If a couple was concerned about their retirement, why could that lead to them having more children if they lived in an agricultural society but fewer chil-dren if they were in an urban society?

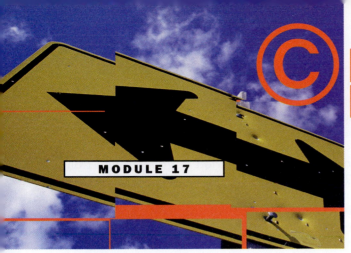

C Determinants of Economic Growth

- What quantifiable factors contribute to economic growth?
- What qualitative factors add to economic growth?
- How can prices of exports affect economic development?

WHAT DO ECONOMISTS BELIEVE LEADS TO ECONOMIC GROWTH?

Many of the great pioneering economists of the eighteenth and nineteenth centuries had theories on the process of economic growth. For example, Adam Smith, in 1776, argued that the wealth of nations derived from the accumulation of capital, which, in turn, resulted from thrift and savings. Capital formation was the key ingredient in Smith's model of economic growth. He also thought that specialization and the division of labor were important, and he criticized the then-accepted ideas of mercantilism, with its emphasis on the need for barriers to trade between people and countries, the accumulation of gold and silver, and various types of governmental regulation.

Other economists emphasized other factors. Karl Marx, for example, argued that all value ultimately derives from labor and that economic growth, therefore, depends on increasing contributions by labor. Some economists, notably the great twentieth century economist Joseph Schumpeter, argued that growth depended to a considerable extent on innovation and technological change, for which the role of managerial or entrepreneurial skills was particularly vital. Schumpeter believed that rewards (temporary monopoly) should go to the innovators, or there would be little incentive to carry out costly and often unsuccessful research projects. A few economists, most notably the Rev. Thomas Robert Malthus, argued that in the long run, per capita economic growth will not occur at all! Still others, including the French philosopher Montesquieu, argued that economic growth and development was a function of climate. Output levels are lower in tropical zones, partly because, or so Montesquieu argued, the work effort is less intense in the heat of the tropics.

WHAT FACTORS ARE BELIEVED TO CONTRIBUTE TO ECONOMIC GROWTH?

In short, many separate explanations of the process of economic growth have been proposed. Which is correct? None of them, by themselves, can completely explain economic growth. However, each of the explanations may be part of a more complicated reality. Economic growth is a complex process involving many important factors, no one of which completely dominates. We can list at least eight factors that nearly everyone would agree have contributed to economic growth in some or all countries:

1. Growth in the quantity and quality of labor resources used;

2. Increase in the use of inputs provided by the land (natural resources);

3. Growth in physical capital inputs (machines, tools, buildings, inventories);

4. Technological advances (new ways of combining given quantities of labor, natural resources, and capital inputs) allowing greater output than previously possible;

5. Economies of scale—efficiencies gained by producing on a larger scale than before (lower input use per unit of output);

6. Greater division of labor (specialization) and trade;

7. Migration of resources from areas of low productivity to areas of high productivity;

8. Government protection of property rights.

HOW CAN CHANGES IN LABOR AFFECT ECONOMIC GROWTH?

We know that labor is needed in all forms of productive activity. But other things being equal, an increase in labor input does not necessarily increase output per capita. If the increase in labor input results from an increase in population, per capita growth might not occur, because the increase in output could be offset by the increase in population. However, if a greater proportion of the population works (that is, the labor force participation rate rises) or if workers put in longer hours, output per capita will increase—assuming that the additional work activity adds something to output. Qualitative improvements in workers (learning new skills, for example) can also enhance output. Indeed, it has become popular to view labor as "human capital" that can be augmented or improved by education and on-the-job training.

WHY ARE NATURAL RESOURCES AN IMPORTANT PART OF ECONOMIC GROWTH?

Greater use of natural resources also can enhance output. The more natural resources (such as more land or better soil) a farmer has to work with, for example, the more he will be able to produce, other things being equal. The abundance of natural resources in the United States has been cited by many observers as a major contributor to U.S. economic growth. Land is obviously an important factor of production in agriculture, and natural resources are also vital as inputs in the manufacture of industrial goods. Resources are, however, not the whole story, as is clear with reference to Japan or especially Hong Kong, both of which have relatively few natural resources.

HOW IMPORTANT IS PHYSICAL CAPITAL TO ECONOMIC GROWTH?

Even in primitive economies, workers usually have some rudimentary tools to further their productive activity. Take the farmer who needs to dig a ditch to improve drainage in his fields. If he used just his bare hands, it might take a lifetime to complete the job. If he used a shovel, he could dig the ditch in hours or days. But with a big earth-moving machine, he could do it in minutes. There is nearly universal agreement that capital formation has played a significant role in the economic development of nations. Perhaps one-third of the economic growth of the United States during its period of great growth from 1840 to 1920 is directly attributable to the growth in per capita capital over time. However, because much technological advance gets "embodied" into new capital, some of the previous estimate may well overstate the critical importance of capital relative to technological advances.

HOW DO TECHNOLOGICAL ADVANCES LEAD TO GROWTH?

Technological advances stem from man's ingenuity and creativity in developing new ways of combining the factors of production to enhance the amount of output from a given quantity of resources. The process of technological advance involves invention and innovation. Innovation is the adoption of the product or process. For example, in the United States, the invention and innovation of the cotton gin, the Bessemer steel-making process, and the railroad were important stimuli to economic growth. New technology, however, must be introduced into productive use by managers or entrepreneurs who must weigh the perceived estimates of benefits of the new technology against estimates of costs.

The wealth of natural resources enhances growth.

The invention and innovation of the elevator was a major contributor to the growth of cities. As a result of the elevator, buildings could be built up as well as out.

Thus, the entrepreneur is an important economic factor in the growth process.

Technological advance permits us to economize on one or more inputs used in the production process. It can permit savings of labor, as occurs when a new machine is invented that does the work of many workers. When this happens, technology is said to be embodied in capital and to be labor saving. Technology, however, can also be land (natural resource) saving or even capital saving. For example, nuclear fission has permitted us to build power plants that economize on the use of coal, a natural resource. The reduction in transportation time that accompanied the invention of the railroad allowed businesses to reduce the capital they needed in the form of inventories. Because goods could be obtained more quickly, businesses could reduce the stock kept on their shelves.

Some scholars believe that the importance of research and development (R & D) is understated. The concept of R & D is broad indeed—it can include new products, management improvements, production innovations, or simply learning-by-doing. However, it is clear that investments in R & D and rewarding innovators with patents have paid big dividends in the past 50 to 60 years. Some would argue that even larger rewards for research and development would spur even more rapid economic growth. In addition, there is an important link between research and development and capital investment. As already noted, when capital depreciates over time, it is replaced with new equipment that embodies the latest technology. Consequently, R & D may work hand-in-hand with investment to improve growth and productivity. In Exhibit 1, we see R & D expenditures as a percentage of GDP in a selected group of industrialized countries.

EXHIBIT 1	RESEARCH AND DEVELOPMENT EXPENDITURES AS A PERCENTAGE OF GDP, 1981–1994	
Country	Non-Defense	Total
United States	2.00	2.49
Japan	2.66	2.69
Germany*	2.26	2.33
France	NA	2.38
United Kingdom	1.88	2.19
Italy	1.14	1.19
Canada	1.53	1.57

*Germany's data for 1981–1990 are for West Germany.

SOURCES: NSF, Division of Science Resources Studies; Organization for Economic Cooperation and Development.

IN THE NEWS

THE NEW ECONOMY?

Microsoft's rise is a testimony to the power of ideas in the new economy. Working with information is very different from working with the steel and glass from which our grandparents built their wealth. Information is easier to produce and harder to control than stuff you can drop on your foot. For a start, computers can copy it and ship it anywhere, almost instantly and almost for free. Production and distribution, the basis of industrial power, can increasingly be taken for granted. Innovation and marketing are all.

So an information economy is more open—it doesn't take a production line to compete, just a good idea. But it's also more competitive. Information is easy not just to duplicate, but to replicate. Successful firms have to keep innovating to keep ahead of copycats nipping at their heels. The average size of companies shrinks. New products and knockoffs alike emerge in months rather than years, and market power is increasingly based on making sense of an overabundance of ideas rather than rationing scarce material goods. Each added connection to a network's pool of knowledge multiplies the value of the whole—one reason for Microsoft's astonishing growth. The result: new rules of competition, new sorts of organization, new challenges for management.

Some zealots talk about a New Economy, capital N, capital E, all too easily caricatured as "there won't be inflation anymore, because of technological change." Alas, as Stanford economist Paul Romer has reminded us, "If a majority of the Fed's board of governors decided to have 20 percent inflation, they could have it in a year, possibly in months." Then there's the idea that recessions are things of the past. This comes up at the end of every expansion.

CONSIDER THIS:
The move to the information economy is shaping the way we think about the future. However, it is difficult to accurately measure the gains computers and telecoms are generating. Almost 75 percent of all computers are used in the service sector, like finance and health. In these areas, productivity gains have been difficult to measure. In addition, many of the benefits come in the form of quality or convenience, like 24-hour-a-day automated bank tellers. Some of these quality-of-life improvements are not accurately measured in macroeconomic data.

SOURCE: John Browning and Spencer Reiss, *Wired Magazine* ONLINE http://www.hotwired.com/special/ene/index.html?word=intro_two

HOW ARE ECONOMIES OF SCALE MOST BENEFICIAL IN ECONOMIC GROWTH?

Sheer size of productive organization might also enhance economic growth. If a firm increases the use of each input by 1.0 percent, but output rises by 1.1 percent, economies of scale are said to exist. This is sometimes referred to as economies of mass production. To the extent that economies of scale exist, they are more likely to be utilized if there are extensive trade and specialization.

HOW IS COMPARATIVE ADVANTAGE USED TO PROMOTE ECONOMIC GROWTH?

Trade can also lead to greater output because of the principle of comparative advantage. Essentially, the principle of comparative advantage suggests that if two nations or individuals with different resource endowments and production capabilities specialize in producing a smaller number of goods and services they are relatively better at and engage in trade, both parties will benefit. Total output will rise. This will be discussed in greater detail in the Module on international trade.

HOW DOES MOBILITY OF RESOURCES ADD TO ECONOMIC GROWTH?

The migration of the factors of production can involve physical movement (geographical mobility) or merely occupational change within a given geographic area. If a man can produce 15 loaves of bread in area A but can increase his output to 25 loaves merely by moving to area B (with its better availability of natural resources needed to make bread), total output in the economy can rise.

HOW DOES THE PROTECTION OF PROPERTY RIGHTS IMPACT ECONOMIC GROWTH?

Economic growth rates tend to be higher in countries where the government enforces property rights. As we discussed in Module 6, property rights give owners the legal right to keep or sell their property—land, labor, or capital. Without property rights, life would be a huge "free-for-all," where people could take whatever they wanted; in this scenario, protection for property, such as alarm systems and private security services, would have to be purchased.

In most developed countries, property rights are effectively protected by the government. However, in developing countries, this is not usually the case. And if the government is not enforcing these rights, the private sector must respond in costly ways that stifle economic growth. For example, an unreliable judiciary system means that entrepreneurs are more often forced to rely on informal agreements that are difficult to enforce. As a result, they may have to pay bribes to get things done, and even then, they may not get the promised services. Individuals will have to buy private security or pay "organized crime" for protection against crime and corruption. In addition, landowners and business owners might be fearful of coups or takeovers from a new government, which might confiscate their property all together. In short, if government is not adequately protecting property rights, the incentive to invest will be hindered, and political instability, corruption, and lower rates of economic growth will be likely.

CONCEPT CHECK

1. The factors that contribute to economic growth are increased quantity of labor, natural resources, physical capital, technological advances, economies of scale, comparative advantage, mobility of resources, and government protection of property rights.

1. Why is no single factor capable of completely explaining economic growth patterns?
2. Why might countries with relatively scarce labor be leaders in labor-saving innovations? In what area would countries with relatively scarce land likely be innovative leaders?
3. Why could an increase in the price of oil increase real GDP growth in oil-exporting countries like Saudi Arabia and Mexico, while decreasing growth in oil-importing countries like the United States and Japan?

4. How is Hong Kong a dramatic example of why abundant natural resources are not necessary to rapid economic growth?
5. Why is the effective use of land, labor, capital, and entrepreneurial activities dependent on the protection of property rights?

D Population Growth and Economic Growth

■ When is population growth beneficial to per capita economic growth?

■ When is population growth detrimental to per capita economic growth?

HOW DOES POPULATION GROWTH AFFECT ECONOMIC GROWTH?

The world's population at the beginning of the English Industrial Revolution around 1750 was perhaps 700 million. It took 150 years, to 1900, for that population to slightly more than double to 1.6 billion. In just 64 years (1964), it had doubled again, to 3.2 billion. By another 40 years, 2004, it is very possible that the population will have doubled again, to 6.4 billion (the world population was 5.8 billion in 1997). We have had economic development amidst all this growth in population, but what role did population play in the economic growth?

The impact of population growth on per capita economic growth is far from obvious. If population were to expand faster than output, per capita output would fall; population growth would be growth-inhibiting. With a greater population, however, comes a greater labor force. Also, economies of large-scale production may exist in some forms of production, so larger markets associated with greater populations lead to more efficient-sized production units. Certainly very rapid population growth—over 3 percent a year—did not seem to impede American economic growth in the mid-nineteenth century. America's economic growth until at least World War I was accompanied by population growth that was among the highest in the world for the time.

There is a general feeling, however, that in many of the less-developed countries today, rapid population growth threatens the possibility of attaining sustained economic

What impact does a large population have on economic growth?

growth. These countries are predominantly agricultural with very modest natural resources, especially land. The land–labor ratio is very low. Why is population growth a threat in these countries? One answer was provided nearly two centuries ago by the English economist, the Rev. Thomas Malthus.

WHAT IS THE MALTHUSIAN PREDICTION?

Malthus formulated a theoretical model that predicted that per capita economic growth would eventually become negative and that wages would ultimately reach an equilibrium at a subsistence level, or just large enough to provide enough income to stay alive. Malthus assumed an agricultural society where goods were produced by two inputs, land and labor. He further assumed that the supply of land was fixed in quantity. Further, he assumed that the sexual desires of humans would work to increase population.

WHAT IS THE LAW OF DIMINISHING RETURNS?

As population increased, the number of workers would increase. Thus with greater labor inputs available, output would also go up. At some point, however, output would increase by diminishing amounts because of the law of diminishing returns, which states that if you add variable amounts of one input (in this case, labor) to fixed quantities of another input (in this case, land), output would rise but by diminishing amounts (as the land–labor ratio falls, there is less land per worker).

HOW CAN AN ECONOMY AVOID MALTHUS' PREDICTION?

Fortunately, Malthus's theory proved spectacularly wrong for much of the world. While the law of diminishing returns is a valid concept, Malthus's other assumptions were unrealistic. Agricultural land is not completely fixed in quantity or quality. Irrigation, fertilizer, and conservation techniques have effectively increased arable land. More important, Malthus implicitly assumed there would be no technological advance, and ignored the real possibility that improved technology, often embodied in capital, could overcome the impact of the law of diminishing returns. Moreover, the Malthusian assumption that sexual desire would necessarily lead to population increase is not even accurate. True, sexual desire may always be with us, but births can be reduced by birth-control techniques.

ARE THERE SOME COUNTRIES THAT FIT MALTHUS' PREDICTION TODAY?

Unfortunately, the Malthusian assumptions are not too widely at variance from reality for several less-developed countries today. Some nations of the world are having substantial population increases, with a virtually fixed supply of land and little technological advance. Population growth has a negative impact on per capita output in this case, since the added output derived from having more workers on the land is very small. In short, for some places in the modern world, the Malthusian model may be relevant.

In this situation, it is scarcely surprising that population control is considered to be of critical importance, not only in India but in many other less-developed countries. The implementation of birth control has been far from routine, however. While greater population, other things equal, may lower per capita output, from the perspective of an individual family, the production of children may mean greater security in old age, more labor for the farm now, and so forth. Governments have sometimes absorbed most or all of the cost of birth control, and even given financial incentives to persons opting for surgical procedures designed to control births. Still, in most countries, efforts to date have been only modestly successful. Population control remains a key factor in the growth patterns in countries with high populations in relation to natural resources and capital equipment.

CONCEPT CHECK

1. Population growth may increase per capita output in resource-rich countries like the United States, Australia, and Saudi Arabia, because they have more resources for each laborer to produce with. They are more likely to be able to exploit economies of large-scale production, and they are more likely to have rapidly expanding technology.

2. In some countries, the Malthusian dilemma posed by population growth and diminishing returns is a problem, and they may suffer as a result of population growth.

1. What happens to per capita real output if population grows faster than output? If population grows more slowly than output?
2. How can economies of large-scale production allow per capita output to rise as population rises?

3. How did Malthus' prediction on population growth follow from the law of diminishing returns?
4. Why is population control a particularly important issue in countries with very low levels of per capita income?

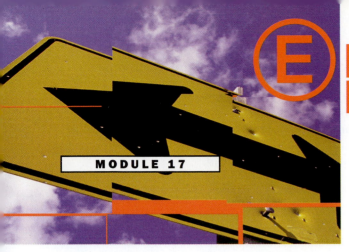

E Desirability of Economic Growth

■ Why are rising expectations detrimental to the desirability of economic growth?

■ How do environmental concerns affect the desirability of economic growth?

IS ECONOMIC GROWTH DESIRABLE?

Our discussions thus far have certainly implied that economic growth is a good thing, something that nations should seek to enhance or maximize. Actually, that contention is debatable. At least two lines of arguments can be used to support the position that economic growth is not necessarily good and indeed may even be harmful.

WHAT ARGUMENTS SUGGEST THAT ECONOMIC GROWTH IS NOT DESIRABLE?

The first argument, which we developed earlier in the text, is that economic growth brings with it increased expectations. Indeed, sometimes it has been said that there is a revolution of rising expectations in newly developing countries. Happiness, or utility, may depend not only on the level of real consumption of goods and services but also on expectations of what you think you want or what you expect to have.

Second, many environmentalists have argued that economic growth is potentially life threatening in the long run, because with economic growth comes not only more goods but also more bads in the form of pollution. Per capita pollution would be expected to rise with per capita output, perhaps to the point where life is seriously threatened. This "pessimistic" view of the world might be a modern equivalent of Malthus's. Economic growth also involves the greater use of physical inputs, including natural resources. The stock of natural resources, however, is relatively fixed. Economic growth may increase the rate of depletion of these resources, again potentially sentencing future generations to death or a life of misery at the subsistence level.

WHAT DO THE CRITICS SAY ABOUT THESE ARGUMENTS?

These arguments are susceptible to criticism. Because utility is difficult to measure, the validity of the first argument can be questioned, although there is at least some crude evidence to support it.[1] At the same time, however, if a nation were unilaterally to decide to endorse policies leading to little or no economic growth, the country would soon be surpassed in income by other nations. In this day of advanced communications, the nation with zero growth might well develop new frustrations as it sees people in other countries with new gadgets, more services, better health, more leisure, and all of the other by-products of economic growth. Moreover, economic growth is important to national security. A nation that declines relative to other nations in its productive capacity is also falling behind in its potential military strength, because output can be converted to military rather than civilian purposes fairly readily (e.g., we can turn auto assembly lines into tank assembly lines, and can make bombers instead of commercial jet aircraft).

The environmental-resource arguments are also debatable. It is not clear, for example, that pollution necessarily rises as output increases. Some of the increasing output can and is used for pollution abatement; air pollution levels in the United States today are far below levels prevailing 40 years ago for nearly all types of pollution. For example, Environmental Protection Agency data suggests that the volume of particulate matter in the air has declined well over 50 percent since 1940. During the same period, however, there has been considerable economic growth. Production techniques can be altered to reduce the level of environmental damage from air, water, noise, or even visual pollution.

The natural resource limitation considered so crucial by some "doomsday" social scientists sounds very similar to the assumption that Malthus made, namely that land is fixed in quantity. In fact, technological advances, changes in relative prices, and new discoveries have led us to

---

[1] Richard A. Easterlin, "Does Economic Growth Improve the Human Lot? Some Empirical Evidence," in Paul David and Melvin Reder, *Nations and Households in Economic Growth* (New York: Academic Press, 1974).

harness new resources, as well as to find more of traditional resources. Thus, nuclear power comes from minerals that had no energy uses just 50 years ago. Solar energy depends upon the sun, a resource that went virtually untapped for millennia. Hence, while it is true that the process of economic growth tends to lead to increased resource use, it does not necessarily follow that a depletion of resources poses any immediate or even longer-term threat. For example, the reserves-to-consumption ratio for oil and other resources has increased despite growth in consumption. The pessimistic arguments may have some validity, but they largely proceed from the same unrealistic assumptions that made Malthus's predictions so spectacularly untrue in the Western world.

CONCEPT CHECK

1. Happiness, or utility, may not depend solely on the amount of real income but also on the increased expectations resulting from economic growth.

2. The desirability of economic growth may be diminished because of the fact that usually with economic growth come economic "bads," such as pollution.

---

1. Is it possible that utility, or happiness, could fall as income rises? Why or why not?
2. Why does economic growth not necessarily lead to environmental damage? How can it lead to environmental improvements?

3. Economic growth leads to increased resource use. Does this mean that economic growth will necessarily lead to a depletion of natural resources in the long run? Why or why not?

Application: Economic Growth and Relative Happiness

Can expectations affect our welfare? Do our expectations change over time?

THE RELATIVE DEPRIVATION PRINCIPLE: HAPPINESS IS RELATIVE TO OTHERS' ATTAINMENTS

Happiness is relative not only to our past experience, but also to our comparisons with others. We are always comparing ourselves to others. And whether we feel good or bad depends on who those others are. . . .

An example: To explain the frustration expressed by U.S. Air Corps soldiers during World War II, researchers formulated the concept of relative deprivation—the sense that we are worse off than others with whom we compare ourselves. Despite a relatively rapid promotion rate for the group, many soldiers were frustrated about their own promotion rates (Merton & Kitt, 1950). Apparently, seeing so many others being promoted inflated the soldiers' expectations. And when expectations soar above attainments, the result is frustration. When the Oakland Athletics signed outfielder José Canseco to a $4.7 million annual salary, his fellow outfielder Rickey Henderson became openly dissatisfied with his $3 million salary and refused to show up on time for spring training (King, 1991).

Such comparisons help us understand why the middle- and upper-income people in a given country tend to be slightly more satisfied with life than the relatively poor, with whom the better-off can compare themselves (Diener, 1984). Nevertheless, once a person reaches a moderate income level, further increases do little to increase happiness. Why? Because as people climb the ladder of success they mostly compare themselves with those who are at or above their current level (Gruder, 1977; Suls & Tesch, 1978). For Rickey Henderson, José Canseco was the standard of comparison. For many American physicians earning an average $170,000, the higher salaries of professional athletes and corporate CEOs become a point of comparison (Associated Press,

1993). As Bertrand Russell (1930, pp. 68–69) observed, "Napoleon envied Caesar, Caesar envied Alexander, and Alexander, I daresay, envied Hercules, who never existed. You cannot, therefore, get away from envy by means of success alone, for there will always be in history or legend some person even more successful than you are."

By "counting our blessings" when we compare ourselves with those less fortunate, we can, however, increase our satisfaction. As comparing ourselves with those better off creates envy, so comparing ourselves with those less well off boosts contentment. Marshall Dermer and his colleagues (1979) demonstrated this by asking University of Wisconsin-Milwaukee women to study others' deprivation and suffering. After viewing vivid depictions of how grim life was in Milwaukee in 1900, or after imagining and then writing about various personal tragedies, such as being burned and disfigured, the women expressed greater satisfaction with their own lives. Similarly, when mildly depressed people read about someone who is even more depressed, they feel somewhat better (Gibbons, 1986).

The effect of comparison with others helps us understand why students of a given level of academic ability tend to have a higher academic self-concept if they attend a school where most other students are not exceptionally able (Marsh & Parker, 1984). If you were near the top of your class in high school, you might feel inferior upon entering a college where everyone was near the top of their class.

SOURCE: David G. Myers, *Exploring Psychology*, Third Edition (Worth Publishers, 1996), pp. 346–350.

"I've got the bowl, the bone, the big yard. I know I should be happy."

As we see in this article, material welfare probably depends not only on the amount people consume in a given period but also on the relationship of their consumption to their expectations as to what they want to consume. If my neighbor buys a new car, puts in a swimming pool, or hires a landscaper, I may have an increased desire to have the same consumer goods and services. "Keeping up with the Joneses" is a reality that confronts many of us. Karl Marx put it well when he said

> A house may be large or small; as long as the surrounding houses are equally small it satisfies all social demand for a dwelling. But if a palace rises besides the little house, the little house shrinks into a hut.[1]

With rising incomes over time, our expectations also rise. That is, a rise in real per capita income or output may not mean an increase in happiness if expected consumption rises as fast or faster than actual consumption expenditures. As incomes rise, a given amount of income may mean less than before. For example, a person in 1949 may have derived more happiness than the same person in 1999 with the same real income per capita. And this unhappiness may be a result of rising expectations. For example, in 1949, our mythical person may have had a new small black-and-white TV, one radio, a small record player, and one car. Today, the same person would expect to have two color TVs, two or three radios, a stereo with both a CD player and a tape deck, a VCR, and two automobiles.

Studies have shown that, at any moment of time, the higher the income of a person, the happier he or she tends to be—that is, there is a movement along the utility curve. On the other hand, similar studies show that *over time*, the level of happiness has not tended to increase in spite of rising incomes—a downward shift in the total utility curve. This phenomenon is graphically illustrated in Exhibit 1, which looks at the relationship between utility, or happiness, and income, or GDP per capita. Looking at the hypothetical curve for 1949, note that the person's utility rose as income rose. But over time, as a result of higher expectations and "bads" like air and water pollution, crime, and traffic congestion, the utility curve might shift down. The result could hypothetically be a situation in which higher per capita income might lead to lower utility.

| EXHIBIT 1 | THE HYPOTHETICAL UTILITY-INCOME RELATIONSHIP |

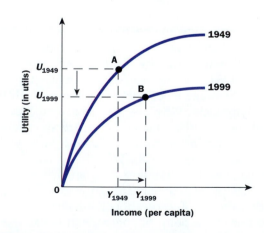

[1] Karl Marx, as quoted in S. M. Lipset, *Political Man: The Social Bases of Politics* (Garden City, NY: Doubleday, 1960), p. 63.

ONE STEP BEYOND

Some people might disagree about the benefits of economic growth, but most would likely agree that economic growth is a complex topic. To test your mastery of the basic ideas related to economic growth, turn to the exercises and problems in your Workbook. Then, follow the links found on your EconActive CD-ROM to get a picture of some of the current research and debates about economic growth.

PHOTO CREDITS MODULE 17

Page **422:** © Larry Brownstein/Rainbow/PNI; Page **423:** left, © Christopher Arnesen/AllStock/PNI; right, © Michael Collier/Stock, Boston/PNI; Page **424:** © Robert Caputo/ Aurora/PNI; Page **428:** left, © George Lepp/Corbis Images; right, © 1998 Don Couch Photography; Page **431:** © Art Wolfe/AllStock/PNI; Page **436:** Drawing by M. Twohy; copyright 1992 *The New Yorker* Magazine, Inc.

Measuring Economic Performance

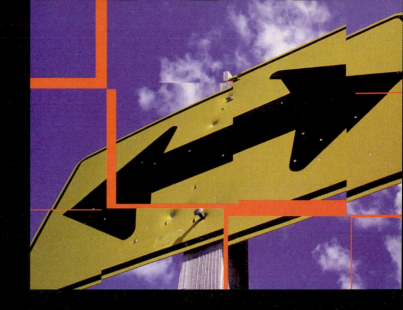

A. The Circular Flow Model
Why does total spending equal total income?

B. National Income Accounting: Measuring Economic Performance
How can we measure our nation's economic performance?

C. The Expenditure Approach to Measuring GDP
What are the four categories of purchases in the expenditure approach?

D. The Income Approach to Measuring GDP
How do we compute GDP using the income approach?

E. Problems in Calculating an Accurate GDP
What factors make it difficult to accurately calculate GDP?

F. Problems with GDP as a Measure of Economic Welfare
How does GDP fail to accurately measure economic welfare?

G. Application: The Declining *Real* Cost of Living
What are the shortcomings of using money prices to calculate the cost of living?

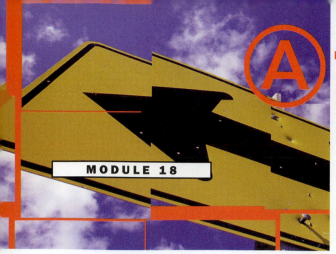

A The Circular Flow Model

■ What are product and factor markets?
■ What is the circular flow model?

WHAT WERE EARLY ECONOMIES LIKE?

In a very primitive society, where there is virtually no trade and persons are almost totally self-sufficient, the analysis of the entire economy—macroeconomics—is very simple. Every household is, in effect, a self-contained economy. The concept of the "domestic" product of an economy is not terribly meaningful because economic activity occurs on a localized basis with no trade.

Human interdependence, of course, does exist, because people have found it mutually beneficial to engage in trade. The institution of money has arisen to meet the needs of trade, as have modern corporate business enterprises and banks and other financial institutions. A whole framework of economic institutions has grown up both in response to the growth in economic interrelationships, and to facilitate their further growth.

WHAT ARE PRODUCT MARKETS?

An **exchange economy,** which uses money as the basis for settling debts incurred in the process of trade, results in a constant flow of goods and services and monetary payments between the various economic institutions in society. The output of goods and services produced by some institutions in society provides income for others in society, namely the persons who provide the labor, capital, and raw material inputs used to produce those goods. Likewise, the producers of goods—business enterprises—receive income payments when they sell the goods they produce to households. Payments flow to businesses at the same time as goods flow to households. These transactions are carried out in what economists call **product markets.**

WHAT ARE FACTOR MARKETS?

Where do the households get the funds to pay businesses for the goods they buy? They get the money from the businesses themselves, as payment for the labor, land, capital,

and entrepreneurship needed to produce goods and services. These payments take the form of wages (salaries), rent, interest payments, and profits. These transactions between businesses and households are carried out in what economists call **factor (or input) markets.**

WHAT IS THE CIRCULAR FLOW MODEL?

There is a continuous flow of goods and payments between the producers of goods and services, which we call businesses, and individuals, who typically live in family units called households. The nature and direction of these

The macroeconomy is relatively simple in an economy with self-sufficiency and little trade.

exchanges are presented in the **circular flow model of income and output.** This model is illustrated in Exhibit 1.

Income and output are flow concepts; that is, they are measured over a span of time. The flow of incomes from businesses to households and vice versa will continue unabated at a stable, or equilibrium, magnitude if income received is utilized or spent at the same rate, and if there is no siphoning of funds (resources) out of the flow. For example, a teacher's supply of services brings in income that can be used to buy automobiles, vacations, food, and other goods. In sum, the total spending is the total amount that households spend and that equals the total amount that buyers of factors had to pay. In other words, total spending equals total income.

EXHIBIT 1 THE CIRCULAR FLOW MODEL OF INCOME AND OUTPUT

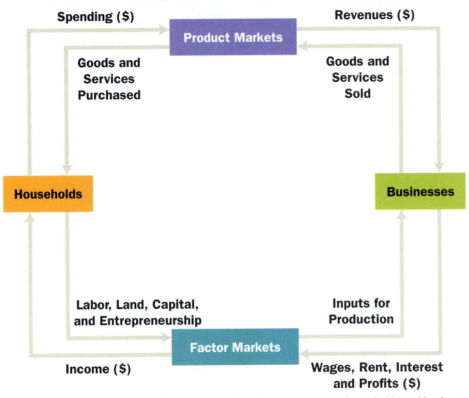

The two major institutional economic arrangements in the private sector—households and business enterprises—continuously trade goods and services and payments between each other. To a considerable extent, households receive income from firms in exchange for working and providing other inputs. Households then recycle that income to the firms in exchange for goods and services.

CONCEPT CHECK

1. Wages, rent, interest, and profits are the payments for the land, labor, capital, and entrepreneurship needed to produce goods and services. These transactions are carried out in factor, or input, markets.

2. The circular flow model illustrates the flow of goods, services, and payments among businesses and households.

1. Why does the circular flow of money move in the opposite direction from the flow of goods and services?

2. Why would an increase in your income in factor markets likely increase your demand in product markets?

3. Why would a decrease in demand for what you produce in product markets decrease your income in factor markets?

B National Income Accounting: Measuring Economic Performance

- What reasons are there for measuring our economy's performance?
- What is gross domestic product?
- What are the different methods of measuring GDP?

WHY DO WE MEASURE OUR ECONOMY'S PERFORMANCE?

There is a great desire to measure the success, or performance, of our economy. Are we getting "bigger" (and hopefully better) or "smaller" (and worse) over time? Aside from reasons of intellectual curiosity, the need to evaluate the magnitude of our economic performance is important to macroeconomic policymakers, who want to know how well the economy is performing so that they can set goals and develop policy recommendations.

Measurement of the economy's performance is also important to private business because inaccurate measurement can lead to bad decision making. Traders in stocks and bonds are continually checking economic statistics—buying and selling in response to the latest economic data.

WHAT IS NATIONAL INCOME ACCOUNTING?

To fulfill the desire for a reliable method of measuring economic performance, **national income accounting** was

We have always had a preoccupation with measurement, whether it is a fastball or the growth in the economy.

born early in the twentieth century. The establishment of a uniform means of accounting for economic performance was such an important accomplishment that one of the first Nobel Prizes in economics was given to the late Simon Kuznets, a pioneer of national income accounting in the United States.

Several measures of aggregate national income and output have been developed, the most important of which is gross domestic product (GDP). We will examine GDP and other indicators of national economic performance in detail later in this Module.

WHAT IS GROSS DOMESTIC PRODUCT?

The measure of aggregate economic performance that gets the most attention in the popular media is **gross domestic product (GDP)**, which is defined as the value of all final goods and services produced within a country during a given period of time. By convention, that period of time is almost always one year. But let's examine the rest of this definition. What is meant by "final good or service" and "value"?

HOW DO WE MEASURE THE VALUE OF GOODS AND SERVICES?

How is the value of a good or service determined? Value is determined by the market prices at which goods and services sell. Underlying the calculations, then, are the various equilibrium prices and quantities for the multitude of goods and services produced.

WHAT IS A FINAL GOOD OR SERVICE?

The word "final" means that the good is ready for its designated ultimate use. Many goods and services that are produced are intermediate goods or services, goods that are used in the production of other goods. For example, suppose United States Steel Corporation produces some steel that it sells to General Motors Corporation for use in making an automobile. If we counted the value of steel used in making the car as well as the full value of the finished auto in the GDP, we would be engaging in **double counting**—adding the value of the steel in twice, first in its raw form and second in its final form, the automobile. Another example is the paper used in this book. The paper is an intermediate good; it is the book, the final good, that is included in the GDP.

MEASURING GROSS DOMESTIC PRODUCT

There are two primary ways of calculating economic output: the expenditure approach and the income approach. Although these methods differ, their result, GDP, is the same, apart from minor "statistical discrepancies." In the following two Concepts, we will examine each of these approaches in turn.

T U N E   U P

DEFINING GDP

Q: Jay Loppy just bought a 10-year-old used car. Will Jay's car be included in this year's GDP figures?

A: No. Only goods and services produced in the current period are included in this year's GDP. Jay's car was included in GDP 10 years ago when it was produced. That is, even though they are still being used this year, houses, cars, CD players, and so forth produced last year are only included in last year's GDP figures. If, however, Jay bought the car from a used car dealer, the value of the service provided would be counted, but that would be quite small relative to the price of the car.

If we count the steel that goes into a car as well as the finished car, are we guilty of double counting?

CONCEPT CHECK

1. We measure our economy's status in order to see how its performance has changed over time. These economic measurements are important to government officials, private businesses, and investors.
2. National income accounting, pioneered by Simon Kuznets, is a uniform means of measuring national economic performance.
3. Gross domestic product (GDP) is the value of all final goods and services produced within a country during a given time period.
4. Two different ways to measure GDP are the expenditure approach and the income approach.

1. Why does GDP measure only *final* goods and services produced, rather than all goods and services produced?
2. Why aren't all of the expenditures on used goods in an economy included in the current GDP?
3. Why do GDP statistics include real estate agents' commissions from selling existing homes and used car dealers' profits from selling used cars but not the value of existing homes and used cars when they are sold?
4. Why are sales of previously existing inventories of hula hoops not included in the current year's GDP?

© The Expenditure Approach to Measuring GDP

- What are the four categories of purchases included in the expenditure approach?
- What are durable and nondurable goods?
- What are fixed investments?
- What types of government purchases are included in the expenditure approach?
- How are net exports calculated?

WHAT IS THE EXPENDITURE APPROACH TO MEASURING GDP?

One approach to measuring GDP is the **expenditure approach.** With this method, GDP is calculated by adding up the expenditures of market participants on final goods and services over a period of time. For convenience and for analytical purposes, economists usually categorize spending into four categories: consumption, identified symbolically by the letter C; investment, I; government spending, G; and net exports (which equals exports (X) minus imports (M), or $X - M$). Following the expenditure method, then

$$GDP = C + I + G + (X - M)$$

WHAT IS CONSUMPTION (C)?

Consumption refers to the purchase of consumer goods and services by households. For most of us, a large percentage of our income in a given year goes for consumer goods and services. The consumption category does not include purchases by business or government. As Exhibit 1 indicates, in 1997, consumption expenditures totaled well over $5 trillion ($5,486 billion). This figure was 68 percent of GDP. In that respect, the 1997 data were fairly typical. In every year since 1929, when GDP accounts began to be calculated annually, consumption has been more than half of total expenditures on goods and services (even during World War II).

Consumption spending, in turn, is usually broken down into three subcategories, nondurable goods, durable consumer goods, and services.

What Are Nondurable and Durable Goods?

Nondurable goods include tangible consumer items that are typically consumed or used up in a relatively short period of time. Food and clothing are examples, as are such quickly consumable items as drugs, toys, magazines, soap, razor blades, light bulbs, and so on. Nearly everything purchased in a supermarket or drug store is a nondurable good.

Durable goods include longer-lived consumer goods, the most important single category of which is automobiles and other consumer vehicles. Appliances, stereos, and furniture are also included in the durable goods category. On occasion, it is difficult to decide whether a good is durable or nondurable, and the definitions are, therefore, somewhat arbitrary.

The distinction between durables and nondurables is important because consumer buying behavior is somewhat different for each of these categories of goods. In boom periods, when GDP is rising rapidly, expenditures on durables often increase dramatically, while in years of stagnant or falling GDP, sales of durable goods often plummet. By contrast, sales of nondurables like food tend to be more stable over time because purchases of such goods are more difficult to shift from one time period to another. You can "make do" with your car for another year, but not your lettuce.

What Are Services?

Services are intangible items of value, as opposed to physical goods. Education, health care, domestic housekeeping, professional football, legal help, automobile repair, haircuts, airplane transportation—all of these are

EXHIBIT 1	U.S. GDP BY TYPE OF SPENDING, 1997

Category	Amount (billions of current dollars)	Percent of GDP
Gross domestic product	$8,080	
Consumption (*C*)	5,486	68%
Investment (*I*)	1,243	15
Government purchases (*G*)	1,453	18
Net exports of goods and services (*X – M*)	–101.1	–1.2

SOURCE: U.S. Bureau of Economic Analysis, *Survey of Current Business*, May 1998.

services. In recent years, service expenditures have been growing faster than spending on goods; the share of total consumption going for services increased from 35 percent in 1950 to almost 60 percent by 1997. As incomes have risen, Americans have devoted an increasing amount of their resources to services, and accordingly, service industries such as health, education, and tourism have grown dramatically.

WHAT IS INVESTMENT (*I*)?

Investment, as used by economists, refers to the creation of capital goods—inputs like machines and tools whose purpose is to produce other goods. This definition of investment deviates from the popular use of that term. It is common for someone to say that he invested in a stock, meaning that he has traded money for a piece of paper, called a stock certificate, that says he owns a share in some company. That transaction was not an investment as defined by economists (i.e., an increase in capital goods), even though that action could provide resources for the business enterprise selling the stock (assuming they were newly issued shares) to finance or pay for new capital goods, which would be counted as investment by economists.

There are two categories of investment purchases measured in the expenditures approach: fixed investment and inventory investment.

What Are Fixed Investments?

Fixed investments include all spending on capital goods—sometimes called **producer goods**—such as machinery, tools, and factory buildings. All of these goods increase our future production capabilities. Residential construction is also included as an investment expenditure in GDP calculations. The construction of a house allows for a valuable consumer service—shelter—to be provided, and is thus considered to be an investment. Residential construction is the only part of investment that is directly tied to household expenditure decisions.

Durable goods include longer-lasting goods, such as major household appliances.

Why are inventories considered a form of investment?

What Is Inventory Investment?

Inventory investment includes all purchases by businesses that add to their inventories—stocks of goods kept on hand by businesses to meet customer demands. Every business needs inventory and, other things equal, the greater the inventory, the greater the amount of goods and services that can be sold to a consumer in the future. Thus, inventories are considered a form of investment. Consider a grocery store. If the store expands and increases the quantity and variety of goods on its shelves, future sales can rise. An increase in inventories, then, is presumed to increase the firm's future sales, and this is why we say it is an investment.

How Stable Are Investment Expenditures?

In recent years, investment expenditures have generally been around 15 percent of gross domestic product. Investment spending is the most volatile category of GDP, however, and tends to fluctuate considerably with changing business conditions. When the economy is booming, investment purchases tend to increase dramatically. In downturns, the reverse happens. In the first year of the Great Depression, investment purchases declined by 37 percent. U.S. expenditures on capital goods have been a smaller proportion of GDP in most recent years than in many other developed nations, a fact that worries some people who are concerned about U.S. GDP growth compared to other countries, because investment in capital goods is directly tied to a nation's future production capabilities.

WHAT PART OF GOVERNMENT SPENDING IS INCLUDED IN GDP (*G*)?

The part of government spending that is included in GDP is expenditures on goods and services. For example, the government must pay the salaries of its employees, and it must also make payments to the private firms with which it contracts to provide various goods and services, such as highway construction companies and weapons manufacturers. All of these payments would be included in GDP. However, transfer payments are not included in government purchases, because that spending does not go to purchase newly produced goods or services, but is merely a transfer of income among that country's citizens (which is why such expenditures are called transfer payments). The government purchase proportion of GDP has grown rapidly over the last 30 years.

HOW DO EXPORTS AFFECT GDP (*X* – *M*)?

Some of the goods and services that are produced in the United States are exported for use in other countries. The fact that these goods and services were made in the United States means that they should be included in a measure of U.S. production. Thus, we include the value of exports when calculating GDP. At the same time, however, some of our expenditures in other categories (consumption and investment in particular) were for foreign-produced goods and services. These imports must be excluded from GDP in order to obtain an accurate measure of American production. Thus, GDP calculations measure net exports, which equals total exports (*X*) minus total imports (*M*). Net exports are a small proportion of GDP and are often negative for the United States.

Highway construction is part of government spending.

1. The expenditure approach to measuring GDP involves adding up the purchases of final goods and services by market participants.
2. Four categories of spending are used in the GDP calculation: consumption (C), investment (I), government spending (G), and net exports (X − M).
3. Consumption spending includes spending on nondurable consumer goods, tangible items that are usually consumed in a short period of time; durable consumer goods, longer-lived consumer goods; and services, intangible items of value that do not involve physical production.
4. Fixed investment includes all spending on capital goods, such as machinery, tools, and buildings. Inventory investment includes the net expenditures by businesses to increase their inventories.
5. The part of government spending that is included in GDP includes purchases of goods and services only. Transfer payments are not included in these calculations, because that spending is not a payment for a newly produced good or service.
6. Net exports are calculated by subtracting total imports from total exports.

---

1. What would happen to GDP if consumption purchases (C) and net exports (X − M) both rose, holding other things equal?
2. Why do you think economic forecasters focus so much on consumption purchases and their determinants?
3. Why are purchases of durable goods more unstable than purchases of nondurable goods?
4. Why does the investment component of GDP include purchases of new capital goods but not purchases of corporate stock?
5. If Mary received a welfare check this year, would that transfer payment be included in this year's GDP? Why or why not?
6. Could inventory investment or net exports ever be negative?

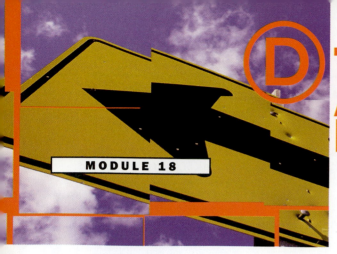

D The Income Approach to Measuring GDP

- How is national income calculated?
- What are factor payments?
- What does personal income measure?

WHAT IS THE INCOME APPROACH TO MEASURING GDP?

In the last Concept, we outlined the expenditure approach to GDP calculation. There is, however, also an alternative method, which is called the **income approach.** This approach involves summing the incomes received by producers of goods and services.

When someone makes an expenditure for a good or service, that spending creates income for someone else. For example, if you buy $10 in groceries at the local supermarket, your $10 in spending creates $10 in income for the grocery store owner. The owner, then, must buy more goods to stock her shelves as a consequence of your consumer purchases; in addition, she must pay her employees, her electricity bill, and so on. Consequently, much of the $10 spent by you will eventually end up in the hands of someone other than the grocer. The basic point, however, is that someone (one person or many) receives the $10 you spent, and that receipt of funds is called income. Therefore, by adding up all of the incomes received by producers of goods and services, we can also calculate the gross domestic product, because output creates income of equal value.

WHAT ARE FACTOR PAYMENTS?

As we stated earlier in this Module in our discussion of the circular flow model, incomes received by persons providing goods and services are actually payments to the owners of productive resources. These payments are sometimes called **factor payments.** Factor payments include wages for the use of labor services, rent for land, payments for the use of capital goods in the form of interest, and profits for entrepreneurs who put labor, land, and capital together.

WHAT ARE NON-INCOME EXPENSE ITEMS?

Although we can identify and sum the various factor payments, the total will not exactly equal GDP. In order to find an accurate GDP, two additional factors must be consid-

ered: indirect business taxes and depreciation. Together, these factors are called **non-income expense items.**

Indirect Business Taxes

Sales taxes that are sent by businesses to the government are **indirect business taxes.** The best example of an indirect business tax is a sales tax. For example, a compact disc may cost $14.95 plus a tax of $1.20, for a total of $16.15. The retail distributor (record store), record producer, and others will share $14.95 in proceeds, even though the actual equilibrium price is $16.15. In other words, the output (compact disc) is valued at $16.15, even though recipients only get $14.95 in income. Besides sales taxes, other important indirect business taxes include excise taxes (e.g., taxes on cigarettes, automobiles, and liquor) and gasoline taxes.

Depreciation

Depreciation payments are annual allowances set aside for the replacement of worn-out plant and equipment. The depreciation factor is also known as the **capital consumption allowance.**

Are gasoline taxes an example of an indirect business tax?

ADDING IT UP: THE STATISTICAL DISCREPANCY FIGURE

As you can see in Exhibit 1, when added together, all of these components in the income approach equal GDP—just as the factors in the expenditure approach equal GDP. However, the sum calculated using the income approach is always slightly different than that found with the spending approach because of errors in collecting data. To make the two GDP calculations identical, a statistical discrepancy figure is added. As shown in Exhibit 1, this figure was $41 billion in 1997.

WHAT ARE NATIONAL INCOME AND PERSONAL INCOME?

National income and personal income are two additional measurements that economists often use.

National Income

National income (NI) is a measure of the income earned by owners of resources used in making final goods and services—factor payments. Accordingly, national income includes payments for labor services (wages, salaries, and fringe benefits), for use of land and buildings (rent), money lent to finance economic activity (interest), and payments for use of capital resources (profits). However, it excludes income earned to pay indirect business taxes, depreciation, and income earned by foreigners in the United States.

Personal Income

Very often, we are interested in the income *received* by persons rather than the income *earned*, because the income received reflects the amount available for spending. **Personal income (PI)** measures the amount of income received by individuals.

Some owners of productive resources do not receive all of the income that they earn. For example, some of the profits earned by stockholders of corporations are retained by the corporations to help finance business expansion. In recent years, only about one-third of before-tax corporate profits have been distributed to the owners of corporations. In addition, workers do not receive that part of their paycheck earmarked as their Social Security contributions. Social Security payroll taxes have been growing steadily in recent years.

EXHIBIT 1	AGGREGATE INCOME, BY TYPE OF INCOME, 1997	
	Amount (billions of current dollars)	Percent of Total
Aggregate income		
Wages	$4,704	58%
Profits	1,350	17
Interest	448	6
Rent	148	2
Indirect business taxes (e.g., Sales taxes)	542.5	7
Depreciation	868	10
Net income of foreigners*	−20	−.3
Statistical discrepancy**	41	0.5
equals GDP	$8,080	

*Net income of foreigners is the income earned abroad by U.S. firms or residents minus income earned by foreign firms or residents in the United States.

**The statistical discrepancy is relatively small at $41 billion; it is added to the components of national income to equal domestic income, which equals GDP.

1. The income approach to measuring GDP involves summing the incomes received by the producers of goods and services. These payments to the owners of productive resources are also known as factor payments.
2. The income approach also takes two non-income expense items into consideration: (1) indirect business taxes, such as sales taxes; and (2) depreciation, payments set aside for the replacement of worn-out capital.

3. National income (NI) is measured by adding together the payments to the factors of production—wages, rent, interest, and profit.
4. Personal income (PI) measures the amount of income received by individuals rather than the amount earned.

1. Why should we expect the total expenditures that go into GDP to equal total income in an economy?
2. What two non-income expense items does the income approach take into consideration?

3. How is personal income different from national income?

E Problems in Calculating an Accurate GDP

MODULE 18

- What are the problems with GDP in measuring output?
- What is the purpose of a price level index?
- What inherent problems exist with a price level index?
- What is per capita GDP?

WHAT PROBLEMS ARE THERE IN CALCULATING AN ACCURATE GDP?

The primary problem in calculating accurate GDP statistics becomes evident when attempts are made to compare the GDP over time. Between 1970 and 1978, a period of relatively high inflation, GDP in the United States rose over 100 percent. What great progress! Unfortunately, however, the "yardstick" used in adding together the values of different products, the U.S. dollar, also changed in value over this period of time. A dollar in 1979, for example, would certainly not buy as much as a dollar in 1970, because the *overall* price level for goods and services increased.

HOW DO WE SOLVE THIS PROBLEM?

One solution to this problem would be to use physical units of output—which, unlike the dollar, don't change in value from year to year—as our measure of total economic activity. The major problem with this approach is that different products have different units of measurement. How do you add together tons of steel, bushels of wheat, kilowatts of electricity, gallons of paint, cubic feet of natural gas, miles of air passenger travel, number of games of bowling, and number of magazines sold? In order to compare GDP values over time, a common or standardized unit of measure, which only money can provide, must be used in the calculations.

HOW CAN A PRICE LEVEL INDEX HELP?

The dollar, then, is the yardstick of value that we can use to correct the inflation-induced distortion of the GDP. We must adjust for the changing purchasing power of the dollar by constructing a **price index.** Essentially, a price index attempts to provide a measure of the trend in prices paid for a certain bundle of goods and services over time. The price index can be used to deflate the nominal or current dollar GDP values to a real GDP expressed in dollars of constant purchasing power.

WHAT ARE THE CONSUMER PRICE INDEX (CPI) AND THE GDP DEFLATOR?

There are many different types of price indices. The most well known index, the **consumer price index (CPI),** provides a measure of the trend in the prices of certain goods and services purchased for consumption purposes. The CPI is the price index that may be most relevant to households trying to evaluate their changing financial position over time.

The price index used to correct GDP statistics for changing prices is an even broader index called the **GDP deflator.** The GDP deflator measures the average level of prices of all consumer goods and services produced in the economy.

HOW IS A PRICE INDEX CREATED?

Constructing a price index is complicated. To begin with, there are literally thousands of goods and services in our economy; attempting to include all of them in an index would be cumbersome, make the index expensive to compute, and would take a long period of time (to gather necessary price data). Therefore, a "bundle" or "basket" of representative goods and services is selected by the index calculators (the Bureau of Labor Statistics of the U.S. Department of Labor for consumer and wholesale price indices; the Office of Business Economics of the Department of Commerce for the GDP deflator).

Unfortunately for our ability to calculate inflation, not all prices move by the same amount or in the same direction, so an average of the many price changes must be calculated. This is complicated by several factors. First, goods and services change in quality over time, so the observed price change may, in reality, reflect a quality change in the product rather than the purchasing power of the dollar. A $500 television set today is dramatically better than a television set in 1950 that cost many times more. Second, new products come on the market and occasionally old products disappear. For example, color TV sets did not exist in 1950 but are a major consumer item now. How do

THE BOX-OFFICE LEADERS

Everyone knows that *Titanic* is one of the biggest box-office hits of all time. But where would it rank if the grosses of old-time releases were adjusted for inflation?

How does *Gone with the Wind* rank when box office receipts are adjusted for inflation?

ALL-TIME LEADERS AS OF AUGUST 3, 1998

Rank	Title (distributor)	Release date	Total domestic gross	Adjusted domestic gross*
1	*Gone with the Wind* (MGM)**	1939	$196,636,563	$866,326,760
2	*Star Wars* (Fox)**	5/25/77	460,935,665	774,992,216
3	*E.T.* (Universal)**	6/11/82	399,804,539	594,267,291
4	*Titanic* (Paramount)	12/19/97	590,489,873	590,489,873
5	*The Ten Commandments* (Paramount)	1956	65,500,000	572,470,000
6	*The Sound of Music* (Fox)	1965	163,214,286	570,597,144
7	*Jaws* (Universal)	6/20/75	260,000,000	559,704,433
8	*Doctor Zhivago* (MGM)	1965	111,721,910	542,471,941
9	*The Jungle Book* (Buena Vista)**	1967	135,475,556	485,269,000
10	*Snow White and the Seven Dwarfs* (RKO/Buena Vista)**	1937	184,925,486	476,330,000
11	*Ben-Hur* (MGM)	1959	70,000,000	470,615,385
12	*101 Dalmatians* (Buena Vista)**	1961	152,551,111	459,757,486
13	*The Empire Strikes Back* (Fox)**	5/21/80	290,158,751	431,710,050
14	*Return of the Jedi* (Fox)**	5/25/83	309,125,409	413,782,013
15	*The Exorcist* (Warner Brothers)	12/26/73	165,000,000	412,028,571

**Gross totals include reissues.

SOURCE: http://www.MrShowbiz.com/reviews/moviereviews/NUMBERS/top100adjusted.html

---

CONSIDER THIS:

In this article, we see the importance of adjusting for prices when ranking the great movies of all time. The left-hand column indicates total box office gross receipts. The problem is that films move up on this list if they were released later in the era of higher-priced tickets. In the right-hand column, Exhibitor Relations, a company that tracks box office receipts, used 1996 dollars to compute inflation-adjusted gross receipts. The central point of this article is that ignoring price changes leads to vastly different rankings of the all-time greatest revenue earning movies. As we have seen in this Module, adjusting for prices is very important when trying to measure the growth of the economy. Imagine if we failed to index for prices when we computed GDP. Because the price level has been rising steadily over the last 30 years, if we failed to index for price level changes, we would certainly overstate the value of goods and services being produced in the economy. And grossly inaccurate GDP figures would make it even more difficult for policy makers to manage the economy, an already difficult task.

you calculate changes in prices over time when some products did not even exist in the earlier period?

Clearly, calculating a price index is not a simple, direct process. As you can see from the *In the News* article, there are many factors that could potentially distort the CPI.

HOW DO WE CALCULATE REAL GDP?

Once the price index has been calculated, the actual procedure for adjusting nominal, or current dollar, GDP to get real GDP figure is not complicated. For convenience, an index number of 100 is assigned to some base year. The base year is arbitrarily chosen—it can be any year.

The formula for converting any year's nominal GDP into real GDP (in base year dollars) is as follows:

$$\text{Real GDP} = \frac{\text{Nominal GDP}}{\text{Price level index}} \times 100$$

Say the GDP deflator (price index) was expressed in terms of 1992 prices (1992 = 100), and the index figure for 1996 was 109.9. This means that prices were 9.9 percent higher in 1996 than they were in 1992. Now, in order to correct the 1996 nominal GDP, we take the nominal GDP figure, $7,576 billion, and divide it by the price level index, 109.9, which results in a quotient of $68.94 billion. We then multiply this number by 100, giving us $6,894 billion, which is the 1996 GDP in 1992 dollars (that is, 1996 real GDP, in terms of a 1992 base year).

IS REAL GDP ALWAYS LESS THAN NOMINAL GDP?

In modern times, inflation has been prevalent. For most readers of this book, the price level (as measured by the consumer price index) has risen in every single year of their lifetime, because the last year of a declining price level was 1955. Therefore, the adjustment of nominal (money) GDP to real GDP will tend to reduce the growth in GDP suggested by nominal GDP figures. Given the distortions introduced by inflation, most news reports about GDP today speak of real GDP changes, although this is not always made explicit.

Which one is more expensive, adjusting for quality and inflation?

HOW ACCURATE IS THE CPI INDEX?

Bill Clinton, Bob Dole, Pat Moynihan, and Newt Gingrich have each hinted they'd like to "correct" the CPI downward. Revamping the CPI is a politician's dream: Seemingly painless tax increases and spending cuts result. The Congressional Budget Office says lowering the CPI by one percentage point would increase the IRS's annual take by $45 billion a decade from now (because tax brackets are adjusted for inflation each year). At the same time, it would reduce the growth of Social Security payments, military pensions, and interest payments by $90 billion. Much of this could even be done in the name of "fairness," since too-high cost-of-living adjustments cause inequitable transfers of wealth from the young (taxpayers) to the old (pensioners). . . .

The basic problem with the CPI is rooted in the way the Bureau of Labor Statistics (BLS) collects and adds up the data. Every day, some 400 government price collectors fan out across the country to note the price of everything from green beans to rent on a house. The BLS weights each product category according to the basket of goods and services a typical American bought in, roughly, 1983.

But the BLS often collects the prices companies charge rather than the prices people actually pay. If you stock up on lower-priced Wal-Mart film instead of the name brand at your local store, the BLS doesn't necessarily count your saving as a reduction in price. Nor does it subtract most coupons. These and similar biases make the CPI overstate the inflation rate by about 0.2, says Michael Boskin, a Stanford professor who heads a panel of economists studying the CPI's upward bias. But even these obvious and comparatively small fixes are controversial. BLS officials say the effect of discount shopping and coupons is so small it's not worth fixing.

A bigger fight is likely to arise over the panel's contention that the whole idea of the CPI—tracking the price of a fixed basket of goods over many years—gives a poor picture of the cost of living. If the price of a favorite cookie, for example, shoots up, some consumers switch to lower-priced substitutes, changing their basket and saving money. And the BLS's fixed basket doesn't fully capture quality improvements and price drops in new products like computers. Substitution and quality improvements probably account for 0.7 of the CPI rate, the panel believes, and all its biases together most likely overstate the rate by between one and 1.5 points.

SOURCE: Kim Clark, "How Best to Measure Inflation? The Glamorous World of Economic Indicators," *Fortune*, November 11, 1996.

If people prefer buying in bulk at discount stores, will the CPI accurately measure inflation?

CONSIDER THIS:
The consumer price index (CPI), the current measure of inflation, may have serious problems. Some economists believe that it might overstate the inflation rate by as much as 1.5 points. That is, an officially measured inflation rate of 5 percent might only really represent 3.5 percent inflation. This has important implications for welfare and Social Security recipients because these programs are adjusted for inflation using the CPI. In other words, we may be overpaying these recipients because the CPI overstates the real rate of inflation.

The problems with the CPI are numerous. It does not adjust accurately for quality changes or new products and services like cellular phones (which may be included in 1998 or 1999). In addition, it does not take into consideration the use of coupons or discount stores. However, most importantly, it does not accurately reveal how consumers will substitute away from higher-priced goods in favor of goods that fall in price. That is, the appropriate "basket" of goods and services is constantly changing, while the CPI continues to use a constant basket.

WHAT IS PER CAPITA GDP?

The measure of economic welfare most often cited is real **per capita gross domestic product.** We use a measure of real GDP for reasons already cited. To calculate per capita GDP, we divide the real GDP by the total population to get the value of real output of final goods and services per person. *Ceteris paribus*, people prefer more goods to fewer, so a higher GDP would seemingly make people better off. Economic growth, then, is usually considered to have occurred anytime the real GDP per capita has risen.

WHY IS THE MEASURE OF PER CAPITA GDP SO IMPORTANT?

Because one purpose of using GDP as a crude welfare measure is to relate output to human desires, we need to adjust for population change. If we do not take population growth into account, we can be misled by changes in real GDP values. For example, in some less-developed countries in some time periods, real GDP has risen perhaps 2 percent a year but the population has grown just as fast. In these cases, the real output of goods and services per person has remained virtually unchanged, but this would not be apparent in an examination of real GDP trends alone.

CONCEPT CHECK

1. It is difficult to compare real GDP over time because of the changing value of money over time.
2. A price index allows us to compare prices paid for goods and services over time by creating a measure of how many dollars it would take to maintain a constant purchasing power over time. The consumer price index (CPI) is the most well-known index.
3. The GDP deflator is a price index that measures the average level of prices of all consumer goods and services produced in the economy.
4. The problems with the consumer price index are that it fails to account for an increase in the quality of goods, new goods introduced, or changes in the relative quantities of goods purchased.
5. Per capita GDP is real output of goods and services per person. In some cases, real GDP may increase, but per capita GDP may actually drop, as a result of population growth.

---

1. If we overestimated inflation over time, would our calculations of real GDP growth likely be over- or underestimated?
2. Why does the consumer price index tend to overstate inflation if the quality of goods and services is rising over time?
3. Why would the growth in real GDP overstate the growth of output per person in a country with a growing population?
4. Why doesn't the consumer price index accurately adjust for the cost-of-living effects of a tripling in the price of bananas relative to the prices of other fruits?

Problems with GDP as a Measure of Economic Welfare

- What are some of the deficiencies of GDP as a measure of economic welfare?
- What are nonmarket transactions?
- What is the underground economy?
- Does GDP reflect the value of externalities?

As we have noted throughout this Module, real GDP is often used as a measure of the economic welfare of a nation. The accuracy of this measure for that purpose is, however, questionable, because several important factors are excluded from its calculations. These factors include nonmarket transactions, the underground economy, leisure, externalities, the types of goods purchased, the distribution of income, and expectations.

WHAT IS THE IMPACT OF NONMARKET TRANSACTIONS ON OUR ECONOMY?

Nonmarket transactions include the provision of goods and services outside of traditional markets for which no money is exchanged. We simply do not have information on this output that is reliable enough to include it in the GDP. The most important single nonmarket transaction omitted from the GDP is the services of housewives or househusbands. These services are not sold in any market, so they are not entered into the GDP, but they are nonetheless performed. For example, if a single woman hires a male housekeeper to clean house for her, those payments enter into the calculation of GDP. Suppose, though, that the woman marries the housekeeper. Now the woman no longer pays her husband for his housekeeping services. Reported GDP falls after the marriage, although output does not change.

In less-developed countries, where a significant amount of food and clothing output is produced in the home, the failure to include nonmarket economic activity in GDP is a serious deficiency. Even in the United States, homemade meals, housework, and the vegetables and flowers produced in home gardens are excluded, even though they clearly represent an output of goods and services.

HOW LARGE IS THE UNDERGROUND ECONOMY?

It is impossible to know for sure the magnitude of the underground economy, which includes unreported income from both legal and illegal sources. For example, illegal gambling and prostitution are not included in the GDP, leading to underreporting of an unknown dimension. The reason these activities are excluded, however, has nothing to do with the morality of the services performed, but rather results from the fact that most payments made for these services are neither reported to governmental authorities nor go through normal credit channels. Likewise, cash payments made to employees "under the table" slip through the GDP net. The estimates of the size of the underground economy vary from less than 4 percent to more than 20 percent of GDP. It also appears that a good portion of this unreported income comes from legal sources, such as self-employment.

CAN WE MEASURE THE VALUE OF LEISURE?

The value that individuals place on leisure is omitted in calculating GDP. Most of us could probably get a part-time job if we wanted to, earning some additional money by working in the evening or on weekends. Yet we choose not

Are her efforts included in the GDP?

Do you think all restaurant tips are declared as income?

DOES GDP MEASURE EXTERNALITIES?

As we discussed in earlier Modules, positive and negative externalities can result from the production of some goods and services. As a result of these externalities, the equilibrium prices of these goods and services—the figure used in GDP calculations—does not reflect their true values to society (unless, of course, the externality has been internalized). For example, if a steel mill produces 100,000 more tons of steel, GDP increases; GDP does not, however, decrease to reflect damages from the air pollution that resulted from the production of that additional steel. Likewise, additional production of a vaccine would be reflected in the GDP, but the positive benefit to others in society than the purchaser would not be included in the calculation. In other words, while GDP measures the goods and services that are produced, it does not adequately measure the "goods" and "bads" that result from the production processes.

DOES GDP ACCOUNT FOR INCOME DISTRIBUTION?

Another problem with real per capita GDP as a welfare measure is that it ignores the distribution of output, or of incomes generated from that output, among members of society. While the welfare implications of income distribution are explored in greater detail in the microeconomic portion of this text, it can be demonstrated that under certain assumptions, a redistribution of income from the very rich to the very poor might raise the welfare of the poorer persons more than it reduces the welfare of the rich, so that, on balance, the redistribution increases overall economic welfare. Redistribution of income from rich to poor

to do so. Why? The opportunity cost is too high—we would have to forego some leisure. If you work on Saturday nights, you cannot see your friends, go to parties, see concerts, watch television, or go to the movies. The opportunity cost of the leisure is the income foregone by not working. Leisure, then, has a positive value that does not show up in the GDP accounts. To put leisure in the proper perspective, ask yourself if you would rather live in Country A, which has a per capita GDP of $20,000 a year and a 30-hour work week, or Country B, with a $20,000 per capita GDP and a 50-hour work week. Non-workaholics might well choose the former. The problem that this omission in GDP poses can be fairly significant in international comparisons, or when one looks at one nation over time, because the amount of leisure varies considerably, usually falling with rising GDP (suggesting an understatement of economic growth).

Is leisure time measured in GDP?

AN INVALUABLE ENVIRONMENT

Environmentalists have long felt cross with the way governments measure national incomes and wealth. These figures for GDP, they point out, fail to value a country's environmental assets, such as fine public parks. They treat the use of natural capital differently from that of man-made capital: a country that depletes its stock of production equipment grows poorer, while one that chops down its forests appears to grow richer. And they treat the costs of cleaning up environmental damage as an addition to national income without subtracting the environmental loss caused by the damage in the first place.

The answer might seem obvious: adjust national accounts to take account of changes in the environment. Statisticians have laboured for more than a decade to find ways to do this. The difficulties of creating environmental statistics that are comparable to national income and wealth statistics are serious. GDP is measured in money, but putting monetary values on environmental assets is a black art. Some assets, such as timber, may have a market value, but that value does not encompass the trees' role in harbouring rare beetles, say, or their sheer beauty. Methods for valuing such benefits are controversial. To get round these problems, the U.N. guidelines suggest measuring the cost of repairing environmental damage. But some kinds of damage, such as extinction, are beyond costing, and others are hard to estimate.

For economists, the average value of a good or service is usually less important than the marginal value—the cost or benefit of one more unit. Marginal value, how-

ever, is a tricky concept to bring into environmental analysis. It may be clear that the cost of wiping out an entire species of beetle would be high, but what value should be attached to the extermination of a few hundred bugs?

Putting environmental concepts into economic terms raises other difficulties as well. Geography weighs differently: a ton of sulphur dioxide emitted in a big city may cause more harm than the same ton emitted in a

rural area, while a dollar's worth of output counts the same wherever it is produced. And the exploitation of natural resources may not always have a cost. Is a country depleting resources if it mines a ton of coal? All other things equal, the mining of that ton might raise the value of the coal that remains in the ground, leaving the value of coal assets unchanged.

SOURCE: *The Economist*, April 18, 1998, p. 75.

CONSIDER THIS:
GDP doesn't measure everything that contributes or detracts from our well-being, because it is very difficult to measure the value of those effects. Environmentalists believe that national income accounts should adjust for changes in the environment. However, this leads to many conceptual problems, such as measuring the marginal values of goods and services that are not sold in markets, and adjusting for geographical differences in environmental damage. The critical issue is whether there are important trends in "uncounted" goods and services that result in questionable conclusions about whether we are getting better or worse off.

---

does not always enhance welfare, however, because redistribution schemes reduce work incentives for productive members of society. Still, the distribution of income does have some bearing on welfare, and the per capita GDP statistics give no indication of what that distribution is.

WHAT IS THE MEASURE OF ECONOMIC WELFARE (MEW)?

Conceptually, we would like a measure of economic activity that adds the value of positive externalities and subtracts the value of negative externalities to GDP. Two

distinguished economists have developed such an indicator, called a **measure of economic welfare,** or MEW. They (and others) have developed broader-based welfare measures that attempt to correct for the deficiencies in GDP, such as the failure to account for the spillover effects of pollution or the value of leisure. Work in the direction of developing a "quality of life" indicator may ultimately reduce reliance on GDP as a measure of performance. One difficulty is that construction of such indicators involves many subjective judgments (e.g., what is the value of leisure?). Given the deficiencies with GDP as a welfare measure, however, the work will no doubt continue.

TUNE UP

PROBLEMS WITH MEASURING GDP

Q: Sally Mander, a biologist, often works in the streams near the automobile plant. Sally claims that every day the company dumps tons of waste into the river. Is the waste included in GDP accounts?

A: The negative effects of environmental externalities are not currently accounted for in GDP measurements. While it may be difficult to accurately assess the damages, many think that if GDP is going to accurately attempt to gauge standard of living, then at least some attempt needs to be made to incorporate economic bads, like pollution and crime.

SHOULD GDP BE USED AS A MEASURE OF OUR WELFARE?

There are severe defects with real GDP as a welfare measure. Nonetheless, at the present time, there is no alternative measure that is generally accepted as better, although it is possible that, in time, a broader-based "quality of life" measure (such as MEW) will be devised that wins wide acceptance. The GDP indicator is, however, useful in making comparisons of the market values over time and across countries, even if we cannot be completely sure of the welfare implications of the comparisons. We can probably even sometimes be fairly confident about the welfare implications of changing GDP. An unexpectedly fast increase in GDP probably will lead to an increase in consumption relative to expectations, almost certainly increasing welfare. Likewise, a sharp fall in GDP leads to reduced consumption—a decline in the ratio of what people have to what they want—and therefore almost certainly a decline in human welfare.

CONCEPT CHECK

1. There are several factors that make it difficult to use GDP as a welfare indicator, including nonmarket transactions, the underground economy, leisure, and externalities.
2. Nonmarket transactions are the exchange of goods and services that do not occur in traditional markets, and so no money is exchanged.
3. The underground economy is the unreported production and income that come from legal and illegal activities.
4. The presence of positive and negative externalities makes it difficult to measure GDP accurately.

---

1. Why do GDP measures omit nonmarket transactions?
2. How would real GDP comparisons between two countries be impacted by the existence of a high level of nonmarket activities in one of the countries?
3. If we choose to decrease our hours worked because we value the additional leisure more, would the resulting change in real GDP accurately reflect the change in our well-being? Why or why not?
4. How do pollution and crime affect GDP? How do pollution- and crime-control expenditures impact GDP?

Application: The Declining *Real* Cost of Living in America

Why is time at work used as a measure of the cost of goods and services? What are the shortcomings of using money prices?

TIME WELL SPENT

As America exits the twentieth century, we'd be hard-pressed to find a five and dime store. Penny candy now goes for a nickel or more. Five cents no longer buys a good cigar. Dime novels can't be found. Even a 3¢ stamp costs 32¢. Over the century, prices have gone up. The buying power of a dollar is down. We know this from statistical measures of inflation. We know it also from Grandpa's stories about paying 15¢ for a ticket to *Gone with the Wind* or 19¢ for a gallon of gasoline. Even a casual observer of the U.S. economy can see that the prices of milk, bread, houses, clothes, cars, and many other goods and services rise from year to year.

The cost of living is indeed going up—in money terms. What really matters, though, isn't what something costs in money; it's what it costs in time. Making money takes time, so when we shop, we're really spending time. The real cost of living isn't measured in dollars and cents but in the hours and minutes we must work to live. American essayist Henry David Thoreau (1817–62) noted this in his famous book, *Walden*: "The cost of a thing is the amount of . . . life which is required to be exchanged for it, immediately or in the long run."

The shortcoming of money prices is that they mean little apart from money wages. A pair of stockings cost just 25¢ a century ago. This sounds wonderful until we learn that a worker of the era earned only 14.8¢ an hour. So paying for the stockings took 1 hour 41 minutes of work. Today a better pair requires only about 18 minutes of work. Put another way, stockings cost an 1897 worker today's equivalent of $22, whereas now a worker pays only about $4. If modern Americans had to work as hard as their forebears did for everyday products, they'd be in a continual state of sticker shock—$67 scissors, $913 baby carriages, $2,222 bicycles, $1,202 telephones.

The best way to measure the cost of goods and services is in terms of a standard that doesn't change—time at work, or real prices. There's a regular pattern to real prices in our dynamic economy.

Americans come in all shapes and sizes. We differ in height and weight, gender, race, and age. We vary in talents, skills, education, experience, determination, and luck. Quite naturally, our paychecks differ, too. Some of us scrape by at minimum wage, while movie stars, corporate chieftains, and athletes sometimes make millions of dollars a year.

Calculations of the work time needed to buy goods and services use the average hourly wage for production and nonsupervisory workers in manufacturing. A century ago this figure was less than 15¢ an hour. By 1997 it had hit a record $13.18, a livable wage, but nothing worthy of *Lifestyles of the Rich and Famous*. What's most important about this wage is that it roughly represents what's earned by the great bulk of American society.

In calculating our cost of living, a good place to start is with the basics—food, shelter, and clothing. In terms of time on the job, the cost of a half-gallon of milk fell from 39 minutes in 1919 to 16 minutes in 1950, 10 minutes in 1975 and 7 minutes in 1997. A pound of ground beef steadily declined from 30 minutes in 1919 to 23 minutes in 1950, 11 minutes in 1975 and 6 minutes in 1997. Paying for a dozen oranges required 1 hour 8 minutes of work in 1919. Now it takes less than 10 minutes, half what it did in 1950. The money price of a 3-pound fryer chicken rose from $1.23 in 1919 to $3.15 in 1997, but its cost in work time fell from 2 hours 37 minutes to just 14 minutes. A sample of a dozen food staples—a market basket broad enough to provide three squares a day—shows that what required 9.5 hours to buy in 1919 and 3.5 hours in 1950 now takes only 1.6 hours.

SOURCE: W. Michael Cox and Richard Alm. *1997 Annual Report: Time Well Spent*, Federal Reserve Bank of Dallas.

EXHIBIT 1	DOMESTIC SERVANTS

Electric Range

1910	1950	1970	1997
$67	$420	$380	$288
345 hr.	292 hr.	113 hr.	22 hr.

Hughes Electric's three-burner stove listed for $40 in 1910 (a separate oven cost $27), the equivalent of about 5 weeks' wages for middle-income Americans. General Electric's midline models today sell for around $288, less than one-tenth the work-time cost of comparable models offered in the 1950s.

EXHIBIT 2	FOOD ON THE GO

Big Mac

1940	1997
$0.30	$1.89
27 min.	9 min.

In the currency of work time, today's 1/5-pound Big Mac costs a third of the McDonald brothers' 1/8-pound burgers in 1940.

Large Pepperoni Pizza

1958	1970	1980	1997
$1.99	$3.99	$7.99	$10.99
57 min.	71 min.	66 min.	50 min.

Compared with the huge initial investment required to start say, long-distance phone service, the outlay for setting up a pizza shop is relatively small. Even with mostly recurring costs—ingredients, labor, rent and so on—Pizza Hut has managed to cut the work-time tab for its large pepperoni pizza from 57 minutes in 1958 to just 50 today.

EXHIBIT 3	FALLING FASTER AT FIRST

VCR

1972	1978	1984	1990	1997
$1,395	$985	$499	$329	$199
365 hr.	160 hr.	54 hr.	30 hr.	15 hr.

Video recorders that used cassettes and would both play and record crept into the market in 1972 at prices ranging from $1,395 to $1,850. Better models today sell for just 4 percent of the 1972 work-time price.

Cellular Phone

1984	1997
$4,195	$120
456 hr.	9 hr.

Motorola introduced the DynaTAC 8000X cellular phone in late 1984 with a suggested retail price range of $3,995–$4,395. Better equipped Motorola models today sell for $120 or less, and monthly service fees are half what they were 13 years ago. The number of cellular subscribers has grown from only one—on the streets of downtown Chicago—to nearly 55 million as the work-time cost of a phone has fallen to under 2 percent of what it was in 1984.

SOURCE: W. Michael Cox and Richard Alm. *1997 Annual Report: Time Well Spent*, Federal Reserve Bank of Dallas.

According to Michael Cox and Richard Alm, the real cost of living measured in the hours and minutes we must work to live is surely falling. That is, what does it cost to buy a particular good or service in terms of time on the job? Many goods like microwaves, cellular phones, and camcorders have fallen in money prices. This, coupled with higher wages and better quality, has been a real boon to the consumer.

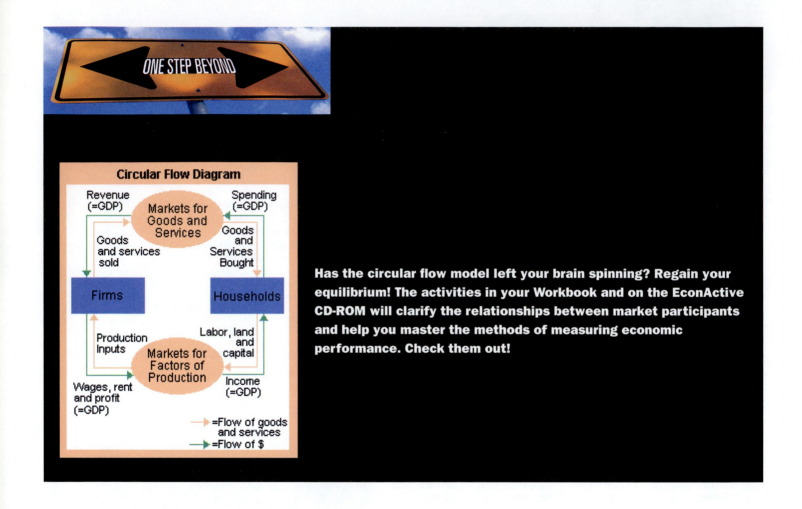

ONE STEP BEYOND

Circular Flow Diagram

Has the circular flow model left your brain spinning? Regain your equilibrium! The activities in your Workbook and on the EconActive CD-ROM will clarify the relationships between market participants and help you master the methods of measuring economic performance. Check them out!

PHOTO CREDITS MODULE 18

Page **440:** © Kevin Schaefer, Martha Hill/AllStock/PNI; Page **442:** © Ron Vesely Photography; Page **443:** © Rob Nelson/Black Star/PNI; Page **445:** left, © David Hautzig/Workbook CO/OP Stock; right, © Charles Gupton/Stock, Boston/PNI; Page **446:** © Billy E. Barnes/Stock, Boston/PNI; Page **448:** © 1998 Don Couch Photography; Page **452:** © The Everett Collection; Page **453:** left, © Albert Rose/Archive Photos/PNI; right, © Associated Press/Lennox McLendon; Page **454:** James Knowles/Stock, Boston/PNI; Page **456:** © Robert Sexton; Page **457:** top, © Frank Siteman/Stock, Boston/PNI; bottom, © Caroline Wood/AllStock/PNI; Page **461:** top, © Chicago Historical Society/PNI; bottom left, © PhotoDisc; bottom right, © 1998 Don Couch Photography.

Aggregate Demand

Ⓐ Consumption: The Primary Determinant of Aggregate Demand

- What is aggregate demand?
- What is the permanent income hypothesis?
- What is the average propensity to consume?
- What is the marginal propensity to consume?

WHAT IS AGGREGATE DEMAND?

Aggregate demand (AD) is the sum of the demand for all goods and services in the economy. It can also be seen as the quantity of real GDP demanded at different price levels. Specifically, aggregate demand reflects the summation of expenditures by household consumers, business investors, government, and foreign buyers on newly produced goods and services. The four major components of aggregate demand are consumption (C), investment (I), government spending (G), and net exports $(X - M)$. Aggregate demand, then, is equal to $C + I + G + (X - M)$.

In this Concept, we will examine the first of these four components—consumption. Investment, government spending, and net exports are covered in detail in Concept B.

HOW IMPORTANT IS CONSUMPTION (C) TO AGGREGATE DEMAND?

Consumption is by far the largest component in aggregate demand. Expenditures for consumer goods and services typically absorb almost 70 percent of total economic activity, as measured by GDP. Understanding the determinants of consumption, then, is critical to an understanding of the forces leading to changes in aggregate demand, which in turn, change total output and income.

DOES HIGHER INCOME MEAN GREATER CONSUMPTION?

The notion that the higher a nation's income, the more it spends on consumer items, has been validated empirically. At the level of individuals, most of us spend more money when we have higher incomes. But what matters most to us is not our total income but our after-tax, or **disposable income.** Moreover, there are other factors that might explain consumption. Some consumer goods are "lumpy"; that is, the expenditures for these goods must come in big amounts rather than in small dribbles. Thus, in years in which a consumer buys a new car, takes the family on a European trip, or has major surgery, consumption may be much greater in relation to income than in years in which

What impact might the purchase of a new car have on consumption in relation to income?

the consumer does not buy such high-cost consumer goods or services. Interest rates also affect consumption because they affect savings. At higher real interest rates, people save more and consume less. At lower real interest rates, people save less and consume more.

WHAT IS THE PERMANENT INCOME HYPOTHESIS?

Milton Friedman, a Nobel laureate in economics who taught for many years at the University of Chicago, observed that consumption is related to permanent income rather than to current income levels. This is called the **permanent income hypothesis.** Studies show, for example, that college students often consume more than their total income; the same is true of very old persons. These groups **dissave.** On the other hand, people in their 30s and 40s tend to save quite a bit and consume relatively less of their income (even so, though, a higher-income person of 40 is likely to consume more than a low-income person of 20 or 70). Why? College-age persons expect to earn more income later, and gauge their consumption in part by their

College-age and elderly individuals tend to dissave, although for different reasons.

expectations of future (lifetime) income. Likewise, middle-age persons expect to retire at some future date on a lower income and save for that eventuality. Older, retired persons expect to die and, accordingly, feel justified in drawing down their savings. A highly paid 35-year-old baseball player may consume less than a 35-year-old lawyer with the same income, because the baseball player expects his income to fall soon, while the lawyer does not. Farmers have "good" years and "bad" years and save more in good

years to maintain consumption in the bad years. People, then, consume on the basis of lifetime income expectations, which are only partly determined by current income. Looking at the economy as a whole, however, we have many groups of people with many different expectations. So, for the economy as a whole, consumption has been shown to be closely related to current income.

WHAT IS THE AVERAGE AND MARGINAL PROPENSITY TO CONSUME?

Households typically spend a large portion of their total income—the rest they save. The fraction of their total income that households spend on consumption is called the **average propensity to consume (APC).** For example, a household that consumes $450 out of $500 total income has an APC of 0.9 ($450/$500). However, households tend to behave differently with additional income than with their income as a whole. How much increased consumption results from an increase in income? That depends upon the **marginal propensity to consume (MPC),** which is the additional consumption that results from an additional dollar of disposable income. If consumption goes from $450 to $600 when disposable income goes from $500 to $700, what is the marginal propensity to consume out of disposable income? First, we calculate the change in consumption: $600 − $450 = $150. Next, we calculate the change in income: $700 − $500 = $200. The marginal propensity to consume, then, equals change in consumption divided by change in disposable income. In this example,

MPC = Consumption/Disposable income = $150/$200 = 3/4 = 0.75

For each additional dollar in after-tax income over this range, this household consumes three-fourths of the addition, or 75 cents.

CONCEPT CHECK

1. Aggregate demand is the sum of the demand for all goods and services in the economy. It can also be seen as the quantity of real GDP demanded at different price levels.
2. The four major components of aggregate demand are consumption *(C)*, investment *(I)*, government spending *(G)*, and net exports *(X − M)*. Aggregate demand, then, is equal to *C + I + G + (X − M)*.
3. Empirical evidence suggests that consumption increases directly with any increase in income.
4. According to the permanent income hypothesis, consumption is more closely related to permanent income than current income.
5. The additional consumption spending stemming from an additional dollar of disposable income is called the marginal propensity to consume (MPC).

---

1. What are the major components of aggregate demand?
2. If consumption is a direct function of disposable income, how would an increase in personal taxes or a decrease in transfer payments affect consumption?
3. What does the permanent income hypothesis imply about consumption as a fraction of income for young and old consumers versus middle-aged consumers?
4. Would you spend more or less on additional consumption if your marginal propensity to consume increased?

B Investment, Government Spending, and Net Exports

- What are induced and autonomous investment?
- What five factors determine investment behavior?
- What is government spending?
- What are net exports?

INVESTMENT (*I*)

Because investment expenditures (purchases of investment goods) are an important component of aggregate demand, which in turn is a determinant of the level of GDP, changes in investment spending are often responsible for changes in the level of economic activity. If consumption is determined largely by the level of disposable income, what determines the level of investment expenditures? As you may recall, investment expenditures is the most unstable category of GDP; it is sensitive to changes in economic, social, and political variables.

Many factors are important in determining the level of investment expenditures. In order to better understand the impact of these factors, it is helpful to distinguish between two types of investment: induced investment and autonomous investment. When businesses decide to proceed with an investment on the basis of increases in income or output, we call this **induced investment.** Good business conditions "induce" firms to invest, because a healthy growth in demand for products in the future seems likely based on current experience. Investment that is not determined by the level of income is called **autonomous (or independent) investment.** Consider some of the key variables that impact these two types of investments.

Factors Impacting Induced Investment

Optimism   Because investment depends so much on expectations as to the future, the mood of the businessperson at the time of the investment decision is crucial. Is he or she optimistic or pessimistic about the future? The more optimistic the person is, the greater the investment. Optimism, in turn, seems to be highly correlated with the rate of economic growth, both in the period in which the investment decisions are being made and in the immediate past. The more rapid the rate of growth in the level of economic activity (GDP) in a period, the greater the investment begun in that period and completed in the next time period. There are some inevitable time lags from the time

decisions are made until the investment is actually completed; it takes time to get machines that have been ordered, to construct buildings, and so on.

Level of and Rate of Change in Profits   A second factor impacting induced investment is the level and rate of change in profits in the present and immediate past. Investment spending is largely carried out by businesses, whose primary motive is to maximize their profits, investing where the expected rate of return on capital assets exceeds the opportunity cost of capital. Generally, when economic growth is high, profits are high and rising. The higher the profits, the greater the expected rate of return on future ventures. Present-day success breeds optimism about the future. This is significant, because capital goods are typically used over a long period, so investment decisions depend largely on expectations of the long-term profit potential of capital expenditures.

Moreover, the existence of large profits eases the problem of obtaining funds to pay for capital expenditures, allowing firms to internally finance investment rather than having to obtain funds from outsiders. Because profits, the difference between total revenue and total cost, are income to the firm, investment is partly a function of firm income, much as consumption is a function of household income. For example, if total revenue rises more rapidly than total cost, the resulting profit enables firms to invest more.

Factors Impacting Autonomous Investment

Interest Rates   One factor affecting autonomous investment is the real interest rate. The higher the interest rate, the higher the opportunity cost of investments in capital; fewer investments will now have benefits greater than the new higher costs. If an investment is expected to return 10 cents in income annually for every dollar invested (a 10 percent rate of return), the project is expected to be profitable if the firm can borrow the money at 6 percent interest, meaning it pays six cents a year for the use of each dollar. Even after paying the lender six cents on every

Are businesses as likely to invest when interest rates are high?

If inventories are excessive, will firms increase their investment in inventories in the next period?

dollar borrowed, the business expects to be four cents ahead. If the interest rate were higher, the business decision maker might decide against the investment, because the expected profit would be lower, or even negative, and there is the possibility that results won't live up to profit expectations. If the interest rate is 12 percent, the potential investor will definitely not proceed, as the investment appears to be unprofitable. Many forms of investment spending are highly sensitive to changing interest rates.

Rate of Capital Utilization A second determinant that impacts autonomous investment is the size of the capital stock of firms, relative to the current demand for goods. When output is low relative to the ability of business capital to produce goods, capital utilization rates are also low, and new investment will be lower than if firms are functioning at or near their productive capacities. The overall magnitude of the capital stock of firms is important in another respect. A large proportion of gross investment is to offset depreciation—replacing old, worn-out, or obsolete capital equipment and structures. The greater the stock of existing capital, the greater the magnitude of investment necessary to replace a depreciating capital stock, just to keep the amount of available productive capital from declining. Depreciation rates tend to be fairly independent of income, and in recent years, over half of gross investment has been accounted for by depreciation, although the relative importance of replacement investment varies considerably from year to year.

Inventories The last determinant of investment spending relates to inventories. When sales are at a level that is different from what was expected for a particular time period, firms' inventories change in unintended ways. If sales were lower in the previous period than intended, for example, inventories will have accumulated above their desired levels and inventory investment will have been greater than intended. What will businesses do now, as a result? Worried about excessive inventories, they may reduce planned investment in the current time period (they may also cut output). Very small inventories in relation to sales can lead to shortages and some foregone sales; very high inventories in relation to sales mean that too much of a firm's capital is tied up in relatively unprofitable excess inventories. Thus, firms try to achieve what they perceive to be an optimal inventory–sales ratio from the standpoint of profit maximization.

GOVERNMENT SPENDING (*G*)

Government spending varies over time for many reasons, some of them relatively noneconomic or quasi-economic in character. In 1996, the federal government accounted for slightly more than 18 percent of total spending. While volatile shifts in government spending are less frequent than volatile shifts in investment spending, they do occasionally occur, often at the beginning or end of wars. In any case, government spending tends to fall with rising income, because higher income means lower welfare payments, less unemployment compensation, and so on. Government tax receipts clearly increase with income. So when income rises over a business cycle, budget deficits automatically get smaller.

NET EXPORTS (*X* − *M*)

The interaction of the U.S. economy with the rest of the world is becoming increasingly important. Up to this

"This should jump-start the economy."

point, for simplicity, we have not included the foreign sector. However, international trade must be incorporated into the framework. Models that include international trade effects are called **open economy** models.

Exports are those goods and services that we sell to foreign customers, like movies, wheat, or Mustangs. Imports are those goods and services that we buy from foreign customers, like BMWs, French wine, or Sony TVs.

Exports and imports can alter aggregate demand. It makes no difference to sellers if the buyers that purchase their goods and services are in this country or in some other country. A buyer is a buyer, foreign or domestic. That is, exports (X) must be added to the demand side of our equation. But what about goods and services that are consumed here but not produced by the domestic economy? When U.S. consumers buy foreign goods and services, it has no direct impact on the total demand for U.S. goods and services. In other words, imports (M) have to be subtracted from our equation.

Exports minus imports is what we call **net exports,** and it represents the balance of trade. When the economy is running a trade surplus, we have positive net exports ($X > M$); exports are greater than imports. And when the economy is running a trade deficit, net exports are negative ($X < M$); imports are greater than exports.

The impact that net exports ($X - M$) have on aggregate demand is similar to the impact that government spending has on aggregate demand. Suppose a country has a balanced trade, with no trade surplus and no trade deficit—zero net exports. Now say that foreign consumers start buying more American goods and services while American consumers continue to buy imports at roughly the same rate. This will lead to positive net exports ($X > M$), and as a result of a greater demand for U.S. goods and services, a higher level of aggregate demand. From a policy standpoint, this might explain why countries that are currently in a recession might like to run a trade surplus by increasing exports.

Of course, it is also very possible that a country could run a trade deficit. Again let us assume that the economy was initially in a position with zero net exports. A trade deficit, or negative net exports ($X < M$), other things equal, would lower aggregate demand in the United States.

CONCEPT CHECK

1. When businesses invest because of positive changes in income or output, it is called induced investment.
2. Investment that is not determined by the level of income is called autonomous investment.
3. The five major factors that determine investment behavior are optimism, profits, interest rates, capital stock, and inventories.
4. Government spending is generally independent of income levels.
5. Trade deficits lower aggregate demand, other things equal; trade surpluses increase aggregate demand, other things equal.

---

1. Why does increased business optimism lead to increased investment?
2. Why do decisions to invest depend largely on the expected rate of return on investments compared to the opportunity cost of borrowed money (the market interest rate)?
3. Why might a larger existing capital stock tend to increase the rate of new capital goods investment?
4. If inventories have risen above the desired level for a firm, what does that tell it about the demand for its product relative to what it expected demand to be?
5. What would an increase in exports do to aggregate demand, other things equal? An increase in imports? An increase in both imports and exports, where the change in exports was greater in magnitude?

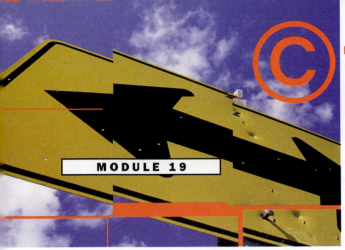

C The Aggregate Demand Curve

■ How is the aggregate demand curve different from the demand curve for a particular good?
■ Why is the aggregate demand curve downward sloping?

WHAT IS THE AGGREGATE DEMAND CURVE?

The **aggregate demand curve** reflects the total amounts of real goods and services that all groups together want to purchase in a given time period. In other words, it indicates the quantities of real gross domestic product demanded at different price levels. Note that this is different from the demand curve for a particular good presented in Module 4, which looked at the relationship between the relative price of a good and the quantity demanded.

HOW IS THE QUANTITY OF REAL GDP DEMANDED AFFECTED BY THE PRICE LEVEL?

The aggregate demand curve slopes downward, which means that there is an inverse (or opposite) relationship between the price level and real gross domestic product (RGDP) demanded. This relationship is illustrated in Exhibit 1, where the quantity of RGDP demanded is measured on the horizontal axis and the overall price level is measured on the vertical axis. As we move from point A to point B on the aggregate demand curve, we see that an increase in the price level causes RGDP demanded to fall. Conversely, if there is a reduction in the price level, a movement from B to A, quantity demanded of RGDP increases. Why do purchasers in the economy demand less real output when the price level rises, and more real output when the price level falls?

WHY IS THE AGGREGATE DEMAND CURVE NEGATIVELY SLOPED?

There are three complementary explanations for the negative slope of the aggregate demand curve: the real wealth effect, the interest rate effect, and the open economy effect.

What Is the Real Wealth Effect?

Imagine that you are living in a period of high inflation on a fixed pension that is not indexed for the changing price

---

EXHIBIT 1   **THE AGGREGATE DEMAND CURVE**

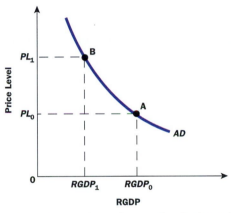

The aggregate demand curve slopes downward, reflecting an inverse relationship between the overall price level and the quantity of real GDP demanded. When the price level increases, the quantity of RGDP demanded decreases; when the price level decreases, the quantity of RGDP demanded increases.

---

level. As the cost of goods and services you buy rises by leaps and bounds, your monthly pension check remains the same. Therefore, the purchasing power of your pension will continue to decline as long as inflation is occurring. The same would be true of any asset of fixed dollar value, like cash. If you had $1,000 in cash stashed under your bed while the economy suffered a serious bout of inflation, the purchasing power of your cash would be eroded by the extent of the inflation. That is, an increase in the price level reduces real wealth and would consequently decrease your planned purchases of goods and services, lowering the quantity of RGDP demanded.

In the event that the price level falls, the reverse would hold true. A falling price level would increase the real value of your cash assets, increasing your purchasing power and increasing RGDP. The connection can be summarized as follows:

If you keep your savings in a cookie jar, what will happen to your real wealth as a result of a price level increase? A price level decrease?

$$\uparrow \text{Price level} \Rightarrow \downarrow \text{Real wealth} \Rightarrow \downarrow \text{Purchasing power} \Rightarrow \downarrow \text{RGDP demanded}$$

and

$$\downarrow \text{Price level} \Rightarrow \uparrow \text{Real wealth} \Rightarrow \uparrow \text{Purchasing power} \Rightarrow \uparrow \text{RGDP demanded}$$

What Is the Interest Rate Effect?

The effect of the price level on interest rates can also cause the aggregate demand curve to have a negative slope. Suppose the price level increases. As a result, most goods and services will now have a higher price tag. Consequently, consumers will wish to hold more dollars in order to purchase those items that they want to buy. That will increase the demand for money. If the demand for money increases and the Federal Reserve System, the controller of the money supply, does not alter the money supply, then interest rates will rise. In other words, if the demand for money increases relative to the supply, then the demanders of dollars will bid up the price of those dollars—the interest rate.

At higher interest rates, the opportunity cost of borrowing rises, and fewer interest-sensitive investments will be profitable, reducing the quantity of investment goods demanded. Businesses contemplating replacing worn-out equipment or planning to expand capacity may cancel or delay their investment decisions unless interest rates decline again. Also, at the higher interest rate, many consumers may give up plans to buy new cars, boats, or houses. The net effect of the higher interest rate, then, is that it will result in fewer investment goods demanded and, consequently, a lower RGDP demanded.

On the other hand, if the price level fell, and people demanded less money as a result, then interest rates would fall. Lower interest rates would trigger greater investment spending, and a larger real GDP demanded would result. We can summarize this process as follows:

$$\uparrow \text{Price level} \Rightarrow \uparrow \text{Money demand (Money supply unchanged)} \Rightarrow \uparrow \text{Interest rate} \Rightarrow \downarrow \text{Investments} \Rightarrow \downarrow \text{RGDP demanded}$$

and

$$\downarrow \text{Price level} \Rightarrow \downarrow \text{Money demand (Money supply unchanged)} \Rightarrow \downarrow \text{Interest rate} \Rightarrow \uparrow \text{Investments} \Rightarrow \uparrow \text{RGDP demanded}$$

What Is the Open Economy Effect of Changes in the Price Level?

Many goods and services are bought and sold in global markets. If the prices of goods and services in the domestic market rise relative to those in global markets due to a

If the domestic price level rises, will domestic consumers buy more foreign goods?

higher domestic price level, consumers and businesses will buy more from foreign producers and less from domestic producers. Because real GDP is a measure of domestic output, the reduction in the willingness of consumers to buy from domestic producers leads to a lower real GDP demanded at the higher domestic price level. And if domestic prices of goods and services fall relative to foreign prices, more domestic products will be bought, increasing real GDP demanded. This relationship can be shown as follows:

$$\uparrow \text{Price level} \Rightarrow \downarrow \text{Demand for domestic goods} \Rightarrow \\ \downarrow \text{RGDP demanded}$$

and

$$\downarrow \text{Price level} \Rightarrow \uparrow \text{Demand for domestic goods} \Rightarrow \\ \uparrow \text{RGDP demanded}$$

CONCEPT CHECK

1. A microeconomic demand curve shows the relationship between the relative price of a good and how much of that good is demanded, while an aggregate demand curve relates the amounts of real goods and services willingly purchased in an economy to the general price level for these goods and services.

2. The aggregate demand curve is downward sloping because of the real wealth effect, the interest rate effect, and the open economy effect.

1. How is the aggregate demand curve different from the microeconomic demand curve?
2. How does an increased price level reduce the quantities of investment goods and consumer durables demanded?
3. What is the real wealth effect, and how does it imply a downward-sloping aggregate demand curve?

4. What is the interest rate effect, and how does it imply a downward-sloping aggregate demand curve?
5. What is the open economy effect, and how does it imply a downward-sloping aggregate demand curve?

Shifts in the Aggregate Demand Curve

- What variables shift the aggregate demand curve to the right?
- What variables shift the aggregate demand curve to the left?
- What is the difference between a movement along and a shift in the aggregate demand curve?

DOES A CHANGE IN THE PRICE LEVEL SHIFT THE AGGREGATE DEMAND CURVE?

As for the supply and demand curves of Module 4, there can be both shifts in and movements along the aggregate demand curve. In the previous section, we discussed three factors—the real wealth effect, the interest rate effect, and the foreign market effect—that result in the downward slope of the aggregate demand curve. Each of these factors, then, generates a movement *along* the aggregate demand curve, because the general price level changed. In this section, we will discuss some of the many factors that can cause the aggregate demand curve to shift to the right or left.

The whole aggregate demand curve can shift to the right or left, as seen in Exhibit 1. Put simply, if some non-price level determinant causes total spending to increase, then the aggregate demand curve will shift to the right. If a non-price level determinant causes the level of total spending to decline, then the aggregate demand curve will shift to the left. Now let's look at some specific factors that could cause the aggregate demand curve to shift.

AGGREGATE DEMAND CURVE SHIFTERS

Anything that changes the amount of total spending in the economy (holding price levels constant) will impact the aggregate demand curve. An increase in any component of GDP (C, I, G, and $X - M$) can cause the aggregate demand curve to shift rightward. Conversely, decreases in C, I, G, or ($X - M$) will shift aggregate demand leftward.

Changing Consumption (*C*) Demand

A whole host of changes could alter consumption patterns. For example, an increase in consumer confidence, an increase in wealth, or a tax cut, each can increase consumption and shift the aggregate demand curve to the right. An increase in population would also increase the aggregate demand, as there are now more consumers spending more money on goods and services.

Of course, the aggregate demand curve could shift to the left due to decreases in consumption demand. For example, if consumers sensed that the economy was headed for a recession or if the government imposed a tax increase, this would result in a leftward shift of the aggregate demand curve. Because consuming less is saving more, an increase in savings, *ceteris paribus*, will shift aggregate demand to the left. Consumer debt may also be a reason that some consumers might put off additional spending. In fact, some economists believe that part of the 1990–1992 recession was due to consumer debt that had built up during the 1980s. Aside from maxing out their credit cards, some individuals also lost equity in their homes and, consequently, had a reduction in their wealth

---

EXHIBIT 1	SHIFTS IN THE AGGREGATE DEMAND CURVE

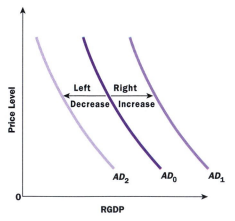

An increase in aggregate demand shifts the curve to the right (from AD_0 to AD_1). A decrease in aggregate demand shifts the curve to the left (from AD_0 to AD_2).

---

and purchasing power—again shifting aggregate demand to the left.

Changing Investment (*I*)

Investment is also an important determinant of aggregate demand. Increases in the demand for investment goods occur for a variety of reasons. For example, if business confidence increases or real interest rates fall, business investment will increase and aggregate demand will shift to the right. A reduction in business taxes would also shift the aggregate demand curve to the right, because businesses would now retain more of their profits to invest. However, if interest rates or business taxes rise, then we would expect to see a leftward shift in aggregate demand.

Changing Government Spending (*G*)

Government spending is also part of total spending and therefore must impact aggregate demand. An increase in

How would a boom in China's economy impact U.S. aggregate demand?

TUNE UP

CHANGES IN AGGREGATE DEMAND

Q: Any aggregate demand category that has the ability to change total purchases in the economy will shift the aggregate demand curve. That is, changes in consumption purchases, investment purchases, government purchases, or net export purchases shift the aggregate demand curve. For each component of aggregate demand (*C, I, G,* and *X − M*), list some changes that can increase aggregate demand. Then, list some changes that can decrease aggregate demand.

A: In Exhibit 1, we list some aggregate demand curve shifters.

INCREASES IN AGGREGATE DEMAND (RIGHTWARD SHIFT)	DECREASES IN AGGREGATE DEMAND (LEFTWARD SHIFT)
Consumption Spending (*C*) —lower income taxes —a rise in consumer confidence —greater stock market wealth	**Consumption Spending (*C*)** —higher income taxes —a fall in consumer confidence —reduced stock market wealth
Investment (*I*) —lower real interest rates —optimistic business forecasts	**Investment (*I*)** —higher real interest rates —a pessimistic economic outlook
Government Spending (*G*) —an increase in government defense outlays —an increase in social security benefits or welfare payments	**Government Spending (*G*)** —a cutback in government defense outlays —a reduction in social security benefits or welfare payments
Net Exports (*X − M*) —income increases abroad, which will likely increase the sale of domestic goods (exports)	**Net Exports (*X − M*)** —income falls abroad, which will lead to a reduction in the sales of domestic goods (exports)

government spending, other things equal, shifts the aggregate demand curve to the right, while a reduction shifts aggregate demand to the left.

Changing Net Exports (X − M)

Global markets are also very important in a domestic economy. For example, if major trading partners are experiencing economic slowdowns (such as is occurring in the Asian market in the late 1990s), then they will demand fewer U.S. imports. This causes U.S. net exports (X − M) to fall, shifting aggregate demand to the left. Alternatively, an economic boom in the economies of major trading partners may lead to an increase in our exports to them, causing net exports (X − M) to rise and aggregate demand to increase.

CONCEPT CHECK

1. A change in the price level causes a movement along the aggregate demand curve, not a shift in the aggregate demand curve.

2. Aggregate demand is made up of total spending, or C + I + G + (X − M). Any change in these factors will cause the aggregate demand curve to shift.

1. How is the distinction between a change in demand and a change in quantity demanded the same for aggregate demand as for the demand for a particular good?

2. What happens to aggregate demand if the demand for consumption goods increases, *ceteris paribus?*

3. What happens to aggregate demand if the demand for investment goods falls, *ceteris paribus?*

4. Why would an increase in the money supply tend to increase expenditures on consumption and investment, *ceteris paribus?*

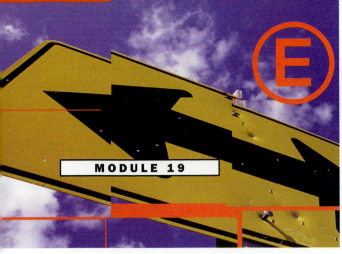

Application: The Consumer Confidence Index

How does consumer confidence impact aggregate demand? How would stock market wealth, joblessness, and inflation alter the aggregate demand curve?

A BRIEF DESCRIPTION OF THE CONSUMER CONFIDENCE SURVEY

The Consumer Confidence Survey measures the level of confidence individual households have in the performance of the economy. Survey questionnaires are mailed to a representative nationwide sample of 5,000 households, of which approximately 3,500 respond. Households are asked five questions that include (1) a rating of current business conditions in the household's area, (2) a rating of expected business conditions in six months, (3) current job availability in the area, (4) expected job availability in six months, and (5) expected family income in six months. The responses are seasonally adjusted. An index is constructed for each response and then a composite index is fashioned based on the responses. Two other indexes, one for an assessment of the present situation and one for expectations about the future, are also constructed. Expectations account for 60 percent of the index, while the current situation is responsible for the remaining 40 percent. In addition, indexes for the present and expected future economic situations

are calculated for each of the nine census divisions. In the base year, 1985, the value of the index was 100.

The Conference Board also tracks consumer buying plans over the next six months. Among the items tracked are automobiles, homes, vacations, and major appliances. If the economy experiences a long-term expansion, buying intentions may eventually decline even if the jobless rate stays low, because of the satisfaction of pent-up demand. Conversely, if inflation begins to accelerate, spending plans may increase for the short-term as consumers buy now to avoid having to pay higher prices later.

Consumer confidence correlates closely with joblessness, inflation, and real incomes. The growth of help wanted advertising (a measure of job prospects) is also correlated with strong consumer confidence. Rising stock market prices also boost consumer confidence.

Dismal Sciences (http://www.dismal.com/toolbox/dict_consumer.stml), 1998.

JUMP IN EXPECTATIONS SPURS NEW GAINS, THE CONFERENCE BOARD REPORTS TODAY

Consumers' expectations for the economy over the next six months climbed sharply. More than 18 percent of all consumers look for business conditions to improve during the next six months, up from 17 percent in March. Nearly 18 percent also expect jobs to become more plentiful, up from about 15 percent in March.

The latest Conference Board probe also reports that nearly 28 percent say their family's income will rise by next fall, up from 25 percent in March.

But there was a modest decline in consumers' assessments of current conditions. The proportion of consumers rating present business conditions as "good" was unchanged, but nearly 10 percent now label business conditions as "bad," up about one point from March. Slightly more consumers (nearly 15 percent vs. 14 percent) say jobs are difficult to find.

The Conference Board (http://www.conference-board.org/search/dpress.cfm?pressid=cciapril98), April 28, 1998.

The consumer confidence index has the potential to reflect important aggregate demand shifters. For example, if inflation is expected, consumers may increase their spending now. This would shift the aggregate demand curve to the right. Also, if the consumer confidence survey shows that consumer and business confidence in the economy is rising, we would also expect to see an increase in aggregate demand. Stock market wealth would increase consumption and shift the aggregate demand curve to the right. Of course, if the consumer confidence survey showed pessimism and signs of a downturn, we would expect the aggregate demand curve to shift to the left. In short, consumers and business perceptions of the economy are often important aggregate demand shifters and can have significant impact on price level, real output, and employment as a result.

Fall is the time of year, when the aspens are bursting with colorful autumn leaves and the excitement of the upcoming ski season at one of the nation's finest ski resorts fills the crisp, clean mountain air. Come to Breckenridge. Mountain setting. Historic past. Colorful present. Special events, activities, and festivals for the whole family. CIRCLE 20 ON REPLY CARD.

Est. 1859
BRECKENRIDGE
Colorado's Kingdom

Airfare and lodging 888-533-9879 • www.gobreck.com

Planning a trip in the next six months? What might this say about your confidence in the economy?

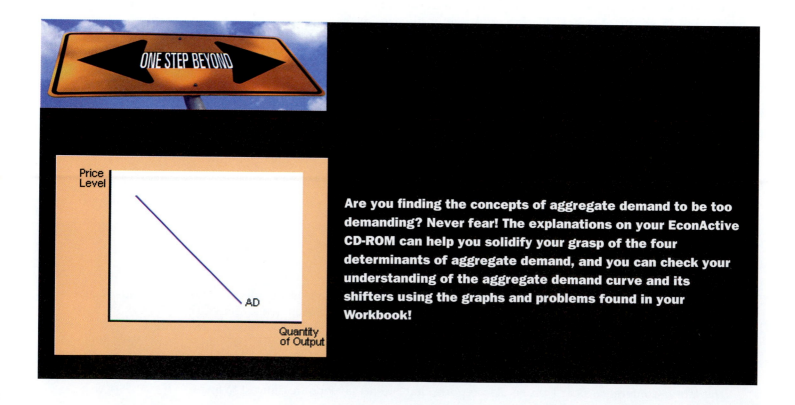

Are you finding the concepts of aggregate demand to be too demanding? Never fear! The explanations on your EconActive CD-ROM can help you solidify your grasp of the four determinants of aggregate demand, and you can check your understanding of the aggregate demand curve and its shifters using the graphs and problems found in your Workbook!

PHOTO CREDITS MODULE 19

Page **466**: © AP Photo/Carlos Osorio; Page **467**: © 1998 Don Couch Photography; Page **469**: left, © Bob Daemmrich/Stock, Boston/PNI; right, © Richard Pasley/Stock, Boston/PNI; Page **470**: © The New Yorker Collection, 1991, Bernard Schoenbaum, from cartoonbank.com. All Rights Reserved; Page **472**: top, © 1998 Don Couch Photography; bottom, © 1998 Don Couch Photography; Page **475**: © Erica Lansner/Black Star/PNI.

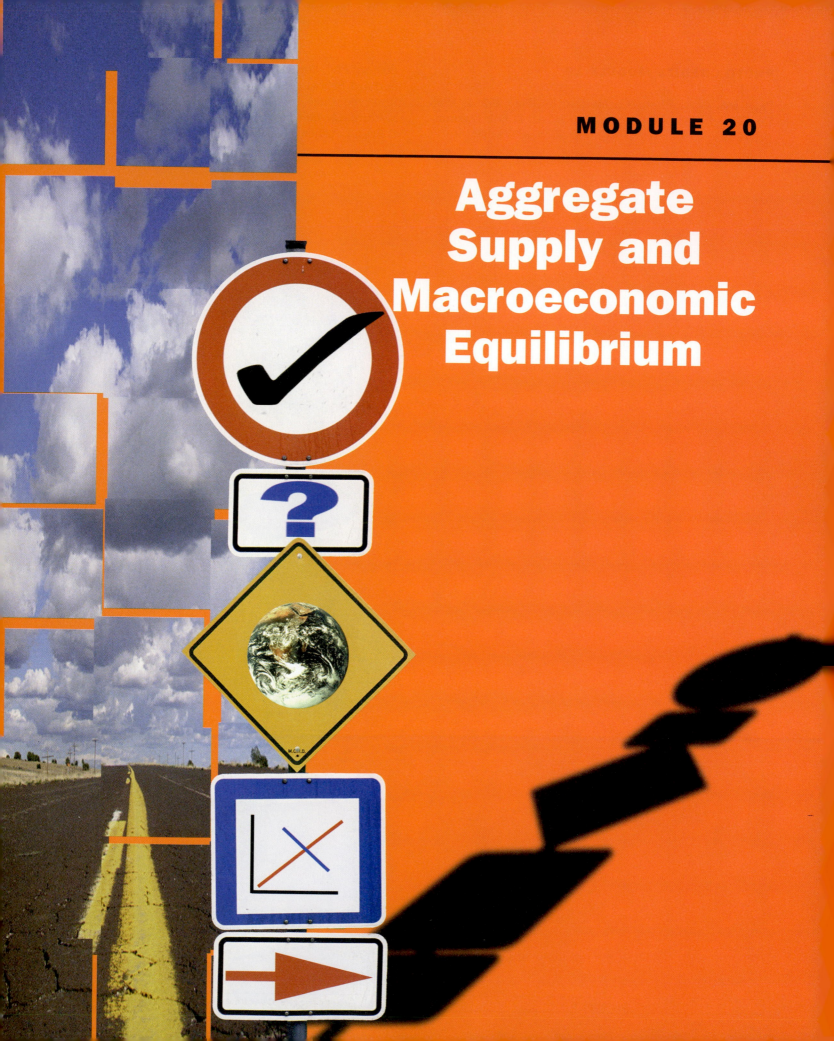

Aggregate Supply and Macroeconomic Equilibrium

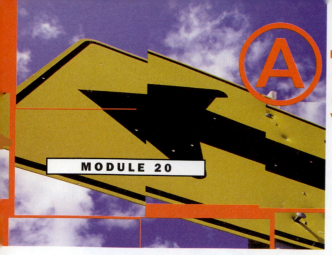

The Aggregate Supply Curve

■ What do the aggregate supply curves represent?

■ Why do producers supply more as the price level increases in the short run?

■ Why do the short-run and the long-run aggregate supply curves differ?

WHAT IS THE AGGREGATE SUPPLY CURVE?

Aggregate supply (AS) is the relationship between the total quantity of final goods and services that suppliers are *willing* and *able* to produce and the overall price level. The aggregate supply curve represents how much RGDP suppliers will be willing to produce at different price levels. In fact, there are two aggregate supply curves—a **short-run aggregate supply curve** and a **long-run aggregate supply curve.** The short-run relationship refers to a period when output can change in response to supply and demand, but input prices have not yet been able to adjust. For example, nominal wages are assumed to adjust slowly in the short run. The long-run relationship refers to a period long enough for the prices of outputs and all inputs to fully adjust to changes in the economy.

WHY IS THE SHORT-RUN AGGREGATE SUPPLY CURVE POSITIVELY SLOPED?

In the short run, the aggregate supply curve is upward sloping, as shown in Exhibit 1. This means that at a higher price level, producers are willing to supply more real output, and at lower price levels, they are willing to supply less real output. Why would producers be willing to supply more output just because the price level increases? There are two possible explanations: the profit effect and the misperception effect.

The Profit Effect

To many firms, input costs—like wages and rents—are relatively constant in the short run. The slow adjustments of input prices are due to the longer-term input contracts that do not adjust quickly to price changes. So when the

EXHIBIT 1	THE SHORT-RUN AGGREGATE SUPPLY CURVE

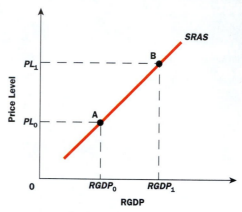

The short-run aggregate supply *(SRAS)* curve is upward sloping. Suppliers are willing to supply more RGDP at higher price levels and less at lower price levels, other things equal.

price level rises, output prices rise relative to input prices (costs), raising producers' short-run profit margins. These increased profit margins make it in the producers' self-interest to expand their production and sales at higher price levels.

If the price level falls, output prices fall and producers' profits tend to fall. Again, this is because many input costs, such as wages and other contracted costs, are relatively constant in the short run. When output prices fall, producers will find it more difficult to cover their input costs and, consequently, will reduce their level of output.

The Misperception Effect

The second explanation of the upward-sloping short-run aggregate supply curve is that producers can be fooled by price changes in the short run. For example, say a cotton rancher sees the price of his cotton rising. If he thinks that the relative price of his cotton is rising (i.e., that cotton is becoming more valuable in real terms), he will supply more. In actuality, however, it might be that it was not just cotton prices that were rising; the prices of many other goods and services could also be rising at the same time as a result of an increase in the price level. The relative price of cotton, then, was not actually rising, although it appeared so in the short run. In this case, the producer was fooled into supplying more based on his short-run misperception of relative prices.

WHY IS THE LONG-RUN AGGREGATE SUPPLY CURVE VERTICAL?

Along the short-run aggregate supply curve, we assume that wages and other input prices are constant. This is not the case in the long run, which is a period long enough for the price of all inputs to fully adjust to changes in the economy. When we move along the long-run supply curve, then we are looking at the relationship between RGDP produced and the

If the price of cotton rises, along with the average of all other prices, cotton ranchers may be fooled into supplying more cotton to the market.

price level, once input prices have been able to respond to changes in output prices. Along the long-run aggregate supply (*LRAS*) curve, two sets of prices are changing—the prices of outputs and the price of inputs. That is, along the *LRAS* curve, a 10 percent increase in the price of goods

TUNE UP

THE SHORT-RUN AGGREGATE SUPPLY CURVE

Q: Why would a firm be willing to supply more if output prices (the price level) are rising?

A: It is critical to remember that along the short-run aggregate supply curve, many input prices are constant even though the output prices are changing. This means two things to producers. One, greater short-run profits can be made if you expand production because the price of the output you are selling is rising faster than what you have to pay for your inputs. Two, in the short run, you can be fooled into producing more because you think the relative price of the good you are selling is rising. Only later do you find out that it's not just your prices that are rising but that the price level (the average of all prices) is rising.

and services is matched by a 10 percent increase in the price of inputs. The long-run aggregate supply curve, then, is insensitive to the price level. As you can see in Exhibit 2, the *LRAS* curve is drawn as perfectly vertical, reflecting the fact that the level of RGDP producers are willing to supply is not affected by changes in the price level. Note that the vertical long-run aggregate supply curve will always be positioned at the natural rate of output, where all resources are fully employed ($RGDP_{FE}$). That is, in the long run, firms will always produce at the maximum level allowed by their capital, labor, and technological inputs, regardless of the price level.

The long-run equilibrium level is where the economy will settle when undisturbed and when all resources are fully employed. Remember that the economy will always be at the intersection of aggregate supply and aggregate demand but that will *not* always be at the natural rate of output, $RGDP_{FE}$. Long-run equilibrium will only occur where the aggregate supply and aggregate demand curves intersect along the long-run aggregate supply curve at the natural, or potential, rate of output.

EXHIBIT 2 **THE LONG-RUN AGGREGATE SUPPLY CURVE**

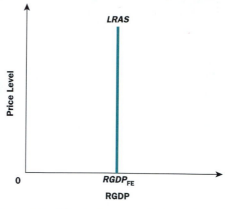

Along the long-run aggregate supply curve, the level of RGDP does not change with the price level. The position of the LRAS curve is determined by the natural rate of output, $RGDP_{FE}$, which reflects the levels of capital, land, labor, and technology in the economy.

CONCEPT CHECK

1. The short-run aggregate supply curve measures how much RGDP suppliers will be willing to produce at different price levels.
2. In the short run, producers supply more as the price level increases because wages and other input prices tend to be slower to change than output prices. For this reason, they can make a profit by expanding production when the price level rises. They also may be fooled into thinking that the relative price of the item they are producing is rising, so they increase production.

3. In the long run, the aggregate supply curve is vertical. In the long run, input prices change proportionally with output prices. The position of the *LRAS* curve is determined by the level of capital, land, labor, and technology at the natural rate of output, $RGDP_{FE}$.

---

1. What relationship does the short-run aggregate supply curve represent?
2. What relationship does the long-run aggregate supply curve represent?
3. Why is focusing on producers' profit margins helpful in understanding the logic of the short-run aggregate supply curve?
4. Why is the short-run aggregate supply curve upward sloping, while the long-run aggregate supply curve is vertical at the natural rate of output?

5. What would the short-run aggregate supply curve look like if input prices always changed instantaneously as soon as output prices changed? Why?
6. If the price of cotton increased 10 percent when cotton producers thought other prices were rising 5 percent over the same period, what would happen to the quantity of real GDP supplied in the cotton industry? What if cotton producers thought other prices were rising 20 percent over the same period?

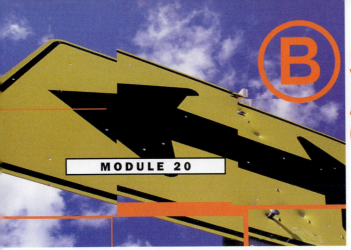

(B) Shifts in the Aggregate Supply Curve

MODULE 20

■ What is the main cause of shifts in aggregate supply?
■ Which factors of production affect aggregate supply?
■ What nonmarket forces affect aggregate supply?

WHAT CAUSES BOTH LONG-RUN AND SHORT-RUN SUPPLY CURVES TO SHIFT?

We will now examine the determinants that can shift the whole aggregate supply curve to the right or left, as shown in Exhibit 1. The underlying determinant of shifts in short-run aggregate supply is production costs. *Ceteris paribus,* lower production costs will motivate producers to produce more at any given price level, shifting the aggregate supply curve rightward. Likewise, higher production costs will motivate producers to produce less at any given price level, shifting the aggregate supply curve leftward.

Any change in the quantity of any factor of production available—capital, entrepreneurship, land, or labor—can cause a shift in both the long-run and short-run aggregate supply curves. In the following paragraphs, we will see how these factors can change the position of the aggregate supply curve.

Exploring and finding new oil supplies can shift the SRAS and LRAS curves.

| EXHIBIT 1 | SHIFTS IN BOTH LONG-RUN AND SHORT-RUN AGGREGATE SUPPLY |

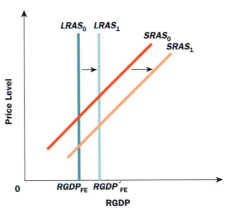

Increases in any of the factors of production—capital, land, labor, or technology—can shift both the *LRAS* and *SRAS* curves to the right.

How Do Changes in Capital Affect Aggregate Supply?

As we learned in the previous module, changes in the stock of capital will alter the amount of goods and services the economy can produce. Investing in capital improves the quantity and quality of the capital stock. And more and better quality capital will lower the costs of production in the short run, shifting the short-run aggregate supply curve rightward, and allow output to be permanently greater than before, shifting the long-run aggregate supply curve rightward, *ceteris paribus.*

Changes in human capital can also alter the aggregate supply curve. Investments in human capital may include educational or vocational programs or on-the-job training. All of these investments in human capital would cause productivity to rise. As a result, the short-run aggregate supply curve would shift to the right, because a more skilled work

Will new technology shift the *LRAS* and *SRAS* curves?

force will lower the costs of production, and the *LRAS* curve would shift to the right because greater output is achievable on a permanent, or sustainable, basis, *ceteris paribus*.

How Do Technology and Entrepreneurship Affect Aggregate Supply?

Bill Gates of Microsoft and Steve Jobs, the founding father of Apple Computer, are just a couple of examples of entrepreneurs who, through inventive activity, can increase both the short-run and long-run aggregate supply curves by lowering costs and expanding real output possibilities. As another example, a few years ago, two scientists claimed that they had found a way to create energy out of cold fusion. Attempts to duplicate their results were futile, but one can only imagine the huge impact that an inexpensive source of energy would have had on production costs and potential output. If entrepreneurial activities lower the costs of production and expand what can be produced with the resources available to the economy, then the aggregate supply curves both shift to the right.

How Do Changes in Land (Natural Resources) Affect Aggregate Supply?

Remember that land is an all-encompassing definition that includes all natural resources. An increase in natural resources, such as successful oil exploration, would presumably lower the costs of production and expand the economy's sustainable rate of output shifting both the

short-run and long-run aggregate supply curves to the right. Likewise, a decrease in the amount of natural resources available would result in a leftward shift of both the short-run and long-run aggregate supply curves. For example, in the 1970s and early 1980s when the OPEC cartel was strong and effective at raising world oil prices, the *AS* curve shifted to the left, as the members of the cartel deliberately controlled the production of oil.

How Do Changes in the Quantity and Quality of the Labor Force Affect Aggregate Supply?

The addition of workers to the labor force, *ceteris paribus*, can increase aggregate supply. For example, during the 1960s, women and baby boomers entered the labor force in large numbers. This increase tended to depress wages and increase short-run aggregate supply, *ceteris paribus*. The expanded labor force also increased the economy's potential output, increasing long-run aggregate supply. Increases or decreases in labor productivity will also affect the aggregate supply curve. Lower output per worker causes production costs to rise and potential real output to fall, resulting in a leftward shift in both the short-run and long-run aggregate supply curves.

How Can Government Regulations Affect Aggregate Supply?

Increases in government regulations can make it more costly for producers. This increase in production costs results in a leftward shift of the short-run aggregate supply curve, and the reduction in society's potential output would shift the long-run aggregate supply curve to the left as well. Likewise, a reduction in government regulations on businesses would lower the costs of production and expand potential real output, causing both the *SRAS* and *LRAS* curves to shift to the right.

WHAT FACTORS SHIFT SHORT-RUN AGGREGATE SUPPLY ONLY?

Some factors shift the short-run aggregate supply curve but do not impact the long-run aggregate supply curve. The most important of these factors are changes in input prices and natural disasters. The impact of these factors on short-run aggregate supply is illustrated in Exhibit 2.

How Do Input Prices Affect Short-Run Aggregate Supply?

The price of factors, or inputs, that go into producing outputs will affect only the short-run aggregate supply curve if they don't reflect permanent changes in the suppliers of some factors of production. For example, if wages increase without a corresponding increase in labor productivity, then it will become more costly for suppliers to produce goods and services at every price level, causing the *SRAS* curve to shift to the left. Long-run aggregate supply will not shift, however, because with the same supply of labor as before, potential output does not change. For example, if the price of steel rises, automobile producers will find it more expensive to do business, because their production costs will rise, again resulting in a leftward shift in the short-run aggregate supply curve. The *LRAS* curve will not shift, however, as long as the capacity to make steel has not been reduced.

It is supply and demand in factor markets (like capital, land, and labor) that cause input prices to change. The reason that changes in input prices only affect short-run aggregate supply and not long-run aggregate supply, unless they reflect permanent changes in the supplies of those inputs lies in our definition of long-run aggregate supply. Recall that the long-run aggregate supply curve is vertical at the natural level of real output, determined by the supplies of the various factors of production. A fall in input prices, which shifts the short-run aggregate supply curve to the right, only shifts long-run aggregate supply to the right if potential output has risen, and that only occurs if the supply of those inputs is increased.

How Do Natural Disasters Affect Aggregate Supply?

Major widespread flooding, earthquakes, droughts, and other natural disasters can increase the costs of production. Any of these disasters could cause the short-run aggregate supply curve to shift to the left, *ceteris paribus*. However, once the temporary effects of these disasters have been felt, no appreciable change in the economy's productive capacity has occurred, so the long-run aggregate supply doesn't shift as a result.

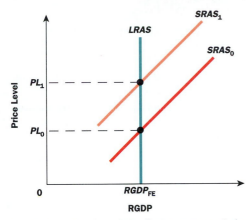

A change in input prices that does not reflect a permanent change in the supply of those inputs will shift the *SRAS* curve but not the *LRAS* curve. Likewise, adverse supply shocks, such as those caused by natural disasters, may cause a temporary change that will only impact short-run aggregate supply.

Temporary natural disasters like droughts can destroy crops and leave land parched like in the picture above. This may shift the *SRAS* curve but not the *LRAS* curve.

T U N E   U P

SHIFTS IN THE SHORT-RUN AGGREGATE SUPPLY CURVE

Q: Bill M. Later works in the auditing department of a big company. He wants to know why wage increases (and other input prices) impact the short-run aggregate supply but *not* the long-run aggregate supply. Can you help Bill out?

A: Remember, in the short run, wages and other input prices are assumed to be constant along the *SRAS* curve. If the firm has to pay more for its workers or any other input, its costs will rise. That is, the *SRAS* curve will shift to the left. This is shown in Exhibit 3 in the shift from $SRAS_0$ to $SRAS_1$. The reason the *LRAS* curve will *not* shift is that unless these input prices reflect permanent changes in input supply, those changes will only be temporary, and output will not be permanently or sustainably different as a result. Other things equal, if an input price is to be permanently higher relative to other goods, its supply must have decreased, but that would mean that potential real output, and hence long-run aggregate supply, would also shift left.

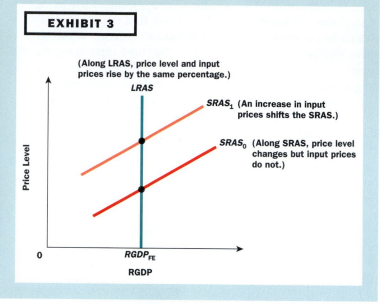

EXHIBIT 3

(Along LRAS, price level and input prices rise by the same percentage.)

LRAS

$SRAS_1$ (An increase in input prices shifts the SRAS.)

$SRAS_0$ (Along SRAS, price level changes but input prices do not.)

Price Level

$RGDP_{FE}$

RGDP

0

CONCEPT CHECK

1. Any increase in the quantity of any of the factors of production—capital, land, labor, or technology—available will cause both the long-run and short-run aggregate supply curves to shift to the right. A decrease in any of these factors will shift both of the aggregate supply curves to the left.

2. Changes in input price and temporary supply shocks shift the short-run aggregate supply curve but do not affect the long-run aggregate supply curve.

---

1. Which of the aggregate supply curves will shift in response to a change in the price level? Why?
2. Why do lower input costs increase the level of real GDP supplied at any given price level?
3. What would discovering huge new supplies of oil and natural gas do to the short-run and long-run aggregate supply curves?
4. What would happen to the short-run and long-run aggregate supply curves if the government required every firm to file explanatory paperwork each time a decision was made?
5. What would happen to the short-run and long-run aggregate supply curves if the capital stock grew and available supplies of natural resources expanded over the same period of time?

6. How can a change in input prices change the short-run aggregate supply curve but not the long-run aggregate supply curve? How could it change both long-run and short-run aggregate supply?
7. What would happen to short- and long-run aggregate supply if unusually good weather led to bumper crops of most agricultural products?
8. If OPEC temporarily restricted the world output of oil, what would happen to short- and long-run aggregate supply? What would happen if the output restriction was permanent?

© Macroeconomic Equilibrium

MODULE 20

- ■ What is short-run macroeconomic equilibrium?
- ■ What is long-run macroeconomic equilibrium?
- ■ What is demand-pull inflation?
- ■ What is cost-push inflation?
- ■ Can both aggregate supply and aggregate demand shift?

HOW IS MACROECONOMIC EQUILIBRIUM DETERMINED?

The short-run equilibrium level of real output and the price level are determined by the intersection of the aggregate demand curve and the short-run aggregate supply curve. When this equilibrium occurs at the potential output level, on the long-run aggregate supply curve the economy is operating at full employment, as seen in Exhibit 1. Only a short-run equilibrium that is at potential output is also a long-run equilibrium. Short-run equilibrium can change when the aggregate demand curve or the short-run aggregate supply curve shifts rightward or leftward, but the long-run equilibrium level of RGDP only changes when the LRAS curve shifts. Sometimes, these supply or demand changes are anticipated; at other times, however, the shifts occur unexpectedly. Economists call these unexpected shifts, **shocks.**

EXHIBIT 1	LONG-RUN MACROECONOMIC EQUILIBRIUM

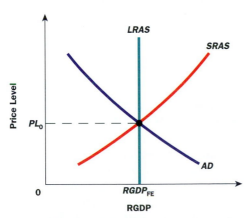

Long-run macroeconomic equilibrium occurs at the level where short-run aggregate supply and aggregate demand intersect at a point on the long-run aggregate supply curve. At this level, real GDP will equal potential GDP at full employment ($RGDP_{FE}$).

WHAT IS DEMAND-PULL INFLATION?

Demand-pull inflation occurs when the price level rises as a result of an increase in aggregate demand. Consider the case in which there is an increase in consumer optimism that results in a corresponding increase in aggregate demand. As shown in Exhibit 2, this increase in aggregate demand causes an increase in the price level and an increase in real output. This is demonstrated in Exhibit 2 in the movement along $SRAS_0$ from point A to point B. Recall that the increase in output as a result of the increase in the price level is a result of its effect on their profits; firms have an incentive to increase real output when the prices of the goods they are selling are rising faster than the costs of the inputs they use in production.

Note that point B in Exhibit 2 is positioned beyond $RGDP_{FE}$. It seems peculiar that the economy can operate beyond its potential, but this is possible, temporarily, as firms encourage workers to work overtime, extend the hours of part-time workers, hire recently retired employees, reduce frictional unemployment through more extensive searches for employees, and so on. However, this level of output and employment cannot be sustained in the long run. Because the price level is now higher, workers become disgruntled with wages that have not yet adjusted to the new price level (if prices have risen, but wages have not risen as much, real wages have fallen). Recall that along the SRAS curve, wages and other input prices are assumed to be constant. Therefore, workers' and input suppliers' purchasing power falls as output prices rise. Real (adjusted for inflation) wages have fallen. Consequently, workers and other suppliers demand higher prices to be willing to supply their inputs. As input prices respond to the higher level of output prices, the short-run aggregate supply curve shifts to the left, from $SRAS_0$ to $SRAS_1$. Suppliers will continually seek higher prices for their inputs until they reach the new long-run equilibrium, point C in Exhibit 2. At point C, input suppliers' purchasing power is now restored at full employment equilibrium. The only difference from point A is the new, higher price level.

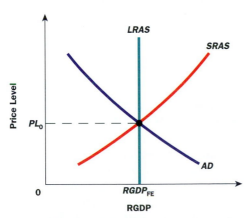

| EXHIBIT 2 | DEMAND-PULL INFLATION |

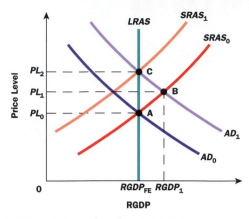

Demand-pull inflation occurs when the aggregate demand curve shifts to the right along the short-run aggregate supply curve. This leads, however, to rising input prices, which raises costs and shifts the SRAS curve to the left, until *AD* and *SRAS* once again intersect on the *LRAS* curve.

| EXHIBIT 3 | COST-PUSH INFLATION |

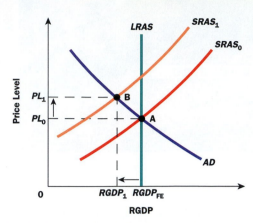

Cost-push inflation is caused by a leftward shift in the aggregate supply curve, from $SRAS_0$ to $SRAS_1$.

WHAT IS COST-PUSH INFLATION?

The 1970s and early 1980s witnessed a phenomenon known as **stagflation,** where lower growth and higher prices occurred together. Some economists believe that this was caused by a leftward shift in the aggregate supply curve, as seen in Exhibit 3. If the aggregate demand curve did not change significantly and the price level increased, then the inflation was caused by supply-side forces, not demand. This is what is called **cost-push inflation.**

The primary culprits responsible for the leftward shift in the aggregate supply curve were OPEC and the price of oil, as oil barrel prices reached record high levels during that period ($40 dollars a barrel as compared to less than $15 today). As we discussed in the last Concept, an increase in input prices can cause the short-run aggregate supply curve to shift to the left, and this spelled big trouble for the U.S. economy—higher price levels, lower output, and higher rates of unemployment. The impact of cost-push inflation is illustrated in Exhibit 3.

In Exhibit 3, we see that the economy is initially at full employment equilibrium at point A. Now suppose there is a sudden increase in input prices, such as the increase in the price of oil. This increase would shift the SRAS curve to the left—from $SRAS_0$ to $SRAS_1$. As a result of the shift in short-run aggregate supply, the price level rises to PL_1 and real output falls to $RGDP_1$ from $RGDP_{FE}$ (point B). Now firms may demand fewer workers as a result of the higher input costs that cannot be passed on to the consumers. The result is higher prices, lower real output, and more unemployment.

WHAT HELPED THE UNITED STATES RECOVER?

As far as energy prices are concerned, the 1980s witnessed falling oil prices as OPEC lost some of its clout due to internal problems. In addition, many non-OPEC oil producers increased production. The net result was a rightward shift in the aggregate supply curve. Holding aggregate demand constant, this rightward shift in the aggregate supply curve would lead to lower prices, greater output, and lower rates of unemployment.

"GO BACK TO SLEEP, ALAN... IF THERE IS A MONSTER IN YOUR CLOSET, IT'S ONLY A LITTLE ONE!"

Could too much money chasing too few goods cause demand-pull inflation?

ANOTHER CAUSE OF RECESSION

Just as cost-push inflation can cause a recession, so can a decrease in aggregate demand. For example, consider the case in which consumer confidence plunges and the stock market "tanks." As a result, aggregate demand would fall, shown in Exhibit 4 as the shift from AD_0 to AD_1. Now, at every price level, households, firms, and governments are buying fewer goods and services. In response to this drop in demand, output would fall from $RGDP_{FE}$ to $RGDP_1$, and the price level would fall from PL_0 to PL_1. So, in the short run, this fall in aggregate demand causes higher unemployment and a reduction in output.

HOW PRECISE IS THE AGGREGATE SUPPLY AND DEMAND MODEL?

In this Module, we have been shifting the aggregate supply and aggregate demand curves around as if we knew exactly what we were doing. But it is very important to mention that the AD/AS model is a crude tool.

In the supply and demand curves covered in Modules 4 and 5, we saw how this simple tool is very rich in explanatory power. But even supply and demand analysis does not always provide precise estimates of the shifts or of the exact price and output changes that accompany those shifts. However, while supply and demand analysis is not perfect, it does provide a framework to predict the direction that certain important variables will change under different circumstances.

The same is true in the AD/AS model, but it is less precise because of the complexities and interrelationships that exist in the macroeconomy. The slopes of the aggregate de-

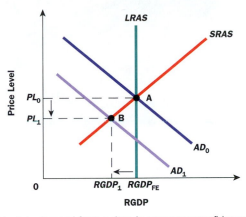

| EXHIBIT 4 | SHORT-RUN DECREASE IN AGGREGATE DEMAND |

A fall in aggregate demand from a drop in consumer confidence can cause a short-run change in the economy. The decrease in aggregate demand (shown in the movement from point A to point B) causes lower output and higher unemployment in the short run.

mand and aggregate supply curves, the magnitudes of the shifts, and the interrelationship of the variables are to some extent a mystery. For example, if a reduction in aggregate demand leads to lower real GDP and, as a result, there are fewer workers that are willing to look for work, it impacts the aggregate supply curve. There are other examples of the interdependence of the aggregate demand and aggregate supply curves that make this analysis not completely satisfactory. Nevertheless, the framework still provides important insights into the workings of the macroeconomy.

CONCEPT CHECK

1. Short-run macroeconomic equilibrium is determined by the intersection of the aggregate demand curve and the short-run aggregate supply curve. A short-run equilibrium is also a long-run equilibrium only if it is at potential output on the long-run aggregate supply curve.
2. Demand-pull inflation occurs when the price level rises as a result of an increase in aggregate demand.

3. Firms have an incentive to increase real output if the price of the goods they are selling is rising faster than the cost of their inputs. As this happens, though, suppliers and workers experience diminished purchasing power. In the long run, input suppliers will demand higher wages or other input prices, and the end result will be a higher price level—inflation.
4. Cost-push inflation is caused by a leftward shift in the short-run aggregate supply curve.

---

1. What is demand-pull inflation?
2. What is cost-push inflation?
3. Starting from long-run equilibrium on the long-run aggregate supply curve, what happens to the price level, real output, and unemployment as a result of cost-push inflation?

4. How would a drop in consumer confidence impact the short-run macroeconomy?
5. What would happen to the price level, real output, and unemployment in the short run if world oil prices fell sharply?

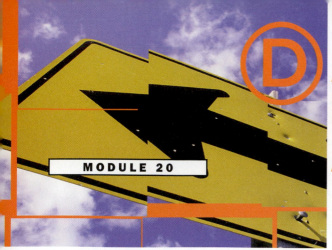

D Application: El Niño and the AD/AS Model

How will a supply shock like El Niño-induced flooding impact short-run aggregate supply? How about long-run aggregate supply?

EFFECTS OF EL NIÑO FELT IN LETTUCE HARVEST, PRICES

SALINAS, California (AP)—The heavy rains have stopped but the effects of El Niño storms on supermarket produce have only begun. Growers in California, the nation's top farm state, say incessant rains earlier this year sharply reduced the supply of lettuce and the shortage will be a problem until at least the middle of May. "El Niño weather conditions out here have created a little havoc with the supply situation," grower-shipper Frank Pinney said last week. "We expect a roller-coaster effect for the next four to five weeks with supply."

California's planting season, December through spring, was interrupted by storms that drenched the region in January and February. "Guys couldn't get the tractors in the field to do proper fertilization, aeration and cultivation," Pinney said. In some instances, farmers couldn't plant for about three weeks.

Shortages will be felt especially among loose leaf lettuce, growers said. "Romaine, red leaf, and green leaf are in very short supply," said Steve Adlesh, sales director at Apio, a grower and lettuce shipper in northern Santa Barbara County. "This is only going to maintain itself for the next two weeks. By the beginning of May, it should improve, but it will be fragmented as far as the supply goes for the next month." Just how short the supply will be remains in question, but Adlesh said it could be as low as 50 percent of normal during some weeks.

The price already has doubled. A box of 24 heads of lettuce, which usually costs $8 to $10, ranged from $16 to $25

Friday, Adlesh said. Although it's difficult to translate the increases into supermarket prices, Adlesh said he thinks lettuce that typically costs 60 to 70 cents a head would be $1 or more.

There are problems other than missing planting season. "Yields will be off due to fungus and other moisture-related diseases," Pinney said. "Plants in general will be weaker with more defects, and they will have shorter shelf life." Growers said they hope the supply will begin leveling out as the peak summer season begins in Salinas Valley. But the effects of earlier losses won't be forgotten quickly. "I have never seen a year like this before and I think it goes across the board for other farmers," said Pinney, who's been in the lettuce business for 25 years.

SOURCE: http://cnn.com/US/9804/21/lettuce.prices.ap/index.html.

In Exhibit 1, we see the impact of bad weather on the aggregate supply curve. These unanticipated adverse effects are called supply shocks. In 1997–1998, the shock was El Niño; in other years, it was major flooding in the Midwest that destroyed a considerable portion of the wheat crop. Unexpected bad weather causes production costs in input markets to rise. As a result of this increase, the aggregate supply curve shifts to the left.

Supply shocks are not always bad news. Unusually good weather can cause production costs to fall, resulting in a rightward shift of the aggregate supply curve. It is also possible that a major oil discovery would have the same effect—lowering production costs and shifting the aggregate supply curve to the right. Unless these shocks permanently alter an economy's productive capacity, however, they will not affect long-run aggregate supply. For example, a bad crop due to unusual weather one year does not imply a reduced output of that crop next year, and the falling of oil prices one year does not guarantee that oil prices will stay down the next year.

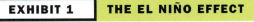

EXHIBIT 1   THE EL NIÑO EFFECT

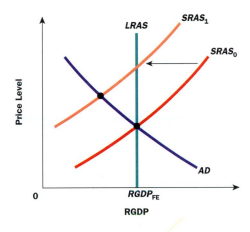

ONE STEP BEYOND

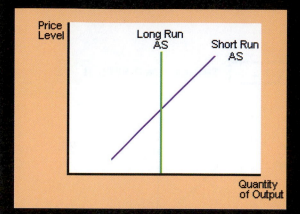

Can you supply all of the answers when it comes to long- and short-term aggregate supply and macroeconomic equilibrium? Test your mastery of these concepts using the exercises in your Workbook and the self-tests on the EconActive CD-ROM!

PHOTO CREDITS MODULE 20

Page 483: © John Running/Stock, Boston/PNI; Page 485: © Ken Graham/AllStock/PNI; Page 486: © Associated Press/Jack Dempsey; Page 487: © Keren Su/AllStock/PNI; Page 490: © Joe Hoffecker. Reprinted with permission from Cincinnati Business Courier; Page 492: © Associated Press/Damian Dovarganes.

Fiscal Policy

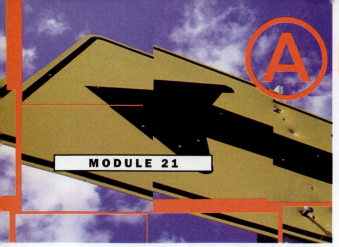

A Fiscal Policy

- What is fiscal policy?
- How does expansionary fiscal policy affect the government's budget?
- How does contractionary fiscal policy affect the government's budget?

WHAT IS FISCAL POLICY?

It is possible that short-run equilibrium real GDP can be accompanied by undesirably high levels of unemployment and/or high price levels. The government can use fiscal policy to change such results. **Fiscal policy** is the use of government purchases, taxes, and transfer payments to alter real GDP and price levels.

When government spending (for purchases of goods and services and transfer payments) exceeds tax revenues, there is a **budget deficit.** When tax revenues are greater than government spending, a **budget surplus** ex-

ists. A balanced budget, where government expenditures equal tax revenues, may seldom occur unless efforts are made to deliberately balance the budget as a matter of public policy.

Deficits and Expansionary Fiscal Policy

In the United States, the federal government has followed a typical practice of running at least a modest deficit, with large deficits in recession years, such as in the early 1980s and early 1990s (see Exhibit 1). From 1970 to 1997, the federal budget was in a deficit in every year. In many of those years, particularly since the 1970s, the deficit was fairly

| EXHIBIT 1 | THE U.S. FEDERAL BUDGET DEFICIT AS A PERCENT OF GDP |

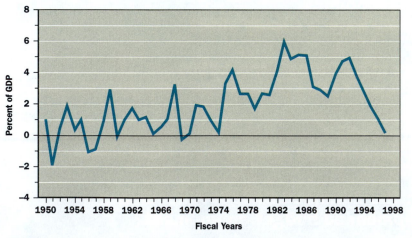

The budget is projected to be in balance in fiscal 1999 for the first time since 1969.

SOURCES: Department of Commerce (Bureau of Economic Analysis) and Office of Management and Budget.

substantial, often exceeding 2 percent of GDP. Thus, federal government policy, until very recently, seems to have gotten away from the notion accepted by many economic policymakers in earlier years that the budget ought to be roughly balanced over the business cycle, running surpluses in good times and offsetting deficits in bad times. While the growing U.S. economy is forecast to generate a federal budget surplus in 1999, and possibly beyond, the size of government has been rising steadily, with increased government spending in this country and other industrial countries as well, as seen in Exhibit 2, financed by a combination of increased taxes and larger budget deficits.

HOW IS THE BUDGET AFFECTED BY FISCAL STIMULUS?

When the government wishes to stimulate the economy by increasing aggregate demand, it will increase government purchases of goods and services, increase transfer payments, lower taxes, or use some combination of these approaches. Any of those options will increase the budget deficit (or reduce the budget surplus). Thus, **expansionary fiscal policy** is associated with increased government budget deficits. Likewise, if the government wishes to dampen a boom in the economy by reducing aggregate demand, it will reduce its purchases of goods and services, increase taxes, reduce transfer payments, or use some combination of these approaches. Thus, **contractionary fiscal policy**, will tend to create or expand a budget surplus, or reduce a budget deficit, if one exists.

"In a compromise move to cut the budget, Congress and the president agreed to move the decimal one point to the left."

GLOBAL WATCH

GOVERNMENT SPENDING AS A PERCENT OF GDP

EXHIBIT 2								
Country	1870	1913	1920	1937	1960	1980	1990	1996
Canada	—	—	13.3	18.6	28.6	38.8	46.0	44.7
France	12.6	17.0	27.6	29.0	34.6	46.1	49.8	54.5
Germany	10.0	14.8	25.0	42.4	32.4	47.9	45.1	49.0
Italy	11.9	11.1	22.5	24.5	30.1	41.9	53.2	52.9
Japan	8.8	8.3	14.8	25.4	17.5	32.0	31.7	36.2
Norway	3.7	8.3	13.7	—	29.9	37.5	53.8	45.5
Sweden	5.7	6.3	8.1	10.4	31.0	60.1	59.1	64.7
Britain	9.4	12.7	26.2	30.0	32.2	43.0	39.9	41.9
United States	3.9	1.8	7.0	8.6	27.0	31.8	33.3	33.3

The United States government spending is a smaller percentage of GDP than that in most other industrial countries. However, there is a clear trend towards bigger government.

SOURCE: IMF.

1. Fiscal policy is the use of government purchases of goods and services, taxes, and transfer payments to affect aggregate demand and alter GDP and price levels.
2. Expansionary fiscal policies will increase the budget deficit (or reduce a budget surplus) through greater government spending, lower taxes, or both.
3. Contractionary fiscal policies will create a budget surplus (or reduce a budget deficit) through reduced government spending, higher taxes, or both.

1. If, as part of its fiscal policy, the federal government increased its purchases of goods and services, would that be an expansionary or contractionary tactic?
2. If the federal government decreased its purchases of goods and services, would the budget deficit increase or decrease?
3. If the federal government increased taxes or decreased transfer payments, would that be an expansionary or contractionary fiscal policy?
4. If the federal government increased taxes or decreased transfer payments, would the budget deficit increase or decrease?
5. If the federal government increased government purchases and lowered taxes at the same time, would the budget deficit increase or decrease?

B The Multiplier Effect

- What is the multiplier effect?
- How does the marginal propensity to consume affect the multiplier effect?
- How does investment interact with the multiplier effect?

WHAT CAN CAUSE A DECREASE IN TOTAL PURCHASES?

The GDP will change anytime the amount of any one of the four forms of purchases—consumption, investment, government purchases, and net exports—changes. If, for any reason, people generally decide to purchase more in any of these categories out of given income, aggregate demand will shift rightward.

WHAT CAN CAUSE A CHANGE IN TOTAL OUTPUT?

Any one of the components of purchases of goods and services (C, I, G, or $X - M$) can initiate changes in aggregate demand, and thus a new short-run equilibrium. Changes in total output are often brought about by alterations in investment plans, because investment purchases are a relatively volatile category of expenditures. However, if policymakers are unhappy with the present short-run equilibrium GDP, perhaps because they consider unemployment too high, they can deliberately manipulate the level of government purchases in order to obtain a new short-run equilibrium value. Similarly, by changing taxes or transfer payments, they can alter the amount of disposable income of households and thus bring about changes in consumption purchases.

WHAT IS THE MULTIPLIER EFFECT?

Usually when an initial increase in purchases of goods or services occurs, the ultimate increase in total purchases will tend to be greater than the initial increase. This is called the **multiplier effect.** But how does this effect work? Suppose the government increases its defense budget by $10 billion to buy aircraft carriers. When the government purchases the aircraft carriers, not only does it add to the total demand for goods and services directly, it also provides $10 billion in added income to the companies that actually construct the aircraft carriers. Those companies will then hire more workers and buy more capital equipment and other inputs in order to produce the new output. The owners of these inputs therefore receive more income because of the increase in government purchases. And what will they do with this additional income? While behavior will vary somewhat among individuals, collectively they will probably spend a substantial part of the additional income on additional consumption purchases, pay some additional taxes incurred because of the income, and save a bit of it as well. The additional consumption purchases made as a portion of the additional income is measured by the **marginal propensity to consume (MPC)**.

HOW DOES THE MULTIPLIER EFFECT WORK?

Suppose that out of every dollar in *added* income generated by increased investment purchases, individuals collectively spend two-thirds, or 67 cents on consumption purchases. In other words, the MPC is 2/3. The initial $10 billion increase in government purchases causes both a $10 billion increase in aggregate demand and an income increase of $10 billion to suppliers of the inputs used to produce aircraft carriers; the owners of those inputs, in turn, will spend an additional $6.67 billion (two-thirds of $10 billion) on additional consumption purchases. A chain reaction has been started. The added $6.67 billion in consumption purchases by those deriving income from the initial investment brings a $6.67 billion increase in aggregate demand and in new income to suppliers of the inputs that produced the goods and services. These persons, in turn, will spend some two-thirds of their additional $6.67 billion in income, or $4.44 billion on consumption purchases. This means a $4.44 billion more in aggregate demand and income to still another group of persons, who will then proceed to spend two-thirds of that amount, or $2.96 billion on consumption purchases.

The chain reaction continues, with each new round of purchases providing income to a new group of persons who, in turn, increase their purchases. At each round, the added income generated and the number of resulting

EXHIBIT 1 | THE MULTIPLIER PROCESS

Round	Increase in Income Generated (billions of dollars)	Increase in Purchases (billions of dollars)	
1	$10.00	$10.00—direct effect on AD	
2	6.67	6.67	
3	4.44	4.44	The sum of the indirect effect on AD, through induced additional consumption purchases is equal to $20 billion
4	2.96	2.96	
5	1.98	1.98	
6	1.32	1.32	
7	.88	.88	
8	.59	.59	
9	.39	.39	
Total all Rounds	$30.00	$30.00 = Total effect on purchases (AD)	

consumer purchases get smaller, because some of each round's increase in income goes to savings and tax payments that do not immediately flow into greater investment or government expenditure. As Exhibit 1 indicates, by the eighth or ninth round of purchases, the magnitude of further rounds of the process are much smaller than the initial round. What is the total impact of the initial increase in purchases, after all the rounds of additional purchases and income have occurred? The multiplier is calculated as follows:

$$\text{Multiplier} = 1/(1 - MPC)$$

In this case,

$$\text{Multiplier} = 1/(1 - 2/3) = 1/(1/3) = 3$$

An initial increase in purchases of goods or services of $10 billion, then, will increase total purchases by $30 billion ($10 billion × 3), as the $10 billion in investment purchases also generates an additional $20 billion in consumption purchases.

HOW DO CHANGES IN THE MPC AFFECT THE MULTIPLIER PROCESS?

Note that the larger the marginal propensity to consume, the larger the multiplier effect, because relatively more additional consumption purchases out of any given income increase generates relatively larger secondary and tertiary income effects in successive rounds of the process. For example, if the MPC is 3/4, the multiplier is 4:

$$\text{Multiplier} = 1/(1 - 3/4) = 1/(1/4) = 4$$

If the MPC is only one-half, however, the multiplier is 2:

$$\text{Multiplier} = 1/(1 - 1/2) = 1/(1/2) = 2$$

THE MULTIPLIER AND THE AGGREGATE DEMAND CURVE

As we discussed earlier, when the Defense Department decides to buy additional aircraft carriers, it affects aggregate demand. It increases the incomes of owners of inputs used to make the aircraft carriers, including profits that go to owners of the firms involved. That is the initial effect. The secondary effect, the greater income that results, will lead to increased consumer purchases. In addition, the higher profits for the firms involved in carrier construction may lead them to increase their investment purchases. So the initial effect of the government's purchases will tend to have a multiplied effect on the economy. In Exhibit 2, we see that the initial impact of a $10 billion additional purchase by the government directly shifts the aggregate demand curve from AD_0 to AD_1. The multiplier effect then causes the aggregate demand to shift out $20 billion further, to AD_2. The total effect on aggregate demand of a $10 billion increase in government purchases is therefore $30 billion, if the marginal propensity to consume equals two-thirds.

EXHIBIT 2 | THE MULTIPLIER AND AGGREGATE DEMAND

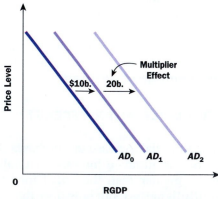

In this hypothetical example, an increase in government purchases of $10 billion for new aircraft carriers will shift the aggregate demand curve to the right by more than the $10 billion initial purchase, other things equal. It will shift aggregate demand by a total of $30 billion, to AD_2. (The shifts are shown larger than they would really be, for visual ease— $30 billion is a small shift in an $8,000 billion economy.)

HOW DO TIME LAGS, TAXES, AND IMPORTS AFFECT THE MULTIPLIER?

The multiplier process is not instantaneous. If I get an additional $100 in income today, I may spend two-thirds of that on consumption purchases eventually, but I may wait six months or even longer to do it. Such time lags mean that the ultimate increase in purchases resulting from an initial increase in purchases may not be achieved for a year or more. The extent of the multiplier effect visible within a

STEALTH BOMBERS AND MULTIPLIERS

DAVE BERRY

So far the B-2 project has cost us taxpayers $45 billion, which has purchased us 21 bombers, which works out to around $2 billion per bomber, making it the most expensive airplane ever built (bear in mind, however, that it comes with floor mats).

Now here's the problem: The General Accounting Office did a big study of the B-2 bomber, concluding that—I will try to put this in layperson's terms—flying is bad for it. Yes. It turns out that the secret stealthy materials are sensitive to moisture, which as luck would have it (Who could have predicted this?) is plentiful in the atmosphere, so according to the GAO, after the B-2 flies, it tends to need lots of costly repairs.

SOURCE: Dave Barry, "At Least the Stealth Bomber Has the Sense to Get Out of the Rain," *The Sacramento Bee,* http://www.sacbee.com/voices/national/barry/barry_oct26.html October 26, 1997

CONSIDER THIS:
In the real world, the multiplier process is important because it may help explain why small changes in consumption, investment, and government purchases can cause larger, multiplied changes in total purchases. These increased purchases, in turn, could lead to increased real output and reduced unemployment when the economy is not already fully employed.

In this application, when the government purchased the stealth bombers, we are assuming that it would not have purchased other goods and services with those same dollars instead. This is important because the purchase of B-2s has the potential to lead to a net increase in demand only so far as it increases total government purchases, which, if the economy is less than fully employed, will increase real output and employment. That is, the increase in demand for stealth bombers, other things equal, will lead to an increase in output for General Dynamics (which builds the B-2). As a result, General Dynamics will hire more employees, who will take their paychecks and spend some of it on clothes, restaurant meals, and other goods and services. Those purchases will result in further growth in those industries, many of which are located far from the B-2 plant. In other words, a government purchase has the potential to have an impact on the economy that is greater than the magnitude of that original purchase. This is the multiplier process at work.

However, if the stealth bomber purchases just replace other government purchases, the multiplied expansion in defense-related industries is offset by a multiplied contraction in industries where government purchases have fallen.

Contrast this example with government purchases of food for a school lunch program. Government purchases of school lunches rise, but private consumption falls as parents now purchase less food—perhaps by the same amount—for their children's lunches. Overall, we would expect only a small change in demand, if any, as government demand replaces private demand. In some real sense, the suppliers of apples, milk, cookies, and chips have just had the names of their customers change.

short time period will be less than the total effect indicated by the multiplier formula. In addition, savings, taxes, and money spent on import goods (which are not part of aggregate demand for domestically produced goods and services) will reduce the size of the multiplier, because each of them reduces the fraction of a given increase in income that will go to additional purchases of domestically produced consumption goods.

CONCEPT CHECK

1. The multiplier effect is a chain reaction of additional income and purchases that results in a final increase in total purchases that is greater than the initial increase in purchases.
2. An increase in the marginal propensity to consume leads to an increase in the multiplier effect.
3. Because of a time lag, the full impact of the multiplier effect on GDP may not be felt until a year or more after the initial investment.

4. An increase in government purchases will also cause an increase in aggregate income and stimulate additional consumer purchases, which will result in a magnified (or multiplying) effect on aggregate demand.

---

1. How does the multiplier effect work?
2. What is the marginal propensity to consume?
3. Why is the marginal propensity to consume always less than one?
4. Why does the multiplier effect get larger as the marginal propensity to consume gets larger?

5. If an increase in government purchases leads to a reduction in private-sector purchases, why could the effect on the economy be less than indicated by the multiplier?

Fiscal Policy and the AD/AS Model

- How can government stimulus of aggregate demand reduce unemployment?
- How can government reduction of aggregate demand reduce inflation?

FISCAL POLICY AND THE AD/AS MODEL

The primary tools of fiscal policy, government purchases, taxes, and transfer payments, can be presented in the context of the aggregate supply and demand model. In Exhibit 1, we have used the AD/AS model to show how the government can use fiscal policy as either an expansionary or contractionary tool to help control the economy.

BUDGET DEFICITS AND FISCAL POLICY

As we discussed earlier, when the government purchases more, taxes less, and increases transfer payments, the size of the government's budget deficit will grow. While budget deficits are often thought to be bad, a case can be made for using budget deficits to stimulate the economy when it is operating at less than full capacity. Such expansionary fiscal policy may have the potential to move an economy out of a recession and closer to full employment.

Expansionary Fiscal Policy at Less Than Full Employment

If the government decides to purchase more, cut taxes, and/or increase transfer payments, other things constant, total purchases will rise. That is, increased government purchases, tax cuts, or transfer payment increases can increase consumption, investment, and government purchases, shifting the aggregate demand curve to the right. The effect of this increase in aggregate demand depends on the position of the macroeconomic equilibrium prior to the government stimulus. For example, in Exhibit 1(a), the initial equilibrium is at E_0, a recession scenario, with real output below potential RGDP. Starting at this point and moving along the short-run aggregate supply curve, an increase in government purchases, a tax cut, and/or increase in transfer payments would increase the size of the budget deficit and lead to an increase in aggregate demand, ideally from AD_0 to AD_1. The result of such a change would be an increase in the price level, from PL_{100} to PL_{115}—an

increase of 15 percent—and an increase in real GDP, from $RGDP_0$ to $RGDP_{FE}$. We must remember, of course, that some of this increase in aggregate demand is caused by the multiplier process, so the magnitude of the change in aggregate demand will be larger than the magnitude of the stimulus package of tax cuts, increases in transfer payments, and/or government purchases. If the policy change is of the right magnitude and timed appropriately, the expansionary fiscal policy might stimulate the economy, pulling it out of recession, resulting in full employment at $RGDP_{FE}$.

Expansionary Fiscal Policy at Full Employment

Now suppose that the economy is currently operating at full employment—$RGDP_{FE}$. This is seen as point E_0 in Exhibit 1(b). An increase in government spending, an increase in transfer payments, and/or a tax cut causes an increase in aggregate demand from AD_0 to AD_1. Moving along short-run aggregate supply curve $SRAS_0$, the price level rises and real output rises to $RGDP_1$ as we reach a short-run equilibrium at E_1. This is not a long-run, or sustainable, equilibrium, however, because at this point, the high level of aggregate demand at beyond full capacity will put pressure on input markets, sending wages and other input prices higher. The higher costs that result from these input price increases will shift the short-run aggregate supply curve leftward from $SRAS_0$ to $SRAS_1$. This, in turn, shifts the short-run equilibrium point from E_1 to E_2, which, because it is on the long-run aggregate supply curve, is a sustainable long-run equilibrium. So we see that real output returns to the full employment level, and the long-term effect is a 20 percent increase in the price level, from PL_{100} to PL_{120}.

BUDGET SURPLUSES AND FISCAL POLICY

When the government purchases less, taxes more, or decreases transfer payments, the size of the government's

EXHIBIT 1   **EXPANSIONARY FISCAL POLICY**

a. At Less Than Full Employment

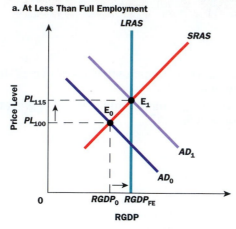

b. At Full Employment

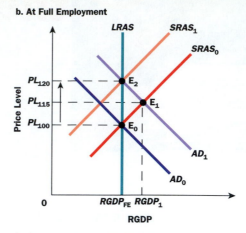

An increase in government purchases, an increase in transfer payments, and/or a tax cut at less than full employment

An increase in government purchases, an increase in transfer payments, and/or a tax cut at full employment

In Exhibit 1(a), the increase in government purchases, a tax cut, and/or an increase in transfer payments leads to a rightward shift in aggregate demand. This results in a change in equilibrium from E_0 to E_1, reflecting a higher price level and a higher RGDP. Because this result is on the LRAS curve, it is a long-run, sustainable equilibrium. In Exhibit 1(b), we see that the same policy change will only lead to a short-run increase in RGDP. Once input owners realize that the price level has changed, they will require higher input prices, raising costs and shifting the SRAS curve to the left. The final long-run equilibrium will only reflect the new higher price level (PL_{120}).

budget deficit will fall or the size of the budget surplus will rise, other things equal. Sometimes such a change in fiscal policy may help "cool off" the economy when it has overheated and inflation has become a serious problem. Then, contractionary fiscal policy has the potential to offset an overheated, inflationary boom.

Contractionary Fiscal Policy beyond Full Employment

Suppose that the price level is at PL_{130} and that short-run equilibrium is at E_0, as shown in Exhibit 2(a). Say that the government decides to reduce its purchases, increase taxes, or reduce transfer payments. A government purchase change may directly affect aggregate demand. A tax increase on consumers or a decrease in transfer payments will reduce households' disposable incomes, reducing purchases of consumption goods and services, and higher business taxes will reduce investment purchases. The reductions in consumption, investment, and/or government purchases will shift the aggregate demand curve leftward, ideally from AD_0 to AD_1. This lowers the price level from PL_{130} to PL_{100} and brings RGDP back to the full employ-

ment level at $RGDP_{FE}$, resulting in a new short- and long-run equilibrium at E_1.

A Contractionary Fiscal Policy at Full Employment

Now consider the case of an initial short- and long-run equilibrium at full employment, as indicated by point E_0, with a price level of PL_{130}, where AD_0 intersects both the SRAS curve and the LRAS curve. This situation is depicted in Exhibit 2(b). A decrease in aggregate demand from AD_0 to AD_1 that results from a reduction in government purchases, higher taxes, or lower transfer payments leads to a short-run equilibrium at E_1, with lower prices and real output reduced below its full employment level at $RGDP_1$. As prices fall, input suppliers then revise their price level expectations downward. That is, laborers and other input suppliers are now willing to take less for the use of their resources, and the resulting reduction in production costs shifts the short-run supply curve from $SRAS_0$ to $SRAS_1$. The resulting eventual long-run equilibrium is a reduction in the price level, with real output returning to its full employment.

EXHIBIT 2

CONTRACTIONARY FISCAL POLICY

a. Beyond Full Employment

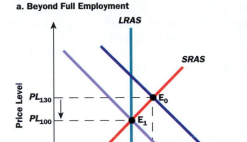

b. At Full Employment

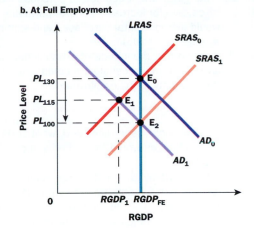

A reduction in government purchases, a decrease in transfer payments, and/or higher taxes beyond full employment

A reduction in government purchases, a decrease in transfer payments, and/or higher taxes at full employment

In Exhibit 2(a), the reduction in government purchases, tax increase, or transfer payment decrease leads to a leftward shift in aggregate demand and a change in the short-run equilibrium from E_0 to E_1, reflecting a lower price level and a return to full employment RGDP ($RGDP_{FE}$). In Exhibit 2(b), the reduction in aggregate demand leads to a short-run equilibrium at E_1, reflecting a lower price level and real output below its full employment level. At this point, input owners change their price level expectations and are now willing to accept lower compensation. This reduces production costs and shifts short-run aggregate supply to the right, from $SRAS_0$ to $SRAS_1$. The final long-run effect is a new lower price level and real output that has returned to $RGDP_{FE}$.

IN THE NEWS

JAPAN'S LEADER FAVORS PERMANENT TAX CUTS

TOKYO—Isolated by growing pressure for quick action to fix its anemic economy, Japan's prime minister on Friday said for the first time that he would support a permanent tax cut to stimulate consumer spending.

"I hope we will have not temporary tax cuts, but so-called permanent tax reforms. I think we'll move in that direction," Ryutaro Hashimoto said. Until now, he had favored one-time tax breaks instead of longer-term tax relief.

Temporary tax cuts failed to stimulate the economy in the past because the Japanese—

known for their high savings rate—simply squirreled away the extra money. Officials contend that a permanent tax break will bolster consumer confidence, lead to greater spending and help Japan out of its worst recession since World War II.

Hashimoto had previously resisted going beyond temporary tax relief measures for fear of ballooning the deficit, which he has pledged to shrink.

SOURCE: "Japan's Leader Favors Permanent Tax Cuts," *Los Angeles Times*, July 4, 1998, p. D1.

CONSIDER THIS:
Japan's former prime minster realized the importance of expansionary fiscal policy—permanent tax cuts to stimulate aggregate demand. However, the Japanese voted Hashimoto and his ruling party out of office as a result of his disastrous decision to *raise* consumption taxes and his tardiness on prescribing permanent tax cuts.

1. If the government decided to purchase more, cut taxes, and/or increase transfer payments, that would increase total purchases and shift out the aggregate demand curve.
2. If the correct magnitude of expansionary fiscal policy is used in a recession, it could potentially bring the economy to full employment.
3. Expansionary fiscal policy at full employment may lead to short-run increases in output and employment, but in the long run, the expansionary effect will only lead to higher price levels.
4. Contractionary fiscal policy has the potential to offset an overheated inflationary boom.

1. If the economy is in recession, what sorts of fiscal policy changes would tend to bring it out of recession?
2. If the economy is at a short-run equilibrium at greater than full employment, what sorts of fiscal policy changes would tend to bring the economy back to a full employment equilibrium?
3. What effects would an expansionary fiscal policy have on the price level and real GDP, starting from a full employment equilibrium?
4. What effects would a contractionary fiscal policy have on the price level and real GDP, starting from a full employment equilibrium?

D Possible Obstacles to Effective Fiscal Policy

■ How does the crowding out effect limit the economic impact of increased government purchases or reduced taxes?

■ What is the Ricardian equivalence theorem?

■ How do time lags in policy implementation affect policy effectiveness?

WHAT IS THE CROWDING OUT EFFECT?

The multiplier effect of an increase in government purchases implies that the increase in aggregate demand will tend to be greater than the initial fiscal stimulus, other things equal. However, this may not be true, because all other things will not tend to stay equal in this case. In particular, when the government borrows money to finance the deficit, it increases the overall demand for loanable funds, driving interest rates up. The increase in the demand for loanable funds sends the interest rate up (from r_0 to r_1), as seen in Exhibit 1(a). The higher interest rate means that

the opportunity cost of borrowing funds has risen. As a result of the higher interest rate, consumers may decide against buying a car, a home, or other interest-sensitive good, and businesses may cancel or scale back plans to expand or buy new capital equipment. In short, the higher interest rate will choke off private spending on goods and services, and as a result, the impact of the increase in government purchases may be smaller than we first assumed. Economists call this the **crowding out effect.** For example, in Exhibit 1(b), say the federal government borrows to finance a deficit created by expansionary fiscal policy. The increase in government spending and the multiplier shifts

---

EXHIBIT 1	THE CROWDING OUT EFFECT

a. Loanable Funds Market

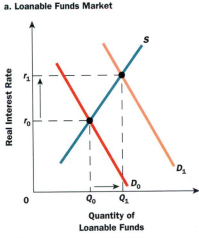

b. Changes in Aggregate Demand

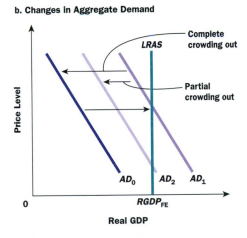

In Exhibit 1(a), we see that if the government's demand for loans is added to the private sector demand for loans, demand increases, shifting from D_0 to D_1. This leads to a higher real interest rate and lower levels of investment and consumption. The lower levels of investment can either partially or completely offset the fiscal policy effect, shifting aggregate demand to the left from AD_1 to AD_2, or all the way back to AD_0.

---

the aggregate demand curve to the right, from AD_0 to AD_1. However, as this process takes place, interest rates are bid up, as seen in Exhibit 1(a). The higher real interest rate leads to a reduction in private-sector spending, because borrowing is now more expensive. This reduction in private spending shifts the aggregate demand curve from AD_1 to AD_2. If every dollar of government purchases crowded out a dollar of private purchases (100 percent crowding out), fiscal policy would have no *net* effect on aggregate demand, shifting the aggregate demand curve all the way back to AD_0.

In Exhibit 1(a), we see that when the government increases its borrowing to pay for increases in government purchases, the demand for loanable funds shifts the curve to the right (from D_0 to D_1), causing the equilibrium interest rate to rise. In Exhibit 1(b), we see that an initial $10 billion increase in government purchases, by itself, would shift aggregate demand right by $10 billion times the multiplier, from AD_0 to AD_1. However, because of the higher interest rates resulting from the additional government borrowing, interest-sensitive investments for consumers and businesses are choked off (seen in Exhibit 1(a)), which, by itself, would cause the aggregate demand curve to shift left by the purchases crowded out times the multiplier, from AD_1 to AD_2. Because both these processes are taking place at the same time, the net effect is an increase in aggregate demand equal to the difference between the added government purchases and the private purchases crowded out by higher interest rates, times the multiplier, or from AD_0 to AD_2.

The Crowding Out Effect in the Open Economy

Another form of crowding out can take place in international markets. For example, say the government cut taxes and is now running a larger budget deficit. To finance the deficit the United States government borrows more money—increasing the demand for loanable funds and driving up the interest rate. This is the basic crowding out effect. However, the higher U.S. interest rate will attract funds from abroad. In order to invest in the U.S. economy, foreigners will have to first convert their currencies into dollars. The increase in the demand for dollars relative to other currencies, will cause the dollar to appreciate in value, making foreign imports relatively cheaper in the U.S. and U.S. exports relatively more expensive in other countries. This will cause net exports $(X - M)$ to fall for two reasons. One, because of the higher relative price of the dollar, foreign imports become cheaper for those in the U.S., and imports will increase. Two, because of the higher relative price of the dollar, U.S.-made goods become more expensive to foreigners, so exports fall. The increase in imports and the decrease in exports causes a reduction in net exports and a fall in aggregate demand. The net effect, is that to the extent net exports are crowded out, fiscal policy

has a smaller effect on aggregate demand than it would otherwise.

WHAT IS THE RICARDIAN EQUIVALENCE THEOREM?

Another related problem undermining the power of fiscal policy to change aggregate demand is expressed in what is called the **Ricardian equivalence theorem.** This theory is named for the famous economist David Ricardo, who first presented this argument in the 1800s. The argument is that an increase in aggregate demand that would be expected as a result of an increase in government purchases will be partially or fully offset by an increase in savings (which is the same as a reduction in consumption purchases). If people realize that the increase in government purchases will lead to higher taxes in the future, they may increase their savings now to pay for those higher future taxes. Thus, the expected increase in aggregate demand as a result of an increase in government spending is offset by the reduction in current consumption as individuals save for the future tax increase. Just as with the crowding out effect, this implies that fiscal policy will have a smaller effect on aggregate demand than otherwise predicted. The more current consumption falls in response to the fiscal policy stimulus, the less effective that stimulus is in raising income. If savings changes exactly offset the fiscal stimulus, there will be no net effect on aggregate demand.

Graphically, this short-run effect looks much the same as the results of the crowding out effect shown in Exhibit 1(b). As a result of the government purchases alone, aggregate demand would shift rightward by the increase in government purchases, times the multiplier, from AD_0 to AD_1. To the extent individuals respond by saving more to pay the greater future tax burden and consuming less, the effect of this on aggregate demand would be to shift it left by the reduction in consumption purchases times the multiplier, or AD_1 to AD_2. The net effect is to increase aggregate demand from AD_0 to AD_2. If consumers fully anticipate the future tax liability, there will be no net effect on aggregate demand. It should be noted, however, that the empirical evidence of the 1980s does not fully support the theory, as large budget deficits were not accompanied with increases in the savings rate. In fact, since the early 1980s decreases in private savings have accompanied the large and growing budget deficits.

WHY ARE THERE TIME LAGS IN POLICY IMPLEMENTATION?

It is important to recognize that in a democratic country, fiscal policy is implemented through the political process, and that process takes time. Often, the lag between the time that a fiscal response is desired and the time an appropriate policy is implemented and its effects felt is considerable. Sometimes a fiscal policy designed to deal with a contracting economy may actually take effect during a period of economic expansion, or vice versa, resulting in a stabilization policy that actually destabilizes the economy.

HOW DOES THE POLICY MAKING PROCESS WORK?

Government tax or spending changes require both congressional and presidential approval. Suppose the economy is beginning a downturn. It may take two or three months before enough data are gathered to indicate the actual presence of a downturn. Sometimes a future downturn can be forecast through econometric models or by looking at the index of leading indicators, but usually decision makers are hesitant to plan policy on the basis of forecasts that are not always accurate.

At some point, however, policymakers may decide that some policy change is necessary. At this point, experts are consulted, and congressional committees have hearings about and listen to testimony on possible policy approaches. During the consultation phase, many decisions have to be made. If, for example, a tax cut is recommended, what form should the cut take and how large should it be? Across-the-board income tax reductions? Reductions in corporate taxes? More generous exemptions and deductions from the income tax (e.g., for child care, casualty losses, education of children)? In other words, who should get the benefits of lower taxes? Likewise, if the decision is made to increase government expenditures, which programs should be expanded or initiated and by how much? These are questions with profound political consequences, so reaching a decision is not always easy and usually involves much compromise and a great deal of time.

Finally, once the House and Senate have completed their separate deliberations and have arrived at a final version of the bill, it is presented to Congress for approval. After congressional approval is secured, the bill then goes to the president for approval or veto.

HOW LONG DOES IT TAKE FOR APPROVED POLICY TO TAKE EFFECT?

Even after legislation is signed into law, it takes time to bring about the actual fiscal stimulus desired. If the legislation provides for a reduction in withholding taxes, for example, it might take a few months before the changes actually show up in workers' paychecks. With respect to changes in government purchases, the delay is usually much longer. If the government increases spending for public works projects like sewer systems, new highways,

or urban renewal, it takes time to draw up plans and get permissions, to advertise for bids from contractors, to get contracts, and then to begin work. And there may be further delays because of government regulations. For example, an environmental impact statement must be completed before most public works projects can begin, a process that often takes many months or even years.

WHY IS TIMING SO IMPORTANT?

The timing of fiscal policy is crucial. Because of the significant lags before the fiscal policy has its impact, the increase in aggregate demand may occur at the wrong time. For example, imagine that we are initially at AD_0 in Exhibit 2. The economy is currently suffering from low levels of output and high rates of unemployment. In response, policymakers decide to increase government purchases and implement a tax cut. But during the period from the time when the policymakers recognized the problem to the time when the policies had a chance to work themselves through the economy, there was a large increase in business and consumer confidence, shifting the aggregate demand curve rightward from AD_0 to AD_1—increasing real GDP and employment. Now when the fiscal policy takes effect, the policies will have the undesired effect of causing inflation, with little permanent effect on output and employment. This is seen in Exhibit 2, as the aggregate demand curve shifts from AD_1 to AD_2.

EXHIBIT 2	TIMING EXPANSIONARY FISCAL POLICY

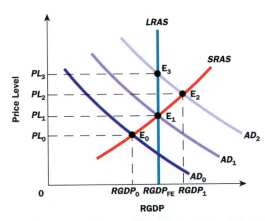

Initially, the macroeconomy is at equilibrium at point E_0. With high unemployment (at $RGDP_0$), the government decides to increase government purchases and cut taxes to stimulate the economy. This shifts aggregate demand from AD_0 to AD_1 over time—perhaps 12 to 16 months. In the meantime, if consumer confidence increases, the aggregate demand curve might shift to AD_2, leading to much higher prices (PL_3) in the long run, rather than at the target level, E_1, at price level PL_1.

TAXATION, GOVERNMENT ACTIVITY, AND ECONOMIC GROWTH

TALKING TAXES

- In terms of the size of its tax burden, the United States is a relatively low-tax nation: It is 21st of the 24 industrialized countries in the Organization for Economic Cooperation and Development.

- In terms of growth in taxes from 1965 to 1993, America was 23rd in the OECD.

- Various economic studies have shown that government taxation produces a drag on the economy that can amount to as much as 50 cents per dollar of tax revenues collected.

- Tax increases are usually accompanied by declines in per capita growth in GDP.

Why does government activity seem to impede economic growth? The reasons include the following:

Few economic incentives for efficiency in the public sector: Managers of government activities seldom receive rewards for initiating cost-reducing or output-enhancing measures. Indeed, in some cases, increases in productivity may mean the manager in question has a smaller budget and also must incur the wrath of fellow employees who suffer from the changes that generate an increase in output per worker.

Government monopolies: For many government services, there is a single provider that does not feel pressure to cut costs to meet competition from other providers of goods and services. The lack of competition may explain why, by most measures, productivity has not risen rapidly in the provision of, for example, education and postal services.

Special-interest groups: As government grows, efforts to use the political process to redistribute income from the general tax-paying public to specific individuals or groups intensify. Highway contractors promote "infrastructure investment," public employees seek large salary increases, businesses lobby for subsidies, and still others favor public assistance of one form or another.

Government regulation: In a world of limited government, private entrepreneurs have incentives to raise productivity—to use fewer resources to produce a given quantity of output. Government regulation, if it is heavy, interferes with this activity, leading to lower productivity. While some regulation may be needed, it can easily become excessive and generate more costs than benefits.

The political process: In the public sector, legislators, in particular, think primarily in terms of the immediate future. They are attuned to the rhythm of electoral cycles. In response to these cycles, they will often take actions that they perceive to be in their electoral interest but which have adverse long-term effects on economic activity.

This is not to say that all government activity is counterproductive. There are valuable things government does to enhance the functioning of an economy, such as providing for the common defense, establishing a legal framework for resolving disputes, constructing a basic infrastructure, and supervising a social safety net. These are the positive works of government.

But there are diminishing returns to government activity. And, as government expands—and so increases the level of taxation to finance its activities—the inefficiencies just described become more and more pronounced.

SOURCE: Lowell Gallaway, "Taxes around the World," *The World & I,* July 1996, pp. 100–105.

CONSIDER THIS:
While taxes may not be high in the United States relative to other countries, there may be other reasons why Americans find taxation and increased government activity burdensome.

CONCEPT CHECK

1. The crowding out effect states that as the government borrows to pay for the deficit, it drives up the interest rates and crowds out private spending and investment.

2. According to the Ricardian equivalence theorem, an increase in government spending will lead to higher taxes in the future, other things equal. If people save for the predictable future tax increase, there will be a reduction in current consumption. This would reduce, and could even completely offset, the effect of a fiscal stimulus.

3. The lag time between when a fiscal policy may be needed and when it is actually implemented is considerable.

---

1. Why does a larger government budget deficit increase the magnitude of the crowding out effect?

2. Why does fiscal policy have a smaller effect on aggregate demand, the greater the crowding out effect?

3. Why does the Ricardian equivalence theorem imply that if people correctly recognize the future tax liability represented by a current budget deficit, and save enough to pay for those future taxes as a result, then fiscal policy may have no effect on aggregate demand?

4. How do time lags impact the effectiveness of fiscal policy?

E Automatic Stabilizers

■ What are automatic stabilizers?
■ Which automatic stabilizers are the most important?

WHAT ARE AUTOMATIC STABILIZERS?

Some changes in government transfer payments and taxes take place automatically as business cycle conditions change, without deliberations in Congress or the executive branch of the government. Changes in government transfer payments or tax collections that automatically tend to counter business cycle fluctuations are called **automatic stabilizers.**

HOW DOES THE TAX SYSTEM STABILIZE THE ECONOMY?

The most important automatic stabilizer is the tax system. For example, with the personal income tax, as incomes rise, tax liabilities also increase automatically. Personal income taxes vary directly in amount with income, and in fact rise or fall by greater percentage terms than income itself rises or falls. Big increases and big decreases in GDP are both lessened by automatic changes in income tax receipts. For example, GDP declines, tax liabilities decline, increasing disposable incomes and stimulating consumption spending, partly offsetting the initial decline in aggregate demand.

There are, of course, other income-related payroll taxes, notably Social Security taxes. In addition, there is the corporate profit tax. Because incomes, earnings, and profits all fall during a recession, the government collects less in taxes. This reduced tax burden partially offsets the magnitude of the recession. Beyond this, the unemployment compensation program is another example of an automatic stabilizer. During recessions, unemployment is usually high

and unemployment compensation payments increase, providing income that will be consumed by recipients. During boom periods, such payments will fall as the number of the unemployed declines. The system of public assistance (welfare) payments tends to be another important automatic stabilizer, as the number of low-income persons eligible for some forms of assistance grows during recessions (stimulating aggregate demand) and declines during booms (reducing aggregate demand).

Automatic stabilizers work without legislative action.

ENTITLEMENT FRAUD GIVES "PRISON SECURITY" NEW MEANING

E.V. KONTOROVICH

William Bonin, California's infamous "freeway killer," spent 14 years on death row—about as long as the entire lives of the 21 boys he confessed to murdering. During his stretch in San Quentin, Bonin was getting monthly checks from the U.S. Treasury, some as high as $589. By the time his sentence was finally carried out in 1996, he had collected about $80,000 in Social Security payments while in prison.

Prisoners are ineligible for Social Security and most other benefit programs. Since the taxpayer already pays for their room, board, medical benefits and sometimes legal counsel, sending them benefit checks would amount to giving the perps pocket money. The Social Security Administration has always said it was vigilant about such fraud,

but its Bonin blunder was spotted only when his death papers were being shuffled.

Embarrassed by the error and hounded by the parents of Bonin's victims, the agency conducted an internal investigation, which concluded that Bonin's benefits were a fluke. Well, not quite. Congress began looking into the matter, and last March—two years after the Bonin mess—the SSA's inspector general, David Williams, admitted that some 60,000 inmates were taking the taxpayer to the tune of $500 million a year in fraudulent benefits.

Social Security isn't the only program from which prisoners profit: A GAO study of four states last year found that roughly 12,000 inmates were receiving illegal food stamp benefits because of the program's

"reliance on client-provided information"— the same obvious error as the SSA's.

SOURCE: E.V. Kontorovich, "Entitlement Fraud Gives 'Prison Security' New Meaning," *Wall Street Journal*, June 15, 1998.

> **CONSIDER THIS:**
> Although Social Security taxes are an automatic stabilizer that can help the economy, some people take advantage of them. Democrats and Republicans both want to get tough on government fraud on transfer programs.

CONCEPT CHECK

1. Automatic stabilizers are changes in government transfer payments or tax collections that happen automatically and whose effects vary inversely with business cycles.

2. The tax system is the most important automatic stabilizer; it has the greatest ability to smooth out swings in GDP during business cycles. Other automatic stabilizers are unemployment compensation and welfare payments.

1. How does the tax system act as an automatic stabilizer?
2. Are automatic stabilizers impacted by a time lag? Why or why not?

3. Why are transfer payments, such as unemployment compensation, effective automatic stabilizers?

F Supply-Side Fiscal Policy

- What is supply-side fiscal policy?
- How do supply-side policies affect long-run aggregate supply?
- What do its critics say about supply-side ideas?

WHAT IS SUPPLY-SIDE FISCAL POLICY?

The debate over short-run stabilization policies has been going on for some time, and there is no sign that it is close to being settled. When policymakers discuss methods to stabilize the economy, the focus since the 1930s has been on managing the economy through demand-side policies. But there is a group of economists who believe that we should be focusing on the supply side of the economy as well, especially in the long run, rather than just on the demand side. In particular, they believe that individuals will save less, work less, and provide less capital when taxes, government transfer payments (like welfare), and regulations are too burdensome on productive activities. In other words, they believe that fiscal policy can work on the supply side of the economy as well as the demand side.

HOW WOULD SUPPLY-SIDE POLICIES IMPACT THE ECONOMY?

Supply-siders would encourage government to reduce individual and business taxes, deregulate, and increase spending on research and development. Supply-siders believe that these types of government policies could cause greater long-term economic growth by stimulating personal income, savings, and capital formation.

DO LOWER TAX RATES AFFECT THE SUPPLY SIDE OF THE ECONOMY?

"Supply-siders" believe that savings and investment could be improved through lowering taxes. Imagine that your family had $100,000 in a savings account with an interest rate of 10 percent per year. At the end of the year, the account would have accrued $10,000 in interest—but the interest is taxable, say at 30 percent. So instead of receiving $10,000, your family would receive only $7,000 in interest after taxes. According to supply-siders, this reduced after-tax return to saving discourages people from saving, and

that has wide-ranging implications, because greater savings encourages greater investment and capital formation.

WHY IS INVESTMENT IMPORTANT?

Workers without capital cannot be very productive. For example, a fisherman with only his hands will not do as well as those with capital such as nets, boats, and sonar equipment. That is, worker productivity (output per worker) depends to a large extent on the capital that is available to the worker. So taxing savings and investment heavily will reduce new capital investment, which will reduce the growth of worker productivity.

Businesses might also get similar relief in the form of **investment tax credits.** These allow businesses to accelerate the speed that businesses can write off some of their new investments for tax purposes, raising after-tax rates of return on investment. This tax break would also encourage firms to invest in new capital, raising worker productivity.

HOW DOES GOVERNMENT REGULATION AFFECT THE SUPPLY CURVE?

As we discussed in Module 6, it is important that government provide certain regulations for the environment, workers' safety, consumer protection, and so on. However, the costs imposed on producers as a result of these regulations have an effect similar to taxes, and as a result, make goods and services more expensive. As a result, these regulations reduce the economy's potential production, reflected in a leftward shift of the aggregate supply curve.

For example, in its attempt to provide health benefits to consumers, the Food and Drug Administration (FDA) often takes years to approve new drugs. These procedures are very costly and increase the price of new drugs. Higher minimum wages, designed to ensure workers a "livable" wage, also increase the cost of doing business and the unemployment rate in the unskilled labor market. This is also true of the Family Leave Act, which allows workers to be absent from work for up to 12 weeks without losing their fringe benefits, such as health care. All of these government regulations shift the short- and long-run aggregate supply curves to the left, because they increase the cost of producing these goods, which drives up prices for consumers, and they reduce the economy's potential real output. For this reason, supply-siders support reductions in government regulations where the benefits don't justify the costs.

WHAT EFFECT DO HIGHER MARGINAL TAX RATES HAVE ON WORKERS?

Some economists emphasize the idea that higher marginal tax rates will discourage people from working as much as they otherwise would. Recall that the *marginal* tax rate is the tax rate on the last, or marginal, dollar earned from additional work, and that workers are concerned with their after-tax earnings. A lower marginal tax rate will raise after tax earnings, improving productive incentives—it may entice more people to seek work, it may encourage workers to postpone their retirement, it may mean that more workers will work longer hours, and it could lead to more two-income families in the labor force. It is also possible that the high tax rates reduce work efforts in the market sector and encourage work efforts in the underground economy instead, where cash and barter transactions are very difficult to observe and tax.

WHAT EFFECT DO HIGHER TAX RATES HAVE ON INVESTORS?

Higher tax rates also discourage investment. In pursuit of higher after-tax returns on investment, both foreign and domestic investors will tend to seek areas where taxes are lower, *ceteris paribus.* Higher marginal tax rates will also lead investors to spend more scarce resources looking for tax shelters, which harms the economy, as high-return but highly taxed investments give way to lower-return tax shelters. For example, tax-free municipal bonds may be substituted for higher-return investments that are taxable.

HOW DOES RESEARCH AND DEVELOPMENT IMPACT THE SUPPLY-SIDE OF THE ECONOMY?

Some economists believe that investment in research and development will have long-run benefits for the economy. In particular, greater research and development will lead to new technology and knowledge, which will permanently shift the short- and long-run aggregate supply curves to the right. The government could encourage investments in research and development by giving tax breaks or subsidies to firms.

HOW DO SUPPLY-SIDE POLICIES AFFECT LONG-RUN AGGREGATE SUPPLY?

We see in Exhibit 1 that rather than being primarily concerned with short-run economic stabilization, supply-side policies are aimed at increasing both the short-run and long-run aggregate supply curves. If these policies are successful and maintained, output and employment will increase in the long run, as seen in the shift from $RGDP_{FE}$ to $RGDP'_{FE}$. Both short- and long-run aggregate supply will increase over time, as the effects of deregulation and major structural changes in plant and equipment work their way through the economy. It takes workers some time to fully respond to improved work incentives.

DO THESE POLICIES ALSO AFFECT THE AGGREGATE DEMAND?

You can see in Exhibit 1 that in addition to the aggregate supply curves, the aggregate demand curve is also shifting to the right. For example, if supply-siders call for a reduction in tax rates, it is quite possible that the demand-side stimulus from the increased disposable income (income after taxes) that results may be equal to, or even greater than may the supply-side effects. This causes higher price levels, and even greater short-run real output levels, although the long-run real output level increases with the long-run aggregate supply curve.

ANDY CAPP By Reggie Smythe

Reprinted by permission of North American Syndicate

Is this an example of fiscal policy operating on the supply side?

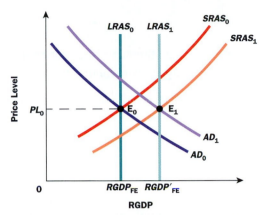

The impact of a reduction in tax rates and regulations and investments in research and development could create long-term effects on income, savings, and capital formation, shifting both the SRAS curve and the LRAS curve rightward. As income rises, it is spent, shifting the aggregate demand curve to the right.

WHAT DO THE CRITICS SAY ABOUT SUPPLY-SIDE ECONOMICS?

Of course, those that believe in the supply-side effects of fiscal policy have their critics. The critics are skeptical of the magnitude of the impact of lower taxes on work effort and the impact of deregulation on productivity. Critics claim that the tax cuts of the 1980s led to moderate real output growth but only through a reduction in real tax revenues, inflation, and large budget deficits.

While real economic growth followed the tax cuts, the critics say that it came as a result of a large budget deficit. And the critics question whether people will save and invest much more if capital gains taxes are reduced (capital gains are increases in the value of an asset). How much more work effort will we see if marginal tax rates are lowered? Will the new production that occurs from deregulation be enough to offset the benefits thought by many to come from regulation?

WHAT IS THE RESPONSE TO THE SUPPLY-SIDE CRITICS?

Defenders of the supply-side approach argue that the real tax revenues of those in the highest marginal tax brackets actually increased as their tax rates fell in the 1980s (as they also had for earlier reductions in tax rates on the most heavily taxed high income groups) and that, compared to other developed countries in the world, the United States had very prosperous growth from 1982 to 1989. In addition, many supply-siders argue that most of their policy prescriptions were never really even tried, for at least three reasons. First, many of supply-siders' proposals for improving productive incentives were ignored, and in some cases, productive incentives were made worse rather than better. Second, the real output effects of the initial tax cuts were minimized by the restrictive, inflation fighting policies of the Federal Reserve in the early 1980s. Third, Congress did not reduce federal expenditures, which was at least partially responsible for the growing deficit.

CONCEPT CHECK

1. Supply-side fiscal policy advocates believe that people will save less, work less, and provide less capital when taxes, government transfer, and regulations are too burdensome.
2. Supply-side policies are designed to increase output and employment in the long run, causing the long-run and short-run aggregate supply curves to shift to the right.

3. Critics of supply-siders question the magnitude of impact of lower taxes on work effort, saving, and investment and the impact of deregulation on productivity.

1. Is supply-side economics more concerned with short-run economic stabilization or long-run economic growth?
2. Why could you say that supply-side economics is really more about after-tax wages and after-tax returns on investment than it is about tax rates?

3. Why do government regulations have the same sorts of effects on businesses as taxes?
4. Why aren't the full effects of supply-side policies seen quickly?
5. If taxes increase, what would you expect to happen to employment in the underground economy? Why?

G Fiscal Policy in Its Prime—The 1960s

- How did Kennedy's fiscal stimulus affect our economy?
- Can a tax cut lead to larger tax revenues?

HOW DID KENNEDY'S EXPANSIONARY POLICY AFFECT OUR ECONOMY?

Real GDP rose only very slowly in 1960 and 1961 and un-employment increased; by 1961, the unemployment rate of 6.7 percent approached the highest rate since the Depression. The new President, John F. Kennedy, was lectured on the need for counter-cyclical fiscal policy by his chairman of the Council of Economic Advisers, Walter Heller, and two future Nobel laureates in economics, James Tobin and Robert Solow. Kennedy accepted the view that a more ex-pansionary policy was needed, and he advocated both some increase in government spending and a tax cut. In short, he wanted to use both fiscal policy mechanisms to

How did President Kennedy fine-tune the economy of the early 1960s?

shift the aggregate demand curve to the right. (Supply-siders believe that the tax cut stimulated work effort—it is sometimes hard to tell "what causes what"!) In fiscal 1962, federal government spending rose by $9 billion, or more than 9 percent, while revenues rose by only $5 billion. The doubling of the federal deficit (from $3 to $7 billion) pro-vided added stimulus to the economy. The 1962 unem-ployment rate fell to 5.5 percent, a major drop from the previous year, and real GDP surged by more than 6 per-cent. Given the substantial slack in the economy, the in-crease in output and employment was not accompanied by massive inflation. The GDP deflator rose by only a bit over 1 percent a year in both 1961 and 1962.

In addition, President Kennedy proposed an invest-ment tax credit plan that lowered taxes for firms that in-vested in new capital equipment. The impact of this move was to shift out the aggregate supply curve. The impact of these policies on the two curves is shown in Exhibit 1.

| EXHIBIT 1 | THE 1961 KENNEDY TAX CUT |

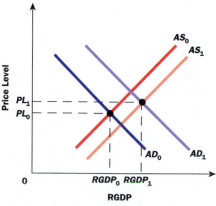

The Kennedy tax cut, increase in government spending, and investment tax credit in the early 1960s led to greater output and employment and only slightly higher price levels (shifting from PL_0 to PL_1).

DID JOHNSON CONTINUE TO FOLLOW TRADITIONAL FISCAL POLICY?

President Lyndon B. Johnson, Kennedy's successor, defied tradition and conventional fiscal policy response by announcing plans in his 1965 inaugural address for a great expansion in governmental social welfare programs in the tradition of Franklin D. Roosevelt's New Deal of three decades earlier. Between fiscal year 1965 and fiscal year 1968, government spending increased by more than $60 billion—over 50 percent. While tax revenues rose as personal income increased, tax rates were not increased, and the increase in tax revenues was much smaller than the growth in expenditures. In fiscal year 1968, the federal government's deficit exceeded $25 billion, roughly 3 percent of GDP. The fiscal stimulus when the economy was at full employment came at a considerable cost, as the inflation rate more than doubled to over 4 percent a year with little effect on real output or unemployment, as seen in Exhibit 2.

WHAT ARE THE DANGERS OF FISCAL POLICY?

The success of the fiscal policy of the early 1960s in reducing unemployment in a largely non-inflationary manner is often cited as an example of how fiscal policy can work. The factual evidence seemed undeniable at the time. It is

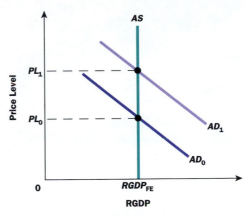

EXHIBIT 2   JOHNSON'S "GREAT SOCIETY"

In the late 1960s, the Johnson Administration pursued a large increase in government spending programs. With tax revenues rising at a slower rate than spending, a large deficit caused the aggregate demand curve to shift to the right, from AD_0 to AD_1. Because the economy was already at full employment, the stimulus program resulted in higher prices with little increases in output and employment.

true, however, that when politicians saw the *political* gains from economic stimulus, it led to excesses, such as the post-1965 stimulus that brought about increasing inflation.

CONCEPT CHECK

1. Kennedy's stimulus (an increase in government spending and a tax cut) led to a large increase in GDP, decreases in unemployment, and only a very small increase in inflation.

2. Johnson's increase in government spending and large budget deficits during full employment led to an increase in the price level with little effect on real output or unemployment.

---

1. When President Kennedy cut tax rates and instituted an investment tax credit, was he using a demand-side or a supply-side strategy?
2. If Kennedy's policy had been adopted during a period of full employment, would it have worked as well? Why or why not?

3. What effect did President Johnson's economic policies have on the economy?

Financing the Deficit

- Is the national debt a problem for our economy?
- Who are the three major types of buyers of federal debt?
- How do the effects of selling Treasury bonds to these three groups vary?

HOW CAN A GOVERNMENT FINANCE A BUDGET DEFICIT?

How has the government run continuous budget deficits for such a long period of time? After all, it has to have some means of paying out the funds necessary to support government expenditures that are in excess of the funds derived from tax payments. One thing the government could do is simply print money—dollar bills. This approach was used to finance much of the Civil War budget deficit, both in the North and in the Confederate States. However, printing money to finance activities is highly inflationary and also undermines confidence in the government. The more respectable and conservative method of financing deficits is by issuing debt. The federal government in effect borrows an amount necessary to cover the deficit by issuing bonds, or IOUs, payable typically at some maturity date. The sum total of the values of all bonds outstanding constitutes the federal debt. As Exhibit 1 indicates, the ten-

dency of the federal government to engage in budget deficits has led to increasing federal debt over time.

The increase in federal government debt since 1945 has actually been much less than the growth in GDP, so the total debt today equals the value of only 5 or 6 months of total U.S. GDP, compared with nearly 15 months of output in 1945.

HOW DOES THE DEBT AFFECT OUR ECONOMY?

Is a national debt of $5 trillion life-threatening to the economy? The answer is surprisingly "no." However, it does have an impact on the economy. To begin, the debt is primarily an obligation of the United States government to its citizens; relatively little of the debt is typically owned by foreigners (10 to 15 percent), although that amount has grown in recent years—foreigners currently own about 17 percent of the debt. Since 1980, the national debt has

Is the national debt a problem?

EXHIBIT 1	PUBLIC DEBT, FEDERAL GOVERNMENT, SELECTED YEARS	
Fiscal Year	Public Debt (billions of dollars)	Public Debt as a Percentage of GDP
1929	$16.9	18%
1940	43.0	45
1945	260.2	120
1950	256.8	94
1955	274.4	69
1960	290.5	56
1965	322.3	47
1970	380.9	38
1975	541.9	35
1980	909.1	33
1985	1,817.5	44
1990	3,206.6	56
1996	5,207.3	71

SOURCES: Office of Management and Budget, 1997.

grown from over 30 percent to roughly 70 percent of GDP, and as a result of large deficits and reduced national savings, both public and private savings fell. When the government borrows to finance the debt, it causes the interest rate to rise. The higher interest rate will crowd out private investment by households and firms. To make interest payments on the debt, the government must use existing tax revenues. Currently, such debt service absorbs only a bit more than 3 percent of GDP. Thus, resources equal to about one week's GDP per year must be taken from the taxpaying public and transferred to the owners of debt. It is when the interest on the debt is very large that the redistribution of income to bondholders by way of higher taxes on productive workers may have damaging disincentive and morale effects.

IS THE NATIONAL DEBT A HUGE PROBLEM?

The public debt does not pose a serious problem for two other reasons. First, a large proportion of the debt (about 30 percent in recent years) is actually "owned" by the government itself, in trust funds supporting such activities as Social Security or federal deposit insurance. The Federal Reserve System, a quasi-governmental agency, owns another 10 percent of the debt. The remaining 60 or 65 percent of the debt is held outside the federal government by state and local governments (roughly 30 percent), financial institutions (10 to 15 percent), foreign investors (10 to 15 percent), and U.S. individuals (5 to 10 percent). Second, the government does not have to repay the debt in the sense that it must reduce its debt obligations to zero. When a bond matures (comes due), the government can issue a new bond to obtain funds to pay off the owner of the maturing bond. The government is constantly refunding its debt just as private corporations often refund theirs. To be sure, the ability of the government to refund depends on the willingness of people to buy its bonds. As long as the federal government retains control over resources with its taxing powers and continues to honor its debt obligations, however, refunding the debt should not be a major problem.

WHO BEARS THE BURDEN OF PUBLIC DEBT?

The "burden" of the debt is a topic that has long interested economists, particularly whether it falls on present or future generations. Arguments can be made that the generation of taxpayers living at the time that the debt is issued shoulders the true cost of the debt, because the debt permits the government to take command of resources that might be available for other, private uses. In a sense, the resources its takes to purchase government bonds might take away from private activities, such as private investment financed by private debt. There is no denying, however, that the issuance of debt does involve some intergenerational transfer of incomes. Long after federal debt is issued, a new generation of taxpayers is making interest payments to persons of the generation that bought the bonds issued to finance that debt. If public debt is created intelligently, however, the "burden" of the debt should be less than the benefits derived from the resources acquired as a result; this is particularly true when the debt allows for an expansion in real economic activity or for the development of vital infrastructure for the future. The opportunity cost of expanded public activity may be very small in terms of private activity that must be foregone to finance the public activity, if unemployed resources are put to work. The real issue of importance is whether the government's activities have benefits that are greater than costs; whether taxes are raised, money is printed, or deficits are run are for the most part "financing issues."

CONCEPT CHECK

1. Our national debt is not a serious problem for our economy. Much of the debt is owned by the government itself; only 10 to 15 percent is owned by foreigners. Also, the benefits of debt in terms of economic expansion may be greater than the opportunity cost of lost private investment activity.
2. The government finances a budget deficit primarily by issuing debt to government agencies, private institutions, and private individuals.

3. Selling new debt issues to public agencies, such as the Federal Reserve System or to private institutions, tends to have a more expansionary impact than selling debt to private individuals because the purchase of government debt by individuals tends to result in reduced consumption.

---

1. Why can't the federal government finance its debt by printing more money?
2. How can the federal government finance the national debt?

3. Should we worry about the national debt?
4. What must be true for Americans to be better off as a result of an increase in the federal debt?

Application: The Balanced Budget Amendment

What are the arguments for and against balancing the budget? If we had a balanced budget, how could we allow the government to run deficits during emergencies?

THE BALANCED BUDGET AMENDMENT

BACKGROUND: The United States has not had a balanced budget since 1969. Over the last quarter of a century, Congress has consistently demonstrated its inability to devise a federal spending plan in which outlays do not exceed revenues. Thus, today, we are faced with a national debt which exceeds $5.32 trillion.

The balanced budget amendment was a significant component of the Republican party's 1994 "Contract with America." The amendment would generally prohibit the federal government from spending more than it receives in revenue in any given year. Such legislation would eliminate the budget deficit and would allow us to begin to work to reduce the nation's long-term debt. The proposal includes an exception to permit Congress to run a deficit during times of war or national emergency if both chambers vote to do so by a three-fifths supermajority. In order for a Constitutional amendment to be ratified, it must receive a two-thirds vote in each chamber of Congress and must be ratified by three-quarters of the states.

STATUS: During the 104th Congress, the House passed the balanced budget amendment by a vote of 300 to 132. However, the Amendment received only 65 votes in the Senate, 1 vote less than the two-thirds required for passage.

In January 1997, Senator Orrin Hatch (R-UT) and 62 co-sponsors introduced the balanced budget amendment in the Senate as S J Res 1. With the election of so many fiscally conservative Democrats to the Senate in 1996, passage there seemed imminent. However, in the weeks prior to the vote, some of the Democrats who promised to vote for the bill defected, arguing that the amendment did not sufficiently protect Social Security. As a result, the balanced budget amendment was defeated in the Senate on March 4, 1997 by a vote of 66 to 34.

Although supporters of the amendment pledged that the fight is not over, the fact that the federal budgets for the next several years are expected to be in surplus has made near-term passage of a balanced budget amendment less likely.

SOURCE: AED Issue Summary, March 27, 1998: The Balanced Budget Amendment http://www.aednet.org/govt/legissue/balbud.htm

From 1960 to 1998, the federal budget has been in deficit every year except one, when the government ran a small balanced surplus in 1969. However, some economists believe the real problem is not the deficit but rather that federal spending is out of control. Some individuals believe that we must control the deficits through responsible fiscal restraint—a belief that has prompted a drive to add a balanced budget amendment to the U.S. Constitution.

But the possibility that the spending activities of the federal government may be constitutionally restricted is terrifying to some. Opponents' arguments can be summarized as follows:

First, at best, a balanced budget amendment would be ineffective because there is no way to guarantee that revenues and expenditures will always match up on an annual basis. Second, at worst, a balanced budget amendment would reduce the fiscal flexibility of the federal government, thereby making it more difficult to respond appropriately to changing economic circumstances. Furthermore, if the public really wants the government to balance its budget, our elected representatives already have the power to respond to this desire.

It is certainly true that no amendment to the Constitution can ensure that the budget will ever be perfectly balanced. It is impossible to predict either revenues or expenditures over a specified interval. And there are circumstances in which budget flexibility can be justified. Finally, it is true that Congress has the control over taxing and spending needed to eliminate the chronic deficits if it chooses to do so. Given that this is the case, why should we clutter up the Constitution with a balanced budget amendment?

Proponents of a balanced budget amendment argue that, in the absence of fiscal restraints, excessive government spending will occur because the private advantages that each of us realizes from spending on our government programs are paid for almost entirely by other taxpayers. Of course, each of us suffers from having to pay for the programs of others, and most of us would be willing to reduce our special-interest demands if others would do the same. But we all recognize that as long as we continue to pay for the programs of others, there is no advantage in reducing our individual demands on the government treasury. In this uncontrolled setting, we are in a spending free-for-all, with penalties for the fiscally responsible and rewards for the fiscally irresponsible.

Of course, if all it took to balance the federal budget was for the American public to want it balanced, it would have been balanced a long time ago. According to public opinion polls, the vast majority of the American public wants the federal government to balance its budget. In an ideal world in which broad public preferences were transmitted effectively through political institutions, there would be no need for a balanced budget amendment to control spending. However, political institutions, even democratic political institutions, can be exploited by the organized few to gain special-interest benefits at the expense of the unorganized many.

Of course, a balanced budget amendment could be written that would allow the government to run deficits in time of special emergencies like military involvement, earthquakes, fires, or floods. In addition, the voters might adopt a plan that would allow for a two-thirds vote to increase the deficit or that would opt for a running average balanced budget instead of balancing the budget every year. Any of these proposals could work towards controlling runaway federal spending to some degree.

The most important issue of all might be at what *level* the budget should be balanced. Many would prefer deficits in a small budget to a much larger, but balanced, budget. However, the real issue, as always, is: Are we getting government goods and services with benefits that are greater than costs?

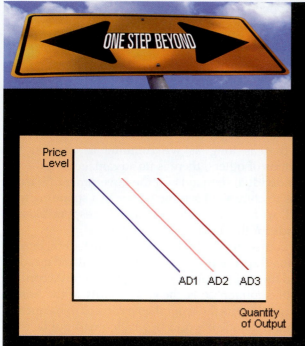

ONE STEP BEYOND

Price Level

AD1 AD2 AD3

Quantity of Output

Is there a deficit in your understanding of how the government impacts the economy through its fiscal policies? Don't worry—there is a surplus of information on expansionary and contractionary fiscal policies, the multiplier effect (shown here), the crowding out effect, and supply-side policies in your Workbook and on the EconActive CD-ROM!

PHOTO CREDITS MODULE 21

Page **499:** From The Wall Street Journal. Reprinted with permission. Cartoon Features Syndicate; Page **503:** © AP Photo/Michael Caulfield; Page **513:** © Associated Press/ Ron Edmonds; Page **516:** Reprinted by permission of North American Syndicate; Page **518:** © Black Star/PNI; Page **520:** © Michael A. Dwyer/Stock, Boston/PNI; Page **523:** © 1997 Draper Hill. Reprinted by permission.

Money and the Banking System

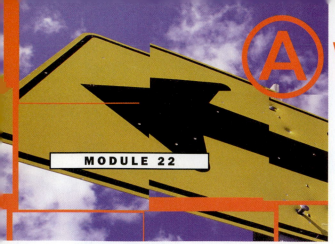

(A) What Is Money?

- What is money?
- In what forms is money held?
- What is included in the money supply?
- Why have demand deposits become less popular?

WHAT IS MONEY?

Money is anything that is generally accepted in exchange for goods or services; it is a medium of exchange. In colonial times, commodities such as tobacco and wampum (Native American trinkets) were sometimes used as money. At some times and in some places, even cigarettes and whiskey have been used as money. But commodities have several disadvantages when used as money, the most im-portant of which is that many commodities deteriorate easily after a few trades. Precious metal coins have been used for money for millennia, partly because of their durability.

WHAT IS CURRENCY?

Currency consists of coins and/or paper that some institution or government has created to be used in the trading of goods and services and the payment of debts. Currency in the form of metal coins is still used as money throughout the world today. But metal currency has a disadvantage: It is bulky. Also, certain types of metals traditionally used in coins, like gold and silver, are not available in sufficient quantities to meet our demands for a monetary instrument. For these reasons, metal coins have for centuries been supplemented by paper currency, often in the form of bank notes. In the United States, the Federal Reserve System issues Federal Reserve Notes in various denominations, and this paper currency, along with coins, provides the basis for most transactions of relatively modest size in the United States today.

Is this money?

What is currency? What makes this paper and metal valuable?

HOW DOES CURRENCY BECOME LEGAL TENDER?

In the United States and in most other nations of the world, metallic coins and paper currency are the only forms of **legal tender**. In other words, coins and paper money have been officially declared to be money—to be acceptable for the settlement of debts incurred in financial transactions. In effect, the government says, "We declare these instruments to be money, and citizens are expected to accept them as a medium of exchange." Legal tender is **fiat money**—a means of exchange that has been established not by custom and tradition, or because of the value of the metal in a coin, but by government fiat, or declaration.

WHAT ARE CHECKABLE DEPOSITS?

Most of the money that we use for day-to-day transactions, however, is not official legal tender. Rather, it is a monetary instrument that has become "generally accepted" in exchange over the years and has now, by custom and tradition, become money. What is this instrument? It is assets in checking accounts in banks, more formally called **demand deposits.**

Demand deposits are defined as deposits in banks that can be withdrawn on demand, by simply writing a check. Some other forms of accounts in financial institutions also have virtually all of the attributes of demand deposits. For example, there are also other checkable deposits that earn interest but have some restrictions, such as higher monthly fees or minimum balance requirements. These interest-earning checking accounts effectively permit the depositors to write "orders" similar to checks and assign the

rights to deposit to other persons, just as we write checks to other parties. Practically speaking, funds in these accounts are the equivalent of demand deposits and have become an important component in the supply of money. Both of these types of accounts are forms of **transaction deposits,** because they can be easily converted into currency or used to buy goods and services directly. **Travelers checks,** like currency and demand deposits, are also easily converted into currency or used directly as a means of payment.

WHY IS THE USE OF DEMAND DEPOSITS AND OTHER CHECKABLE DEPOSITS SO POPULAR?

Why have demand deposits and other checkable deposits replaced paper and metallic currency as the major source of money used for larger transactions in the United States and in most other relatively well-developed nations? There are several reasons, including ease and safety of transactions, lower transaction costs, and transaction records.

Ease and Safety of Transactions

Paying for goods and services with a check is easier (meaning cheaper) and less risky than paying with paper money. Paper money is readily transferable: If someone takes a $20 bill from you, it is gone, and the thief can use it to buy goods with no difficulty. If, however, someone steals a check that you have written to the telephone company to pay a monthly bill, that person probably will have great difficulty using it to buy goods and services, because the individual has to be able to identify himself as a representative of the telephone company. If your checkbook is stolen, a person can use your check as money only if he or

IN THE NEWS

SHOULD WE GET RID OF THE PENNY?

Americans know where to find pennies—in jars and fountains and on the countertops of convenience stores. What's not known is just what ought to be done about the nation's lowliest coin. At a House hearing last week, lobbyists for the penny—Americans for Common Cents—reported a poll showing that 73 percent of the American public wants the government to keep circulating pennies. The Treasury wants to do that, although the government's General Accounting Office reported that penny production costs taxpayers over $8

million a year. The U.S. Mint disputed this, saying penny production nets the U.S. government between $17.9 and $26.6 million.

The GAO found that only about a third of existing pennies are in circulation. And a poll commissioned by the GAO showed that most Americans (52 percent) would prefer that prices be rounded to the nearest nickel. Penny backers responded with an estimate by Penn State economist Raymond Lombra, who said that rounding prices would result in overcharges costing consumers at least $600 million extra a year.

SOURCE: "Whither the Penny?" *U.S. News & World Report,* July 29, 1996, p. 8.

CONSIDER THIS:
While a penny doesn't seem like much, rounding up could cost U.S. consumers approximately $600 million a year.

she can successfully forge your signature and provide some identification. Hence, transacting business by check is much less risky than using legal tender; there is, then, an element of insurance or safety in the use of transaction deposits instead of currency.

Lower Transaction Costs

Suppose that you decide that you want to buy a compact disc player from the current J.C. Penney's mail-order catalogue that costs $81.28. It is much cheaper, easier, and safer for you to send a check for $81.28 rather than four $20 bills, a $1 bill, a quarter, and three pennies. Transaction deposits are a popular monetary instrument precisely because they lower transaction costs compared with the use of metal or paper currency. In very small transactions, the gains in safety and convenience of checks are outweighed by the time and cost required to write and process them; in these cases, transaction costs are lower with paper and metallic currency. For this reason, it is unlikely that the use of paper or metallic currency will disappear entirely.

Transaction Records

Another useful feature of transaction deposits is that they provide a record of financial transactions. Each month, the bank sends the depositor canceled checks and/or a statement recording the deposit and withdrawal of funds. In an age where detailed records are often necessary for tax purposes, this is a useful feature. Of course, it can work both ways. Paper currency transactions are also popular, in part, probably because a substantial amount of business activity is going on with cash payments so that no record will be available for the tax collectors to review.

ARE CREDIT CARDS A FORM OF MONEY?

Credit cards are "generally acceptable in exchange for goods and services." At the same time, however, credit card payments are actually guaranteed loans available on demand to users, which merely defers customer payment for transactions using a demand deposit. Ultimately, things purchased with a credit card must be paid for with

T U N E   U P

DEMAND DEPOSITS

Q: In recent years, we have moved increasingly towards a "checkless" society. Do you think that this means that demand deposits will eventually be abolished?

A: No. Increasingly, deposits and withdrawals are handled electronically, through electronic impulses sent from store cash registers to bank computers, for example. Thus, the physical effort of writing and processing checks, an expensive and labor-intensive task, has been largely eliminated, and people are actually paying for many of their goods with bank credit cards and automated teller machine (ATM) cards.

Calvin and Hobbes

by Bill Watterson

USING CREDIT CARDS ON THE INTERNET

KURT DAHL

Enough is enough. The public is being badly served by the hysterical reporting about credit-card security on the Internet. The reality is far different from the picture painted in the press. The reality is this. Using your credit card in a secured browser on the Internet is hundreds, if not thousands, of times more secure than any other way you use it. A secured Internet transaction goes from your computer to the commercial Web site without any human intervention. This is true of virtually no other credit-card transactions. We all give our credit cards willingly to waiters, cashiers, bank tellers, gas station attendants and phone operators at catalog companies. Every day, somewhere around 10 million people handle close to 100 million credit cards in the course of their jobs. Talk about a security risk!

But do we see headlines like: "Two Berkeley graduate students discover they can steal credit-card numbers by going to work for Wal-Mart." I suppose the press is interested in security on the Internet because of the intriguing and somewhat scary idea that remote hackers can magically steal your card number as it zooms past on the phone network. But if a hacker had a mind to steal credit-card numbers from the phone network, there are significantly more fertile grounds than the Internet. How do you suppose the credit card that you give to the cashier at Wal-Mart or any other retailer gets authorized and transferred to the bank? In most cases it is over the same kind of phone network as the Internet.

Here is another one. What percentage of credit-card fraud is a result of lost or stolen cards? I'm sure it is quite high, but it is virtually impossible to lose your credit card while doing business in your home or at work. Once again, Internet commerce is far more secure. How about this headline: "Police recommend leaving your purse at home; you might lose it." The press coverage about commerce on the Internet has made the public think it is not safe to use your credit card on the Internet. That's just plain wrong. If you want to use your credit card in the most secure way possible, by far, use a secure browser on the Internet.

SOURCE: Kurt Dahl, "Internet Is Safest Way to Use Your Credit Card," *Seattle Times*, September 24, 1995.

> **CONSIDER THIS:**
> Credit cards have certainly become a convenient way of purchasing goods. Over 30 percent of large purchases ($100 or more) are done with credit cards. The ease and safety of using the credit card will inevitably lead to even greater use in the future.

a check; monthly payments on credit card accounts are required in order to have continued use of the card. Credit cards, then, are not money, but rather a convenient means to carry out transactions that minimizes the physical transfer of checks and currency. In that sense, they are substitutes for the use of money in exchange; they also allow any given amount of money to facilitate more exchanges.

ARE SAVINGS ACCOUNTS "MONEY"?

Economists are not completely in agreement on what constitutes money for all purposes. Coins, paper currency, demand and other checkable deposits, and travelers checks are certainly forms of money, because all are accepted as direct means of payment for goods and services. There is nearly universal agreement on this point. Some economists, however, argue that for some purposes "money" should be more broadly defined to include **nontransaction deposits.** Nontransaction deposits are fund accounts against which the depositor *cannot* directly write checks— hence the name. If these funds cannot be used directly as a means of payment, but must first be converted into money, then why do people hold such accounts? People use these accounts primarily because they generally pay higher interest rates than transaction deposits.

Two primary types of nontransaction deposits exist—savings accounts and time deposits (sometimes referred to as certificates of deposit, or CDs). Most purists would argue that nontransaction deposits are **near money** assets but not money itself. Why? Savings accounts and time deposits cannot be used directly to purchase a good or service. They are not a direct medium of exchange. For example, you cannot go into a supermarket, pick out groceries, and give the clerk the passbook to your savings account. You must convert funds from your savings account into currency or demand deposits before you can buy goods and services. So, strictly speaking, nontransaction deposits do not meet the formal definition of money. At the same time, however, savings accounts are assets that can be quickly converted into money at the face value of the account. In the jargon of finance, savings accounts are highly liquid assets. True, under federal law, commercial banks legally can require depositors to request withdrawal of funds in writing, and then can defer making payment for several weeks. But in practice, no bank prohibits instant withdrawal, although early withdrawal from some time deposits, especially certificates of deposit, may require the depositor to forgo some interest income as a penalty.

WHY ARE MONEY MARKET MUTUAL FUNDS CONSIDERED NEAR MONEY?

Money market mutual funds are interest-earning accounts provided by brokers who pool funds into investments like Treasury bills. These funds are invested in short-term securities, and the depositor is allowed to write checks against his or her account subject to certain limits. This type of fund has experienced tremendous growth over the last 20 years. Money market mutual funds are highly liquid assets. They are considered to be near money because they are relatively easy to convert into money for the purchases of goods and services.

ARE NONMONETARY ASSETS SUCH AS STOCKS AND BONDS CONSIDERED MONEY?

There are many other forms of financial assets that virtually everyone agrees are not "money." Stocks and bonds are good examples. Suppose you buy 100 shares of Gen-

Is this money?

eral Motors common stock at $70 per share, for a total of $7,000. The stock is traded daily on the New York Stock Exchange and elsewhere; you can readily sell the stock and get paid in legal tender or a demand deposit. Why, then, is this stock not considered money? First, it takes a few days to receive payment for the sale of stock; the asset cannot be turned into cash as quickly as a savings deposit in a financial institution. Second and more important, the value of the stock fluctuates over time, and there is no guarantee that the owner of the asset can obtain its original nominal value at any moment in time. Thus, stocks and bonds are not sufficiently liquid assets to be considered "money."

WHAT IS THE MONEY SUPPLY?

Because a good case can be made both for including and for excluding savings accounts, certificates of deposits (CDs), and money market mutual funds from our operational definition of the money supply for different purposes, we will compromise and do both. Economists call the narrow definition of money—currency, checkable deposits, and travelers checks—**M1.** The broader definition of money, encompassing M1, plus saving accounts, time deposits (except for some large-denomination certificates of deposits), and money market mutual funds, is called **M2.**

The difference between M1 and M2 is striking, as evidenced by the varying size of the total stock of money using different definitions as seen in Exhibit 1. M2 is more than three times the magnitude of M1. This means that people prefer to keep the bulk of their liquid assets in the form of savings accounts of various kinds, rather than as currency or in transactions accounts.

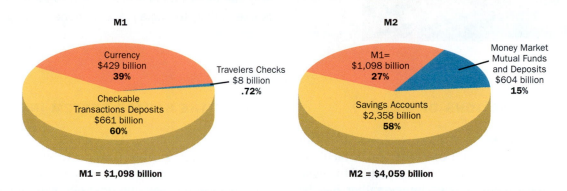

| EXHIBIT 1 | TWO DEFINITIONS OF THE MONEY SUPPLY: M1 AND M2 |

M1

Currency
$429 billion
39%

Travelers Checks
$8 billion
.72%

Checkable
Transactions Deposits
$661 billion
60%

M1 = $1,098 billion

M2

M1 =
$1,098 billion
27%

Money Market
Mutual Funds
and Deposits
$604 billion
15%

Savings Accounts
$2,358 billion
58%

M2 = $4,059 billion

SOURCE: Board of Governors, Federal Reserve System, *Federal Reserve Bulletin,* May 1998.

CONCEPT CHECK

1. Money is anything used as a medium of exchange for goods or services.
2. Coins, paper currency, demand and other checkable deposits, and travelers checks are all forms of money.
3. M1 is made up of currency, checkable deposits, and travelers checks. M2 is made up of M1, plus savings accounts, time deposits, and money market mutual funds.

1. If everyone in an economy accepted poker chips as payment in exchange for goods and services, would poker chips be money?
2. If you were buying a pack of gum, would using currency or a demand deposit have lower transactions costs? What if you were buying a house?
3. What is the main advantage of a transaction deposit for tax purposes? What is its main disadvantage for tax purposes?
4. Are credit cards money?
5. What are M1 and M2?
6. How have interest-earning checking accounts and overdraft protection led to the relative decline in demand deposits?

- Is using money better than barter?
- How does money lower the costs of making transactions?
- Why can money be an efficient way to store value?
- Is it less risky to make loans of money or of goods?

WHAT ARE THE FUNCTIONS OF MONEY?

We have already indicated that the primary function of money is to serve as a medium of exchange, to facilitate transactions, and to lower transactions costs. However, money is not the only medium of exchange; rather, it is the only medium that is generally accepted for most transactions. How would people trade with one another in the absence of money? They would **barter** for goods and services they desire.

THE FAR SIDE   By GARY LARSON

New York 1626: Chief of the Manhattan Indians addresses his tribe for the last time.

WHY IS THE BARTER SYSTEM INEFFICIENT?

Under a barter system, individuals pay for goods or services by offering other goods and services in exchange. Suppose I am a farmer who needs some salt. I go to the merchant selling salt and offer her 30 pounds of wheat for 2 pounds of salt. The wheat that I use to buy the salt is not money, because the salt merchant may not want wheat and therefore may not accept it as payment. That is one of the major disadvantages of barter: The buyer may not have appropriate items of value to the seller. The salt merchant may reluctantly take the wheat that she does not want, later bartering it away to another customer for something that she does want. In any case, barter is inefficient because several trades may be necessary in order to receive the desired goods.

Moreover, barter is extremely expensive over long distances. What would it cost me, living in California, to send wheat to Maine in return for an item in the L.L. Bean catalogue? It is much cheaper to mail a check. Finally, barter is time consuming, because of difficulties in evaluating the value of the product that is being offered for barter. For example, the person that is selling the salt may wish to inspect the wheat first to make sure that it is pure and not filled with dirt or other unwanted items. Barter, in short, is expensive and inefficient and generally prevails only where limited trade is carried out over short distances, which generally means in relatively primitive economies. The more complex the economy (e.g., the higher the real per capita GDP), the greater the economic interactions between people, and consequently, the greater the need for one or more universally accepted assets serving as money. Only in a Robinson Crusoe economy, where people live in isolated settlements and are generally self-sufficient, is the use of money unnecessary.

THE BARTER SYSTEM

Q: Ann Chovie owns a pizza parlor in a college town. She has decided that she is no longer going to take cash for the sale of pizzas; instead, she is going to work on a barter system. Is Ann making a time-consuming, costly mistake?

A: Imagine this: Last week, after 15 minutes of haggling, you traded Ann a pair of slightly used hiking boots for a deep dish supreme pizza. What will your next pizza cost you, and how long will it take the two of you to figure it out? Bartering can be a costly and tedious process, and for those reasons, Ann is undoubtedly going to regret her decision.

Bartering lacks a standard measure of value.

HOW IS MONEY A STANDARD OF VALUE?

Besides serving as a medium of exchange, money is also a standard of value. With a barter system, one does not know precisely what 30 pounds of wheat are worth relative to 2 pounds of salt. With money, a common "yardstick" exists so that the values of diverse goods and services can be very precisely compared. Thus, if wheat cost 50 cents a pound and salt costs $1 a pound, we can say that a pound of salt is valued precisely two times as much as a pound of wheat ($1 divided by 50 cents = 2). By providing a universally understood measure of value, money serves to lower the information costs involved in making transactions. Without money, a person might not know what a good price for salt is, because so many different commodities can be bartered for it. With money, there is but one price of salt, and that price is readily available as information to the potential consumer.

HOW IS MONEY A STORE OF VALUE?

Money also serves as a store of value. It can provide a means of saving or "storing" things of value in an efficient manner. The farmer in a barter society who wants to save for retirement might accumulate enormous inventories of wheat, which he would then gradually trade away for other goods in his old age. This is a terribly inefficient way to save. Storage buildings would have to be constructed to hold all of the wheat, and the interest payments that the farmer would earn on the wheat would actually be negative, as rats will eat part of it or it will otherwise deteriorate. Most important, physical goods of value would be tied up in unproductive use for many years. With money, the farmer saves pieces of paper that can be used to purchase goods and services in old age. It is both cheaper and safer to store paper rather than wheat.

HOW IS MONEY A MEANS OF DEFERRED PAYMENT?

Finally, money is a **means of deferred payment.** Money makes it much easier to borrow and to repay loans. With barter, lending is cumbersome and subject to an added problem. If a wheat farmer borrows some wheat and agrees to pay it back in wheat next year, what if the value of wheat soars because of a poor crop resulting from drought? The debt will be paid back in wheat that is far more valuable than that borrowed, causing a problem for the borrower. Of course, fluctuations in the value of money can also occur, and indeed, inflation has been a major problem in our recent past and continues to be a problem in many countries. But the value of money fluctuates far less than the value of many individual commodities, so lending in money imposes fewer risks on buyers and sellers than lending in commodities.

1. Barter is inefficient compared to money because a person may have to make several trades before receiving something that is truly wanted.
2. By providing a universally understood measure of value, money serves to lower the information costs involved in making transactions.
3. Money is both cheaper and easier to store than other goods.
4. Because the value of money fluctuates less than specific commodities, it imposes fewer risks on borrowers and lenders.

---

1. Why does the advantage of monetary exchange over barter increase as an economy becomes more complex?
2. How can uncertain and rapid rates of inflation erode money's ability to perform its functions efficiently?
3. In a world of barter, would useful financial statements, like balance sheets, be possible? Would stock markets be possible? Would it be possible to build cars?
4. Why do you think virtually all societies create something to function as money?

C The Demand for Money

- ■ Why do people choose to hold money?
- ■ How is money "backed"?

WHY DO PEOPLE HOLD MONEY?

Money has several functions, but what stimulates persons to hold money as opposed to other financial assets? There are at least three motives: transaction purposes, precautionary reasons, and asset purposes.

Transaction Purposes

First, money is demanded for transactions purposes, to facilitate exchange. The higher one's income, the more transactions a person will make (because consumption is income related), the greater will be GDP and the greater the demand for money for transactions purposes, other things equal.

Precautionary Reasons

Second, people like to have money on hand for precautionary reasons. If unexpected medical or other expenses

People might keep money around for unexpected expenses.

require an unusual outlay of cash, people like to be prepared. The extent to which people demand cash for precautionary reasons depends partly on an individual's income and partly on the opportunity cost of holding money, which is determined by market rates of interest. The higher market interest rates are, the higher the opportunity cost of holding money instead, and people will hold less of their financial wealth as money.

Asset Purposes

Third, money has a trait (liquidity) that makes it a desirable asset. Other things equal, people desire more-liquid assets in preference to less-liquid assets. That is, they would like to easily convert some of their money into goods and services. For this reason, most people wish to have some of their portfolio in money form. At higher interest rates on other assets, the amount of money desired for this purpose will be smaller because the opportunity cost of holding money desired for this purpose will be smaller. Why? Because the opportunity cost of holding money will have risen.

HOW IS MONEY "BACKED"?

Until fairly recent times, coins in most nations were largely made from precious metals, usually gold or silver. These metals had a considerable intrinsic worth: If the coins were melted down, the metal would be valuable for use in jewelry, industrial applications, dentistry, and so forth. Until 1933, the United States was on an internal **gold standard,** meaning that the dollar was defined as equivalent in value to a certain amount of gold, and paper currency or demand deposits could be freely converted to gold coin. The U.S. left the gold standard, however, eventually phasing out gold currency. Some silver coins and paper money convertible into silver remained, but by the end of the 1960s, even this tie of the monetary system to precious metals ended, in part because the price of silver soared so high that the metal in coins had an intrinsic worth greater

At one time, cash was backed by gold. What backs our money now?

than its face value, leading people to hoard coins or even melt them down. When there are two forms of money available, people prefer to spend the form of money that is less valuable. This is a manifestation of **Gresham's Law:** "Cheap money drives out dear money."

WHAT REALLY BACKS OUR MONEY?

Consequently, today, there is no meaningful precious metal "backing" to give our money value. Why, then, do people accept dollar bills, for example, in exchange for goods? After all, a dollar bill is a piece of generally wrinkled paper about 6 inches by 2.5 inches in size, with virtually no inherent utility or worth. Do we accept these bills because it states on the front of the bills, "This note is legal tender for all debts, public and private"? Perhaps, but we accept some forms of currency and money in the form of demand deposits without that statement, which says, in effect, that by fiat the U.S. government has declared the instrument to be money.

The true backing behind our money is our faith in the government's ability to provide an instrument people will take in exchange for goods and services. We accept with great eagerness these small pieces of green paper with pictures of long deceased individuals with funny looking hair simply because we believe that they will be exchangeable for goods and services with an intrinsic value. If you were to drop two pieces of paper of equal size on the floor in front of 100 students, one a blank piece of paper and the other a $100 dollar bill, and then leave the room, the group would probably start fighting for the $100 dollar bill while the blank piece of paper would be ignored. Such is our faith in the green paper's practical value that some will even fight for it. As long as people have confidence in something's convertibility into goods and services, "money" will exist and no further backing is necessary.

Because governments represent the collective will of all the people, they are the institutional force that traditionally defines money in the legal sense. People are willing to accept pieces of paper as money only because of their faith in the government. When people lose faith in the exchangeability of pieces of paper that the government decrees as money, even legal tender loses its status as meaningful money. Something is money only if people will generally accept it. While governments play a key, vital role in defining money, much of it is actually created by private businesses in the pursuit of profit. A majority of our money, whether M1 or M2, is in the form of deposits at privately owned financial institutions.

People who hold money, then, must not only have faith in their government, but also in banks and other financial institutions as well. If I accept a check drawn on a regional bank, I believe that bank or, for that manner, any bank will be willing to convert that check into legal tender (currency) enabling me to buy goods or services that I want to have. Thus I have faith in the bank as well. One Nobel laureate in economics, the late Friedrich von Hayek, has even gone so far as to suggest that all money could be created by privately owned businesses and that governmental participation is unnecessary and possibly undesirable. While few economists would go that far, the fact remains that our "money" is money because of confidence that we have in private financial institutions as well as our government.

How do these institutions create (and destroy) the money that we use? That is the major question addressed in the next Concept.

1. Three motives exist for demanding money: transaction purposes, precautionary reasons, and asset purposes.

2. Money is no longer backed by gold. The true backing is our faith that others will accept it from us in exchange for goods and services.

1. If the earnings available on other financial assets rose, would you want to hold more or less money? Why?

2. For the economy as a whole, why would individuals want to hold more money as GDP rises?

3. If in an era of very rapid inflation, many people stopped accepting a country's currency for payment, would that currency still be money?

4. Why might people who expect a major market "correction" (a fall in the value of stock holdings) wish to increase their holdings of money?

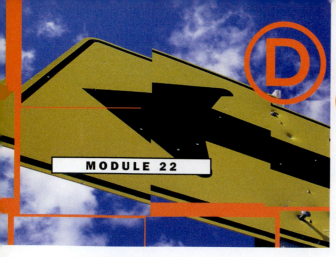

How Banks Create Money

- How is money created?
- What is a reserve requirement?
- How do reserve requirements affect how much money can be created?

WHO ARE THE PLAYERS IN THE BANKING INDUSTRY?

The biggest players in the banking industry are **commercial banks.** Commercial banks are distinct from most other financial institutions in that they can create demand deposits. The right to create money by increasing demand deposits is a valuable right, and persons wanting to engage in commercial banking practices must seek a charter from the state or federal government. Commercial banks account for more than two-thirds of all of the deposits in the banking industry; they maintain almost all of the demand deposits and close to half of the savings accounts.

There are nearly 1,000 commercial banks in the United States. This number is in marked contrast to most other nations, where the leading banks operate throughout the country and where a large proportion of total bank assets are held in a handful of banks. Until recently, banks were restricted by federal law from operating in more than one state. This has now changed, and the structure of banking as we now know it will inevitably change with the emergence of interstate banking, mergers, and "hostile" takeovers.

Aside from commercial banks, the banking system includes two other important financial institutions: **Savings and Loan Associations** and **Credit Unions.** Savings and loan associations provide many of the same services as commercial banks, including checkable deposits, a variety of time deposits, and money market deposit accounts. The almost 2,000 members of savings and loan associations have typically invested most of their savings deposits into home mortgages. Credit unions are cooperatives, made up of depositors with some common affiliation, like the same employer or union.

WHAT ARE THE FUNCTIONS OF FINANCIAL INSTITUTIONS?

Financial institutions offer a large number of financial functions. For example, they often will pay an individual's monthly bills by automatic withdrawals, administer estates, rent safe deposit boxes, and so on. Most important, though, they are depositories for savings and liquid assets that are used by individuals and firms for transaction purposes. They can create money by making loans. In making loans, financial institutions act as intermediaries (middlemen) between savers, who supply funds, and borrowers seeking funds to invest.

HOW DO BANKS CREATE MONEY?

As we have already learned, most money, narrowly defined, is in the form of transaction deposits, assets that can be directly used to buy goods and services. But how did the assets in, say, a checking account get there in the first place? Perhaps it was through a loan made by a commercial bank. When a bank lends to a person, it does not typically give the borrower cash (paper and metallic currency). Rather, it gives the person the funds by a check or by adding funds to an existing checking account of the borrower. If you go into a bank and borrow $1,000, the bank probably will simply add $1,000 to your checking account at the bank. In doing so, a new checkable deposit—money—is created.

HOW DO BANKS MAKE PROFITS?

Banks make loans and create checkable deposits in order to make a profit. How do they make their profit? By collecting higher interest payments on the loans they make than they pay their depositors for those funds. If I borrow $1,000 from Loans R Us National Bank, the interest payment I make, less the expenses the bank incurs in making the loan, including their costs of acquiring the funds, represents profit to the bank.

WHAT ARE RESERVE REQUIREMENTS?

Because the way to make more profit is to make more loans, banks want to make a large volume of loans. Stockholders of banks want the largest profits possible, so what keeps banks from making nearly infinite quantities of loans? Primarily, government regulatory authorities limit the loan issuance of banks by imposing **reserve requirements.** Reserve requirements require banks to keep on hand a quantity of cash or reserve accounts with the Federal Reserve equal to a prescribed proportion of their checkable deposits.

WHAT IS A FRACTIONAL RESERVE SYSTEM?

Even in the absence of regulations restricting the creation of checkable deposits, a prudent bank would put some limit on their loan (and therefore deposit) volume. Why? For people to accept checkable deposits as money, the checks written must be generally accepted in exchange for goods and services. People will accept checks only if they know that they are quickly convertible at par (face value) into legal tender. For this reason, banks must have adequate cash reserves on hand (including reserves at the Fed that can be almost immediately converted to currency, if necessary) to meet the needs of customers who wish to convert their checkable deposits into currency or spend them on goods or services.

Our banking system is sometimes called a **fractional reserve system,** because banks, by law as well as by choice, find it necessary to keep cash on hand and reserves at the Federal Reserve equal to some fraction of their checkable deposits. If a bank were to create $100 in demand deposits for every $1 in cash reserves that it had, the bank might well find itself in difficulty before too long. Why? Consider a bank with $10,000,000 in demand and time deposits and $100,000 in cash reserves. Suppose a couple of large companies with big accounts decide to withdraw $120,000 in cash on the same day. The bank would be unable to convert into legal tender all of the funds requested. The word would then spread that the bank's checks are not convertible into lawful money. This would cause a so-called "run on the bank." The bank would have to quickly convert some of its other assets into currency, or it would be unable to meet its obligations to convert its deposits into currency, and it would have to close.

Therefore, even in the absence of reserve regulations, few banks would risk maintaining fewer reserves on hand than they thought prudent for their amount of deposits (particularly demand deposits). Reserve requirements exist primarily to control the amount of demand and time deposits, and thus the size of the money supply; they do not exist simply to prevent bank failures.

While banks must meet their reserve requirements, they do not want to keep any more of their funds as additional reserves than necessary for safety, because cash assets do not earn any interest. In order to protect themselves but also earn some interest income, banks usually keep some of their assets in highly liquid investments such as United States government bonds. These types of highly liquid, interest-paying assets are often called **secondary reserves.**

WHAT IS A BALANCE SHEET?

Earlier in this Module, we learned that money is created when banks make loans. We will now look more closely at the process of bank lending and its impact on the stock of money. In doing so, we will take a closer look at the structure and behavior of our hypothetical bank, the Loans R Us National Bank. To get a good picture of the size of the bank, what it owns, and what it owes, we look at its **balance sheet,** which is sort of a financial "photograph" of the bank at a single moment in time. Exhibit 1 presents a balance sheet for the Loans R Us Bank.

WHAT ARE A BANK'S ASSETS?

The assets of a bank are those things of value that the bank owns (e.g., cash, reserves at the Federal Reserve, bonds, and its buildings), including contractual obligations of individuals and firms to pay funds to the bank (loans). The largest asset item for most banks is loans. Banks maintain most of their assets in the form of loans because interest payments on loans are the primary means by which they earn revenue. Some assets are kept in the form of non-interest-bearing cash and reserve accounts at the Federal Reserve, in order to meet legal reserve requirements (and secondly, to meet the cash demands of customers). Typically, relatively little of a bank's reserves, or cash assets, is physically kept in the form of paper currency in the bank's vault or at tellers' windows. Most banks keep a majority of their reserves as reserve accounts at the Federal Reserve. As previously indicated, banks usually also keep some assets in the form of bonds that are quickly convertible into cash if necessary (secondary reserves).

WHAT ARE A BANK'S LIABILITIES?

All banks have substantial liabilities, which are financial obligations that the bank has to other people. The predominant liability of virtually all banks is deposits. If you have money in a demand deposit account, you have the right to demand cash for that deposit at any time. Basically, the bank owes you the amount in your checking account. Time deposits similarly constitute a liability of banks.

WHAT IS A BANK'S CAPITAL?

For a bank to be healthy and solvent, its assets, or what it owns, must exceed its liabilities, or what it owes others. In other words, if the bank were liquidated and all the assets converted into cash and all the obligations to others (liabilities) paid off, there would still be some cash left to distribute to the owners of the bank, its stockholders. This difference between a bank's assets and its liabilities constitutes the bank's capital. Note that this definition of capital differs from the earlier definition, which described capital as goods used to further production of other goods (machines, structures, tools, etc.). As you can see in Exhibit 1, capital is included on the right side of the balance sheet so that both sides (assets and liabilities plus capital) are equal in amount. Any time the aggregate amount of bank assets changes, the aggregate amount of liabilities and capital also must change by the same amount, by definition.

WHAT IS A REQUIRED RESERVE RATIO?

Suppose for simplicity that the Loans R Us National Bank faces a reserve requirement of 10 percent on all deposits. That percentage is often called the **required reserve ratio.** But what does a required reserve ratio of 10 percent mean? This means that the bank *must* keep cash on hand or at the Federal Reserve Bank equal to one-tenth (10 percent) of its deposits. For example, if the required reserve ratio was 10 percent, banks would be required to hold $100,000 in required reserves for every $1 million in deposits. The remaining 90 percent of cash is called **excess reserves.**

Reserves in the form of cash and reserves at the Federal Reserve earn no revenue for the bank; there is no profit to be made from holding cash. Whenever excess reserves appear, banks will invest the excess reserves in interest-earning assets, sometimes bonds but usually loans.

WHAT HAPPENS WHEN A BANK LOANS ITS EXCESS RESERVES?

To see what happens to new demand deposits of $100,000, let's return to the Loan R Us Bank. We will continue to assume that the required reserve ratio is 10 percent. That is, the bank is required to hold $10,000 in required reserves for this new deposit of $100,000. The remaining 90 percent, or $90,000, becomes excess reserves, and most of this will likely become available for loans for individuals and businesses.

However, this is not the end of the story. Let us say that the bank loans out all of its new excess reserves of $90,000 to an individual who is remodeling her home. At the time that the loan is made, the money supply will increase by $90,000. Specifically, no one has less money—the original depositor still has $100,000 and the bank now adds $90,000 to the borrower's checking account (demand deposit). A

EXHIBIT 1	BALANCE SHEET, LOANS R US NATIONAL BANK		

Assets		Liabilities and Capital	
Cash (reserves)	$2,000,000	Transaction deposits (Checking deposits)	$5,000,000
		Savings and time deposits	4,000,000
Loans	6,100,000	Total Liabilities	9,000,000
Bonds (U.S. govt. and municipal)	1,500,000		
		Capital	1,000,000
Bank building, equipment, fixtures	400,000		
Total Assets	**$10,000,000**	**Total Liabilities and Capital**	**$10,000,000**

new demand deposit, or checking acount, of $90,000 has been created. Since demand deposits are money, the issuers of the new loan have created money.

Furthermore, borrowers are not likely to keep the money in their checking accounts for long, since you usually take out a loan to buy something. Say that the loan is used for remodeling; then the borrower pays the construction company and the owner will likely deposit the money into his account at another bank to add even more funds to additional money expansion. This whole process is summarized in Exhibit 2.

In short, banks create money when they increase demand deposits through the process of creating loans. In the next Concept, we will see how the process of loans and deposits has a multiplying effect throughout the banking industry.

EXHIBIT 2   **FRACTIONAL RESERVE BANKING SYSTEM**

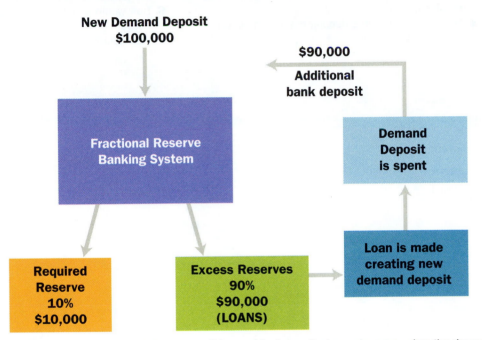

When a new deposit enters the banking system, much of that money will be used for loans. Banks create money when they increase demand deposits through the process of creating loans.

1. Money is created when banks make loans. Borrowers receive newly created demand deposits.
2. Required reserves are the amount of cash or reserves—equal to a prescribed proportion of their deposits—that banks are required to keep on hand or in reserve accounts with the Federal Reserve.
3. A balance sheet is a financial record that indicates the balance between a bank's assets and its liabilities plus capital.
4. Banks create money by increasing demand deposits through the process of making loans.

---

1. How did laws against interstate banking lead to a large number of U.S. banks? What is happening to the number of banks now that interstate banking is allowed?
2. In what way is it true that "banks make money by making money"?
3. How do legal reserve deposit regulations lower bank profits?
4. Is a demand deposit an asset or a liability?
5. If the Bonnie and Clyde National Bank's only deposits were demand deposits of $20 million, and it faced a 10 percent reserve requirement, how much money would it be required to hold in reserves?
6. How would a new deposit into your demand deposit account create a situation of excess reserves at your bank?

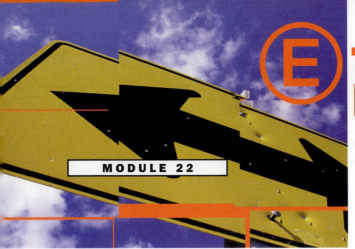

E The Money Multiplier

■ How does the multiple expansion of the money supply process work?

■ What is the money multiplier?

WHAT IS THE MULTIPLE EXPANSION EFFECT?

You learned in Concept D that banks can create money (demand deposits) by making loans and that the monetary expansion of an individual bank is limited to its excess reserves. While this is true, it ignores the further effects of a new loan and the accompanying expansion in the stock of money. New loans create new money directly, but they also create excess reserves in other banks, which leads to still further increases in both loans and the stock of money. There is a multiple expansion effect, where a given volume of bank reserves creates a multiplied amount of money.

HOW DO BANK DEPOSITS LEAD TO MULTIPLE EXPANSIONS?

To see how the process of multiple expansion works, let us extend our earlier example. Say Loans R Us Bank receives a new cash deposit of $100,000. (In the next Module we will discuss in detail how this deposit happens to arrive at the bank.) For convenience, say the bank was only required to keep new cash reserves equal to one-tenth (10 percent) of new deposits. With that, Loans R Us is only required to hold $10,000 of the $100,000 deposit for required reserves. Thus, Loans R Us Bank now has $90,000 in excess reserves as a consequence of the new cash deposit.

Loans R Us Bank, being a profit maximizer, will probably put its newly acquired excess reserves to work in some fashion earning income in the form of interest. Most likely, it will make one or more new loans totaling $90,000.

WHEN DOES THE MULTIPLE EXPANSION PROCESS STOP?

The process does not stop there. When the borrowers from Loans R Us Bank get their loans, the borrowed money will almost certainly be spent on something—such as new machinery, a new house, a new car, or greater store inventories. The new money will lead to new spending.

The $90,000 spent by persons borrowing from Loans R Us Bank likely will end up in bank accounts in still other banks, such as Bank A shown in Exhibit 1. Bank A now has a new deposit of $90,000 with which to make more loans and create still more money. This process continues with Bank B, Bank C, Bank D, and others. Loans R Us Bank's initial cash deposit, then, has a chain reaction impact that ultimately involves many banks and a total monetary impact that is far greater than suggested by the size of the original deposit of $100,000. That is, every new loan gives rise to excess reserves, which lead to still further lending and deposit creation. Each round of lending is smaller than the preceding one, because some (we are assuming 10 percent) of the new money created must be kept as required reserves.

WHAT IS THE MONEY MULTIPLIER?

The following formula can be used to measure the total maximum potential impact on the supply of money:

$$\text{Potential money creation} = \text{Initial deposit} \times \text{Money multiplier}$$

The **money multiplier** is simply 1 divided by the reserve requirement. The larger the reserve requirement, the smaller the money multiplier. Thus, a reserve requirement of 25 percent, or one-fourth, means a money multiplier of four. Likewise, a reserve requirement of 10 percent, or one-tenth, means a money multiplier of 10.

In the example in Exhibit 1, where Loans R Us Bank (facing a 10 percent reserve requirement) receives a new $100,000 cash deposit, initial deposit equals $100,000. Potential money creation, then, equals $100,000 (initial deposit) multiplied by 10 (the money multiplier), or $1,000,000. Using the money multiplier, we can calculate that the total potential impact of the initial $100,000 deposit is some $1,000,000 in money being created. In other words, the final monetary impact is 10 times as great as the initial deposit. Most of this increase, $900,000, has been created by the increase in demand deposits generated

EXHIBIT 1   **THE MULTIPLE EXPANSION PROCESS**

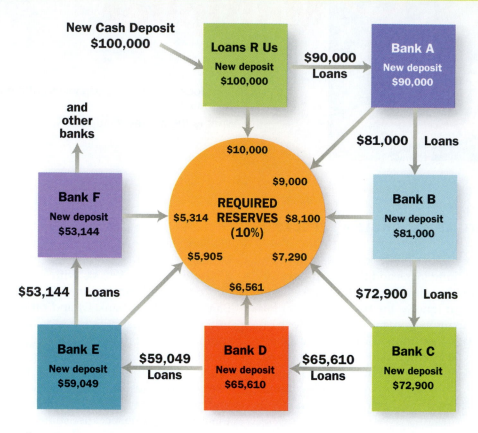

New Cash Deposit $100,000

Loans R Us
New deposit
$100,000

$90,000 Loans

Bank A
New deposit
$90,000

$81,000 Loans

and other banks

Bank F
New deposit
$53,144

Bank B
New deposit
$81,000

REQUIRED RESERVES (10%)
$10,000
$9,000
$5,314 $8,100
$5,905 $7,290
$6,561

$53,144 Loans

$72,900 Loans

Bank E
New deposit
$59,049

$59,049 Loans

Bank D
New deposit
$65,610

$65,610 Loans

Bank C
New deposit
$72,900

A $100,000 new cash deposit in Loans R Us Bank has the potential to create $1,000,000 in a chain reaction that involves many banks. The process repeats itself, as the money lent from one bank becomes a new deposit in another bank.

when banks make loans; the remaining $100,000 is from the initial deposit.

WHY IS IT ONLY "POTENTIAL" MONEY CREATION?

Note that the expression "potential money creation" was used in describing the impact of creating loans and deposits out of excess reserves. Why "potential"? Because it is possible that some banks will choose not to lend all of their excess reserves. Some banks may simply be extremely conservative and keep some extra newly acquired cash assets in that form. When that happens, the chain reaction effect is reduced by the amount of excess reserves not loaned out.

Moreover, some borrowers may not spend all of their newly acquired bank deposits, or they may wait a considerable period of time before doing so. Others may put their borrowed funds into time deposits rather than checkable deposits, which would reduce the M1 expansion process

but not the M2 money expansion process. Still others may choose to keep some of their loans as currency in their pockets. Such leakages and time lags in the bank money

TUNE UP

THE MULTIPLE EXPANSION PROCESS

Q: Holden Reserves is a banker. If someone borrows money from Holden's bank and doesn't spend it, will the money supply increase through the banking multiplier?

A: No. If the borrower keeps the money, a new account does not get created and the multiple expansion process will not work.

expansion process usually mean that the actual monetary impact of an initial deposit created out of excess reserves within a short time period is less than indicated by the money multiplier. Still, the multiplier principle does work, and a multiple expansion of deposits will generally occur in a banking system that is characterized by fractional reserve requirements.

HOW IS MONEY DESTROYED?

The process of money creation can be reversed, and in the process, money is destroyed. When a person pays a loan back to a bank, she usually does so by writing a check to the bank for the amount due. As a result, demand deposits decline, directly reducing the money stock.

IN THE NEWS

CHANGES IN THE BANKING INDUSTRY

More competition or bigger is better? It looks like the financial industry is going for the bigger is better idea.

Two more bank mega-mergers have been announced. The largest is the nearly $60 billion deal with BankAmerica Corp., and NationsBank Corp. At the same time Banc One is joining with First Chicago in a nearly $30 billion deal.

As usual they promise better service and more products for consumers. It usually comes at a cost.

NationsBank Corp., Chairman Hugh McColl and BankAmerica Corp., Chairman David Coulter shook hands on a deal that will create the nation's biggest bank, in yet another banking merger that will affect millions of banking customers and thousands of employees. The merger will include some 29 million households and two million business accounts in 22 states.

They'll keep the BankAmerica name and will operate in 22 states, with 4,800 branches and 15,000 automated teller machines. The banks have 180,000 employees and the merger could eliminate 5,000 to 8,000 positions.

BankAmerica has been a California fixture and San Francisco based institution for 94 years. The two banks say it will be good for their customers but there's always a downside to mergers.

The cost consumers often pay when banks merge are:

- The costs of checking accounts often go up.
- There may be branch closings.
- Account terms often change.
- There are often higher banking fees.
- There are sometimes new fees in larger banks.
- Sometimes accounts have to be restructured.
- And mergers cause account computer confusion.

Yet during the news conference to announce the merger there were no hints of the potential confusion from the leaders of the two banks. Hugh McColl of NationsBank said, "The resources that such a bank can put together for customers and shareholders alike is a good one. We're here because in the words of Victor Hugo an invasion of armies can be resisted but not an idea whose time has come."

Whether it's good for the consumer or not the makeover of the nation's banking industry is moving very quickly and it is a fact of life, a fact of life that will affect all of us.

SOURCE: J. D. Kohn, ed., "How Will the Latest Bank Merger Affect Consumers?" http://www.abcnews.com/local/kabc/news/7200_4131998.html

CONSIDER THIS:
Are there economies of scale in the banking industry? That is, can the merger of two banks bring about lower costs? The banks claim the mergers will lead to better service and more products.

1. New loans mean new money (demand deposits), which can increase spending as well as the stock of money.

2. The banking system as a whole can potentially create money equal to several times the amount of total reserves or new money equal to several times the amount of excess reserves, the exact amount determined by the money multiplier, which is equal to one divided by the reserve requirement.

1. Why do the stock of money and the volume of bank loans both increase or decrease at the same time?

2. Why would each bank in the money supply multiple expansion process lend out a larger fraction of any new deposit it receives, the lower the reserve requirement?

3. If a particular bank with a reserve requirement of 10 percent has $30,000 in a new cash deposit, how much money could it create through making new loans?

4. Why do banks choosing to hold excess reserves or borrowers choosing to hold some of their loans in the form of currency reduce the actual impact of the money multiplier to a level below that indicated by the multiplier formula?

The Collapse of America's Banking System, 1920–1933

- What caused the collapse of the banking system between 1920 and 1933?
- How are bank failures avoided today?

WHAT LED TO THE COLLAPSE OF THE BANKING SYSTEM BETWEEN 1920 AND 1933?

Perhaps the most famous utterance from Franklin D. Roosevelt, the President of the United States from 1933 to 1945, was made on the day he assumed office, when he declared, "The only thing we have to fear is fear itself." Those 10 words succinctly summarize the problems that led the world's leading economic power to a near total collapse in its system of commercial banking and, with that, to an abrupt and unprecedented decline in the stock of money. The decline in the money stock, in turn, contributed to an economic downturn that had dire consequences for many, especially for the one-fourth of the labor force unemployed at the time of Roosevelt's first inaugural address.

WHAT HAPPENED TO THE BANKING INDUSTRY?

In 1920, there were 30,000 banks in the United States; by 1933, the number had declined to about 15,000. What happened? During the prosperous 1920s, nearly 6,000 banks closed their doors. In some cases, bank failure reflected imprudent management or even criminal activity on the part of bank officers (stealing from the bank). A few banks had a sufficient amount of resources stolen by others to make them insolvent (the Bonnie and Clyde effect). More often, though, banks in rural areas closed as a consequence of having large sums of assets tied up in loans to farmers who, because of low farm prices, were not in a position to pay off the loans when they came due. Rumors spread that a bank was in trouble, and these rumors, even if false, became self-fulfilling prophecies. Bank "runs" developed and even conservatively run banks with cash equal to 15 or 20 percent of their deposit liabilities found themselves with insufficient cash reserves to meet the withdrawal requests of panicky depositors.

The bank failures of the 1920s, while numerous, were generally scattered around small towns in the country. Confidence in banks actually generally increased in that decade, and by the fall of 1929, there were $11 in bank deposits for every $1 in currency in circulation.

The first year following the stock market crash of 1929 saw little dramatic happen to the banking system, but in late 1930, a bank with the unfortunately awesome sounding name of the Bank of the United States failed, the largest bank failure in the country to that time. This failure had a ripple effect. More bank "runs" occurred as depositors began to get jittery. Banks, fearing runs, began to not lend their excess reserves, thereby aggravating a fall in the money stock and reducing business investment.

As depositors converted their deposits to currency, bank reserves fell, and with that the ability of banks to support deposits. The situation improved a bit in 1932, when a newly created government agency, the Reconstruction Finance Corporation (RFC), helped banks in distress with loans. By early 1933, however, the depositor confidence decline had reached such a point that the entire banking system was in jeopardy. On March 4, newly inaugurated President Roosevelt declared a national bank holiday, closing every bank in the country for nearly two weeks. Then, only the "good" banks were allowed to reopen, an action that increased confidence. By this time the deposit–currency ratio had fallen from 11 to 1 (in 1929) to 4 to 1. Passage of federal deposit insurance in mid-1933 greatly strengthened depositor confidence and led to money reentering the banks. The recovery process began.

WHAT CAUSED THE COLLAPSE?

The collapse occurred for several reasons. First, the nation had thousands of relatively small banks. Customers believed that depositor withdrawals could force a bank to close, and the mere fear of bank runs made them a reality. Canada, with relatively few banks that were mostly very large with many branches, had no bank runs. Second, governmental attempts to stem the growing distress were weak and too late. Financial aid to banks was nonexistent; the Federal Reserve System and other governmental efforts began only in 1932—well into the decline. Third, deposit insurance, which would have bolstered customer confidence, did not exist. The financial consequences of bank failures were correctly perceived by the public to be great. Fourth, growing depositor fear was enhanced by the fact that the economy was in a continuous downward spiral—there was no basis for any optimism that bank loans would be safely repaid.

WHY DON'T WE HAVE BANK FAILURES TODAY?

The combination of the Federal Deposit Insurance Corporation (FDIC) and the government's greater willingness to assist distressed banks has largely eliminated bank runs and failures in recent times. Now, when a bank runs into financial difficulty, the FDIC may assist another bank in taking over the assets and liabilities of the troubled bank so that no depositor loses a cent. Thus, changes in the money supply resulting from a loss of deposits from failed banks are no longer a big problem. Better bank stability means a greater stability in the money supply, which means, as will be more explicitly demonstrated in the next Module, a greater level of economic stability.

What changes have been made to prevent this from happening today?

CONCEPT CHECK

1. The entire banking system was in jeopardy by 1933.
2. The banking collapse occurred because of customers' fears and the government's weak attempt to correct the problem.

3. The creation of the Federal Deposit Insurance Corporation has largely eliminated bank runs in recent times.

---

1. How did the combination of increased holding of excess reserves by banks and currency by the public lead to bank failures in the 1930s?

2. What are the four reasons cited in the text for the collapse of the U.S. banking system in this period?
3. What is the FDIC, and how did its establishment increase bank stability and reassure depositors?

MODULE 22

What are the cost-saving advantages of Internet banking? How can smaller banks compete with multi-billion-dollar banks?

INTERNET BANKING

AMY OLMSTEAD

NEW YORK, August 14—Internet banks have started to chip away at their concrete and steel competitors' business.

Net.Bank, Security First Network Bank (which has one walk-in customer service center), *TeleBank* and Principal Bank have more than 64,000 accounts combined. At least one—Net.Bank—is turning a profit.

They're winning customers largely because of their lower cost structures. Physical branches are expensive to staff and operate. Without those costs, Internet banks can offer higher interest rates on accounts and lower fees.

It's often enough to entice customers to open an account. But cyberbanking's inconveniences mean many consumers are reluctant to completely convert to branchless banking.

Internet banks push their cost advantages. Net.Bank CEO D. R. Grimes says his bank can offer 95 percent of the services traditional banks offer at almost half the cost. (Net.Bank is changing its name from Atlanta Internet Bank.)

"In the most recent quarter, our expenses—everything except interest—were about 40 percent less than a traditional bank of our size," says Grimes. "That's a very significant advantage."

Better interest rates on accounts and CDs are the top selling point. Net.Bank offers interest checking accounts with annual interest rates from 3.0 to 3.93 percent on a deposit of at least $100. TeleBank offers rates starting at 3.10 percent on interest checking accounts of $2,500.

In comparison, interest checking accounts at two East Coast *Citibank* branches offer rates of 1.0 to 1.14 percent, with no minimum balance. Interest checking accounts at two *Bank of America* branches in the West offered rates of 1.0 percent on accounts with $2,000 or more. The difference in fees is substantial, too.

"It costs pennies for any bank to do transactions over the Internet," says Aileen Lopez Pugh, CFO of TeleBank, "but you don't see large banks offering any benefits to their customers. We pass on our cost savings."

There are other obstacles for Internet banks. They can't offer some bank services, like safety deposit boxes, without a physical location.

The paper trail can be even more burdensome. Checks that are traditionally slipped into an ATM have to be mailed. Wire transfers replace cash deposits. Funds not withdrawn at an ATM are sent as cashiers checks or wire transfers.

. . . Despite the uncertainties, Internet banks believe there's at least one market that will be a cinch to convert—expatriates. Many Americans living abroad still have bills to pay back home. With an Internet bank, they can do their banking from their laptop at a cafe.

SOURCE: ABCNEWS.com fromTheStreet.com. Copyright 1998 ABCNEWS and Starwave Corporation.

The financial industry is looking at some new very large bank mergers. Why would one bank merge with another? The obvious reason is that there are sometimes economies of scale in mergers. That is, two companies may be able to lower their production costs by joining forces. However, consolidation is not the only way to cut costs in an increasingly competitive financial world. Internet banking looks like it is here to stay and it can cut costs with low overhead—no tellers, expensive buildings, or security guards. Many experts believe that we are not far from a cashless society in which one debit credit card will be used to take care of all transactions.

How does Internet banking allow small banks to compete with large banks?

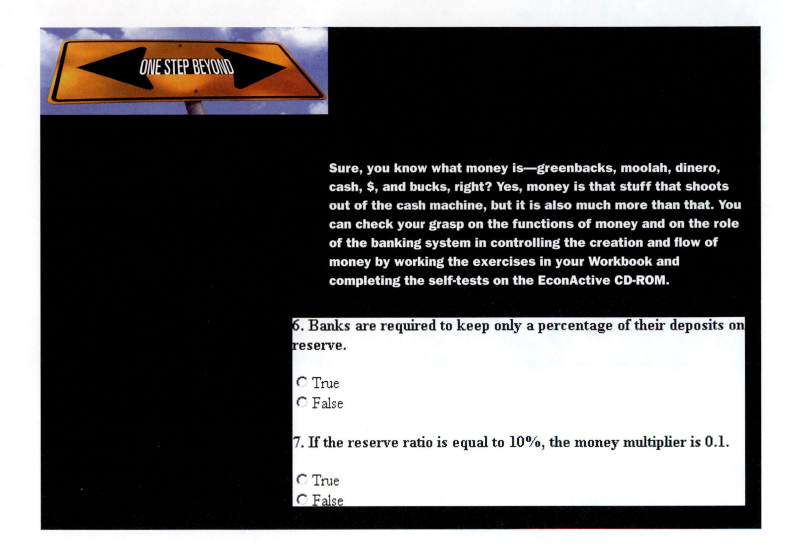

ONE STEP BEYOND

Sure, you know what money is—greenbacks, moolah, dinero, cash, $, and bucks, right? Yes, money is that stuff that shoots out of the cash machine, but it is also much more than that. You can check your grasp on the functions of money and on the role of the banking system in controlling the creation and flow of money by working the exercises in your Workbook and completing the self-tests on the EconActive CD-ROM.

6. Banks are required to keep only a percentage of their deposits on reserve.

○ True
○ False

7. If the reserve ratio is equal to 10%, the money multiplier is 0.1.

○ True
○ False

PHOTO CREDITS MODULE 22

Page **528**: left, © Barbara Alper/Stock, Boston/PNI; right, © 1998 Don Couch Photography; Page **530**: CALVIN AND HOBBES © 1992 & 1993 Watterson. Reprinted with permission of UNIVERSAL PRESS SYNDICATE. All rights reserved; Page **531**: © Mark Burnett/Stock, Boston/PNI; Page **532**: © T.J. Florian/Rainbow/PNI; Page **534**: THE FAR SIDE © 1991 FARWORKS, INC. Used by permission. All rights reserved; Page **535**: © Burke: Triolo/Food Pix/PNI; top inset, © 1998 Don Couch Photography; Page **537**: © 1998 Don Couch Photography; Page **538**: © PhotoDisc; Page **550**: © Library of Congress/Corbis Images; Page **552**: Photo courtesy of Atlanta Internet Bank.

The Federal Reserve System and Monetary Policy

A. The Federal Reserve System
What is the role of a central bank?

B. The Equation of Exchange
How does the equation of exchange help our understanding
of the role of money in the economy?

C. Implementing Monetary Policy: Tools of the Fed
What are the three major tools of the Fed?

D. Money, Interest Rates, and Aggregate Demand
How do changes in money supply and money demand
affect interest rates in the money market?

E. Problems in Implementing Monetary Policy
What factors can limit the effectiveness of monetary policy?

F. Application: The Independence of the Fed
Should the Fed be independent from the administration and Congress?

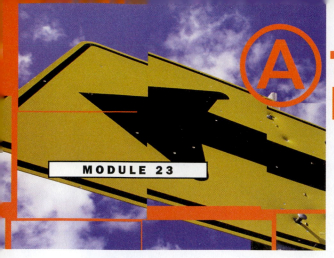

A The Federal Reserve System

- What are the functions of a central bank?
- Who controls the Federal Reserve System?
- How is the Fed tied to Congress and the executive branch?

WHAT ARE THE FUNCTIONS OF A CENTRAL BANK?

In most countries of the world, the job of manipulating the supply of money belongs to the central bank. A central bank has many functions. First, a central bank is a "banker's bank." It serves as a bank where commercial banks maintain their own cash deposits—their reserves. Second, a central bank performs a number of service functions for commercial banks, such as transferring funds and checks between various commercial banks in the banking system. Third, the central bank typically serves as the major bank for the central government, handling, for example, its payroll accounts. Fourth, the central bank buys and sells foreign currencies and generally assists in the completion of financial transactions with other countries. Fifth, it serves as a "lender of last resort" that helps banking institutions in financial distress. Sixth, the central bank is concerned with the stability of the banking system and the supply of money, which as you have already learned, results from the loan decisions of banks. The central bank can and does impose regulations on private commercial banks; it thereby regulates the size of the money supply and influences the level of economic activity. The central bank also implements monetary policy, which along with fiscal policy, forms the basis of efforts to direct the economy to perform in accordance with macroeconomic goals.

WHERE IS THE FEDERAL RESERVE SYSTEM LOCATED?

In most countries, the central bank is a single bank; for example, the central bank of Great Britain, the Bank of England, is a single institution located in London. In the United States, however, the central bank is 12 institutions, closely tied together and collectively called the Federal Reserve System. The Federal Reserve System, or Fed, as it is nicknamed, has separate banks in Boston, New York, Philadelphia, Richmond, Atlanta, Dallas, Cleveland, Chicago, St. Louis, Minneapolis-St. Paul, Kansas City, and

Commercial banks keep reserves with the Central Bank.

San Francisco. As Exhibit 1 shows, these banks and their branches are spread all over the country, but they are most heavily concentrated in the Eastern states.

Each of the 12 banks has branches in key cities in its district. For example, the Federal Reserve Bank of Cleveland serves the fourth Federal Reserve district and has branches in Pittsburgh and Cincinnati. Each Federal Reserve bank has its own board of directors and, to some limited extent, can set its own policies. Effectively, however, the 12 banks act largely in unison on major policy issues, with effective control of major policy decisions resting with the Board of Governors and the Federal Open Market Committee of the Federal Reserve System, headquartered in Washington, D.C. The Chairman of the Federal Reserve Board of Governors (currently Alan Greenspan) is generally regarded as

The letter indicates which of the Fed banks issued the $20 bill. A "B" and the number 2 indicate that the bill was issued in New York, the second Federal Reserve District.

one of the most important and powerful economic policy-makers in the country.

WHAT IS THE FED'S RELATIONSHIP TO THE FEDERAL GOVERNMENT?

The Federal Reserve was created in 1913 because the U.S. banking system had so little stability and no central direc-

tion. Technically, the Fed is privately owned by the banks that "belong" to it. All banks are not required to belong to the Fed; however, since the passage of new legislation in 1980, virtually no difference exists between the requirements of member and nonmember banks.

The private ownership of the Fed is essentially meaningless, because the Board of Governors of the Federal Reserve, which controls major policy decisions, is appointed by the president of the United States, not by the stockholders. The owners of the Fed have relatively little control over its operations and receive only small fixed dividends on their modest financial stake in the system. Again, the private ownership but public control feature was a compromise made to appease commercial banks opposed to direct public (government) regulation.

WHAT ARE THE FED'S TIES TO THE EXECUTIVE BRANCH?

An important aspect of the Fed's operation is that, historically, it has had a considerable amount of independence from both the executive and legislative branches of government. True, the president appoints the seven members of the Board of Governors, subject to Senate approval, but the term of appointment is 14 years. This means that no member of the Federal Reserve Board will face reappointment from the president who initially made the appointment, because presidential tenure is limited to two four-year terms. Moreover, the terms of board members are staggered, so a new appointment is made only every two years. It is practically impossible for a single president to appoint a majority of the members of the board, and

---

| EXHIBIT 1 | BOUNDARIES OF FEDERAL RESERVE DISTRICTS AND THEIR BRANCH TERRITORIES |

NOTE: Both Hawaii and Alaska are in the Twelfth District.

even if it were possible, members have little fear of losing their jobs as a result of presidential wrath. The Chair of the Federal Reserve Board is a member of the Board of Governors and serves a four-year term. The Chair is truly the chief executive officer of the system, and he effectively runs it with considerable help from the presidents of the 12 regional banks.

HOW DOES THE FED OPERATE?

Many of the key policy decisions of the Federal Reserve are actually made by its Federal Open Market Committee (FOMC), which consists of the seven members of the Board of Governors; the President of the New York Federal Reserve Bank, and four other presidents of Federal Reserve Banks, who serve on the committee on a rotating basis. The FOMC makes most of the key decisions influencing the direction and size of changes in the money stock, and their regular, secret meetings are accordingly considered very important by the business community and government.

The chair of the Fed is truly the chief executive officer of the system.

CONCEPT CHECK

1. Of the six major functions of a central bank, the most important is its role in regulating the money supply.
2. There are 12 Federal Reserve banks in the Federal Reserve System. Although these banks are independent institutions, they act largely in unison on major policy decisions.
3. The Federal Reserve Board of Governors and the Federal Open Market Committee are the prime decision makers for monetary policy in the United States.

4. The Fed is tied to the president in that he appoints the members of the Board of Governors to a 14-year term, with only one appointment made every two years. The president also selects the Chair of the Federal Reserve Board, who serves a four-year term. The only other government intervention in the Fed can come from legislation passed in Congress.

1. What are the six primary functions of a central bank?
2. What is the FOMC and what does it do?

3. How is the Fed tied to the executive branch? How is it insulated from executive branch pressure to influence monetary policy?

B The Equation of Exchange

- What is the equation of exchange?
- What is the velocity of money?
- How is the equation of exchange useful?

As we discussed in the previous Concept, perhaps the most important function of the Federal Reserve is its ability to regulate the money supply. In order to fully understand the significant role that the Federal Reserve plays in the economy, we will first examine the role of money in the national economy.

WHAT IS THE EQUATION OF EXCHANGE?

The role that money plays in determining equilibrium GDP, the level of prices, and real output of goods and services has attracted the attention of economists for generations. In the early part of this century, economists noted a useful relationship that helps our understanding of the role of money in the national economy, called the **equation of exchange.** The equation of exchange can be presented as follows:

$$MV = PQ$$

where M is the money supply, however defined (usually M1 or M2), V is the income velocity of money, P is the average level of prices of final goods and services, and Q is the physical quantity of final goods and services produced in a given period (usually one year).

We have previously defined M. V, the velocity of money, refers to the "turnover" rate, or the intensity with which money is used. Specifically, V represents the average number of times that a dollar is used in purchasing final goods or services in a one-year period. Thus, if individuals are hoarding their money, velocity will be low; if individuals are writing lots of checks on their checking accounts and spending currency as fast as they receive it, velocity will tend to be high.

The expression PQ represents the dollar value of all final goods and services sold in a country in a given year. Does that sound familiar? It should, because that is the definition of nominal gross domestic product (GDP). Thus, for our purposes, we may consider the average level of prices (P) times the physical quantity of final goods and services (Q) to be equal to nominal GDP. We could say then, that

$$MV = \text{Nominal GDP}$$

or,

$$V = \text{Nominal GDP} / M$$

That, in fact, is the definition of velocity: The total output of goods in a year divided by the amount of money is the same thing as the average number of times a dollar is used in final goods transactions in a year.

The actual magnitude of V will depend on the definition of money that is used. For example, using M1, the velocity of money in 1993 equaled

$$V = \text{Nominal GDP} / \text{M1} = \$6{,}374 \text{ billion} / \$1{,}128 \text{ billion} = 5.65$$

Using the broader definition of money, M2, the velocity of money in 1993 equaled

$$V = \text{Nominal GDP} / \text{M2} = \$6{,}374 \text{ billion} / \$3{,}566 \text{ billion} = 1.79$$

Velocity is the average number of times a dollar is used in final goods transactions in a year.

The average dollar of money, then, turns over a few times in the course of a year, with the precise number depending on the definition of money.

HOW IS THE EQUATION OF EXCHANGE USEFUL?

The equation of exchange is a useful tool when we try to assess the impact in a change in the stock of money (M) on the aggregate economy. If M increases, then one of the following must happen:

1. V must decline by the same magnitude, so that MV remains constant, leaving PQ unchanged.
2. P must rise.
3. Q must rise.
4. P and Q must each rise some, so that the product of P and Q remains equal to MV.

In other words, if the money stock increases and the velocity of money does not change, there will be either higher prices (inflation), greater output of final goods and services, or a combination of both. If one considers a macroeconomic policy to be successful if output is increased but unsuccessful if the only effect of the policy is inflation, then an increase in M is a good policy if Q increases but a bad policy if P increases.

Likewise, dampening the rate of increase in M or even causing it to decline will cause nominal GDP to fall, unless the change in M is counteracted by a rising velocity of money. Intentionally decreasing M can also either be good or bad, depending on whether the declining money GDP is reflected mainly in falling prices (P) or in falling output (Q).

Therefore, expanding the money supply, unless counteracted by increased hoarding of currency (leading to a decline in V), will have the same type of impact on aggregate demand as an expansionary fiscal policy—increasing government purchases, reducing taxes, or increases in transfer payments. Likewise, policies designed to reduce the money supply will have a contractionary impact (unless offset by a rising velocity of money) on aggregate demand, similar to the impact obtained from increasing taxes, decreasing transfer payments, or decreasing government purchases.

In sum, what these relationships illustrate is that monetary policy can be used to obtain the same objectives as fiscal policy. Some economists, often called monetarists, believe that monetary policy is the most powerful determinant of macroeconomic results.

HOW VOLATILE IS THE VELOCITY OF MONEY?

Economists once considered the velocity of money a given. We now know that it is not constant, but often moves in a fairly predictable pattern. Thus, the connection between money supply and GDP is still fairly predictable. Historically, the velocity of money has been quite stable over a long period of time, and it has been particularly stable using the M2 definition. However, velocity is less stable when measured using the M1 definition and over shorter periods of time. For example, an increase in velocity can occur with anticipated inflation. When individuals expect inflation, they will spend their money more quickly. They don't want to be caught holding money that is going to be worth less in the future. Also, an increase in the interest rates will cause people to hold less money. That is, people want to hold less money when the opportunity cost of holding money increases. This, in turn, means that the velocity of money increases.

CONCEPT CHECK

1. The equation of exchange is $MV = PQ$, where M is the money supply, V is the velocity of money, P is the average level of prices of final goods and services, and Q is the physical quantity of final goods and services produced in an economy in a given year.

2. The velocity of money (V) represents the average number of times that a dollar is used in purchasing final goods or services in a one-year period.

3. The equation of exchange is a useful tool when analyzing the effects of a change in the stock of money on the aggregate economy.

1. If the money stock is $10 billion and velocity is 4, what is the product of the price level and output? If the price level is 2, what does output equal?
2. If nominal GDP is $200 billion and the money stock is $50 billion, what must velocity be?

3. If the money stock increases and velocity does not change, what will happen to nominal GDP?
4. If velocity is unstable, does stabilizing the money stock help stabilize the economy? Why or why not?

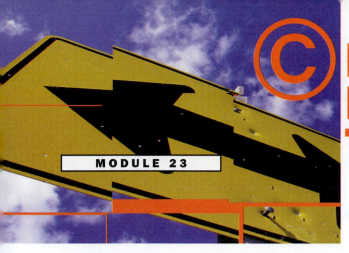

© Implementing Monetary Policy: Tools of the Fed

- What are the three major tools of the Fed?
- What is the purpose of the Fed's tools?
- What other powers does the Fed have?

HOW DOES THE FED MANIPULATE THE SUPPLY OF MONEY?

As noted previously, the Board of Governors of the Fed and the Federal Open Market Committee are the prime decision makers for monetary policy in the United States. They decide whether to expand the stock of money and, hopefully, the real level of economic activity, or to contract the money stock, hoping to cool inflationary pressures. How does the Fed control the stock of money, particularly when, as we discussed in the previous Module, it is the privately owned commercial banks that actually create and destroy money by making loans?

The Fed has three major methods that it can use to control the supply of money: It can engage in open market operations, change reserve requirements, or change its discount rate. Of these three tools, the Fed uses open market operations the most. It is by far the most important device used by the Fed to influence the money supply.

WHAT ARE OPEN MARKET OPERATIONS?

Open market operations involve the purchase and sale of government securities by the Federal Reserve System. Decisions regarding whether to buy or sell government bonds are made by the Federal Open Market Committee at its regular meetings. For several reasons, open market operations are the most important method the Fed uses to change the stock of money. To begin, it is a device that can be implemented quickly and cheaply—the Fed merely calls an agent who buys or sells bonds. It can be done quietly, without a lot of political debate or a public announcement. It is a rather powerful tool, as any given purchase or sale of securities has an ultimate impact several times the amount of the initial transaction.

When the Fed buys bonds, it pays the seller of the bonds by a check written on one of the 12 Federal Reserve banks. The person receiving the check will likely deposit it in his or her bank account, increasing the money stock in the form of added transactions deposits. More importantly, the commercial bank, in return for crediting the account of the bond seller with a new deposit, gets cash reserves or a higher balance in their reserve account at the Federal Reserve Bank in its district.

For example, suppose the Loans R Us National Bank has no excess reserves and that one of its customers sells a bond for $10,000 through a broker to the Federal Reserve System. The customer deposits the check from the Fed for $10,000 in his or her account, and the Fed credits the Loans R Us Bank with $10,000 in reserves. Suppose the reserve requirement is 10 percent. The Loans R Us Bank, then, only needs new reserves of $1,000 ($10,000 × .10) to support its $10,000, meaning that it has acquired $9,000 in new excess reserves ($10,000 new actual reserves minus $1,000 in new required reserves). Loans R Us can, and probably will, lend out its excess reserves of $9,000, creating $9,000 in new deposits in the process. The recipients of the loans, in turn, will likely spend the money, leading to still more new deposits and excess reserves in other banks, as discussed in the previous Module.

In other words, the Fed's purchase of the bond directly creates $10,000 in money in the form of bank deposits, and indirectly permits up to $90,000 in additional money to be created through the multiple expansion in bank deposits. (The money multiplier is the reciprocal of 1/10, or 10. 10 × $9,000 = $90,000.) Thus, if the reserve requirement is 10 percent, a total of up to $100,000 in new money is potentially created by the purchase of one $10,000 bond by the Fed.

The process works in reverse when the Fed sells a bond. The individual purchasing the bond will pay the Fed by check, lowering demand deposits in the banking system. Reserves of the bank where the bond purchaser has a bank account will likewise fall. If the bank had zero excess reserves at the beginning of the process, it will now have a reserve deficiency that must be met by selling secondary reserves or by reducing loan volume, either of which will lead to further destruction of deposits. A multiple contraction of deposits will begin.

TUNE UP

OPEN MARKET OPERATIONS

Q: Cass Sheer is a worker at a branch of the Federal Reserve. She is trying to explain to her mother, who owns several government bonds, how the money supply can increase as result of open market operations. Can you help Cass?

A: Cass explains that in order for people to want to put more money in banks and less in government bonds, the Fed must offer bond holders an attractive price. If the Fed's price is high enough, it will tempt some investors to sell their government bonds. When those individuals place the proceeds from the sale in the bank, new deposits are created, increasing reserves in the banking system. The excess reserves can then be loaned by the banks, creating more new deposits and increasing the excess reserves in still other banks.

EXHIBIT 1	MONEY AND INFLATION (PERCENT PER YEAR)

Years	M₂	Inflation*
1960–69	7.0	2.5
1970–79	9.6	7.6
1980–89	7.7	3.5
1990–96	2.9	3.2
1960–96	7.4	4.5

Inflation and the growth in money supply (M₂) tend to move together.

*Inflation based on GDP deflector.
SOURCE: DRI/McGraw-Hill Macroeconomic Database.

HOW DO THE FED'S OPEN MARKET ACTIVITIES AFFECT THE EQUATION OF EXCHANGE?

Generally, in a growing economy where the real value of goods and services is increasing over time, an increase in the supply of money is needed even to maintain stable prices. If the velocity of money (V) in the equation of exchange is fairly constant and real GDP (denoted by Q in the equation of exchange) is rising between 3 and 4 percent a year (as it has over the period since 1840), then a 3 or 4 percent increase in M is consistent with stable prices. We would expect, then, that over long time expanses, the Fed's open market operations would more often lead to monetary expansion than monetary contraction. In other words, the Fed would more often purchase bonds than sell them. Moreover, in periods of rising prices, if V is fairly constant, the growth of M likely will exceed the 3 to 4 percent annual growth that appears to be consistent with long-term price stability.

WHAT IS THE RELATIONSHIP BETWEEN INFLATION AND THE GROWTH IN THE MONEY SUPPLY?

From 1970 to 1979, the United States experienced considerable inflation, reflecting in part a sizeable increase in the growth in the money supply (M2). This is documented in Exhibit 1. Note that inflation tended to rise more in periods of rapid monetary expansion (reflecting, to a considerable extent, open market operations) than in periods of slower growth in the money supply. The positive correlation between money growth (M2) and inflation is not perfect, however; inflation during the early 1960s rose slowly despite a fairly large growth in the money supply. This reflected the fact that real output (measured by Q in the equation of exchange) rose quite substantially; also V declined somewhat to offset increases in the money supply.

There is also international support for the relationship between higher money growth and higher inflation. This data is presented in Exhibit 2.

EXHIBIT 2

MONEY SUPPLY GROWTH AND INFLATION RATES, 1985–1994

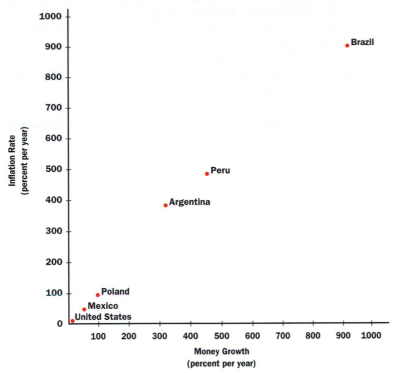

There is often a strong positive correlation between a country's average annual inflation rate and its annual growth in money supply.

SOURCE: Data from World Bank, *World Development Report 1996*.

HOW DOES CHANGING THE RESERVE REQUIREMENTS IMPACT A BANK'S ABILITY TO CREATE MONEY?

While open market operations are the most important and widely utilized tool that the Fed has to achieve its mone-tary objectives, it is not its potentially most powerful tool. The Fed possesses the power to change the reserve requirements of member banks by altering the reserve ratio. This can have an immediate, significant impact on the ability of member banks to create money. Suppose the banking system as a whole has $500 billion in deposits and $60 billion in reserves, with a reserve ratio of 12 percent. Because $60 billion is 12 percent of $500 billion, the system has no excess reserves. Suppose now that the Fed lowers reserve requirements by changing the reserve ratio to 10 percent. Now, banks are required to keep only $50 billion in reserves ($500 billion × .10), but they still have $60 billion. Thus, the lowering of the reserve requirement gives banks $10 billion in excess reserves. The banking system as a whole can expand deposits and the money stock by a multiple of this amount, in this case 10 (10 percent equals 1/10; the banking multiplier is the reciprocal of this, or 10). The lowering of the reserve requirement in this case, then, would permit an expansion in deposits of $100 billion, which represents a 20 percent increase in the stock of money, from $500 to $600 billion.

WHEN DOES THE FED USE THIS TOOL?

Relatively small reserve requirement changes, then, can have a big impact on the potential supply of money. The tool is so potent, in fact, that it is used relatively seldom. Carpenters don't use sledge hammers to hammer small nails or tacks; the tool is too big and powerful to use effectively. Similarly, the Fed changes reserve requirements rather infrequently for the same reason, and when it does make changes, it is by very small amounts. For example, between 1970 and 1980, the Fed changed the reserve requirement twice, and less than 1 percent on each occasion. The Fed did make an out-of-the-ordinary move in 1992 when it lowered the reserve requirement from 12 to 10 percent.

Frank and Ernest

© 1988 Thaves/Reprinted with permission.

TOOLS OF THE FED

Q: Chase Manhattan, a New York banker, argued that required reserve ratios are a potentially more powerful tool for the Fed than open market operations. Do you agree? If so, why isn't this tool used as often as open market operations?

A: The advantage of the reserve requirement is that it is a very powerful tool. However, this is also its disadvantage because a very small reduction in the reserve requirement, for example, can make a huge change in the number of dollars that are in excess reserves in banks all over the country. Such huge changes in required reserves and excess reserves have the potential to be disruptive to the economy.

WHAT IS THE DISCOUNT RATE AND HOW DOES IT AFFECT BANKS?

Banks having trouble meeting their reserve requirement can borrow funds directly from the Fed. The interest rate the Fed charges on these borrowed reserves is called the **discount rate.** If the Fed raises the discount rate, it makes it more costly for banks to borrow funds from it to meet their reserve requirements. The higher the interest rate banks have to pay on the borrowed funds, the lower the potential profits from any new loans made from borrowed reserves, and fewer new loans will be made and less money created. If the Fed wants to contract the money stock, it will raise the discount rate, making it more costly for banks to borrow reserves; if the Fed is promoting an expansion of money and credit, it will lower the discount rate, making it cheaper for banks to borrow reserves.

The discount rate changes fairly frequently, often several times a year. Sometimes the rate will be moved several times in the same direction within a single year, which has a substantial cumulative effect.

WHAT IS THE SIGNIFICANCE OF THE DISCOUNT RATE?

The discount rate is a relatively unimportant tool, mainly because member banks do not rely heavily on the Fed for borrowed funds in any case. There seems to be some stigma among bankers about borrowing from the Fed; borrowing from the Fed is something most bankers believe should be reserved for real emergencies. When banks have short-term needs for cash to meet reserve requirements, they are more likely to take a very short-term (often overnight) loan from other banks in the **federal funds market.** For that reason, many people pay a lot of attention to the interest rate on federal funds.

The discount rate's main significance is that changes in the rate are commonly viewed as a signal of the Fed's intentions with respect to monetary policy. Unlike open market operations, which are carried out in secret, with the operations being announced in the minutes of the FOMC published only several weeks after the decisions have been made, discount rate changes are widely publicized. People look to these changes for clues as to the type of monetary policy the Fed is pursuing, although increasingly in recent years, the Fed has announced publicly its "target" rates of growth for the stock of money (although actual monetary growth sometimes is outside the "target" range).

HOW DOES THE FED REDUCE THE MONEY STOCK?

Summarizing the previous discussion, the Fed can do three things if it wants to reduce the money stock. It can: (1) sell bonds ("buy" money from the economy), (2) raise reserve requirements, or (3) raise the discount rate. Of course, the Fed could also opt to use some combination of these three tools in its approach.

These moves would tend to reduce nominal GDP, hopefully through a decrease in P rather than Q. These actions would be the monetary policy equivalent of a fiscal policy of raising taxes, lowering transfer payments, and/or lowering government purchases.

THE WALL STREET JOURNAL

"You want to know what Alan Greenspan is thinking? Hey. I'm good, but I'm not that good."

TUNE UP

THE DISCOUNT RATE

Q: Rhonda has just finished a report on banking, and she says that the discount rate is more of a signal than it is an opportunity to borrow from the Fed. Why might this be the case?

A: Banks do not want to reveal any weaknesses or signs of reckless behavior to the Fed because they fear the dreaded audit. This is why banks tend to borrow from other banks in the federal funds market rather than borrowing from the Fed. However, the discount rate is an important signal to banks. If the Fed lowers the discount rate, it is essentially telling banks to be more expansionary. If you get in trouble, I will bail you out with cheap loans. On the other hand, if the Fed raises the discount rate, then the message it is sending banks is to be more cautious in their lending practices—and if banks heed this message, then the money supply will tend to contract.

TUNE UP

TOOLS OF THE FED

Q: It is 11:00 P.M. and Stella D. Knight is cramming for her macro final tomorrow morning. She is almost sure that her economics teacher is going to ask about the three possible methods the Fed can use to reduce the money supply (or its rate of growth) and the three ways it can increase the money supply. Can you help Stella?

A: In the case of persistent, high inflation, the Fed would pursue a contractionary policy. To decrease the money supply, it would sell bonds, raise the discount rate, and/or raise the reserve requirement. If the Fed wanted to pursue an expansionary policy, because of a severe recession, it would increase the money supply by buying bonds, lowering the reserve requirement, and/or lowering the discount rate.

HOW DOES THE FED INCREASE THE SUPPLY OF MONEY?

If the Fed is concerned about underutilization of resources (e.g., unemployment), it would engage in precisely the opposite policies: (1) buy bonds, (2) lower reserve requirements, or (3) lower the discount rate. The government could use some combination of these three approaches.

These moves would tend to raise nominal GDP, hopefully through an increase in Q (in the context of the equation of exchange) rather than P. Equivalent expansionary fiscal policy actions would be to lowering taxes, increasing transfer payments, and/or increasing government purchases.

HOW ELSE CAN THE FED INFLUENCE ECONOMIC ACTIVITY?

The Fed's control of the money supply is largely exercised through the three methods outlined above, but it can influence the level and direction of economic activity in numerous less important ways as well. First, the Fed can attempt to influence banks to follow a particular course of action by the use of **moral suasion.** For example, if the Fed thinks the money supply and credit are growing too fast, it might write a letter to bank presidents urging them to be more selective in making loans, and suggesting that good banking practices mandate that banks maintain some excess reserves. During business contractions, the Fed may urge bankers to lend more freely, hoping to promote an increase in the stock of money.

The Federal Reserve also has at its command some selective controls, meaning regulatory authority over specific types of economic activity. For example, the Federal Reserve Board of Governors establishes margin requirements for the purchase of common stock. This means that the Fed specifies the proportion of the purchase price of stock that a purchaser must pay in cash. By allowing the Fed to control limits on borrowing for stock purchases, Congress believes that the Fed can limit speculative market dealings in securities and reduce instability in securities markets (although whether the margin requirement rule has in fact helped achieve such stability is open to question).

In the last few decades or so, the Federal Reserve regulatory authority has been extended to new areas. Beginning in 1969, the Fed began enforcing provisions of the Truth in Lending Act, which requires lenders to state actual interest rate charges when making loans. Similarly, in the mid-1970s, the Fed assumed the authority of enforcing provisions of the Equal Lending Opportunity Act, designed to eliminate discrimination against loan applicants.

THE FED AND THE MEDIA

May 19—The Federal Reserve met again this week to decide whether or not to alter interest rates. But just how did the world's most powerful central bank let everyone from Wall Street to Main Street know its decision?

. . . Just how is this information, which can change the economic landscape and impact everything from the rate on new car loans to the interest on credit cards, disseminated to the public at large?

WAITING FOR THE CALL

. . . shortly before 2 P.M. ET Wednesday, members of the financial press squeeze into a small, poorly lit, dingy room at the Treasury Department across town and wait for a phone call from the influential Fed. Indeed, the room is so small that some of the 25 or so reporters who turn up have to wait in a back room.

At 2, the doors to the pressroom are closed. Then, sometime between 2 and 2:15 P.M., a phone rings in the room—and what happens next has to be seen to be believed.

On the phone is Joseph Coyne, assistant to the Board of Governors of the Federal Reserve. Coyne tells the one reporter who takes the call in the Treasury pressroom that either a fax is en route or that the Federal Open Market Committee meeting ended at a certain time and there will be no further announcement. (By the way, the reporter that takes the call is nearly always the Dow Jones reporter since Dow Jones is regarded as the leading disseminator of financial news in the United States.)

If Coyne tells the reporter that the FOMC meeting ended and there'll be no further announcement, this means the central bank is leaving interest rates right where they are, although Coyne doesn't specifically say that.

AT THE SOUND OF THE BELL

After thanking Coyne, the reporter will then tell the others in the pressroom and they'll all hurriedly fine-tune their stories to say, "Fed leaves interest rates unchanged," or words to that effect. Then, when they're all ready—yes, when the press are all ready, not when the Fed says the news can be released—one of the reporters rings a bell,

and all the news stories are electronically filed to thousands of information news screens around the world.

Bizarre eh? Well . . . it gets stranger.

Let's say Coyne calls over to the Treasury pressroom and tells the reporter who takes the call that a fax is en route. Knowing that a fax is coming means the Fed has decided to change interest rates, since the Fed only issues a press release if it has opted to raise or lower rates. But that's all the press knows at this point—which way rates are going is unknown.

The reporters wait for the fax. But sometimes the fax machine jams and the vital in-

formation they're all waiting for has to be resent to another fax machine down the hall. Finally, the fax arrives. One reporter then makes copies and hands them out to the reporters present. The pre-written stories are adjusted to reflect either an increase or decrease in rates, and then the one reporter on "bell" duty asks if everyone is ready. Once all the reporters give the thumbs up, the bell is rung and the news goes out to the world.

SOURCE: Colin Hurlock, "How Does the Fed Spread the Word?" *MSNBC,* May 19, 1998 from http://www.msnbc.com/news/104317.asp

---

CONSIDER THIS:

Decisions made by the Federal Reserve affect just about everyone. They influence car loans, mortgage rates, and stock markets, just to mention a few. It is no surprise, then, that journalists hover over the phone in a tiny little room in the Treasury Department awaiting the call from the assistant to the Board of Governors of the Federal Reserve. As you have read in this Module, changes in the money supply can drastically alter the course of the economy, so those in the financial markets are particularly interested in any actions or inactions taken by the Fed. Many consider the chair of the Federal Reserve System to be the second most important leader (and perhaps the most powerful single economic policymaker) in the country because of the importance of the money supply.

1. The three major tools of the Fed are open market operations, changing reserve requirements, and changing the discount rate.
2. If the Fed wants to stimulate the economy, it will increase the money supply by buying government bonds, lowering the reserve ratio, and/or lowering the discount rate.
3. If the Fed wants to restrain the economy, it will lower the money supply by selling bonds, increasing the reserve ratio, and/or raising the discount rate.

4. The Fed has some lesser tools that can influence specific sectors of the economy, such as the authority to establish and change margin requirements on the purchase of common stock (thus hopefully controlling excess speculation).

---

1. What three main tactics could the Fed use in pursuing a contractionary monetary policy?
2. What three main tactics could the Fed use in pursuing an expansionary monetary policy?
3. Would the money stock rise or fall if the Fed made an open market purchase of government bonds, *ceteris paribus?*

4. If the Fed raised the discount rate from 12 to 15 percent, what impact would that have on the money supply?
5. What is moral suasion, and why would the Fed use this tactic?

Money, Interest Rates, and Aggregate Demand

■ What causes the demand for money to change?

■ What is the banking system's role in money market equilibrium?

■ How do changes in income change the money market equilibrium?

WHAT IS THE MONEY MARKET?

The Federal Reserve's policies with respect to the supply of money has a direct impact on short-run real interest rates, and accordingly, on the components of aggregate demand. The **money market** is the market where money demand and money supply determine the equilibrium interest rate. When the Fed acts to change the money supply by changing one of its policy variables, it alters the money market equilibrium.

WHAT AFFECTS THE DEMAND FOR MONEY?

In an earlier Module, we learned that people have three basic motives for holding money instead of other assets: for the purpose of carrying out transactions, for precautionary reasons, and for asset reasons. The quantity of money demanded varies inversely with the rate of interest. When interest rates are higher, the opportunity cost—in terms of the interest income on alternative assets foregone—of holding monetary assets is higher, and persons will want to hold less money for each of these reasons. At the same time, the demand for money, particularly for transactions purposes, is highly dependent on income levels, because the transactions volume varies directly with income.

The previous discussion is summarized graphically in Exhibit 1. At lower interest rates, the quantity of money demanded is greater, a movement from A to B in Exhibit 1. An increase in income will lead to an increase in the demand for money, depicted by a rightward shift in the money demand curve, a movement from A to C in Exhibit 1.

WHY IS THE SUPPLY OF MONEY RELATIVELY INELASTIC?

The supply of money is largely governed by the regulatory policies of the central bank. Whether interest rates are 4 percent or 14 percent, banks seeking to maximize profits will increase lending as long as they have reserves above their desired level, because even a 4 percent return on loans provides more profit than maintaining those assets in non-interest-bearing cash or reserve accounts at the Fed. Given this fact, the supply of money is effectively almost perfectly inelastic with respect to interest rates over their plausible range, controlled by Federal Reserve policies that determine the level of bank reserves (through open market purchases or sales of government bonds and changes in the discount rate) and the money multiplier (through changes in reserve requirements). Therefore, we draw the money supply curve as vertical, other things equal, in Exhibit 2, with changes in Federal Reserve policies acting to shift the money supply curve.

WHAT IS MONEY MARKET EQUILIBRIUM?

Combining the money demand and money supply curves (Exhibit 2), money market equilibrium occurs at that inter-

EXHIBIT 1	MONEY DEMAND, INTEREST RATES, AND INCOME

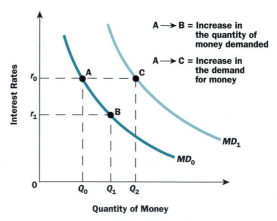

An increase in the level of income will increase the amount of money that people want to hold for transactions purposes at any given interest rate; therefore it shifts the demand for money to the right, from MD_0 to MD_1. The demand for money curve is downward sloping because at lower interest rates, the opportunity cost of holding money is lower.

EXHIBIT 2

MONEY MARKET EQUILIBRIUM

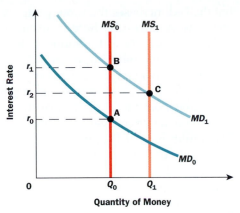

An increase in income will shift the money demand curve to the right, from MD_0 to MD_1, raising interest rates from r_0 to r_1. This results in a new equilibrium at point B. An increase in the money supply resulting from expansionary monetary policies (e.g., the Fed buying bonds or lowering the discount rate or required reserves) will shift the money supply curve to the right (from MS_0 to MS_1), lowering the rate of interest (from r_1 to r_2) and shifting the equilibrium to point C.

est rate (r_0) where the quantity of money demanded equals the quantity of money supplied, at point A. At a below-equilibrium interest rate, people try to hold more money than is available from the banking system, given the level of bank reserves and reserve requirements. The result is that the quantity of money demanded at that interest rate exceeds the quantity supplied—a shortage. Competition for funds will then lead financial institutions to raise interest rates in response making it more costly to hold or bor-

row money. At an above-equilibrium interest rate, the quantity of money banks would like to supply by making loans at that interest rate, given their level of reserves and reserve requirements, exceeds the quantity of money demanded at that interest rate—a surplus. Competition to make loans will then lead to lower interest rates, until people are willing to hold the amount of money banks are able to create by making loans to borrowers.

HOW DO INCOME CHANGES AFFECT THE EQUILIBRIUM POSITION?

Rising national income increases the demand for money, shifting the money demand curve to the right from MD_0 to MD_1, and leading to a new higher equilibrium interest rate.

HOW WOULD AN INCREASE IN THE STOCK OF MONEY AFFECT EQUILIBRIUM INTEREST RATES AND AGGREGATE DEMAND?

A Federal Reserve policy change that increased the money supply would be depicted by a shift in the money supply curve to the right. As a result of this shift, the equilibrium quantity of money demanded increases and equilibrium interest rates fall. The immediate impact of expansionary monetary policy is to decrease real interest rates. The lower interest rate, or the fall in the cost of borrowing money, then leads to an increase in aggregate demand for goods and services at the current price level. The lower interest rate will increase home sales, car sales, business investments, and so on. That is, an increase in the money supply will lead to lower interest rates and an increase in aggregate demand, as seen in Exhibit 3. In contrast, a

EXHIBIT 3

THE IMPACT OF AN INCREASE IN THE STOCK OF MONEY

a. Impact on the Money Market

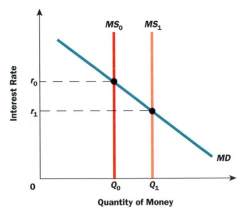

b. Impact on Aggregate Demand

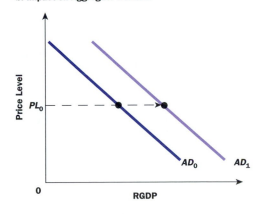

The increase in the money stock in the money market causes the real interest rate to fall in the short run, as seen in Exhibit 3(a). At lower interest rates, households and businesses invest more and buy more goods and services, shifting the aggregate demand curve to the right, as shown in Exhibit 3(b).

fiscal policy or other change that increases aggregate demand, and therefore income, will have the immediate effect of increasing interest rates (unless offset by monetary policy).

EXPANSIONARY MONETARY POLICY AT LESS THAN FULL EMPLOYMENT

An increase in aggregate demand through monetary policy can lead to an increase in real GDP if the economy is currently operating at less than full employment, the output level to the left of $RGDP_{FE}$ in Exhibit 5. The initial equilibrium is E_0, the point at which AD_1 intersects the short-run aggregate supply curve. At this point, output is equal to $RGDP_0$ and the price level is PL_0. If the Fed engages in an expansionary monetary policy, it can shift the aggregate demand curve from AD_0 to AD_1, expanding output to $RGDP_{FE}$ and increasing the price level to PL_1.

EXPANSIONARY MONETARY POLICY AT FULL EMPLOYMENT

Suppose that the Fed increases the money supply via open market operations. As a result, there is an increase in the money supply. This increase in the money supply will increase aggregate demand, shifting it from AD_0 to AD_1 as shown in Exhibit 6. However, if the economy is initially at full employment, $RGDP_{FE}$, the increase in aggregate demand moves the economy to a temporary short-run equilibrium at E_1, where the price level is PL_1 and real output is $RGDP_1$. This equilibrium at E_1 is *not* sustainable, because the economy is beyond full capacity. This puts pressure on input markets, sending wages and other input prices higher. The higher input costs shift the short-run aggregate supply curve leftward, from $SRAS_0$ to $SRAS_1$. As a result of this shift in aggregate supply, a new equilibrium, E_2, is reached. Because this new equilibrium is on the long-run aggregate supply curve, it is a sustainable long-run equilibrium. So we see that real output returns to the full employment output level, but at a higher price level, PL_2 rather than PL_0.

TUNE UP

MONEY AND THE AD/AS MODEL

Q: During the Great Depression in the United States, the price level fell, real GDP fell, and unemployment reached 25 percent. Investment fell, and as banks failed, the money supply fell dramatically. Can you show the effect of these changes from a vibrant 1929 economy to a battered 1932 economy using the AD/AS model?

A: The 1929 economy was at PL_{1929} and $RGDP_{1929}$ in Exhibit 4. The lack of consumer confidence coupled with the large reduction in the money supply and falling investment sent the aggregate demand curve reeling. As a result, the aggregate demand curve fell from AD_{1929} to AD_{1932}, real GDP fell to $RGDP_{1932}$, and the price level fell to PL_{1932}—deflation.

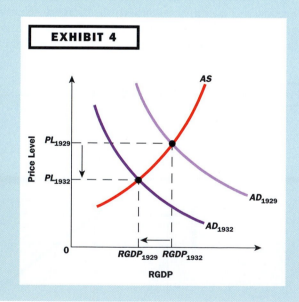

EXHIBIT 4

EXHIBIT 5	EXPANSIONARY MONETARY POLICY AT LESS THAN FULL EMPLOYMENT

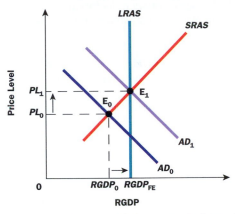

Expansionary monetary policy can shift the aggregate demand curve to the right, from AD_0 to AD_1, causing an increase in output and in the price level.

EXHIBIT 6	EXPANSIONARY MONETARY POLICY AT FULL EMPLOYMENT

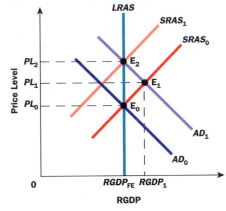

Expansionary monetary policy shifts the aggregate demand curve from AD_0 to AD_1. At the short-run equilibrium, E_1, the economy is operating beyond full capacity, which puts pressure on input markets. The higher cost in input markets causes the short-run aggregate supply curve to shift from $SRAS_0$ to $SRAS_1$. The resulting new long-run equilibrium, E_2, is at a higher price level, PL_2.

IN THE NEWS

FED LEAVES INTEREST RATES ALONE

. . . The much-advertised slowdown in U.S. economic growth has arrived. Employment rose a moderate 205,000 in June, while wages advanced just a penny, the slowest rate in more than two years. The National Association of Purchasing Management's index fell below 50%, indicating factory activity slowed for the first time in 22 months. Inventories are high. Exports are slowing. New orders for durable goods are off. All of this spells one thing: Steady Fed policy. "After months of hoping and waiting, the Fed is getting some very comforting news," says Anthony Karydakis, senior economist at First Chicago.

It's not that the Fed isn't concerned about the outlook for growth and inflation. A summary of the May 19 FOMC meeting released Thursday shows that two district Fed presidents—hard-line monetarists Jerry Jordan of Cleveland and William Poole of St. Louis—wanted higher short-term rates to slow money-supply growth. The Fed is still biased toward higher rates and there's pressure on Fed Chairman Alan Greenspan to discard his growing faith in the New Economy.

Still, the Fed held its fire last week. Clearly, Greenspan isn't about to okay a tightening with Asia still in the throes of crisis and growth softening at home.

Another sign the Fed is not about to add liquidity to the economy came last week. The central bank took the unusual step of warning banks against lowering lending standards on business loans. Greenspan has cautioned in recent months that loans ex-

tended in the latter years of an expansion— for instance, right now—are the ones banks usually wind up regretting. So, the Fed told bankers to avoid any assumption that "unusually favorable economic environment of the last few years will continue indefinitely."

SOURCE: William Pesek Jr., "Fed Holds Rates Steady Amid Signs of Slowing; Will the Second Half Bring Continued Stability?" *Barron's* Online, July 6, 1998.

CONSIDER THIS:
The Board of Governors is not always in agreement. There are several key terms in this box that are important. For example, the Fed finds the slowdown in economic growth to be "comforting news," because it may help eliminate the fears of unsustainable real output growth that can lead to increasing inflation. In addition, the "Fed is biased towards higher rates" implies that Fed policymakers are leaning towards higher interest rates to safeguard against inflationary pressures. "Greenspan is not about to okay a tightening with Asia" means that he does not want to follow a restrictive policy—that is, why increase interest rates if it may not be necessary. Finally, liquidity means adding money to banking reserves; the Fed doesn't want banks to be too aggressive in their lending practices.

1. The quantity of money demanded varies inversely with interest rates (a movement along the money demand curve) and directly with income (a shift of the money demand curve). Monetary policies that increase the supply of money will lower interest rates in the short run, other things equal. Fiscal policy or other changes that increase aggregate demand and incomes will increase the demand for money and raise interest rates, other things equal.
2. The competition to make or acquire additional loans when interest rates are not at their equilibrium level in the money market causes interest rates to move toward their equilibrium levels.

3. Rising incomes increase the demand for money. This will lead to a new higher equilibrium interest rate, other things equal.
4. An expansionary monetary policy at less than full employment can cause an increase in real GDP and price level.
5. An expansionary monetary policy at full employment can *temporarily* increase real GDP, but in the long run, only the price level will rise.

---

1. Who controls the supply of money in the money market?
2. How does an increase in income or a decrease in the interest rate increase the demand for money?
3. What Federal Reserve policies would shift the money supply curve to the left?
4. Will an increase in the money stock increase or decrease the short-run equilibrium real interest rate, other things equal?

5. Will an increase in national income increase or decrease the short-run equilibrium real interest rate, other things equal?
6. What is the relationship between interest rates and aggregate demand in monetary policy?
7. How will an expansionary monetary policy impact real GDP and the price level at less than full employment?
8. How will an expansionary monetary policy impact real GDP and the price level at full employment?

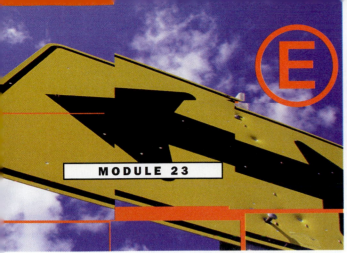

E Problems in Implementing Monetary Policy

- What problems exist in implementing monetary policy?
- What problems exist in coordinating monetary and fiscal policies?

WHAT PROBLEMS EXIST IN CONDUCTING MONETARY POLICY?

The lag problem inherent in adopting fiscal policy changes is much less acute for monetary policy, largely because the decisions are not slowed by the same budgetary process. The FOMC of the Federal Reserve, for example, can act quickly (in emergencies, almost instantly, by conference call) and even secretly to buy or sell government bonds, the key day-to-day operating tool of monetary policy. However, the length and variability of the impact lag before its effects on output and employment are felt are still significant—roughly 12 to 20 months in most cases—and the time before the full price level effects are felt is even longer and more variable.

HOW DO COMMERCIAL BANKS IMPLEMENT THE FED'S MONETARY POLICIES?

One limitation of monetary policy is that it ultimately must be carried out through the commercial banking system. The Central Bank (Federal Reserve System in the United States) can change the environment in which banks act, but the banks themselves must take the steps necessary to increase or decrease the stock of money. Usually, when the Fed is trying to constrain monetary expansion, there is no difficulty in getting banks to make appropriate responses. Banks must meet their reserve requirements, and if the Fed raises bank reserve requirements, sells bonds, and/or raises the discount rate, banks must obtain the necessary cash or reserve deposits at the Fed to meet their reserve requirements. In response, they will call in loans that are due for collection, sell secondary reserves, and so on, to obtain the necessary reserves, and in the process of contracting loans, they lower the stock of money.

When the Federal Reserve wants to induce monetary expansion, however, it can provide banks with excess reserves (e.g., by lowering reserve requirements or buying government bonds), but it cannot force the banks to make loans, thereby creating new money. Ordinarily, of course, banks want to convert their excess reserves to work earning interest income by making loans. But in a deep recession or depression, banks might be hesitant to make enough loans to put all those reserves to work, fearing that they will not be repaid. Their pessimism might lead them to perceive that the risks of making loans to many normally credit-worthy borrowers outweigh any potential interest earnings (particularly at the low real interest rates that are characteristic of depressed times). Some have argued that banks maintaining excess reserves rather than loaning them out was, in fact, one of the monetary policy problems that arose in the Great Depression.

HOW CAN BANKS THAT ARE NOT PART OF THE FEDERAL RESERVE SYSTEM AFFECT ITS POLICY IMPLEMENTATION?

A second problem with monetary policy relates to the fact that the Fed can control deposit expansion at member banks, but it has no control over global and nonbank institutions that also issue credit (loan money) but are not subject to reserve requirement limitations, like pension funds and insurance companies. Therefore, while the Fed may be able to predict the impact of its monetary policies on member bank loans, the actions of global and nonbanking institutions can serve to alter the impact of monetary policies adapted by the Fed on the money market or equivalently, the loanable funds market. Hence, there is a real question of how precisely the Fed can control the short-run real interest rates through its monetary policy instruments.

WHY ARE THERE FISCAL AND MONETARY COORDINATION PROBLEMS?

Another possible problem that arises out of existing institutional policy making arrangements is the coordination of fiscal and monetary policy. Decision making with respect to fiscal policy is made by Congress and the president, while monetary policy decision making is in the hands of the Federal Reserve System. A macroeconomic problem arises if the federal government's fiscal decision makers differ on policy objectives or targets with the Fed's monetary decision makers. For example, the Fed may be more concerned about keeping inflation low, while fiscal policymakers may be more concerned about keeping unemployment low.

HOW ARE THE COORDINATION PROBLEMS ALLEVIATED?

In recognition of potential macroeconomic policy coordination problems, the Chairman of the Federal Reserve Board has participated for several years in meetings with top economic advisers of the president. An attempt is made in those meetings to reach a consensus on the appropriate policy responses, both monetary and fiscal. Still, there is often some disagreement, and the Fed occasionally works to partly offset or even neutralize the effects of fiscal policies that it views as inappropriate. Some people believe that monetary policy should be more directly controlled by the president and Congress, so that all macroeconomic policy will be determined more directly by the political process. Also, it is argued that such a move would enhance coordination considerably. Others, however, argue that it is dangerous to turn over control of the nation's money stock to politicians, rather than allowing decisions to be made by technically competent administrators who are focused more on price stability and more insulated from political pressures from the public and from special interest groups.

OVERALL PROBLEMS WITH MONETARY AND FISCAL POLICY

Much of macroeconomic policy in this country is driven by the idea that the federal government can counteract economic fluctuations: stimulating the economy (with increased government purchases, tax cuts, transfer payment increases, and easy money) when it is weak, and restraining it when it is overheating. But policymakers must adopt the right policies in the right amounts at the right time for such "stabilization" to do more good than harm. And for this, government policymakers need far more accurate and timely information than experts can give them.

First, economists must know not only which way the economy is heading, but also how rapidly. And the unvarnished truth is that in our incredibly complicated world, no one knows exactly what the economy will do, no matter how sophisticated the econometric models used. It has often been said, and not completely in jest, that the purpose of economic forecasting is to make astrology look respectable.

But let's assume that economists can outperform astrologers at forecasting. Indeed, let's be completely unrealistic and assume that economists can provide completely accurate economic forecasts of what will happen if macroeconomic policies are unchanged. Even then, they could not be certain of how to best promote stable economic growth.

If economists knew, for example, that the economy was going to dip into another recession in six months, they would then need to know exactly how much each possible policy would spur activity in order to keep the economy stable. But such precision is unattainable, given the complex forecasting problems faced. Furthermore, despite assurances to the contrary, economists aren't always sure what effect a policy will have on the economy. Will an increase in government purchases quicken economic growth? It is widely assumed so. But how much? And increasing government purchases increases the budget deficit, which could send a frightening signal to the bond markets. The result can be to drive up interest rates and choke off economic activity. So even when policymakers know which direction to nudge the economy, they can't be sure which policy levers to pull, or how hard to pull them, to fine-tune the economy to stable economic growth.

But let's further assume that policymakers know when the economy will need a boost, and also which policy will provide the right boost. A third crucial consideration is how long it will take a policy before it has its effect on the economy. The trouble is that, even when increased government purchases or expansionary monetary policy does give the economy a boost, no one knows precisely how

Some economists believe that fine-tuning the economy is like driving a car with an unpredictable steering lag on a winding road.

long it will take to do so. The boost may come very quickly, or many months (or even years) in the future, when it may add inflationary pressures to an economy that is already overheating, rather than helping the economy recover from a recession.

In this way, macroeconomic policy making is like driving down a twisting road in a car with an unpredictable lag and degree of response in the steering mechanism. If you turn the wheel to the right, the car will eventually veer to the right, but you don't know exactly when or how much. In short, there are severe practical difficulties in trying to fine-tune the economy. Even the best forecasting models and methods are far from perfect. Economists are not exactly sure where the economy is or where or how fast it is going, making it very difficult to prescribe an effective policy. Even if we do know where the economy is headed, we cannot be sure how large a policy's effect will be or when it will take effect.

CONCEPT CHECK

1. Monetary policy faces somewhat different implementation problems than fiscal policy. Both face difficult forecasting and lag problems. But the Fed can take action much more quickly. But its effectiveness depends largely on the reaction of the private banking system to its policy changes, and those effects can be offset by global and nonbank financial institutions, over which the Fed lacks jurisdiction.

2. In the United States, monetary and fiscal policy are carried out by different decision makers, thus requiring cooperation and coordination for effective policy implementation.

1. Why is the lag time for adopting policy changes shorter for monetary policy than for fiscal policy?
2. Why would a banking system that wanted to keep some excess reserves rather than lending them all out hinder the Fed's ability to increase the money stock?
3. How can the activities of global and nonbank institutions weaken the Fed's influence on the money market?

4. If fiscal policy was expansionary, but the Fed wanted to counteract the fiscal policy effect on aggregate demand, what could it do?
5. What are the arguments for and against having monetary policy be more directly controlled by the political process?
6. How is fine-tuning the economy like driving a car with an unpredictable steering lag on a winding road?

Application: The Independence of the Fed

Should the Fed be independent from Congress and the Administration? Is there any evidence that the Fed does act independently?

FEDERAL RESERVE CHIEF SHOWS HIS POLICY INDEPENDENCE

When Federal Reserve Board chairman Alan Greenspan raised short-term interest rates earlier this month, he did so, he said, to head off inflation.

Many Fed-watchers also believe he was asserting independence from the Clinton administration, which has implored the central banker to maintain a monetary policy loose enough to stimulate the consumer purchases and business investments that help the economy grow and generate jobs.

. . . Fed chairmen are used to pressure. "All the way back to the beginning, the head of the Federal Reserve Board who served during the same term as the president who appointed him was the tool of the White House," recalls a monetary official, offering a historical review of Federal Reserve Board-Executive Branch dynamics.

Perhaps the most obvious example in relatively recent history, he says, was President Nixon's appointment of Arthur Burns to the top Fed position in 1970. Mr. Burns then "helped set wage and price controls and served as chairman of the wage and price-control review panel, carrying out essentially a Cabinet-level duty." He was "widely believed to have pumped up the money supply during 1972 to help reelect Nixon."

Paul Volcker, appointed by President Carter in 1979, "essentially asked for a mandate from Carter to be as independent as he needed to combat inflation," recounts the monetary official. But President Reagan, who inherited Mr. Volcker as Fed chairman, "feared Volcker's tight monetary policy during a time when he wanted a stimulative policy," he says. Volcker's conduct under Mr. Carter, and Mr. Reagan's distrust of him "did much to build up the idea of an independent Fed," the official says.

Mr. Greenspan, he adds, "is not close to the White House at all, notwithstanding the 1993 State of the Union address," when the Fed chairman occupied the symbolically important seat next to Hillary Rodham Clinton—a placement many observers said was designed to show a close working relationship between Greenspan and the president. . . .

SOURCE: Amy Kaslow, "Federal Reserve Chief Shows His Policy Independence," *The Christian Science Monitor,* February 24, 1994.

While the Fed is an independent agency, it is hard to imagine that it is not subject to, and potentially responsive to, pressure from the Administration and Congress. However, because the Fed is responsible for maintaining price stability, it is important that it is not manipulated to generate gains for a political party.

The Fed is not very dependent on Congress, either. For example, while federal agencies must ask Congress for an annual appropriation, the Fed does not, as it owns a large portfolio of government securities (whose purchases and sales are used to alter bank reserves) that provides enough interest income to make the Fed entirely self-supporting. Hence, the Fed is somewhat insulated from political pressures, such as threats of withholding budget appropriations, from both the president and from Congress, although the mere threat of legislation that would curb its independence usually keeps the Fed from following a policy too much at variance from the wishes of the executive and/or legislative branches of government. Still, it is true that monetary policy is implemented by a privately owned, quasi-public institution that has a considerable amount of political independence from the federal government.

What relationship exists between the Fed and Congress?

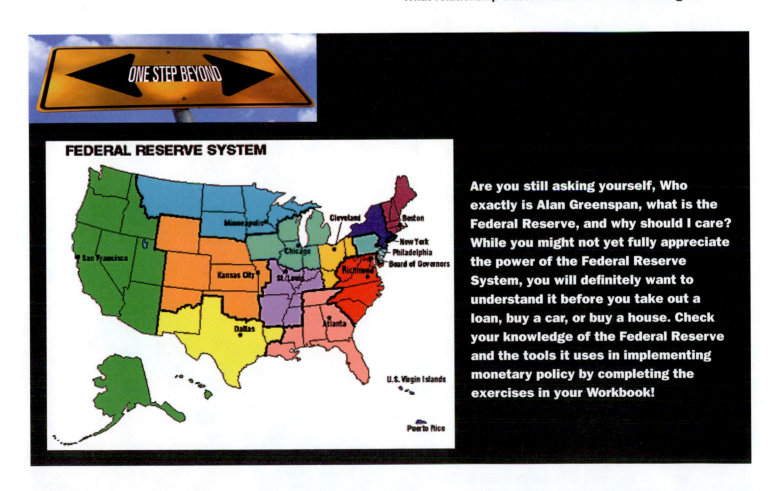

Are you still asking yourself, Who exactly is Alan Greenspan, what is the Federal Reserve, and why should I care? While you might not yet fully appreciate the power of the Federal Reserve System, you will definitely want to understand it before you take out a loan, buy a car, or buy a house. Check your knowledge of the Federal Reserve and the tools it uses in implementing monetary policy by completing the exercises in your Workbook!

PHOTO CREDITS MODULE 23

Page **556:** © 1998 Don Couch Photography; Page **557:** © AP Photo/Dan Loh; Page **558:** © Dennis Brack/Black Star; Page **559:** © 1998 Don Couch Photography; Page **563:** © 1988 Thaves/ Reprinted with permission; Page **564:** From *The Wall Street Journal*. Reprinted with permission, Cartoon Features Syndicate; Page **566:** © Ed Stein. Reprinted with permission of Rocky Mountain News; Page **574:** © Vincent DeWitt/Stock, Boston/PNI; Page **577:** © AP Photo/Dennis Cook.

Inflation, Unemployment, and Expectations

A. The Phillips Curve
Is there a relationship between
unemployment and inflation?

B. The Phillips Curve Over Time
Why does the Phillips curve shift?

C. Rational Expectations
What is the rational expectations theory?

D. Wage and Price Controls and Indexing
What purpose do wage and price controls and indexing serve?

E. Application: The Role of Expectations in Macroeconomics
Are rational expectations the same as perfect information?

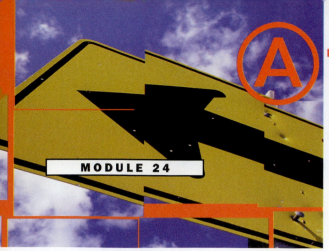

The Phillips Curve

- What is the Phillips curve?
- How does the Phillips curve relate to the aggregate supply and demand model?

WHAT IS THE HISTORY OF UNEMPLOYMENT AND INFLATION?

Despite legislation committing the federal government to the goal of full employment and the development of macroeconomic theory arguing that full employment can be achieved by manipulating aggregate demand, periods of high unemployment still occur.

Similarly, price stability, which had been achieved for long periods before the 1930s, has not been consistently observed since that time. In every year in the lifetimes of most readers of this book, the general level of prices has risen.

HOW DO INFLATION AND UNEMPLOYMENT INTERACT?

We usually think of inflation as an evil—higher prices mean lower real incomes for persons on fixed incomes, while those with the power to raise the prices charged for goods or services they provide may actually benefit. Some economists believe that inflation could actually help eliminate unemployment. For example, if output prices rise but money wages do not go up as quickly or as much, real wages fall. At the lower real wage, unemployment is less because the lower wage makes it profitable to hire more, now cheaper, employees than before. The result is real wages that are closer to the full employment equilibrium wage that clears the labor market. Hence, with increased inflation, one might expect lower unemployment.

WHAT IS A PHILLIPS CURVE?

In fact, an inverse relationship between the rate of unemployment and the changing level of prices has been observed to have in fact occurred in many periods and places

in history. Credit for identifying this relationship generally goes to British economist A.H. Phillips, who in the late 1950s published a paper setting forth what has since been called the Phillips curve. Phillips, and many others since, have suggested that at higher rates of inflation, the rate of unemployment is lower, while during periods of relatively stable or falling prices, there is substantial unemployment. In short, the cost of lower unemployment appears to be greater inflation, and the cost of greater price stability appears to be higher unemployment.

The actual inflation–unemployment relationship for the United States for the 1960s is shown in Exhibit 1. The points in this graph represent the combination of the inflation rate and the rate of unemployment in each of the 10 years of the decade. The curved line—the Phillips curve—is the smooth line that best "fits" the data points.

WHY IS THE SLOPE OF THE PHILLIPS CURVE NOT CONSTANT?

In examining Exhibit 1, it is evident that the slope of the Phillips curve is not the same throughout its length. The curve is steeper at higher rates of inflation and lower levels of unemployment. This suggests that once the economy has relatively low unemployment rates, further reductions in the unemployment rate can occur only by accepting larger increases in the inflation rate. Once unemployment is low, it takes larger and larger doses of inflation to eliminate a given quantity of unemployment. Presumably, at lower unemployment rates, an increased part of the economy is already operating at or near full capacity, and further fiscal or monetary stimulus primarily triggers inflationary pressures in sectors already at capacity, while eliminating decreasing amounts of unemployment in those sectors where some excess capacity and unemployment still exist.

| EXHIBIT 1 | THE PHILLIPS CURVE RELATIONSHIP, UNITED STATES, 1960s |

THE PHILLIPS CURVE AND AGGREGATE SUPPLY AND DEMAND

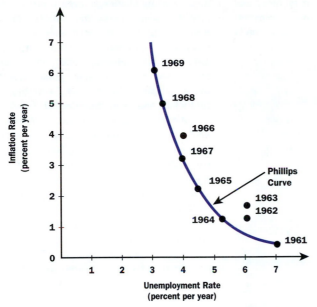

In Exhibit 2, we see the relationship between aggregate supply and demand analysis and the Phillips curve. Imagine that the economy has moved from a 2 percent annual inflation rate to a 4 percent inflation rate and that the unemployment rate has simultaneously fallen from 5 percent to 4 percent. In the Phillips rate curve we see this as a move up the curve from point A to point B in Exhibit 2(a). We can see the same relationship in the AD/AS model in Exhibit 2(b). Imagine that there is an increase in aggregate demand. Consequently, the price level increases from PL_{102} to PL_{104} and output increases from $RGDP_0$ to $RGDP_1$. To increase output, firms employ more workers, so employment increases and unemployment falls from 5 percent to 4 percent. This drop in unemployment is shown in the movement from point A to point B in Exhibit 2(b).

The Phillips curve illustrates an inverse relationship between the rate of unemployment and the rate of inflation. The slope of the Phillips curve becomes more steep as the unemployment rate drops, indicating that at very low unemployment rates, further decreases in unemployment can occur by accepting much larger increases in inflation rates.

| EXHIBIT 2 | THE PHILLIPS CURVE AND THE AD/AS CURVES |

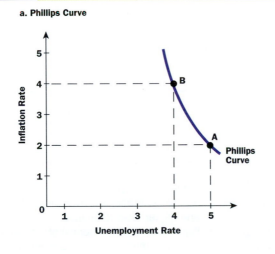

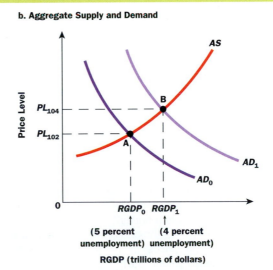

As shown in Exhibit 2(b), if the aggregate supply curve is positively sloped, an increase in aggregate demand will cause higher prices and higher output (lower unemployment); a decrease in aggregate demand will cause lower prices and lower output (higher unemployment). This same trade-off is illustrated in the Phillips curve in Exhibit 2(a) in the shift from point A to point B.

TIGHT LABOR MARKET MAKING IT HARD FOR FAIR TO FIND TEMPORARY WORKERS

CARY STEMLE

The Kentucky State Fair doesn't have a musical theme, but if it did, this year's might be "Help!" With Louisville-area unemployment at 4.0 percent in June, and with stiff competition among employers, finding enough workers for the 11-day run is an increasing challenge, organizers say. Geralyn Clements, personnel director for the Kentucky State Fair Board, said about 500 temporary workers are needed to work gates, handle cleanup and setup, drive trams and serve as tour guides for the event, which begins August 14 at the Kentucky Fair and Exposition Center.

"We do experience difficulty," Clements said. "The low unemployment rate is definitely a factor. We do a lot of recruiting, and we work with temporary services and other organizations, like schools or softball teams. But usually, by the end of the fair, we're short-staffed."

One result of the tight labor market is pressure on wages. This year's salary is generally $5.50 an hour, up 25 cents an hour from last year. . . . Turnover is always a problem, he said. It can run as high as 150 percent. . . .

SOURCE: http://www.amcity.com/louisville/stories/081197/story4.html August 11, 1997

In tight labor markets, even temporary workers can bargain for higher wages.

CONSIDER THIS:
When unemployment falls to very low levels, competition for workers will tend to drive wages up.

CONCEPT CHECK

1. The inverse relationship between the rate of unemployment and the rate of inflation is called the Phillips curve.

2. The Phillips curve relationship can also be seen indirectly from the AD/AS model.

1. How does the rate of inflation affect real wage rates, if nominal wages rise less or more slowly than output prices?

2. How does the change in real wage rates (relative to output prices) as inflation increases affect the unemployment rate?

3. What is the argument for why the Phillips curve is relatively steeper at lower rates of unemployment and higher rates of inflation?

4. For a given upward-sloping short-run aggregate supply curve, how does an increase in aggregate demand correspond to a movement up and to the left along a Phillips curve?

B The Phillips Curve Over Time

- How reliable is the Phillips curve?
- Is the Phillips curve stable over time?
- What is the difference between the long-run and short-run Phillips curves?

WAS THE PHILLIPS CURVE WELL ACCEPTED IN THE 1960S?

It became widely accepted in the 1960s that policy makers merely had to decide on the combination of unemployment and inflation they wanted from the Phillips curve, and then simply pursue the appropriate economic policies. To be sure, a reduction in the rate of unemployment came at a cost (more inflation), as did a reduction in the amount of inflation (more unemployment). Nonetheless, policy makers believed they could influence economic activity so that some goals could be met, though with a trade-off in terms of other macroeconomic goals. The empirical evidence on prices and unemployment seemed to fit the Phillips curve approach so beautifully at first that it is not surprising that it was embraced so rapidly and completely. Economists like Milton Friedman and Edmund Phelps who questioned the long-term validity of the Phillips curve were largely ignored in the 1960s. These economists believed there might be a short-term trade-off between unemployment and inflation but not a permanent trade-off. According to Friedman, the short-run trade-off comes from *unanticipated* inflation.

IS THE PHILLIPS CURVE STABLE?

Unfortunately, in the 1970s (and 1980s and 1990s also) economists recognized that macroeconomic decision-making was not as simple as picking a point on a stable Phillips curve. As shown in Exhibit 1, the data from the 1970s indicates that the Phillips curve starts to break down.

In fact, since 1969, every data point has been to the right of the 1960s Phillips curve, meaning a worsening trade-off between inflation and unemployment. In 1975, for example, the unemployment rate was 8.5 percent, the worst for any full year since the Great Depression. Moreover, in that year, prices rose 9.1 percent. In short, the 1970s experienced more of both inflation and unemployment than existed in the 1960s.

EXHIBIT 1	THE PHILLIPS CURVE, 1960–1979

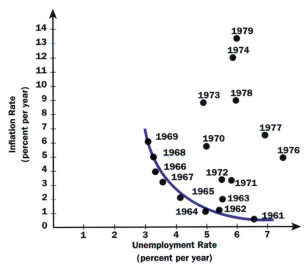

The Phillips curve relationship breaks down in the 1970s; it no longer neatly fits the observations, and it does not have a consistent, pronounced negative slope, calling into question the notion that one can continue to "buy" full employment with inflation.

THE SHORT-RUN AND LONG-RUN PHILLIPS CURVE

The **long-run Phillips curve** shows the relationship between the inflation rate and the unemployment rate when the actual and expected inflation rates are the same. In Exhibit 2, we see that the long-run Phillips curve is vertical at the natural rate of unemployment. This is equivalent to the vertical long-run aggregate supply curve introduced in an earlier Module. Along the long-run Phillips curve we see that the natural rate of unemployment can occur at any rate of inflation. That is, regardless of fiscal and monetary stimulus output and employment will be at the natural rate in the long run.

EXHIBIT 2 | THE LONG-RUN PHILLIPS CURVE

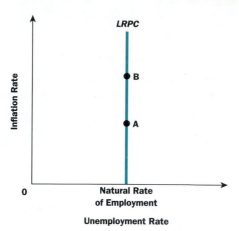

The long-run Phillips curve shows the relationship between the inflation rate and the unemployment rate when the actual and expected inflation rates are the same. Along the long-run Phillips curve we see that the natural rate of unemployment can occur at any rate of inflation.

HOW IS THE SHORT-RUN PHILLIPS CURVE RELATED TO THE LONG-RUN PHILLIPS CURVE?

Suppose the economy is at point A in Exhibit 3(a). At that point, the inflation rate is 3 percent and the unemployment rate is at the natural rate, 5 percent. Now suppose the growth rate of the money supply increases. The increase in the growth rate of money supply will stimulate aggregate demand. In the short run, the increase in aggregate demand will increase output and decrease unemployment, as the economy moves up along the short-run Phillips curve, from point A to point B, where the actual inflation rate has increased from 3 percent to 6 percent and the unemployment rate has fallen below the natural rate to 3 percent.

Because the increase in inflation was unanticipated, real wages fall. Firms are now receiving higher prices relative to their input costs, so they expand output. Consequently, unemployment rates fall, seen in Exhibit 3(a) as a movement along the short-run Phillips curve from A to B. Eventually, workers (and other input owners) realize that their real wage has fallen because of the increase in the inflation rate that was not initially anticipated. Workers now vigorously negotiate for higher wages. This increases costs to

producers, and as a result, they reduce output and unemployment rises—rightward shift in the short-run Phillips curve from point B to point C in Exhibit 3(a).

In short, the higher expected inflation rate shifts the short-run Phillips curve up. If the 6 percent inflation rate continues, the adjustment of expectations will move the economy to point C, where the expected and actual inflation rates are equal at the natural level of output and the natural rate of unemployment.

In the long run, the economy moves from A to C as inflation increases from 3 percent to 6 percent. This reveals that there is no trade-off between the inflation rate and the unemployment rate in the long run. The policy implication is that the use of fiscal or monetary policy to alter real output from the natural level of real output or unemployment from the natural rate of unemployment is ineffective in the long run.

Alternatively, say there was a decrease in the rate of growth in the money supply as a result of the Federal Reserve System's inflationary concerns. The decrease in the rate of growth in the money supply would reduce aggregate demand. In the short run, the decrease in aggregate demand moves the economy down along the short-run Phillips curve from point C to point D, where the actual inflation rate has decreased from 6 percent to 3 percent and the unemployment rate has risen above the natural rate, to 7 percent. The decrease in aggregate demand has led to lower production and a higher unemployment rate.

Initially, the reduction in the inflation rate is not anticipated and real wages rise; firms are now receiving lower prices relative to their input costs, so they reduce their output. This leads to a higher unemployment rate, as seen in the movement from point C to point D in Exhibit 3(b). If this new inflation rate remains steady at 3 percent, the actual and expected inflation rates will eventually become the same. The growth in wages will slow, lowering the cost of production, increasing output, and lowering the unemployment rate as the short-run Phillips curve shifts leftward from point D to point E in Exhibit 3(b).

In short, when people recognize that prices are not rising as rapidly as before, at only 3 percent rather than 6 percent, they adjust their expectations to reflect that fact, and the short-run Phillips curve shifts leftward, moving from point D to point E in Exhibit 3(b). The inflation rate is now lower, and unemployment and output have returned to their natural rates. In this scenario, the economy's road to lower inflation rates has come at the expense of higher unemployment in the short run, until people's expectations adapt to the new lower inflation rate in the long run.

EXHIBIT 3 | THE SHORT-RUN AND LONG-RUN PHILLIPS CURVES

a. An Increase in the Growth of the Money Supply

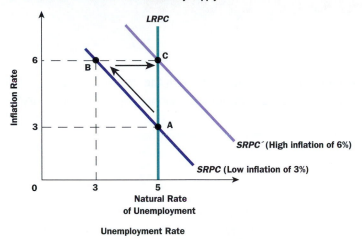

b. A Reduction in the Growth of the Money Supply

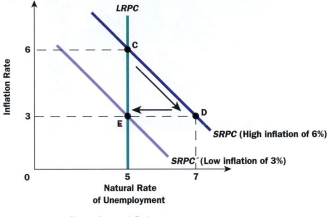

The economy initially moves along the short-run Phillips curve as actual inflation deviates from expected inflation. When expected inflation rates then adapt to take into account actual inflation rates, the short-run Phillips curve shifts back to the natural level of real output and to the natural rate of unemployment at that inflation rate on the long-run Phillips curve.

CONCEPT CHECK

1. The Phillips curve depicting the period of high inflation and unemployment in the 1970s no longer suggests the strong inverse relationship between the two variables that was evident in the 1960s.

2. The short-run Phillips curve relationship is seen as unstable and not a permanent relationship between unemployment and inflation rates.

3. The long-run Phillips curve shows the relationship between the inflation rate and the unemployment rate when the actual and expected inflation rates are the same.

4. Along the long-run Phillips curve, the natural rate of unemployment can occur at any rate of inflation.

---

1. Is the Phillips curve stable over time?

2. Why would you expect there to be no relationship between inflation and unemployment in the long run?

3. Why is the economy being on the long-run Phillips curve equivalent to its being on the long-run aggregate supply curve?

4. Why would inflation have to accelerate over time to keep unemployment below its natural rate (and real output above its natural level) for a sustained period of time?

5. What does the long-run Phillips curve say about the relationship between macroeconomic policy stimulus and unemployment in the long run?

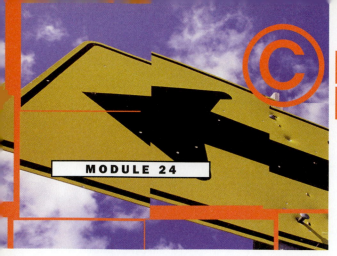

Rational Expectations

- What is the rational expectations theory?
- What do critics say about the rational expectations theory?

CAN HUMAN BEHAVIOR COUNTERACT GOVERNMENT POLICY?

Is it possible that people can anticipate the plans of policy makers and alter their behavior quickly, to neutralize the intended impact of government action? For example, if workers see that the government is allowing the money supply to expand rapidly, they may quickly demand higher money wages in order to offset the anticipated inflation. In the extreme form, if people could instantly recognize and respond to government policy changes, it might be impossible to alter real output or unemployment levels through policy actions, because government policymakers could no longer surprise consumers and businesses. An increasing number of economists believe that there is at least some truth to this point of view. At a minimum, most economists accept the notion that real output and the unemployment rate cannot be altered with the ease that was earlier believed; some believe that the unemployment rate can seldom be influenced by fiscal and monetary policies.

WHAT IS RATIONAL EXPECTATIONS THEORY?

The relatively new extension of economic theory that leads to this rather pessimistic conclusion regarding macroeconomic policy's ability to achieve our economic goals is called the **theory of rational expectations.** The notion that expectations or anticipations of future events are relevant to economic theory is not new; for decades, economists have incorporated expectations into models analyzing many forms of economic behavior. Only in the recent past, however, has a theory evolved that tries to incorporate expectations as a central factor in the analysis of the entire economy.

The interest in rational expectations has grown rapidly in the last decade. Acknowledged pioneers in the develop-

ment of the theory include Professor Robert Lucas of the University of Chicago and Professor Thomas Sargent of the University of Minnesota. In 1995, Professor Lucas won the Nobel Prize for his work in rational expectations.

Rational expectation economists believe that wages and prices are flexible, and that workers and consumers incorporate the likely consequences of government policy changes quickly into their expectations. In addition, rational expectation economists believe that the economy is inherently stable after macroeconomic shocks, and that tinkering with fiscal and monetary policy cannot have the desired effect unless consumers and workers are caught "off guard" (and catching them off guard gets harder the more you try to do it).

HOW DO RATIONAL EXPECTATIONS AFFECT THE CONSEQUENCES OF GOVERNMENT MACROECONOMIC POLICIES?

Rational expectations theory, then, suggests that government economic policies designed to alter aggregate demand to meet macroeconomic goals are of very limited effectiveness. When policy targets become public, it is argued, people will alter their own behavior from what it would otherwise have been, in order to maximize their own utility, and in so doing, they largely negate the intended impact of policy changes. If government policy seems tilted towards permitting more inflation in order to try to reduce unemployment, people start spending their money faster than before, become more adamant in their wage and other input price demands, and so on. In the process of quickly altering their behavior to reflect the likely consequences of policy changes, they make it more difficult (costly) for government authorities to meet their macroeconomic objectives. Rather than fooling people into changing real wages, and therefore unemployment, with inflation "surprises," changes in inflation are quickly reflected into expectations with little or no effect on unemployment or real output even in the short run. As a consequence, policies intended to reduce unemployment through stimulating aggregate demand will often fail to have the intended effect. Fiscal and monetary policy, according to this view, will work only if the people are caught off guard or fooled by policies so that they do not modify their behavior in a way that reduces policy effectiveness.

HOW DOES ANTICIPATION OF AN EXPANSIONARY MONETARY POLICY AFFECT THE AD/AS MODEL?

Consider the case in which there is an increase in aggregate demand as a result of an expansionary monetary policy. This increase is reflected in Exhibit 1 in the shift from AD_0 to AD_1. As a result of anticipating the predictable inflationary consequences of that expansionary policy, the price level will immediately adjust to a new price level at PL_1. Consumers, producers, workers, and lenders who have anticipated the effects of the expansionary policy simply built the higher inflation rates into their product prices, wages, and interest rates. That is, consumers, producers, and workers realize that expansionary monetary policy can cause inflation if the economy is working close to capacity. Consequently, in an effort to protect themselves from the higher anticipated inflation, workers ask for higher wages, suppliers increase input prices, and producers raise their product prices. Because wages, prices, and interest rates are assumed to be flexible, the adjustments take place immediately. This increase in input costs for wages, interest, and raw materials causes the aggregate supply curve to shift up or leftward, shown as the movement from AS_0 to AS_1 in Exhibit 1. So the desired policy effect of greater real output and reduced unemployment from a shift in the aggregate demand curve is offset by an upward or leftward shift in the aggregate supply curve caused by an increase in input costs.

WHAT HAPPENS IF A DECLINE IN AGGREGATE DEMAND IS ANTICIPATED?

A decline in the aggregate demand curve would have the opposite effect. Consider the case in which the Fed wants to fight inflation with a reduction in the money supply. If consumers and producers anticipate the reduced inflation that will accompany a reduction in the money supply, wages and input prices will quickly fall to reflect the new lower price levels. As a result of the lower input prices, the

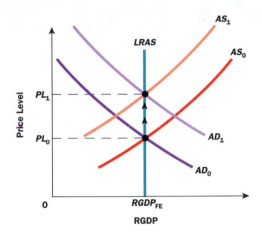

| EXHIBIT 1 | RATIONAL EXPECTATIONS AND THE AD/AS MODEL |

aggregate supply curve shifts down or rightward, shown in Exhibit 1 as the shift from AS_0 to AS_1. The price level quickly falls back to PL_0 without a change in real output or unemployment. Of course, the same would be true if we used fiscal policy rather than monetary policy in an expansionary or contractionary effort. The upshot of this discussion is that changed policy prescriptions that one expected cannot alter real output and unemployment. That is, stimulus policies proposed by the government are ineffective because consumers and producers anticipate the consequences of those changes and rapidly adjust their expectations, neutralizing the desired policy effects.

WHAT DO CRITICS SAY ABOUT RATIONAL EXPECTATIONS THEORY?

Of course, rational expectations theory does have its critics. Critics want to know if consumers and producers are completely informed about the impact that say, an increase in money supply will have on the economy. In general, all citizens will be completely informed, but key players like corporations, financial institutions, and labor organizations may well be informed about the impact of these policy changes. But there are other problems, too. For example, are wages and other input prices really that flexible? That is, even if decision makers could anticipate the eventual effect of policy changes on prices, those prices may still be slow to adapt (e.g., what if you had just signed a three-year labor or supply contract when the new policy is implemented?).

1. Rational expectation economists believe that wages and prices are flexible and thus should be left alone. They also believe that workers and consumers form rational expectations that essentially negate the desired effect of a policy change.

2. Critics of rational expectations theory believe that most people are truly not informed about the effects of a policy change and therefore do not adjust their behavior. Additionally, they question whether prices and wages are really that flexible.

1. What is the rational expectations theory?
2. Why could an unexpected change in inflation change real wages and unemployment, while an expected change in inflation could not?
3. Why can the results of rational expectations be described as generating the long-run results of a policy change in the short run?
4. In a world of rational expectations, why is it harder to reduce unemployment below its natural rate but potentially easier to reduce inflation rates?

5. Even if people could quickly anticipate the consequences of government policy changes, how could long-term contracts (e.g., 3-year labor agreements and 30-year fixed-rate mortgages) and the costs of changing price lists and catalogs result in unemployment still being affected by those policy changes?
6. Why do expected rainstorms have different effects on people than unexpected rainstorms?

Wage and Price Controls and Indexing

- How are wage and price controls imposed and what purpose do they serve?
- What are some problems associated with wage and price controls?
- What is indexing and how can it be used?

WHAT PURPOSE DO WAGE AND PRICE CONTROLS SERVE?

If monetary and fiscal policy are ineffective or counterproductive, what policies are left to control inflation? It is possible that the federal government could set up a comprehensive program over nominal wages and prices—this is often called **incomes policy.** One method to deal with existing inflationary pressures is to impose controls on wages and/or prices. We have imposed such controls three times in modern American history, during World War II, during the Korean War, and in 1971 near the end of the Viet Nam War. Wage and price controls involve either a complete freeze on wages and prices at pre-control levels or some rigid limits as to the increases in wages and prices that will be permitted. One or more government agencies are created to monitor the program.

HOW CAN PRICE CONTROLS BE IMPLEMENTED WITHOUT GOVERNMENT REGULATION?

Sometimes it is felt that it is more desirable to establish voluntary guidelines or guideposts than to force companies and unions to limit their price and wage levels. This approach avoids the expense and political acrimony associated with establishing a control bureaucracy. Sometimes the "jawboning," the verbal pressuring or persuasion, gets pretty intense. The one memorable instance of jawboning in modern history came in the early 1960s, when President Kennedy became angered when major steel producers announced price increases. All sorts of pressures were placed on steelmakers, who were summoned to Washington, pleaded with, and even threatened with possible legal action under the antitrust laws. Finally, one company decided not to go along with the price increases, and then other companies quickly fell in line. In 1978, voluntary wage and price guidelines were imposed by the Carter administration. Those guidelines explicitly stated that pressure would be used by the government to insure compliance, making them virtually mandatory controls.

WHAT ARE THE JUSTIFICATIONS FOR WAGE AND PRICE CONTROLS?

There are two justifications given for wage and price controls. First, by limiting price increases by law, the government directly reduces the rate of inflation legally allowed. In this connection, it is interesting to note that during the four years of direct U.S. involvement in World War II, when price controls were in effect, consumer prices rose only a bit more than 20 percent, despite a huge increase in aggregate demand. Second, especially with respect to wage controls, it is argued that wage and price controls lower the inflationary expectations of workers and their unions, reducing the "inflation psychology" that contributes to cost-push inflation.

IF WAGE AND PRICE CONTROLS HAVE THESE ADVANTAGES, WHY ARE THEY NOT USED MORE OFTEN?

Wage and price controls also have several major disadvantages, which are very likely to be viewed as being greater than the advantages, except possibly during wartime situations when aggregate demand is growing very rapidly. The problem of enforcing the controls has already been mentioned. With millions of businesses, products, and workers in our economy, the administrative problem of monitoring wages and prices is immense, and any effective enforcement is likely to be costly. Black markets (illegal sales) often develop. These problems are often very hard to solve.

To give one example, suppose the price administrators say that next year's models of automobiles can be priced 4 percent higher than this year's. Suppose now that an automaker brings out a new model selling for only 3 percent more than the old model. At the same time, however, suppose that the new model is slightly smaller than the old one, has less "frills" than the previous model, has a slightly smaller engine, and so forth. Is the automaker in violation of the price control? The company would say no, because the price is up only 3 percent. Others might say yes, because the new product is inferior to the old one in several ways.

Another even more fundamental problem with wage and price controls is that they lead to shortages of goods, services, and workers. With these controls, inflationary pressures are not eradicated but rather disguised, manifesting themselves not as price increases but as a lack of desired goods or human resources. As a result, severe and prolonged controls can lead to a very serious misallocation of resources.

HOW DO PRICE CONTROLS LEAD TO A MISALLOCATION OF RESOURCES?

Straightforward supply and demand analysis indicates the misallocation of resources due to wage and price controls, as illustrated in Exhibit 1. Suppose the demand and supply for refrigerators are indicated by D_0 and S in Exhibit 1. The equilibrium price of refrigerators, P_0, is determined by the intersection of the demand and supply curves. Suppose that recent stock market wealth has led to higher income and an increase in demand for refrigerators to D_1. If the market is allowed to work without intervention, the price of refrigerators would increase to the new equilibrium price of P_1, where D_1 intersects S. But suppose wage and price controls are imposed and the price controllers consider an increase in price from P_0 to P_1 to be unacceptably large, declaring instead that the price can only rise to the government ceiling price, $P_{CEILING}$. At the price ceiling, however, the quantity demanded exceeds the quantity supplied and shortages arise.

EXHIBIT 1	THE IMPACT OF PRICE CONTROLS

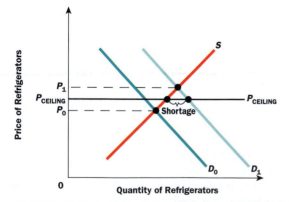

Suppose that price controls exist and the ceiling price on refrigerators is set at $P_{CEILING}$. Suppose for some reason the demand for refrigerators rises from D_0 to D_1. Without controls, price would be P_1. Price controls lead to a quantity demanded that is greater than quantity supplied, resulting in a shortage.

WHAT ARE SOME EXAMPLES OF PROBLEMS WITH PRICE CONTROLS?

During the 1973 Arab oil boycott, the federal government imposed price ceilings on gasoline that prevented gas prices from rising as they normally would have in response to reduced supply. At the ceiling price, quantity demanded exceeded quantity supplied; gas stations ran out of gas, were often closed, or placed a limit on the amount of gas they would sell. When drivers were able to buy gas, they often not only filled their tanks but also several containers they carried along to reduce the risk of being unable to buy gas when they needed it. In the former Soviet Union, where price-control-related shortages were commonplace, citizens typically carried briefcases or even suitcases and large quantities of cash, in case they were able to purchase a normally unavailable good. Rather than just buy the product for themselves, they would buy several items for their friends and relatives as well, to keep them from having to stand in line for hours, often in vain, trying to buy it. Winston Churchill once aptly termed a society with rigid price controls as a "queuetopia." (The British commonly used the term "queue" to refer to long lines.)

WHAT ARE EXAMPLES OF PROBLEMS CREATED BY WAGE CONTROLS?

In the case of prolonged wage controls, shortages of personnel can occur. Wages serve as market signals. Rising wages in an occupation increase an occupation's attractiveness, leading to new entrants of workers. In the early 1970s, for example, newly trained accountants were earning much more than other new college graduates. Predictably, there was a supply response, as accounting majors became much more numerous in colleges. By the late 1970s, the salary (or price) of accountants started to fall a bit relative to other occupations. If, however, the government had decreed that the salaries of new accountants in the five years after 1972 could not rise above, say, $12,000 a year, the increase in the quantity of new accountants supplied would not have occurred and an accountant shortage would have developed, causing all sorts of problems for businesses needing an accurate evaluation of their financial performance, individuals needing their tax returns prepared, and so forth.

Whether the gains from wage and price controls in the form of reduced inflation outweigh the costs in the form of shortages and inefficient resource allocation is debatable. This is a normative issue where honest, informed persons can differ in their perceptions of costs and benefits. The classic illustration of this was the monumental, prolonged debate in the U.S. Congress in 1977 over the removal of price controls on natural gas, with one side arguing that controls should be removed to end shortages and enhance long-term supply, while the other side argued that removing controls would lead to inflated prices for gas and inflated profits for gas producers, while causing hardships to lower-income users of gas. Eventually the issue was resolved by easing, but not completely removing, the controls until 1993.

HOW CAN PRICES BE KEPT DOWN WITHOUT THE USE OF PRICE CONTROLS?

The attempt to control prices politically can take another form. The presence of monopolistic elements in an industry can lead to higher prices for that industry's products than would be the case for a more competitive industry. By stimulating price competition among private firms, the government may be able to help in reducing inflationary pressures. In recent years, the possibility of using the antitrust laws to attack alleged monopoly influences in certain industries with rapidly increasing prices—such as the prescription drug industry—has been considered. However, despite much talk, there has been relatively little actual use of antitrust laws to try to reduce inflation pressures. Moreover, monopoly power can also be artificially created by government regulations; such has been the case in transportation. The relaxation of price regulation of airlines, for example, led to lower air fares in the late 1970s.

HOW COULD INDEXING REDUCE THE COSTS OF INFLATION?

Another approach to some of the problems posed by inflation is **indexing.** As you recall, inflation poses substantial equity and distributional problems only when it is unanticipated or unexpected. One means of protecting parties against unanticipated price increases is to write contracts that automatically change prices of goods or services whenever the overall price level changes, effectively rewriting agreements in terms of dollars of constant purchasing power. Wages, loans, and mortgage payments—everything possible—would be changed every month or so by an amount equal to the percent change in some broad-based price index. Thus, if prices rise by 1.2 percent this month and my last month's wage was $1,000, my wage this month will be $1,012 ($1,000 × 1.012). By making as many contracts as possible payable in dollars of constant purchasing power, those involved can protect themselves against unanticipated changes in inflation.

WHY ISN'T INDEXING MORE EXTENSIVELY USED?

Indexing seems to eliminate most of the wealth transfers associated with unexpected inflation. Why then is it not more commonly used? One main argument against indexing is that it could well worsen inflation. As prices go up, wages and certain other contractual obligations (e.g., rents) would also automatically increase. This immediate and comprehensive reaction to price increases will lead to greater inflationary pressures. One price increase likely might lead to a second, which in turn will lead to a third, and so on.

WHAT OTHER PROBLEMS EXIST WITH INDEXING?

One might say, so what? If prices are rising rapidly but wages, rents, and so forth are also moving up with prices, real wages and rents are remaining constant. Yet if the inflation gets bad enough, it may become almost impossible administratively to maintain the indexing scheme. The index, to be effective, might have to be changed every few days, but the information to make such changes is not currently readily available. To get such quick information, then, might be quite expensive, involving a small army of price-checking bureaucrats and a massive electronic communications system. There are other inefficiencies as well. During the German hyperinflation of the early 1920s, prices at one point rose so rapidly that workers demanded to be paid twice a day, at noon and at the end of work. During their lunch hour, workers would rush money to their wives, who would then run out and buy real goods before prices increased further.

Other big problems include the fact that indexing reduces the ability for relative price changes to allocate resources where they are more valuable. Not everything can be indexed, so indexing would cause wealth redistribution. In addition, costs would necessarily be incurred as a result of renegotiating cost-of-living (COLA) clauses.

Excessive inflation, then, leads to great inefficiency, as well as to a loss of confidence in the issuer of money—namely, the government. Furthermore, inflation influences world trade patterns. Limited indexing, in fact, has already been adopted, as some wage and pension payments are changed with changes in the cost-of-living index. Whether on balance those escalator clauses are "good" or "bad" is a debatable topic, a normative judgment that we will leave to the reader to make.

1. Wage and price controls can be imposed by government regulation or "voluntarily" with the use of moral suasion. The purpose of such controls is to reduce inflation and lower future inflation expectations.
2. Besides the problems of enforcing wage and price controls, these policies lead to shortages of goods and personnel as well as misallocations of goods.

3. Indexing is a process of adjusting payment contracts to automatically adjust for changes in inflation. Indexing reduces the impact of inflation on the distribution of income but may also intensify the inflationary effects of expansionary monetary policy by increasing inflationary pressures.

1. In what ways might "voluntary" government inflation guidelines not be completely voluntary?
2. If holding down legal price increases through price controls reduces official inflation rates, why are black markets likely to arise?
3. How might wage and price controls lead to shortages of goods and services (a "queuetopia")?

4. How might wage and price controls lead to the production of inferior products over time?
5. If every possible good was indexed to changes in the general price level, would it be very easy for relative price changes to signal changing relative scarcities? Why or why not?

Application:
The Role of
Expectations in
Macroeconomics

Policy makers agree that the art of economic forecasting is a different one. One important aspect of policy making is how consumers, producers, and investors form their expectations. Do consumers, producers, and investors have rational expectations about the future of the economy? If so, do those expectations impact the economy? In this article, we see the contribution that Professor Lucas has made in the area of expectations.

GETTING IT RIGHT

ROBERT BARROW

. . . Bob Lucas's contributions to macroeconomics in the 1970s permanently changed the very center of the discipline. Moreover, his influence has been as great on critics, primarily Keynesians, as on supporters, who tend to represent market-clearing or equilibrium-style approaches.

In some key articles published from 1972 to 1975, Bob applied John Muth's insights on rational expectations to monetary theories of the business cycle. Previous analyses had relied on simplistic Phillips curve models in which increased inflation led mechanically to lower unemployment and higher output. But these theories assumed that workers and firms did not exploit available information and thereby would commit the same mistakes time after time. For instance, higher inflation was assumed to raise the willingness to work because workers were continually fooled into thinking that their real wage was higher than it was.

In Bob's theory, where expectations are formed rationally, people can be confused temporarily by monetary surprises. (Rational expectations are not the same as complete information or perfect foresight.) In particular, an unanticipated expansion of money and the general price level may temporarily fool workers into thinking that their real wage had risen and producers into believing that the relative price of their product had gone up. Through these channels, a monetary stimulus may cause a temporary boom, but one that must end soon after the errors in expectations are recognized.

In the older style theory, the permanent trade-off between inflation and unemployment meant that monetary policy had a key role in fine-tuning the economy. The revised theory has dramatically different implications because the monetary authority has its main influence when it does something surprising. Thus, it is not enough to print more money when the economy is contracting and to print less when the economy is expanding. The expectations of this policy pretty much neutralize the real effects. . . .

Unfortunately, the easiest way for the monetary authority to create surprises is to behave erratically, an approach that has effects that are real but harmful. Therefore, an important policy influence from Lucas's theory is that the central bank ought to relinquish the idea of fine-tuning and instead concentrate on long-run objectives such as price stability. . . .

The role of expectations is not limited to monetary policy but is crucial in many areas of economics, as Bob showed in his later research on investment, unemployment, taxation, public debt management, and asset pricing. In all of these situations, the appropriate evaluation of policy must take account of the way that expectations would be rationally formed; the older analyses, which failed to consider this exceptional adjustment, are now described as failing the "Lucas critique. . . ."

SOURCE: Robert Barrow, *Getting It Right*, MIT Press, 1996, pp. 168–170.

The rational expectations hypothesis is that consumers, producers, and investors can forecast the future as well as economic forecasters and that people are continuously updating their information and revising their expectations so that they will not be continuously surprised. The real point is that people are influenced by expectations and policy makers must anticipate the impact of changing expectations on a policy proposal like a tax cut. The implications are important, because if Lucas and his supporters are correct, then the macroeconomic policy that is anticipated will be offset by workers and businesses who anticipate these changes.

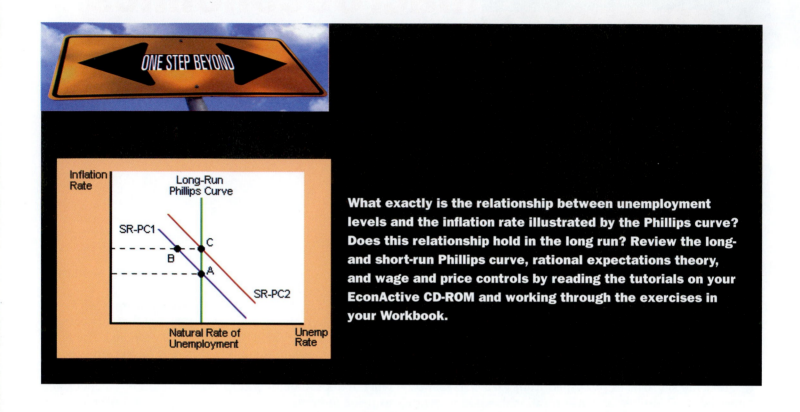

ONE STEP BEYOND

What exactly is the relationship between unemployment levels and the inflation rate illustrated by the Phillips curve? Does this relationship hold in the long run? Review the long- and short-run Phillips curve, rational expectations theory, and wage and price controls by reading the tutorials on your EconActive CD-ROM and working through the exercises in your Workbook.

PHOTO CREDITS MODULE 24

Page **582:** © Nik Wheeler/Corbis Images.

International Trade

A. The Growth in World Trade
How important is international trade?

B. Comparative Advantage and Gains from Trade
What is the difference between comparative advantage and absolute advantage?

C. Supply and Demand in International Trade
Who gains and who loses from exports and imports?

D. Tariffs, Import Quotas, and Subsidies
How do tariffs, import quotas, and subsidies impact the domestic economy?

E. Application: Common Misperceptions on Trade
Are the welfare gains associated with trade overstated?

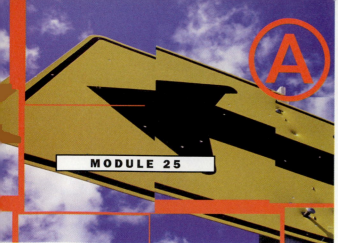

(A) The Growth in World Trade

- What has happened to the volume of international trade over time?
- Who trades with the United States?

HOW IMPORTANT IS INTERNATIONAL TRADE?

In a typical year, about 15 percent of the world's output is traded in international markets. Of course, the importance of the international sector varies enormously from place to place on the planet. Some nations are almost closed economies, with foreign trade equaling only a very small proportion (perhaps 5 percent) of total output. In the United States, in the mid-1990s, exports were over 11 percent of gross domestic product (GDP), while imports were a little higher, at almost 13 percent of GDP. In Germany, by contrast, nearly 33 percent of all output produced was exported, while in Belgium exports accounted for over 70 percent of GDP.

The volume of international trade has increased substantially in the United States over the last 50 years, in which time exports and imports have gone from less than 5 percent of GDP to over 10 percent of GDP. There has also been an explosion of trade in world markets since the 1950s. From 1950 to 1990, world output rose over 400 percent and world exports rose over 1,000 percent. Exports of one nation are imports to another, so world exports are conceptually equal in magnitude to world imports. During this 40-year period, the world exhibited remarkable rates of economic growth (in part because of trade), but the growth in world trade was faster than output growth generally, so trade as a proportion of gross world product more than doubled.

WITH WHOM DOES THE U.S. TRADE?

In its early history, U.S. international trade was largely directed towards Europe and to Great Britain in particular. In recent years, however, trade has become highly multidirectional, with no one nation or small geographic area being of dominant importance. This is indicated in Exhibit 1, which suggests that our most important single trading partner, Canada, accounts only for around one-fifth of our imports and exports. Trade with Japan, Germany, China, Taiwan, and Italy are also particularly important.

Canada is the United States' most important trading partner.

EXHIBIT 1 | MAJOR U.S. TRADING PARTNERS

Top Five Trading Partners—Exports of Goods in 1996

Rank	Country	Value of Goods (billions of dollars)	Percent of Total
1	Canada	$133.7	21.4
2	Japan	67.5	10.8
3	Mexico	56.8	9.1
4	United Kingdom	30.9	4.9
5	Korea	26.6	4.3

Top Five Trading Partners—Imports of Goods in 1996

Rank	Country	Value of Goods (billions of dollars)	Percent of Total
1	Canada	$156.5	19.8
2	Japan	115.2	14.6
3	Mexico	73.0	9.2
4	China	51.5	6.5
5	Germany	38.9	4.9

SOURCE: U.S. Census Bureau, *Wall Street Almanac,* 1998, p. 183.

IN THE NEWS

BAYWATCH IS WORLD WATCHED

In the world of entertainment exports, the syndicated series *Baywatch* is like the Boeing 747. You can see *Baywatch* in Bangladesh, Barbados, Bolivia, Brunei, and 140 other countries. Produced by a small, independent Los Angeles production company, the weekly dose of sun, sand, sea, and skin, with muscled lifeguards rescuing drowning damsels (and vice versa), earns about $100 million per year, 67 percent of which is currently from foreign distribution.

Baywatch is currently riding the crest of a wave being surfed by all of the Hollywood studios and production companies. At the Walt Disney Company in Burbank, Calif., CFO Richard Nanula says that while the Magic Kingdom has had a presence in some foreign markets for up to 50 years, the international demand for Disney products is now growing at an accelerated pace. This is especially true in film and television where international business now accounts for about 40 percent of revenue, but growth is twice that of domestic.

"The international markets really help the performance of a movie in its profit statement—substantially more than they used to," Nanula says. Overseas box office receipts used to add perhaps 20 percent to a film's gross. Now some movies, particularly animation and action-adventure, that make $100 million at home might eventually make twice as much internationally.

SOURCE: Steve Barth, "Exporting Fantasy," *World Trade*, March 1998, pp. 41–42.

CONSIDER THIS: The international marketplace has become very important in the television and movie industry.

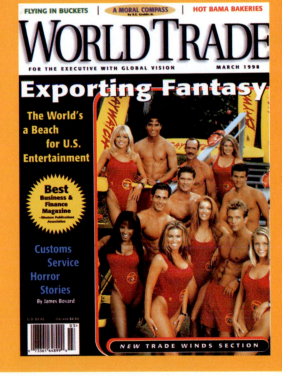

1. The volume of international trade has increased substantially in the United States over the last 50 years. During that time, exports and imports have grown from less than 5 percent to over 10 percent of GDP.

2. Our most important single trading partner, Canada, accounts only for around one-fifth of our imports and exports. Trade with Japan, Germany, China, Taiwan, and Italy is also particularly important to the United States.

1. Why is it important to understand the effects of international trade?

2. Why would producers and consumers in the United States be more concerned about Canadian trade restrictions than Swedish trade restrictions?

B Comparative Advantage and Gains from Trade

- Does economic growth result from greater specialization?
- What is the principle of comparative advantage?
- What benefits are derived from specialization?

DOES ECONOMIC GROWTH LEAD TO A DECLINE IN SELF-SUFFICIENCY?

One of the most striking characteristics of any relatively poor nation undergoing a substantial amount of economic growth is the decline in self-sufficiency and the rise in specialization. Before growth begins, a large proportion of output produced in traditional agricultural societies is produced by family units, who also consume those goods and services. A relatively small proportion of goods are traded to others. Families are "Jacks and Jills of all trades," economic units that, in addition to producing a wide variety of foodstuffs, also engage in the manufacture of clothing items, the construction of buildings, and so on. The family's workers are, in addition to being farmers, part-time carpenters, plumbers, shoemakers, seamstresses, candle makers, soap makers, bakers, and even physicians. Household manufacturing tends to die out to a considerable extent, however, with economic growth, and even in their agricultural functions, farmers tend to specialize more and more in a few individual crops or forms of livestock, exporting surplus output from the farm in exchange for other goods that the farmer no longer produces. Why does this decline in self-sufficiency occur?

Using simple logic, we conclude that the very existence of trade suggests that trade is economically beneficial. This is true if one assumes that people are utility maximizers and are rational, intelligent, and engage in trade on a voluntary basis. Because almost all trade is voluntary, it would seem that trade occurs because the participants feel that they are better off because of the trade. Both participants of an exchange of goods and services anticipate an improvement in their economic welfare. Sometimes, of course, anticipations are not realized (because the world is uncertain), but the motive behind trade remains an expectation of some enhancement in utility or satisfaction by both parties.

Going beyond this rather simplistic explanation that "trade must be good because people do it," the classical economist David Ricardo is usually given most of the credit for developing the economic theory that more precisely explains how trade can be mutually beneficial to both parties, raising output and income levels in the entire trading area.

THE PRINCIPLE OF COMPARATIVE ADVANTAGE

Ricardo's theory of international trade centers on the concept of comparative advantage. A nation, geographic area, or even a person can gain from trade if it (the area or the person) produces a good or service relatively cheaper than other areas or persons can produce it. Put slightly differently, an area should specialize in producing and selling those items that it can produce at a lower opportunity cost than can other countries.

Comparative advantage analysis does not mean that nations or areas that export goods will necessarily be able to produce those goods or services more cheaply than other nations in an absolute sense. What is important is comparative advantage, not absolute advantage. For example, the United States may be able to produce more cotton cloth per worker than India, but that does not mean the United States should necessarily sell cotton cloth to India. Indeed, the United States has an absolute advantage or productive superiority over India in nearly every good, given the higher levels of output per person in the United States. Yet India's inferiority in producing some goods is much less than for others. In goods where India's productivity is only slightly less than that of the United States, such as perhaps in cotton cloth, it probably has a comparative advantage over the United States. How? For a highly productive nation to produce goods in which it is only marginally more productive than other nations, the nation must take resources from the production of other goods in which its productive abilities are markedly superior. As a result, the opportunity costs in India of making cotton cloth may be less than in the United States. With that, both can gain from trade, despite potential absolute advantages for every good in the United States.

If the U.S. can produce more shirts per year than India, should it necessarily do so?

COMPARATIVE ADVANTAGE AND THE PRODUCTION POSSIBILITIES CURVE

In Exhibit 1, we show the production possibilities curves for two individuals, Wendy and Calvin. Wendy and Calvin can produce either food or clothing. In Exhibit 1, we see that if Wendy devotes all of her resources to producing food, she can produce 30 pounds of food; if she devotes all of her resources to producing clothes, she can produce 10 yards of clothing. In Exhibit 1, we see that when Calvin uses all of his resources to produce food, he only produces 10 pounds; but when he uses all of his resources to produce clothing, he can produce 30 yards. In this example, Wendy actually has an absolute advantage in food, while Calvin has an absolute advantage in clothing, but as we shall see, it would not affect the result if Calvin could only produce 2 pounds of food and 6 yards of clothing.

For simplicity, we will assume each producer operates on a straight line production possibilities curve (*PPC*) and each initially chooses to produce 7.5 pounds of food and 7.5 yards of clothing, although any amount of each good could have been produced.

Wendy can produce food at a lower opportunity cost than Calvin. When Wendy produces 30 pounds of food, it costs only 10 yards of clothing. However, when Calvin produces only 10 pounds of food, it costs 30 yards of clothing. Wendy, then, is the lowest-cost producer of food. However, Calvin can produce clothing at a lower opportunity cost than Wendy. When Calvin produces 30 yards of clothing, it costs him 10 pounds of food. And when Wendy

produces 10 yards of clothing, it costs 30 pounds of food. Calvin, then, is the lowest-cost producer of clothing.

To demonstrate our point about comparative advantage, we have overlapped the two production possibility curves in Exhibit 1. At point A, we see that Wendy produces 7.5 pounds of food and 7.5 yards of clothing and Calvin produces 7.5 yards of clothing and 7.5 pounds of food. Together they would produce 15 pounds of food and 15 yards of clothing, point B. However, if each specialized and pursued his or her comparative advantage, the goods each can produce at the lowest opportunity cost, then Wendy could produce 30 pounds of food and Calvin could produce 30 yards of clothing, point C. That is, by specializing, Wendy and Calvin have produced 30 units of each good rather than 15 units. Now if Wendy does not want all food and Calvin does not want all clothing, they can trade with each other. In fact, if Wendy trades half of her food for half of the clothing Calvin has produced, then each will have 15 units of food and clothing. This is 7.5 more pounds of food and 7.5 more yards of clothing than they had before specialization and trade. Exhibit 1 also shows that as a result of specialization and trade, Wendy gains D to B in additional clothing and Calvin gains E to B in additional

| **EXHIBIT 1** | **SPECIALIZATION AND TRADE** |

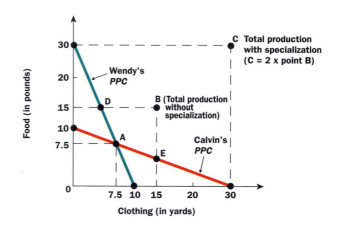

Before Trade

Point A—Without specialization, say that Wendy and Calvin each choose to produce 7.5 pounds of food and 7.5 yards of clothing.

Point B—Wendy and Calvin's total production if they do not specialize: Collectively they produce 15 pounds of food and 15 yards of clothing.

Point C—Wendy and Calvin's total production if they specialize: Wendy produces 30 pounds of food and Calvin produces 30 yards of clothing.

Specialization and Trade

Point B—If Wendy and Calvin split their total production after specialization equally, they will each have 15 pounds of food and 15 yards of clothing.

Point D—As a result of specialization and trade, Wendy gains D to B in additional clothing.

Point E—As a result of specialization and trade, Calvin gains E to B in additional food.

COMPARATIVE ADVANTAGE

Q: Surrey A. List, a famous artist, can complete one painting in each 40-hour workweek. Each painting sells for $2,000. As a result of his enormous success, however, Surrey is swamped in paperwork. To solve the problem, Surrey hires Dave to handle all of the bookkeeping and typing associated with buying supplies, answering inquiries from prospective buyers and dealers, writing art galleries, and so forth. Surrey pays Dave $300 per week for his work. After a couple of weeks in this arrangement, Surrey realizes that he handled the secretarial chores more quickly than Dave does. In fact, he estimates that he is twice as fast as Dave, completing in 20 hours what it takes Dave 40 hours to complete. Should Surrey fire Dave?

A: Clearly Surrey has an absolute advantage over Dave in both painting and paperwork because he can do twice as much paperwork in 40 hours as Dave can, and Dave can't paint well at all. Still, it would be foolish for Surrey to do his own secretarial work. If Surrey did his own secretarial work, 20 hours per week would be involved in secretarial chores, leaving him only 20 hours to paint. Because each watercolor takes 40 hours to paint, Surrey's output would fall from one painting per week to one painting per two weeks. Instead of getting $2,000 a week, he would only earn $1,000 a week.

When he had his own secretary, Surrey's net income was $1,700 ($2,000 minus $300 in secretarial wages); now it is only $1,000. While Surrey is both a better painter and a better secretary than Dave, it pays for him to specialize in painting, in which he has a comparative advantage, and allow Dave to do the typing. The opportunity cost to Surrey of secretarial work is high. For Dave, who lacks skills as a painter, the opportunity costs of being a secretary are much less.

---

food. The point is the differences in opportunity costs provided an incentive to gain from specialization and trade.

REGIONAL COMPARATIVE ADVANTAGE

In the last section, using a production possibilities curve, we saw how Wendy and Calvin could benefit from specialization and trade. The principle of comparative advantage can be applied to regional markets as well. In fact, trade has evolved in large part because different geographic areas have different resource endowments, and therefore different production possibilities. The impact of trade between two areas with differing factor endowments is shown in Exhibit 2. To keep the analysis simple, suppose two trading areas exist that can produce just two commodities, grain and computers. A "trading area" may be a locality, a region, or even a nation, but for our example, suppose we think in terms of two hypothetical regions, Grainsville and Techland.

Grainsville and Techland have various potential combinations of grain and computers that they can produce. For each region, the cost of producing more grain is the output of computers that must be foregone, and vice versa. Observe in this table that Techland has the capability of producing more of both grain (40 bushels) and computers (100 units) than Grainsville can (30 bushels; 30 units), reflecting perhaps superior resources (more or better labor, more land, and so on); this means that Techland has an absolute advantage in both products.

| EXHIBIT 2 | PRODUCTION POSSIBILITIES, TECHLAND AND GRAINSVILLE |

Region	Grain (bushels per day)	Computers (units per day)
Techland	0	100
	10	75
	20	50
	30	25
	40	0
Grainsville	0	30
	6	24
	12	18
	18	12
	24	6
	30	0

Before Specialization

Region	Grain (bushels per day)	Computers (units per day)
Techland	10	75
Grainsville	18	12
Total	28	87

After Specialization

Region	Grain (bushels per day)	Computers (units per day)
Techland	0	100
Grainsville	30	0
Total	30	100

Suppose that, before specialization Techland chooses to produce 75 computers and 10 bushels of grain per day. Similarly, suppose Grainsville decides to produce 12 computers and 18 bushels of grain. Collectively, then the two areas are producing 87 computers (75 + 12) and 28 bushels of grain (10 + 18) per day before specialization.

Now, suppose the two nations specialize. Techland decides to specialize in computers and devotes all of its resources to making that product. As a result, computer output in Techland rises to 100 units per day, some of which is sold to Grainsville. Grainsville, in turn, devotes all of its resources to grain, producing 30 bushels of grain per day and selling some of it to Techland. Together, the two areas are producing more of both grain and computers than before—100 instead of 87 computers and 30 instead of 28 bushels of grain. Both areas could, as a result, have more of both products than before they began specializing and trading.

How can that happen? In Techland, the opportunity cost of producing grain is very high—25 computers must be foregone to get 10 more bushels of grain. The cost of one bushel of grain, then, is 2.5 computers (25 divided by 10). In Grainsville, by contrast, the opportunity cost of producing six more units of grain is six units of computers that must be foregone, so the cost of one unit of grain is one unit of computers. In Techland, a unit of grain costs 2.5 computers, while in Grainsville the same amount of grain

costs only one computer. Grain is more costly in Techland in terms of the computers foregone than in Grainsville, so Grainsville has the comparative advantage in the production of grain, even though Techland has an absolute advantage in grain.

With respect to computers, an increase in output by 25 units, say from 25 to 50 units, costs 10 bushels of grain foregone in Techland. The cost of one more computer is .4 bushels of grain (10 divided by 25). In Grainsville, an increase in computer output of six units, say from 12 to 18, is accompanied by a decrease in grain production by six bushels as resources are converted from grain to computer manufacturing. The cost of one computer is one bushel of grain. Computers are more costly (in terms of opportunity cost) in Grainsville and cheaper in Techland, so Techland should specialize in the production of computers.

Thus, by specializing in products in which it has a comparative advantage, an area has the potential of having more goods and services, assuming it trades the additional output for other desirable goods and services others can produce at a lower opportunity cost. In the scenario presented here, the people in Techland would specialize in computers, and the people in Grainsville would specialize in farming (grain). As you can see from this example, specialization increases the division of labor and increases the interdependence of one group of people on others.

THE MIRACLE OF TRADE

It is mere common sense that if one country is very good at making hats, and another is very good at making shoes, then total output can be increased by arranging for the first country to concentrate on making hats and the second on making shoes. Then, through trade in both goods, more of each can be consumed in both places.

That is a tale of absolute advantage. . . . Each country is better than the other at making a certain good, and so profits from specialization and trade. Comparative advantage is different: a country will have it despite being bad at the activity concerned. Indeed, it can have a comparative advantage in making a certain good even if it is worse at making that good than any other country.

This is not economic theory, but a straightforward matter of definition: a country has a comparative advantage where its margin of superiority is greater, or its margin of inferiority smaller.

. . . [W]hen people say of Africa, or Britain, or wherever, that it has no comparative advantage in anything, they are simply confusing absolute advantage (for which their claim may or may not be true) with comparative advantage (for which it is certainly false).

Why does this confusion over terms matter? Because the case for free trade is often thought to depend on the existence of absolute advantage and is therefore thought to collapse whenever absolute advantage is absent. But economics shows that gains from trade follow, in fact, from comparative advantage. Since comparative advantage is never absent, this gives the theory far broader scope than more popular critics suppose.

In particular, it shows that even countries which are desperately bad at making everything can expect to gain from international competition. If countries specialize according to their comparative advantage, they can prosper through trade regardless of how inefficient, in absolute terms, they may be in their chosen specialty.

SOURCE: *The Economist*, January 27, 1996, pp. 61, 62.

> **CONSIDER THIS:**
> Even countries that are not very good at producing anything can prosper from free trade.

1. As economic growth occurs, regions and countries tend to specialize in what they produce best.
2. A nation, geographic area, or even a person can gain from trade if the area produces for sale a good or service relatively cheaper than other areas or persons can produce it; that is, an area should specialize in producing and selling those items that it can produce at a lower opportunity cost than others.

3. Through trade and specialization in products in which it has a comparative advantage, a country can enjoy a greater array of goods and services at a lower cost.

---

1. Why do people voluntarily choose to specialize and trade?
2. How could a country have an absolute advantage in producing one good or service without also having a comparative advantage in its production?

3. Why do you think the introduction of the railroad reduced self-sufficiency in the United States?
4. If you can do the dishes in two-thirds the time it takes your younger sister, do you have a comparative advantage in doing the dishes compared to her?

Supply and Demand in International Trade

- What is consumer surplus?
- What is producer surplus?
- Who benefits and who loses when a country becomes an exporter?
- Who benefits and who loses when a country becomes an importer?

THE IMPORTANCE OF TRADE: PRODUCER AND CONSUMER SURPLUS

The difference between the most a consumer would be willing to pay for a quantity of a good and what a consumer actually has to pay is called **consumer surplus**. The difference between the least a supplier is willing to supply a quantity of a good or service for and the revenues a supplier actually receives for selling it is called **producer surplus.** With the tools of consumer and producer surplus, we can better analyze the impact of trade. Who gains? Who loses? What happens to net welfare?

The demand curve represents a collection of maximum prices that consumers are willing and able to pay for different quantities of a good or service while the supply curve represents a collection of minimum prices that suppliers require to be willing to supply different quantities of that good or service, as seen in Exhibit 1. For example, for the first unit of output, the consumer is willing to pay up to $7 and the producer would demand at least $1 for producing that unit. However, the equilibrium price is $4, as indicated by the intersection of the supply and demand curves. It is clear that the two would gain from getting together and trading that unit because the consumer would receive $3 of consumer surplus ($7 – $4) and the producer would receive $3 of producer surplus ($4 – $1). Both would also benefit from trading the second and third unit of output—in fact, from every unit up to the equilibrium output. Once the equilibrium output is reached at the equilibrium price, all of the mutually beneficial opportunities from trade between suppliers and demanders will have taken place; the sum of consumer surplus and producer surplus is maximized.

It is important to recognize that the total gains to the economy from trade is the sum of consumer and producer surplus. That is, consumers benefit from additional amounts of consumer surplus and producers benefit from additional amounts of producer surplus.

EXHIBIT 1 CONSUMER AND PRODUCER SURPLUS

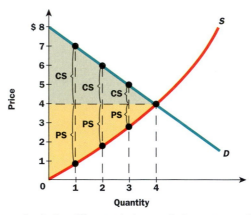

Consumer surplus is the difference between what a consumer has to pay ($4) and what the consumer is willing to pay. For unit 1, consumer surplus is $3 ($7 – $4). Producer surplus is the difference between what a seller receives for selling a good or service ($4) and the price at which he is willing to supply that good or service. For unit 1, producer surplus is $3 ($4 – $1).

FREE TRADE AND EXPORTS—DOMESTIC PRODUCERS GAIN MORE THAN DOMESTIC CONSUMERS LOSE

Using the concepts of consumer and producer surplus, we can graphically show the net benefits of free trade. Imagine an economy with no trade, where the equilibrium price, P_{BT}, and the equilibrium quantity, Q_{BT}, of wheat are determined exclusively in the domestic economy, as seen in Exhibit 2. Say that this imaginary economy decides to engage in free trade. You can see that the world price, P_W, is higher than the domestic price before trade, P_{BT}. In other words, the domestic economy has a comparative advan-

| EXHIBIT 2 | FREE TRADE AND EXPORTS |

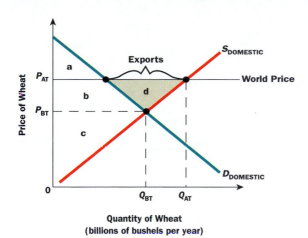

Domestic Gains and Losses from Free Trade (exports)

	Area
Domestic producers gain	+ b + d
Domestic consumers lose	− b
Net domestic gain from trade	+ d

Domestic producers gain more than domestic consumers lose from exports when there is free trade. On net, domestic wealth rises by area d.

tage in wheat, because it can produce wheat at a lower relative price than the rest of the world. So this wheat-producing country sells some wheat to the domestic market and some wheat to the world market, all at the going world price.

The price after trade (P_{AT}) is higher than the price before trade (P_{BT}). Because the world market is huge, the demand from the rest of the world at the world price (P_W) is assumed to be perfectly elastic. That is, domestic wheat farmers can sell all the wheat they want at the world price. If you were a wheat farmer in Nebraska, would you rather sell all of your bushels of wheat at the higher world price or the lower domestic price? As a wheat farmer, you would surely prefer the higher world price. But this is not good news for domestic cereal and bread eaters, who now have to pay more for products made with wheat, because P_{AT} is greater than P_{BT}.

Graphically, we can see how free trade and exports affect both domestic consumers and domestic producers. At the higher world price, P_{AT}, domestic wheat producers are receiving larger amounts of producer surplus. Before trade, they received a surplus equal to area c; after trade, they received surplus c + b + d, for a net gain of area b + d. However, part of the domestic producer's gain comes at domestic consumer's expense. Specifically, consumers had a consumer surplus equal to a + b before the trade (at P_{BT}), but they now only have area a (at P_{AT})—a loss of area b.

Area b reflects a redistribution of income, because producers are gaining exactly what consumers are losing. Is that good or bad? We can't say objectively whether consumers or producers are more deserving. However, the net benefits from allowing free trade and exports are clearly visible in area d. Without free trade, no one gets area d. That is, on net, members of the domestic society gain when domestic wheat producers are able to sell their wheat at the higher world price. While domestic wheat consumers lose from the free trade, those negative effects are more than offset by the positive gains captured by producers. On net, export trade increases domestic wealth.

"You like protectionism as a 'working man.' How about as a consumer?"

FREE TRADE AND IMPORTS

Now suppose that our economy does not produce shirts relatively as well as other countries of the world. In other words, other countries have a comparative advantage in producing shirts. This means that the domestic price for shirts is above the world price. This scenario is illustrated in Exhibit 3. At the new, lower, world price, the domestic producer will supply quantity Q_S. However, at the lower world price, the domestic producers will not produce the entire amount demanded by domestic consumers, Q_D. At the world price, reflecting the world supply and demand for shirts, the difference between what is domestically supplied and what is domestically demanded is supplied by imports.

At the world price, we assume the world supply curve to the domestic market is perfectly elastic—that the producers of the world can supply all that domestic consumers are willing to buy at the going price. At the world price, Q_S is supplied by domestic producers and the difference between Q_D and Q_S is imported from other countries.

Who wins and who loses from free trade and imports? Domestic consumers benefit from paying a lower price for shirts. In Exhibit 3, before trade, consumers only received area a in consumer surplus. But after trade, the price fell and quantity purchased increased, causing the area of consumer surplus to increase from area a to area a + b + d, a gain of b + d. Domestic producers lose because they are now selling their shirts at the lower world price, P_{AT}. The producer surplus before trade was b + c. After trade, the producer surplus falls to area c, reducing producer surplus by area b. Area b, then, represents a redistribution from producers to consumers, but area d is the net increase in domestic wealth from free trade and imports.

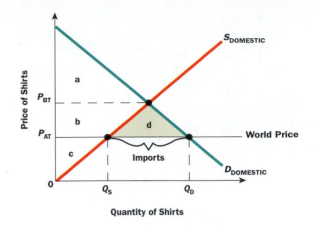

EXHIBIT 3   FREE TRADE AND IMPORTS

Domestic Gains and Losses from Free Trade (imports)

	Area
Domestic producers lose	− b
Domestic consumers gain	+ b + d
Net domestic gain from trade	+ d

Domestic consumers gain more than domestic producers lose from imports when there is free trade. On net, domestic wealth rises by area d.

CONCEPT CHECK

1. The difference between what a consumer is willing to pay and what a consumer actually has to pay is called consumer surplus.
2. The difference between what a supplier is willing to supply and the price a supplier receives for selling a good or service is called producer surplus.

3. With free trade and exports, domestic producers gain more than domestic consumers lose.
4. With free trade and imports, domestic consumers gain more than domestic producers lose.

---

1. How does voluntary trade generate both producer and consumer surplus?
2. If the world price of a good is greater than the domestic price prior to trade, why does that imply that the domestic economy has a comparative advantage in producing that good?
3. If the world price of a good is less than the domestic price prior to trade, why does that imply that the domestic economy has a comparative disadvantage in producing that good?

4. When a country has a comparative advantage in the production of a good, why do domestic producers gain more than domestic consumers lose from free international trade?
5. When a country has a comparative disadvantage in the production of a good, why do domestic consumers gain more than domestic producers lose from free international trade?
6. Why do U.S. exporters, such as farmers, favor free trade more than U.S. producers of domestic products who face competition from foreign imports, such as the automobile industry?

D Tariffs, Import Quotas, and Subsidies

■ What are tariffs?
■ What are the effects of a tariff?
■ What is an import quota?
■ What is the economic impact of subsidies?

WHAT ARE TARIFFS?

A tariff is a tax on imported goods. Tariffs are usually relatively small revenue producers that retard the expansion of trade. They bring about higher prices and revenues to domestic producers, and lower sales and revenues to foreign producers. Moreover, tariffs lead to higher prices to domestic consumers. In fact, the gains to producers are more than offset by the loss to consumers.

WHAT PURPOSE DO TARIFFS SERVE?

One factor in the growth in international trade has been the reduction in tariffs over time, lowering transaction costs of cross border trade. Because tariffs restrict trade and thus reduce the gains attributable to specialization and comparative advantage, why do nations levy them in the first place? One reason, of course, is to obtain revenue to run the government. In relatively underdeveloped countries, custom duties often provide a major part of the revenue of the central government. Custom duties are collected on trade passing through a generally small number of ports and are, therefore, relatively easy to collect. Taxes on income, sales, or property may be much harder to administer efficiently and equitably in such countries, particularly when much economic activity occurs outside markets and thus is not objectively and openly valued.

In the United States, up to the Civil War of the 1860s, nearly all federal government revenue came from custom duties. Even on the eve of World War I, nearly half of all the revenue of the federal government was derived from tariffs, although custom duties accounted for only 10 to 15 percent of the revenues of all governments (because state and local governments could not levy tariffs). Today, in most developed countries, custom duties are relatively unimportant as a revenue producer. In the United States, for example, duties account for less than 2 percent of all federal revenues, and less than 1 percent of all government revenue. Today, in most countries, tariffs exist mainly as a means of protecting domestic industry from foreign com-

petition. Even in earlier years, duties were considered to be an effective means of helping domestic industry and the employees in domestic industry withstand the adverse economic effects of foreign competition.

WHAT IS THE DOMESTIC ECONOMIC IMPACT OF TARIFFS?

The domestic economic impact of tariffs is presented in Exhibit 1, which illustrates the supply and demand curves for domestic consumers and producers of shoes. In a typical international supply and demand illustration, the intersection of the world supply and demand curves would determine the domestic market price. However, with import tariffs, the domestic price of shoes is greater than the world price, as in Exhibit 1(a). We consider the world supply curve (S_{WORLD}) to domestic consumers to be perfectly elastic; that is, we can buy all we want at the world price (P_W). At the world price, domestic producers are only willing to provide quantity Q_S, but domestic consumers are willing to buy quantity Q_D—more than domestic producers are willing to supply. The difference is made up with imports.

As you can see in Exhibit 1, the imposition of the tariff shifts up the perfectly elastic supply curve from foreigners to domestic consumers from S_{WORLD} to $S_{WORLD + TARIFF}$, but it does not alter the domestic supply or demand curve. At the resulting higher domestic price ($P_{W + T}$), domestic suppliers are willing to supply more, Q_S, but domestic consumers are willing to buy less, Q_D. At the new equilibrium, the domestic price ($P_{W + T}$) is higher and the quantity of shoes demanded (Q'_D) is smaller. But at the new price, the domestic quantity demanded is lower and the quantity supplied domestically is greater, reducing the quantity of imported shoes. Overall, then, tariffs lead to (1) a smaller total quantity sold, (2) a higher price for shoes for domestic consumers, (3) greater sales of shoes at higher prices for domestic producers, and (4) lower sales of foreign shoes.

While domestic producers do gain more sales and higher earnings, consumers lose much more. The increase in price from the tariff results in a loss in consumer surplus, as shown in Exhibit 1. After the tariff, shoe prices rise to P_{W+T}, and, consequently, consumer surplus falls by area a + b + c + d, representing the welfare loss to consumers resulting from the tariff. Area A in Exhibit 1 shows the gain to domestic producers as a result of the tariff. That is, at the higher price, domestic producers are willing to supply more shoes, representing a welfare gain to producers resulting from the tariff. As a result of the tariff, government gains area c. This is the import tariff—the revenue government collects from foreign countries on imports. However, we see from Exhibit 1 that consumers lose more than producers and government gain from the tariff.

ARGUMENTS FOR TARIFFS

Despite the preceding arguments against tariffs, tariffs continue to be levied. Some rationale for their existence is necessary. Four common arguments for the use of tariffs deserve our critical examination.

Tariffs Help Infant Industries Grow

The most enduring argument for tariffs is that tariff protection will allow a new industry to more quickly reach a scale

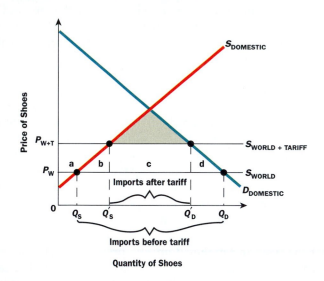

| EXHIBIT 1 | THE IMPACT OF TARIFFS |

Gains and Losses from Tariffs

	Area
Domestic consumers lose	−(a + b + d + d)
Domestic producers gain	+ a
Government gains (Imports × Tariff)	+ c
Net domestic loss from tariffs	−(b + d)

In the case of a tariff, we see that consumers lose more than producers and government gain.

of operation at which economies of scale and production efficiencies can be realized. It is presumed that without this protection, the industry could never get on its feet. At first hearing, the argument sounds valid, but there are many problems with it. How do you identify "infant industries" that genuinely have potential economies of scale and will quickly become efficient with protection? We do not know the long-run average total cost curves of industries, a necessary piece of information. Moreover, if firms and governments are truly convinced of the advantages of allowing an industry to reach a large scale, would it not be wise to make massive loans to the industry, allowing it to instantly begin large-scale production rather than slowly and at the expense of consumers? In other words, the goal of allowing the industry to reach its efficient size can be reached without a protective tariff. Finally, the history of infant industry tariffs suggests that the tariffs often linger long after the industry is mature and no longer in "need" of protection.

Tariffs Can Reduce Domestic Unemployment

Exhibit 1 showed how tariffs increase output by domestic producers, thus leading to increased employment and reduced unemployment in industries where tariffs were imposed. Yet the overall employment effects of a tariff imposition are not likely to be positive; the argument is incorrect. Why? First, the imposition of a tariff by the United States on, say, foreign steel, is going to be noticed in the countries adversely affected by the tariff. If a new tariff on steel lowers Japanese steel sales to the United States, the Japanese very likely will retaliate by imposing tariffs on American exports to Japan, say, on machinery exports. The retaliatory tariff will lower American sales of machinery and thus employment in the U.S. machinery industries. As a result, the gain in employment in the steel industry will be offset by a loss of employment elsewhere.

Even if the other countries did not retaliate, U.S. employment would likely suffer outside the industry gaining the tariff protection. The way that other countries pay for U.S. goods is by getting dollars from sales to the United States—imports to us. If new tariffs lead to restrictions on imports, fewer dollars will be flowing overseas in payment for imports, which means that foreigners will have fewer dollars available to buy our exports. Other things equal, this will tend to reduce our exports, thus creating unemployment in the export industries.

Tariffs Are Necessary for National Security Reasons

Sometimes it is argued that tariffs are a means of preventing a nation from becoming too dependent on foreign suppliers of goods vital to national security. For example, if oil is vital to running planes and tanks, a cutoff of foreign supplies of oil during wartime could cripple a nation's defenses.

The national security argument is usually not valid. If a nation's own resources are depletable, tariff-imposed reliance on domestic supplies will hasten depletion of domestic reserves, making the country even *more* dependent in the future. If we impose a very high tariff on foreign oil to protect domestic producers, we will increase domestic output of oil in the short run, but in the process, we will deplete the stockpile of available reserves. Thus, the defense argument is often of questionable validity. From a defense standpoint, it makes more sense to use foreign oil in peacetime and perhaps stockpile "insurance" supplies so that larger domestic supplies would be available during wars.

THE POLITICAL ECONOMY OF TARIFFS

Except in rather unusual circumstances, then, the arguments for tariffs are rather suspect. Tariffs lower total world output and real income and involve income redistribution from domestic consumers, who are forced to pay higher prices, and foreign producers, who sell fewer goods they have a comparative advantage in, to domestic producers, who benefit from protection. Why, if tariffs are typically harmful to the whole economy, are they so widespread?

Tariff legislation, like other forms of legislation, is enacted largely in response to the actions of pressure groups. In the case of tariffs, a larger group of voters, consumers, have on the whole more to lose from the new tariffs than the gains received by domestic producers and workers in protected industries. Yet the producer lobbying efforts are often more effective than the consumer efforts. Why?

Suppose an industry has five producers who will equally share $100 million in gains from a new tariff, while 200 million consumers will equally share losses of $400 million from the tariff. On balance, the losses exceed the gains and, on net, society loses ($300 million). Yet each single producer stands to gain $20 million ($100 million divided by five). For each one, the potential gains if the law is adopted are enormous. Moreover, each producer knows it is a significant proportion of the total group lobbying for the tariff, and each is therefore likely to cooperate in the effort, perhaps through an industry association.

For consumers, though, the situation is often quite different. The losses from tariffs, while a considerable aggregate sum, average only $2 per consumer ($400 million divided by 200 million). The cost of fighting a tariff—even writing letters to a few members of Congress—is far greater to the average consumer than the expected benefits. Moreover, each individual consumer is such a small proportion of the total consuming population that he or she might doubt whether any lobbying effort on his or her part will have any real impact. Given the existence of spillover effects in lobbying, the consumer's attitude often is "let someone else do the lobbying." As a consequence,

there are not too many who complain effectively on the consumer side. Using a cost–benefit approach, it pays the producer to lobby for tariffs, but it does not pay the consumer to lobby against them. Thus, many tariffs may be enacted that are not truly in the overall public interest but are rather due to the power of special interests.

WHAT IS AN IMPORT QUOTA?

Despite the fact that the politics of tariffs work in their favor, the benefits of free trade have been sufficiently recognized by citizens and politicians that tariff barriers have been significantly reduced in recent years. The protectionist forces have other weapons to attempt to restrict entry of foreign goods. While tariffs have generally fallen over time, various nontariff barriers have actually increased in use. Chief among these is the **import quota.** An import quota gives producers from another country a maximum number of units of the good in question that can be imported within any given time span. For example, the U.S. government might tell Japanese steel-makers that they can sell no more than 11 million tons of steel a year to the United States, or television-set manufacturers that they can sell no more than 3 million sets. Sometimes these quotas are "voluntary" in that they are negotiated with foreign governments.

The case for quotas is probably even weaker than the case for tariffs. Like tariffs, quotas directly restrict imports, leading to reductions in trade and thus preventing nations from fully realizing their comparative advantage. But tariffs at least use the price system as the basis of restricting trade, while quotas do not. Suppose that the Japanese have been sending 4 million TV sets annually to the United States but now are told that, because of quota restrictions, they can only send 3 million sets. If the Japanese manufacturers are allowed to determine how the quantity reduction is to occur, they will likely collude, leading to higher prices. Suppose that each producer is simply told to reduce sales by 25 percent. They will substantially raise the price of the sets to Americans above what the 4 million original buyers would have paid for them.

DOES THE GOVERNMENT COLLECT REVENUES FROM IMPORT QUOTAS?

Unlike what occurs with a tariff, the U.S. government does not collect any revenue as a result of the import quota. Despite the higher prices, the loss in consumer surplus, and the loss in government revenue, quotas come about because people often view them as being less "protectionist" than tariffs—the traditional, most maligned form of protection.

Besides the rather blunt means of curtailing imports by using tariffs and quotas, nations have devised still other, more subtle means to restrict international trade. For example, nations sometimes impose product standards ostensibly designed to protect consumers against inferior merchandise, but which in effect are sometimes a means to restrict foreign competition. For example, France might keep certain kinds of wine out of the country on the grounds that they were made with allegedly inferior grapes or had an inappropriate alcoholic content. Likewise, the United States might prohibit automobile imports that do not meet certain standards in terms of pollutants, safety, and gasoline mileage. Even if these standards are not intended to restrict foreign competition, the regulations may nonetheless have that impact, restricting consumer choice in the process.

WHAT IS THE ECONOMIC IMPACT OF SUBSIDIES?

Working in the opposite direction, governments sometimes try to encourage exports by subsidizing producers. With a subsidy, revenue is given to producers for each exported unit of output. This stimulates exports. While not a barrier to trade like tariffs and quotas, subsidies can be objected to on the ground that they distort trade patterns and lead to ones that are inefficient. How does this happen? With subsidies, producers will export goods not because their costs are lower than that of a foreign competitor, but because their costs have been artificially reduced by government action transferring income from taxpayers to the exporter. The actual labor, raw material, and capital costs of production are not reduced by the subsidy—society has the same opportunity costs as before. A nation's taxpayers end up subsidizing the output of producers who, relative to producers in other countries, are inefficient. The nation, then, exports products in which it does not have a comparative advantage. Gains from trade in terms of world output are eliminated or reduced by such subsidies. Thus, subsidies, usually defended as a means of increasing exports and improving a nation's international financial position, are usually of dubious worth to the world economy and even to the economy doing the subsidizing.

CONCEPT CHECK

1. A tariff is a tax on imported goods.
2. Tariffs bring about higher prices and revenues to domestic producers, and lower sales and revenues to foreign producers. Tariffs lead to higher prices and reduce consumer surplus for domestic consumers.
3. Arguments for the use of tariffs include: tariffs help infant industries grow, tariffs can reduce domestic unemployment, new tariffs can help finance our international trade, and tariffs are necessary for national security reasons.
4. Like tariffs, import quotas restrict imports, lowering consumer surplus and preventing countries from fully realizing their comparative advantage.
5. Sometimes government tries to encourage production of a certain good by subsidizing its production with taxpayer dollars. Because subsidies stimulate exports, they are not a barrier to trade like tariffs and import quotas. However, they do distort trade patterns and cause overall inefficiencies.

1. Why do tariffs increase domestic producer surplus but decrease domestic consumer surplus?
2. How do import tariffs increase employment in "protected" industries, but at the expense of a likely decrease in employment overall?
3. Why is the national security argument for tariffs questionable?
4. Why is the domestic argument for import quotas weaker than the case for tariffs?
5. Why would foreign producers prefer import quotas to tariffs, even if they resulted in the same reduced level of imports?
6. Why does subsidizing exports by industries that lack a comparative advantage tend to harm the domestic economy, on net?

Ⓔ Application: Common Misperceptions on Trade

In this Module, we have stressed the economic gains associated with trade. However, there are still many skeptics who believe that there is a difference between theory and reality. In particular, they argue that freer trade will lead to problems because of national differences in factor endowments (like cheaper labor) and environmental standards. Professor Jagdish Bhagwati, an expert in international economics, addresses these issues. However, before reading this article, think of the following questions: If labor costs were the sole determining production factor, then why aren't all of the world's products produced in countries like Haiti and Portugal? Why are BMWs and Mercedes Benzs produced in Germany? Why are intricate computer parts produced in the United States?

FAST TRACK: NOT SO FAST

JAGDISH BHAGWATI

- *Trade is "unfair" if trading nations have different pollution and labor standards.* The truth, however, is that a diversity of standards is perfectly legitimate. The reason is simple: Different nations have different conditions and preferences. Thus, if Chile already has cleaner air and worse water than the U.S. does, it would only be sensible for it to have stiffer penalties for polluting water than the U.S., and smaller penalties for polluting air. Different regulatory burdens for an industry in different countries are therefore to be expected.

- *In competing to attract multinationals, countries will lower their standards.* This "race to the bottom" argument says the U.S. must seek harmonized international regulations in order to safeguard our own standards. The empirical evidence for this claim, however, is negligible. In fact, the economist Arik Levinson has shown that multinationals mostly use the most environmentally friendly technology. There are excellent economic reasons, including harm to their reputations, for companies not to exploit weaker standards. In addition, most poor countries are now democratic and have elements of an articulate civil society. It is hard to imagine their elected leaders trying to attract multinationals by inviting them to pollute their nations.

- *Products made with lower labor standards are morally unacceptable.* At first blush, it seems reasonable that we should want to exclude products made, for instance, in sweatshops. Shouldn't we then be able to say we will not trade with countries that fail to conform to our labor standards? Such "values"-based denials of access to the U.S.

market can surely open a Pandora's box, seriously disrupting trade. Because we think only of our values being imposed on others, we fail to see that the single worst aspect of some of our industries would be cited in efforts to curtail their international trade. For instance, many Americans strenuously object to the use of purse seine nets in tuna fishing because they kill dolphins. But what about the crowded U.S. hog farms? Or what if other nations want to suspend U.S. agricultural imports because of abuses against migrant workers in this country? Protectionist interests in other countries would quickly seize on such arguments, causing ever more economic damage.

- *Trade with poor countries is driving down U.S. workers' wages.* By now it has become commonplace to assert that up to 20 percent of the decline in real U.S. wages since the 1970s is due to international trade. Yet nearly all trade economists who have examined the issue conclude the adverse impact is negligible. The conventional view is that U.S. wages must move in tandem with the prices of labor-intensive goods, which are increasingly produced in low-wage countries. Yet my latest research shows that real U.S. wages rose in the 1970s even though the prices of labor-intensive goods produced abroad fell, and U.S. wages fell in the 1980s while these prices rose. Indeed, I conclude that trade with poor countries has likely benefited U.S. workers.

SOURCE: Jagdish Bhagwati, "Fast Track: Not So Fast," *The Wall Street Journal,* September 10, 1997.

The Clinton Administration has garnered some impressive victories in the name of free trade: the North American Free Trade Agreement (NAFTA) and the Uruguay Round of General Agreement on Tariffs and Trade (GATT). However, despite these impressive gains, there are still some important steps that most economists believe should be made. For example, sanctions have been imposed on both Mexico and Canada to protect domestic agricultural interests. In addition, U.S. citrus and sugar producers are among several domestic industries that have the political clout to maintain their tariff protection.

With public sentiment behind the president on NAFTA, this was an excellent opportunity to reduce protectionism in global markets. Individuals are finally realizing that the argument for trade protection based on the notion that world trade has cost us jobs does not sit well with the facts. Furthermore, protection against imports will have the undesirable effect of protecting less productive jobs at the expense of more productive jobs. A typical job that is "saved" costs Americans thousands of dollars.

Should we refuse to trade with countries that fail to conform to U.S. labor standards?

International trade increases our wealth by allowing us to specialize in those products we produce best and trade for those products that others produce best. As Professor Bhagwati points out, some argue that without import restrictions we cannot compete with foreign producers because their costs are too low and because they are government-subsidized. Some products can be produced more cheaply in foreign countries than here. The United States cannot be the most efficient producer of everything. But neither are we the least efficient producer of everything. Indeed, the reason why wages are so low in many foreign countries is that workers are not as productive, lacking capital infrastructure and training.

It is true that foreign producers often receive government subsidies to ship goods to the United States. That is an unfortunate practice because it encourages inefficient production, but it is certainly no reason to fear that we are unable to compete successfully against other countries. It is impossible for a government to subsidize all goods. Subsidizing some goods requires imposing taxes on other goods, and our consumers benefit from lower prices on the subsidized goods.

But won't some people lose their jobs if we take full advantage of international trade? In the short run, yes. Consider, however, that we are a rich country because businesses have been forced to compete for the consumer's dollar by providing better products at lower prices. Every time some firms become more successful in this competition, other firms lose sales and are forced to reduce their work forces. The result is unemployment in the short run but the movement of capital and labor into more valuable employment in the long run.

In short, free trade should facilitate a more efficient economy, faster growth, more high-paying jobs, and higher standards of living. In addition, trade can lower inflationary pressure by increasing the supply of goods and services competing for consumers' dollars. In the case of the automobile, we have seen that free trade and international competition have led to higher quality vehicles.

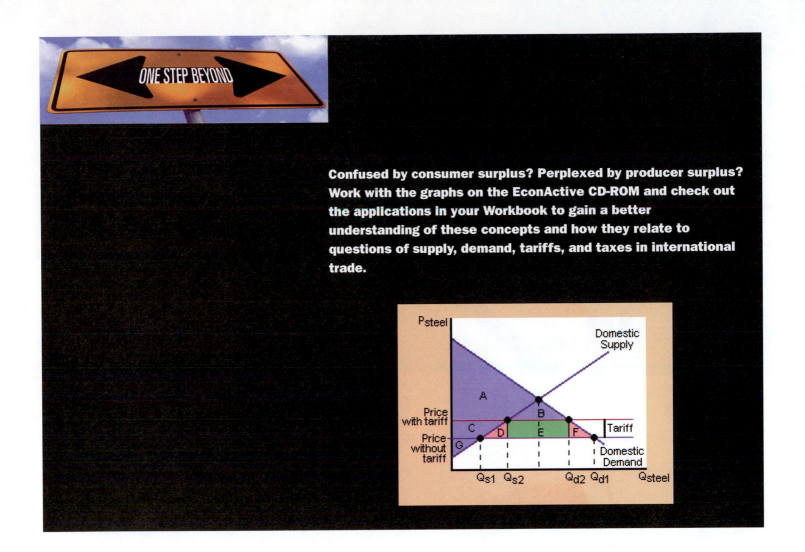

ONE STEP BEYOND

Confused by consumer surplus? Perplexed by producer surplus? Work with the graphs on the EconActive CD-ROM and check out the applications in your Workbook to gain a better understanding of these concepts and how they relate to questions of supply, demand, tariffs, and taxes in international trade.

PHOTO CREDITS MODULE 25

Page **598**: left, AP Photo/Chiaki Tsukoms, right, Harcourt Brace; Page **599**: World Trade Magazine; Page **602**: © Bill Bachmann/Stock, Boston/PNI; Page **607**: BERRY'S WORLD reprinted by permission of United Feature Syndicate; Page **614**: © Owen Franken/Stock Boston/PNI

International Finance

A The Balance of Payments

- What is the balance of payments?
- What are the three main components of the balance of payments?
- What is the balance of trade?
- What are the four types of official reserve assets?

WHAT IS THE BALANCE OF PAYMENTS?

The record of all of the international financial transactions of a nation over a year is called the **balance of payments**. The balance of payments is a statement that records all the exchanges those in a nation engaged in that required an outflow of funds to foreign nations or an inflow of funds from other nations. Just as an examination of gross domestic product accounts gives us some idea of the economic health and vitality of a nation, the balance of payments provides information about a nation's world trade position. The balance of payments is divided into three main sections: the current account, the capital account, and the official reserve assets. It also includes an "error term" called the statistical discrepancy.

WHAT IS THE CURRENT ACCOUNT?

The current account is made up of current imports and exports of goods and services. Any time a foreign buyer buys a good from a U.S. producer, the foreign buyer must pay the U.S. producer for the good. Usually, the foreigner must pay for the good in U.S. dollars, because the seller wants to pay for his workers and other inputs with dollars. This requires the foreign buyer to exchange units of his currency at a foreign exchange dealer for U.S. dollars. Because the United States gains claims over foreign buyers by obtaining foreign currency in exchange for the dollars needed to buy exports, all exports of U.S. goods abroad are considered a credit or plus (+) item in the U.S. balance of payments. Those foreign currencies are later exchangeable for goods and services made in the country that purchased the U.S. exports.

HOW DO IMPORTS AFFECT THE CURRENT ACCOUNT?

When a U.S. consumer buys an imported good, however, the reverse is true: The U.S. importer must pay the foreign producer, usually in that nation's currency. Typically, the U.S. buyer will go to a foreign exchange dealer and exchange dollars for units of that foreign currency. Imports are thus a debit (–) item in the balance of payments, because the dollars sold to buy the foreign currency add to foreign claims against U.S. buyers, which are later exchangeable for goods and services made in the U.S. Our imports, then, provide the means by which foreigners can buy our exports.

HOW DO SERVICES AFFECT THE CURRENT ACCOUNT?

While imports and exports of merchandise (goods) are the largest components of the balance of payments, they are not the only ones. Nations import and export services as well. A particularly important service is tourism. When a tourist from the U.S. goes abroad, he or she is buying foreign-produced services in addition to those purchased by citizens there. Those services include the use of hotels, sightseeing tours, restaurants, and so forth. In the current account, these services are included in imports. On the other hand, foreign tourism in the United States provides us with foreign currencies and claims against foreigners, so they are included in exports. Airline and shipping services also affect the balance of payments. When someone from Italy flies American Airlines, that person is making a payment to a U.S. company. Because the flow of international financial claims is the same, this payment is treated just like a U.S. merchandise export in the balance of payments. If an American flies on Alitalia, however, Italians acquire claims against the U.S., and so it is included as a debit (import) item in the U.S. balance of payments accounts.

WHAT ELSE AFFECTS THE CURRENT ACCOUNT?

Another major type of import or export expenditure is income from financial investments. These payments can be viewed as compensation for the use of capital services. In the past, the United States has made huge financial

How is the current account affected when a foreign tourist rides a sightseeing bus in the United States?

porting capital services. Similarly, when a foreign company, such as Royal Dutch Shell or Mercedes Benz makes profits in the United States, they obtain their profits in dollars. This creates claims against the United States and is recorded as a debit item in the U.S. balance of payments, similar to the import of merchandise.

HOW DOES THE GOVERNMENT AFFECT THE CURRENT ACCOUNT?

One other item that affects the current account is government grants to other countries. When the U.S. gives foreign aid to another country, this creates a debit in the U.S. balance of payments because it gives foreigners added claims against the United States in the form of dollars. Private donations, such as individuals sending money to relatives or friends in foreign countries, shows up in the current account as debit items as well.

WHAT IS THE BALANCE ON CURRENT ACCOUNT?

The balance on current account is the net amount of credits or debits after adding up all transactions of goods (merchandise imports and exports), services (including investment income), and fund transfers (e.g., foreign aid). If the sum of credits exceeds the sum of debits, the nation is said to run a balance of payments surplus on current account. If debits exceed credits, however, the nation is running a balance of payment deficit on current account.

investments abroad, both through the establishment of U.S. corporations overseas and by purchasing securities of foreign business enterprises or governments. By doing this, the U.S. obtains claims on foreign countries just as it does when it exports goods, only in this case, we are ex-

HOW IS THE BALANCE OF TRADE RELATED TO THE BALANCE ON CURRENT ACCOUNT?

The balance of payments of the United States for 1996 is presented in Exhibit 1. Note that exports and imports of

EXHIBIT 1	U.S. BALANCE OF PAYMENTS, 1996 (BILLIONS OF DOLLARS)

Type of Transaction

Current Account		Capital Account	
1. Merchandise exports	$612	7. U.S. capital inflow	$547
2. Merchandise imports	−803	8. U.S. capital outflow	−351
Balance of Trade (lines 1–2)	−191	Capital Account Balance (lines 7–8)	194
3. Service exports	237	9. Statistical discrepancy	−46
4. Service imports	−157	Net Balance (lines 1–9)	0
5. Investment income (net)	3		
6. Unilateral transfers (net)	−40		
Current Account Balance (lines 1–6)	−148		

SOURCE: *Survey of Current Business*, May 1998, Table F.3, p. D-53.

goods and services are by far the largest credits and debits. Note also that the U.S. merchandise exports were $191 billion less than merchandise imports. The merchandise import/export relationship is often called the balance of trade. The U.S. therefore experienced a balance of trade deficit that year of $191 billion. A historical balance on current account table is presented in Exhibit 2. How could the U.S. buy more goods abroad than it sold? Note that total imports were only $108 billion more than total exports, because a good deal of the $191 billion trade deficit was offset by credits from an $80 billion surplus in service exports and $3 billion in net investment income. Then, when $40 billion of net unilateral transfers from the U.S. is included, the total deficit on current account was $148 billion.

WHAT IS THE CAPITAL ACCOUNT?

How was this deficit on current account financed? Remember that U.S. credits give us the financial means to buy foreign goods, and that our credits were $194 billion less than our debits from our imports and net unilateral transfers to foreign countries. This deficit on current account balance is settled by movements of financial, or capital, assets. These transactions are recorded in the capital account, so that a current account deficit is financed by a capital account surplus.

WHAT DOES THE CAPITAL ACCOUNT RECORD?

These capital account transactions include items such as international bank loans, purchases of corporate securities, government bond purchases, and direct investments in

foreign subsidiary companies. In 1996, the U.S. made new foreign financial investments of nearly $351 billion, which was a further debit because it provided foreigners with U.S. dollars. On the other hand, foreign investments in the U.S. were over $547 billion, most of which were purchases of U.S. government securities. On net, then, foreigners made about $194 billion more new financial investments in the U.S. than Americans did abroad. On balance, then, there was a surplus (positive credit) in the Capital account from capital movements of $194 billion, offsetting the $148 billion deficit on current account.

WHAT IS THE STATISTICAL DISCREPANCY?

In the final analysis, it is true that the balance of payments account must balance so that credits and debits are equal. Why is this so? Due to the reciprocal aspect of trade, every credit eventually creates a debit of equal magnitude. But, in 1996, the measured $194 net capital inflow didn't match the measured $148 deficit on current account. If debits and credits do not come out equal, as in 1996, it is because of some errors and/or omissions of accounting. These errors are often rather large ($46 billion, or $194 billion minus $148 billion, in 1996), and are entered into the balance of payments as the statistical discrepancy. Including the errors and omissions recorded as the statistical discrepancy, the balance of payments do balance.

HOW DO NATIONS MEET THEIR BALANCE OF PAYMENTS DEFICITS?

Transactions are used to equalize a nation's balance of payments account and provide debits equal to credits. For example, if the U.S. lacks adequate foreign currency to meet its international financial requirements, it can seek to borrow funds from other countries or from an international financial institution. In this manner, nations with balance of payments difficulties have often gone to nations with balance of payments surpluses and borrowed from them to meet their deficit.

Balance of Payments: A Useful Analogy

The international balance of payments is very similar conceptually to the personal financial transactions of individuals. Each individual has his own "balance of payments," reflecting his trading with other economic units: other individuals, corporations, or governments. People earn income or credits by "exporting" their labor service to other economic units, or by receiving investment income (a return on capital services). Against that, they "import" goods from other economic units; we call these imports "consumption." This debit

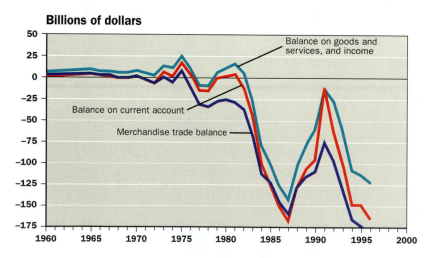

| EXHIBIT 2 | U.S. BALANCE OF TRADE, 1960–1996 |

Billions of dollars

SOURCE: Chart prepared by the U.S. Bureau of the Census.

item is sometimes augmented by payments made to outsiders (e.g., banks) on loans, and so forth. Fund transfers, such as gifts to children or charities, are other debit items (or credit items if persons are recipients of this assistance).

As individuals, if our spending on our consumption exceeds our income from our exports of our labor and capital services, we have a "deficit" that must be financed by borrowing or selling assets. If we "export" more than we "import," however, we can make new investments and/or increase our "reserves" (savings and investment holdings). Like nations, individuals who run a deficit in daily transactions must make up for it through accommodating transactions (e.g., borrowing or reducing one's savings or investment holdings) to bring about an ultimate balance of credits and debits to their personal account.

TUNE UP

TRADE GAPS

Q: Would a trade deficit widen if domestic consumer confidence picked up?

A: The increase in consumer confidence in the domestic economy will lead to an increase in demand for domestic and foreign goods. Holding the other economies of the world constant in the short run, this would widen the trade deficit.

CONCEPT CHECK

1. The balance of payments is the record of all the international financial transactions of a nation for any given year.
2. The balance of payments is made up of the current account, the capital account, as well as an "error term" called the statistical discrepancy.
3. The balance of trade refers strictly to the imports and exports of merchandise (goods) with other nations. If our imports of foreign goods are greater than our exports, we are said to have a balance of trade deficit.

1. What is the balance of payments?
2. Why would a British purchaser of U.S. goods or services have to first exchange pounds for dollars?
3. How is it true that U.S. imports provide the means by which foreigners can buy U.S. exports?
4. What would have to be true in order for the U.S. to have a balance of trade deficit and a balance of payments surplus?
5. What would have to be true in order for the U.S. to have a balance of trade surplus and a current account deficit?
6. If there are no errors or omissions in the recorded balance of payments accounts, what should the statistical discrepancy equal?
7. A Nigerian family visiting Chicago enjoys a Chicago Cubs baseball game at Wrigley Field. How would that expense be recorded in the balance of payments accounts? Why?

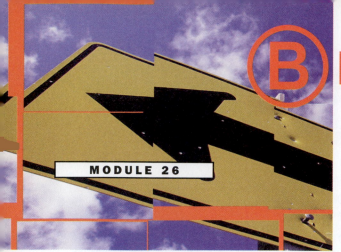

(B) Exchange Rates

- What are exchange rates?
- How are exchange rates determined?
- How do exchange rates affect the demand for foreign goods?

WHY DO WE NEED FOREIGN CURRENCIES?

When U.S. consumers buy goods from persons in other countries, the sellers of those goods want to be paid in their own domestic currencies. The U.S. consumers, then, must first exchange U.S. dollars for the seller's currency in order to pay for those goods. American importers must therefore constantly buy yen, Euros, pesos, and other currencies in order to finance their purchases. Similarly, persons in other countries buying goods made in the United States must sell their currencies to obtain U.S. dollars in order to pay for those goods.

WHAT ARE EXCHANGE RATES?

The price of a unit of one foreign currency in terms of another is called the **exchange rate.** If an importer in the U.S. has agreed to pay Euros (the new currency of the European Union) to buy a cuckoo clock made in the Black Forest in Germany, he or she would then have to exchange U.S. dollars for Euros. If it takes $1.00 to buy one Euro, then the exchange rate is $1.00 per Euro. From the German perspective, the exchange rate is one Euro per U.S. dollar.

HOW DO CHANGES IN EXCHANGE RATES AFFECT THE DOMESTIC DEMAND FOR FOREIGN GOODS?

Prices of goods in their currencies combine with exchange rates to determine the domestic price of foreign goods. Suppose the cuckoo clock sells for 100 Euros in Germany. What is the price to U.S. consumers? Let us assume that tariffs and other transactions costs are zero. If the exchange rate is $1 = 1 Euro, then the equivalent U.S. dollar price of the cuckoo clock is 100 Euros times $1 per Euro, or $100. If the exchange rate were to change to $2 = 1 Euro, fewer clocks would be demanded in the United States. This is be-

cause the effective U.S. dollar price of the clocks would rise to $200 (100 Euros times $2 per Euro). The new higher relative value of a Euro compared to the dollar (or equiva-

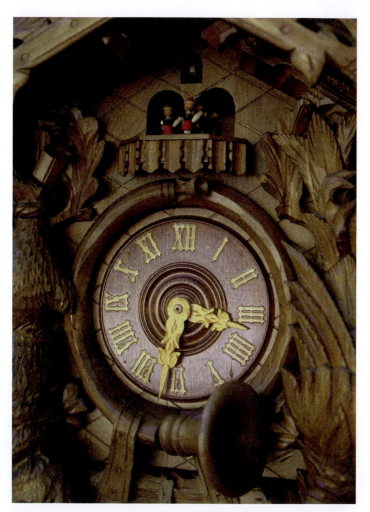

If the Euro becomes relatively more expensive in terms of dollars (it costs more dollars to buy a Euro), what will happen to the domestic demand for European goods?

lently, the lower the relative value of a dollar compared to the Euro) would lead to a reduction in U.S. demand for German-made clocks.

HOW DO CHANGES IN THE DEMAND FOR GOODS AFFECT EXCHANGE RATES?

The demand for foreign currencies is what economists call a derived demand. This is because the demand for a foreign currency derives directly from the demand for foreign goods and services or for foreign capital. The more foreign goods are demanded, the more of that foreign currency that will be needed to pay for those goods. Such an increased demand for the currency will push up the exchange value of that currency relative to other currencies.

WHAT DETERMINES THE SUPPLY OF A FOREIGN CURRENCY?

Similarly, the supply of foreign currency is provided by foreigners who want to buy the exports of a particular nation. For example, the more that foreigners demand U.S. products, the more of their currencies they will supply in exchange for U.S. dollars, which they use to buy our products.

HOW ARE EXCHANGE RATES DETERMINED?

We know that the demand for foreign currencies is derived from the demand for foreign goods, but how does that af-

How is the equilibrium price of the Euro determined?

fect the exchange rate? Just as in the product market, the answer lies with the forces of supply and demand. In this case, it is the supply of and demand for a foreign currency that determine the equilibrium price (exchange rate) of that currency.

WHY DOES THE DEMAND CURVE FOR A FOREIGN CURRENCY SLOPE DOWNWARD?

As Exhibit 1 shows, the demand curve for a foreign currency—Euros, for example—is downward sloping, just as it is in product markets. In this case, however, the demand curve has a negative slope because as the price of the Euro falls relative to the dollar, European products become relatively more inexpensive to U.S. consumers, who therefore buy more European goods. To do so, the quantity of Euros demanded by U.S. consumers will increase to buy more European goods as the price of the Euro falls. This is why the demand for foreign currencies is considered to be a derived demand.

WHY DOES THE SUPPLY CURVE FOR FOREIGN CURRENCY SLOPE UPWARD?

The supply curve for a foreign currency is upward sloping, also just as it is in product markets. In this case, as the price, or value, of the Euro increases relative to the dollar, American products will become relatively more inexpensive to European buyers and increase the quantity of dollars they demand. Europeans will, therefore, increase the quantity of Euros supplied to the U.S. by buying more U.S. products. Hence, the supply curve is upward sloping. (Note: The supply curve here is upward sloping because we have assumed that the European demand for U.S. goods is price elastic.)

WHERE IS EQUILIBRIUM IN THE FOREIGN EXCHANGE MARKET?

Equilibrium is reached where the demand and supply curves for a given currency intersect. In Exhibit 1, equilibrium price of a Euro is $1.20. As in the product market, if the dollar price of Euros is higher than the equilibrium price, there will be an excess quantity of Euros supplied at that price, or a surplus of Euros, and competition among Euro sellers will push the price of Euros down toward equilibrium. Likewise, if the dollar price of Euros is lower than the equilibrium price, there will be an excess quantity of Euros demanded at that price, or a shortage of Euros. Competition among Euro buyers will push the price of Euros up toward equilibrium.

EXHIBIT 1 — EQUILIBRIUM IN THE FOREIGN EXCHANGE MARKET

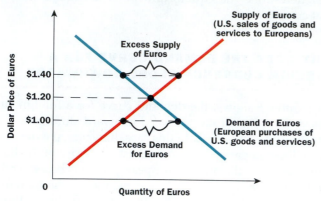

The foreign exchange market is in equilibrium at 1 Euro = $1.20. At any price higher than $1.20, there will be a surplus of Euros. At any price lower than $1.20, there will be a shortage of Euros.

EXCHANGE RATES

Q: Why is a strong dollar a mixed blessing?

A: A strong dollar will lower the price of imports and make trips to foreign countries less expensive. However, it makes U.S. exports more expensive. Consequently, foreigners will buy fewer U.S. goods and services. The net effect is a fall in exports and a rise in imports—net exports fall. Note that some Americans are helped (vacationers going to foreign countries and those preferring foreign goods), while others are harmed (producers of U.S. exports, operators of hotels dependent on foreign visitors in the U.S.).

CONCEPT CHECK

1. The exchange rate is the price in one country's currency of one unit of another country's currency.
2. The exchange rate for a currency is determined by the supply of and demand for that currency in the foreign exchange market.
3. If the dollar appreciates in value relative to foreign currencies, foreign goods become more inexpensive to U.S. consumers, increasing U.S. demand for foreign goods.

---

1. What is an exchange rate?
2. When a U.S. dollar buys relatively more French francs, why does the cost of imports from France fall in the U.S.?
3. When a U.S. dollar buys relatively fewer Austrian shillings, why does the cost of U.S. exports fall in Austria?
4. How does an increase in domestic demand for foreign goods and services increase the demand for those foreign currencies?
5. As Euros get cheaper relative to U.S. dollars, why does the quantity of Euros demanded by Americans increase? Why doesn't the demand for Euros increase as a result?
6. Who competes exchange rates down when they are above their equilibrium value? Who competes exchange rates up when they are below their equilibrium value?

Equilibrium Changes in the Foreign Exchange Market

- What factors cause the demand curve for a currency to shift?
- What factors cause the supply curve for a currency to shift?

WHAT FACTORS SHIFT THE DEMAND FOR AND SUPPLY OF A CURRENCY?

The equilibrium exchange rate of a currency changes many times daily. Sometimes, these changes can be quite significant. Any force that shifts either the demand for or supply of a currency will shift the equilibrium in the foreign exchange market, leading to a new exchange rate. These factors include changes in tastes for goods, changes in income, changes in relative real interest rates, and changes in relative inflation rates.

HOW DO TASTE CHANGES AFFECT THE EQUILIBRIUM EXCHANGE RATE?

Because the demand for foreign currencies is derived from the demand for foreign goods, any change in the demand for foreign goods will shift the demand schedule for foreign currency in the same direction. For example, if a cuckoo clock revolution sweeps through the U.S., German producers would have reason to celebrate, knowing that many U.S. buyers will turn to Germany for their cuckoo clocks. The Germans, however, will only accept payment in the form of Euros, and so U.S. consumers and retailers must convert their dollars into Euros before they can purchase their clocks. The increased tastes for European goods in the U.S. would, therefore, lead to an increased demand for Euros. As shown in Exhibit 1, this increased demand for Euros shifts the demand curve to the right, resulting in a new, higher equilibrium price for Euros.

HOW DO CHANGES IN INCOME OR REDUCTIONS IN U.S. TARIFFS AFFECT THE EQUILIBRIUM EXCHANGE RATE?

Any change in the average income of U.S. consumers will also change the equilibrium exchange rate, *ceteris paribus*.

If on the whole, incomes increased in the U.S., Americans would buy more goods, including imported goods, so more European goods would be bought. This increased demand for European goods would lead to an increased demand for Euros, resulting in a higher exchange rate for Euros. A decrease in U.S. tariffs on European goods would tend to have the same affect as an increase in incomes by making European goods more affordable. As Exhibit 1 shows, this would again lead to an increased demand for European goods and a higher short-run equilibrium exchange rate for Euros.

EXHIBIT 1	IMPACT OF U.S. TASTE OR INCOME INCREASE, OR TARIFF DECREASE, ON THE FOREIGN EXCHANGE MARKET

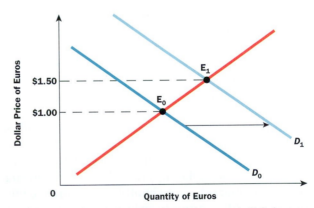

An increase in taste for European goods, an increase in U.S. income, and a decrease in U.S. tariffs all have the potential to cause an increase in demand for Euros, shifting the demand for Euros to the right and leading to a higher equilibrium exchange rate.

What impact will an increase in travel to Paris by U.S. consumers have on the Euro?

WHAT IF EUROPEAN TASTES, TARIFFS, OR INCOME CHANGED?

If European incomes rose, European tariffs on U.S. goods fell, or their tastes for American goods increased, the supply of Euros in the Euro foreign exchange market would increase. Any of these changes would cause Europeans to demand more U.S. goods, and therefore more U.S. dollars in order to purchase those goods. To obtain those added dollars, Europeans must exchange more of their Euros, increasing the supply of Euros on the Euro foreign exchange market. As Exhibit 2 demonstrates, the effect of this would be a rightward shift in the Euro supply curve, leading to a new equilibrium at a lower exchange rate for Euros.

HOW DO CHANGES IN INTEREST RATES AFFECT EXCHANGE RATES?

If interest rates in the United States were to increase relative to say European interest rates, other things equal, the rate of return on U.S. investments would increase relative to that on European investments. European investors would thus increase their demand for U.S. investments, and therefore offer Euros for sale to buy dollars to buy U.S. investments, shifting the supply curve for Euros to the right, from S_0 to S_1 in Exhibit 3.

In this scenario, U.S. investors would also shift their investments away from Europe by decreasing their demand for Euros relative to their demand for dollars, from D_0 to D_1 in Exhibit 3. Exhibit 3 shows the subsequent lower equilibrium price ($1.50) that would result for the Euro due to an increase in the U.S. interest rate. That is, there will be a depreciation of the Euro because Euros can now buy fewer units of dollars than before. In short, the higher interest rate in the United States attracted more capital to the U.S. and led to a relative appreciation of the dollar and a relative depreciation of the Euro.

HOW DO CHANGES IN THE RELATIVE INFLATION RATES AFFECT THE EQUILIBRIUM EXCHANGE RATE?

If Europe experienced an inflation rate greater than that experienced in the United States, other things equal, what would happen to the exchange rate? In this case, European products would become more expensive to U.S. consumers. Americans would decrease the quantity of European goods demanded and, therefore, decrease their demand for Euros. The result would be a leftward shift of the demand curve for Euros.

On the other side of the Atlantic, U.S. goods would become relatively cheaper to Europeans, leading Europeans to increase the quantity of U.S. goods demanded, and therefore, to demand more U.S. dollars. This increased demand for dollars translates into an increased supply of Euros, shifting the supply curve for Euros outward. Exhibit 4 shows the shifts of the supply and demand curves and the new lower equilibrium price for the Euro resulting from the higher European rate.

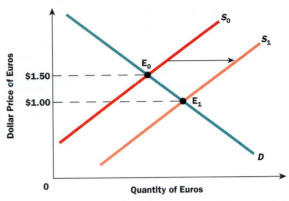

| EXHIBIT 2 | IMPACT OF EUROPEAN TASTE OR INCOME INCREASE, OR TARIFF DECREASE, ON THE FOREIGN EXCHANGE MARKET |

If European incomes increased, European tariffs on U.S. goods fell, or European tastes for American goods increased, the supply of Euros would increase. The increase in demand for dollars would cause an increase in the supply of Euros, shifting it to the right, from S_0 to S_1.

| EXHIBIT 3 | IMPACT OF U.S. INTEREST RATE INCREASE ON THE FOREIGN EXCHANGE MARKET |

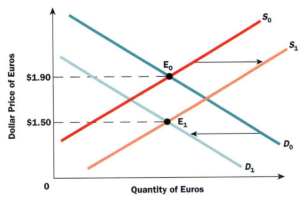

When interest rates increase in the United States, European investors will increase their supply of Euros to buy dollars—the supply curve of Euros increases from S_0 to S_1. In addition, U.S. investors will also shift their investments away from Europe, decreasing their demand for Euros and shifting the demand curve from D_0 to D_1. This will lead to a depreciation of the Euro; that is, Euros can now buy fewer units of dollars.

| EXHIBIT 4 | IMPACT OF EUROPEAN INFLATION RATE INCREASE ON THE FOREIGN EXCHANGE MARKET |

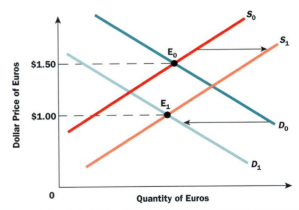

If Europe experienced a higher inflation rate than the U.S., European products would become more expensive to U.S. consumers. As a result, those consumers would demand fewer Euros, shifting the demand for Euros to the left, from D_0 to D_1. At the same time, U.S. goods would become relatively cheaper to Europeans, who would then buy more dollars by supplying Euros, shifting the Euro supply curve to the right, from S_0 to S_1. The result: a new lower equilibrium price for the Euro.

BIG MACCURRENCIES

As the yen plunges and sterling soars, economists are being forced to revise their currency forecasts. To help them get their teeth into the subject, The Economist has updated its Big Mac index, which seeks to make exchange-rate theory a bit more digestible.

The Big Mac index is based upon the theory of purchasing-power parity (PPP), the notion that a dollar should buy the same amount in all countries. That is, the exchange rate between any two currencies reflects the differences in the price level. In the long run, purchasing power parity theory states that the exchange rate between two currencies should move towards the rate that would equalize the prices of an identical basket of goods and services in each country. Many economists believe that there are many factors that are more important than the price level in exchange rate determination in the short run. However, in the long run, purchasing power parity is very important in exchange rate determination.

Our "basket" is a McDonald's Big Mac, produced in 110 countries. The Big Mac PPP is the exchange rate that would leave hamburgers costing the same in America as abroad. Comparing actual rates with PPPs signals whether a currency is under- or overvalued.

The first column of the table shows local-currency prices of a Big Mac; the second converts the prices into dollars. The cheapest Big Macs are now in Indonesia and Malaysia, where they cost $1.16. At the other extreme, Big Mac fans in Switzerland have to pay $3.87. Given that Americans in four cities pay an average of $2.56, the rupiah and the ringgit look massively undervalued, the Swiss franc massively overvalued.

The third column calculates Big Mac PPPs. For example, dividing the Japanese price by the American price gives a dollar PPP of ¥109. On April 6th, the exchange rate was ¥135, implying that the yen is 19% undervalued against the dollar. Three years ago the index suggested that the yen was 100% overvalued against the dollar. Likewise, the D-mark is now only 5% overvalued, against 50% in April 1995.

Thanks to the dollar's rise—long predicted by burgernomics—it is now closer to its PPP against other big currencies than for many years. Indeed, only five currencies in the table are now significantly overvalued against the greenback, among them Britain's, Sweden's, and Denmark's. All three countries have decided not to adopt Europe's single currency, the Euro, next year. The pound is 19% overvalued against the dollar, which implies it is 14% overvalued against the D-mark. In contrast, the currencies of the Euro-block countries are close to Mcparity against the D-mark.

The most dramatic changes in the index over the past year are in East Asia, where devaluations have left currencies significantly undervalued. This competitive advantage, however, is being eroded by inflation. In Indonesia, the price of a Big Mac has more than doubled over the past year. East European currencies also look cheap, with the Hungarian forint 52% undervalued against the dollar.

The Big Mac index is not a perfect measure of PPP. Price differences may be distorted by trade barriers on beef, sales taxes, local competition and changes in the cost of non-traded inputs such as rents. But despite its flaws, the Big Mac index produces PPP estimates close to those derived by more sophisticated methods. A currency can deviate from PPP for long periods, but several studies have found that the Big Mac PPP is a useful predictor of future movements—enabling the hungry investor to get rich by putting his money where his mouth is.

SOURCE: http://www.economist.com/editorial/justforyou/11-4-98/fn7226.html

---

CONSIDER THIS:
Since 1989, *The Economist* magazine has been tracking the values of different currencies around the world with their "Big Mac index." This index is based on the theory of purchasing power parity (PPP). This theory suggests that one unit of currency (a dollar) would buy the same amount of a traded good anywhere in the world. PPP therefore suggests that a Big Mac, for example, should cost the same amount of dollars all around the world. The index shows, however, that this is not the case.

EXHIBIT 5	BIG MAC INDEX

The hamburger standard

	Big Mac prices		Implied PPP* of the dollar	Actual $ exchange rate 6/4/98	Under (-)/over(+) valuation against dollar, %
	in local currency	in dollars			
United States†	**$2.56**	**2.56**	–	–	–
Argentina	Peso2.50	2.50	0.98	1.00	-2
Australia	A$2.65	1.75	1.04	1.51	-32
Austria	Sch34.0	2.62	13.28	12.96	+2
Belgium	BFr109	2.87	42.58	38.00	+12
Brazil	Real3.10	2.72	1.21	1.14	+6
Britain	£1.84	3.05	1.39‡	1.66‡	+19
Canada	C$2.79	1.97	1.09	1.42	-23
Chile	Peso1,250	2.75	488	455	+7
China	Yuan9.90	1.20	3.87	8.28	-53
Czech Republic	CKr54.0	1.57	21.1	34.4	-39
Denmark	DKr23.8	3.39	9.28	7.02	+32
France	FFr17.5	2.84	6.84	6.17	+11
Germany	DM4.95	2.69	1.93	1.84	+5
Hong Kong	HK$10.2	1.32	3.98	7.75	-49
Hungary	Forint259	1.22	101	213	-52
Indonesia	Rupiah9,900	1.16	3,867	8,500	-55
Israel	Shekel12.50	3.38	4.88	3.70	+32
Italy	Lire4,500	2.47	1,758	1,818	-3
Japan	¥280	2.08	109	135	-19
Malaysia	M$4.30	1.16	1.68	3.72	-55
Mexico	Peso17.9	2.10	6.99	8.54	-18
Netherlands	Fl5.45	2.63	2.13	2.07	+3
New Zealand	NZ$3.45	1.90	1.35	1.82	-26
Poland	Zloty5.30	1.53	2.07	3.46	-40
Russia	Rouble12,000	2.00	4,688	5,999	-22
Singapore	S$3.00	1.85	1.17	1.62	-28
South Africa	Rand8.00	1.59	3.13	5.04	-38
South Korea	Won2,600	1.76	1,016	1,474	-31
Spain	Pta375	2.40	146	156	-6
Sweden	SKr24.0	3.00	9.38	8.00	+17
Switzerland	SFr5.90	3.87	2.30	1.52	+51
Taiwan	NT$68.0	2.06	26.6	33.0	-20
Thailand	Baht52.0	1.30	20.3	40.0	-49

*Purchasing-power parity: local price divided by price in United States
†Average of New York, Chicago, San Francisco and Atlanta   ‡Dollars per pound
Source: McDonald's

TUNE UP

DETERMINANTS OF EXCHANGE RATES

Q: How will the following events impact the foreign exchange market?

 A. American travel to Europe increases.

 B. Japanese investors' money flows into U.S. stock market.

 C. U.S. real interest rates abruptly increase relative to world interest rates.

 D. Other countries become less political and economically stable than the United States.

A: A. Demand for Euro increases (demand shifts right in the Euro market), the dollar will depreciate and the Euro will appreciate, *ceteris paribus.*

 B. Demand for dollars increases (demand shifts right in the dollar market), the dollar will appreciate and the Yen will depreciate, *ceteris paribus.* Alternatively, you could think of this as an increase in supply in the yen market.

 C. International investors will increase their demand for dollars in the dollar market to take advantage of the higher interest rate. The dollar would appreciate relative to other foreign currencies, *ceteris paribus.*

 D. More foreign investors will want to buy U.S. assets, causing an increase in demand for dollars.

CONCEPT CHECK

1. Any force that shifts either the demand or supply curves for a foreign currency will shift the equilibrium in the foreign exchange market and lead to a new exchange rate.

2. Any changes in tastes, income levels, relative real interest rates, or relative inflation rates will cause the demand for and supply of a currency to shift.

1. Why will the exchange value of a foreign currency relative to U.S. dollars decline when U.S. domestic tastes change, reducing the demand for foreign-produced goods?

2. Why does the demand for foreign currencies shift in the same direction as domestic income? What happens to the exchange value of those foreign currencies in terms of dollars?

3. How would increased U.S. tariffs on imported European goods affect the exchange value of Euros in terms of dollars?

4. Why do changes in tastes, incomes, or tariffs in the U.S. change the demand for Euros, while similar changes in Europe change the supply of Euros?

5. What would happen to the exchange value of Euros in terms of U.S. dollars if incomes rose in both Europe and the U.S.?

6. Why does an increase in interest rates in Germany relative to U.S. interest rates increase the demand for Euros but decrease their supply?

7. What would an increase in U.S. inflation relative to Europe do to the supply and demand for Euros and to the equilibrium exchange value (price) of Euros in terms of U.S. dollars?

D Flexible Exchange Rates

MODULE 26

- How are exchange rates determined today?
- How are exchange rate changes different under a flexible-rate system than in a fixed system?
- What major problems exist in a fixed-rate system?
- What are the major arguments against flexible rates?

HOW WAS THE FLEXIBLE EXCHANGE RATE SYSTEM DEVELOPED?

Since 1973, the world has essentially operated on a system of flexible exchange rates. Flexible exchange rates mean that currency prices are allowed to fluctuate with changes in supply and demand, without governments stepping in to prevent those changes. Before that, governments operated under what was called the Bretton Woods fixed exchange rate system, in which they would maintain a stable exchange rate by buying or selling currencies or reserves to bring demand and supply for their currencies together at the fixed exchange rate. The present system evolved out of the Bretton Woods fixed-rate system, and occurred by accident, not design. Governments were unable to agree on an alternative fixed-rate approach when the Bretton Woods system collapsed, so nations simply let market forces determine currency values.

ARE EXCHANGE RATES MANAGED AT ALL?

To be sure, governments sensitive to sharp changes in the exchange value of their currencies do still intervene from time to time to prop up their currency's exchange rate was if it considered to be too low or falling too rapidly, or to depress its exchange rate if it was considered to be too high or rising too rapidly. Such was the case as the U.S. dollar declined in value in the late 1970s, but the U.S. government intervention appeared to have little if any effect in preventing the dollar's decline. However, present-day fluctuations in exchange rates are not determined solely by market forces. Economists sometimes say that the current exchange rate system is a "dirty float" system, meaning that fluctuations in currency values are partly determined by market forces and partly influenced by government intervention. Over the years, however, such governmental support attempts have been insufficient to dramatically alter exchange rates for long, and currency exchange rates have changed dramatically. These rather drastic fluctuations in exchange rates are indicated in Exhibit 1, which shows how exchange rates for the U.S. dollar have changed over the years.

HOW DO THESE CHANGES AFFECT TRADE?

When exchange rates change, they affect not only the currency market but the product markets as well. For example, if U.S. consumers were to receive fewer and fewer British pounds and Japanese yen per U.S. dollar, the effect would be an increasing price of foreign imports, *ceteris paribus*, because it would now take a greater number of dollars to buy a given number of yen or pounds, which U.S. consumers use to purchase those foreign products. It would, however, lower the cost of U.S. exports to foreigners. And if the dollar increased in value relative to other currencies, then this would lower the relative price of foreign goods, *ceteris paribus*. However, foreigners would find that U.S. goods were more expensive in terms of their own currency prices, and, as a result, would import fewer U.S. products.

WHAT ARE THE ADVANTAGES OF FLEXIBLE RATES?

As mentioned earlier, the present system of flexible exchange rates was not planned. Indeed, most central bankers thought that a system where rates were not fixed would lead to chaos. What in fact has happened? Since the advent of flexible exchange rates, world trade has not only continued, but expanded. Over a one-year time period, the world economy adjusted to the shock of a four-fold increase in the price of its most important internationally traded commodity, oil. Although the OPEC oil cartel's price increase certainly had adverse economic impacts, it did so without paralyzing the economy of any one nation.

The most important advantage of the flexible-rate system is that the recurrent crises that led to speculative rampages and major currency revaluations under the fixed Bretton Woods system have significantly diminished. Under the fixed-rate system, price changes in currencies

Japanese Yen per U.S. Dollar

German Marks per U.S. Dollar

British Pound in U.S. Dollars

SOURCE: *The Wall Street Journal Almanac*, 1998, p. 361.

came infrequently, but when they came, they were of a large magnitude: 20 or 30 percent changes overnight were fairly common. Today, price changes occur daily or even hourly, but each change is much smaller in magnitude, with major changes in exchange rates typically occurring only over periods of months or years.

HOW CAN FIXED EXCHANGE RATES LEAD TO CURRENCY SHORTAGES?

Perhaps the most significant problem with the fixed-rate system is that it can result in currency shortages, just as

domestic price and wage controls lead to shortages. Suppose we had a fixed-rate system with the price of one Euro set at $1.00, as shown in Exhibit 2. In this example, the original quantity of Euros demanded and supplied is indicated by curves D_0 and S, so that $1.00 is the equilibrium price. That is, at a price of $1.00, the quantity of Euros demanded (by U.S. importers of European products and others wanting Euros) equals the quantity supplied (by European importers of U.S. products and others).

Suppose that some event happens to increase U.S. demand for Dutch goods. For this example, let us assume that Royal Dutch Shell discovers new oil reserves in the North Sea and thus has a new product to export. As U.S.

Under a flexible-rate system, small changes in exchange rates occur daily or even hourly.

consumers begin to demand Royal Dutch Shell oil, the demand for Euros increases. That is, at any given dollar price of Euros, U.S. consumers want more Euros, shifting the demand curve to the right, to D_1. Under a fixed exchange rate system, the dollar price of Euros must remain at $1, where the quantity of Euros demanded (Q_0) now exceeds the quantity supplied, Q_1. The result is a shortage of Euros—a shortage that must be corrected in some way. As a solution to the shortage, the U.S. may borrow Euros from the Netherlands, or perhaps ship the Netherlands some of its reserves of gold. The ability to continually make up the shortage (deficit) in this manner, however, is limited, particularly if the deficit persists for a substantial period of time.

HOW DO FLEXIBLE RATES SOLVE THE CURRENCY SHORTAGE?

Under flexible exchange rates, a change in the supply or demand for Euros does not pose a problem. Because rates are allowed to change, the rising U.S. demand for Euro-

pean goods (and thus for Euros) would lead to a new equilibrium price for Euros, say at $1.50. At this higher price, European goods are more costly to buyers in the U.S. Some of the increase in demand for European imports, then, is offset by a decrease in quantity demanded resulting from higher import prices. Similarly, the change in the exchange rate will make U.S. goods cheaper to Europeans, thus increasing U.S. exports and, with that, the quantity of Euros supplied. For example, a $40 software program that cost Europeans 40 Euros when the exchange rate was $1 per Euro, costs less than 27 Euros when the exchange rate increases to $1.50 per Euro ($40 divided by 1.50).

HOW DO FLEXIBLE RATES AFFECT MACROECONOMIC POLICIES?

With flexible exchange rates, the imbalance between debits and credits arising from shifts in currency demand and/or supply is accommodated by changes in currency prices, rather than through the special financial borrowings or reserve movements necessary with fixed rates. In a pure

EXHIBIT 2 | HOW FLEXIBLE EXCHANGE RATES WORK

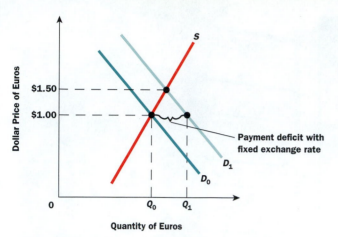

As increase in demand for Euros shifts the demand curve to the right, from D_0 to D_1. Under a fixed-rate system, this increase in demand results in a shortage of Euros at the equilibrium price of $1, because the quantity demanded at this price (Q_1) is greater than the quantity supplied (Q_0). If the exchange rate is flexible, however, no shortage develops. Instead, the increase in demand forces the exchange rate higher, to $1.50. At this higher exchange rate, the quantity of Euros demanded doesn't increase as much, and the quantity of Euros supplied increases as a result of the now relatively lower cost of imports from the United States.

flexible exchange rate system, balance of payments deficits and surpluses tend to disappear automatically. The market mechanism itself is able to address world trade imbalances, dispensing with the need for bureaucrats attempting to achieve some administratively determined price. Moreover, the need to use restrictive monetary and/or fiscal policy to end such an imbalance while maintaining a fixed exchange rate is alleviated. Nations are thus able to feel less constraint in carrying out internal macroeconomic policies under flexible exchange rates. For these reasons, many economists welcomed the collapse of the Bretton Woods system and the failure to arrive at a new system of fixed or quasi-fixed exchange rates.

WHAT ARE THE DISADVANTAGES OF FLEXIBLE RATES?

Despite the fact that world trade has grown and dealing with balance of payments problems has become less difficult, flexible exchange rates have not been universally endorsed by everyone. Several disadvantages of this system have been cited.

Have flexible rates hurt world trade?

Traditionally, the major objection to flexible rates was that they introduce considerable uncertainty into international trade. For example, if you order some perfume from France with a commitment to pay 1,000 Euros in three months, you are not certain what the dollar price of Euros, and therefore, of the perfume, will be three months from now, because the exchange rate is constantly fluctuating. Because people prefer certainty to uncertainty and are generally risk averse, this uncertainty raises the costs of international transactions. As a result, flexible exchange rates can reduce the volume of trade, thus reducing the potential gains from international specialization.

Proponents of flexible rates have three answers to this argument. First, the empirical evidence shows that international trade has, in fact, grown in volume faster since the introduction of flexible rates. The exchange rate risk of trade has not had any major adverse impact. Second, it is possible to, in effect, buy insurance against the proposed adverse impact of currency fluctuations. Rather than buying currencies for immediate use in what is called the "spot" market for foreign currencies, one can contract today to buy foreign currencies in the future at a set exchange rate in the "forward" or "futures" market. By using this market, a perfume importer can buy Euros now for delivery to her in three months; in doing so, she can be certain of the dollar price she is paying for the perfume. Since floating exchange rates began, booming futures markets in foreign currencies have opened in Chicago, New York, and in foreign financial centers. The third argument is that the alleged certainty of currency prices under the old Bretton Woods system was fictitious, because the possibility existed that nations might, at their whim, drastically revalue their currencies to deal with their own fundamental balance of payments problems. Proponents of flexible rates, then, argue that they are therefore no less disruptive to trade than fixed rates.

Do flexible rates lead to inflation?

A second, more valid criticism of flexible exchange rates is that they can contribute to inflationary pressures. Under fixed rates, domestic monetary and fiscal authorities have an incentive to constrain their domestic prices, because lower domestic prices increase the attractiveness of exported goods. This discipline is not present to the same extent with flexible rates. The consequence of a sharp monetary or fiscal expansion under flexible rates would be a decline in the value of one's currency relative to those of other countries. Yet even that may not seem to be as serious a political consequence as the Bretton Woods solution of an abrupt devaluation of the currency in the face of a severe balance of payments problem.

Advocates of flexible rates would argue that inflation need not occur under flexible rates. Flexible rates do not cause inflation; rather it is caused by the expansionary macroeconomic policies of governments and central banks.

Actually, flexible rates give government decision makers greater freedom of action than fixed rates; whether they act responsibly is determined by exchange rates, but rather by domestic policies.

CONCEPT CHECK

1. While rates are free today to fluctuate based on market transactions, governments occasionally intervene to increase or depress the price of their currencies.
2. Changes in exchange rates occur more often under a flexible-rate system, but the changes are much smaller than the drastic, overnight revaluations of currencies that occurred under the fixed-rate system.
3. Under a fixed rate system, as the supply and demand for currencies shift, currency prices are not allowed to shift to the new equilibrium, leading to surpluses and shortages of currencies.
4. The main arguments presented against flexible exchange rates are that international trade levels will be diminished due to the uncertainty of future currency prices and that the flexible rates would lead to inflation. Proponents of flexible exchange rates have strong counter-arguments to those views.

1. What are the arguments for and against flexible exchange rates?
2. When the U.S. dollar starts to exchange for fewer Japanese yen, other things equal, what happens to U.S. and Japanese imports and exports as a result?
3. Why is the system of flexible exchange rates sometimes called a "dirty float" system?
4. Were exchange rates under the Bretton Woods system really stable? How could you argue that exchange rates were more uncertain under the fixed rate system than with floating exchange rates?
5. What is the uncertainty argument against flexible exchange rates? What evidence do proponents of flexible exchange rates cite in response?
6. Do flexible exchange rates cause higher rates of inflation? Why or why not?

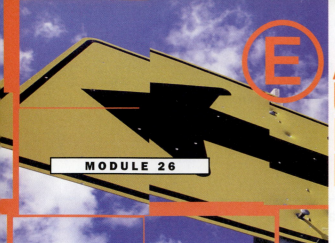

Application: The United States Intervenes to Boost the Yen

In this Module we have examined the interworkings of the exchange market. In this application, we see that the United States recently intervened in the foreign exchange market to bolster another country's currency—the Japanese yen. Why would the United States do this? How would a further fall in the value of the yen impact the global economy?

U.S. INTERVENES IN ASIAN CRISIS

WASHINGTON, June 17—In the latest sign of the seriousness of the Asian crisis, the United States intervened in currency markets Wednesday, selling dollars and buying yen in an effort to bolster the value of the sagging Japanese currency. The sales of dollars for yen marked the first time the Clinton administration has sold dollars to support another currency and underscored concerns about the deepening economic troubles of the world's second-largest economy.

The move was also the first time the administration had tried directly to influence exchange rates since August 1995.

The dollar immediately responded, tumbling against the yen. Dollar/yen screeched past several key support levels, falling rapidly from its 142.03 yen level in early New York trading to a session low of 136.18.

In early Tokyo trading on Thursday, the dollar continued to skid, falling to 135.72, more than 6 yen below its close Wednesday on Asian markets. The foreign exchange action was also having an uplifting effect on Asia's stock exchanges. In early morning trading, Japan's 225-share Nikkei average jumped 4.23 percent, or 621.83 points, to 15,337.21; South Korea's main index was up some 8 percent; and Hong Kong's 6 percent.

Dealers in New York said the United States likely spent up to $2 billion during the intervention on Wednesday. "We have been hearing the figure is around $2 billion," one market source said. Others said the total intervention, including that spent by the Bank of Japan, was likely in the $6 billion range. It was the first U.S. intervention on behalf of the yen in more than six years.

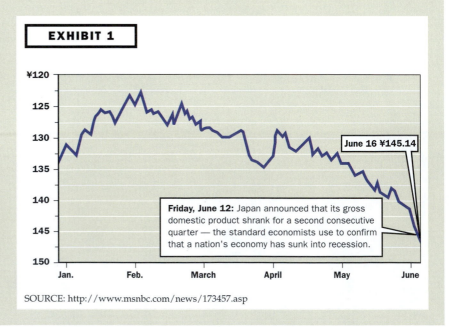

EXHIBIT 1

June 16 ¥145.14

Friday, June 12: Japan announced that its gross domestic product shrank for a second consecutive quarter — the standard economists use to confirm that a nation's economy has sunk into recession.

SOURCE: http://www.msnbc.com/news/173457.asp

The yen in recent weeks had fallen to its lowest level in 8 years amid mounting concern over Japan's economic recession. President Clinton said Wednesday he had offered U.S. support for Japan's yen after Japanese Prime Minister Ryutaro Hashimoto had pledged "aggressive" financial system reform and other economic steps.

"I was very encouraged by the prime minister's statement that he intends to pursue aggressive reform of their banking institutions and intends to do the things that were necessary to get their economy going again, and therefore I thought it was important that we support them," Clinton said in response to a reporter's question during a White House Rose Garden appearance.

. . . "Japan is very important to the world, especially to the United States, and to the efforts we're making to support an economic recovery in Asia, which is very important to keeping our own economic progress going," Clinton said.

"It is important that they take some critical steps, and as they do them, we will support them," he said. "We've got a chance to turn that situation in Asia around before it gets any worse."

A leading currency expert agreed. Fred Bergsten, director of the Institute for International Economics, told CNBC Wednesday that "what was needed was intervention of this type" given that there was a risk that "a continued free-fall of the yen would trigger falls in other currencies . . . and literally cause a global financial crisis." . . .

The U.S. government is concerned with the weakening yen. The government is concerned that if the yen falls any more, it will have substantial implications in other East Asian countries and, ultimately, in the United States. The depreciating yen has broad implications for both consumers and producers. For example, a lower exchange rate will lead to lower prices for Japanese computer chips and the computers made with those chips, as well as other Japanese goods, like cars, camcorders, and car stereos. On the other hand, higher relative prices for U.S. goods means that Japanese buyers will look elsewhere. This may keep inflation from rising but could lead to a reduction in manufacturing job growth in the United States.

ONE STEP BEYOND

What would happen to the exchange rate for the Euro if pizzas made with special imported Italian cheeses, sausages, spices, and sauces suddenly became all of the rage on college campuses across the United States? Can you identify other factors that impact the foreign exchange market? Use the problems in your Workbook to gauge your understanding of these topics, and then check out recent data and information about U.S. exports by following the links provided on your EconActive CD-ROM.

PHOTO CREDITS MODULE 26

Page **619:** © Sandy Felsenthal/Corbis Images; Page **622:** © Dave G. Houser/Corbis Images; Page **623:** © Associated Press/Bob Edme; Page **626:** © Jonathan Blair/Corbis Images; Page **633:** © PhotoDisc; Page **637:** © Steve Lindstrom, Duluth News-Tribune.

Module 1: Economics: Ten Powerful Ideas
Concept A

1. What is the definition of economics?

Economics is the study of the allocation of our scarce resources to satisfy our unlimited wants for goods and services.

2. Why does scarcity force us to make choices?

Scarcity, the fact that our wants exceed what our resources can produce, means that we are forced to make choices on how best to use those limited resources.

3. Why are choices costly?

In a world of scarcity, whenever we choose one option, we also choose to do without something else that we also desire. This want that we choose not to satisfy is the opportunity cost of that choice.

4. Why do even "non-economic" issues have an economic dimension?

Even apparently non-economic issues have an economic dimension because economics concerns anything worthwhile to some human being (including love, friendship, charity, etc.) and the choices we make among those things we value.

5. If a genie gave you three wishes, would that solve the problem of scarcity for you?

No. You couldn't satisfy all of your wants with three wishes if we assume that none of your wishes could be used for more wishes. That is, wishes would still be scarce.

Concept B

1. What are resources?

Resources are the scarce inputs that are used to produce the goods and services we want. They include both man-made (e.g., machinery) and natural (e.g., land) inputs, labor, and the entrepreneurship that puts the other resources together.

2. How do finite resources impact our ability to produce goods and services?

The fact that resources are finite (limited) means that the things that can be produced from them—the goods and services we want—are also limited as a result.

3. What must be true for something to be an economic good?

An economic good, tangible or intangible, is any good or service that we value or desire. This definition includes the reduction of things we don't want, bads, as a good (e.g., trash is a bad, while trash clean-up is a good).

4. Does wanting more tangible and intangible goods and services make us selfish?

No. Among the goods many of us want more of is helping others (charity), so to say that we all want more goods does not imply that we are selfish, merely that we are "self-interested."

5. Why might sunshine be scarce in Seattle but not in Tucson?

For a good to be scarce, we must want more of it than we are able to have freely available from nature. Residents of Tucson typically have all of the sunshine they desire, while rain may be something that is very scarce relative to residents' desires. For residents of Seattle, where the sun shines much less and it rains much more, the opposite might well be true.

Concept C

1. Does everyone face scarcity?

Because no one can have all the goods and services that he or she desires, we all face scarcity as a fact of life.

2. Why does scarcity affect each of us differently?

Because our desires and the extent of the resources we have available to meet those desires vary, scarcity affects each of us differently.

3. Why can't a country become so technologically advanced that its citizens won't have to choose?

No matter how productive a country becomes, its citizens' desires will continue to outstrip their ability to satisfy them. As we get more productive and incomes grow, we discover new wants that we would like to satisfy, so our ability to produce never catches up with our wants.

4. If Penny Pincher became a billionaire after winning the largest lotto ever, would she still face scarcity?

Becoming a billionaire does make some goods more available to an individual, but it does not eliminate scarcity. Among other very scarce goods, it can't guarantee us as long a lifespan, as many friends, or as much happiness as we might like.

Concept D

1. Would we have to make choices if we had unlimited resources?

We would not have to make choices if we had unlimited resources, because we would then be able to produce all of the goods and services we wanted, and having more of one thing would not require having less of other goods or services. However, unlimited resources also means unlimited time—most of us would always desire more leisure time—meaning that labor is likely to remain scarce, regardless of what happens to other inputs.

2. What is given up when we make a choice?

When you make a choice, you give up the opportunity to pursue other valued alternatives with the same time or resources.

3. What do we mean by opportunity cost?

The opportunity cost of a choice is the highest valued foregone opportunity resulting from a decision. It can usefully be thought of as the value of the opportunity a person would have chosen if their most-preferred option was taken away.

4. Why is there no such thing as a free lunch?

There is no such thing as a free lunch because the production of any good uses up some of society's resources. As a result, those resources are then no longer available for use in the production of other goods and services we want.

5. How are prices and costs different?

A price reflects the monetary value of the good; it is an objective fact. Costs are personal and subjective, reflecting the relative values of foregone goods and services to individuals that result from choices made. Because individuals have different preferences and face different circumstances, the costs they incur from making a choice will be different.

6. Why was the opportunity cost of staying in college higher for Tiger Woods than for most undergraduates?

The alternative to Tiger Woods of staying in school—starting a very highly paid professional golf career sooner than he could have otherwise—was far more lucrative than the alternatives facing most undergraduates. Because the alternative was more valuable for Tiger Woods, his opportunity cost of staying in school was higher than for most.

7. Why is the opportunity cost of time spent getting an MBA typically lower for a 22-year-old straight out of college than for a 45-year-old experienced manager?

The opportunity cost of time for a 45-year-old experienced manager—the earnings he would have to give up to spend a given period of time getting an MBA—is higher than that of a 22-year-old straight out of college, whose income-earning alternatives are far less.

Concept E

1. What are marginal choices? Why does economics focus on them?

Marginal choices are choices of how much of something to do, not choices of whether to do something or not. Economics focuses on marginal choices because those are the sort of choices we most frequently face: Should I do a little more of this or a little less of that?

2. What is the rule of rational choice?

The rule of rational choice is that in trying to make themselves better off, people alter their behavior if the expected marginal benefits from doing so outweigh the expected marginal costs they will bear as a result. If the expected marginal benefits of an action exceed the expected marginal costs, a person will do more of that action; if the expected marginal benefits of an action are less than the expected marginal costs, a person will do less of that action.

3. Why does rational choice involve expectations?

Because the world is uncertain in many important respects, we can seldom know for certain whether the marginal benefits of an action will in fact exceed the marginal costs. Therefore, the rule of rational choice deals with expectations that decision makers hold at the time they make their decisions, recognizing that mistakes can be made.

4. Why do students often stop taking lecture notes when a professor announces that the next few minutes of material will not be on any future test or assignment?

The benefit, in terms of grades, from taking notes in class falls when the material discussed will not be tested or "rewarded," and because the marginal benefits of note taking are now smaller in this situation relative to the unchanged marginal costs, students do less of it.

5. If you decide to speed to get to a doctor's appointment and then get into an accident as a result, does your decision to speed invalidate the rule of rational choice?

No. Remember, the rule of rational choice deals with expectations at the time decisions are made. If you thought you would get into an accident due to speeding in this situation, you would not have decided to speed. The fact that you got in an accident doesn't invalidate the rule of rational choice; it only means that your expectations at the time you decided to speed proved to be incorrect.

Concept F

1. What is the difference between positive incentives and negative incentives?

Positive incentives are those that either increase the benefits or decrease the costs of an action, thus encouraging the action.

Negative incentives are those that either decrease the benefits or increase the costs of an action, thus discouraging the action.

2. According to the rule of rational choice, would you do more or less of something if its expected marginal benefits increased?

If the expected marginal benefits of an activity increased, you would do more of that activity, because you would get a higher overall benefit level by doing so.

3. According to the rule of rational choice, would you do more or less of something if its expected marginal costs increased?

If the expected marginal costs of an activity increased, you would do less of that activity, because you would incur fewer costs (and therefore have a higher overall benefit level) by doing so.

4. How does the rule of rational choice imply that young children are typically more likely to misbehave at a supermarket checkout counter than at home?

When a young child is at a supermarket checkout counter, the benefit of misbehaving (the potential payoff to pestering Mom or Dad for candy) is greater. Also, because his parents are less likely to punish him, or to punish him as severely, in public as in private for his misbehavior, the costs are lower as well. Because the benefits of misbehavior are higher and the costs are lower at a supermarket checkout counter, more child misbehavior is to be expected there.

5. Why do many parents refuse to let their children have dessert before they eat the rest of their dinner?

Children often find that the costs of eating many foods at dinner exceed the benefits (e.g., "If it's green, it must be yucky"), but that is seldom true of dessert. If parents let their children eat dessert first, they would often not eat the food that was "good for them." But by adding the benefit of getting dessert to the choice of eating their other food, parents can get their children to eat the rest of their dinner also.

Concept G

1. Why do people specialize?

People specialize because by concentrating their energies on the activities to which they are best suited, individuals incur lower opportunity costs. That is, they specialize in doing those things that they can do at lower opportunity costs than others, and they let individuals who can do other things at lower opportunity costs than they can specialize in doing those activities.

2. What do we mean by comparative advantage?

A person, region, or country has a comparative advantage in producing a good or service when it can produce it at a lower opportunity cost than other persons, regions, or countries.

3. Why does the combination of specialization and trade make us better off?

Trade increases wealth by allowing a person, region, or a nation to specialize in those products that it produces relatively better than others and to trade for those products that others produce relatively better than it does. Exploiting our comparative advantages and then trading allows us to produce, and therefore consume, more than we could otherwise from our scarce resources.

4. If you can mow your lawn in half the time it takes your younger brother to do it, do you have a comparative advantage in mowing the lawn?

No, not necessarily. Your faster speed at mowing the lawn does not establish that you have a comparative advantage in mowing. That can only be established relative to other tasks. The person with a comparative advantage in mowing lawns is the one with the lowest opportunity cost, and that could be your younger brother in this case. For instance, if you could earn $12 an hour, mowing the lawn in half an hour implies an opportunity cost of $6 of foregone output elsewhere. If your brother could only earn $5 per hour (he was less than half as productive in doing other things compared to you), the opportunity cost of him mowing the lawn in an hour is $5. In this case, your younger brother has a comparative advantage in mowing the lawn.

5. If you became far more productive than before in completing yard chores, could that eliminate your current comparative advantage in doing the dishes?

The opportunity cost of you doing the dishes is the value of other chores you must give up to do the dishes. Therefore, an increase in your productivity in doing yard chores would increase the opportunity cost of doing the dishes, and could well eliminate your current comparative advantage in doing the dishes compared to other members of your family.

6. Could a student who gets a C in one class but a D or worse in everything else have a comparative advantage in that class over someone who gets a B in that class but an A in everything else?

A student who gets a C in a class is less good, in an absolute sense, at that class than a student who gets a B in it. But if the C student gets Ds in other classes, he is relatively, or comparatively, better at the C class, while if the B student gets As in other classes, he is relatively, or comparatively, worse at that class.

7. How can Michael Jordan help feed more poor people by playing basketball than by serving meals in a homeless shelter?

Michael Jordan could earn a great deal of money by playing two hours of basketball (his comparative advantage), which he could then donate to feed a large number of people in a homeless shelter. The result would be to feed far more people than if he spent those two hours serving meals at the shelter himself.

Concept H

1. Why must every society choose some manner by which to allocate its scarce resources?

Every society must choose some manner by which to allocate its scarce resources because the collective wants of its members always far outweighs what can be produced from those resources.

2. How does a market system allocate resources?

A market system allows individuals, both as producers and consumers, to indicate their wants and desires through their actions (how much they are willing to buy or sell at various prices). The market then acts to bring about that level of prices which coordinates the plans of the buyers and sellers.

3. What do market prices communicate to others in society?

The prices charged by suppliers communicate the relative availability of products to consumers; the prices consumers are willing to pay communicate the relative values consumers place on products to producers. That is, market prices provide a way for both consumers and suppliers to communicate about the relative value of goods, services, and resources.

4. How do price controls undermine the market as a communication device?

Price controls, price floors, price ceilings, and overall caps on all prices (as during war) prevent the market from communicating relevant (changing) information between consumers and suppliers.

A price floor set above the market price prevents suppliers from communicating their willingness to sell for less to consumers. A price ceiling set below the market price prevents consumers from indicating their willingness to pay more to suppliers. And price controls don't allow expressions of willingness-to-pay to operate throughout an economy.

5. Why can markets sometimes fail to allocate resources efficiently?

Markets can sometimes fail to allocate resources efficiently. Such situations, called market failures, represent situations such as externalities, where costs can be imposed on some individuals without their consent (e.g., from dumping "crud" in their air or water), where information in the market may not be communicated honestly and accurately, and where firms may have market power to distort prices in their favor (against consumers' interests).

Concept I

1. What justifications are there for government involvement in the economic decision-making process?

At least seven reasons have been used to justify government involvement in the economic decision-making process: (1) To provide a legal framework to enforce and protect property rights; (2) to provide goods and service that are inherently public in character, like national defense; (3) to overcome inefficiencies due to a lack of competition in some markets; (4) to provide information to help market participants make better choices; (5) to correct inappropriate market signals in cases of externalities, like pollution; (6) to change a market-determined income distribution considered unfair or undesirable; and (7) to improve the overall level of output, employment, or prices from what might result from the market mechanism alone. (Note: Not all of these justifications receive universal support nor are they of equal importance.)

2. What are property rights?

Property rights are the powers granted owners of property to use, sell, rent, dispose of, and enhance the value of those goods or resources.

3. How do different property rights alter incentives?

Different property rights alter incentives because they change the expected marginal benefits and the expected marginal costs of a wide range of actions. For example, private property serves as a powerful incentive for individuals to maintain and conserve their resources, because they will be able to benefit from any future increase in the value of those resources. Under public ownership, individuals cannot benefit from future increases in the value of those resources, and as a result, they have less incentive to maintain and conserve those goods and resources.

4. What is the law of unintended consequences?

The law of unintended consequences is the term used to remind us that the results of actions are not always as they appear, because the secondary effects of an action often include many consequences that were not part of what was intended. Indeed, the unintended consequences of an action often work counter to the original intent.

5. Why is the law of unintended consequences so important in making public policy?

It is impossible to change just one incentive to achieve a particular result through a government policy. A policy will change the incentives facing multiple individuals making multiple decisions, and changes in all of those effected choices will result. Sometimes, the unintended consequences can be so substantial that they completely undermine the intended effects of a policy.

6. Why is the shared, common area of a dormitory often messier than the students' individual rooms?
When cleaning her own area, a student gets all of the benefits and bears all the costs of cleaning. But when cleaning the common area, she gets only a small part of the benefits, which are shared with others, while still bearing all of the costs of that cleaning. The result is less effort spent cleaning common areas.

Concept J

1. Why do we want economic growth to take place?
In a world of scarcity, we would rather have more goods and services to consume than less, and economic growth expands the amount of consumption possible in the future.

2. Can economic growth have negative side effects?
Economic growth in the amounts of goods and services available for consumption can potentially have negative side effects, including environmental damage, increased economic inequality, and so forth. However, it is important to realize that expanding economic opportunities do not necessarily result in these negative side effects. Indeed, properly measured, growth incorporates any negative side effects.

3. What sorts of policies can encourage economic growth?
Economic growth can be encouraged by policies that increase capital formation, encourage new technology development, and lead to the discovery of more efficient methods of doing things.

4. Is it possible for economic growth to increase the quality of the environment?
Yes. Economic growth indicates that more of many goods can be produced than before. One of those goods that we could produce more of with economic growth is environmental quality. That is, economic growth can produce more environmental quality, but it may not do so because environmental quality is usually supplied in a political setting where the proper amounts of many things may not always be forthcoming because political incentives differ from economic incentives.

5. If a country is building a bridge or road that nobody uses, will that kind of investment contribute to economic growth?
It is valuable investments, not just investments per se, that add to the future productive capacity of the economy. Investments in bridges and roads that nobody uses do not add to the economy's productivity and thus do not add to its economic growth. Indeed, the opportunity cost of using a country's resources in this particular way are very high.

Concept K

1. What is inflation?
Inflation describes the situation where overall prices are rising (even though some prices may be falling).

2. What is deflation?
Deflation describes the situation where overall prices are falling (even though some prices may be rising).

3. Why is price stability useful?
Price stability is useful because it enables producers and consumers to more accurately predict the general level of prices in the society and thus allows them to better coordinate their plans and decisions through the market.

4. How can inflation distort price signals?
With inflation, not all prices change at the same time and in the same amount. As a result, inflation distorts relative prices, undermining their ability to communicate accurately about relative scarcities in the economy.

5. Why is the mere *possibility* of inflation costly to society?
Just the possibility of inflation is costly to society because it increases the uncertainty, and the costs of that uncertainty, about what the general price level will be in the future. The less one can be sure about the future price level, the harder it is to determine the appropriate prices to charge or pay in market negotiations.

6. Why does writing a five-year supply agreement for coal become more difficult when the future price level becomes more uncertain?
Setting an agreed-upon price for a five-year supply agreement requires the parties involved to estimate today the price level over the next five years. The more uncertain the future price level, the riskier it becomes to lock in prices today and the more difficult it is to negotiate such a long-term agreement.

Module 2: The Role and Method of Economics
Concept A

1. What makes economics a social science?
Economics is a social science because it is concerned with reaching generalizations about human, or social, behavior.

2. What distinguishes macroeconomics from microeconomics?
Macroeconomics deals with the economy as a whole, analyzing issues such as inflation, unemployment, business cycles, and economic growth. Microeconomics deals with smaller units within the economy, such as the behavior of individuals, households, firms, and industries. Both, however, ultimately strive to understand people's behavior.

3. Why is it worth studying economics?
Perhaps the best reason to study economics is that so many of the things that concern us are at least partly economic in character. Economics helps us intelligently evaluate our options and determine the most appropriate choices in given situations; it helps develop a disciplined method of thinking about problems. Economics also helps us to understand how the many choices made by economic "actors" are coordinated in the market.

4. Why is the market for running shoes considered a microeconomic topic?
Because a single industry is small relative to the economy as a whole, the market for running shoes (or the running shoe industry) is a microeconomic topic.

5. Why is inflation considered a macroeconomic topic?
Because inflation—a change in the overall price level—has effects throughout the entire economy rather than just in certain small areas of the economy, it is a macroeconomic topic.

Concept B

1. What do economists mean by self-interest?
By self-interest, economists simply mean that people try to improve their own situation (as they see it, not necessarily as others see it).

2. What does rational behavior involve?

Economists consider individuals to be acting rationally if they are striving to do their best to achieve their goals with their limited income, time, and knowledge, given the prices they face and their expectations of the likely future consequences (both benefits and costs) of their behavior.

3. Why are observation and prediction more difficult in the social sciences?

Observation and prediction are more difficult in the social sciences than in physical sciences because social sciences are concerned with human behavior, which is more variable and often less readily predictable than the behavior of experiments observed in a laboratory. Social scientists can seldom run truly "controlled" experiments like those of the biological scientists.

4. Why do economic predictions refer to the behavior of groups of people rather than individuals?

Economists' predictions usually refer to the collective behavior of large groups rather than individuals because looking at the behaviors of a large group of individuals allows economists to discern general patterns of actions and therefore make more reliable generalizations.

5. Why is it typically rational for students to make some mistakes (get less than 100 percent) on a test?

Rational behavior reflects benefits and costs at the margin. A student who expects to get in the high 90 percent range on a test expects to get an A on the test. In that circumstance, the marginal benefit of continued studying to get closer to 100 percent is normally very small, so that the marginal costs of additional studying typically exceed the marginal benefits of added studying before 100 percent mastery is expected.

6. Can you sometimes get a high grade on a test without studying? Does that mean that additional studying does not lead to higher grades?

There may be some instances where a student can get a high grade on an exam without studying. However, because additional studying increases mastery of the material, additional studying will typically increase test performance and grades. That is, while there are some unusual situations (for example, an unusually intelligent person who can absorb most of the material from just going to class) where added studying will not raise grades, additional studying does, in general, lead to higher grades.

Concept C

1. What are economic theories?

A theory is an established explanation that accounts for known facts or phenomena. Economic theories are statements or propositions about patterns of human behavior that are expected to take place under certain circumstances.

2. What is the purpose of a theory?

The purpose of a theory is primarily to explain and predict well. They are necessary because the huge number of potential facts of a complex world do not organize themselves.

3. Why must economic theories be abstract?

Economic theories must be abstract because they could not possibly include every possible event, circumstance, or factor that might affect behavior. Like a road map, an economic theory abstracts from some issues to focus more clearly and precisely on the central questions it is designed to explain. It is actually unde-

sirable for a theory to be realistic, because if it were, it would be just as hard to understand as the world we are trying to understand (for example, a map showing the way from Los Angeles to San Francisco would be hundreds of miles long).

4. What is a hypothesis? How do we determine if it is tentatively accepted?

A hypothesis is a testable proposal that makes some type of predictions about behavior in response to certain changed conditions. An economic hypothesis is a testable proposal about how people will behave or react to a change in economic circumstances. It is tentatively acceptable if its predictions are consistent with what actually happens. In economics, empirical analysis is often used to see if the hypothesis is supported by the facts.

Concept D

1. Why do economists hold other things constant (*ceteris paribus*)?

The *ceteris paribus* assumption is used in economics because, in trying to assess the effect of one variable on another, we must isolate their relationship from other important events or variables that might also influence the situation the theory tries to explain or predict. This way of thinking is the analog of the controlled experiment in biology, where everything is held constant but the variable of interest.

2. What is the relationship between association and causation?

Association means that two things are related; causation means that one thing caused the other to occur. While causation implies association, association does not necessarily imply causation.

3. To what types of misinterpretations does confusing association and causation lead?

Mistaking association between variables as causation can lead to three types of misinterpretations: (1) It can lead a person to "see" causation between two variables or events where there is none; (2) it can lead a person to "see" causation between two variables or events when a third variable or event is actually responsible for causing both of them; and (3) it can lead a person to "see" one variable or event causing the other, when in fact the causation runs in the opposite direction.

4. What is the fallacy of composition?

The fallacy of composition is the sometimes incorrect idea that if something is true for an individual, it must also always be true for many individuals as a group.

5. If U.S. consumers bought more gasoline in 1998, when prices averaged $1.20 per gallon, than they did in 1970, when prices averaged $0.30 per gallon, does that mean that people buy more gas at higher prices? Why or why not?

No. Other things were far from constant between these two years. The overall price level changed dramatically, as did people's incomes, the safety and convenience of automobiles, distances between home and work, and so forth. Only if people bought more gas at a higher price, holding these and all other important determinants of gasoline purchases constant, could we conclude that higher gas prices lead people to buy more gas.

6. If rain dancing is correlated with rain, does that mean that rain dancing causes rain? Why or why not?

No. The causation is more likely that both rain dancing and rain are caused by the onset of an area's traditional rainy season. When rains come later than normal, this could lead to rain dancing to appease "the rain gods" who are not sending the rain on time. If those dances last long enough in the rainy season, it will rain, but because it is the rainy season rather than because of the rain dancing.

7. Why could getting up earlier to beat the other fishermen to the fish lead anglers to catch the same number of fish at 5 A.M. as they would at noon?

A fisherman gets up earlier hoping to beat the other fishermen to the fish. That would likely lead him to catch more fish, provided none of the other fishermen do the same thing. If they all get up earlier to beat the crowd, however, they may catch no more fish than before as a result. This is an example of the fallacy of composition.

Concept E

1. What is positive analysis? Must positive analysis be testable?

Positive analysis focuses on how people actually behave, rather than on how people should behave; it deals with how variable A impacts variable B. Positive analysis must be testable in order to determine whether its predictions are borne out by the evidence.

2. What is normative analysis? Is normative analysis testable?

Normative analysis focuses on what should be or what ought to happen; it involves opinions about the desirability of various actions or results. Normative analysis is not testable, because there is no scientific way to establish whether one value judgment is better than another value judgment.

3. Why is the positive–normative distinction important?

It is important to distinguish between positive and normative analysis because many controversies in economics revolve around policy considerations that contain both. Deciding whether a policy is good requires both positive (what will happen) and normative (is what happens good or bad) analysis.

4. Why are there policy disagreements among economists?

As with most disciplines, economists do disagree. However, the majority of those disagreements stem from differences in normative analysis, because the evidence cannot establish whether one set of value judgments is better or more appropriate than other sets of value judgments.

5. Is the statement, "UFOs land in my back yard at least twice a week," a positive statement? Why or why not?

A positive statement need not be true; it simply needs to be testable in order to determine whether it is borne out by the evidence. Assuming that the UFOs in question are visible or otherwise detectable, this statement is a positive one because it can be verified or proven false.

6. Is there any way to scientifically determine if the "rich" pay their "fair share" of taxes? Why or why not?

No. There is no scientific way to determine to who qualifies as "rich" or what would constitute their "fair share" of taxes. Such issues necessarily involve value judgements that cannot be proven right or wrong.

Module 3: Scarcity and the Economizing Problem
Concept A

1. What are factors of production?

Factors of production are the resources, or inputs, that are used to produce outputs of final goods and services. They include capital, land, labor, and entrepreneurship.

2. What do economists mean by land? Labor? Capital? Entrepreneurship?

Land refers to all natural resources. Labor refers to the physical and mental effort expended by people in the economy. Capital refers to human-made resources used to produce final goods. Entrepreneurship refers to the process of looking for new possibilities, new products, and new methods of production. The entrepreneur is the one who "puts it all together," hoping to make a profit.

3. What is the difference between capital goods and money capital?

Capital goods are produced goods that are used to produce further goods. Money capital is an instrument of exchange—a means by which other commodities are acquired.

4. Why do you think economists often refer to training that increases the quality of workers' skills as "adding to human capital"?

Training increases a worker's ability to produce goods, just as capital goods increase an economy's ability to produce goods. Because of this similarity in their effects on productive abilities, training is often referred to as adding to workers' human capital.

5. What are some of the ways that students act as entrepreneurs as they seek higher grades?

There are a wide variety of ways that students are entrepreneurs in seeking higher grades. They sometimes form study groups, often even assigning different material to different members. They often share notes. They study harder for those questions they believe will be more likely to be tested. Sometimes they try to get hold of old tests or to cheat. All of this and more is part of different students' efforts to discover the lowest-cost way to get higher grades.

Concept B

1. What does a production possibilities curve illustrate?

The production possibilities curve illustrates the potential output combinations of any two goods in an economy that is operating at full capacity, given the inputs and technology available to the economy.

2. What distinguishes consumption goods and investment goods?

Consumption goods are goods that give us immediate satisfaction. Investment goods do not give immediate satisfaction, but they increase our future ability to produce goods and services.

3. How are opportunity costs shown by the production possibilities curve?

Opportunity cost, the foregone output of one good necessary to increase output of another good, is illustrated by the slope between the two goods at a given point on the production possibilities curve.

4. Why do the opportunity costs of added production increase with output?

Opportunity costs of added production increase with output because some resources cannot be easily adapted from their current uses to alternative uses. At first, easily adaptable resources can be switched to producing more of a good. But once those easily adapted resources have been switched, producing further output requires the use of resources that are less well adapted to expanding that output, thus raising the opportunity cost of output.

5. How does the production possibilities curve illustrate increasing opportunity costs?

Increasing opportunity costs are illustrated by a bowed (concave from below) production possibilities curve. It shows that initial units of one good can be produced by giving up little of another good, but progressive increases in output will require greater and greater sacrifices of the other good.

6. If people reduced their saving (thus reducing the funds available for investment), what would that do to society's production possibilities curve over time?

Reduced savings reduces investment. Investment acts to shift labor's productivity over time, as each unit of labor has more capital with which to work, so reduced savings reduces the growth of the capital stock, which slows the growth of the production possibilities curve over time (and in extreme cases, it could cause the capital stock and the production possibilities curve to fall over time).

7. If Robin's son Crusoe could produce 20 fishing nets in a day or catch 60 fish in a day, while Robin could produce only 10 fishing nets a day or catch 20 fish in a day, who would you pick to begin making fishing nets first? Why?

You would choose the lower opportunity cost producer of fishing nets first, according to the principle of increasing cost. Robin is the lower opportunity cost producer of fishing nets, because he gives up catching two fish with the time and resources it takes him to produce one fishing net, while Crusoe gives up catching three fish with the time and resources it takes him to produce one fishing net.

Concept C

1. Why does scarcity force us to decide what to produce?

Because our wants exceed the amount of goods and services that can be produced from our limited resources, it must be decided which wants should have (marginal) priority over others.

2. How is a command economy different from a market economy?

A command economy makes decisions about what and how much to produce centrally by members of a planning board or organization. In a market economy, those decisions are the result of decentralized decision making by individual producers and consumers, coordinated by their offers to buy and sell on markets.

3. How does consumer sovereignty determine production decisions in a market economy?

Consumer sovereignty determines production decisions in a market economy because producers make those goods and services that they believe consumers will "vote" for by being willing to pay for them.

4. Do you think that what and how much an economy produces depends on who will get the goods and services produced in that economy? Why or why not?

Who will get the goods produced in an economy affects the incentives of the producers. The less a producer will benefit from increased production, the smaller are his incentives to increase his production, and the smaller will be total output in an economy.

5. Why do consumers have to "vote" for a product with their dollars for it to be a success?

Unlike in the political sector, where politicians typically need the votes of a majority to win, many products can be profitable even if they attract only a small number of possible dollar votes in the market sector. A wide variety of niche products exist in the market sector as a result.

Concept D

1. Why must we choose among multiple ways of producing the goods and services we want?

We must choose among multiple ways of producing the goods and services we want because goods can generally be produced in several ways, using different combinations of resources. That requires a decision to be made about how to produce the goods and services we want.

2. Why might production be labor intensive in one economy, but be capital intensive in another?

Production will tend to be labor intensive where labor is relatively plentiful, and therefore relatively less expensive; it will tend to be capital intensive where capital is relatively plentiful, and therefore relatively less expensive. Because the factors of production have different relative prices in different situations, different manners of production can be efficient in different situations (for example, a hand-sewn necktie made in Thailand versus a machine-made necktie made in the United States).

3. If a tourist from the United States notices on an overseas trip that other countries don't produce crops "like they do back home," would he be right to conclude that farmers in the other country produce crops less efficiently than U.S. farmers?

No. The different ways of farming in different areas reflect the different relative scarcities of land, labor, and capital faced by farmers in those areas. Those factors of production that are relatively scarce in an economy are also relatively costly there as a result. Producers will economize on the use of those more costly resources by using more of relatively less scarce, and less costly, resources instead. For example, where land is very scarce, it is very intensively cultivated with relatively cheaper (less scarce) labor and capital, but where capital is very scarce, relatively cheaper (less scarce) land and labor are substituted for capital.

4. Why are the golf tee areas on driving ranges in Japan often multileveled, while they are usually on a single level in the United States?

Because land is relatively more scarce, and thus relatively more costly, in Japan than in the United States, the tee areas on Japanese driving ranges are often multileveled to conserve on that relatively more scarce land.

Concept E

1. In a market economy, what determines "who gets what"?

In a market economy, "who gets what" depends on people's willingness to pay. This willingness to pay is limited by individuals' incomes, which are determined by the quantity, quality, and value of the scarce resources they supply to others.

2. In what way does scarcity determine income?

Relative scarcity determines the market values of the scarce resources people offer to others in exchange for income.

Concept F

1. Why are we concerned with unemployed or underemployed resources in a society?

We are concerned with unemployed or underemployed resources in a society because, if we could reduce the extent of unemployed or underemployed resources, people could have more scarce goods and services available for their use.

2. What do we mean by efficiency, and how is it related to underemployment of resources?

Efficiency means getting the most we can out of our scarce resources. Underemployment of resources means that a society is not getting the most it can out of its resources, either because they are not fully employed or because they are not matched to their best uses.

3. How are efficiency and inefficiency illustrated with a production possibilities curve?

Efficient combinations of outputs are illustrated by points on the production possibilities curve, along which more of one good can be produced if less of some other good is also produced. Inefficient combinations of outputs are illustrated by points inside the production possibilities curve, because more of both goods could then be produced with the resources available to the economy.

4. Will a country that makes being unemployed illegal be more productive than one that does not? Why or why not?

A more productive economy is one that makes the best use of those who wish to work. Making unemployment illegal (as was true in the old USSR) does not eliminate underemployment, nor does it guarantee that people and other resources are employed where they are most productive (especially because it is more difficult to search for a better job when you are working than when you are not working).

5. If a 68-year-old worker in the United States chooses not to work at all, does that mean that the United States is functioning inside its production possibilities curve? Why or why not?

A person who chooses retirement rather than work must consider himself better off not working, when all of the relevant considerations are taken into account. He is therefore as fully employed, given his circumstances, as he would like to be, and so there is no implication that the United States would be inside its production possibilities curve as a result. However, if such workers became more willing to work, that would shift the United States' production possibilities curve outward.

Concept G

1. What is the essential question behind issues of economic growth?

The essential question behind issues of economic growth is: How much are we willing to give up today to get more in the future?

2. What is the connection between sacrifices and economic growth?

The more current consumption is sacrificed in an economy, the larger the fraction of its current resources it can devote to producing investment goods, which will increase its rate of economic growth.

3. How is economic growth shown in terms of production possibilities curves?

Economic growth, the expansion of what an economy can produce, is shown as an outward shift in the production possibilities curve, with formerly unattainable output combinations now made possible.

4. Why doesn't economic growth eliminate scarcity?

Economic growth doesn't eliminate scarcity, because people's wants still exceed what they are capable of producing, so that trade-offs among scarce goods must still be made.

5. What would happen to the production possibilities curve in an economy where a new innovation greatly increased its ability to catch fish but did not change its ability to make fishing nets?

If fishing nets are on the vertical axis and fish are on the horizontal axis of the production possibilities curve, such a technological change would leave the vertical intercept unchanged, but make it less steep (reflecting the reduced opportunity cost of producing additional fish), shifting out the curve's intercept with the horizontal axis.

Module 4: Supply and Demand

Concept A

1. What are transaction costs?

Transactions costs are the costs of making exchanges. Markets and middlepersons arise to reduce transactions costs.

2. Why is it hard to precisely define a market?

Every market is different. There is an incredible variety of exchange arrangements, with different types of products, different degrees of organization, different geographical limits, and so forth.

3. Why do you get your produce at a supermarket rather than directly from farmers?

Supermarkets act as middlepersons between growers of produce and consumers of produce. You hire them to do this task for you when you buy produce from them, rather than directly from growers, because they conduct those transactions at lower costs than you could (if you could do this more cheaply than supermarkets, you would buy directly from farmers rather than from supermarkets).

4. Why do the prices people pay for similar items at garage sales vary more than the prices they pay for similar items in a department store?

Items for sale at department stores are more standardized, easier to compare, and more heavily advertised, which makes consumers more aware of the prices at which they could get a particular good elsewhere, reducing the differences in price that can persist among department stores. Garage sale items are non-standardized, costly to compare, and not advertised, which means that people are often quite unaware of how much a given item could be purchased for elsewhere, so that price differences for similar items at different garage sales can be substantial.

Concept B

1. How are money prices and relative prices different?

Money prices are what are paid in dollars and cents (or other currency); relative prices are the prices of goods relative to (or in terms of) the prices of other goods and services.

2. Why are economists so concerned about relative prices?

Relative prices—the prices of goods relative to other goods and services—reflect the tradeoffs people face in making choices among those goods and services in markets. Changing relative prices alter the opportunity costs of choices, changing the choices that are made.

3. The money price of most goods has risen over time. What does that mean?

Most prices have risen in money terms. However, the relative prices of all goods cannot rise, because if the price of good A rises relative to the price of good B, the price of good B must fall relative to the price of good A. The fact that most goods have risen in money price really means that the value of money has fallen relative to the value of goods.

4. If Motel 6 began by charging $6 per night for a room but now charges $36 per night, what would have to be true for the relative price of its motel rooms to have fallen in that period?

If Motel 6's room prices have gone up six times since it began, its relative price is lower than before only if other prices have gone up more than six times over the same period.

Concept C

1. What is an inverse, or negative, relationship?

An inverse, or negative, relationship is one where one variable changes in the opposite direction from the other. For example, if one variable increases, the other decreases.

2. How do lower prices change buyers' incentives?

A lower price for a good means that the opportunity cost to buyers of purchasing it is lower than before, and self-interest leads buyers to buy more of it as a result.

3. How do higher prices change buyers' incentives?

A higher price for a good means that the opportunity cost to buyers of purchasing it is higher than before, and self-interest leads buyers to buy less of it as a result.

4. How does demand represent willingness to pay?

Demand reflects the value of other things someone would be willing to give up for each unit of a good or service. Expressed in terms of dollars for convenience, this represents that person's willingness to pay for each unit of that good or service.

5. Why do economists prefer talking about wants and desires rather than needs?

By definition, needs are goods for which there are no substitutes. But there are usually many substitutes for a particular good or service. Therefore, to analyze choices in a world with large numbers of substitution possibilities, we must focus on wants and desires (reflected in willingness to pay) rather than needs.

6. If even a minor cheating infraction was punished by expulsion, what would happen to the extent of cheating on campus?

By raising the "price" of cheating on campus, this policy would decrease the amount of cheating.

7. Assume that we "need" water, food, clothing, and shelter to survive. Why is talking about these as needs not very helpful in analyzing choices that must be made among them?

We must often choose among quantities of different goods we need (in some amount) to survive. Talking in terms of need seems to imply that there could be no such choices, which doesn't help us to understand the tradeoffs among the goods that are involved or to analyze those choices.

Concept D

1. What is an individual demand schedule?

An individual demand schedule reveals the different amounts of a good or service a person would be willing to buy at various possible prices in a particular time interval.

2. What difference is there between an individual demand curve and a market demand curve?

The market demand curve shows the total amounts of a good or service that all of the buyers as a group are willing to buy at various

possible prices in a particular time interval. The market quantity demanded at a given price is just the sum of the quantities demanded by each individual buyer at that price.

3. Why does the amount of dating on campus tend to decline just before and during finals?

The opportunity cost of dating—in this case, the value to students of the studying time foregone—is higher just before and during finals than during most of the rest of an academic term. Because the cost is higher, students do less of it.

Concept E

1. What is the difference between a change in demand and a change in quantity demanded?

A change in demand shifts the entire demand curve, while a change in quantity demanded refers to a movement along a given demand curve.

2. If the price of zucchini increases and it causes the demand for yellow squash to rise, what do we call the relationship between zucchini and yellow squash?

Whenever an increased price of one good increases the demand for another, they are substitutes. This reflects the fact that some people consider zucchini as an alternative to yellow squash, so that as zucchini becomes more costly, some people substitute into buying now relatively cheaper yellow squash instead.

3. If income rises and, as a result, demand for jet skis increases, how do we describe that good?

If income rises and, as a result, demand for jet skis increases, we call jet skis a normal good, because for most (or normal) goods, we would rather have more of them than less, so an increase in income would lead to an increase in demand for such goods.

4. How do expectations about the future influence the demand curve?

Expectations about the future influence the demand curve because buying a good in the future is an alternative to buying it now. For example, if higher future prices for a good are expected, future purchases become less attractive. As a result, we would expect current demand for that good to increase, as people will buy more now when it is expected to be cheaper, rather than later, when it is expected to be more costly.

5. Would a change in the price of ice cream cause a change in the demand for ice cream? Why or why not?

No. The demand for ice cream represents the different quantities of ice cream that would be purchased at different prices. In other words, it represents the relationship between the price of ice cream and the quantity of ice cream demanded. Changing the price of ice cream does not change this relationship, so it does not change demand.

6. Would a change in the price of ice cream likely cause a change in the demand for frozen yogurt, a substitute?

Yes. Changing the price of ice cream, a substitute for frozen yogurt, would change the quantity of frozen yogurt demanded at every price.

7. If plane travel is a normal good and bus travel is an inferior good, what will happen to the demand curves for plane and bus travel if people's incomes increase?

The demand for plane travel and all other normal goods will increase if incomes increase, while the demand for bus travel and all other inferior goods will decrease if incomes increase.

Concept F

1. What is a direct, or positive, relationship?

A direct, or positive, relationship is one where both variables involved change in the same direction at the same time if one increases, the other increases.

2. What are the two reasons why a supply curve is positively sloped?

A supply curve is positively sloped because (1) the benefits to sellers from selling increase as the price they receive increases, and (2) the opportunity costs of supplying additional output rise with output (the law of increasing opportunity costs), so it takes a higher price to make increasing output in the self-interest of sellers.

3. What is the difference between an individual supply curve and a market supply curve?

The market supply curve shows the total amounts of a good that all of the sellers as a group are willing to sell at various prices in a particular time period. The market quantity supplied at a given price is just the sum of the quantities supplied by each individual seller at that price.

4. When we say that the supply curve for economics tutoring services is upward sloping, what relationship does that statement represent?

An upward-sloping supply curve for economics tutoring services simply means that there will be more hours of economics tutoring offered for sale—a higher quantity supplied—at a higher price than at a lower price, other things constant.

Concept G

1. What is the difference between a change in supply and a change in quantity supplied?

A change in supply shifts the entire supply curve, while a change in quantity supplied refers to a movement along a given supply curve.

2. What causes a movement along a supply curve?

A movement along a supply curve is caused by a change in the price of that good (called that good's own-price).

3. What causes a shift in the entire supply curve?

A shift in the supply curve is cause by anything that changes the quantity of that good supplied except a change in its own-price. These supply curve shifters are summarized by the term SPENT: (S) supplier input prices; (P) prices of related goods; (E) expectations of sellers; (N) the number of sellers; and (T) technology, taxes, tampering, and temperature.

4. If a seller expects the price of a good to rise in the near future, how will that affect his current supply curve?

Selling a good in the future is an alternative to selling it now. Therefore, the higher the expected future price relative to the current price, the more attractive future sales become and the less attractive current sales become. This will lead sellers to reduce (shift left) the current supply of that good, as they will want to sell later, when the good is expected to be more valuable, rather than now.

5. Would a change in the price of wheat change the supply of wheat? Would it change the supply of corn, if wheat and corn can be grown on the same type of land?

The supply of wheat represents the different quantities of wheat that would be offered for sale at different prices. In other words, it represents the relationship between the price of wheat and the quantity of wheat supplied. Changing the price of wheat does not change this relationship, so it does not change the supply of wheat. However, a change in the price of wheat changes the relative attractiveness of raising wheat instead of corn, which changes the supply of corn.

6. If a guitar manufacturer had to increase its wages in order to keep its workers, what would happen to the supply of guitars as a result?

An increase in wages (or any other input price) raises the opportunity cost of producing guitars. This would decrease (shift left) the supply of guitars, making fewer guitars available for sale at any given price.

7. What happens to the supply of baby-sitting services in an area when many teenagers get their driver's licenses at about the same time?

When teenagers get their drivers licenses, their increased mobility expands their alternatives to baby-sitting substantially, thus raising the opportunity cost of babysitting. This decreases (shifts left) the supply of baby-sitting services.

Module 5: Markets in Motion
Concept A

1. How does the intersection of supply and demand indicate the equilibrium price and quantity in a market?

The intersection of supply and demand indicates the equilibrium price and quantity in a market, because at higher prices, sellers would be frustrated by their inability to sell all they would like, leading sellers to compete by lowering the price they charge; at lower prices, buyers would be frustrated by their inability to buy all they would like, leading buyers to compete by increasing the price they offer to pay.

2. What can cause a change in the supply and demand equilibrium?

Changes in any of the PYNTE demand curve shifters or the SPENT supply curve shifters will change the supply and demand equilibrium.

3. What must be true about the price charged for there to be a shortage?

The price charged must be less than the equilibrium price, with the result that buyers would like to buy more at that price than sellers are willing to sell.

4. What must be true about the price charged for there to be a surplus?

The price charged must be greater than the equilibrium price, with the result that sellers would like to sell more at that price than buyers are willing to buy.

5. Why do market forces tend to eliminate both shortages and surpluses?

Market forces tend to eliminate both shortages and surpluses because of the self-interest of the market participants. A seller is better off successfully selling at a lower equilibrium price than not being able to sell at a higher price (the surplus situation), and a buyer is better off successfully buying at a higher equilibrium price than not being able to buy at a lower price (the shortage situation). Therefore, we expect market forces to eliminate both shortages and surpluses.

6. Why do economists refer to the "invisible hand" of the market?

Economists refer to the "invisible hand" of the market because no one person or group (a visible hand) determines the market outcome. Rather, the interaction of all of the demanders and suppliers is the invisible hand that determines the market outcome.

7. If tea prices were above their equilibrium level, what force would tend to push tea prices down? If tea prices were below their equilibrium level, what force would tend to push tea prices up?

If tea prices were above their equilibrium level, sellers, frustrated by their inability to sell as much tea as they would like at those prices, would compete the price of tea down, as they tried to make more attractive offers to tea buyers. If tea prices were below their equilibrium level, buyers, frustrated by their inability to buy as much tea as they would like at those prices, would compete the price of tea up, as they tried to make more attractive offers to tea sellers.

8. Why does the time you spend in supermarket checkout lines tend to be about the same, regardless of which line you are in?

If you knew that you could check out faster in one line than the others, you would choose that line. But the same is true of other shoppers. The result of self-interested shoppers all looking to save time is that the time spent checking out tends to be about the same for all the checkout lines.

Concept B

1. When demand increases, does that create a shortage or a surplus at the original price?

An increase in demand increases the quantity demanded at the original equilibrium price, but it does not change the quantity supplied at that price, meaning that it would create a shortage at the original equilibrium price.

2. What happens to equilibrium price and quantity as a result of a demand increase?

Frustrated buyers who are unable to buy all they would like at the original equilibrium price will compete the market price higher, and that higher price will induce suppliers to increase their quantity supplied. The result is a higher market price and a larger market output.

3. When supply increases, does that create a shortage or surplus at the original price?

An increase in supply increases the quantity supplied at the original equilibrium price, but it does not change the quantity demanded at that price, meaning that it would create a surplus at the original equilibrium price.

4. What happens to equilibrium price and quantity as a result of a supply increase?

Frustrated sellers who are unable to sell all they would like at the original equilibrium price will compete the market price lower, and that lower price will induce demanders to increase their quantity demanded. The result is a lower market price and a larger market output.

5. Why do heating-oil prices tend to be higher in the winter?

The demand for heating oil is higher in cold winter months. The result of this higher winter heating oil demand, for a given supply curve, is higher prices for heating oil in the winter.

6. Why are evening and weekend long-distance calls cheaper than weekday long-distance calls?

The demand for long-distance calls is greatest during weekday business hours, but far lower during other hours. Because the demand for "off-peak" long-distance calls is lower, for a given supply curve, prices during those hours are lower.

Concept C

1. What would have to be true for both supply and demand to shift in the same time period?

For both supply and demand to shift in the same time period, one or more of both the SPENT supply curve shifters and the PYNTE demand curve shifters would have to change in that same time period.

2. How do we "add up" the effects of simultaneous changes in both supply and demand on equilibrium prices and quantities?

Adding up simultaneous changes in both supply and demand considers the effects of each of the shifts on the market price and quantity separately, then "adds up" the directions of those changes to see the net change in each variable. If both shifts change a variable in the same direction, that will also be the net effect, but if they push a variable in opposite directions, the net effect will be indeterminate without knowing the relative magnitudes of the shifts.

3. When both supply and demand shift, what added information do we need to know in order to determine in which direction the indeterminate variable changes?

When both supply and demand shift, we need to know which of the shifts is of greater magnitude, so we can know which of the opposing effects in the indeterminate variable is larger; the larger effect will determine the direction of the net effect on the indeterminate variable.

4. If both buyers and sellers of coffee expect coffee prices to rise in the near future, what will happen to coffee prices and sales today?

If coffee buyers expect coffee prices to rise in the near future, it will increase their current demand to buy coffee, which would tend to increase current prices and increase the current quantity of coffee sold. If coffee sellers expect coffee prices to rise in the near future, it will decrease their current supply of coffee for sale, which would tend to increase current prices and decrease the current quantity of coffee sold. Because both of these effects tend to increase the current price of coffee, coffee prices will rise. However, the supply and demand curve shifts tend to change current sales in opposing directions, so without knowing which of these shifts was of a greater magnitude, we do not know what will happen to current coffee sales. They could go up, down, or even stay the same.

5. If demand for peanut butter increases and supply decreases, what will happen to equilibrium price and quantity?

An increase in the demand for peanut butter increases the equilibrium price and quantity of peanut butter sold. A decrease in the supply of peanut butter increases the equilibrium price and quantity of peanut butter sold. The result is an increase in peanut butter prices and an indeterminate effect on the quantity of peanut butter sold.

Concept D

1. What happens in a market when demand is greater than anticipated?

When demand is greater than anticipated, there is a temporary disequilibrium shortage, leading to competition among frustrated buyers bidding the price up, and those higher prices lead sellers to increase output. These responses drive the market to a new higher market equilibrium price and output.

2. How do market adjustments resolve the temporary disequilibrium that results when demand is incorrectly estimated?
Temporary shortages and surpluses set in motion competitive processes in which frustrated market participants compete the price toward the new equilibrium level, and the incentives caused by that change in price moves the market output to its new equilibrium level.

3. If the maker of Beanie Babies found that its inventories were plummeting, what kind of temporary disequilibrium would that indicate?
Plummeting Beanie Baby inventories would indicate that the quantity demanded at the current price is greater than sellers expected and had produced for sale at that price. In other words, it indicates a temporary shortage at the current price, which leads to Beanie Baby price and output increases until the temporary disequilibrium is eliminated.

Concept E

1. How is rent control an example of a price ceiling?
A price ceiling is a maximum price set below the equilibrium price by the government. Rent control is an example because the controlled rents are held below the market equilibrium rent level.

2. What predictable effects result from price ceilings like rent control?
The predictable effects resulting from price ceilings include shortages, reduced amounts of the controlled good being made available by suppliers, reductions in the quality of the controlled good, and increased discrimination by sellers among potential buyers of the good.

3. How is the minimum wage law an example of a price floor?
A price floor is a minimum price set above the equilibrium price by the government. The minimum wage is an example because the minimum wage is set above the market equilibrium wage level for some low-skill workers.

4. What predictable effects result from price floors like the minimum wage?
The predictable effects resulting from price floors include surpluses, reduced amounts of the controlled good being purchased by demanders, increases in the quality of the controlled good, and increased discrimination by demanders among potential suppliers of the good.

5. What may happen to the amount of discrimination against groups such as families with children, pet owners, smokers, or students when rent control is imposed?
Rent control laws prevent prospective renters from compensating landlords through higher rents for any characteristic landlords find less attractive, whether it is bothersome noise from children or pets, odors from smokers, increased numbers of renters per unit, or risks of non-payment by lower-income tenants such as students, and so forth. As a result, it lowers the cost of discriminating against anyone possessing what landlords consider unattractive characteristics, as there are other prospective renters without those characteristic who are willing to pay the same controlled rent.

6. Why does rent control often lead to condominium conversions?
Rent control applies to rental apartments but not to apartments owned by their occupants. Therefore, one way to get around rent control restrictions on apartment owners' ability to receive the market value of their apartments is to convert those apartments to condominiums by selling them to tenants instead. Then, what was once a controlled rent becomes part of an uncontrolled mortgage payment. This effect harms poor individuals the most, which is ironic, in that concern for the welfare of lower-income individuals motivates the politics of rent control.

Module 6: Government and the Economy
Concept A

1. What are the arguments for government intervention in the economy?
Seven arguments for government intervention are given in the text: (1) enforcement of property rights, (2) externalities, (3) provision of public goods, (4) information costs, (5) imperfect competition in markets, (6) macroeconomic goals, and (7) income redistribution.

2. How is government enforcement of property rights necessary to a market economy?
The definition and enforcement of property rights—the power to use, sell, rent, dispose of, or enhance the value of one's resources—is necessary to a market economy because such property rights act as incentives for owners to use their resources efficiently and because trade is far more costly to conduct without clear property rights.

3. How does the government right of eminent domain affect property rights?
Eminent domain gives the government the power to force you to sell your property, so citizens do not have the right to maintain ownership against the government. However, under eminent domain, government must compensate owners for that property, so citizens retain the right to be paid for their property. But only if that payment is equal to the market value of the property are property rights not damaged by eminent domain.

4. Would many bicycles be produced in a country where a person maintained his ownership of a bicycle only as long as he was sitting on it? Why?
Without clear, enforceable property rights in bicycles, a buyer would not be willing to pay very much to buy a bicycle (perhaps only the value placed on riding the bicycle once). With buyers willing to pay so little, bicycle sellers would not find it profitable to produce bicycles, and there would be few if any bicycles produced in that country.

5. How do laws against selling stolen property make private property rights more secure?
Laws against stolen property reduce the payoff to potential thieves from stealing (they get less money from their "fence," who must bear greater risks to sell the stolen goods), leading to less theft and making property rights more secure as a result.

Concept B

1. Why are externalities also called spillover effects?
An externality exists whenever the benefits or costs of an activity impact individuals outside the market mechanism. That is, some of the effects spill over to those who have not voluntarily agreed to bear them or compensate others for them, unlike the voluntary exchange of the market.

2. How are externalities related to property rights?

Externalities tend to involve goods for which there are not clearly defined property rights. For example, if you could demand, and receive, compensation for the costs that dirtier air imposes on you, you would have an effective property right to clean air, which you would give up voluntarily only if you were sufficiently compensated. But if your voluntary agreement is required, the effect is no longer an externality because it is internalized by the market mechanism.

3. How do external costs affect the price and output of a polluting activity?

Because the owner of a firm that pollutes does not have to bear the external costs of pollution, he can ignore those real costs of pollution to society. The result is that the private costs he must pay are less than the true social costs of production, so that the market output of the polluting activity is greater, and the resulting market price lower, than it would be if producers did have to bear the external costs of production.

4. How can the government intervene to force producers to internalize external costs?

If the government could impose on producers a tax or fee equal to the external costs imposed on people without their consent, producers would have to take into account those costs. The result would be that those costs would no longer be external costs because they would be internalized by producers.

5. How does internalizing the external costs improve efficiency?

Internalizing external costs eliminates those trades where the marginal benefits to society (measured by the willingness to pay along the market demand curve) exceeds the private marginal costs but are less than the social marginal costs (including the external costs). The resulting net gain in efficiency is that illustrated by the triangle in Exhibit 1 in this concept.

6. How do external benefits affect the output of an activity that causes them?

External benefits are benefits that spill over to others that are not involved in producing or consuming the good. That is, the total benefits of an activity are not fully reflected in the private demand curve; the private demand curve lies further to the left than it would if all spillover benefits were taken into consideration by the market. The result is that the market produces too little of the good—an underallocation from society's standpoint.

7. How can the government intervene to force external benefits to be internalized?

Just as taxes can be used to internalize external costs imposed on others, subsidies can be used to internalize external benefits generated for others. For example, education is subsidized by virtually all developed countries for this reason.

8. Why do most cities have more stringent noise laws for the early morning and late evening hours than for during the day?

The external costs to others from loud noises in residential areas are higher early in the morning and late in the evening (because residents are home and trying to sleep) than in the daytime (when many people are gone at work or are already awake). Given those higher potential external costs, most cities impose more restrictive noise laws for nighttime hours to reduce them.

Concept C

1. How are public goods different from private goods?

Private goods are rival in consumption (we cannot both consume the same unit of a good) and exclusive (non-payers can be prevented from consuming the good unless they pay for it). Public goods are nonrival in consumption (more than one person can consume the same good) and nonexclusive (non-payers can't be effectively kept from consuming the good, even if they don't voluntarily pay for it).

2. Why does the free rider problem arise in the case of public goods?

The free rider problem arises in the case of public goods because people cannot be prevented from enjoying the benefits of public goods once they are provided. Therefore, people have an incentive to not voluntarily pay for those benefits, because they know that their specific contribution will not be important in determining whether they get the good. Thus, it is very difficult or even impossible to finance the efficient quantity of public goods through voluntary market arrangements.

3. How does the free rider problem relate to property rights?

The free rider problem arises in cases where property rights to goods are not easy to prescribe and enforce, as with externalities and public goods.

4. In what way can government provision of public goods solve the free rider problem?

The government can overcome the free rider problem by forcing people to pay for the provision of a public good through taxes.

5. Why is it difficult for the government to determine the proper amount of a public good to produce?

Unlike the case for private goods, people do not reveal the values they place on public goods through the prices they are willing to pay in markets. As a result, there is no way for the government to accurately measure and take into account the magnitudes of the relevant benefits and costs of a public good to individuals.

6. How does a TV broadcast have characteristics of a public good?

An over-the-air broadcast can be watched by a viewer without reducing other viewers' ability to watch the same broadcast, and a viewer of such broadcasts cannot be excluded from watching if he refuses to pay for it. Note that cable broadcasts, in contrast, can exclude non-payers, so they don't have both characteristics of a public good.

7. Can lighthouse services be privately provided if all of the boats using the services of a lighthouse are heading for the port nearest that lighthouse? Why or why not?

If boats that used the port could be charged a docking fee to pay for the lighthouse services, that would create a mechanism to pay for the private provision of lighthouse services. (There must, of course, not be another port sufficiently close that the boats could use the lighthouse to navigate safely to the other port.)

Concept D

1. How long should you continue to seek more information before making a decision?

As with any other choice, one should seek more information before making a decision as long as the expected marginal benefits from having added information exceed the marginal expected costs of acquiring that information. This implies that it is often rational to be less than completely informed when making decisions.

2. What is the rationale for government provision of information?
In some cases, the government might be able to gather or communicate information at lower costs than citizens could otherwise. By lowering information costs, more information is acquired before choices are made, and citizens benefit by making better-informed choices (i.e., making fewer mistakes).

3. What are the objections to government provision of information?
Government-provided information may be more costly to acquire than through market channels, it may be inaccurate or misleading, and it can be manipulated by special interest groups for their own advantages rather than to benefit consumers.

4. Why do consumers spend more time researching a home purchase than an electric can opener purchase?
The likely benefits from an additional hour researching a home purchase is likely to be far larger, whether in terms of a better price or a better match for your preferences, than the likely benefits from spending that hour researching an electric can opener purchase.

5. If someone argues that we need occupational licensing of gardeners to guarantee that misinformed consumers don't get shoddy service, is that person more likely to be a (highly trained) gardener or a homeowner who uses a gardening service? Why?
Occupational licensing has very often been advocated by existing producers of the services involved as a way to reduce competition from potential new producers who would otherwise enter and reduce the profits of the existing producers. Most homeowners, on the other hand, feel sufficiently protected from serious problems with gardening services because of the market information conveyed by gardeners' reputations and the large number of alternative gardeners available.

Concept E

1. Why would the government want to prevent market conditions of insufficient competition?
When there is insufficient or restricted competition, outputs are lower and prices paid by consumers are higher than they would be with more effective competition. By encouraging competition and discouraging monopoly, then, consumers can benefit.

2. What are the macroeconomic goals of government intervention in the economy?
The primary macroeconomic goals of government intervention in the economy include full employment, price stability, and economic growth.

3. What government policy changes might be effective in increasing employment in recessions?
Government policies to stimulate the economy, such as decreasing taxes or increasing government purchases, could potentially increase employment in recessions.

4. What government policy changes might be effective in controlling inflation?
Government policies to control inflation can include increasing taxes, decreasing government purchases, and reducing the growth in the money supply through the banking system.

Concept F

1. What is the basic argument in favor of government redistribution of income?
The basic argument in favor of government redistribution of income is that some believe the market-determined distribution of income is unfair or inequitable. Therefore, the government could improve equity or fairness by redistributing income toward those who are needier.

2. What are the objections to government intervention intended to redistribute income?
The central objection to government intervention to redistribute income is that not everyone agrees about what is fair (e.g., helping someone get their "fair share" through the government means taking those resources from someone else, and they might not consider the result fair). Another objection is that there is no way to redistribute income without undermining incentives to work hard and be productive.

3. How does the government use taxes, subsidies, and transfer payments to redistribute income toward lower-income groups?
Taxes, particularly progressive ones such as the individual income tax, are borne more heavily by higher-income citizens than lower-income citizens, while most subsidy and transfer payment programs are primarily focused on lower-income citizens.

4. If a government wanted to make the distribution of income more equal, would it be more effective to impose a tax on luxury cars or on food?
To equalize the distribution of income, a tax would have to be borne more heavily by higher-income individuals than by lower-income individuals. A tax on luxury cars achieves this result far better than a tax on food.

Concept G

1. What principles does the public choice analysis of government behavior share with the economic analysis of market behavior?
Public choice analysis of government behavior is based on the principle that the behavior of individuals in politics, just like that in the marketplace, is influenced by self-interest. That is, it applies basic economic theory to politics, looking for differences in incentives to explain people's behavior.

2. Why is it rational to be relatively less informed about most political choices than about your own market choices?
It is rational to be relatively less informed about most political choices than about your own market choices because the costs of becoming more informed about political choices tend to be higher and the benefits of becoming more informed about political choices tend to be lower than for your own market choices.

3. Why can't the majority of citizens effectively counter the political power of special-interest groups?
The majority of citizens can't effectively counter the political power of special interest groups because even if the special interest group is successful in getting everyone else to pay for a project that benefits it, the cost to each citizen will be small. In fact, this cost is very likely far smaller than the cost to a member of the majority of becoming informed and active to successfully oppose it.

4. According to public choice theorists, what is the primary advantage of government? What is the biggest threat from government?
The primary advantage of government is its ability to establish a legal and economic environment that provides general opportunity for people to benefit from their own efforts through productive cooperation with others. The biggest threat from government is the risk that its power can be captured by special interests and used to advance their objectives at the expense of the general public.

5. Why are college students better informed about their own teachers' and schools' policies than about national education issues?

The benefits from "local knowledge" of teachers and school policies to students can be large, say, in a higher GPA, and the costs of acquiring that information is typically low for those on campus. On the other hand, the benefits from being more informed on national educational issues are typically much lower, because your actions are very unlikely to change those policies, and the costs of acquiring that information can be very large for what are far more complex national educational issues. The result is that students are better informed about their own teachers and school policies than national educational issues.

6. How can you be forced to pay for something you do not want to "buy" in the political sector? Is this sometimes good?

The government can use its power to tax to force you to pay for services they provide, even if you do not want to pay for those services. This can be useful, such as in overcoming the free rider problem in financing public goods or solving externality problems, as well as bad, as in the case of special interest dominance.

7. Why do you think news reporters are more informed than average citizens about public policy issues?

The benefits news reporters receive from being more informed about public policy issues are greater than for most citizens, because being better informed allows reporters to do a better job, which they benefit from in higher wages, greater honors, and so forth. Because the benefits of being better informed are typically higher for news reporters, they are better informed than average citizens.

Concept H

1. What accounts for most of the growth of government spending as a share of total output since 1965?

Most of the growth of government spending as a share of total output since 1965 has come from an increase in transfer payments, for programs such as Social Security and welfare.

2. What options are available for a government to finance its spending?

A government can finance its spending through taxes, borrowing, or inflation.

3. What is the difference between a progressive tax and a regressive tax?

A progressive tax is one that takes a higher proportion of income from higher income individuals than from lower income individuals; a regressive tax is one that takes a smaller proportion of income from higher income individuals than from lower income individuals.

4. What are some advantages and disadvantages of a flat tax? Would it be progressive?

With a flat tax, everyone would be taxed the same percentage of their income above a stipulated income level. A flat tax would be simpler than the current tax system, and traditional exemptions, along with their abuses, would be eliminated. A flat tax would be progressive as long as there was some initial level of income exempt from the tax. Higher-income people would then pay the flat tax rate on a larger share of their incomes than lower-income people.

Module 7: Consumer Choice and Elasticities
Concept A

1. How do economists define utility?

Economists define utility as the level of satisfaction or well-being an individual receives from consumption of a good or service.

2. Why can't interpersonal utility comparisons be made?

We can't make interpersonal utility comparisons because it is impossible to measure the relative satisfaction of different people in comparable terms.

3. What is the relationship between total utility and marginal utility?

Marginal utility is the increase in total utility from increasing consumption of a good or service by one unit.

4. Why could you say that Rich, who is a millionaire, gets less marginal utility from a second piece of pizza than from the first piece, but you couldn't say whether he got more or less marginal utility from a second piece of pizza than Les, who has a very low income?

Rich gets less marginal utility from a second piece of pizza than from the first piece because of the law of diminishing marginal utility. However, it is impossible to measure the relative satisfaction of different people in comparable terms, even when we are comparing rich and poor people, so we cannot say whether Rich or Les got more marginal utility from a second slice of pizza.

5. How would it be possible for someone to get negative marginal utility from consuming an additional piece of pizza for dinner?

It is possible to have eaten so much that an additional piece of pizza would leave you with less total utility. For instance, the last piece eaten in a pizza eating contest is very likely to have negative marginal utility. Because he must pay a positive price for each good or service he consumes, a rational person would not, as a general rule, consume something that gives him negative utility.

6. Are you likely to get as much marginal utility from your last piece of chicken at an all-you-can-eat restaurant as a restaurant where you pay $2 per piece of chicken?

No. If you pay $2 per piece, you only eat another piece as long as it gives you more marginal utility than spending the $2 on something else. But at an all-you-can-eat restaurant, the dollar price of one more piece of chicken is zero, so you consume more chicken and get less marginal utility out of the last piece of chicken you eat. Indeed, you would consume chicken until it had a zero marginal utility to you.

Concept B

1. What do economists mean by consumer equilibrium?

Consumer equilibrium means that a consumer is consuming the optimum, or utility-maximizing, combination of goods and services for a given level of income.

2. How could a consumer raise his total utility if the ratio of his marginal utility to the price for good A was greater than that for good B?

Such a consumer would raise his total utility by spending less on good B and more on good A, because a dollar less spent on B would lower his utility less than a dollar more spent on A would increase it.

3. What must be true about the ratio of marginal utility to price for each good consumed in consumer equilibrium?

In consumer equilibrium, the ratio of marginal utility to price for each good consumed must be the same, otherwise the consumer could raise his total utility by changing his consumption pattern to increase consumption of those goods with higher marginal utility per dollar and decrease consumption of those goods with lower marginal utility per dollar.

4. How does the law of demand reflect the law of diminishing marginal utility?

In consumer equilibrium, the marginal utility per dollar spent is the same for all goods and services consumed. Starting from that point, reducing the price of one good increases its marginal utility per dollar, resulting in increased consumption of that good. This is what the law of demand states: The quantity of a good demanded will increase, the lower its price, *ceteris paribus*.

5. Why doesn't consumer equilibrium imply that the ratio of total utility per dollar is the same for different goods?

It is the additional, or marginal, utility per dollar spent for different goods, not the total utility you get per dollar spent, that matters in determining whether consuming more of some goods and less of others will increase total utility.

6. Why does the principle of consumer equilibrium imply that people would tend to buy more apples when the price of apples is reduced?

A fall in the price of apples will increase the marginal utility per dollar spent on the last apple a person was willing to buy before their price fell. This means a person could increase his or her total utility for a given income by buying more apples and less of some other goods.

7. If the price of walnuts is $6 per pound and the price of peanuts is $2 per pound, if a person gets 20 units of added utility from eating the last pound of peanuts he consumes, how many units of added utility would that person have to get from eating the last pound of walnuts in order to be in consumer equilibrium?

Because consumer equilibrium requires that the marginal utility per dollar spent must be the same across goods that are consumed, the last pound of walnuts would have to provide 60 units of added, or marginal, utility in this case ($60 \div 6 = 20 \div 2$).

Concept C

1. What is consumer surplus?

Consumer surplus is defined as the monetary difference between what a consumer is willing to pay for a good and what he is required to pay for it.

2. Why do the first units consumed at a given price add more consumer surplus than the last units consumed?

Because what a consumer is willing to pay for a good declines as more of that good is consumed, the difference between what he is willing to pay and the price he must pay also declines for later units.

3. Why does a decrease in a good's price increase the consumer surplus from consumption of that good?

A decrease in a good's price increases the consumer surplus from consumption of that good by lowering the price for those goods that were bought at the higher price and by increasing consumer surplus from increased purchases at the lower price.

4. Why might the consumer surplus from purchases of mink coats, which are very expensive, be less than the consumer surplus from purchases of far less expensive leather coats?

Consumer surplus is the difference between what people would have been willing to pay for the amount of the good consumed

and what they must pay. Even though the marginal value of a leather coat is lower than the marginal value of a mink coat to buyers, the difference between the total value of the leather coats purchased and what consumers had to pay may well be larger than that difference for mink coats. In fact, the consumer surplus could be negative for the mink coats (hence, they are not purchased) despite their giving a higher utility than a leather coat, because their price is higher yet!

Concept D

1. What question is the price elasticity of demand designed to answer?

The price elasticity of demand is designed to answer the question: How responsive is quantity demanded to changes in the price of a good?

2. How is the price elasticity of demand calculated?

The price elasticity of demand is calculated as the percentage change in quantity demanded, divided by the percentage change in the price that caused the change in quantity demanded.

3. What is the difference between a relatively elastic demand curve and a relatively inelastic demand curve?

Quantity demanded changes relatively more than price along a relatively elastic segment of a demand curve, while quantity demanded changes relatively less than price along a relatively inelastic segment of a demand curve.

4. What is the relationship between the price elasticity of demand and the slope at a given point on a demand curve?

At a given initial price and quantity, the flatter the demand curve, the more quantity demanded changes for a given change in price (which means that percentage change must also be larger), so the greater the elasticity of demand.

5. What factors tend to make demand curves more elastic?

Demand curves tend to become more elastic, the larger the number of close substitutes there are for the good, the larger proportion of income spent on the good, and the greater the amount of time that buyers have to respond to a change in the good's price.

6. Why would a tax on a particular brand of cigarettes be less effective at reducing smoking than a tax on all brands of cigarettes?

A tax on one brand of cigarettes would allow smokers to avoid the tax by switching brands rather than by smoking less, but a tax on all brands would raise the cost of smoking any cigarettes. A tax on all brands of cigarettes would therefore be more effective in reducing smoking.

7. Why is the elasticity of demand for products at a 24-hour convenience store likely to be lower at 2 A.M. than at 2 P.M.?

There are fewer alternative stores open at 2 A.M. than at 2 P.M., and because there are fewer good substitutes, the demand for products at 24-hour convenience stores is greater at 2 A.M.

8. Why is the elasticity of demand for turkeys likely to be lower, but the elasticity of demand for turkeys at a *particular* store likely to be greater, at Thanksgiving than at other times of the year?

For many people, there are far fewer good substitutes for turkey at Thanksgiving than at other times, so the demand for turkeys is more inelastic at Thanksgiving. But grocery stores looking to attract customers for their entire large Thanksgiving shopping trip also often offer and heavily advertise turkeys at far better prices than normal, which means that during the Thanksgiving season, there are more good substitutes and a more elastic demand for buying a turkey at a particular store than normal.

Concept E

1. Why does total revenue vary inversely with price if demand is relatively elastic?

Total revenue varies inversely with price if demand is relatively elastic, because the quantity demanded (which equals the quantity sold in equilibrium) changes relatively more than price along a relatively elastic demand curve. This means that total revenue, which equals price times quantity demanded (sold) at that price, will change in the opposite direction from the change in price.

2. Why does total revenue vary in the same direction as price if demand is relatively inelastic?

Total revenue varies in the same direction as price if demand is relatively inelastic, because the quantity demanded (which equals the quantity sold in equilibrium) changes relatively less than price along a relatively inelastic demand curve. This means that total revenue, which equals price times quantity demanded (sold) at that price, will change in the same direction as price.

3. Why is a linear demand curve more elastic at higher price ranges than at lower price ranges?

Along the upper half of a linear (constant-slope) demand curve, total revenue increases as the price falls, indicating that demand is relatively elastic. Along the lower half of a linear (constant-slope) demand curve, total revenue decreases as the price falls, indicating that demand is relatively inelastic.

4. If demand for some good was perfectly inelastic, how would total revenue from its sales change as its price changed?

A perfectly inelastic demand curve would be one where the quantity sold did not vary with the price. In such an (imaginary) case, total revenue would increase proportionately with price: A 10 percent increase in price with the same quantity sold would result in a 10 percent increase in total revenue.

5. Assume that both you and Art, your partner in a picture-framing business, want to increase your firm's total revenue. You argue that in order to achieve this goal, you should lower your prices; Art, on the other hand, thinks that you should raise your prices. What assumptions are each of you making about your firm's elasticity of demand?

You are assuming that a lower price will increase total revenue, which implies that you think the demand for your picture frames is relatively elastic. Art is assuming that an increase in your price will increase your total revenue, which implies that he thinks the demand for your picture frames is relatively inelastic.

Concept F

1. How does the cross elasticity of demand tell you whether two goods are substitutes? Complements?

Two goods are substitutes when a higher price for one increases the demand for the other good at a given price. But if a higher price of one good increases the demand for the other good, they have a positive cross elasticity of demand. Two goods are complements when a higher price for one decreases the demand for other good at a given price. But if a higher price of one good decreases the demand for the other good, they have a negative cross elasticity of demand.

2. How does the income elasticity of demand tell you whether a good is normal? Inferior?

A good is normal when an increase in income increases the quantity of the good demanded at a given price. But if a higher income increases the quantity of a good demanded, it has a positive income elasticity. A good is inferior when an increase in income decreases the quantity of the good demanded at a given price. But if a higher income decreases the quantity of a good demanded, it has a negative income elasticity.

3. What does it mean to say that the elasticity of supply for one good is greater than that for another?

For the elasticity of supply for one good to be greater than for another, the percentage increase in quantity supplied that results from a given percentage change in price will be greater for the first good than for the second.

4. How do the relative elasticities of supply and demand determine who bears the greater burden of a tax?

When demand is more elastic than supply, the tax burden falls mainly on producers; when supply is more elastic than demand, the tax burden falls mainly on consumers.

5. If the cross elasticity of demand between potato chips and popcorn was positive and very large, would popcorn makers benefit from a tax imposed on potato chips?

A large positive cross elasticity of demand between potato chips and popcorn indicates that they are close substitutes. A tax on potato chips, which would raise the price of potato chips as a result, would also substantially increase the demand for popcorn, increasing the price of popcorn and the quantity of popcorn sold, increasing the profits of popcorn makers.

6. As people's incomes rise, why will they spend an increasing portion of their incomes on goods with income elasticities greater than one (CDs) and a decreasing portion of their incomes on goods with income elasticities less than one (food)?

An income elasticity of one would mean that people spend the same fraction or share of their income on a particular good as their incomes increase. An income elasticity greater than one would mean that people spend an increasing fraction or share of their income on a particular good as their incomes increase. An income elasticity less than one would mean that people spend a decreasing fraction or share of their income on a particular good as their incomes increase.

7. If people spent three times as much on restaurant meals and four times as much on CDs as their incomes doubled, would restaurant meals or CDs have a greater income elasticity of demand?

CDs would have a higher income elasticity of demand (4) in this case than restaurant meals (3).

Module 8: Production and Costs
Concept A

1. What is the difference between explicit costs and implicit costs?

Explicit costs are those costs readily measured by the money spent on the resources used, such as wages. Implicit costs are those that do not represent an explicit outlay of money but do represent opportunity costs, such as the opportunity cost of your time when you work for yourself. Usually, explicit costs are contractually required of the firm, while implicit costs are not.

2. Are both explicit costs and implicit costs relevant in making economic decisions?

In making economic decisions, where expected marginal benefits must be weighed against expected marginal costs, all relevant costs must be included, whether they are explicit or implicit.

3. How do we measure profits?

Profit is measured as total revenue minus total cost.

4. What is the difference between economic profits and accounting profits?

Accounting profit equals total revenue minus total explicit cost. Economic profit equals total revenue minus both explicit and implicit cost, including the opportunity cost (foregone earnings) of financial resources invested in the firm. To be earning economic profits means that a firm is earning an above-normal rate of return on capital invested in the firm.

5. If you turn down a job offer of $45,000 per year to work for yourself, what is the opportunity cost of working for yourself?

Other things equal, you incur a $45,000 per year implicit cost of working for yourself in this case, because that is what you gave up when you chose to turn down the alternative job offer. If you turned down even better offers, your opportunity cost of working for yourself would be even higher.

6. What happens to the cost of growing strawberries on your own land if a housing developer offers you three times what you thought your land was worth?

The implicit opportunity cost of growing strawberries on your own land increases, because the value of an alternative use of the land has increased.

7. As a farmer, you work for yourself, using your own tractor, equipment, and farm structures, and you cultivate your own land. Why might it be difficult to calculate your profits from farming?

All of your owned inputs—your own time, tractor, equipment, structures, and land—have opportunity costs that are not revealed in explicit dollar payments. Correctly assigning implicit costs to all of these owned inputs, so that a correct measure of the economic profits from farming can be made, could be very difficult.

Concept B

1. What is the difference between fixed and variable inputs?

Fixed inputs are those, such as plant and equipment, that *cannot* be changed in the short run; variable inputs are those, such as hourly labor, that *can* be changed in the short run.

2. Why do we call the long run a planning horizon?

The long run is a period of time long enough to allow the firm to adjust all of its inputs. However, at any point in time, some inputs are fixed in amount, so that a firm never operates in the long run. The long run, therefore, refers to however long a period it would take for all inputs to be variable—in other words, the planning horizon.

3. Why are all inputs variable in the long run?

All inputs are variable in the long run by definition, because the long run is defined as that time period necessary to allow all inputs to be varied.

4. What relationship does a production function represent?

A production function represents the relationship between different combinations of inputs and the maximum output of a product that can be produced with those inputs, with given technology.

5. What is the law of diminishing marginal product? What causes it?

The law of diminishing marginal product states that as the amount of a variable input is increased, the amount of other inputs being held constant, a point ultimately will be reached beyond which marginal product will decline. This effect is caused by reductions in the amount of fixed inputs that can be combined with each unit of a variable input, as the amount of that variable input used increases.

6. Why is entering an industry a long-run decision, while once you have entered the industry, you operate in the short run?

Prior to entering an industry, none of your inputs are yet fixed, and decisions when no inputs are fixed are long-run decisions. Once you have entered an industry, some of your inputs are fixed in amount at any given point in time, and decisions when some inputs are variable are short-run decisions.

7. Say that your firm's total product curve includes the following data: 1 worker can produce 8 units of output; 2, 20 units; 3, 34 units; 4, 50 units; 5, 60 units; 6, 70 units; 7, 76 units; 8, 78 units; and 9, 77 units.

a) What is the marginal product of the seventh worker?
b) When does the law of diminishing product set in?
c) Under these conditions, would you ever choose to employ nine workers?

a) The marginal product of the seventh worker is the increase in total product when the seventh worker is added, or 6 units (76 units with seven workers, minus 70 units with six workers).

b) The law of diminishing marginal product sets in with the fifth worker, when the addition to total product from one more worker of 10 (60-50) first falls below that for adding earlier workers (8, 12, 14, and 16 for the first four workers, respectively).

c) No, you would never employ nine workers, because you must pay for workers, and the ninth worker actually decreases your output. Only if someone actually paid you to hire the worker would you consider it.

Concept C

1. What is the difference between fixed costs and variable costs?

Fixed costs are the expenses associated with fixed inputs (which therefore only exist in the short run), which are constant regardless of output. Variable costs are the expenses associated with variable inputs, which change as the level of output changes.

2. How are average fixed cost, average variable cost, and average total cost calculated?

For a given level of output, any average cost is calculated as the relevant total cost divided by the level of output (the cost per unit). Average fixed cost is therefore total fixed cost divided by output; average variable cost is total variable cost divided by output; and average total cost is total cost (fixed cost plus variable cost) divided by output.

3. Why is marginal cost the relevant cost to consider when one is deciding whether to produce more or less of a product?

Marginal cost is the additional cost of increasing output by one unit. That is, it is the cost relevant to the choice of whether to produce and sell one more unit of a good. For producing and selling one more unit of a product to increase profits, the addition to revenue from selling that output (marginal revenue) must exceed the addition to cost from producing it (marginal cost).

4. If the average variable cost curve was constant over some range of output, why would the average total cost be falling over that range of output?

Average total cost is the sum of average variable cost and average fixed cost. Average fixed costs fall over the entire possible range of output. Therefore, if the average variable cost curve was constant over a range of output, the average total cost curve must be falling over that range of output.

5. If your season batting average going into a game was .300 (3 hits per 10 at bats) and you got 2 hits in 5 at bats during the game, would your season batting average rise or fall as a result?

Your "marginal" batting average in the game was .400 (2 hits per 5 at bats), which was higher than your previous batting average. As a consequence, because that game's marginal outcome was above your previous average, it raises your season batting average as a result.

6. As a movie exhibitor, you can choose between paying a flat fee of $5,000 to show a movie for a week or paying a fee of $2 per customer. Will your choice affect your fixed and variable costs? How?

A flat fee arrangement would imply a fixed cost of $5,000 per showing, with the marginal cost of showing it to one more customer equal to zero. A per-customer fee would result in zero fixed costs to show the movie, but a $2 variable cost per customer. Your decision clearly depends on whether or not you expect to have more than 2,500 customers during the week.

7. If your university pays lecture note takers $20 per hour to take notes in your economics class, and then sells subscriptions for $15 per student, is the cost of the lecture note taker a fixed or variable cost of selling an additional subscription?

Because the cost of the lecture note taker does not change as the number of subscriptions "produced" changes, it is a fixed cost to be considered in the decision of how many subscriptions to sell.

Concept D

1. What is the primary reason that average total cost falls as output expands over low output ranges?

The primary reason that average total cost falls as output expands over low output ranges is that average fixed costs decline sharply with output at low levels of output.

2. Why does average total cost rise at some point as output expands further?

Average total cost begins to rise at some point as output expands further, because of the law of diminishing marginal product, also called the law of increasing costs. Over this range of output, adding more variable inputs does not increase output by the same proportion, so that the average cost of production increases over this range of output, ultimately driving up average total costs.

3. When marginal cost is not equal to average total cost, why does average total cost change in the direction of marginal cost?

When the marginal cost of a unit of output exceeds its average total cost, including the higher cost unit will raise the average (just as getting higher marginal grades this term will increase your GPA). Similarly, a marginal cost below the current average cost will pull down the average.

4. Why does the law of diminishing marginal productivity imply the law of increasing costs?

Over the range of output subject to diminishing marginal productivity, adding more of a variable input will increase output by less than the same proportion. But for a given increase in cost (the increase in the variable input times its price) to add less to output than before means that the added cost of those additional units of output rises.

5. What is likely to happen to your marginal costs when adding output requires working beyond an eight-hour day, if workers must be paid time-and-a-half wages beyond an eight-hour day?

Because your marginal cost of labor becomes much higher once time-and-a-half wages begin, other things equal, your marginal cost curve will rise sharply as you exceed an eight-hour work day.

6. A one-day ticket to visit the Screaming Coasters theme park costs $36, but you can also get a two-consecutive-day ticket for $40. What is the average cost per day for the two-day ticket? What is the marginal cost of the second consecutive day?

The average cost per day of the two-consecutive-day ticket is $20 ($40 ÷ 2). However, the marginal cost of the second consecutive day is $4 ($40 − $36). Note that the lower marginal cost pulled down the average cost from $36 to $20.

Concept E

1. Why is the law of diminishing returns a short-run, rather than a long-run, concept?

The law of diminishing returns is a short-run, rather than a long-run, concept, because it refers to changes in output resulting from changes in a variable input, for a given level of fixed inputs, and inputs are fixed only in the short run.

2. What are economies of scale, diseconomies of scale, and constant returns to scale?

Each of these terms refers to average, or per-unit, costs, as output expands in the long run. Economies of scale means that long-run average cost falls as output expands; diseconomies of scale means that long-run average cost rises as output expands; and constant returns to scale means that long-run average cost is constant as output expands.

3. How might cooking for a family dinner be subject to falling average total cost in the short run as the size of the family grows?

Many of the costs of cooking are virtually the same (e.g., the cost of cleaning the pots and pans involved and following the recipe) whether you are cooking for one more family member or not. These fixed costs imply that the average fixed cost per meal served falls with the number of meals, which tends to make the average total cost per meal fall with the number of meals, other things equal. This is one reason that you would expect larger families to eat a higher percentage of their meals at home.

4. How might a university cafeteria cooking for 400 students rather than 4 be subject to economies of scale in the long run?

Once the appropriate larger-scale cooking technology has been adopted (i.e., in the long run, when all inputs can be varied), such as larger ovens, and that larger scale allows more productivity by increasing the specialization of workers' tasks, the average cost per meal served is likely to be lower when cooking for 400 than for 4.

Module 9: Perfect Competition
Concept A

1. Why do perfectly competitive markets involve homogeneous goods?

For there to be a large number of sellers of a particular good, so that no seller can appreciably affect the market price (i.e., sellers are price takers), the goods in question must be the same, or homogeneous.

2. Why does the absence of significant barriers to entry tend to result in a large number of suppliers?

With no significant barriers to entry, it is fairly easy for entrepreneurs to become suppliers of a product. With such easy entry, as long as an industry is profitable, it will attract new suppliers, typically resulting in large numbers of sellers.

3. Why does the fact that perfectly competitive firms are "small" relative to the market make them price takers?

Because a perfectly competitive firm sells only a small amount relative to the total market supply, even sharply reducing or increasing its output will make virtually no difference in the market quantity supplied; therefore, it will make virtually no difference in the market price. Because a firm is able to sell all it wants at the market equilibrium price but is unable to appreciably affect that price, it takes the market equilibrium price as given—it is a price taker.

4. Why is the market for used furniture unlikely to be perfectly competitive?

Perfectly competitive markets require large numbers of sellers and buyers of a homogeneous good. But used furniture by its nature cannot be standardized to the point where there can be a large number of sellers of identical pieces of used furniture.

Concept B

1. Why would a perfectly competitive firm not try to raise or lower its price?

A perfectly competitive firm is able to sell all it wants at the market equilibrium price. Therefore, it has no incentive to lower prices (sacrificing revenues and therefore profits) in an attempt to increase sales. Because other firms are willing to sell perfect substitutes for each firm's product (because goods are homogeneous) at the market equilibrium price, trying to raise price would lead to the firm losing all its sales. Therefore, it has no incentive to try to raise its price, either.

2. Why can we represent the demand curve of a perfectly competitive firm as perfectly elastic (horizontal) at the market price?

Because a perfectly competitive firm can sell all it would like at the market equilibrium price, the demand curve it faces for its output is perfectly elastic (horizontal) at that market equilibrium price.

3. How does an individual perfectly competitive firm's demand curve change when the market price changes?

Because a perfectly competitive firm can sell all it would like at the market equilibrium price, it faces a perfectly elastic demand curve at the market equilibrium price. Therefore, anything that changes the market equilibrium price (any of the PYNTE market demand curve shifters or the SPENT market supply curve shifters) will change the price at which each perfectly competitive firm's demand curve is perfectly elastic (horizontal).

4. If the marginal costs facing every producer of a product shifted up, would the position of the perfectly competitive firm's demand curve be likely to change as a result?

Yes. If the marginal cost curves facing each producer shifted up, there would be a decrease (leftward shift) in the industry supply curve. That would result in a higher market price that each producer takes as given, which would shift up each producer's horizontal demand curve to that new market price.

Concept C

1. How is total revenue calculated?

Total revenue is equal to the price times the quantity sold. However, because the quantity sold at that price must equal the quantity demanded at that price (because to sell a product, you need a willing buyer), it can also be described as price times quantity demanded at that price.

2. How is average revenue derived from total revenue?

Average, or per-unit revenue for a given quantity of output is just the total revenue from that quantity of sales divided by the quantity sold.

3. How is marginal revenue derived from total revenue?

Marginal revenue is the change in total revenue from the sale of one more unit of output. It can be either positive (total revenue increases with output) or negative (total revenue decreases with output).

4. Why is marginal revenue equal to price for a perfectly competitive firm?

Because a perfectly competitive firm can sell all it would like at the market equilibrium price, it can sell one more unit at that price without having to lower its price on the other units it sells (which would require sacrificing revenues from those sales). Therefore, its marginal revenue from selling one more unit equals the market equilibrium price, and its horizontal demand curve is the same as its horizontal marginal revenue curve. Recall that when any marginal curve is equal to the average curve, the latter is neither rising nor falling (for example, if your marginal grade this term is the same as your GPA, your GPA won't change).

5. Why must a perfectly competitive firm's marginal cost curve be rising at its profit-maximizing level of output?

Because a perfectly competitive firm can sell all it would like at the market equilibrium price, its marginal revenue from each additional unit sold is constant and equal to that same market price. But because a profit-maximizing firm will sell as long as marginal revenue exceeds marginal cost, a perfectly competitive firm would continue to expand its output indefinitely unless its marginal cost curve at some point rose to intersect its horizontal marginal revenue curve.

Concept D

1. How is the profit-maximizing output quantity determined?

The profit-maximizing output is the output where marginal revenue equals marginal cost (because profits increase for every unit of output for which marginal revenue exceeds marginal cost), when marginal cost is rising.

2. How do we determine total revenue and total cost for the profit-maximizing output quantity?

At the profit-maximizing quantity, total revenue is equal to average revenue (price) times quantity (because average revenue is total revenue divided by quantity), and total cost is equal to average cost times quantity (because average cost equals total cost divided by quantity).

3. If a profit-maximizing, perfectly competitive firm is earning a profit because total revenue exceeds total cost, why must the market price exceed average cost?

If total revenue exceeds total cost, total revenue divided by the quantity of output, which is average revenue or price, must also exceed total cost divided by the same quantity of output, which is average cost, for that level of output.

4. If a profit-maximizing, perfectly competitive firm is earning a loss because total revenue is less than total cost, why must the market price be less than average cost?

If total revenue is less than total cost, total revenue divided by the quantity of output, which is average revenue or price, must also be less than total cost divided by the same quantity of output, which is average cost, for that level of output.

5. If a profit-maximizing, perfectly competitive firm is earning zero economic profits because total revenue equals total cost, why must the market price be equal to the average cost for that level of output?

If total revenue equals total cost, total revenue divided by the quantity of output, which is average revenue (or price), must also be equal to total cost divided by the same quantity of output, which is average cost, for that level of output.

6. Why would a profit-maximizing, perfectly competitive firm shut down rather than operate if price was less than its average variable costs?

If a firm shuts down, its losses will equal its fixed costs (because there is no revenue or variable costs). If a firm operates and revenues exactly cover variable costs, it will also suffer losses equal to fixed costs. But if a firm cannot even cover all of its variable costs with its revenues, it will lose its fixed costs plus part of its variable costs. Because those losses are greater than the losses incurred from shutting down, a firm would choose to shut down rather than continue to operate in this situation.

7. Why would a profit-maximizing, perfectly competitive firm continue to operate for a period of time if price was greater than average variable cost but less than average total cost?

If price was greater than average variable cost but less than average total cost, a firm is earning losses and will eventually go out of business if that situation continues. However, in the short run, as long as revenues more than cover variable costs, losses from operating will be less than the losses from shutting down (these losses equal total fixed cost), as at least part of fixed costs are covered by revenues, so a firm will continue to operate in the short run in this situation.

Concept E

1. Why do firms enter profitable industries?

Profitable industries generate a higher rates of return to productive assets than other industries. Therefore, firms will enter such industries in their search for more profitable uses for their assets.

2. Why does entry eliminate positive economic profits in a perfectly competitive industry?

Entry eliminates positive economic profits (above-normal rates of return) in a perfectly competitive industry, because as firms enter, the increased supply will drive down prices, ultimately causing a fall in profits. Entry will continue as long as economic profits remain positive (rates of return are higher than in other industries).

3. Why do firms exit unprofitable industries?

Unprofitable industries generate lower rates of return to productive assets than other industries. Therefore, firms will exit such industries in their search for more profitable uses for their assets elsewhere.

4. Why does exit eliminate economic losses in a perfectly competitive industry?

Exit eliminates negative economic profits (below-normal rates of return) in a perfectly competitive industry because as firms exit the industry, the reduction in supply causes the prices to rise, ultimately eliminating the losses. Exit will continue as long as economic profits remain negative (rates of return are lower than in other industries).

5. Why is a situation of zero economic profits a stable long-run equilibrium situation for a perfectly competitive industry?

A situation of zero economic profits is a stable long-run equilibrium situation for a perfectly competitive industry because, in that situation, there are no profit incentives for firms either to enter or leave the industry. The price, which equals the (minimum) average total cost, will have no tendency to rise or fall.

6. Say that there are a large number of small producers in an industry but very large barriers to entry to new firms. After a large, permanent increase in industry demand, would producers in the industry again earn zero economic profits in long-run equilibrium?

In a perfectly competitive industry, any short-run profits are eroded by the entry of new producers into the industry. A permanent increase in industry demand would lead to positive short-run profits, but the barriers to entry would prevent new producers from entering and driving economic profits back to zero in the industry. As a result, positive economic profits could persist in such an industry.

Concept F

1. What must be true about input costs as industry output expands for a constant-cost industry?

Input costs remain constant as industry output expands for a constant-cost industry (which is why it is a constant-cost industry).

2. What must be true about input costs as industry output expands for an increasing-cost industry?

Input costs increase as industry output expands for an increasing-cost industry (which is why it is an increasing-cost industry).

3. What would be the long-run equilibrium result of an increase in demand in a constant-cost industry?

The long-run equilibrium result of an increase in demand in a constant-cost industry is an increase in industry output with no change in price, because output will expand as long as price exceeds the constant level of long-run average cost.

4. What would be the long-run equilibrium result of an increase in demand in an increasing-cost industry?

The long-run equilibrium result of an increase in demand in an increasing-cost industry is an increase in industry output (but a smaller increase than in the constant-cost case) and a higher price. Output will expand as long as price exceeds long-run average cost, but that expansion of output increases costs by raising input prices, so that in the long run, prices just cover the resulting higher costs of production.

Module 10: Monopoly
Concept A

1. Why are the industry and firm demand curves the same for a monopoly?

The industry and firm demand curves the same for a monopoly because a monopoly is the only seller of the product under consideration. Because a monopolist is the only seller in the industry, its demand curve is the industry demand curve.

2. Why is a monopoly a price maker but a perfectly competitive firm a price taker?

A perfectly competitive firm is a price taker because it cannot appreciably change the quantity offered for sale on a market, and therefore it cannot change the equilibrium market price appreciably. However, because a monopoly controls the quantity offered for sale, it can alter the price by changing its output; it "makes" the price through its decision of how much to produce.

3. Why is monopoly as a stable market structure dependent on the existence of barriers to entry?

If a monopoly was unusually profitable (earning a higher than normal rate of return), entry by other firms would occur, driving its economic profits down and increasing the number of sellers, unless some barrier to entry prevented it.

4. Why is a pure monopoly a rarity?

Pure monopolies are a rarity because there are very few goods or services for which there are no close substitutes and for which there is only one producer.

5. Why is marginal revenue less than price for a profit-maximizing monopolist?

For a monopolist, selling an additional unit requires it to reduce its price, and reducing its price reduces its revenues from units it was selling before at its previous higher price. Therefore, the monopolist's marginal revenue equals price minus this lost revenue from the reduced price on other units, and is less than price as a result.

6. Why does the marginal revenue curve decline at a more rapid rate than the linear demand curve from which it derives?

The marginal revenue curve declines at a more rapid rate than the demand curve because marginal revenue equals price minus the lost revenue from the reduced price on other units. Marginal revenue falls as price falls (output increases), but it also falls because the lower the price, the more previous units that would have been sold at a higher price must also be lowered in price, sacrificing more revenues from the units that would have been sold without the price reduction. (Note that it is assumed here that all units are sold at a common price.)

7. Why does a monopolist always operate on the elastic portion of its demand curve?

To maximize its profits, a monopolist will produce the output where marginal revenue equals marginal cost. But because marginal cost will be positive, this requires that marginal revenue is also positive at the profit maximizing level. Because a positive marginal revenue means that total revenue increases as quantity sold increases along a demand curve, and this only occurs if demand is relatively elastic (elasticity of demand greater than one), this means that a monopolist will always choose to operate on the elastic portion of its demand curve.

8. If a monopolist had zero production costs, would it operate at a point where its demand curve was relatively elastic?

A profit-maximizing monopolist will produce that quantity where marginal revenue equals marginal cost. When marginal cost is positive, marginal revenue must also be positive at the equilibrium output level, which in turn requires that its demand curve is relatively elastic at that point. But if marginal cost was zero, marginal revenue must also be zero at the equilibrium output level, which in turn requires that its demand curve is unit elastic (elasticity of demand equals 1) at that point.

Concept B

1. What is a monopolist's principle for choosing the profit-maximizing output?

A monopolist's principle for choosing the profit-maximizing output is the same as for a perfectly competitive firm: produce all of those units for which marginal revenue exceeds marginal cost, resulting in a profit-maximizing equilibrium quantity where marginal revenue equals marginal cost. The differences between a monopoly and a perfectly competitive firm arise because marginal revenue also equals price for a perfectly competitive firm but marginal revenue is less than price for a monopolist.

2. How do you find the profit-maximizing price for a monopolist?

A monopolist produces the quantity where marginal revenue equals marginal cost. The height of its demand curve at that quantity indicates the price at which that profit-maximizing quantity can be sold.

3. For a monopolist making positive economic profits, what must be true about the relationship between price and average total cost?

Just as for a perfectly competitive firm, for a monopoly to be earning economic profits, its total revenue must exceed total cost at the profit-maximizing output. But this must mean that price (average revenue) must also exceed average cost at the profit-maximizing output level for positive economic profits to be earned.

4. For a monopolist making negative economic profits, what must be true about the relationship between price and average total cost?

Just as for a perfectly competitive firm, for a monopoly to be earning negative economic profits, its total revenue must be less than its total cost at the profit-maximizing output. But this must mean that price (average revenue) must also be less than average cost at the profit-maximizing output level for negative economic profits to be earned.

5. Why, unlike perfectly competitive firms, can a monopolist continue to earn positive economic profits over time?

Unlike perfectly competitive firms, a monopolist can continue to earn positive economic profits over time, because barriers to entry keep entrants, whose entry would erode those economic profits, from entering the industry.

Concept C

1. Why does the reduced output under monopoly cause inefficiency?

The reduced output and higher prices under monopoly causes inefficiency because some units for which the marginal value (indicated by willingness to pay along the demand curve) exceeds the marginal cost are no longer exchanged (unlike in perfect competition), eliminating the net gains that such trades would have generated.

2. Does monopoly power retard innovation?

Monopoly has been claimed to retard innovation, but many near-monopolists are important innovators. Therefore, the incentive to innovate exists in monopolistic as well as competitive market structures.

3. What does the welfare cost of monopoly represent? How is it measured?

The welfare cost of monopoly represents the net gains from trade (the difference between the marginal values of those goods indicated by the demand curve and the marginal costs of producing them) from those units of a good that would have been traded but that are no longer traded because of the output restriction of monopoly. It is measured by the area between the demand curve and the marginal cost curve for those units that are no longer traded because of the monopoly output restriction.

4. How can economies of scale lead to monopoly? How can it result in monopoly increasing rather than decreasing market output relative to the competitive market structure?

Economies of scale can lead to monopoly because output can be produced at lower costs on a larger scale than on a smaller scale, and this efficiency (cost) advantage can result in a larger firm outcompeting a large number of smaller firms. Industries with economies of scale over the entire range of market demand therefore tend toward monopoly. But if the production cost savings are greater than the price-increasing effect of monopoly output restriction, the result of such a monopoly would be a lower price and a higher quantity than would be the case with a larger number of firms (i.e., a more competitive market structure).

5. Can monopoly be the result of a new innovation that leaves consumers better off than before?

A new innovation may result in its innovator having a monopoly on it, which would give its creator incentives to raise prices and reduce outputs like any other monopoly. But for that monopoly innovator to attract customers away from the products customers currently purchase, those customers must expect to be made better off buying it at the price charged. This means that such a monopoly has no ability to harm consumers compared to their earlier situation.

Concept D

1. What alternative ways of dealing with the monopoly problem are commonly used?

The monopoly problem (with respect to efficiency, equity, and power) is commonly dealt with through antitrust policies, regulation, and public ownership.

2. How do antitrust laws promote more price competition?

Antitrust laws promote more price competition by making monopolistic practices and restrictions on price competition illegal.

3. What price and output are ideal for allocative efficiency for a regulated natural monopolist? Why is an unregulated natural monopolist unlikely to pick this solution?

The efficient price and output is where demand (marginal value) equals marginal cost, because this guarantees that every mutually beneficial trade takes place. However, with economies of scale (falling average cost curves), marginal cost is less than average cost for a natural monopolist, so that marginal cost prices would result in economic losses. An unregulated natural monopolist would not choose such a solution.

4. What is average cost pricing? How is it different from marginal cost pricing?

Average cost pricing is a regulatory approach to natural monopoly that permits the regulated natural monopolist to earn a normal rate of return on capital investment (zero economic profits). Zero economic profits requires that total revenues equal total costs, which requires that average revenue, or price, equals average cost. Forcing a natural monopolist to charge prices equal to marginal cost would require a price below average cost, because marginal cost is less than average cost for a natural monopolist, implying losses to the producer, which is not sustainable over the long run.

5. What are some difficulties encountered when regulators try to implement average cost pricing on natural monopolies?

Difficulties encountered when regulators try to implement average cost pricing include difficulties in calculating costs, eroded incentives for regulated firms to keep costs down, and the risk that the regulatory agency will make decisions on a political basis rather than on an economic basis.

6. Why might a job with a regulated natural monopolist that is allowed to earn a "fair and reasonable" return tend to have more perks (non-cash forms of compensation) than a comparable job in a non-regulated firm?

A regulated natural monopolist that is allowed to earn a "fair and reasonable" rate of return has no incentive to keep costs down, because reducing costs won't allow them to earn higher profits as a result. Those potential profits the monopolist is not allowed to keep instead get converted into business expenses that benefit the management, such as lavish perks (first-class air travel, hotels and meals, etc.).

Concept E

1. What is the argument most commonly made in favor of government monopoly?

The argument most commonly made in favor of government monopoly is that in some industries, it is inherently inefficient to have more than one firm producing the good or service (i.e., that the good or a service is a natural monopoly).

2. What arguments are commonly made against government monopoly?

Arguments commonly made against government monopoly include questioning whether the good or service in question is really a natural monopoly and concerns about reduced incentives for government monopolies to be efficient.

3. What is the argument in favor of the government enforcing patents and copyrights?

By enforcing patents and copyrights, which give limited monopoly power to their holders, the government provides incentives for innovators to invest in research and development and other creative activities, because they can capture the profits from such innovations.

4. How can government licensing act as a barrier to entry?

Government licensing acts as a barrier to entry by limiting the number of licenses available. Those who are unable to acquire a license are barred from the industry.

5. How can government licensing result in higher prices than would otherwise be the case?

By artificially restricting the number of producers in such an industry, government licensing reduces industry supply and increases prices in the industry.

Concept F

1. How do we define price discrimination?

Price discrimination is defined as charging different customers different prices for the same good or service.

2. Why does price discrimination arise from the profit-maximization motive?

Price discrimination arises from the profit-maximization motive because different customers react differently to price changes (i.e., they have different elasticities of demand). Therefore, profit maximization implies treating these different customers differently.

3. What principle will a profit-maximizing monopolist use in trying to price discriminate among different groups of customers?

A profit-maximizing monopolist will attempt to sell the output where marginal revenue equals marginal cost for each group of customers. That is, it wants to maximize profits for each group of customers separately.

4. Why will a price-discriminating monopolist charge a higher price to relatively inelastic demanders than to relatively elastic demanders?

Marginal revenue is closer to price for customers with more elastic demand curves, so prices charged those customers are lower, closer to cost, than for customers with more inelastic demand curves, whose marginal revenue is much further below price.

5. Why is preventing resale the key to successful price discrimination?

If customers who are being charged different prices for the same goods can resell the good among themselves, the lower-price group will resell to the higher-price group, undermining the seller's ability to charge a higher price to the groups with more inelastic demand curves.

6. Why is it generally easier to price discriminate for services than for goods?

Preventing resale is a key to successful price discrimination, and it is typically easier to prevent resale of services provided directly to customers than for goods sold to them (e.g., it is harder to resell a gall bladder surgery or plumbing repairs than to resell a computer).

Module 11: Monopolistic Competition
Concept A

1. How is monopolistic competition a mixture of monopoly and perfect competition?

Monopolistic competition is like monopoly in that sellers' actions can change the price. It is like competition in that there is competition from substitute products, there are many sellers, and entry is relatively free.

2. Why is product differentiation necessary for monopolistic competition?

Product differentiation is the source of the monopoly power that each monopolistically competitive seller (a monopolist of its own brand) has. If products were homogeneous, others' products would be perfect substitutes for the products of any particular firm, and such a firm would have no market power as a result.

3. What are some common forms of product differentiation?

Forms of product differentiation include physical differences, prestige differences, location differences, and service differences.

4. Why are many sellers necessary for monopolistic competition?

Many sellers are necessary in the monopolistic competition model because it means that a particular firm has little control over what other firms do; if there were few firms, they would begin to consider competitors as individuals (rather than only as a group) whose policies would be influenced by their own actions.

5. Why is free entry necessary for monopolistic competition?

Free entry is necessary in the monopolistic competition model because entry in this type of market is what tends to eliminate economic profits in the long run, as in perfect competition.

6. List three ways that a grocery store might differentiate itself from its competitors.

A grocery could differentiate itself by locating closer to customers, doubling coupons, having a wider variety of products, providing fresher produce, providing a faster checkout, delivering groceries to customers, and so forth.

7. What might make you choose one gas station over another?

In addition to the gas price charged, gas station choices can be determined by location (e.g., being on the way to work or even on the right side of the road, where getting in and out are easier), service, credit card acceptance, the cleanliness of the restroom facilities, whether they sell tires and batteries or offer repair services, whether you can use the air and water hoses for free, whether they offer a full-service option, and so forth.

Concept B

1. How is the short-run profit-maximizing policy of a monopolistically competitive firm like that of a monopoly?

Just as for a monopoly, a monopolistic competitor maximizes its short-run profits by producing the quantity (and corresponding price along the demand curve) at which marginal revenue equals marginal cost. The only difference is that a monopolistic competitor faces a more elastic downward-sloping demand curve than a monopolist, because it competes with others who produce close substitute products.

2. How is the choice of whether to operate or shut down in the short run the same for a monopolistic competitor as for either a monopoly or a perfectly competitive firm?

Because a firm will lose its fixed costs if it shuts down, it will shut down if price is expected to remain below average variable cost, regardless of market structure, because operating in that situation results in even greater losses than shutting down.

3. How is the long-run equilibrium of monopolistic competition like that of perfect competition?

The long-run equilibrium of monopolistic competition is like that of perfect competition in that entry (when the industry makes short-run economic profits) and exit (when it makes short-run economic losses) drive economic profits to zero in the long run.

4. How is the long-run equilibrium of monopolistic competition different from that of perfect competition?

For there to be zero economic profits in long-run equilibrium at the same time each seller faces a downward-sloping demand curve, a firm's downward-sloping demand curve must be just tangent to its average cost curve (because that is the situation where a firm earns zero economic profits and that is the best the firm can do), resulting in costs greater than the minimum possible average cost. This same tangency to long-run cost curves characterizes the long-run zero economic profit equilibrium in perfect competition, but because firm demand curves are horizontal in perfect competition, that tangency comes at the minimum point of firm average cost curves.

5. If Frank's hot dog stand was very profitable when he first opened, why should he expect those profits to fall over time?

Because entry into the hot dog stand industry is very easy, if Frank's hot dog stand was profitable at first and others found out about it, new competitors would enter, which would reduce Frank's profits.

6. Why do you think there are some restaurants that are highly profitable while other restaurants in the same general area are going out of business?

Some restaurants may have such strong consumer preferences that others in the restaurant industry may not be able to easily replicate the reason for those strong preferences. Even though others are able to enter the industry freely, they may not take enough business away from well-established restaurants to eliminate their economic profits. At the same time, some new restaurants that tried unsuccessfully to attract customers away from established rivals, and existing restaurants that couldn't keep their old customers from leaving to patronize rivals instead, may well be going out of business.

Concept C

1. Why is a monopolistic competitor's demand curve more elastic than a monopolist's demand curve?

A monopolistic competitor has a downward-sloping demand curve because of product differentiation, but because of the large number of good substitutes for its product, its demand curve is more elastic than that of a monopolist, for whose product there are no good substitutes.

2. Why do monopolistically competitive firms produce at less than the efficient scale of production?

Because monopolistically competitive firms have downward-sloping demand curves, their long-run zero profit equilibrium tangency between demand and long-run average total cost must occur along the downward-sloping part of the long-run average total cost curve. Because this level of output does not allow the full realization of all economies of scale, it results in a less than efficient scale of production.

3. Why do monopolistically competitive firms operate with excess capacity?

Monopolistically competitive firms operate with excess capacity because the zero profit tangency equilibrium occurs along the downward-sloping part of a firm's short-run average cost curve, so that the firm's plant has the capacity to produce more output at lower average cost than it actually is. That is what is meant by excess capacity in monopolistically competitive industries.

4. Why does the fact that price exceeds marginal cost in monopolistic competition lead to allocative inefficiency?

The fact that price exceeds marginal cost in monopolistic competition lead to the same sort of allocative inefficiency as for monopoly: Some goods for which the marginal value (measured by willingness to pay along a demand curve) exceeds the marginal cost are not traded, and the net gains that would have resulted from those trades are therefore lost. However, the degree of that inefficiency is smaller under monopolistic competition than under monopoly, because firms face more elastic demand curves than in monopoly, so the resulting output restriction is less.

5. What is the price we pay for differentiated goods under monopolistic competition?

Under monopolistic competition, excess capacity can be considered the price we pay for differentiated goods, because while costs, and therefore prices, might be greater than under perfect competition, that is the "price" we pay for the value we get from the additional choices and variety offered by differentiated products.

6. Why is the difference between the long-run equilibrium under perfect competition and monopolistic competition likely to be relatively small?

Even though monopolistically competitive firms face downward-sloping demand curves, which is the cause of the excess capacity and higher than necessary costs in these markets, those demand curves are likely to be highly elastic because of the large numbers of close substitutes. Therefore, the deviation from perfectly competitive results is likely to be relatively small.

7. Suppose that half of the restaurants in a city are closed so that the remaining eateries can operate at full capacity. What "cost" might restaurant patrons incur as a result?

Because there would be fewer remaining restaurants and they will be operating at capacity, you would expect longer waiting lines at restaurants; more people who eat at "off-peak" hours, when restaurants will be less crowded; fewer choices as to cuisine, quality levels, and ambiance; less concern at restaurants about losing diners to other restaurants as a result of shoddy service or high prices; and so forth.

Concept D

1. How can advertising make a firm's demand curve more inelastic?

Advertising is intended to increase a firm's demand curve by increasing consumer awareness of a firm's products and improving its image. It is intended to make its demand curve more inelastic by convincing buyers that its products are truly different (better) than alternatives (remember that the number of good substitutes is the primary determinant of a firm's elasticity of demand).

2. What are the arguments made against private sector advertising?

Some people argue that private sector advertising manipulates consumer tastes and creates artificial "needs" for unimportant products, taking resources away from more valuable uses.

3. What are the arguments made for private sector advertising?

The essential argument for private sector advertising is that it conveys valuable information to potential customers about the products and options available to them, and the prices at which they are available, helping them to make choices that better match their situations and preferences

4. Can advertising actually result in lower costs? How?

Advertising can lower costs by increasing sales and thus lowering production costs if there are economies of scale. Overall costs and prices can be lowered as a result, if the savings in production costs are greater than the additional costs of advertising.

5. Why is advertising more important for the success of chains such as Toys R Us and Office Depot than for the corner barber shop?

Large-scale advertising of their wide selection and low prices can allow chains such as Toys R Us and Office Depot to attract a large number of customers and sell a very large volume of products, which allows them to receive large quantity discounts from their suppliers and exploit substantial economies of scale in handling, service, advertising, and so forth. Because these large quantity discounts or extensive economies of scale are not achievable for local barber shops, advertising is less important for them.

Module 12: Oligopoly
Concept A

1. Why is oligopoly characterized by mutual interdependence?
Because there are few sellers in oligopoly, any change in output or price by one of them is likely to appreciably impact the sales of competing firms. Each of the sellers recognizes this fact, so that what each firm should do to maximize its profits depends on what other firms do, and their choices and policies therefore reflect this mutual interdependence.

2. Why do economies of scale result in few sellers in oligopoly models?
Where there are substantial economies of scale relative to market demand, reasonably low costs of production cannot be obtained unless a firm produces a large fraction of the market output. If each firm, to produce at low costs, must supply a substantial fraction of the market, only a few such firms can produce efficiently in such an industry.

3. How do economies of scale result in barriers to entry in oligopoly models?
Low-cost entry must take place on a large scale in industries with substantial economies of scale. Therefore, existing firms could be profitable at their current prices and outputs without leading to entry. The great increase a large-scale entrant would cause in the market output, and the resulting decrease in the market price, could make that entrant unprofitable at those lower post-entry prices, even if current firms are profitable at current prices.

4. Why does an oligopolist have a difficult time in finding its profit-maximizing price and output?
An oligopolist has more difficulty in discovering its profit-maximizing price and output because its demand curve is dramatically affected by the price and output policies of its rivals. This causes great deal of uncertainty about the location and shape of its demand and marginal revenue curves, because they depend on what policies rivals actually adopt.

5. Why would an automobile manufacturer be more likely to be an oligopolist than your corner baker?
There are very substantial economies of scale relative to market demand in the automobile industry, so that lower-cost automobile production can be obtained by a firm that produces a substantial fraction of the market output. As a result, there is only "room" in the automobile industry for relatively few efficient-scale producers. In contrast, the bakery industry does not have substantial economies of scale relative to market demand, so that there is "room" in the industry for a large number of efficient-scale bakeries.

Concept B

1. How does having a price leader reduce pricing uncertainty in oligopolistic industries?
Having one or more firms that traditionally lead price changes in oligopolistic industries reduces uncertainty about whether a price change will be followed, minimizing the potentially serious consequences of misjudging the behavior of others in the industry.

2. How is a collusion or a cartel like a monopoly?
A collusion is an attempt to achieve monopoly profits in an industry by getting producers not to compete with each other, but rather to act jointly in pricing and other matters. The resulting disadvantages are the same as in a monopoly situation: lower outputs and higher prices that harm consumers, and a misallocation of resources.

3. Why are collusive agreements typically unstable and short-lived?
Collusive agreements are typically unstable and short-lived (1) because they are strictly illegal under antitrust laws in the United States and in many other countries, and (2) because there is a great temptation for firms to cheat on collusive agreements by increasing their output and decreasing prices, which undermines any collusive agreement.

4. Why is the temptation to collude greater when the industry's demand curve is relatively more inelastic?
The more inelastic the demand curve, the greater the increase in profits from colluding to jointly restrict output from its current level and raise prices in the industry, and so the greater the temptation to collude.

Concept C

1. What impact does easy entry have on the profitability of oligopolies?
Economic profits in oligopolistic industries will attract entrants, if entry is easy. Entrants may break down existing price agreements by cutting prices in an attempt to establish themselves in the industry, forcing existing firms to reduce their prices and suffer reduced market shares, undermining the profitability of the oligopoly.

2. Why are barriers to entry necessary for successful, ongoing collusion?
Because easy entry erodes economic profits where they are positive, barriers to entry are necessary for oligopolists to continue to earn economic profits in the long run.

3. Why might oligopolists charge less than their short-run profit-maximizing price when threatened by entry?
When entry threatens to undermine the economic profits of an oligopolistic industry, firms in the industry may lower their prices below the level that would maximize their short-run profits in order to deter entry by making it less profitable.

4. A group of colluding oligopolists incur costs of $10 per unit, and their profit-maximizing price is $15. If they know that potential market entrants could produce at a cost of $12 per unit, what price are the colluders likely to charge?
If the colluding oligopolists are afraid of attracting entrants who will expand market output and reduce market prices and the colluders' profits, they might price below their short-run profit-maximizing price in order make it unprofitable to new entrants. In this case, colluding oligopolists might well charge $12 or just below, rather than the $15 they would otherwise charge.

Concept D

1. How is noncollusive oligopoly like a military campaign or a poker game?
Noncollusive oligopoly is like a military campaign, a poker game, or other strategic games in that firms take certain actions not because they are necessarily advantageous in themselves but because they improve the position of the oligopolist relative to its competitors, with the intent of improving its ultimate position.

Firm actions take into account the likely countermoves that rivals will make in response to those actions.

2. What is the difference between cooperative and noncooperative games?

Noncooperative games are those where actions are taken independently, without consulting others; cooperative games are those where players can communicate and agree to binding contracts with each other.

3. How does the prisoners' dilemma illustrate a dominant strategy for noncolluding oligopolists?

The prisoners' dilemma illustrates a dominant strategy for noncolluding oligopolists because it is in each player's interest to make the same choice regardless of the choice of the other player. Where a strategy is optimal regardless of opponents' actions, that strategy will dominate (be chosen over) others.

4. What is a Nash equilibrium?

A Nash equilibrium is one where each firm is doing as well as it can, given the actions of its competitors. A Nash equilibrium is self-enforcing because once it is established, there is no incentive for any firm to change its policies or its actions.

5. In the prisoners' dilemma, if each prisoner believed that the other prisoner would deny the crime, would each choose to deny the crime?

The prisoners' dilemma illustrates a dominant strategy in which it is in the interest of each of the two prisoners to confess, regardless of whether the other prisoner confesses: Prisoner A gets a lighter sentence if he confesses (3 years) than if he does not (6 years) when Prisoner B confesses, but he also gets a lighter sentence if he confesses (6 months) than if he does not (1 year) when Prisoner B does not confess; and the same is true for Prisoner B. The result is that, given the payoff matrix, each prisoner will confess regardless of what he expects the other prisoner to do.

6. Suppose Pepsi is considering an ad campaign aimed at rival Coca-Cola. What is the dominant strategy if the payoff matrix is similar to the one shown in Exhibit 3?

Exhibit 3 illustrates a game without a dominant strategy, in which the best thing for Pepsi to do depends on what Pepsi expects Coca-Cola to do. Say that Coca-Cola is firm A and Pepsi is firm B. If Coca-Cola chooses to advertise, Pepsi makes higher profits if it advertises ($16,000) than if it does not advertise ($12,000). But if Coca-Cola chooses not to advertise, Pepsi makes higher profits if it does not advertise ($12,000) than if it advertises ($10,000). As a result, Pepsi will advertise if it believes Coca-Cola will advertise, but it will not advertise if it believes Coca-Cola will not advertise.

7. Suppose your professor announces that each student in your large lecture class who receives the highest score (no matter how high or how low) on a take-home exam will get an A in the course. She points out that if the entire class colludes, everyone will get the same score. Is it likely that everyone in the class will get an A?

What is the likelihood that an attempted collusion that requires everyone in the class to participate and not one to "cheat" will work? Your professor thinks the odds are low, because she thinks that cheating on such a collusion will be likely (versus not cheating). If a student believes that others will cheat, replacing any of the agreed-upon answers with the correct answer, he knows that he will get a higher grade by answering correctly than by giving the agreed-upon answer, so he will cheat. However, if he believes others will not cheat, he will get an A if he does not cheat, but he will still get an A if he does cheat (because he will then get the sole high score in the class). Only if all students believe that all of the others will not cheat on such a collusion, and no one answers any questions correctly rather than giving the agreed-upon answers as "insurance" for their A, will the collusion work.

Module 13: Supply and Demand in Input Markets
Concept A

1. Why is the demand for productive inputs derived from the demand for the outputs those inputs produce?

The demand for productive inputs is derived from the demand for the outputs produced by those inputs because the value to a firm of the services of a productive input depends on the value of the outputs produced, and the value of the output depends on the demand for that output.

2. Why is the demand for tractors and fertilizer derived from the demand for agricultural products?

The reason farmers demand tractors and fertilizer is that they increase the output of crops they grow. But the value to farmers of the additional crops they can grow as a result is greater, the higher the price of those crops. Therefore, the greater the demand for those crops, other things equal, the higher the price of those crops, which increases the demand for tractors and fertilizer by increasing the value to farmers of the added output they make possible.

Concept B

1. Why is the marginal revenue product of labor the demand curve for labor?

Because the marginal revenue product of labor is the additional revenue that a firm obtains from utilizing one more unit of labor, that determines the maximum amount it would be willing to pay for each additional unit of labor. This is what the demand for labor schedule represents.

2. Would a firm hire another worker if the marginal revenue product of labor exceeded the marginal factor cost of labor? Why or why not?

A firm would hire another worker if the marginal revenue product of labor exceeded the marginal factor cost of labor, because doing so would add more to its total revenue than it would add to its total costs, raising profits.

3. How does the law of diminishing returns imply that the marginal product of labor must eventually fall?

As more and more units of the variable input labor are added to a given quantity of the fixed input capital, the additional output from each additional unit of labor must begin to fall at some point.

4. Why does the eventually falling marginal product of labor mean that the marginal revenue product of labor must also eventually fall?

Because marginal revenue product equals marginal product times the price of the output, the eventually falling marginal product of labor mean that the marginal revenue product of labor must also eventually fall, even if the price of the output did not fall with increasing output. If the price of the output falls with increasing output, that will also cause marginal revenue to fall.

5. Why is a firm hiring in a competitive labor market a price (wage) taker for a given quality of labor?

A perfectly competitive seller cannot by its output choices appreciably affect the market quantity, and thereby the market price of that output, and so it takes the output market price as given. In just the same way, a firm hiring in a competitive labor market cannot by its input (hiring) choices appreciably affect the quantity, and therefore the market price if that input, and so it takes the input (labor) market price (wage) as given.

6. Why are wages in different fields not necessarily related to how important people think those jobs are?

Wages are determined by the marginal revenue product of labor interacting with the decisions of individual suppliers of that labor in the market, and this does not bear any necessary relationship to how important or critical people consider that job to be in some absolute sense. Thus, a famous sports or entertainment figure can earn millions of dollars, while a cardiac nurse doing "important" things makes a small fraction of that amount.

7. Would the owner of University Pizza Parlor hire another worker for $60 per day if that worker added 40 pizzas a day and each pizza added $2 to University Pizza Parlor's revenues? Why or why not?

Assuming for simplicity that there were no costs of producing pizzas other than labor, the pizza parlor would hire another worker, because the marginal revenue product is $80 (40 more pizzas at $2 per pizza), which is more than the $60 marginal cost of hiring the additional worker, so that the profits would rise $20 by hiring that worker.

Concept C

1. If wages were above their equilibrium level, why would they tend to fall toward the equilibrium level?

If wages were above their equilibrium level, the quantity of labor supplied at that price would exceed the quantity of labor demanded at that price. The resulting surplus of labor would lead workers frustrated by their ability to get jobs to compete the wage for those jobs down toward the equilibrium level.

2. If wages were below their equilibrium level, why would they tend to rise toward the equilibrium level?

If wages were below their equilibrium level, the quantity of labor demanded at that price would exceed the quantity of labor supplied at that price. The resulting shortage of labor would lead employers frustrated by their ability to find workers to compete the wage for those jobs up toward the equilibrium level.

3. Why do increases in technology or increases in the amounts of capital or other complementary inputs increase the demand for labor?

Increases in technology or increases in the amounts of capital or other complementary inputs increase the demand for labor by increasing the productivity of labor; as labor productivity increases, the marginal revenue product of labor (the demand for labor) increases.

4. Why can any of the PYNTE shifters of demand in output markets shift the demand for labor and other inputs used to produce that output in the same direction?

When any of the PYNTE shifters of demand in output markets change the price of that output, it changes the marginal revenue product (marginal product times price) of labor and other inputs used to produce that output in the same direction.

5. Explain why increases in immigration or population growth, increases in workers' willingness to work at a given wage, decreases in nonwage income, or increases in workplace amenities will increase the supply of labor.

Increases in immigration or population growth increases the number of potential workers; increases in willingness to work at a given wage increase hours worked; decreases in nonwage income lowers workers incomes, increasing their willingness to work at any given wage; and an increase in workplace amenities makes working more desirable (less undesirable), also increasing workers' willingness to work at a given wage.

6. What would happen to the supply of labor if nonwage incomes increased and workplace amenities also increased over the same time period?

Higher nonwage incomes would reduce the supply of labor, but better workplace amenities would increase the supply of labor. The net effect would depend on which of these effects was of greater magnitude.

7. If the private market wage of engineers was greater than that of sociologists, what would happen if a university tried to pay all its faculty the same salary?

Say the university based its salaries on the average salaries elsewhere for all fields. Other things equal, the resulting salaries would be below the equilibrium salary level for engineers, resulting in a shortage of engineering professors at that university (e.g., the university would lose current engineering faculty and have a hard time hiring new engineering faculty), but above the equilibrium salary level for sociologists, resulting in a surplus of sociology professors at that university.

8. If a competitive firm was paying $8 per hour (with no fringe benefits) to its employees, what would tend to happen to its equilibrium wage if the company began to give on-the-job training or free health insurance to its workers?

A competitive firm cares about what it costs it to hire a worker in total compensation costs, not just wages alone. If the equilibrium compensation per hour for workers with the skills needed at that company is $8, the addition of on-the-job training or health insurance that added $1 to the cost of a worker per hour would cause the wage to fall by an equal amount, to $7 per hour, other things equal.

Concept D

1. How can acting together as a group increase workers' bargaining power?

Workers acting together to reduce the competition between them for jobs reduces competition among workers, and therefore gives them increased bargaining power.

2. Why are service industries harder to unionize than manufacturing industries?

Service industries tend to be harder to unionize than manufacturing industries because service industry jobs tend to be less standardized and service industry firms tend to be smaller.

3. How do union restrictions on membership or other barriers to entry affect the wages of members?

Union restrictions on membership or other barriers to entry reduce the quantity of labor services offered to employers, reducing the number of such jobs and increasing their wages.

4. What would increasing unionization do to the wages of those who were not in unions?

Increasing unionization would reduce the number of jobs in industries that became more unionized, increasing the supply of workers in industries that were still nonunion and lowering the wages that those jobs pay.

5. How can unions potentially increase worker productivity?

Unions can potentially increase worker productivity by providing a collective voice that workers can use to communicate their discontents more effectively, which can reduce the number of workers that quit, reducing employee training costs. They could also improve worker motivation and morale by better handling worker grievances.

6. Why does data indicating that unionization tends to lower firm profits weaken the argument that the primary effect of unionization is increased worker productivity?

If increased worker productivity was the primary effect of unionization, unionized firms should have lower costs and therefore higher profits than nonunion firms. But the data seems to indicate that the opposite is true.

Concept E

1. If labor demand rises faster than labor supply, what will happen to real wages?

An increase in labor demand would increase real wages, but an increase in labor supply would decrease real wages. If the labor demand shift is greater, that effect on wages will dominate the supply effect, and real wages will rise.

2. What will either a slowdown in the growth rate of labor demand or an increase in the growth rate of labor supply do to the growth rate of real wages?

A slowdown in the growth rate of demand for any good will slow the growth of its relative price, *ceteris paribus;* an increase in the growth rate of supply for any good will reduce the relative price of such a good, *ceteris paribus.* Both of these effects will reduce the growth rate of real wages from what they would otherwise have been.

3. Say there are completely different "men's jobs" and "women's jobs." If the labor supply of women grows faster than the labor supply of men, what will happen to the average wage of a woman versus the average wage of a man?

If the labor supply of women grows faster than the labor supply of men, other things equal, the equilibrium wage in women's jobs will fall relative to those for men's jobs.

4. If a large number of skilled workers retire at about the same time, what will happen to the wages of skilled workers, other things equal?

If a large number of skilled workers retire at about the same time, that will reduce the supply of skilled labor relative to demand, and raise the equilibrium wages of skilled workers, other things equal.

Concept F

1. Why is the demand curve for capital downward sloping?

The demand for capital is downward sloping because the lower the interest rate, the lower the opportunity cost of borrowed funds, and the more projects that can profitably be pursued with those funds (there are more capital investment projects when rates of return are higher than the opportunity cost of borrowing).

2. Why is the supply curve for capital upward sloping?

The interest rate represents the benefit savers get from saving (deferring consumption). A higher interest rate means an increase in the benefits of saving, resulting in increased saving and therefore an increase in the supply of funds available for capital investment projects.

3. Why does the price of agricultural land so closely reflect the prices of what is produced on the land?

The value of an asset reflects the value of what it produces. The more valuable the crop that can be grown on a parcel of land, the higher is that land's marginal revenue product, and the resulting higher demand for the land increases its price.

4. If a new machine would earn a 12 percent rate of return in your firm, and you could borrow the funds to finance it at an interest rate of 15 percent per year, would you borrow the money to buy it? Why or why not?

You would not borrow the money to buy the machine, because the opportunity cost of the funds (15 percent per year) exceeds the expected returns (benefits) from investing in the machine (12 percent).

Module 14: Income Distribution and Poverty
Concept A

1. Why might patterns in the measured income distribution give an incorrect impression?

The measured income distribution may give an inaccurate impression because it does not include all forms of income. For instance, it does not include nonmonetary income.

2. Why might measured income shares understate the degree of income inequality?

Measured income shares may understate the degree of income inequality because they do not include the nonmonetary income and privileges of the relatively well-to-do.

3. Why might measured income shares overstate the degree of income inequality?

Measured income shares may overstate the degree of income inequality because they don't adjust for predictable differences in incomes by age, demographic trends such as the growth of both divorce and two-earner families, taxes, in-kind income from the government (e.g., food stamps), the benefits of government programs, or movement within the income distribution over time.

4. How does the fraction of the population that is middle aged, rather than young or old, affect measurements of income inequality?

The more people are in their peak earning middle-age years, the higher their earnings appear relative to their lifetime incomes; the more people who are young or old, in their low earning years, the lower their earnings appear relative to their lifetime income.

5. How does the growth of both two-earner families and divorced couples increase measured income inequality?

Combining two incomes as the income of one family and increasing the number of lower-income, female-headed households due to divorce increase the number of families counted at both the upper and lower ends of the income distribution, increasing measured income inequality.

6. Why is it important to take account of the substantial mobility of families within the income distribution over time when evaluating the degree of income inequality in the United States?

The substantial income mobility within the income distribution means that someone who has a low income today will not necessarily have a low income for a long period of time; there may continue to be low-income people, but they are likely to be different people.

Concept B

1. How is the principle of diminishing marginal utility used to justify income redistribution?

The idea that the marginal utility of income falls with income has been used to argue that by taking income from those with higher incomes (and therefore low marginal utility of income) and giving it to those with lower incomes (and therefore high marginal utility of income), total utility in society could be increased.

2. Why is the idea that redistributing income from rich to poor will increase society's utility not provable?

Utility is not comparable between people. Even if an individual's marginal utility of income falls with income, that means his marginal utility is lower for higher incomes than for lower incomes; it does not mean that a higher income person's marginal utility of income is lower than the marginal utility of income of a different person with a lower income.

3. What are the fairness and incentive arguments against government redistribution of income?

The fairness argument against government redistribution of income is that it is unfair to take a substantial part of someone's income (given to them voluntarily by others) to give to others. The incentive argument is that there is no way for the government to redistribute income without undermining the earning incentives of both those taxed and those subsidized.

4. How might lower tax rates sometimes increase both incomes and government tax revenues?

Lower tax rates will increase incomes because they increase incentives to earn income. They might increase government tax revenues if the magnitude of the effect of the increase in reported income as a result of improved incentives to earn, as well as decreased incentives to move income into the underground economy to avoid taxes, was greater than the magnitude of the reduction in tax rates.

5. Why are there likely to be trade-offs between income redistribution and economic growth?

Because there is no way for the government to redistribute income without undermining the incentives of both those taxed and those subsidized to earn income, attempts to make the distribution of income more equal can also slow the rate of economic growth through reduced work effort and reduced capital formation (due to reduced saving).

6. If high-income individuals must pay increased income-tax rates in order to provide subsidies for low-income individuals (and the subsidies are phased out as income increases), are the productive incentives of both high- and low-income individuals reduced? Why or why not?

Increased income tax rates on high-income individuals reduce their take-home (after-tax) pay from the marginal hours of work involved, giving them less incentive to work those hours. Subsidies to low-income individuals whose benefits are phased out as their incomes grow act as income taxes (benefit reductions) on those individuals, giving them less incentive to work as well.

Concept C

1. What is the difference between job-entry discrimination and wage discrimination?

Job-entry discrimination refers to a worker denied employment due to discrimination; wage discrimination refers to those who are employed, but at lower wages, due to discrimination.

2. Explain how earnings differences could reflect either discrimination or productivity differences.

If employers discriminated among workers for reasons other than productivity, that would result in earnings differences. But employers are also willing to pay more to more productive workers (e.g., those with more education), resulting in earnings differences. The difficulty is determining how much each accounts for differences in earnings.

3. What is the environmental explanation for differences in earnings across the sexes and races?

The environmental explanation for differences in earnings across the sexes and races is that women and minorities are not as productive because they have been prevented from gaining the necessary training and skills and because women are more likely to interrupt their careers to have and care for children.

4. How do firms' incentives to maximize profits tend to reduce the extent of discrimination?

A firm that chooses not to hire an employee that has a higher marginal revenue product than his or her wage because of some preference for discrimination, sacrifices profits as a result. Those sacrificed profits make discriminating costly, reducing its occurrence.

5. How can discrimination reflect imperfect information and the costs of acquiring more information about potential employees?

If an employer's past experience with a particular group has been worse than that with other groups, he or she might prefer not to hire people from that group because the probability that they will perform well is lower. But this use of past experience as a screening device for new employees only makes sense if it is costly for employers to discover the productivity of individual potential employees, rather than the average of some group, prior to hiring them.

6. Say you now only hire purple workers. If purple workers strongly prefer to work with one another instead of with other groups, why might you prefer to hire a less-productive purple worker than a more-productive non-purple worker at the same wage?

Say each of your 20 current purple workers would demand $1 more per hour to work with a non-purple worker than with another purple worker. You would then have to compare how much more productive your prospective non-purple worker was at a given wage than a purple worker, or how much less he would have to be paid for a given level of productivity, against how much more you would have to pay your other workers to work next to him. In this case, if the productivity or wage difference exceeds $20 per hour of work, the non-purple worker would be hired, but if it was less than $20 per hour of work, he would not be hired.

7. Why would subsidizing employers for hiring minority workers give employers greater incentives to expand minority job opportunities than imposing implicit hiring quotas for minority workers?

An implicit minority hiring quota would raise employers' costs by making them hire workers they find less productive than those they would otherwise have hired. This reduces the profits of those firms, tending to reduce their size and number, and reducing the number of job opportunities they offer. Subsidizing the hiring of minority workers, however, lowers the cost to employers (they would not hire them unless the subsidy more than compensated them for any reduction in productivity) of hiring minority workers, increasing their profits and expanding the number of job opportunities for minority workers.

Concept D

1. How are absolute and relative measures of poverty different?

An absolute measure of poverty is one based on whether income is sufficient to provide the basic necessities of life (food, clothing, etc.) in minimum quantities; a relative measure of poverty is based on having lower incomes relative to others (e.g., earning half the median income).

2. Why could economic growth potentially eliminate absolute measures of poverty but not relative measures of poverty?

Economic growth increases output, making it possible to bring every citizen up to some minimal absolute level of income. It does not, however, eliminate the fact that some will still have relatively lower incomes than others.

3. Some people have argued that poverty could be eliminated by "rich" countries. Can both absolute and relative poverty be eliminated by "rich" countries? Why or why not?

Absolute poverty could possibly be eliminated providing all citizens the basic necessities of life in minimum quantities. However, unless a country completely equalized the incomes of all its citizens, some would continue to have lower incomes than others, and such relative poverty would persist to some degree.

Module 15: The Environment
Concept A

1. What is the difference between private and social costs?

Social costs include all of the relevant opportunity costs of production, whether they must be paid for by the decision maker or not. Private costs include only those social costs that must be borne by the decision maker.

2. Why do decision makers tend to ignore external costs?

Decision makers pay attention to their private costs because they are forced to compensate others for those costs; they tend to ignore external costs because they are not forced to compensate those who bear the costs.

3. How can internalizing the external costs of production move us closer to the efficient level of output?

A decision maker will produce the quantity where the marginal benefit of production (the price he sells his output for) equals his marginal private costs, in order to maximize profits. But the marginal social costs of those last units, which equal the sum of marginal private and marginal external costs, must exceed their marginal benefits. Internalizing external costs will make the private and social cost of production the same, and will lead profit-maximizing decision makers to reduce their output to the efficient level.

4. Why is it particularly difficult to measure the value of external costs or benefits?

Because there are few markets in which externalities are traded, there are few market prices to reveal their relative values to us. Even in cases where there are markets (e.g., houses in a clean part of town versus those in a dirty part of town, with the price differential representing the willingness to pay for environmental quality, *ceteris paribus*), the participants may not have very good information about all of the costs and benefits of the externality. Therefore, estimating the values of external costs or benefits is much more difficult than for goods traded in ordinary markets.

5. Say that the last ton of steel produced by Remington's Steel imposes three types of costs: labor costs of $25; additional equipment costs of $10; and the cost of additional "crud" dumped into the air of $15. What costs will Remington's Steel consider in deciding whether to produce another ton of steel?

Remington's Steel would consider only $35 ($25 for labor plus $10 for equipment rental) of the $50 total cost (including $15 for "crud") of producing its last ton of steel, because those are the only costs it is forced to pay.

6. Why can a homeowner make a better argument for compensation for noise pollution if a local airport was built after he moved in than if it was already there when he moved in? Would it matter whether or not he knew it was going to be built?

If the airport was already there or the homeowner knew it was going to be built before he bought the house, the lowered price he had to pay for the house as a result already compensated him for the expected noise pollution, and he has no real argument for compensation. But if the airport was not expected, a homeowner would have a better claim for compensation for the damages imposed on him (compared to the peace and quiet he expected when he bought the house).

Concept B

1. How do compliance standards act to internalize external costs?

By forcing companies to find less pollution-intensive ways of production rather than imposing the costs of additional pollution on others, they are forced to internalize those costs formerly imposed on others.

2. How does pollution control lead to both rising marginal costs and falling marginal benefits?

The marginal costs of pollution control rise for the same reason as with other goods. Pollution will be reduced in the lowest-cost manner first. Once lower-cost pollution control methods are exhausted, if we wish to reduce pollution further, we will have to turn to progressively more costly methods. The marginal benefits from pollution controls will fall, because the value of reducing crud in the atmosphere is higher, the more crud there is. As controls reduce the level of crud in the air, the marginal benefit of further crud reductions will fall.

3. How is the optimal amount of pollution control determined, in principle? Why is it so difficult to achieve agreement on what that optimal level of pollution is?

In principle, the optimal amount of pollution control is the amount at which the marginal social benefit of pollution reduction equals the marginal cost of pollution reduction. But there is no clear agreement about what those marginal benefits or costs are, leading to disagreements about the optimal amount of pollution.

4. How could transferable pollution rights lead to pollution being reduced at the lowest possible opportunity cost?

Transferable pollution rights would create a market for pollution reduction. Every polluter would then find it profitable to reduce pollution as long as they could do it more cheaply than the price of a pollution right. Therefore, producers would employ the lowest-cost pollution control methods for a given amount of pollution reduction.

5. What are the objectives of an ideal pollution-control policy from the perspective of economists interested in resource allocation?

An ideal pollution control strategy from the perspective of economists interested in resource allocation would reduce pollution to the efficient level, it would do so at the lowest possible opportunity cost, and it would create incentives to motivate advances in pollution-abatement technology.

6. Why might an efficient pollution tax be lower in Fargo, North Dakota, than in Los Angeles, California?

The more polluted an area already is and the more people that are breathing that pollution, the greater the marginal social cost of an additional unit of pollution. Therefore, the marginal social benefit from pollution reduction is greater, and therefore the optimal pollution tax will also be greater, in such circumstances.

7. If a firm can reduce its sulfur dioxide emissions for $30 per ton, but it owns tradable emissions permits that are selling for $40 per ton, what will the firm want to do if it is trying to maximize profits?

This firm can reduce its emissions more cheaply ($30 per ton) than other firms (reflected in the $40 price of tradable emissions permits). It would choose to sell emissions permits (for $40 per ton of marginal revenue) and reduce its own emissions further instead (for $30 per ton of marginal cost), raising its profits by $10 for each ton of emissions reduced. This would continue as long as the cost for the firm to reduce pollution was cheaper than the price of emissions permits.

Concept C

1. Why can externalities be considered a property rights problem?

If the rights to clean air, water, and so forth were clearly owned, those that infringed on those rights could be forced to compensate the owners. Such costs would be internalized, rather than external, to the relevant decision makers. Therefore, externalities are the result of the absence of clear and enforceable property rights in certain goods.

2. Why, according to the Coase Theorem, will externalities tend to be internalized when property rights are clearly defined and information and transaction costs are low?

When property rights are clearly defined and information and transactions cost are low, whoever wants to exercise their right faces an opportunity cost of what others would pay for that right.

That opportunity cost, represented by the potential payment from others to sell the right, is what forces decision makers to internalize what would otherwise be an externality.

3. How do transactions costs and the free rider problem limit the market's ability to efficiently solve externality problems?

Transactions costs limit the ability of the market mechanism to internalize externalities, because trading becomes more difficult. The free rider problem where those who benefit from some action cannot be forced to pay for it also hinders the ability for voluntary trade across markets to generate efficient levels of goods such as cleaner air.

Module 16: Introduction to the Macroeconomy
Concept A

1. What are the three major macroeconomic goals of most societies?

The three major macroeconomic goals of most societies are full employment (so that jobs are relatively plentiful and financial suffering from lack of income is relatively uncommon), price stability (so consumers and producers can make better decisions), and economic growth (so output, and therefore income and consumption, increases over time).

2. What is the Employment Act of 1946? Why was it significant?

The Employment Act of 1946 was a law that committed the federal government to policies designed to reduce unemployment in a manner consistent with price stability. It was significant because it was the first formal acknowledgment of government's primary macroeconomic goals.

Concept B

1. What happens to the unemployment rate when the number of unemployed people increases, *ceteris paribus*? When the labor force grows, *ceteris paribus*?

The unemployment rate is defined as the number of people officially unemployed divided by the labor force. Therefore, the unemployment rate rises as the number of unemployed people increases, and it falls when the labor force grows, as long as the increase in the labor force takes the form of added employment. An increase in the labor force may increase both the unemployed and the employed, leaving the impact on the unemployment rate ambiguous.

2. How might the official unemployment rate understate the "true" degree of unemployment? How might it overstate it?

The official unemployment rate understates the "true" degree of unemployment by not including discouraged workers as unemployed, by counting part-time workers who cannot find full-time jobs as "fully" employed, and by counting those employed in jobs that underutilize worker skills as "fully" employed. It overstates the "true" degree of unemployment by not counting those working overtime or multiple jobs as "overemployed," by counting those employed in the underground economy as unemployed, and by including those just "going through the motions" of job search to maintain unemployment benefits or other government benefits as unemployed.

3. Why might the fraction of the unemployed who are job leavers be higher in a period of strong labor demand?

In a period of strong labor demand, people would be more

confident of their ability to find other jobs, and therefore they would be more likely to leave (quit) their current jobs.

4. Suppose you live in a community of 100 people where no one was unwilling or unable to work. If 80 people are over 16 years old and 72 people are employed, what is the unemployment rate in that community?

The unemployment rate in this community is the number of unemployed (8) divided by the labor force (80), or 10 percent.

5. What would happen to the unemployment rate if a substantial group of unemployed people started going to school full time? What would happen to the size of the labor force?

Full-time students are not considered part of the labor force, so the labor force, the number officially unemployed, and the unemployment rate would all fall if unemployed people became full-time students.

6. What happens to the unemployment rate when unemployed people become discouraged workers? Does anything happen to employment in this case?

When unemployed workers become discouraged workers, they stop seeking jobs and are no longer counted as either part of the labor force or as unemployed, reducing the unemployment rate. However, because they do not find jobs, there is no effect on employment as a result.

Concept C

1. Why do we want some frictional unemployment?

We want some frictional unemployment because we want human resources employed in areas of higher productivity, and some period of job search (frictional unemployment), rather than taking the first job offered, can allow workers to find more productive employment through better matching of jobs with worker skills, which takes some time.

2. Why might a job retraining program be a more useful policy to address structural unemployment than to address frictional unemployment?

Structural unemployment reflects people who lack the necessary skills for the jobs available. A job retraining program to develop skills to match the jobs available addresses such structural unemployment, not frictional unemployment, which reflects a temporary period of search between jobs. This presumes, of course, that the job retraining programs are "effective" in that the training is relevant to potential job prospects.

3. What is the traditional government policy "cure" for cyclical unemployment?

The traditional government policy "cure" for cyclical unemployment is to adopt policies designed to increase aggregate demand for goods and services.

4. Does new technology increase unemployment?

New technology can increase unemployment among those whose skills are replaced by that technology. However, it also creates new jobs manufacturing, servicing, and repairing the new equipment, and by lowering costs, new technology frees up more income to demand other goods and services, creating jobs in those industries.

5. What types of unemployment are present at full employment (at the natural rate of unemployment)?

At full employment (at the natural rate of unemployment), both frictional and structural unemployment, but not cyclical unemployment, are present.

6. Why might frictional unemployment be higher in a period of plentiful jobs (low unemployment)?

In a period of plentiful jobs, frictional unemployment can be higher because job opportunities are plentiful, which stimulates mobility between jobs, thus increasing frictional unemployment.

7. If the widespread introduction of the automobile caused a very productive maker of horse-drawn carriages to lose his job, would he be structurally or frictionally unemployed?

If the carriage maker's skills were in demand in other industries, this would result in frictional unemployment, but if his skills were not in demand in other industries, this would result in structural unemployment.

8. If a fall in demand for domestic cars causes auto workers to lose their jobs in Michigan, while there are plenty of jobs for lumberjacks in Montana, what kind of unemployment results?

This would be an example of structural unemployment, resulting from skills mismatched to the jobs available.

Concept D

1. How does price level instability increase the difficulties buyers and sellers have in coordinating their plans?

Price level instability increases the difficulties buyers and sellers have in coordinating their plans by reducing their certainty about what price changes mean: Do they reflect changes in relative prices or changes in inflation? Eliminating this uncertainty makes the meaning of price changes clearer, allowing buyers and sellers to better coordinate their plans through the price system.

2. What will happen to the nominal interest rate if the real interest rate rises, *ceteris paribus*? What if expected inflation increases, *ceteris paribus*?

The nominal interest rate is the sum of the real interest rate and the expected inflation rate. If either the real interest rate or the expected rate of inflation increases, nominal interest rates will also increase.

3. Say you owe money to the River Bank. Will you gain or lose from an unanticipated decrease in inflation?

An unanticipated decrease in inflation will mean that the dollars you must pay back on your loan will be worth more than you expected, raising the real interest rate you must pay on that loan, which makes you worse off.

4. How does a variable interest rate loan "insure" the lender against unanticipated increases in inflation?

With a variable interest rate loan, an unanticipated increase in inflation does not reduce the real interest rate received by the lender, but instead increases the nominal interest rate on the loan to compensate for the increased inflation.

5. Why will neither creditors nor debtors lose from inflation if it is correctly anticipated?

Correctly anticipated, inflation will be accurately reflected in the terms to which creditors and debtors agree, so that neither will lose from inflation. Only unexpected inflation can redistribute wealth between debtors and creditors.

6. How can inflation make people turn to exchange by barter?

If inflation is very rapid, people lose faith in the value of their monetary unit, and this can lead to exchange by barter, because goods can then have a more predictable value than their country's money.

7. What would happen in the loanable funds market if suppliers of loanable funds expected a substantial fall in inflation, while demanders of funds expected a substantial rise in inflation?

If suppliers of loanable funds expected a substantial fall in inflation, they would demand a smaller "inflation premium" to loan money, increasing the supply of loanable funds. If demanders of funds expected a substantial rise in inflation, they would be willing to offer a greater "inflation premium" to borrow, increasing the demand for loanable funds. The increased supply of loanable funds would push down interest rates, while the increased demand for loanable funds would push up interest rates; the net effect on interest rates is unknown, without further information about the relative sizes of the shifts in the curves, but the quantity of loanable funds exchanged would definitely increase.

Concept E

1. In what way does the desire for economic growth arise from scarcity?

In a world of scarcity, we are unable to have or consume as many or as much of goods and services as we would like. This leads to the desire for economic growth, which increases the amounts of goods and services that are available for consumption.

2. How does encouraging capital investment or educational training enhance economic growth?

Both capital investment and educational training can enhance economic growth by increasing worker productivity.

3. Why do we use purchasing power parity to compare per capita GDP across countries?

Purchasing power parity allows us to estimate how much of one currency it would take in one country to buy what one unit of a different currency would buy in another country. This allows us to compare per capita GDP across countries in terms of a common unit of measurement.

4. If a country increased its rate of capital formation, what would happen to its current consumption possibilities? What would happen to its consumption possibilities 15 years from now?

At any point in time, increasing capital formation reduces current consumption possibilities, assuming that we are near full employment. But that current investment increases the future consumption possibilities of a country, as the production possibilities curve shifts outward due to the impact of more capital on worker productivity.

Concept F

1. Why would you expect unemployment to tend to fall during an economy's expansionary phase and to rise during a contractionary phase?

Output increases during an economy's expansion phase. To produce that increased output in the short term requires more workers, which increases employment and reduces the unemployment rate, other things equal.

2. Why might a politician want to stimulate the economy prior to his or her reelection bid?

A politician may want to stimulate the economy prior to his or her reelection bid because there is a strong correlation between the performance of the economy and the fate of an incumbent's bid for reelection.

3. Why is the output of investment goods and durable consumer goods more sensitive to the business cycle than that of most goods?

When output is growing and business confidence is high, investment rises sharply because it appears highly profitable; when incomes and consumer confidence are high, the demand for durable goods, purchases of which are often delayed in less prosperous times, rises sharply. In recessions, investment and consumer durables purchases fall sharply, as such projects no longer appear profitable, and plans are put on hold until better times.

4. Why might the unemployment rate fall after output starts recovering during the expansion phase of the business cycle?

Often unemployment remains fairly high well into the expansion phase, because it takes a period of recovery before businesses become convinced that the increasing demand for their output is going to continue, making it profitable to hire added workers.

Module 17: Economic Growth
Concept A

1. Why does the production possibilities curve shift out with economic growth?

Economic growth means the ability of an economy to produce more goods and services than before. An outward shift in a country's production possibilities curve simply illustrates that fact graphically.

2. Even if "in the long run we are all dead," are you glad that earlier generations of Americans worked and invested for economic growth?

The fact that earlier generations of Americans worked and invested for economic growth means that there is currently a greater stock of capital in the U.S. than there would have been otherwise. If you have more tools with which to work, you are more productive, resulting in a higher income and greater consumption possibilities.

3. If long-run consequences were not important, would many students go to college or participate in internship programs without pay? Why or why not?

No. These are two of many examples where people sacrifice in the short run in order to benefit in the long run. Saving and research and development are other obvious examples.

4. When the Dutch "created" new land with their system of dikes, what did it do to their production possibilities curve? Why?

Building dikes in Holland increased the quantity of usable land the Dutch had to work with, and an increase in the amount of usable natural resources shifts a country's production possibilities curve out.

Concept B

1. Why does knowing what factors are correlated with economic growth not tell us what causes economic growth?

Knowing what factors are correlated with economic growth does not tell us what causes economic growth because correlation does not prove causation. A factor may cause changes in economic growth, or economic growth could cause changes in it, or changes in both the factor and economic growth may be caused by yet another variable.

2. How does increasing the capital stock lead to economic growth?

Increasing the capital stock adds to the tools workers have to work with, increasing their productivity over time, which in turn increases output over time.

3. How do increases in savings affect long-run economic growth?

Increases in savings provide more funds for capital investment, and greater capital investment (which often also embodies advances in technology) increases productivity and output growth.

4. Why would you expect an inverse relationship between self-sufficiency and real GDP per capita?

Because of different endowments and abilities, both people and countries have different opportunity costs of production for large numbers of goods and services (different comparative advantages). Specialization and large-scale production, combined with domestic and international trade, allow an expansion of productive and consumption possibilities by taking advantage of lower-cost production, while self-sufficiency sacrifices those potential gains.

5. If a couple was concerned about their retirement, why could that lead to them having more children if they lived in an agricultural society, but fewer children if they were in an urban society?

In an agricultural society, children can typically "earn their own keep," making them financially "profitable" investments. In an urban society, however, children are a substantial financial liability to their parents.

Concept C

1. Why is no single factor capable of completely explaining economic growth patterns?

No single factor is capable of completely explaining economic growth patterns because economic growth is a complex process involving many important factors, no one of which completely dominates.

2. Why might countries with relatively scarce labor be leaders in labor-saving innovations? In what area would countries with relatively scarce land likely be innovative leaders?

Countries with relatively scarce, and therefore more costly, labor would benefit more from labor-saving innovations, and so would be likely to be leaders in such innovations. Similarly, countries with relatively scarce, and therefore more costly, land would likely be leaders in innovative ways to conserve on land.

3. Why could an increase in the price of oil increase real GDP growth in oil-exporting countries like Saudi Arabia and Mexico, while decreasing growth in oil-importing countries like the United States and Japan?

Because GDP measures the market value of goods and services produced, an increase in the price of a country's exports adds to its GDP. However, an increase in the price of oil will raise costs and reduce output in oil-importing countries, other things equal.

4. How is Hong Kong a dramatic example of why abundant natural resources are not necessary to rapid economic growth?

Although Hong Kong has virtually no natural resources, it has long been among the fastest growing economies in the world, proving that abundant natural resources are not necessary to rapid economic growth.

5. Why is the effective use of land, labor, capital, and entrepreneurial activities dependent on the protection of property rights?

Without protected property rights, both production and exchange become far more difficult, costly, and uncertain, undermining the ability of market incentives to induce the effective use of the factors of production. Similarly, without protected property rights, the rewards to investors and those who seek new and better ways of doing things are also more uncertain, reducing the incentives to make such investments and innovations.

Concept D

1. What happens to per capita real output if population grows faster than output? If population grows more slowly than output?

If population grows faster than real output, per capita real output falls; if population grows more slowly than real output, per capita real output rises.

2. How can economies of large-scale production allow per capita output to rise as population rises?

Economies of large-scale production mean that output can expand more than proportionately to an increase in inputs, so that the increasing labor force that accompanies a larger population may increase output enough through more efficient-sized production units that per capita real output rises as population rises.

3. How did Malthus' prediction on population growth follow from the law of diminishing returns?

Malthus' prediction that population growth results in a subsistence level of wages was based on the assumption of an agricultural society with land and labor as the only factors of production. Assuming that the amount of land was fixed, population and the labor force would grow to the point at which production exhibited the law of diminishing returns, with output growing more slowly than the geometrically increasing variable input, labor, which would reduce per capita incomes, eventually to the point of subsistence.

4. Why is population control a particularly important issue in countries with very low levels of per capita income?

In countries with a fixed supply of land and little if any technological advance, Malthus' assumptions are not far from the reality. Population control is one way to hold down the rate of population increase and thus to prevent the Malthusian subsistence wage result. It is, of course, a possibility that, even for very poor countries, the problem is not population growth but "something else" (e.g. bad government policies or other institutional problems).

Concept E

1. Is it possible that utility, or happiness, could fall as income rises? Why or why not?

Utility, or happiness, depends on both real income and expectations. Therefore, if real income increases faster than one's expectations, utility could rise, while if real income increases more slowly than one's expectations, utility could fall as a result.

2. Why does economic growth not necessarily lead to environmental damage? How can it lead to environmental improvements?

Economic growth can lead to increasing market output at the expense of environmental damage. But economic growth (illustrated by an outward shift in a production possibilities curve with market goods on one axis and environmental quality on the other axis) also makes it possible to have more of both market goods and environmental quality over time. People would become willing to spend more on environmental quality as economic growth raises their incomes, and devoting those added resources to the environment can improve it at the same time more market goods and services are being produced.

3. Economic growth leads to increased resource use. Does this mean that economic growth will necessarily lead to a depletion of natural resources in the long run? Why or why not?

Economic growth increases resource use, but it also increases the incentives to discover and develop new natural resource supplies, as well as to conserve and develop new substitutes for those natural resources. It also generates more and better resources for such discovery and development. The result need not be a depletion of usable natural resources in the long run.

Module 18: Measuring Economic Performance
Concept A

1. Why does the circular flow of money move in the opposite direction from the flows of goods and services?

The circular flow of money moves in the opposite direction from the flows of goods and services because the money flows are the payments made in exchange for the goods and services received by buyers.

2. Why would an increase in your income in factor markets likely increase your demand in product markets?

As your income rises, your demand for goods and services in product markets will also increase (remember that most goods are normal goods, for which demand increases as income increases). Also, saving tends to flow into investment demand.

3. Why would a decrease in demand for what you produce in product markets decrease your income in factor markets?

The value of an input's services is derived from the market value of the outputs produced by that input. When the demand for what you produce in product markets decreases, the price of what you produce decreases, and so does the market value of those services. Therefore, your income in factor markets also decreases.

Concept B

1. Why does GDP measure only *final* goods and services produced, rather than all goods and services produced?

If the market value of every good and service sold was included in GDP, the same output would be counted more than once in many circumstances (as when the sales price of, say bread, includes the value of the flour that was used in making the bread, and the flour, in turn, includes the value of the wheat that was used to make the flour). Only final goods and services are included in GDP to avoid such double counting.

2. Why aren't all of the expenditures on used goods in an economy included in the current GDP?

Current GDP does not include expenditures on used goods because GDP is intended to measure the value of currently produced goods and services in the economy. Used goods are not currently produced, and were already counted the year they were newly produced.

3. Why do GDP statistics include real estate agents' commissions from selling existing homes and used car dealers' profits from selling used cars but not the value of existing homes and used cars when they are sold?

Existing homes and used cars were both produced in the past and therefore aren't counted as part of current GDP. However, the services provided this year by real estate agents and used car lots are currently produced, so the market value of those services, measured by real estate agent commissions and the profits earned by used car lots, are included in GDP.

4. Why are sales of previously existing inventories of hula hoops not included in the current year's GDP?

Previously existing inventories of any product are not newly produced and are therefore not included in current year GDP. They were already produced and counted in an earlier period.

Concept C

1. What would happen to GDP if consumption purchases (*C*) and net exports (*X – M*) both rose, holding other things equal?

Because GDP is the sum of consumption purchases (*C*), investment purchases (*I*), government purchases (*G*), and net exports (*X – M*), an increase of any of those components of GDP will increase GDP, other things being equal. Because either an increase in consumption (*C*) or an increase in net exports (*X – M*) increases GDP, both changes in the same time period will also increase GDP, other things being equal.

2. Why do you think economic forecasters focus so much on consumption purchases and their determinants?

Economic forecasters focus so much on consumption purchases and their determinants because consumption purchases are by far the largest component (roughly two-thirds) of GDP, so that what happens to consumption purchases is crucial to what happens to GDP.

3. Why are purchases of durable goods more unstable than purchases of nondurable goods?

Purchases of durable goods are more unstable than purchases of nondurable goods because nondurable goods are used up in a relatively short period of time, so that their purchase is hard to shift from one time period to another. Durable goods, on the other hand, provide services for several periods, so that consumer durable purchases can be significantly delayed to "make do" during economic hard times and can be significantly accelerated during good times.

4. Why does the investment component of GDP include purchases of new capital goods but not purchases of corporate stock?

New capital goods are newly produced goods, by definition, so they are included in GDP. However, sales of company stock do not involve a newly produced good or service (although the services of the broker, measured by the transaction fee, are included as a newly produced service). When someone buys shares of stock from someone else, no goods are being newly produced. Instead, already existing ownership claims on the future income of the company are simply being transferred from one person to another.

5. If Mary received a welfare check this year, would that transfer payment be included in this year's GDP? Why or why not?

GDP includes only currently produced goods and services. But because transfer payments are not payments in exchange for newly produced goods and services, they are not included in GDP.

6. Could inventory investment or net exports ever be negative?
Yes. If year-end inventories are smaller than beginning of the year inventories, inventory investment is negative, and if the value of exports is smaller than the value of imports, net exports are negative.

Concept D

1. Why should we expect the total expenditures that go into GDP to equal total income in an economy?
Every dollar of purchases that goes into GDP must be paid out to the factors of production that produced it (categorized as wages, rents, interest, and profits). Therefore, total expenditures, properly measured, must equal total income, properly measured.

2. Which two non-income expense items does the income approach take into consideration?
The income approach takes indirect business taxes into consideration, because they are uses to which income is devoted, even though they are not payments for newly produced goods and services. It also takes depreciation, or the capital consumption allowance into consideration, because depreciation represents the amount of income that must be set aside to replace existing capital equipment as it wears out.

3. How is personal income different from national income?
Personal income, the amount of income available to consumers to spend, is not the same as national income, because owners of productive resources do not receive all of the income that they earn and because they receive "unearned" transfer payments. Undistributed corporate profits and social insurance taxes, which are not received by the factors of production, must be subtracted from, and transfer payments must be added to, national income to get personal income.

Concept E

1. If we overestimated inflation over time, would our calculations of real GDP growth likely be over- or underestimated?
Nominal GDP is deflated by the measure of inflation being used to calculate real GDP and real GDP growth. Therefore, for a given nominal GDP growth rate, overestimating inflation over time would result in underestimating real GDP growth over time.

2. Why does the consumer price index tend to overstate inflation if the quality of goods and services is rising over time?
The consumer price index does not adjust for most quality increases that take place in goods and services. Therefore, higher prices that actually reflect increased quality are counted as higher prices for a given quality, so that the consumer price index overstates increases in the cost of living.

3. Why would the growth in real GDP overstate the growth of output per person in a country with a growing population?
Real GDP growth measures what happens to output for the economy as a whole. But if the population is growing, real GDP is being split among an increasing number of people, and real GDP growth exceeds per capita real GDP growth.

4. Why doesn't the consumer price index accurately adjust for the cost-of-living effects of a tripling in the price of bananas relative to the prices of other fruits?

The consumer price index assumes that people continue to consume the same number of bananas as in the base year (survey period). Therefore, the cost of the banana component of the consumer price index triples when the price of bananas triples. However, in fact, consumers will substitute other fruits, which become relatively cheaper as a result of the banana price increase, for bananas so that this component of their cost of living has not actually increased as fast as banana prices.

Concept F

1. Why do GDP measures omit nonmarket transactions?
GDP measures omit nonmarket transactions because there is no accurate way to measure the values of those transactions, unlike the case for normal market transactions, where market prices can be used to measure the values involved.

2. How would real GDP comparisons between two countries be impacted by the existence of a high level of nonmarket activities in one of the countries?
Because nonmarket activities are not included in GDP, GDP would understate the true value of total output more for a country with a relatively high level of nonmarket activities than for a country with a smaller proportion of nonmarket activities, making countries with smaller shares of nonmarket activities look richer relative to countries with larger shares of nonmarket activities.

3. If we choose to decrease our hours worked because we value the additional leisure more, would the resulting change in real GDP accurately reflect the change in our well-being? Why or why not?
Decreasing hours worked would reduce real GDP, other things equal. But if we choose to do so voluntarily, that would mean we place a higher value on the leisure time (which is not counted in GDP) than on the market output (that is counted in GDP) foregone by reducing hours worked, so the change in real GDP would not accurately reflect the change in our well-being. That is, GDP would be going down, but well-being would be actually be going up!

4. How do pollution and crime affect GDP? How do pollution- and crime-control expenditures impact GDP?
Neither pollution nor crime are included (as "bads" to be subtracted) in GDP calculations. However, market expenditures for pollution and crime control are included in GDP, as currently produced goods and services.

Module 19: Aggregate Demand
Concept A

1. What are the major components of aggregate demand?
The major components of aggregate demand are consumption, planned investment, government purchases, and net exports.

2. If consumption is a direct function of disposable income, how would an increase in personal taxes or a decrease in transfer payments affect consumption?
Either an increase in taxes or a decrease in transfer payments decreases the disposable income of households, which would normally be expected to reduce their demands for consumption goods.

3. What does the permanent income hypothesis imply about consumption as a fraction of income for young and old consumers versus middle-aged consumers?

The young and the old earn less at those ages than their lifetime, or average, income, so they consume a higher percentage of their income at those ages; those in middle age earn more at those ages than their lifetime, or average, income, so they consume a lower fraction of their income during those years.

4. Would you spend more or less on additional consumption if your marginal propensity to consume increased?

Because the definition of the marginal propensity to consume is the fraction of an increase in disposable income one would spend on additional consumption purchases, you would spend more, the higher your marginal propensity to consume.

Concept B

1. Why does increased business optimism lead to increased investment?

Increased business optimism increases the expected rates of return on investment projects, increasing the number of such projects that are expected to be profitable, and therefore increasing purchases of investment goods for those projects.

2. Why do decisions to invest depend largely on the expected rate of return on investments compared to the opportunity cost of borrowed money (the market interest rate)?

If the expected rate of return on an investment project exceeds the opportunity cost of funds to finance it, pursuing it will generate economic profits; if the expected rate of return on an investment project is less than the opportunity cost of funds to finance it, pursuing it will generate economic losses.

3. Why might a larger existing capital stock tend to increase the rate of new capital goods investment?

The greater the capital stock for a given output, the lower is capacity utilization, and the smaller would be the rate of new capital goods investment. However, for a given capacity utilization rate, the greater the capital stock, the greater will be the amount of depreciation in any given time period, and the more investment is necessary just to offset depreciation.

4. If inventories have risen above the desired level for a firm, what does that tell it about the demand for its product relative to what it expected demand to be?

Inventories that are rising above desired levels mean that the demand for that firm's output is lower than anticipated.

5. What would an increase in exports do to aggregate demand, other things equal? An increase in imports? An increase in both imports and exports, where the change in exports was greater in magnitude?

An increase in exports would increase aggregate demand, other things equal, because net exports are part of aggregate demand. An increase in imports would decrease aggregate demand, other things equal, by reducing net exports (demand shifts from domestic producers to foreign producers). An increase in both imports and exports will increase aggregate demand if the increase in exports exceeds the increase in imports, other things equal, because the combination will increase net exports.

Concept C

1. How is the aggregate demand curve different from the microeconomic demand curve?

The microeconomic demand curve reflects what happens to the quantity of a particular good demanded as its price relative to other goods changes, with substitution among alternative goods the primary mechanism at work. Aggregate demand, on the other hand, reflects what happens to the total quantity of all real goods and services demanded in the economy as a whole as the overall price level changes, so substitution among goods is not the primary mechanism at work.

2. How does an increased price level reduce the quantities of investment goods and consumer durables demanded?

An increased price level increases the demand for money, which, in turn, increases interest rates. Higher interest rates increase the opportunity cost of financing both investment goods and consumer durables, reducing the quantities of investment goods and consumer durables demanded.

3. What is the real wealth effect, and how does it imply a downward-sloping aggregate demand curve?

A reduced price level increases the real value of people's currency holdings, and as their real wealth increases, so does the quantity of real goods and services demanded, particularly consumption goods. Therefore, the aggregate demand curve, which represents the relationship between the price level and the quantity of real goods and services demanded, slopes downward as a result.

4. What is the interest rate effect, and how does it imply a downward-sloping aggregate demand curve?

A reduced price level reduces the demand for money, which lowers interest rates and thus increases the quantity of investment goods and consumer durable goods people are willing to purchase. Therefore, the aggregate demand curve, which represents the relationship between the price level and the quantity of real goods and services demanded, slopes downward as a result.

5. What is the open economy effect, and how does it imply a downward-sloping aggregate demand curve?

The open economy effect occurs because a higher domestic price level raises the prices of domestically produced goods relative to the prices of imported goods. That reduces the quantity of domestically produced goods demanded (by both citizens and foreigners), as now relatively cheaper foreign-made goods are substituted for them. The result is again a downward-sloping aggregate demand curve, as a higher price level results in a lower quantity of domestic real GDP demanded, other things—in particular, exchange rates—held constant.

Concept D

1. How is the distinction between a change in demand and a change in quantity demanded the same for aggregate demand as for the demand for a particular good?

Just as a change in the price of a particular good changes its quantity demanded, but not its demand, a change in the price level changes the quantity of real GDP demanded, but not aggregate demand. Just as a change in any of the PYNTE demand curve shifters (other factors than the price of the good itself) changes the demand for a particular good, a change in any of the components of aggregate demand (C, I, G, and $X - M$) not caused by a change in the price level changes aggregate demand.

2. What happens to aggregate demand if the demand for consumption goods increases, *ceteris paribus*?

Because consumption purchases are part of aggregate demand, an increase in the demand for consumption goods increases aggregate demand, *ceteris paribus*.

3. What happens to aggregate demand if the demand for investment goods falls, *ceteris paribus*?
Because planned investment purchases are part of aggregate demand, a falling demand for investment goods makes aggregate demand fall, *ceteris paribus*.

4. Why would an increase in the money supply tend to increase expenditures on consumption and investment, *ceteris paribus*?
An increase in the money supply would lead to two effects. First, it would tend to lower interest rates, leading to more investment demand (and perhaps more consumption demand). Second, some individuals would directly spend excess money balances on goods, increasing consumption demand directly.

Module 20: Aggregate Supply and Macroeconomic Equilibrium
Concept A

1. What relationship does the short-run aggregate supply curve represent?
The short-run aggregate supply curve represents the relationship between the total quantity of final goods and services that suppliers are willing and able to produces (the quantity of real GDP supplied) and the overall price level, before all input prices have had time to completely adjust to the price level.

2. What relationship does the long-run aggregate supply curve represent?
The long-run aggregate supply curve represents the relationship between the total quantity of final goods and services that suppliers are willing and able to produce (the quantity of real GDP supplied) and the overall price level, once all input prices have had time to completely adjust to the price level (actually, it shows there is no relationship between these two variables, once input prices have had sufficient time to completely adjust to the price level).

3. Why is focusing on producers' profit margins helpful in understanding the logic of the short-run aggregate supply curve?
Profit incentives are important to understanding what happens to real output as the price level changes in the short run (before input prices completely adjust to the price level). When the prices of outputs rise relative to the prices of inputs (costs), as when aggregate demand increases in the short run, it increases profit margins, which increases the incentives to produce, leading to increased real output. When the prices of outputs fall relative to the prices of inputs (costs), as when aggregate demand decreases in the short run, it decreases profit margins, which decreases the incentives to produce, leading to decreased real output.

4. Why is the short-run aggregate supply curve upward sloping, while the long-run aggregate supply curve is vertical at the natural rate of output?
The short-run aggregate supply curve is upward sloping because in the short run, before input prices have completely adjusted to the price level, an increase in the price level increases profit margins by increasing output prices relative to input prices, which leads producers to increase real output. The long-run aggregate supply curve is vertical because in the long run, when input prices have completely adjusted to changes in the price level, input prices as well as output prices have adjusted to the price level, so that profit margins in real terms do not change as the price level changes; thus, there is no relationship between the price level and real output in the long run. The long-run aggregate supply curve is vertical at the natural rate of real output because that is the maximum output level allowed by capital, labor, and technological inputs at full employment (that is, given the determinants of the economy's production possibilities curve), which is therefore sustainable over time.

5. What would the short-run aggregate supply curve look like if input prices always changed instantaneously as soon as output prices changed? Why?
If input prices always changed instantaneously as soon as output prices changed, the short-run aggregate supply curve would look the same as the long-run aggregate supply curve—vertical at the natural rate of real output. That is because both input and output prices would then change proportionately, so that real profit margins (the incentives facing producers), and therefore real output, would not change as the price level changes.

6. If the price of cotton increased 10 percent when cotton producers thought other prices were rising 5 percent over the same period, what would happen to the quantity of real GDP supplied in the cotton industry? What if cotton producers thought other prices were rising 20 percent over the same period?
If the price of cotton increased 10 percent when cotton producers thought other prices were rising 5 percent over the same period, the quantity of real GDP supplied in the cotton industry would increase, because with other prices (including input prices) falling relative to cotton prices, the profitability of growing cotton would be rising. If the price of cotton increased 10 percent when cotton producers thought other prices were rising 20 percent over the same period, the quantity of real GDP supplied in the cotton industry would decrease, because with other prices (including input prices) rising relative to cotton prices, the profitability of growing cotton would be falling.

Concept B

1. Which of the aggregate supply curves will shift in response to a change in the price level? Why?
The short-run aggregate supply curve shifts in response to a change in the expected price level by changing the expected production costs, and therefore the expected profitability, of producing output at any given output price level. Remember that the long-run aggregate supply curve assumes that people have had enough time to completely adjust to a changing price level, so a change in the expected price level does not change expected profit margins along the long-run aggregate supply curve.

2. Why do lower input costs increase the level of real GDP supplied at any given price level?
Lower input costs increase the level of real GDP supplied at any given (output) price level by increasing the profit margin for any given level of output prices.

3. What would discovering huge new supplies of oil and natural gas do to the short-run and long-run aggregate supply curves?
Discovering huge new supplies of oil and natural gas would increase both the short-run and long-run aggregate supply curves, because those additional resources would allow more to be produced in the short-run, at any given output price level, as well as on a sustainable, long-run basis (because such a discovery would shift the economy's production possibilities curve outward).

4. What would happen to the short-run and long-run aggregate supply curves if the government required every firm to file explanatory paperwork each time a decision was made?

This would shift both the short-run and long-run supply curves to the left. It would permanently raise producers' costs of producing any level of output, which would reduce how much producers would produce in the short run at any given price level, as well as on a sustainable, long-run basis (because such a requirement would shift the economy's production possibilities curve inward).

5. What would happen to the short-run and long-run aggregate supply curves if the capital stock grew and available supplies of natural resources expanded over the same period of time?

Both an increase in the capital stock and increased available supplies of natural resources would shift both the short-run and long-run aggregate supply curves to the right (shifting the economy's production possibilities curve outward), increasing both short-run and sustainable levels of real output.

6. How can a change in input prices change the short-run aggregate supply curve but not the long-run aggregate supply curve? How could it change both long-run and short-run aggregate supply?

A temporary change in input prices can change the short-run aggregate supply curve by changing profit margins in the short run. However, when input prices return to their previous levels (reflecting a return to their previous relative scarcity) in the long run, the sustainable level of real output will be no different than before. If, on the other hand, input price changes reflect a permanently changed supply of inputs (lower input prices reflecting an increased supply), a change in input prices would increase both the short-run and long-run aggregate supply curves by increasing the real output producible both currently and on an ongoing basis (permanently shifting out the economy's production possibilities curve).

7. What would happen to short- and long-run aggregate supply if unusually good weather led to bumper crops of most agricultural products?

Because this reflects only a temporary change in output, it would increase the short-run aggregate supply curve but not the long-run aggregate supply curve.

8. If OPEC temporarily restricted the world output of oil, what would happen to short- and long-run aggregate supply? What would happen if the output restriction was permanent?

A temporary oil output restriction would temporarily increase oil (energy input) prices, reducing the short-run aggregate supply curve (shifting it left) but not the long-run aggregate supply curve. If the oil output restriction was permanent, the oil price increase would also reduce the level of real output producible on a sustainable basis, and so would shift both short-run aggregate supply and long-run aggregate supply to the left.

Concept C

1. What is demand-pull inflation?

Demand-pull inflation occurs when price levels increase as a result of an increase in aggregate demand.

2. What is cost-push inflation?

Cost-push inflation is output price inflation caused by an increase in input prices (that is, by supply-side forces, rather than demand-side forces). It is illustrated by a leftward, or upward, shift of the short-run aggregate supply curve, for given long-run aggregate supply and demand curves.

3. Starting from long-run equilibrium on the long-run aggregate supply curve, what happens to the price level, real output, and unemployment as a result of cost-push inflation?

Starting from long-run equilibrium on the long-run aggregate supply curve, cost-push inflation causes the price level to rise, real output to fall, and unemployment to rise in the short run.

4. How would a drop in consumer confidence impact the short-run macroeconomy?

A drop in consumer confidence would decrease the demand for consumer goods, other things equal, which would reduce (shift left) the aggregate demand curve, resulting in a lower price level, lower real output, and increased unemployment in the short run for a given short-run aggregate supply curve.

5. What would happen to the price level, real output, and unemployment in the short run if world oil prices fell sharply?

If world oil prices fell sharply, it would increase (shift right) the short-run aggregate supply curve, resulting in a lower price level, greater real output, and reduced unemployment in the short run, for a given aggregate demand curve.

Module 21: Fiscal Policy
Concept A

1. If, as part of its fiscal policy, the federal government increased its purchases of goods and services, would that be an expansionary or contractionary tactic?

An increase in government purchases of goods and services would be an expansionary tactic, increasing aggregate demand, other things equal.

2. If the federal government decreased its purchases of goods and services, would the budget deficit increase or decrease?

If the federal government decreased its purchases of goods and services, for a given level of tax revenue, a budget deficit (the difference between government spending and government revenues) would decrease.

3. If the federal government increased taxes or decreased transfer payments, would that be an expansionary or contractionary fiscal policy?

Either an increase in taxes or a decrease in transfer payment would be a contractionary tactic, decreasing aggregate demand by decreasing people's disposable incomes and therefore reducing the demand for consumption goods.

4. If the federal government increased taxes or decreased transfer payments, would the budget deficit increase or decrease?

If the federal government increased taxes or decreased transfer payments, for a given level of government purchases, a budget deficit (the difference between government spending and government revenues) would decrease.

5. If the federal government increased government purchases and lowered taxes at the same time, would the budget deficit increase or decrease?

Increased government purchases would increase a budget deficit, other things equal. Lowered taxes would also increase a budget deficit, other things equal. Therefore, both changes together would increase a budget deficit.

Concept B

1. How does the multiplier effect work?

The multiplier effect arises because the increased purchases during each "round" of the multiplier process generates increased incomes to the owners of the resources used to produce the goods purchased, which leads them to increase consumption purchases in the next "round" of the process. The result is a final increase in total purchases, including the induced consumption purchases, that is greater than the initial increase in purchases.

2. What is the marginal propensity to consume?

The marginal propensity to consume is the proportion of an additional dollar of income that would be spent on additional consumption purchases.

3. Why is the marginal propensity to consume always less than one?

This is true because all expenditures have to ultimately be financed out of income, so that each dollar of added income cannot lead to more than a dollar of added purchases. In addition, taxes and savings also have to be financed out of income, and these do not directly increase aggregate demand.

4. Why does the multiplier effect get larger as the marginal propensity to consume gets larger?

The larger the marginal propensity to consume, the larger the fraction of increased income in each "round" of the multiplier process that will go to additional consumption purchases. Because each round of the multiplier process will therefore be larger the greater the marginal propensity to consume, the multiplier will also be larger, other things equal.

5. If an increase in government purchases leads to a reduction in private-sector purchases, why could the effect on the economy be less than indicated by the multiplier?

At the same time that the increased government purchases are leading to a multiple expansion of income and purchases for one set of citizens, the "crowded out" private sector purchases are causing a multiple contraction of income and purchases for other citizens. The net effect on the economy will therefore be less than the increase in government purchases times the multiplier.

Concept C

1. If the economy is in recession, what sorts of fiscal policy changes would tend to bring it out of recession?

If the economy is in recession, aggregate demand intersects short-run aggregate supply to the left of the long-run aggregate supply curve. Expansionary fiscal policy—increased government purchases, decreased taxes, and/or increased transfer payments—addresses a recession by shifting aggregate demand to the right.

2. If the economy is at a short-run equilibrium at greater than full employment, what sorts of fiscal policy changes would tend to bring the economy back to a full employment equilibrium?

If the economy is at a short-run equilibrium at greater than full employment, aggregate demand intersects short-run aggregate supply to the right of the long-run aggregate supply curve. Contractionary fiscal policy—decreased government purchases, increased taxes, and/or decreased transfer payments—addresses a short-run equilibrium at greater than full employment by shifting aggregate demand to the left.

3. What effects would an expansionary fiscal policy have on the price level and real GDP, starting from a full employment equilibrium?

Starting from a full employment equilibrium, an expansionary fiscal policy would increase aggregate demand, increasing the price level and real GDP in the short run. However, in the long run, real GDP will return to its full-employment long-run equilibrium level as input prices adjust (the short-run aggregate supply curve shifts up or left), and only the price level will end up higher.

4. What effects would a contractionary fiscal policy have on the price level and real GDP, starting from a full employment equilibrium?

Starting from a full employment equilibrium, a contractionary fiscal policy would decrease aggregate demand, decreasing the price level and real GDP in the short run. However, in the long run, real GDP will return to its full-employment long-run equilibrium level as input prices adjust (the short-run aggregate supply curve shifts down or right), and the price level will end up lower.

Concept D

1. Why does a larger government budget deficit increase the magnitude of the crowding out effect?

A larger government budget deficit increases the demand for loanable funds, increasing the magnitude of the increase in interest rates, crowding out more private sector investment as a result.

2. Why does fiscal policy have a smaller effect on aggregate demand, the greater the crowding out effect?

The greater the crowding out effect, the smaller the net effect (the increase in government purchases minus the private sector purchases crowded out) fiscal policy has on aggregate demand. For example, if each dollar of added government purchases crowds out 50 cents worth of private sector purchases, fiscal policy will have only half the effect on aggregate demand that it would if there was no crowding out effect.

3. Why does the Ricardian equivalence theorem imply that if people correctly recognize the future tax liability represented by a current budget deficit, and save enough to pay for those future taxes as a result, then fiscal policy may have no effect on aggregate demand?

The Ricardian equivalence theorem implies that if people correctly recognize the future tax liability represented by a current budget deficit, they will save enough today to pay for those added future taxes. But this increase in savings requires an equal reduction in consumption for a given income, and this reduction in consumption completely offsets the effect of expansionary fiscal policy (which increases the size of a budget deficit) on aggregate demand.

4. How do time lags impact the effectiveness of fiscal policy?

The time lag between when a policy change is desirable and when it is adopted and implemented (for data gathering, decisionmaking, etc.), as well as the time lag between when a policy is implemented and when it has its effects, make it difficult for fiscal policy to have the desired effect at the desired time, particularly given the difficulty in forecasting the future course of the economy.

Concept E

1. How does the tax system act as an automatic stabilizer?

Some taxes, such as progressive income taxes and corporate

profits taxes, automatically increase as the economy grows, and this increase in taxes restrains disposable income and the growth of aggregate demand below what it would have been otherwise. Similarly, they automatically decrease in recessions, and this decrease in taxes increases disposable income and acts as a partial offset to the fall in aggregate demand. The result is reduced business cycle instability.

2. Are automatic stabilizers impacted by a time lag? Why or why not?

Because automatic stabilizers respond to business cycle changes without the need for legislative or executive action, there is no appreciable lag between when business cycle conditions justify a change in them and when they do change. However, there is still a lag between when those stabilizers change and when their full effects are felt.

3. Why are transfer payments, such as unemployment compensation, effective automatic stabilizers?

Some transfer payment programs, such as unemployment compensation, act as automatic stabilizers, because when business cycle conditions worsen, people can start receiving increased transfer payments as soon as they become eligible (lose their jobs, in the case of unemployment compensation). The same is true of some other welfare type programs, such as food stamps. As a consequence of these automatic stabilizers, aggregate demand does not fall as much as it otherwise would have, partially offsetting any recessionary tendencies.

Concept F

1. Is supply-side economics more concerned with short-run economic stabilization or long-run economic growth?

Supply-side economics is more concerned with long-run economic growth than short-run economic stabilization. It is focused primarily on adopting policies that will increase the long-run aggregate supply curve (society's production possibilities curve) over time, by improving incentives to work, save, and invest.

2. Why could you say that supply-side economics is really more about after-tax wages and after-tax returns on investment than it is about tax rates?

It is changes in after-tax wages and after-tax returns on investment that are the incentives that change people's behavior, not changes in the tax rates themselves.

3. Why do government regulations have the same sorts of effects on businesses as taxes?

To the extent that government regulations impose added costs on businesses, the effects of those added costs are the same as a decrease (leftward or upward shift) in supply—as if a tax of that amount was imposed on the business. (In important respects, the regulations are "worse" than taxes because they involve real resource usage (foregone other goods), while the tax revenue is merely a transfer to whomever benefits from the taxes raised.)

4. Why aren't the full effects of supply-side policies seen quickly?

It will often take a substantial period of time before improved productive incentives will have their complete effects. For instance, an increase in the after-tax return on investment will increase investment, but it will take many years before the capital stock has completed its adjustment. The same is true for human capital investments in education, research and development, and

so forth; if a student or researcher learns more today, the full effect won't be observed immediately.

5. If taxes increase, what would you expect to happen to employment in the underground economy? Why?

The primary benefit of employment in the underground economy is the savings from not having to pay taxes (or bear some of the costs of regulations imposed on "legitimate" employment). The cost includes the risk of being caught, the difficulty of dealing on a cash-only or barter basis, and so forth. As tax rates increase, the benefits of working in the underground economy increase relative to the costs, and employment in the underground economy will tend to increase, other things equal.

Concept G

1. When President Kennedy cut tax rates and instituted an investment tax credit, was he using a demand-side or a supply-side strategy?

Both. Cutting tax rates and instituting an investment tax credit increased aggregate demand. But because those policies also improved productive incentives to work harder, save and invest more, and so forth, they also increased aggregate supply, though perhaps over a longer time frame.

2. If Kennedy's policy had been adopted during a period of full employment, would it have worked as well? Why or why not?

Kennedy used expansionary fiscal policy to get out of a recession. However, if a similar expansionary policy had been used during a period of full employment, the resulting increase in real output and accompanying decrease in unemployment would have only been temporary, with the long-run effect being higher prices.

3. What effect did President Johnson's economic policies have on the economy?

President Johnson also used expansionary fiscal policy, but he did so with the economy already at full employment. The result was very little effect on real GDP or employment but a considerable increase in inflation.

Concept H

1. Why can't the federal government finance its debt by printing more money?

Printing money to finance a deficit or the debt is inflationary and undermines confidence in the government.

2. How can the federal government finance the national debt?

The federal government must ultimately finance the national debt by borrowing (which represents future taxes). Attempting to finance the debt through money creation will eventually break down.

3. Should we worry about the national debt?

The national debt is a potential source of worry, because as the interest on the debt becomes large relative to the economy, the crowding out and disincentive effects can be very substantial. However, the privately held federal debt is not now large enough relative to the size of the economy to be a serious concern.

4. What must be true for Americans to be better off as a result of an increase in the federal debt?

For Americans to be better off as a result of an increase in the federal debt, the value of the investments and other spending financed by the debt must be greater than the cost of financing it.

Module 22: Money and the Banking System
Concept A

1. If everyone in an economy accepted poker chips as payment in exchange for goods and services, would poker chips be money?

Because money is anything that is generally accepted in exchange for goods or services (a medium of exchange), if everyone in an economy accepted poker chips as payment in exchange for goods and services, poker chips would be money.

2. If you were buying a pack of gum, would using currency or a demand deposit have lower transactions costs? What if you were buying a house?

If you were buying a pack of gum, or making any other such small purchase, using currency would generally have lower transactions costs than a demand deposit (checking account). However, if you were buying a house, or making any other very large purchase, using a demand deposit would generally have lower transactions costs than paying with currency; it would be cheaper, easier, and safer, and it would generate a more reliable financial record.

3. What is the main advantage of a transaction deposit for tax purposes? What is its main disadvantage for tax purposes?

The main advantage of transactions deposits for tax purposes is that they provide more reliable financial records for complying with record-keeping requirements for tax purposes. The financial records that transaction deposits generate, on the other hand, are their main disadvantage for those who wish to hide their financial activities from tax authorities.

4. Are credit cards money?

Credit cards are not money. They are actually guaranteed loans available on demand to users, which can be triggered by consumers; they are convenient substitutes for making transactions directly with money. That is, they are substitutes for the use of money in exchange. Credit cards do, however, have an important impact on how much money is demanded by consumers and how rapidly that money "turns over" in transactions.

5. What are M1 and M2?

M1 is a narrow definition of money that focuses on money's use as a means of payment (for transactions purposes). M1 includes currency in circulation, checkable deposits, and travelers checks. M2 is a broader definition of money that focuses on money's use as a highly liquid store of purchasing power or savings. M2 equals M1 plus other "near moneys," including savings accounts, small denomination time deposits, and money market mutual funds.

6. How have interest-earning checking accounts and overdraft protection led to the relative decline in demand deposits?

Interest-earning checking accounts provide the same ability to make transactions as non-interest-earning demand deposit accounts, but they are more attractive to many consumers because they earn interest. Overdraft protection means that consumers do not have to keep as much money in demand deposit accounts "just in case," to protect against overdrawing their accounts.

Concept B

1. Why does the advantage of monetary exchange over barter increase as an economy becomes more complex?

As the economy becomes more complex, the number of exchanges between people in the economy grows very rapidly. This means that the transaction cost advantages of using money over barter for those exchanges also grows very rapidly as the economy becomes more complex.

2. How can uncertain and rapid rates of inflation erode money's ability to perform its functions efficiently?

Uncertain and rapid rates of inflation erode money's ability to perform its functions efficiently because money lowers transaction costs most effectively when its value is stable, and therefore more predictable. Uncertain and rapid rates of inflation reduce the stability and predictability of the value of money, reducing its usefulness as a universally understood store of value. It therefore reduces money's ability to reduce transaction costs.

3. In a world of barter, would useful financial statements, like balance sheets, be possible? Would stock markets be possible? Would it be possible to build cars?

In a world of barter, there is no common store of value to allow comparisons of all the "apples and oranges" that must be summarized in financial statements, making such statements virtually impossible. Without money to act as a common store of value, stock and other financial markets, as well as very complex (many transactions) production processes, would also be virtually impossible.

4. Why do you think virtually all societies create something to function as money?

Having some good function as money lowers transactions costs, allowing increasing specialization and exchange to create increasing wealth for a society. That increase in wealth made possible by using money is why virtually all societies create something to function as money.

Concept C

1. If the earnings available on other financial assets rose, would you want to hold more or less money? Why?

Because holding wealth in the form of other financial assets is the alternative to holding it in the form of money, non-money financial assets are substitutes for holding money. When the earnings (interest) available on alternative financial assets rise, the opportunity cost of holding money instead also rises, so that you would want to hold less money, other things equal.

2. For the economy as a whole, why would individuals want to hold more money as GDP rises?

Americans conduct a larger volume of transactions as GDP rises. Therefore, they would want to hold more money as GDP rises in order to keep the costs of those increasing transactions down.

3. If in an era of very rapid inflation, many people stopped accepting a country's currency for payment, would that currency still be money?

If in an era of very rapid inflation, many people stopped accepting a country's currency for payment, that currency could no longer function as meaningful money.

4. Why might people who expect a major market "correction" (a fall in the value of stock holdings) wish to increase their holdings of money?

When the value of alternative financial assets is expected to fall, holding money, which will not similarly fall in value, becomes more attractive. Therefore, in the case of an expected fall in the value of stocks, bonds, or other financial assets, people would want to increase their holdings of money as a precaution.

Concept D

1. How did laws against interstate banking lead to a large number of U.S. banks? What is happening to the number of banks now that interstate banking is allowed?

Laws against interstate banking prevented the formation of large, interstate banking organizations, resulting in a large number of banks in the United States. However, now that interstate banking is allowed, mergers are resulting in fewer, larger, interstate banks.

2. In what way is it true that "banks make money by making money"?

Banks make money (profits) by loaning out their deposits at a higher interest rate than they pay their depositors. However, it is the extension of new loans in search of profits that creates new demand deposits, increasing the stock of money.

3. How do legal reserve deposit regulations lower bank profits?

Unlike other bank assets, legal reserves do not earn interest. Therefore, requiring a larger portion of bank assets to be held in reserve than prudent banking practice would dictate reduces bank earnings and profits.

4. Is a demand deposit an asset or a liability?

A demand deposit is an asset for its owner but a liability of the bank at which the account is kept.

5. If the Bonnie and Clyde National Bank's only deposits were demand deposits of $20 million, and it faced a 10 percent reserve requirement, how much money would it be required to hold in reserves?

The Bonnie and Clyde National Bank would have to hold 10 percent of its $20 million in demand deposits, or $2 million, as reserves.

6. How would a new deposit into your demand deposit account create a situation of excess reserves at your bank?

A new deposit adds that amount to your demand deposit account and to the reserves of your bank. But only a fraction of the added reserves are required by the addition to your demand deposit account. The rest are excess reserves, which the bank will look to convert to interest-earning loans or other assets.

Concept E

1. Why do the stock of money and the volume of bank loans both increase or decrease at the same time?

The stock of money and the volume of bank loans both increase or both decrease at the same time because issuing new bank loans adds to the money stock, while calling in existing bank loans reduces the money stock, by reducing demand deposits.

2. Why would each bank in the money supply multiple expansion process lend out a larger fraction of any new deposit it receives, the lower the reserve requirement?

Each bank in the money supply multiple expansion process can lend up to the amount of its excess reserves. But the excess reserves created by each dollar deposited in a bank equals 1 minus the required reserve ratio. The lower this reserve requirement, the greater the excess reserves created by each new deposit, and therefore the greater the fraction of any new deposit that will be loaned out in this process.

3. If a particular bank with a reserve requirement of 10 percent has $30,000 in a new cash deposit, how much money could it create through making new loans?

Using the money multiplier formula, a $30,000 cash deposit could add $300,000 to the money supply ($30,000 × 10 = $300,000), with $30,000 coming from the initial deposit and $270,000 through the multiple expansion effect.

4. Why do banks choosing to hold excess reserves or borrowers choosing to hold some of their loans in the form of currency reduce the actual impact of the money multiplier to a level below that indicated by the multiplier formula?

If banks choose to hold excess reserves, each bank in the money supply expansion process will lend out less, and therefore create less new money, than if it loaned out all of its excess reserves. The result will be a smaller money supply than that indicated by the multiplier formula, because that formula assumes that banks lend out all of their excess reserves. If borrowers hold some of their loans as currency, that would reduce the amount of vault cash, which counts as a reserve, at banks. This would reduce the amount that could be loaned at each stage of the money supply creation process, and would therefore reduce the actual money multiplier below the level indicated by the multiplier formula.

Concept F

1. How did the combination of increased holding of excess reserves by banks and currency by the public lead to bank failures in the 1930s?

The desire by the public for increased currency holdings, caused largely by the fear of bank failures, also forced banks to sharply increase excess reserves and reduce lending, together causing a sharp fall in the money stock. Despite substantial excess reserves, however, bank runs led to the failure of even many conservatively run banks.

2. What are the four reasons cited in the text for the collapse of the U.S. banking system in this period?

The cited reasons include: 1) the large number of small banks, which were more at risk from bank runs; 2) governmental attempts to stem the distress in the banking industry that were both weak and too late; 3) the absence of deposit insurance, which would have bolstered consumer confidence; and 4) fear that the economy was in a continuous downward cycle, so that there was little basis for optimism that bank loans would be safely repaid.

3. What is the FDIC, and how did its establishment increase bank stability and reassure depositors?

The Federal Deposit Insurance Corporation insures bank deposits. That guarantee of deposits eliminated the risk to depositors if their bank failed, thus eliminating the bank runs that resulted from the fear of bank insolvency. No longer facing the risk of bank runs, banks were more stable. Note, however, that the elimination of that risk reduces depositor interest in how risky the bank's investments are—an important cause of many bank crises throughout the world today.

Module 23: The Federal Reserve System and Monetary Policy
Concept A

1. What are the six primary functions of a central bank?

A central bank: 1) is a "banker's bank," where commercial banks maintain their own deposits; 2) provides services, such as transferring funds and checks, for commercial banks; 3) serves as the major bank for the federal government; 4) buys and sells foreign currencies and assists in transactions with other countries; 5) serves as a "lender of last resort" for banking institutions in financial distress; and 6) regulates the size of the money supply.

2. What is the FOMC and what does it do?
The Federal Open Market Committee is a committee of the Federal Reserve System, made up of the seven members of the Board of Governors, the President of the New York Federal Reserve Bank, and four other presidents of Federal Reserve Banks. It makes most of the key decisions influencing the direction and size of changes in the money stock.

3. How is the Fed tied to the executive branch? How is it insulated from executive branch pressure to influence monetary policy?
The president selects the seven members of the Board of Governors, subject to Senate approval, one every two years, for 14-year terms. He also selects the Chair of the Board of Governors for a four-year term. However, because the president can only select one member every two years, he cannot appoint a majority of the Board of Governors for his term in office. Also, the president cannot use reappointment of his nominees or threats of firing members to pressure the Fed on monetary policy.

Concept B

1. If the money stock is $10 billion and velocity is 4, what is the product of the price level and output? If the price level is 2, what does output equal?
If the money stock is $10 billion and velocity is 4 (so that $MV = \$40$ billion), the product of the price level and real output (PQ, or nominal output), must also be $40 billion. If the price level was 2 in this case, real output would equal the $40 billion nominal output divided by the price level of 2, or $20 billion.

2. If nominal GDP is $200 billion and the money stock is $50 billion, what must velocity be?
Because $MV = PQ$, $V = PQ/M$. $V = \$200$ billion/$50 billion, or 4, in this case.

3. If the money stock increases and velocity does not change, what will happen to nominal GDP?
If M increases and V does not change, MV must increase. Because $MV = PQ$, and PQ equals nominal GDP, nominal GDP must also increase as a result.

4. If velocity is unstable, does stabilizing the money stock help stabilize the economy? Why or why not?
If V is unstable, stabilizing M does not stabilize MV. Because MV will not be stabilized, PQ, or nominal GDP, will not be stabilized either.

Concept C

1. What three main tactics could the Fed use in pursuing a contractionary monetary policy?
The Fed could conduct an open market sale of government securities (bonds), increase reserve requirements, and/or increase the discount rate if it wanted to pursue a contractionary monetary policy.

2. What three main tactics could the Fed use in pursuing an expansionary monetary policy?
The Fed could conduct an open market purchase of government securities (bonds), decrease reserve requirements, and/or decrease the discount rate if it wanted to pursue an expansionary monetary policy.

3. Would the money stock rise or fall if the Fed made an open market purchase of government bonds, *ceteris paribus*?
An open market purchase of government bonds by the Fed would increase banking reserves, thereby increasing the money stock, *ceteris paribus*, in an amount dependent on the money multiplier.

4. If the Fed raised the discount rate from 12 to 15 percent, what impact would that have on the money supply?
Raising the discount rate makes it more costly for banks to borrow reserves directly from the Fed. To the extent that banks borrow fewer reserves directly from the Fed, this reduces total banking reserves, thereby decreasing the money stock, *ceteris paribus*.

5. What is moral suasion, and why would the Fed use this tactic?
Moral suasion is the term used to describe Federal Reserve attempts to persuade or influence banks to follow a particular course of action (e.g., be more selective in making loans) they might not otherwise take.

Concept D

1. Who controls the supply of money in the money market?
The banking system, through the loan expansion process, directly determines the supply of money in the money market. However, the Fed, through the policy variables it controls (primarily open market operations, reserve requirements, and the discount rate), indirectly controls the money supply by controlling the level of reserves and the money multiplier.

2. How does an increase in income or a decrease in the interest rate increase the demand for money?
An increase in income increases (shifts to the right) the demand for money, as people want to hold down the transactions costs on the increasing volume of transactions taking place. A decrease in interest rates, on the other hand, increases the quantity of money demanded (moving down along the money demand curve) but not the demand for money.

3. What Federal Reserve policies would shift the money supply curve to the left?
An open market sale of government securities (bonds), an increase in reserve requirements, and/or an increase in the discount rates would shift the money supply curve to the left.

4. Will an increase in the money stock increase or decrease the short-run equilibrium real interest rate, other things equal?
An increase in the money stock would decrease the short-run equilibrium real interest rate, other things equal, as the rightward shift of the money supply curve pushes the money market equilibrium down along the money demand curve.

5. Will an increase in national income increase or decrease the short-run equilibrium real interest rate, other things equal?
An increase in national income would shift the money demand curve to the right, which would increase the short-run equilibrium real interest rate, other things equal.

6. What is the relationship between interest rates and aggregate demand in monetary policy?

Lower interest rates will tend to stimulate aggregate demand for goods and services, other things equal.

7. How will an expansionary monetary policy impact real GDP and the price level at less than full employment?
An expansionary monetary policy shifts aggregate demand to the right. Starting from less than full employment, the result will be an increase in the price level, an increase in real output, and a decrease in unemployment, as the economy moves up along the short-run aggregate supply curve. This increased output would be sustainable if it did not exceed the natural level of real output.

8. How will an expansionary monetary policy impact real GDP and the price level at full employment?
An expansionary monetary policy shifts aggregate demand to the right. Starting from full employment, the result in the short run will be an increase in the price level, an increase in real output, and a decrease in unemployment. However, because the increase in real output is not sustainable, the long-run result will be real output returning to its natural level, but prices that have risen even more, where the new aggregate demand curve intersects the long-run aggregate supply curve.

Concept E

1. Why is the lag time for adopting policy changes shorter for monetary policy than for fiscal policy?
The lag time for adopting monetary policy changes is shorter than for fiscal policy because those decisions are not slowed by the budgetary process that fiscal tax and expenditure policy changes must go through.

2. Why would a banking system that wanted to keep some excess reserves rather than lending them all out hinder the Fed's ability to increase the money stock?
A desire by the banking system to keep some excess reserves would reduce the money stock, other things equal. Therefore, such a change would at least partly offset the effects of the Fed's expansionary policy changes, which would hinder the Fed's ability to successfully use expansionary monetary policy to increase the money stock.

3. How can the activities of global and nonbank institutions weaken the Fed's influence on the money market?
The Fed has no control over global and nonbank institutions that issue credit (loan money); these institutions are not subject to reserve requirement limitations. Thus, the Fed cannot control their behavior, nor the resulting effects of their activities on the economy, through its policies.

4. If fiscal policy was expansionary, but the Fed wanted to counteract the fiscal policy effect on aggregate demand, what could it do?
Expansionary fiscal policy would increase aggregate demand. To counteract that fiscal policy effect on aggregate demand, the Fed would want to adopt contractionary monetary policy (through an open market sale of government securities, an increase in reserve requirements, and/or an increase in the discount rate), which would tend to reduce aggregate demand, other things equal.

5. What are the arguments for and against having monetary policy be more directly controlled by the political process?
The argument for having monetary policy be more directly controlled by the political process is basically that because fiscal policy is already determined by the political process, and monetary policy (which is not determined by the same political process) can offset or even neutralize the macroeconomic effects of fiscal policy, it would be better for all macroeconomic policy to be directly controlled by the political process. The argument against having monetary policy be more directly controlled by the political process is that it would be dangerous to turn over control of the nation's money stock to politicians, rather than allowing monetary policy decisions made by technically competent administrators who are focused more on price stability and are more insulated from political pressures from the public and special interest groups.

6. How is fine-tuning the economy like driving a car with an unpredictable steering lag on a winding road?
Fine-tuning the economy is like driving a car with an unpredictable steering lag on a winding road, because to steer the economy successfully requires that policy makers have an accurate map of both which way and how rapidly the economy is headed; that they know exactly how much each possible policy would affect the economy, so that they "turn the policy wheels" just the right amount; and that they know how long it will take each possible policy before it actually "turns" the economy.

Module 24: Inflation, Unemployment, and Expectations
Concept A

1. How does the rate of inflation affect real wage rates, if nominal wages rise less or more slowly than output prices?
When nominal wages rise less or more slowly than output prices, real wages (adjusted for inflation) fall.

2. How does the change in real wage rates (relative to output prices) as inflation increases affect the unemployment rate?
The fall in real wage rates (relative to output prices) as inflation increases reduces the unemployment rate, because the lower real wage rates make it profitable to hire more, now relatively cheaper, employees than before. This presumes that workers are not fully aware that their wages have fallen in real terms, however.

3. What is the argument for why the Phillips curve is relatively steeper at lower rates of unemployment and higher rates of inflation?
The argument is that once capacity utilization is high and unemployment is low, an increased part of the economy is already operating at or near full capacity, and further fiscal or monetary policy stimulus primarily triggers inflationary pressures in sectors already at capacity, while eliminating decreasing amounts of unemployment in those fewer sectors where excess capacity and high unemployment still exist.

4. For a given upward-sloping short-run aggregate supply curve, how does an increase in aggregate demand correspond to a movement up and to the left along a Phillips curve?
For a given upward-sloping short-run aggregate supply curve, an increase in aggregate demand moves the economy up along the short-run aggregate supply curve to an increased price level and increased real GDP. The increase in the price level is an increase in inflation and the increase in real GDP is accompanied by a decrease in unemployment, so the same effects are shown by a move up (higher inflation) and to the left (lower unemployment) along a Phillips curve.

Concept B

1. Is the Phillips curve stable over time?
No. While the short-run Phillips curve was once considered to be stable, economists now recognize that it is unstable and that it does not represent a permanent relationship between unemployment and inflation rates.

2. Why would you expect there to be no relationship between inflation and unemployment in the long run?
You would expect there to be no relationship between inflation and unemployment in the long run because the long run represents what happens once people have completely adjusted to changed conditions. Therefore, in the long run, actual and expected rates of inflation are the same, and change rates of inflation do not change people's "real" behavior (reflected in unemployment and real GDP) because those changes are not unexpected.

3. Why is the economy being on the long-run Phillips curve equivalent to it being on the long-run aggregate supply curve?
Unemployment equals its natural rate along the long-run Phillips curve. Real GDP is equal to its natural level along the long-run aggregate supply curve. But the natural level of real GDP is the output level consistent with unemployment equal to its natural rate, so points on both curves illustrate the same results.

4. Why would inflation have to accelerate over time to keep unemployment below its natural rate (and real output above its natural level) for a sustained period of time?
Inflation would have to accelerate over time to keep unemployment below its natural rate (and real output above its natural level) for a sustained period of time, because over time, people would adapt to any given level of inflation. Therefore, at a given rate of inflation, unemployment would return to its natural rate over time. To keep people "fooled" into unemployment below its natural rate requires more inflation than people expected, and to maintain this requires accelerating inflation over time.

5. What does the long-run Phillips curve say about the relationship between macroeconomic policy stimulus and unemployment in the long run?
The vertical long-run Phillips curve indicates that there is no relationship between macroeconomic policy stimulus and unemployment in the long run, once people have had time to completely adapt to it. Unemployment will equal its natural rate in the long run, and macroeconomic policy will therefore only change the inflation rate in the long run.

Concept C

1. What is the rational expectations theory?
Rational expectations theory incorporated expectations as a central factor in the analysis of the entire economy. It is essentially the idea that people will rationally anticipate the predictable future consequences of present decisions, and change their behavior today to reflect those future consequences. For example, this would mean that people can anticipate the inflationary long-run consequences of macroeconomic policies adopted today, and that anticipation leads them to change their current behavior in a way that can quickly neutralize the intended impact of a government action.

2. Why could an unexpected change in inflation change real wages and unemployment, while an expected change in inflation could not?

An unexpected change in inflation could change real wages and unemployment precisely because it was unexpected, and people were "fooled" into changing their behavior (in the short run). An expected change in inflation would not change real wages and unemployment because no one is fooled, so no one changes their real behavior as a result.

3. Why can the results of rational expectations be described as generating the long-run results of a policy change in the short run?
The long run refers to the situation once people have had time to completely adjust their behavior to current circumstances. But under rational expectations, the long-run consequences will be anticipated and responded to today, so that people have completely adjusted their behavior to new policies in the short run. Therefore, the results of rational expectations can be described as generating the long-run results of a policy change in the short run.

4. In a world of rational expectations, why is it harder to reduce unemployment below its natural rate but potentially easier to reduce inflation rates?
Reducing unemployment below its natural rate requires that inflation is greater than expected. But under rational expectations, people are not fooled by inflationary policies (unless they are surprises), so this is very hard to do. It is potentially easier to reduce inflation rates under rational expectations, though, because people will be more quickly convinced that inflation will fall when credible government policies are put in place, and it will not take an extended period of high unemployment before they adapt to the lower inflation rate that results.

5. Even if individuals could quickly anticipate the consequences of government policy changes, how could long-term contracts (e.g., 3-year labor agreements and 30-year fixed-rate mortgages) and the costs of changing price lists and catalogs result in unemployment still being affected by those policy changes?
Even if individuals could quickly anticipate the consequences of government policy changes, long-term contracts can't be instantly adjusted, so the real prices and wages subject to such contracts will be at least temporarily changed by inflation "surprises," at least until such contracts can be rewritten. Similarly, price lists and catalogs will not be changed instantly when new policies are adopted because of the cost of doing so, and those prices will not instantly adapt to new inflationary expectations. Because these prices will be "wrong" for a period after new policies are adopted, real wages and prices, and therefore unemployment, can still be affected by policy changes for a period of time.

6. Why do expected rainstorms have different effects on people than unexpected rainstorms?
Expected rainstorms don't catch you by surprise, so you prepare for them in a way that minimizes their effects (umbrellas, jackets, etc.). Unexpected rainstorms catch you by surprise and have much greater effects, because you haven't prepared for them.

Concept D

1. In what ways might "voluntary" government inflation guidelines not be completely voluntary?
"Voluntary" government inflation guidelines are not completely voluntary because such guidelines are backed up with threats of involuntary controls or other consequences for those that don't comply with them.

2. If holding down legal price increases through price controls reduces official inflation rates, why are black markets likely to arise?

Price controls hold official prices below their equilibrium levels, creating shortages at those prices. The shortages at official prices leads to black markets, where unofficial prices can move up toward their equilibrium levels.

3. How might wage and price controls lead to shortages of goods and services (a "queuetopia")?

For wage and price controls to restrain price increases, they must be held below their equilibrium levels. But below-equilibrium prices will lead to shortages of those goods and services, which can result in queues.

4. How might wage and price controls lead to the production of inferior products over time?

Wage and price controls lead to shortages at official prices. Because prices for given quality goods are not allowed to rise, the same sort of adjustment to a higher price per "unit" of quality is accomplished by lowering quality instead.

5. If every possible good was indexed to changes in the general price level, would it be very easy for relative price changes to signal changing relative scarcities? Why or why not?

When all prices tend to change together (e.g., when one price goes up, the price level goes up, and so other indexed prices also go up as a result), it is harder for relative prices to change to reflect changing relative scarcity.

Module 25: International Trade
Concept A

1. Why is it important to understand the effects of international trade?

All countries are affected by international trade, although the magnitude of the international trade sector varies substantially by country. International connections mean that any of a large number of disturbances that originate elsewhere will have important consequences for the domestic economy.

2. Why would producers and consumers in the United States be more concerned about Canadian trade restrictions than Swedish trade restrictions?

The United States and Canada are the two largest trading partners in the world. That means the effects of trade restrictions into Canada would have a far larger magnitude effect on the United States than similar restrictions imposed by Sweden (although for certain items, we have a larger magnitude of trade with Sweden than with Canada, so Swedish restrictions would then be of more concern for such items).

Concept B

1. Why do people voluntarily choose to specialize and trade?

Voluntary specialization and trade among self-interested parties only takes place because all of the parties involved expect that their benefits from that specialization (according to comparative advantage) and exchange will exceed their costs.

2. How could a country have an absolute advantage in producing one good or service without also having a comparative advantage in its production?

If one country was absolutely more productive at everything than another country, but it wasn't equally more productive at

everything, there would still be some things it had a comparative disadvantage in. For instance, if country A was three times as productive in making X and two times as productive in making Y as country B, it would have a comparative advantage in making X (it gives up less Y for each X produced) and a comparative disadvantage in making Y (it gives up more X for each Y produced), relative to country B.

3. Why do you think the introduction of the railroad reduced self-sufficiency in the United States?

Prior to the introduction of the railroad, the high cost of transportation overwhelmed the gains from specializing according to comparative advantage in much of the United States (production cost differences were smaller than the costs of transportation). The railroads reduced transportation costs enough that specialization and exchange became beneficial for more goods and services, and self-sufficiency caused by high transportation costs declined.

4. If you can do the dishes in two-thirds the time it takes your younger sister, do you have a comparative advantage in doing the dishes compared to her?

We can't know the answer to this question without more information. It is not the time taken to do the dishes that matters in determining comparative advantage, but the opportunity cost of the time in terms of foregone value elsewhere. If your younger sister is less than two-thirds as good at other chores than you, she is relatively better at doing the dishes, and so would have a comparative advantage in doing the dishes. If she is more than two-thirds as good at other chores, she is relatively better at those chores, and so would have a comparative disadvantage in doing the dishes.

Concept C

1. How does voluntary trade generate both producer and consumer surplus?

Voluntary trade generates consumer surplus because a rational consumer will not purchase a good if he does not value the benefits of that purchase at greater than its cost, and consumer surplus is the difference between that value and the cost consumers are forced to pay. Voluntary trade generates producer surplus because a rational producer will not sell additional units unless the price he receives is greater than his marginal cost, and producer surplus is the difference between the revenues received and the costs producers must bear to produce the goods that generate those revenues.

2. If the world price of a good is greater than the domestic price prior to trade, why does that imply that the domestic economy has a comparative advantage in producing that good?

If the world price of a good is greater than the domestic price prior to trade, that implies that the domestic marginal opportunity cost of production is less than the world marginal opportunity cost of production. This means that the domestic economy has a comparative advantage in that good.

3. If the world price of a good is less than the domestic price prior to trade, why does that imply that the domestic economy has a comparative disadvantage in producing that good?

If the world price of a good is less than the domestic price prior to trade, this implies that the domestic marginal opportunity cost of production is greater than the world marginal opportunity cost of production. This means that the domestic economy has a comparative disadvantage in that good.

4. When a country has a comparative advantage in the production of a good, why do domestic producers gain more than domestic consumers lose from free international trade?

When a country has a comparative advantage in the production of a good, the marginal benefit from exporting is the world price, which is greater than the foregone value domestically (along the domestic demand curve) for those units of domestic consumption "crowded out," and greater than the marginal cost of the expanded output. Therefore, there are net domestic gains to international trade (the gains to domestic producers exceeds the losses to domestic consumers).

5. When a country has a comparative disadvantage in the production of a good, why do domestic consumers gain more than domestic producers lose from free international trade?

When a country has a comparative disadvantage in producing a good, the marginal cost of importing is the world price, which is less than the additional value (along the domestic demand curve) for those units of expanded domestic consumption and less than the marginal cost of the domestic production "crowded out." Therefore, there are net domestic gains to international trade (the gains to domestic consumers exceeds the losses to domestic producers).

6. Why do U.S. exporters, such as farmers, favor free trade more than U.S. producers of domestic products who face competition from foreign imports, such as the automobile industry?

Exporters favor free trade over restrictions on what they sell in other countries because that increases the demand, and therefore the prices, for their products, which raises their profits. Those who must compete with importers want those imports restricted rather than freely traded, because that increases the demand, and therefore the prices, for their domestically produced products, raising their profits.

Concept D

1. Why do tariffs increase domestic producer surplus but decrease domestic consumer surplus?

Tariffs raise the price of imported goods to domestic consumers, which also results in higher prices received by domestic producers. The higher price reduces domestic consumer surplus but increases domestic producer surplus.

2. How do import tariffs increase employment in "protected" industries, but at the expense of a likely decrease in employment overall?

Import tariffs increase employment in "protected" industries because the barriers to lower-priced imports increase the demand faced by domestic producers, increasing their demand for workers. However, imports are the means by which foreigners get the dollars to buy our exports, so restricted imports will mean restricted exports (even more so if other countries retaliate with import restrictions of their own). In addition, by raising the prices domestic consumers pay for the protected products (remember that domestic consumers lose more than domestic producers gain from protectionism), consumers are made poorer in real terms, which will reduce demand for goods, and therefore the labor to make them, throughout the economy.

3. Why is the national security argument for tariffs questionable?

The national security argument for tariffs is questionable because tariffs increase current reliance on domestic supplies, which depletes the future stockpile of available reserves. With fewer domestic reserves, the country will be even more dependent on

foreign supplies in the future. Buying foreign supplies and stockpiling them makes more sense as a way of reducing reliance on foreign supplies in wartime.

4. Why is the domestic argument for import quotas weaker than the case for tariffs?

Tariffs at least use the price system as the basis of trade. Tariff revenues end up in a country's treasury, where they can be used to produce benefits for country's citizens or to reduce the domestic tax burden. Import quotas, however, transfer most of those benefits to foreign producers as the higher prices they receive.

5. Why would foreign producers prefer import quotas to tariffs, even if they resulted in the same reduced level of imports?

Restricting imports reduces supply, which increases the price foreign producers receive on the units they sell, benefiting them. Tariffs, on the other hand reduce the after-tariff price foreign producers receive. If both reduce foreign sales the same amount, foreign producers would clearly prefer import restrictions over tariffs.

6. Why does subsidizing exports by industries that lack a comparative advantage tend to harm the domestic economy, on net?

Subsidizing industries where a country has a comparative disadvantage (higher costs) must, by definition, require shifting resources from where it has a comparative advantage (lower costs) to where it has a comparative disadvantage. The value of the output produced from those resources (indirectly in the case of specialization and exchange) is lower as a result.

Module 26: International Finance
Concept A

1. What is the balance of payments?

The balance of payments is the record of all of the international financial transactions of a nation—both those involving inflows of funds and those involving outflows of funds—over a year.

2. Why would a British purchaser of U.S. goods or services have to first exchange pounds for dollars?

Because U.S. goods and services are priced in dollars, a British consumer who wanted to buy U.S. goods would have to first buy dollars in exchange for English pounds before he could buy the U.S. goods and services with dollars. Ultimately, this is because input suppliers want to be paid in dollars so they can buy goods in the U.S. with their incomes.

3. How is it true that U.S. imports provide the means by which foreigners can buy U.S. exports?

The domestic currency Americans supply in exchange for the foreign currencies to buy imports also supplies the dollars with which foreigners can buy U.S. exports.

4. What would have to be true in order for the U.S. to have a balance of trade deficit and a balance of payments surplus?

A balance of trade deficit means that we imported more merchandise (goods) than we exported. A balance of payments surplus means that the sum of our goods and services exports exceeded the sum of our goods and services imports, plus funds transfers from the U.S. For both to be true would require a larger surplus of services (including net investment income) and/or net fund transfer inflows than our trade deficit in merchandise (goods).

5. What would have to be true in order for the U.S. to have a balance of trade surplus and a current account deficit?

A balance of trade surplus means that we exported more merchandise (goods) than we imported. A current account deficit means that our exports of goods and services (including net investment income) were less than the sum of our imports of goods and services, plus net fund transfers. For both to happen would require that the sum of our deficit in services plus net transfers must be greater than our surplus in merchandise (goods) trading.

6. If there are no errors or omissions in the recorded balance of payments accounts, what should the statistical discrepancy equal?

If there were no errors and/or omissions in the recorded balance of payments accounts, the statistical discrepancy should equal zero, because properly recorded, credits and debits must be equal, because every credit creates a debit of equal value.

7. A Nigerian family visiting Chicago enjoys a Chicago Cubs baseball game at Wrigley Field. How would that expense be recorded in the balance of payments accounts? Why?

This would be counted as an export of services, because it would provide Americans with foreign currency (a claim against Nigeria) in exchange for those services.

Concept B

1. What is an exchange rate?

An exchange rate is the price in one country's currency of one unit of another country's currency.

2. When a U.S. dollar buys relatively more French francs, why does the cost of imports from France fall in the United States?

When a U.S. dollar buys relatively more French francs, the cost of imports from France falls in the United States because it takes fewer U.S. dollars to buy a given number of French francs in order to pay French producers. In other words, the price in U.S. dollars of French goods and services has fallen.

3. When a U.S. dollar buys relatively fewer Austrian schillings, why does the cost of U.S. exports fall in Austria?

When a U.S. dollar buys relatively fewer Austrian schillings, the cost of U. S. exports falls in Austria because it takes fewer Austrian schillings to buy a given number of U.S. dollars in order to pay U.S. producers. In other words, the price in Austrian schillings of U.S. goods and services has fallen.

4. How does an increase in domestic demand for foreign goods and services increase the demand for those foreign currencies?

An increase in domestic demand for foreign goods and services increases the demand for those foreign currencies because the demand for foreign currencies is derived from the demand for foreign goods and services and foreign capital. The more foreign goods and services are demanded, the more of that foreign currency will be needed to pay for those goods and services.

5. As Euros get cheaper relative to U.S. dollars, why does the quantity of Euros demanded by Americans increase? Why doesn't the demand for Euros increase as a result?

As Euros get cheaper relative to U.S. dollars, European products become relatively more inexpensive to Americans, who therefore buy more European goods and services. To do so, the quantity of Euros demanded by U.S. consumers will rise to buy them, as the price (exchange rate) for Euros falls. The demand (as opposed to quantity demanded) of Euros doesn't increase, because this represents a movement along the demand for Euros caused by a change in exchange rates, rather than a change in demand for Euros caused by some other factor.

6. Who competes exchange rates down when they are above their equilibrium value? Who competes exchange rates up when they are below their equilibrium value?

When exchange rates are greater than their equilibrium value, there will be a surplus of the currency and frustrated sellers of that currency will bid its price (exchange rate) down. When exchange rates are less than their equilibrium value, there will be a shortage of the currency and frustrated buyers of that currency will bid its price (exchange rate) up.

Concept C

1. Why will the exchange value of a foreign currency relative to U.S. dollars decline when U.S. domestic tastes change, reducing the demand for foreign-produced goods?

When U.S. domestic tastes change, reducing the demand for foreign-produced goods, the reduced demand for foreign-produced goods will also reduce the demand for the foreign currencies to buy them. This reduced demand for those foreign currencies will reduce their exchange rates, relative to U.S. dollars.

2. Why does the demand for foreign currencies shift in the same direction as domestic income? What happens to the exchange value of those foreign currencies in terms of U.S. dollars?

An increase in domestic income increases the demand for goods and services, including imported goods and services. This increases the demand for those foreign currencies to buy those additional imports, which increases their exchange rates (the exchange value of those currencies), relative to U.S. dollars.

3. How would increased U.S. tariffs on imported European goods affect the exchange value of Euros in terms of dollars?

Increased U.S. tariffs on imported European goods would make them less affordable in the U.S. This would lead to a reduced demand for European goods in the U.S., and therefore a reduced demand for Euros. This would reduce the exchange value of Euros in terms of dollars.

4. Why do changes in tastes, incomes, or tariffs in the United States change the demand for Euros, while similar changes in Europe change the supply of Euros?

Changes in U.S. tastes, incomes, or tariffs change the demand for Euros because it changes U.S. demand for European goods and services, which changes the demand for Euros to buy them. Similar changes in Europe change the supply of Euros because they change the European demand for U.S. goods and services, thus changing their demand for dollars with which to buy those goods and services. This requires them to change their supply of Euros in order to get those dollars.

5. What would happen to the exchange value of Euros in terms of U.S. dollars if incomes rose in both Europe and the United States?

These changes would increase both the demand (higher incomes in the U.S.) and supply (higher income in Europe) of Euros. The effect on the exchange value of Euros would be determined by whether the supply or demand for Euros shifted more (rising if demand shifted relatively more and falling if supply shifted relatively more).

6. Why does an increase in interest rates in Germany relative to U.S. interest rates increase the demand for Euros but decrease their supply?

An increase in interest rates in Germany relative to U.S. interest rates increases the rates of return on German investments relative to U.S. investments. U.S. investors therefore increase their demand for German investments, increasing the demand for Euros to make those investments. This would also reduce the demand by German investors for U.S. investments, decreasing the supply of Euros with which to buy the dollars to make the investments.

7. What would an increase in U.S. inflation relative to Europe do to the supply and demand for Euros and to the equilibrium exchange value (price) of Euros in terms of U.S. dollars?

An increase in U.S. inflation relative to Europe would make U.S. products relatively more expensive to European customers, decreasing the U.S. goods and services demanded by European customers, and therefore decreasing the supply of Euros to buy the dollars necessary for those purchases. It would also make European products relatively cheaper to U.S. consumers, increasing the European goods and services demanded by U.S. consumers, and therefore increasing the demand for Euros necessary for those purchases. The decreased supply of and increased demand for Euros results in an increasing exchange value of Euros in terms of U.S. dollars.

Concept D

1. What are the arguments for and against flexible exchange rates?

The arguments for flexible exchange rates include: the large expansion of world trade under flexible exchange rates; the fact that they allowed the economy to adjust to a quadrupling in the price of the world's most important internationally traded commodity—oil; and especially that it diminished the recurring crises that caused speculative rampages and currency revaluations, allowing the market mechanism to address currency shortages and world trade imbalances. The arguments against flexible exchange rates are that it increases exchange rate uncertainty in international trade and can contribute to inflationary pressures, due to the lack of the fixed-rate system's incentives to constrain domestic policies that would erode net exports.

2. When the U.S. dollar starts to exchange for fewer Japanese yen, other things equal, what happens to U.S. and Japanese imports and exports as a result?

When the U.S. dollar starts to exchange for fewer Japanese yen, other things equal, the U.S. cost of Japanese imports rises, de-

creasing the value of Japanese exports to the United States. It also decreases the cost to the Japanese of buying U.S. goods, increasing the value of U.S. exports to Japan.

3. Why is the system of flexible exchange rates sometimes called a "dirty float" system?

The system of flexible exchange rates is sometimes called a "dirty float" system because governments do intervene at times in foreign currency markets to alter their currencies' exchange rates, so that exchange rates are partly determined by market forces and partly by government intervention.

4. Were exchange rates under the Bretton Woods system really stable? How could you argue that exchange rates were more uncertain under the fixed-rate system than with floating exchange rates?

Exchange rates under the Bretton Woods system were not really stable. While exchange rate changes were infrequent, they were large, with large effects. It could be argued that the less frequent but larger exchange rate changes that were common under the Bretton Woods system generated more uncertainty than the more frequent but smaller exchange rate changes that occur with the floating exchange rate system.

5. What is the uncertainty argument against flexible exchange rates? What evidence do proponents of flexible exchange rates cite in response?

The uncertainty argument against flexible exchange rates is that flexible exchange rates add another source of uncertainty to world trade, which would increase the cost of international transactions, reducing the magnitude of international trade. Proponents of flexible exchange rates cite the faster growth of international trade since the introduction of flexible exchange rates, the fact that markets exist on which to hedge exchange rate risks (through forward, or futures, markets), and that the alleged exchange rate certainty was fictitious, because large changes could take place at a nations' whim.

6. Do flexible exchange rates cause higher rates of inflation? Why or why not?

Flexible exchange rates do not cause higher rates of inflation. However, they do reduce the incentives to constrain domestic inflation for fear of reducing net exports under the fixed exchange rate system. Inflation, though is ultimately caused by expansionary macroeconomic policies adopted by governments and their central banks.

GLOSSARY

accounting profits   Profits as accountants record them based on actual cash receipts (revenues) and actual expenditures of cash (explicit costs).

aggregate demand (AD)   The sum of the demand for all goods and services in the economy. It reflects the total amounts of real goods and services that all groups together want to purchase in a given time period.

aggregate supply (AS)   The relationship between the total quantity of final goods and services that suppliers are willing and able to produce and the overall price level.

allocative efficiency   The situation where no resources are wasted—the output at which price equals marginal cost.

assets   Something of value held by a person or a firm.

asset demand   Money individuals hold as a store of value.

association   A relationship.

automatic stabilizers   Changes in government transfer payments or tax collections that automatically tend to counter business cycle fluctuations.

autonomous (independent) investment   Investment not determined by the level of income.

average cost pricing   A regulatory method that sets price equal to average total costs.

average fixed costs (AFC)   Total fixed costs divided by output.

average propensity to consume (APC)   The fraction of total income that households spend on consumption.

average revenue (AR)   The total revenue divided by the number of units sold of the product.

average total cost (ATC)   Total cost divided by output.

average variable cost (AVC)   Total variable cost divided by output.

bads   Items that we do not desire or want.

balance of payments   A statement that records all of the exchanges that those in a nation engaged in that required an outflow of funds to foreign nations or an inflow of funds from other nations.

balance sheet   A financial record that indicates the balance between a bank's assets and its liabilities plus capital.

balanced budget   A situation in which current government revenues are equal to current government expenditures.

barriers to entry   Factors that prevent firms from entering an industry.

barter   Trade in goods and services without the use of money.

boom   A prolonged expansion in economic activity.

budget deficit   What occurs when government spending exceeds tax revenue during a particular time period, usually a year.

budget surplus   When tax revenues are greater than government spending during a particular time period, usually a year.

business cycles   Short-term fluctuations in the level of economic activity, relative to the long-term trend in output.

capital consumption allowance   Another name for depreciation.

capital   Human-made resources used to produce final goods (e.g., office buildings, tools, machines, and factories).

capital intensive   A method of production using a relatively large amount of capital.

cartel   Collection of firms making an agreement on sale, pricing, and other decisions.

ceteris paribus   Let everything else be equal; holding everything else constant.

circular flow model of income and output   A method that illustrates continuous flow of goods, services, and payments among businesses and households.

command economics   Highly centralized economic systems (e.g., Cuba, North Korea, China).

commercial banks   Banks organized chiefly to handle everyday financial transactions of businesses through demand deposit accounts and short-term commercial loans.

comparative advantage   A condition in which a person, a region, or a country can produce a good or service at a lower opportunity cost than others.

complementary goods   Things that go together and are often consumed and used simultaneously.

compliance standards   Government-mandated regulations that require private enterprise to produce their output in a manner that would reduce the negative externality below the amount that would persist in the absence of regulation.

constant-cost industry   An industry where the cost curves of the firm are not affected by changes in the output of the entire industry.

constant returns to scale   A situation where long-run average costs remain stable as output grows. There are neither economies of scale nor diseconomies of scale.

consumer equilibrium   The point at which the optimum utility-maximizing level of each good has been purchased.

consumer price index (CPI)   The standard measure of inflation; it provides a measure of the trend in the prices of certain goods and services purchased for consumption.

consumer sovereignty   The consumer is "king" concept that individuals control the production decisions in mixed-market economies by "voting" with their dollars.

consumer surplus   The difference between the maximum amount the consumer is willing to pay and what the consumer is required to pay.

consumption goods   Goods we consume that bring us immediate satisfaction, like food and clothing.

cooperative game   A situation in which two firms decide to collude in order to improve their profit-maximizing position.

corporate income taxes   Income taxes levied on corporations.

cost-push inflation   Inflation caused by a leftward shift in the short-run aggregate supply curve.

credit union   Corporation made up of depositors with a common affiliation.

cross price elasticity of demand   The percentage change in the quantity demanded of one good divided by the percentage change in the price of another good.

crowding out effect   The theory that as the government borrows to pay for the deficit, it drives up the interest rates and crowds out private spending and investment.

currency   Coins and/or paper that some institution or government has created to be used in the trading of goods and services and the payment of debts.

cyclical unemployment   Unemployment due to a drop in the demand for labor caused by a recession.

deflation   A decrease in the overall price level of goods and services in the economy.

demand deposits   Non-interest earning in checking deposits.

demand-pull inflation   A price level increase resulting from an increase in aggregate demand.

dependent variable   A variable that depends on the independent variables.

depreciation   Annual allowance set aside for the replacement of wornout plant and equipment.

depressions   Severe recessions.

derived demand   The demand for an input derived from consumers' demand for the good or service produced with that input.

direct relationship   Variables move in the same direction. (See *positive relationship*.)

discount rate   The interest rate that the Fed charges commercial banks.

discouraged worker   Individuals who give up looking for a job because they believe they will not find a suitable one.

diseconomies of scale   Long-run average total costs rise as output grows.

disposable income   Individual income available after personal taxes.

dissave   Persons consume more than their total income.

division of labor   When production is broken down into specific taxes.

dominant strategy   A strategy that will be optimal regardless of the opponents' actions.

durable goods   Longer-lived consumer goods, including automobiles, appliances, and furniture.

economic costs   Explicit plus implicit costs.

economic goods   Scarce goods that are created from scarce resources.

economic growth   An upward trend in the real output of goods and services.

economic theories   Statements or propositions about patterns of human behavior that are expected to take place under certain circumstances.

economics   The study of the allocation of our scarce resources to satisfy our unlimited wants for goods and services.

economies of scale   A production condition where the long-run average total costs fall as output expands.

efficiency   Getting the most from scarce resources.

efficient scale   The lowest point of average total cost.

elastic demand   A situation in which the percentage change in quantity demanded is greater than the percentage change in price.

eminent domain   Right of the government to assume ownership of private property if compensation is made to the original owners.

Employment Act of 1946   Act passed that committed the United States to policies designed to reduce unemployment in a manner consistent with price stability.

entrepreneur   Decision maker who decides how to combine land, labor, and capital together, which goods or services to produce, how many to produce, and so on.

entrepreneurship   Decision-making input that is concerned with the application of resources and with identifying new possibilities, new products, and new methods of production.

equation of exchange M (money supply) times V (velocity of circulation) = P (average level of prices of final goods and services times Q (physical quantity of final goods and services produced in a given period).

equilibrium price   The price at which quantity demanded equals the quantity supplied.

equilibrium quantity   The quantity bought and sold at the equilibrium price.

excess capacity   A situation where the firm produces below the level where average total cost is at a minimum.

excess reserves   The actual reserves of a bank minus its required reserves.

exchange economy   An economy that uses money as the basis for settling debts incurred in the process of trade, resulting in a constant.

exchange rate   The price in one country's currency of one unit of another country's currency.

excludability The ability to exclude individuals from using a particular good.

expenditure approach A method of measuring GDP in which GDP is calculated by adding up the expenditures of market participants on final goods and services over a period of time.

explicit costs Costs that are highly visible, readily measured by the money spent on the resources used, and contractual in nature.

externality Occurs whenever there are physical impacts (benefits or costs) of an activity on individuals not directly involved in the activity.

factor markets A market where the factors of production (e.g., land, labor, and capital) are bought and sold.

factor payments Payments to the owners of productive resources.

fallacy of composition Even if something is true for an individual, it is not necessarily true for many individuals as a group.

federal funds market A market in which banks that provide cash to other banks who have short-term needs for cash to meet reserve requirements.

fiat money A means of exchange that has been established by government declaration, not by custom or tradition.

fiscal policy The use of government purchases, taxes, and transfer payments to alter equilibrium GDP and price levels.

fixed costs Expenses that a firm has that exist at a level independent of the level of output.

fixed investments All new spending on capital goods by producers.

flat tax A tax designed so that everyone is charged the same percentage of income above some certain stipulated income level.

fractional reserve banking A system in which banks are required to keep reserves in the Federal Reserve equal to some fraction of their deposits.

free rider A person who does not pay for the benefits received from a public good.

frictional unemployment Unemployment resulting from constant changes in the economy that make it difficult to match qualified unemployed workers with current job openings.

game theory An approach to analyzing oligopoly behavior that presents a firm's and its rival's alternative strategies and consequent outcomes.

GDP deflator A price index that helps to measure the average level of prices of all consumer goods and services produced in the economy.

gold standard The dollar is defined as equivalent in value to a certain amount of gold, and paper currency or demand deposits could be freely converted to gold coin.

goods Objects that can be seen, held, heard, tasted, or smelled.

Gresham's Law "Cheap money drives out dear money." When there are two forms of money available, people prefer to spend the form of money that is less valuable.

gross domestic product (GDP) The value of all final goods and services produced within a country during a given period of time.

human capital People used as resources in production.

implicit costs The opportunity costs of the resources that firms use.

import quota The maximum number of units of a good that can be imported within any given time span.

income approach A method of measuring GDP in which GDP is calculated by summing the incomes received by producers of goods and services.

income elasticity of demand A measure of the relationship between a relative change in income and the consequent relative change in quantity demanded, *ceteris paribus;* percentage change in quantity demanded divided by the percentage change in income.

increasing-cost industry A production condition in which increases in input prices occur as larger quantities of factors are employed in the industry.

independent variable A variable that is not influenced by any other variable; it is determined outside the relationship in question.

indeterminate Change in price or quantity that cannot be determined without additional information about the size of the relative shifts in supply and demand.

indexing The process of adjusting payment contracts to automatically adjust for changes in inflation.

indirect business taxes Taxes, like sales taxes, that are levied on goods that are sold.

individual-consumption-payment link In a private market, an individual selects what he or she wants and is willing to pay for it.

induced investment An investment that results when businesses decide to proceed with an investment on the basis of increases in income or output.

inelastic demand The percentage change in quantity demanded is less than the percentage change in price.

inferior goods Goods for which rising income leads to reduced demand.

inflation A situation in which the overall price level is rising, resulting in a fall of the purchasing power of money.

intangible goods Goods that are less overtly visible, such as friendship, knowledge, security, intelligence, and health.

interest rate The price of borrowed funds.

inventory investment Includes all purchases by businesses that add to their inventories.

inverse relationship Two variables move in different directions. (See *negative relationship*.)

investment Refers to the creation of capital goods.

investment goods Goods that help increase the output of goods and services in future time periods, thus providing us with satisfaction at a later date.

investment tax credits Allow businesses to accelerate the speed that they can write off some of their new investments for tax purposes, raising after-tax rates of return on investment.

job-entry discrimination A situation in which a worker is denied employment on the basis of some non-economic factor, such as race, religion, sex, or ethnic origin.

joint profit maximization The determination of price is based on the marginal revenue function derived from the total (or market) demand schedule for the product and the marginal cost schedules.

labor Resource that includes the total of physical and mental effort expended by people in the economy.

labor force The number of people over the age of 16 who are either employed or unemployed.

labor intensive Production that uses a relatively high level of labor input.

land Resource that includes all natural resources coming from the earth (e.g., trees, animals, water, and minerals), as well as physical space.

law of demand The quantity of a good or service demanded varies inversely with its price, *ceteris paribus*. Other things being equal, when the price of a good or service falls, the quantity demanded increases, and conversely, if the price of a good or service rises, the quantity demanded decreases.

law of diminishing marginal product As the amount of a variable input is increased, the amount of other (fixed) inputs being held constant, a point ultimately will be reached beyond which marginal product will decline.

law of diminishing marginal utility Each successive unit of a good that is consumed generates less satisfaction than did the previous unit.

law of supply The quantity supplied will vary directly with the price of the good, other things being equal.

law of unintended consequences The results of actions are not always as initially intended.

legal tender Instrument declared by a government to be acceptable for the settlement of debts incurred in financial transactions.

long run A time period in which all factors of production can be varied.

long-run aggregate supply Refers to a period long enough for the prices of outputs and all inputs to fully adjust to changes in the economy.

long-run Phillips curve Shows the relationship between the inflation rate and the unemployment rate when the actual and expected inflation rates are the same.

M1 Narrow definition of money that includes currency, checkable deposits, and travelers checks.

M2 Broader definition of money encompassing M1 plus savings accounts, time deposits, and money market mutual funds.

macroeconomics Branch of economics that deals with the total economy and looks at economic problems as they influence the whole of society.

marginal costs The change in total costs associated with a change in output by one unit.

marginal product (MP) The change in total product resulting from a small change in the amount of input used.

marginal propensity to consume (MPC) The additional consumption that results from an additional dollar of income.

marginal resource cost (MRC) The amount that an extra unit of an input adds to the firm's total costs.

marginal revenue Additional revenue derived from the production of one more unit of the good.

marginal revenue product (MRP) The additional revenue that a firm obtains from utilizing one more unit of input.

marginal utility Additional satisfaction generated by the last unit of a good that is consumed.

market A set of rules or an arrangement for the negotiation of exchange between buyers and sellers.

market demand curve The horizontal summing of the demand curves of many individuals.

market economy An economy that uses a decentralized decision-making process to determine what to produce.

market failure Situation in which the economy fails to allocate resources efficiently on its own.

market power Power possessed by some firms to distort prices in their favor.

market supply curve The horizontal summation of the supply curves for individual firms.

measure of economic welfare (MEW) A measure of economic activity that adds the value of positive externalities and subtracts the value of negative externalities to GDP.

Medicare A federal health insurance plan for the elderly and other qualified individuals.

menu costs A cost of inflation that firms incur as a result of being forced to change posted prices.

microeconomics Branch of economics that deals with the smaller units within the economy, attempting to understand the decision-making behavior of firms and households and their interaction in markets for particular goods or services.

minimum-wage rate Standard wage set by the federal government.

mixed economies Economies in which some production decisions are made centrally by the government, while other decisions are made through the interaction of individual producers and purchasers.

money Anything that is generally accepted in exchange for goods or services.

money market The market where money demand and money supply determine the equilibrium interest rate.

money market mutual funds Interest-earning accounts provided by brokers who pool funds into investments like Treasury bills.

money multiplier The reciprocal of the reserve ratio. It is equal to 1 divided by the required reserve ratio.

money price The price that consumers would pay in dollars and cents for a good or service.

monopolistic competition A market structure that allows many producers of somewhat different products to compete with one another.

monopoly A market characterized by only one seller of a product for which no close substitute is available.

moral suasion Federal Reserve's influence upon banks to follow a particular course of action.

multiplier effect Chain reaction of additional income and purchases that results in a final increase in total purchases that is greater than the initial increase in purchases.

Nash equilibrium Point at which each firm is said to be doing as well as it can given the actions of its competitor.

national income (NI) The total of factor payments to the owners of resources.

national income accounting Uniform means of measuring national economic performance.

natural monopoly Situation in which one large firm can provide a good or service at a lower cost than two or more smaller firms.

natural rate of unemployment The sum of frictional unemployment and structural unemployment when they are at a maximum.

near money Nontransaction deposits that are not money but that can be quickly converted into money.

negative externality A cost that spills over to an outside party not involved in the production or consumption of the good or service.

negative incentives Incentives that either reduce benefits or increase costs, resulting in a decrease in the level of the related activity or behavior.

negative relationship Two variables move in different directions. (See *inverse relationship*.)

nominal interest rate Interest rate not corrected for inflation.

noncooperative game Each firm sets its own price without consulting other firms.

nondurable goods Tangible consumer items that are typically consumed or used up in a relatively short period of time, such as food.

non excludable A condition where no one else can be prevented from consuming the good; a characteristic of a public good.

non-income expense items Indirect taxes and depreciation.

nonpecuniary No outlay of money occurs.

non rivalrous A condition where people can consume a good without diminishing the amount available to other consumers.

nontransaction deposits Fund accounts against which the depositor cannot directly write checks.

normal good A good that is in greater demand as a result of higher incomes.

normative statements Opinions expressed about the desirability of various actions.

oligopoly A market structure characterized by a few sellers.

open economy A model that includes international trade effects.

open market operations The purchase and sale of government securities by the Federal Reserve system.

opportunity cost The highest or best foregone opportunity resulting from a decision.

own-price The price of a good or service.

payoff matrix A summary of the possible outcomes from various strategies.

payroll taxes Taxes levied on payrolls (work-related income).

per capita gross domestic product Real output of goods and services per person.

perfect competition A market structure characterized by many buyers and sellers, a homogeneous product, and easy market entry and exit.

personal income (PI) The amount of income received by individuals before they pay personal income taxes.

permanent income hypothesis A theory that consumption is related to permanent income rather than to current income levels.

personal income taxes Income taxes levied on individuals.

Phillips curve A curve showing the relationship between the annual rate of increase in the price level and the unemployment rate.

pollution tax Tax levied on a firm for polluting the environment.

positive analysis Objective, value-free approach that uses the scientific method.

positive externality A market activity that has a positive physical impact on an outside party.

positive incentives Incentives that either increase benefits or reduce costs, resulting in an increase in the level of the related activity or behavior.

positive relationship Variables move in the same direction. (See *direct relationship*.)

precautionary demand An individual's inclination to hold money in case of emergency or other unexpected expenses.

price The amount of money one has to pay for a good or service.

price ceiling Government-imposed maximum prices set for goods deemed important.

price controls Government policies forcing prices above or below what they would be in a market economy.

price discrimination Producers charge different customers different prices for the same good or service when the cost of providing that good or service does not differ among the customers.

price elasticity of demand A measure of the percentage that quantity demanded changes relative to the percentage the price changed to cause that change in quantity demanded.

price elasticity of supply A measure of the percentage that quantity supplied changes relative to the percentage the price changed to cause that change in quantity supplied.

price floor Government-imposed minimum prices set for goods.

price followers Competitors that go along with the pricing decisions of the price leader.

price index A measurement that attempts to provide a measure of the trend in prices paid for a certain bundle of goods and services over time.

price leader Firm that initiates price changes.

price level The average level of all prices in the economy.

price takers Competitive firms that must take the price given by the market because their influence on price is insignificant.

prisoners' dilemma A game that has a dominant strategy and demonstrates the basic problem confronting noncolluding oligopolists.

producer goods Capital goods, such as machinery and factory buildings, that increase future production capabilities.

producer surplus The difference between the least a supplier is willing to supply a quantity of a good or service for and the revenues a supplier actually receives for selling it.

product differentiation The accentuation of unique product qualities—real or perceived—to develop a specific product identity.

production function The maximum amount of a product that a firm can produce with each combination of inputs, using existing technology.

production possibilities curve Curve that represents the potential total output combinations of any two goods for an economy.

productive efficiency The operating level that permits the lowest average cost of production.

profits Difference between the total revenues (TR) of a firm and its total costs (TC).

progressive tax Tax designed so that those with higher incomes pay a greater proportion of their income in taxes.

property rights The broad powers individuals have to use, sell, rent, dispose of, or enhance the value of their goods.

public choice theory The theory that the behavior of individuals in politics is influenced by self-interest.

public good Good with properties of being nonrival in consumption (one person's usage of it does not diminish another's ability to

use it) and nonexclusive (no one can be excluded from using it) such as national defense.

purchasing power parity Allows us to estimate the number of units of currency needed in one country to buy the same amount of goods and services that one unit of currency will buy in another country.

rational ignorance Condition in which voters choose to be relatively uninformed about political issues because of high information costs and low benefits of being politically informed.

real interest rate Interest rate corrected for inflation.

regressive tax Tax that takes a greater proportion of the income of lower-income groups than higher-income groups.

relative price The price of one good relative to others.

required reserve ratio Percentage of deposits that a bank must keep at the Federal Reserve Bank.

resources Inputs, like land, labor, and capital, that are used to make goods and services

Ricardian equivalency theorem Theory that an increase in government spending will lead to higher taxes in the future, other things equal.

rule of rational choice People alter their behavior if the expected marginal benefits to them from doing so outweigh the expected marginal costs they will bear.

savings and loan associations Cooperative associations organized to hold savings of members in the form of dividend-bearing shares and to invest chiefly in home mortgage loans.

scarcity The result that occurs when our wants exceed what our resources can produce.

seasonal unemployment Unemployment that occurs because certain types of jobs are seasonal in nature.

secondary reserves Highly liquid, interest-paying assets.

self-interest Motivation that causes people to improve their own situation.

services Intangible items of value, such as education and health care, as opposed to physical goods.

shocks Unexpected aggregate supply or aggregate demand changes.

shoe leather cost The inflation cost of going to and from the bank to check on your assets.

shortage A condition where the quantity demanded is greater than the quantity supplied at the current price.

short-run A time period in which it is impossible to change some of the inputs, like plant size.

short-run aggregate supply curve Refers to a period when output can change in response to supply and demand, but input prices have not yet been able to adjust.

shutdown point The point where price just covers average variable costs.

social costs The full resource cost of an activity including the external cost.

special-interest groups Political pressure groups formed by individuals with common political objectives to influence decision makers.

specialization Concentrating production in the hands of the most efficient producers.

stagflation Phenomenon caused when lower growth and higher prices occur together.

structural unemployment Reflects the existence of persons who lack the necessary skills for jobs that are available.

subsidy A payment to a producer from the government.

substitute good A good that can replace another good.

substitution effect At higher prices, buyers increasingly substitute other goods for the good that now has a higher relative price.

surplus A condition where the quantity supplied is greater than the quantity demanded at the current price.

tariff A tax on imports.

theory of rational expectations Belief that wages and prices are highly flexible and that workers and consumers quickly incorporate the likely consequences of government policy changes into their expectations.

time-series graph A graph that shows changes over time.

total costs Total fixed costs plus total variable costs.

total product The total output of a particular good or service.

total revenue The total number of dollars generated from the sale of a good or service.

total utility Amount of satisfaction derived from all units of goods and services consumed.

transaction accounts Accounts that can be easily converted into currency or used to buy goods and services directly.

transaction costs The costs of making exchanges or transactions in a market.

transactions demand The tendency for individuals to keep cash on hand for the purposes of exchange.

travelers checks Transaction instruments that can be easily converted into currency.

underground economy Unreported cash and barter transactions.

unemployment rate Percent of the population over the age of 16 who are willing and able to work but are unable to obtain a job; calculated by dividing the number of people unemployed by the number in the labor force.

unit elastic The percentage change in quantity demanded is the same as the percentage change in price that caused it.

util The equivalent of one unit of satisfaction.

utility Level of satisfaction an individual receives from consumption of a good or service.

variable A quantity that can take on different numeric values.

variable costs Costs that are not fixed and therefore change as the level of output changes.

wage The price paid for the use of labor services.

wage and price controls Legislation limiting wage and price increases.

wage discrimination A situation in which workers are given employment at wages lower than those of other workers on some basis other than productivity differences such as race or sex.

economic growth and, 427–428
labor force
    unemployment rate and, 392
    U.S. (1997), 393
labor intensive, 76
labor market
    demand curve for, 322, 323, 325
    determining equilibrium in, 328–329
    employment rates and, 324–325
    immigration and, 332, 342–343
    supply curve for, 327
    supply and demand for, 326, 328
    temporary workers and, 582
    unemployment and imperfections of, 399
    unemployment statistics and, 393–394
    See also markets
labor productivity
    changes in, 330–331
    labor unions and, 335–336
    wage discrimination and, 360
    wages and, 337–338, 350
labor unions, 334–336
Laffer, Arthur, 355
Laffer curve, 355–356
Lamotte, Greg, 385
land
    capital and, 339–340
    described, **66–67**
    supply and demand for, 340
Larson, Gary, 47
law of demand
    law of diminishing marginal utility and, 184–185
    overview of, **92–95**
    See also demand
law of diminishing marginal product, 218
law of diminishing marginal utility, 181, 184–185
laws
    California's smoke-free bars, 385
    California's three strikes, 226
    debate over helmet, 174–175
    enforcement costs and, 34–35
    occupational licensing, 153–154
Lawson, Robert, 414, 415
law of supply, 108–109
law of unintended consequences, 28
Lee, D., 382
legal tender, 529
leisure value, 456–457
Levy, Frank, 350
liabilities (commercial bank), 542, 543
licenses, 274
lighthouses, 402
linear curves, 62–63
linear demand curve, 198–199
    See also demand curve
Lipset, S. M., 436

literary rates, 424
L.L.Bean Inc., 287
location differentiating factor, 286
Loews Cineplex Entertainment, 230
long-distance calls, 130
long-run aggregate supply curve (LRAS), 483–484, 485, 487, 516
long-run average total cost curve (LRATC), 228–229
long-run competitive equilibrium, 249
long-run cost curves, 228–229
long-run industry supply, 250–251
long-run Phillips curve, 583–585
Los Angeles Times, 304
losses
    evaluating short run, 244–246
    for a monopoly, 261
    when there is market exit, 289
Lucas, Robert, 586, 593

M

M1, 532–533, 546
M2, 533, 546
macroeconomic equilibrium, 489–491
macroeconomics
    described, **40**
    flexible rates and, 633–634
    goals of, 390–391
    rational expectations and policies of, 586–587
    role of expectations in, 593–594
Magic Johnson Theatres, 230
Malthusian prediction, 432
Malthus, Robert, 427, 432, 434
Mankoff, Robert, 181
marginal costs
    average total costs and, 225–226
    defining, **221**
    marginal product and, 224–225
    of three strikes law, 226
marginal product
    defining, **217**–218
    law of diminishing, 218
    marginal costs and, 224–225
marginal product (MP), 323
marginal propensity to consume (MPC), 467, 501
marginal resource cost (MRC), 322
marginal revenue (MR)
    demand and, 258
    described, **241**–242
    of monopolist, 256–258
marginal revenue product (MRP), 322, 324
marginal utility, 181, 183, 353
market demand curve, 97–98
market disequilibrium, 133–134
market economy, 73–74
market entry/exit
    in the long run, 289

oligopolists and, 310–311
    profits when firms guard against, 290
    See also barriers to entry or exit
market equilibrium price
    defining, 120
    shortages/surpluses and, 120–121, 122
    See also prices
market failures, 25–26, 75
market labor supply, 327
market power, 25
market profits. *See* profits
markets
    barriers to entry or exit to, 235–236
    capital, 339
    compared to nonrush-hour traffic, 122
    cybergambling and profits of gaming, 252–253
    defining, **88–89**
    economic freedom and emerging, 415
    factor (or input), 440, 441
    foreign exchange, 623–627
    income distribution by, 159
    input, 320–321, 340
    monopoly of, 157
    perfectly competitive, 234–236, 238, 241, 248–249
    product, 440, 441
    See also labor market
market structures
    monopolies as, 157, 256–258, 260–261, 263–265, 267–274, 278–279
    monopolistic competition as, 284–287, 288–290, 292–293, 295
    oligopolies as, 304–315
    perfect competition as, 234, 238, 242–243, 263, 293, 295
    reviewing four types of, 314–315
market supply curve, 109
market supply (hypothetical), 120
market system
    failures of, 25–26
    price system and, 24–25
Marx, Karl, 427, 436
Matthews, Merrill, Jr., 155
means of deferred payment, 535
measure of economic welfare (MEW), 458–459
media, 566
Medicaid, 160
Medicare, 160, **169**
Medoff, James, 335
Melzer, Bruce, 252
menu costs, 405
microeconomics, 40
Microsoft, 5, 68, 264, 266, 268, 429
Miller Brewing Co., 306
minimum wage rate, 25, 137–138
minorities
    affirmative action and, 361
    job-entry discrimination and, 358

wage discrimination and, 359–360
misperception effect, 483
mixed economies, 74
mobility of resources, 425–426, 430
Mobil Oil, 381
monetary policy
    implemented by the Fed, 561–566
    problems with implementing, 573–575
money
    creation of, 540–544
    demand for, 537–538
    described, **528**–530
    destruction of, 547
    equation of exchange and, 559–560
    functions of, 534–535
    interest rates/aggregate demand and, 568–571
    and prices in the long run (1889–1993), 562
    velocity of, 559, 560
money capital, 67
money market, 568
money market equilibrium, 568–569
money market mutual funds, 532
money multiplier, 545–546
money price, 90–91
money stock, 564, 569
money supply, 532–533, 564–565
monopolies
    antitrust policies on, 268–271
    application of, 278–279
    case against, 263–265
    case for, 265, 267
    demand, marginal revenue, total revenue curves of, 256–258
    described, **157,** 256
    government, 272–274
    losses for, 261
    natural, 267
    price determined by, 260
    profit-maximizing output of, 260
    profits of, 261
monopolistic competition
    comparing perfect competition and, 293, 295
    long-run equilibrium in, 289–290
    overview of, **284**–287
    real costs of, 292–293
    short-run equilibrium in, 288
    See also competition
Montana fish and game laws, 34
Montesquieu, Baron de, 427
Moore, Steve, 35
movie ticket prices, 91, 276
Moynihan, Pat, 454
multiple expansion effect, 545
multiplier effect, 501–504, 509
Muth, John, 593
mutual interdependence, 304–305, 310
Myers, David G., 436

N

Nash equilibrium, 313
national debt, 498, 505, 520–521
National Football League (NFL), 140–141
national income accounting, 442–443
national income (NI), 449
national security argument, 610–611
national security/tariff argument, 400–401
NationsBank Corp., 547
natural disasters, 487
natural monopoly, 267
natural rate of unemployment, 401
natural resources, 4, 428, 486
NBA (National Basketball Association), 279
NCAA (National Collegiate Athletic Association), 279
near money, 532
needs, 93–95
negative externalities, 146–147, 372–375
negative incentives, 17
negative relationship, 60–61, 92
Net.Bank, 552
net exports, 470, 476
Netscape, 268
New Balance, Inc., 299–300
New Deal programs, 519
The New Yorker, 5
New York Stock Exchange, 235
New York Times, 304
New York Yankees, 166
Nike, Inc., 299, 300
Nixon, Richard, 576
noise pollution, 374, 380
Noll, Roger G., 166
nominal gross domestic product, 429
nominal interest rate, 405
noncooperative games, 312
nondurable goods, 444
non-income expense items, 448
nonlinear curve, 63
nonmarket transactions, 456
nonmonetary assets, 532
nonpecuniary costs, 373
nontransaction deposits, 531–532
nonwage income, 332–333
Nordhaus, William, 56
normal good, 103
normative statements, 52–53
North American Free Trade Agreement (NAFTA), 614

O

occupational licensing laws, 153–154
O'Connor, Anne-Marie, 116
oeconomicus, 4
oil industry supply shifters, 113
oligopoly
    game theory/strategic behavior and, 312–315

market entry and, 310–311
    mutual interdependence in, 310
    OPEC as collusive, 316–318
    overview of, 304–306
    pricing decisions in, 307–309
O'Neal, Brian, 412
O'Neal, Shaquille, 226
OPEC cartel, 278, 316–317
open economy models, 470, 472–473
open market operations, 561–562
opportunity costs
    considering, 12–13
    increasing, 71
    specialization and, 21
    See also costs
optimism, 468
option demand, 166
Oscar Mayer "Wienermobile," 100
own-price, 100, 105

P

patents, 273–274
payoff matrix, 312–314
payroll taxes, 169
    See also taxation
Peapod, 286
Peltzman, Sam, 154
Pepsi, 100
per capital gross domestic product, 455
Pereira, Joseph, 299
perfect competition
    comparing monopolistic competition and, 293, 295
    cost and revenue calculations for, 243
    defining, **234**
    firm output in, 242
    market and individual firm demand curves in, 238
    monopoly vs., 263
    See also competition
perfectly competitive market
    characteristics of a, 234–236, 238
    profits in a, 248–249
    revenues in a, 241
    See also markets
permanent income hypothesis, 466–467
personal income (PI), 449
personal income taxes, 169
    See also taxation
PETA (People for the Ethical Treatment of Animals), 100
Phelps, Edmund, 583
Philip Morris Co., 306
Phillips, A. H., 580
Phillips curve
    described, 580–582
    over time, 583–585
physical capital, 428
Pirsig, Robert, 46, 47